WITHDRAWN

The Design of Animal Communication

The Design of Animal Communication

edited by Marc D. Hauser and Mark Konishi

A Bradford Book
The MIT Press
Cambridge, Massachusetts
London, England

This book was set in Times New Roman by Asco Typesetters, Hong Kong and was printed and bound in the United States of America.

Library of Congress Cataloging-in-Publication Data

The design of animal communication / edited by Marc D. Hauser and Mark Konishi.
    p.   cm.
"A Bradford book."
Based on a symposium which took place on March 22 and 23, 1997 at the University of California Davis.
Includes bibliographical references and index.
ISBN 0-262-08277-2 (hc : alk. paper)
1. Animal communication—Congresses. I. Hauser, Marc D. II. Konishi, Mark.
QL776.D47   1999
591.59—dc21   99-13959
                                                         CIP

Contents

Preface

Mark Konishi

The present volume is the result of a symposium in honor of Peter Marler which took place on March 22 and 23, 1997 at the University of California Davis. Peter has been a great leader in the study of animal communication. He defined and articulated many of the most important issues in the study of animal communication. He is a man of ideas, a superb synthesizer, and an effective catalyst for connecting different disciplines. The aim of the symposium was to examine the current state of some of the areas that he pioneered.

Animal communication has provided interesting problems and instructive examples in all areas of ethology including ontogeny, mechanisms, function, and evolution. Many of the classical ethological ideas emerged or crystallized from the study of animal communication, for example, the concepts of stereotypy in behavior, species-specific repertoires of movements, species-specificity in animal signals, releasers, sign stimuli, imprinting, and critical period owe their origin largely to observations of social behavior and to comparative studies of animal signals. However, the study of animal communication as an independent discipline became established only in the early 1950s. Peter played a pivotal role in this new development. In one of his earliest papers, those which originated from his thesis research, Peter used the title "The voice of the chaffinch and its function as a language" (1956, *Ibis* 98:231–221). Here lies the foundation of his several quests, which he has vigorously pursued for almost half a century. He set out to find principles of animal communication. One of his earliest and most celebrated discoveries concerns common design features in the alarm calls of birds. He explained how one design makes the signal hard to localize and another easy to localize. This idea emerged in sharp contrast with the then-prevailing one that placed no functional significance on signal designs.

Birds, frogs, fishes, and insects were the favorite animals groups for the students of animal communication, because their signals, particularly visual and auditory signals, can be easily described and studied. Peter's first major review article on animal communication, which appeared in 1959 (in *Darwin's Biological Work*, Cambridge University Press), covered not only these groups but also mammals, including apes and humans. Six years later he wrote a review on vocal communication in monkeys and apes after attending a conference on primate field research. This review stimulated field research on vocal communication in apes and monkeys, research in which he and his students became major players. In this article, he asked if the rules that govern the design of vocal signals in other animals might apply to primate vocalizations. One of the rules was species-specificity in signals used for species recognition. His own field study of two sympatric species of cercopithecine monkeys in

Uganda showed a high degree of species-distinctiveness in adult male calls. In contrast, the alarm calls of the two species were similar. This is exactly what he had found earlier in his comparison of avian vocalizations. Work on vervet monkeys by him and his associates (see chapter 14) produced a discovery that brought him back to his most fundamental question about what animal signals convey. Vervet monkey use different alarm calls for leopards, snakes, and eagles. Human words refer to different objects, events, and ideas. The referential method of communication is, therefore, not unique to human language. This finding has had a significant impact on the thinking of anthropologists, linguists, and psychologists.

Another aspect of communication that is thought to be unique to humans is the brain lateralization of language. Peter and his associates, in collaboration with auditory psychophysicists, found that Japanese macaque monkeys discriminate between their own vocalizations much better than between the vocalizations of another species. Moreover, the macaques discriminated these calls much better with their right ear in much the same way that humans prefer using the right ear for listening to speech (see chapter 22). This right-ear advantage, implicating left hemisphere specialization, showed for the first time that brain lateralization of perception of vocal signals is not unique to humans. In more recent years, another human behavioral trait drew Peter's attention. To attract hens, roosters utter a special call upon discovering edible or even inedible objects. Peter and his coworker showed that roosters produce food calls much more readily when they are with hens than when they are with other roosters or alone. Thus animal vocalizations are mediated by the composition of the social group, a phenomenon that Peter eloquently coined the "audience effect."

How animal signals and responses to them develop raises many interesting questions. Birdsong is an ideal behavior through which to analyze these questions. Peter has been the most influential leader in birdsong research. He has put forth new ideas and revisited old ideas with new perspectives. His discussion of such concepts as innateness versus learning, song templates, and selection versus instruction in song learning enriched the field and stimulated new research (see chapters 10, 11, 12, 13). He was the first to point out the similarities between the development of human speech and that of birdsong. For example, early auditory experience greatly affects the development of speech in human infants and that of song in young birds (see chapter 15). Evidence shows that both young humans and birds learn vocal patterns even before they themselves can produce them. Babies and young birds go through a similar stage of vocal development known as babbling and subsong, respectively. The most important attribute that birds and humans share is the need to control voice by hearing themselves vocalize. It should be pointed out that this ability evolved only in several of the many animal groups that use acoustic signals, including humans, whales, dolphins, and some bats, among mammals, and oscine songbirds, parrots, and some hummingbirds.

The mechanisms of behavior have been an important component of ethology since its early days. Those who have taken Peter's courses or read his book, coauthored with Bill Hamilton, *The Mechanisms of Animal Behavior* (1966), appreciate his interest and knowledge in this aspect of ethology. He would discuss with great enthusiasm such topics as central control of motor coordination and peripheral filtering of stimuli. Much progress has been made in this field since 1966. Many animal sound signals are periodic and the source of this rhythm has been identified in the central nervous system (see chapters 1, 17). Filtering and processing of biologically relevant stimuli by sense organs and central circuits are well understood particularly in simpler systems of invertebrates, fishes, and amphibians. Warm-blooded animals are by no means unsuitable for mechanistic studies, as exemplified by work on bats (see chapter 5), songbirds (see chapter 12), and owls. In general, the integration of ethological and neurophysiological approaches has yielded the most satisfactory results, in which we understand both the neural mechanisms of behavior and the functional significance of neural structure and physiology.

In his book, *Sociobiology: The New Synthesis* (1975), Edward O. Wilson predicted that ethology would be split into sociobiology and neurophysiology. This has happened. Fortunately, neuroethology emerged to occupy the niche of ethology for those whose interests are in mechanisms. However, the rapid advent of neuroscience is having a profound impact on neuroethology in that the uniqueness of neuroethology is slowly eroding. The study of neural mechanisms of natural behavior is the central theme of neuroethology. Peter has been deeply concerned with these trends and constantly reminds us of this aim in the study of neural mechanisms. Even after his official retirement he continues to point the way we should be going. On behalf of the Marler laboratory alumni, I would like to take this opportunity to thank Peter for his guidance, inspiration, and generosity.

I am grateful to Dr. Israel Lederhendler of NIMH for his efforts in funding the symposium, and to Dr. Robert Boughman of NINDS and Dr. Lynn Huerta of NIDCD for making contributions to the grant from their respective institutes. I also thank Professor Thomas W. Schoener and Provost Robert D. Grey of the University of California, Davis, for making the lecture hall available, and the present Marler laboratory members and alumni and Jeni Trevitt for their assistance. Judith Marler deserves our special thanks for many memorable occasions on field trips and at her home, and for making our recent visit to Davis so pleasant.

I MECHANISMS OF COMMUNICATION

Mark Konishi

Animals use many different methods to produce communication signals even within a single sensory modality. For example, sounds may be produced by the passage of air through special organs as in the mammalian larynx and avian syrinx, by rubbing appendages against each other like insect legs and wings, and by striking objects in the environment as in woodpeckers.

Recording bodily movements or their products in naturally behaving animals has been the main method of studying how signal-producing organs work. For example, the spectral and temporal analyses of sound signals can reveal some of the properties of sound production as exemplified by the discovery of the simultaneous production of two different sounds by birds, which led to the two voice theory (Greenewalt 1968; Stein 1968). In the study of insects, fish, and frogs, this approach has progressed to the neuromuscular level. Chapter 1 by Kelley and Tobias is a good example of this approach (see also chapter 17 by Bass et al.). In the past, this level of analysis appeared unobtainable in songbirds despite extensive descriptive and developmental studies of birdsong. This situation has, however, changed dramatically in recent years. Use of an angioscope for inspecting the inside of human blood vessels allows viewing of the inside of the syrinx during phonation. This approach has revealed that the labia instead of the internal tympaniform membranes produce sounds (Goller and Larsen 1997). This finding radically changes the long-held view that these membranes are the source of sounds. Suthers reviews these and other deveopments in the study of avian phonation in chapter 2.

Of many issues, the relationships between respiration and vocalization are particularly interesting. Suthers and his associates succeeded in recording simultaneously song, air flow, and sounds in the trachea or bronchi, pressure in the air sac system, and electrical activities in abdominal and syringeal muscles. Their results have resolved some of the outstanding questions and hypotheses concerning the methods of breathing during song and also uncovered many interesting new facts. The two-voice theory is one of the hypotheses. Simultaneous recordings of air flow and sound in the left and right bronchi of catbirds, brown thrashers, canaries, and cowbirds show that birds do produce different sounds from the left and right halves of their syrinx. The two sides often generate different sounds either simultaneously or in sequence within a syllable. The timing relationships between the two sides are particularly interesting. Birds can close one side while singing with the other side, and they can rapidly switch from one side to the other between syllables and within a syllable (Suthers 1990). This dynamic control of respiration during song suggests that the vocal system sends control signals to the respiratory system. The anatomical bases for this control involve neural pathways from the forebrain song-control circuit to the hindbrain respiratory center (review in Wild 1997).

Lateralization is another important phenomenon for which physiological evidence has become available. In Wasserschlaeger canaries, cutting the left syringeal nerve or lesioning the left nucleus HVC causes the disappearance of a majority of song syllables (Nottebohm and Nottebohm 1976; Nottebhom et al. 1976). This finding led Nottebohm to the hypothesis that there is hemispheric lateralization in song production as in human speech. Air flow and sound recording does show that a majority of syllables are produced by the left side. However, examination of the brain areas that control song production shows no size differences between the hemispheres, whereas the left half of the syrinx is much larger than the right half. Suthers and his coworker found that while a bird is singing with the left side, the dorsal syringeal muscles contract to stop the air flow in the right side (Goller and Suthers 1995). Since other muscles are active on both sides, the difference is not reflected in the size of the song nuclei.

The "mini breath" theory is yet another hypothesis that has been confirmed. Calder (1970) used behavioral methods to show that canaries take a short breath before each song syllable when they are singing fast. Air flow and pressure measurements clearly showed the validity of this interpretation. Suthers and his coworker further demonstrated that canaries produce fast-song syllables without inspiring between the syllables (Hartley and Suthers 1989). They can sing using the air stored in the air sac system. This finding is important for understanding the evolution of vocal signals in birds. It is safe to assume that vocalization evolved from respiration. The question then is how the vocal system was "emancipated" from the constraints of the respiratory rhythm. The air sac system working as a bellow partly frees the vocal system from these limitations.

Only a few years ago we knew more about the brain mechanisms of birdsong than about its syringeal mechanisms. Now, we have many interesting findings about the syrinx, some of which need to be explained in terms of central mechanisms. The discovery of the song control system by Nottebohm and his associates in 1976 marked a new era in birdsong research. It brought birdsong research into the realm of neuroscience. Few vertebrate neural systems with known function are so discrete as the song system. This property allows the investigator to compare the song system between different species, sexes, ages, seasons, and normal and experimentally manipulated individuals. All these comparisons have yielded exciting results including the absence of the forebrain song nuclei in suboscine birds, the rudimentary state of the forebrain song nuclei in the female of species in which only the male sing, developmental and seasonal changes in song nuclei, and growth and differentiation of forebrain song nuclei by hormonal manipulation. Finer analyses of song nuclei have also produced surprising results such as the migration of new neurons into forebrain song nuclei in the adult brain, formation of new synapses in response to testosterone in the adult brain, and the expression of early immediate genes that is correlated with song behavior. Nottebohm (chapter 3) and Ball (chapter 8) provide extensive discussions of these topics.

One aspect of the song system that has received much attention is its role in song imitation. The forebrain part of the system including HVC, RA, X, and LMAN occurs only in oscine songbirds (which can imitate song) and is absent in suboscine songbirds (which sing but do not imitate song). Oscines include such birds as canaries, finches, and sparrows, whereas suboscines include flycatchers and many South American passerines. This observation led Nottebohm (1980) to suggest that the forebrain song nuclei evolved to accommodate song learning (cf. Kroodsma and Konishi 1991). If this theory is true, this example is the only case in which conspicuous differences in the brain are correlated with the ability and inability to learn. Thus the song system is a good model for the study of learning. Some of the changes in the song system mentioned in the preceding paragraph are likely to be involved in song imitation, although ultimately one has to discriminate between maturational and renewal processes, and those that are essential for song imitation. In chapter 3, Nottebohm discusses the significance of anatomical and physiological changes with reference to the critical period of song learning (see also chapter 12).

The discovery of seasonal changes and the effects of sex hormones made the song system a very attractive subject for neuroendocrinological research. In chapter 8, Ball reviews recent advances in this field. In addition to endogenous circannual rhythm, photoperiod plays an important role in avian reproductive behavior of which song is a component. Long spring days following short winter days stimulate the secretion of gonadotropine-releasing hormone from the hypothalamus, gonadtropines from the pituitary, and eventually sex steroids from the gonads. Measurement of testosterone in wild songbirds shows a strong correlation between hormone levels and different phases of the reproductive cycle including singing. Since an increase in testosterone is known to induce the growth of song nuclei, long days should have the same effects. Indeed, relatively short exposure, such as one week, to long days increases the volume of some of the song nuclei. This growth may involve an increase in cell number, growth of dendrites, somata, and intercellular distance. Ball carefully analyzes the existing results to determine which of these events really occur. The action of a single hormone on the song system is, however, by no means simple. For example, growth and regression in the song system can occur without changes in testosterone titre. Some of the song nuclei grow in response to testosterone in the absence of steroid receptor containing cells. This is because cells with steroid receptors influence the growth of other cells by transsynaptic action.

The discovery of gender difference and plasticity in the adult avian brain surprised everyone and stimulated new efforts to look for the same phenomena in other animals, particularly laboratory mammals. Both neurogenesis and seasonal changes in the adult brain were subsequently found in mammals (Gaulin and FitzGerald 1986; Louis and Alvarez-Buyalla 1994; Jacobs and Spencer 1994). Large gender differences were also found in the brain and spinal cord of laboratory mammals (review in Breedlove 1993). Wherever there are innate gender differences in behavior, there are gender differences in the nervous system. Kelley and Tobias review their work on the African clawed frog *Xenopus laevis*, whose males and females produce different calls. Both the vocal organ and the neural circuits for vocal control are different between the sexes in terms of cell number, biochemical properties, and connectivity. One of the most interesting findings discussed in this chapter is the fact that sex differences in the larynx and its muscles can explain why males and females produce different calls. The male larynx is equipped with fast-twitch muscles to produce fast trills, whereas the female larynx is controlled by slow-twitch muscles to accommodate only slow clicks. During development the laryngeal muscles change from slow to fast type in the male under the influence of androgen. However, this conversion does not occur in other muscles of the body. This difference is due to a special gene that is expressed in the laryngeal muscles. The synapses between the motor neurons for these muscles are also different in the sexes. Male synapses have a property suitable for producing male-specific amplitude-modulated trills. The sex difference in laryngeal synapses emerges during ontogeny. Here male synapses retain the juvenile state, whereas female synapses undergo changes in response to estrogen. This body of work constitutes the most thoroughly studied example of sexual differentiation of signaling behavior and its neural substrates.

The methods of signal detection match the diversity of signal production. For example, relevant auditory signals may be detected by the resonant property of peripheral sensors as in the antennae of mosquitoes (Roth et al. 1966), by specialized segments of the basilar membrane as in certain bats (Suga et al. 1975), and by higher-order neurons as in space-specific neurons of barn owls (Konishi 1995).

Mechanistic studies can be carried out on several different levels. Behavior is the first level at which signal detection can be analyzed. For example, in his classic work, von Frisch showed how honey bees communicate through dance the direction and distance of food sources. The "waggle run" part of waggle dances indicates the direction of a food source relative to the sun. Bees can communicate this information by dancing on a vertical surface of their hive in total darkness. In chapter 4, Michelsen addresses the problem of how new recruits extract this information from the dancing bee. Recruits may derive it from the vibration of the comb by the dancing bee or from touching this individual. These methods do not seem likely. Michelsen casts doubt on even his own theory in which rhythmic airflows created by wing movements are supposed to provide the information. If one could manipulate either dancers or new recruits, one could analyze the dance language; therefore, it had been a dream to build a robotic bee. Most models had failed until Michelsen designed and built one. Studies of this robotic bee showed once again that bees need not use odors to locate food sources (cf. Gould 1975). The robotic bee also allowed the investigator to manipulate different components of dances, such as the direction and duration of waggle runs and sounds produced by the wings. The results confirmed the original hypothesis that the direction and duration of waggle runs encode the direction and distance of food sources, respectively. However, the direction of simple runs with sounds was also interpreted to indicate the direction of food sources. Thus bee dances appear to contain coding redundancy. This is an exciting first step in elucidating how new recruits read the codes contained in the dance language.

To communicate one's emotional states to other individuals is perhaps the oldest function of animal communication. Following on the footsteps of Darwin's major treatise on this topic, ethologists have studied the communicative function of facial and bodily expressions. The elaborate ethograms showing expression of threat and fear in wolves and cats are well known (Schenkel 1947; Leyhausen 1956). The recent advent of brain-imaging techniques has made it possible to correlate human sensory perception with the brain areas involved. Adolph reviews work on people whose amygdala is bilaterally lesioned for various reasons. These people fail to recognize facial expressions showing fear, although they have no problem in discriminating between individuals by face. The study of people with lesions in specific areas is likely to yield much information about the functional organization of the human brain. There are, however, constraints on this approach. One of them is the impracticality of single neuron recording in the human brain, although there have been a number of cases in which single neurons were recorded in patients during preoperative explorations. In fact, some studies show that the human amygdala contains neurons selective for faces expressing fear (see chapter 6).

It would seem naive to expect to find neurons selective for faces, because these stimuli could be encoded by ensembles of neurons in which each member is not specialized for any stimuli. Encoding of complex stimuli by single neurons appears to be the dominant method at least in the visual and auditory systems (see chapter 12). However, the reader must first understand how selectivity for such complex stimuli is created. These sensory systems use parallel pathways to process different components of the stimulus. The codes for complex stimuli are then synthesized by collecting processed information from all parallel pathways. These "complex" neurons, therefore, represent the results of all processes that take place in the pathways leading to them. Since these pathways are designed to process biologically relevant stimuli, it is not surprising to find neurons selective for these stimuli at nodal loci of the entire network. The temporal cortex of the macaque monkey contains neurons selective for facial expressions and bodily movements. This makes sense, because facial expressions and bodily movements are biologically important signals in the social life of primates, as Perrett points out in chapter 6.

The biological relevance of stimuli is the most important prerequisite for sensory physiology. To show or infer biological relevance is relatively easy in animals that are adapted for extreme lifestyles such as hunting in the dark. Since bats navigate and hunt by echolocation, processing sonar signals must be important for them. This simple logic has led Suga and his associates to the fruitful exploration of the auditory cortex of bats (Suga 1992). In moustached bats, they charted the auditory cortex according to the stimulus selectivity of neurons. This map is now well known. However, auditory signaling in bats is not restricted to echolocation, as many species, including the moustached bat, have a substantial repertoire of social calls. How are these signals represented in the brain? Are there separate brain areas for echolocation and communication? Kanwal reviews the results of preliminary work to answer these questions. Two of the areas in the sonar map contain neurons that respond well to some of the calls. Some of these neurons are selective for a specific call or a class of calls, either because these calls contain an appropriate combination of excitatory and inhibitory frequencies or because they contain particular temporal patterns or both. These findings raise important questions as to how the bat interprets the response of these neurons, because they appear to represent both sonar and social signals.

Social relationships influence many aspects of communication. The nature of this influence and what mediates it have mostly been studied in laboratory settings and captive animals. For example, the effects of serotonin in establishing and maintaining social hierarchy have been extensively studied in captive animals including crayfish, lobsters, and monkeys (Raleigh et al. 1991; Edwards and Kravitz 1997). Wingfield and his associates (chapter 9) have made heroic and successful efforts to dissect the relationships between the sex hormones and the reproductive behavior of wild songbirds. One of the most interesting findings is the effects of behavior on the serum concentration of testosterone. The testosterone titre of territorial males rises when old neighbors are replaced by new ones and when their mates show precopulatory soliciting behavior in response to injection of estrogen. This rise in testosterone titre occurs even when it is normally low, as during the care of nestlings. These and other findings indicate that the interactions between the endocrine and behavioral control systems change dynamically in different stages of the life cycle and that communication plays an important role in these regulatory mechanisms.

References

Breedlove, S. M. (1993) Sexual differentiation of the brain and behavior. In *Behavioral Endocrinology*, ed. by B. Becker, S. M. Breedlove, and D. Crews, pp. 39–70. Cambridge, MA: MIT Press.

Calder, W. A. (1970) Respiration during song in the canary (*Serinus canaria*). *Comp. Biochem. Physiol.* 32:251–258.

Edwards, D. H. and Kravitz, E. A. (1997) Serotonin, social-status, and aggression. *Cur. Op. Neuro.* 7:812–819.

Gaulin, S. J. C. and FitzGerald, R. W. (1986) Sex differences in spatial ability: An evolutionary hypothesis and test. *Am. Nat.* 127:74–88.

Goller, F. and Larsen, O. N. (1997) A New mechanism of sound generation in songbirds. *Proc. Natl. Acad. Sci. USA* 94:1487–1491.

Goller, F. and Suthers, R. A. (1995) Implications for laterization of birdsong from unilateral gating of bilateral motor patterns. *Nature* 373:63–66.

Gould, J. L. (1975) Honey bee recruitment. *Science* 189:685–693.

Greenewalt, C. H. (1968) *Bird Song: Acoustics and Physiology.* Washington D.C.: Smithsonian Inst. Press.

Hartley, R. S. and Suthers, R. A. (1989) Airflow and pressure during canary song: Evidence for mini-breaths. *J. Comp. Physiol.* A 165:15–26

Jacobs, L. F. and Spencer, W. D. (1994) Natural space-use patterns and hippocampal size in kangaroo rats. *Brain, Behav., Evol.* 44:125–132.

Konishi, M. (1995) Neural mechanisms of auditory image formation. In *The Cognitive Neurosciences*, ed. M. S. Gazzaniga, pp. 269–277. Cambridge, MA: MIT Press.

Kroodsma, E. D. and Konishi, M. (1991) A Suboscine bird (eastern phoebe, Sayornis phoebe) develops normal song without auditory feedback. *Anim. Behav.* 42:477–487.

Leyhausen, P. (1956) Das Verhalten der Katzen (Felidae). *Handbuch Zool.* Vol. 8, 10 (21):1–34.

Louis, C. and Alvarez-Buyalla, A. (1994) Long distance neuronal migration in the adult mammalian brain. *Science* 264:1145–1148.

Nottebohm, F. (1980) Brain pathways for vocal learning in birds: A Review of the first ten years. *Prog. Psychobiol. Physiol. Psychol.* 9:85–124.

Nottebohm, F. and Nottebohm, M. E. (1976) Left hypoglossal dominance in the control of canary amd white-crowned sparrow song. *J. Comp. Physiol.* 108:171–192.

Nottebohm, F., Stockes, T. M., and Leonard, C. M. (1976) Central control of song in the canary, *Serinus canarius. J. Comp. Neurol.* 165:457–486.

Raleigh, M. J., Mcquire, M. T., Brammer, G. L., Pollack, D. B., and Yuwiler, A. (1991) Serotonergic mechanisms promote dominance acquisition in adult male vervet monkeys. *Brain Res.* 559:181–190.

Roth, M. L., Roth, M., and Eisner, T. E. (1966) The Allure of the female mosquito. *Natural History* 75:27–31.

Schenkel, R. (1947) Ausdrucksstudien an Woelfen. *Behaviour* 1:81–129.

Stein, R. C. (1968) Modulation in bird sounds. *Auk* 85: 229–243.

Suga, N. (1992) Philosophy and stimulus design for neuroethology of complex-sound processing. *Phil. Trans. Roy Soc.* 336:423–428.

Suga, N., Simmons, J. A., and Jen, P. H.-S (1975) Peripheral specialization for fine analysis of Doppler-shifted echoes in the auditory system of the "CF-FM" bat Pteronotus parnellii. *J. Exp. Biol.* 63:161–192.

Suthers, R. A. (1990) Contributions to birdsong from the left and right sides of the intact syrinx. *Nature* 347:473–477.

Wild, M. J. (1997) Neural pathways for the control of birdsong production. *J. Neurobiol.* 33:653–670.

1 Vocal Communication in *Xenopus laevis*

Darcy B. Kelley and Martha L. Tobias

Sexual selection (Darwin 1871; Andersson 1994) is thought to play a major role in the evolution of sex differences in vocal communication both with respect to production and perception. A primary function of vocal communication between the sexes—intersexual communication—is to bring males and females together to coordinate their reproduction. Vocal behaviors also serve in intrasexual communication particularly during competition for mates and territorial defense. The developmental and physiological mechanisms underlying sexually differentiated vocal communication systems have been the focus of our research. We have studied an anuran model system, the South African clawed frog, *Xenopus laevis*, which has the double advantages of exhibiting a relatively simple mechanism for vocal production and the powerful control of vocal behaviors by steroid hormones. Sex differences in vocal production have been traced to the action of gonadal steroid hormones, which act during development to control the morphogenesis of the vocal organ and during adulthood to control how the system produces male- and female-specific songs. More recently we have sought to understand how reproductive communication functions in the natural environments of *X. laevis*, how vocal behaviors are perceived, how and why they differ in the sexes, and how communication is tied to the reproductive state of the signaler and the receiver.

Xenopus laevis: Natural History

Xenopus laevis belongs to the family *Pipidae*, a group that currently includes 29 species in several genera; the genus *Xenopus* is the largest in the family with 15 species (Trueb 1996; Graf 1996). *X. laevis* is totally aquatic throughout its life cycle and is nocturnal; the current range is confined to Southern Africa. The species is somewhat opportunistic in habitat (Tinsley et al. 1996); provided that the water does not freeze solid (Tinsley and McCoid 1996), any still body, including sewers, fish ponds, and swimming pools, is readily colonized by adults. Adult *Xenopus* are proficient swimmers but can also travel short distances over ground. The preferred habitat for the species, as judged by population density, is turbid, murky ponds. Most predators are diurnal; wading birds and the algae provide fodder for the tadpoles. This preferred habitat accounts for the dearth of information about the natural history of *X. laevis*.

   X. laevis is represented throughout sub-Saharan Africa by a number of subspecies. Here we concentrate on the subspecies most common in South Africa and now bred commercially for laboratory use, *X. laevis laevis* (which we will refer to simply as *X. laevis*). In the southern parts of South Africa these frogs begin to breed at the end of winter—in Cape Town, for example, from July to November—while in more northern regions, such as areas surrounding Johannesburg, the population breeds in the African summer. The onset and the duration of the breeding season are determined largely by rainfall—within a permissive temperature range (Kalk 1960; Balinsky 1969)—a factor that contributes, despite the retention of some circannual patterns of sexual activity (Kelley 1996), to success in laboratory-based breeding.

The Vocal Repertoire of *Xenopus laevis*

Both oviposition and spermiation are exquisitely sensitive to human chorionic gonadotropin excreted by pregnant women, and reproductive behaviors can be induced at any time of the year by administration of this hormone (reviewed in Kelley 1996). This characteristic facilitated the laboratory-based study of reproductive vocalization in *X. laevis* begun in the early 1950s at Oxford. Influenced by a desire to illuminate basic tenets of human psychotherapy with an ethological approach to animal behavior, W. M. S. Russell characterized the reproductive behaviors of uninjected and gonadotropin-injected frogs (Russell 1954). His descriptions included verbal characterizations assigned to each sex largely on the basis of behavioral context since no outwardly visible movements accompany vocal production.

Russell described the "croaking" given by gonadotropin-injected (and thus sexually active) males and "ticking" given by uninjected (and thus sexually inactive) females. Croaking was said to accompany the initiation of clasping of the female by the male (amplexus) and clasp maintenance; isolated males were also said to croak. When males were paired, another vocal behavior, "sawing," was produced. Croaking was described as a chirping sound ("rather like the word 'Figaro' in the 'Largo al factotum'") and sawing as continuous and low pitched; ticking was described as resembling the sound made by winding a watch (Russell 1954).

Beginning with the field observations of Vigny (1979) who described a male call ("ion-ion-ion"), the characterization of *X. laevis* vocal behaviors was clarified by the use of hydrophones and spectrographic analyses of taped vocalizations. Picker (1980, 1983) and Wetzel and Kelley (1983) also used this form of analysis in laboratory studies to characterize the "ion-ion-ion" mating or *advertisement call*. The calls given by male *Xenopus laevis* are illustrated in figure 1.1. The advertisement call consists of alternating fast and slow trills and is given both by isolated males and by males paired with female conspecifics. During amplexus the male produces a two- or three-

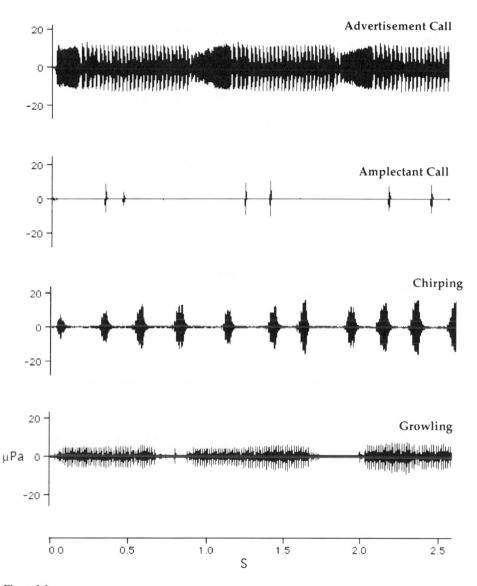

Figure 1.1

Vocal behaviors of male *Xenopus laevis*. The *advertisement call* is a continuous series of alternating fast (70Hz) and slow (35Hz) trills. The *amplectant call* consists of a two or three clicks separated by 1s silent intervals. *Chirping* consists of a short series of clicks, usually 5 or 6, separated by brief intervals (0.2–0.4s). *Growling* is a low-pitched, prolonged trill with relatively short (0.5s) intertrill intervals.

note call, the *amplectant call* (Picker 1980), which accompanies characteristic tremors of the male's body in the early phases of amplexus. Since it is also given by an isolated male after an amplectant pair is separated (Evans and Kelley unpublished data), the call appears to be a male vocal behavior. Two additional distinct calls accompany male/male interactions: *chirping* (Horng and Kelley unpublished data) and *growling* (terminology of Picker 1980; probably corresponds to Russell's "sawing"). *Chirping* consists in brief trill bouts, and *growling* is a rapid, prolonged, low pitched trill.

Two female-specific vocal behaviors have been analyzed: *ticking* (called "tapping" by Picker 1980) and *rapping* (Tobias et al. 1998). *Ticking* (figure 1.2a, inset), a low,

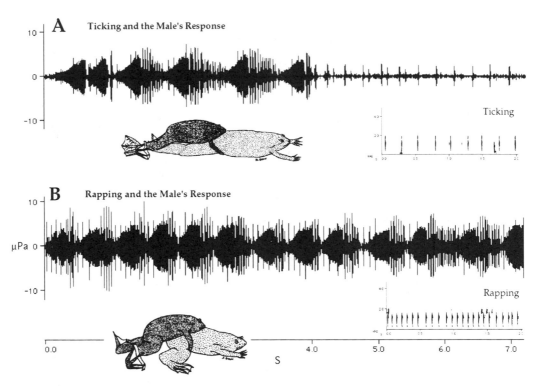

Figure 1.2
Male/female duets and vocal behaviors of female *Xenopus laevis*. (A) *Ticking* (inset) is a slow (7Hz) trill given by sexually unreceptive females. *Ticking* suppresses and outlasts male calling. (B) *Rapping* (inset) is a rapid (16Hz) and irregular trill which stimulates male calling in general and the *answer call* in particular. The answer call resembles the *advertisement call* in consisting of alternating fast and slow trills. However, the fast trill portion is longer and the short trill portion shorter than the *advertisement call*; amplitude modulation of the fast trill is pronounced.

monotonous trill, is given by a sexually unreceptive female when she is clasped by a male or when, after multiple clasp attempts, she is approached by a vocalizing male. *Rapping* (figure 1.2b, inset) is a more rapid and variable trill that acoustically resembles the response of a Geiger counter to ionizing radiation. *Rapping* is given by a sexually receptive female just prior to oviposition (Tobias et al. 1998).

The evidence to date suggests that each of these calls is sex-specific. Females *rap* and *tick*; males produce *advertisement* and *amplectant calls*, *chirps* and *growls*. The vocal repertoire thus provides a rich investigative arena in which to examine the functions of sex-specific calls in social communication as well as the cellular and molecular mechanisms that participate in confining specific calls to females or to males.

Acoustic Analyses of Vocal Communication

The basic unit of vocal behaviors in *X. laevis* is a click, a brief and noisy burst of sound. The component frequencies of the click range from 0.5 to 2kHz with sex-specific characteristic spectral peaks (Wetzel and Kelley 1983; Watson and Kelley 1992). Fast fourier transform analyses suggest that the component frequencies of clicks from *rapping* and *ticking* are identical (peak frequencies ∼1.2kHz). The clicks in *advertisement calling* contain higher frequency components (∼1.8kHz; Wetzel and Kelley 1983) but the clicks in *growling* are made up of lower frequencies (<1kHz). How the frequency of each click is modulated is not known.

Each call consists of a series of clicks in rapid succession (a trill). Temporal pattern, rate, and duration acoustically distinguish different calls (see figure 1.1). Male *advertisement calling* consists in alternating fast (70Hz) and slow (35Hz) trills. The beginning of a calling bout is often characterized by an initial, slower trill (see Picker 1980). *Advertisement calling* is a high intensity vocal behavior: measurements of calling males in glass aquaria reveal a peak sound pressure level of 120dB re 20mNewtons/m^2 (Paton et al. 1982). The *amplectant call*, in contrast, is a lower intensity vocal behavior consisting in two or three individual clicks given at 4–7Hz. *Chirping* is a series of very short trills, typically consisting of 5 clicks; each bout is separated from the next by a short interval (200–400ms). *Growling* consists of ∼700ms bouts of a very rapid (100Hz) trill. *Ticking* (figure 1.2A, inset) is a slower (∼4Hz) series of clicks that is typically less intense than *rapping*. *Rapping* (figure 1.2B, inset) is a rapid (∼16Hz) series of individual clicks which can be as intense as the clicks in *advertisement calling* (Tobias et al. 1998).

Call durations depend on conspecific vocalizations and behaviors. The duration of *ticking* and *rapping*, for example, depends strongly on the male's response. Multiple or prolonged clasp attempts by males elicit more rapid and prolonged bouts of *ticking* in females (Hannigan and Kelley 1986). Because *ticking* is evoked by clasping (during which males can be silent) and suppresses male calling, it can be produced unaccompanied by male vocal behaviors (figure 1.2A; Tobias et al. 1998). *Rapping*, however, evokes intense calling from males and is seldom heard alone in paired animals (figure 1.2b). *Rapping* duets are produced by sexually active pairs that are physically separated by a barrier. Whether females would continue *rapping* without contingent calling from a male (i.e., during a tape of advertisement calling) has not been studied. Sexually active males *advertisement call* for prolonged periods; under laboratory conditions an individual male will call, on average, for 45m out of a 90m observation period (Wetzel and Kelley 1983). While *chirping* and *growling* have not been studied intensively, they are given during male/male interactions and it would be surprising if their durations did not also depend on the partner's response.

Functional Studies of Vocal Communication

How this rich vocal repertoire is used in social communication (Wells 1977) is a current focus of our work. *Advertisement calling* attracts sexually receptive females (Picker 1980, 1983); whether the call also functions in male/male communication has not been studied. Picker (1980) comments that *growling* accompanies male/male clasping and may function as a release call. *Chirping* accompanies *growling* during male/male clasping but both vocalizations occur in male/male pairs that are not clasping (Horng and Kelley unpublished data). In South Africa, the beginning of the breeding season is accompanied by a complex series of vocal behaviors that include some of the male/male calls described above (Tobias unpublished data). We are examining the hypothesis that the complex vocal repertoire of males is used in establishing a male vocal hierarchy tied to reproductive status.

With respect to female-specific vocal behaviors, *ticking* is part of a suite of behaviors, evoked from sexually unreceptive females by male clasp attempts, that elicit release from amplexus (Weintraub et al. 1985). *Ticking* is thus considered to be a release call (Wells 1977), but we do not know whether broadcasts of *ticking* alone would be sufficient, in the absence of other behavioral cues, for the male to release the female from amplexus. *Ticking* (either given by a female or broadcast from a taped recording) suppresses male calling (figure 1.2a; Tobias et al. 1998). *Rapping* is a female advertisement call produced just prior to oviposition (Tobias et al. 1998). *Rapping* stimulates and alters male vocalizations. In response to a *rapping* female or to a broadcast of taped *rapping*, males increase the amount of time spent calling and alter their calls such that the fast portion of the *advertisement call* trill is lengthened, its amplitude modulation is increased, and the slow portion of the trill is shortened (figure 1.2b). The changes produced in the male's advertisement call are stereotyped and constitute the *answer call*. As long as the female *raps*, the male answers; if *rapping* decreases, the male reverts to the *advertisement call*. The reciprocal signaling between a *rapping* female and an *answering* male resembles the duetting seen between male/female pairs of neotropical birds (Farabaugh 1982).

Males also *answer call* to *ticking* females or to tapes of *ticking*. Unlike the response to *rapping*, however, *ticking* suppresses all calling in males and males do not revert to *advertisement calling*. The acoustic cues available to males for distinguishing *rapping* from *ticking* include rate and duration (Tobias et al. 1998). What cues the male actually uses are not yet known. The time required for a male to switch from *advertisement* to *answer calling* in response to either female vocalization can be short (<100ms), a time window that places some constraints on the recognition of these calls by acoustically activated regions of the central nervous system (see below).

The Development of Neuroethological Approaches

The work of Hutchison at the University of Natal in South Africa during the 1960s first brought the study of *X. laevis* into the neuroethological fold. Hutchison was concerned primarily with the neural basis for clasping, a prominent component of amplexus in the male (Hutchison 1964), rather than vocal behavior. However, his study of the neural basis of the clasp reflex together with Russell's (1954) descriptions of sex-typical calls suggested to us that *X. laevis* might be a useful system for neuroethological studies of vocal communication. In particular, we wished to account for the marked sex differences in vocal behaviors. Why, for example, is *advertisement calling* confined to males? Answering this question has required an understanding of the mechanisms of vocal production—particularly the "vocal circuitry" in the central nervous system and the control of vocal behaviors by vocal muscles and motor neurons —and an understanding of the differences in the functions of these elements produced by differences in exposure to gonadal steroids during development and in adulthood.

Mechanisms of Vocal Production

Hormonal Control of Reproductive Vocalizations

The courtship vocalizations of *Xenopus laevis*, like other reproductive behaviors, are under the control of gonadal steroids, particularly androgens and estrogens. The role of gonadal steroids was first suggested by the observation that gonadotropin injections are ineffective in gonadectomized animals (Russell 1954; Kelley and Pfaff 1976). Male *advertisement calling* is abolished by castration and restored by treatment with exogenous androgens; dihydrotestosterone is particularly effective (Wetzel and Kelley 1983). Androgen replacement, however, is not sufficient to completely restore *advertisement calling* to precastrate levels. A synergistic effect of gonadotropin and androgen on *advertisement calling* in castrated males supports the idea that while steroids are necessary for the production of reproductive behaviors, these agents act in concert with other nonsteroidal hormones that include gonadotropin-releasing hormones, gonadotropins, thyrotropin, and prostaglandins (Kelley 1982; Wetzel and Kelley 1983; Weintraub et al. 1985; Taylor and Boyd 1991).

The endocrine control of *rapping* has not yet been thoroughly studied. *Rapping* is induced by treatment with gonadotropin which also induces ovulation and oviposition. Hormones associated with ovulation, such as estradiol 17β released by the ovary, or oviposition, such as prostaglandins synthesized within the oviduct (reviewed in Kelley 1996), are candidates for possible endocrine modulation of *rapping*. *Ticking* is suppressed by prostaglandin administration (Weintraub et al. 1985) or by androgen treatment (Hannigan and Kelley 1986); neither estrogen nor progesterone suppresses *ticking*. Estradiol secretion from the ovary does appear to be responsible for female-specific characteristics of the functional physiology of the vocal organ (see below; Tobias and Kelley 1995; Tobias et al. 1998) and is thus an endocrine candidate for the vocalizations associated with changes from sexually unreceptive (*ticking*) to sexually receptive (*rapping*) states.

Sound Production and Sound Reception

Clicks are produced by the vocal organ or larynx (Ridewood 1898). The larynx (figure 1.3) is a box-like structure of muscle and cartilage that is highly modified in the genus *Xenopus* for the production of sounds underwater. It communicates with the buccal cavity anteriorly, via the glottis, and with lungs posteriorly, via paired tracheae. The cartilages of the laryngeal skeleton are complex, the major structural elements being composed of hyaline and thyohyral cartilages while the sound-producing disks are arytenoid cartilage (Yager 1992). In males, and in androgen-treated females, the larynx also contains elastic cartilage (Fischer et al. 1995).

The detailed mechanism of sound production by the larynx in *X. laevis* is not yet understood; however, in another species within the genus, *borealis*, Yager (1992) has observed that movements of the apposed, paired arytenoid disks are associated with click production. Each disk is attached via a tendon to a pair of intrinsic laryngeal muscles, the bipennate or laryngeal dilator muscles. Yager hypothesizes that when

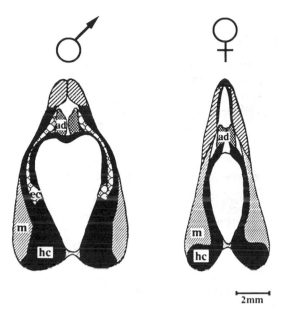

Figure 1.3
The larynx or vocal organ of *Xenopus laevis* is sexually dimorphic in adulthood. The major structural components of the larynx include hyaline cartilage (hc) which forms the cartilaginous box, arytenoid cartilage which forms the sound producing arytenoid disks (ad), surrounded (in males) by elastic cartilage (ec). Sounds are produced when the laryngeal bipennate muscles contract and, acting via tendonous insertions onto the arytenoid disks, pull the disks apart. From Fischer and Kelley 1991.

the force of muscle contraction exceeds the surface tension of the mucopolysaccharide liquid separating the disks, the resultant implosion of air constitutes a click. The larynx is bilaterally symmetrical and the movements of the arytenoid disks are mechanically coupled, a feature that may increase the efficiency of sound production. The mechanism of sound production in the *Xenopus* larynx is thus a relatively simple one that does not, presumably because of its production underwater, require concommitant respiration. This feature has greatly facilitated analysis of the neural and muscular control of vocal production.

Each click in a call is thought to be produced by contraction of the laryngeal muscles in response to action potentials in the laryngeal nerves. These nerves originate in the laryngeal motor nucleus (N. IX–X) located in the posterior brainstem just rostral to the spinal cord (figure 1.4; Kelley 1980). Nucleus IX–X contains both motor neurons and a population of interneurons, neurons whose axons do not exit the central nervous system (Kelley et al. 1989; Watson and Kelley 1989). Neuro-anatomical studies suggest that N. IX–X receives at least two inputs: one from the

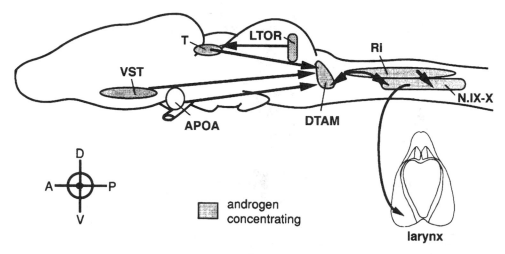

Figure 1.4
Vocal nuclei in the central nervous system of *Xenopus laevis*. Motor neurons in cranial nerve nucleus IX-X
(N. IX-X) project via the laryngeal nerve to the bipennate muscles. N. IX-X contains motor neurons and
interneurons and receives projections from adjacent inferior reticular formation (Ri) and a superior retic-
ular nucleus, the dorsal tegmental area of the medulla (DTAM); in males this connection is reciprocal.
DTAM receives input from the dorsal diencephalon (auditory thalamus: T) and ventral telencephalon
(APOA: anterior preoptic area; VST, ventral striatum). The laminar nucleus of the torus semicircularis
(LTOR) provides auditory input to the thalamus.

adjacent inferior reticular formation (Ri) and another from a group of neurons
located in the superior reticular formation, nucleus DTAM (Wetzel et al. 1985).
Nucleus DTAM in turn receives input from auditory regions of the diencephalon
(see below) and from the ventral forebrain (figure 1.4).

The tympanum in *X. laevis* is located beneath the skin in the fascia covering the
musculature of the head; the tympanic disk is, relative to the size of the skull, twice
as large in males as in females (Elephandt 1996). The auditory papillae (reviewed in
Elephandt 1996) are innervated by a branch of the VIIIth nerve (Wever 1985) which
enters the medulla and synapses on second-order neurons within a dorsomedial zone,
the dorsal acoustic medulla (Altman and Dawes 1983; Simpson et al. 1986). These
project contralaterally to the auditory midbrain or *torus semicircularis*; toral nuclei
including the laminar nucleus respond to auditory stimuli in *X. laevis* (Kelley 1980;
Paton et al. 1982; Kelley and Capranica unpublished data). Midbrain neurons project anteriorly to thalamic nuclei, including the central nuclei of the dorsal thalamus,
and thalamic cells project to ventral striatum in the telencephalon, where cells can be
driven by auditory stimuli (Birkhofer et al. 1994). The response characteristics of

auditory neurons in *Xenopus laevis* have not been studied and we do not yet know which are involved in the discrimination of salient features in the vocal communication system. In previous studies on *Ranid* frogs, Capranica demonstrated that thalamic neurons can be selectively activated by acoustic features present in *advertisement calls* (Mudry and Capranica 1987). We do not yet know which CNS regions are involved in acoustically mediated behaviors such as phonotaxis nor have we yet identified those that participate in discriminating *rapping* from *ticking*.

Sex Difference in Vocal Neuroeffectors

Male and Female Vocal Effectors

Both the vocal organ itself and the neural circuitry underlying vocal production are sexually differentiated in number, biochemical and morphological characteristics, and connectivity. In the central nervous system of adults, males have more laryngeal motor neurons than females (Kelley and Dennison 1990) and the dendritic arbors of interneurons in the male N. IX–X are longer and more complex in males (Kelley et al. 1988). Nucleus DTAM stains more intensely for succinic dehydrogenase (a mitochondrial enzyme associated with metabolic activity) in males (Haerter and Kelley unpublished data), and the projection from N. IX–X to DTAM appears to be absent in females as is the APOA to DTAM projection (Wetzel et al. 1985). Two unresolved questions are the origins of these sex differences in the adult and to what extent they are responsible for sex differences in the vocal repertoire. We do not know whether sex differences in connectivity reflect the ongoing actions of gonadal steroids; for example, the APOA to DTAM connection might require the high levels of circulating androgen characteristic of the adult and be absent in females with their low androgen levels (Kang et al. 1995). Alternatively, connectivity within the vocalization circuit might be permanently established by different developmental programs in the sexes. With respect to behavior, we do not know how the circuitry identified using neuroanatomical tracing methods actually generates the vocal patterns of male- and female-typical behaviors. How does the male brain generate the *advertisement calling* pattern or the female brain the *rapping* pattern? Do sex differences in connectivity of vocal nuclei contribute to sex differences in vocal production? Some insight into the relation between CNS sex differences and behavior has come, however, from examining the isolated laryngeal synapses of males and females; these studies are described below (*Vox in vitro*).

The vocal organ of *X. laevis* is also characterized by a dramatic sexual dimorphism (figure 1.3): the male and female larynx differ markedly in structural, functional, biochemical, and synaptic elements. The sexes share the basic laryngeal elements of the cartilaginous box of hyaline cartilage, the longitudinally running thyohyral rods which provide stiffness, and the laryngeal dilator muscles, bipennate pairs which pull apart the arytenoid disks. The larynx is, however, larger in males than in females due to greater cartilage and muscle mass. The male larynx contains a type of cartilage, elastic cartilage, present in the female only as an undeveloped precursor zone (Fischer et al. 1995). The function of elastic cartilage is not clear, but its apposition to the arytenoid disks and its presence in males suggest that it might contribute to the male's ability to produce rapid clicks (Yager 1992). To the same end, male laryngeal muscle is entirely fast twitch whereas female muscle is predominantly slow twitch (Sassoon et al. 1987).

Vox in vitro: Singing in the Isolated Larynx

When the larynx is removed from the animal and the laryngeal nerves are stimulated electrically, clicks very similar to the clicks of actual vocalizations are produced (figure 1.5; Tobias and Kelley 1987). This characteristic reflects the emancipation of underwater vocal production from airflow and has allowed us to analyze the relation between sex differences in laryngeal characteristics and sex-typical calls.

A vocalization that resembles *advertisement calling* can be produced by isolated male larynges when the nerve is stimulated with the appropriate pattern, 250ms at 35Hz and 750ms at 70Hz. Each shock delivered to the nerve produces muscle activity (muscle action potentials are recorded as the electromyogram or EMG); the resultant muscle contraction produces a tension transient via the tendons that insert onto the arytenoid disks. When suprathreshold transients are produced, the resultant movements of the arytenoid disks produce a series of clicks that resemble the clicks found in actual calls (Tobias and Kelley 1987). The male laryngeal muscle can faithfully follow rates of nerve stimulation up to 100Hz. The female larynx, however, cannot produce clicks in response to rapid (>25Hz) nerve activity. At 33Hz, for example, the male larynx produces an EMG and a tension transient in response to each shock delivered to the nerve; clicks are produced after the third shock and increase in loudness throughout the stimulus train (figure 1.5, upper panel). At 33Hz, the female larynx also produces an EMG response and a change in tension for each shock delivered to the nerve. However, only a single click is produced (figure 1.5, lower right-hand panel). The tension record reveals that female laryngeal muscle responds to 33Hz nerve stimulation with tetany. The female muscle cannot relax sufficiently between stimuli at this rate to return the tension transients to baseline. The arytenoid disks open once, producing a click, but are then held open by continued muscle contraction preventing further click production. When the rate of

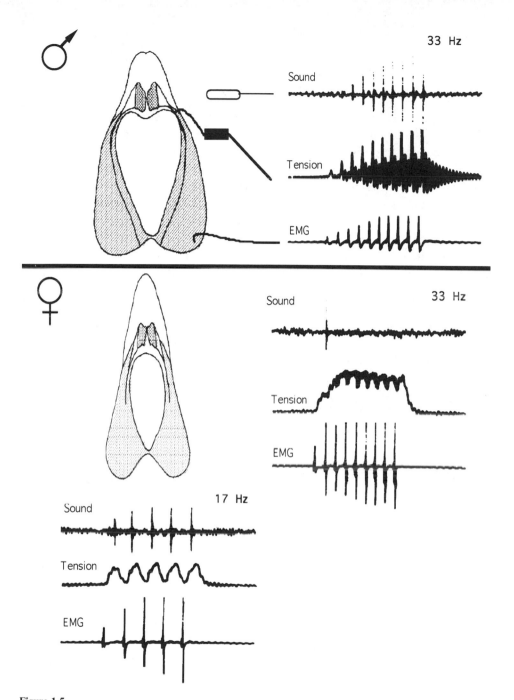

Figure 1.5
Vox in vitro. Sound, tension, and electromyographic (EMG) recordings from isolated male (upper panel) and female (lower panels) larynges in response to nerve stimulation at 33 (male) or 17 and 33Hz (female).

nerve stimulation is decreased to 17Hz (the average rate, for example, of *rapping*) complete tension transients that return to baseline are produced and a click follows each muscle contraction (figure 1.5, lower left-hand panel).

Thus even if the female laryngeal nerve conveyed rapid activity (at, for example, *advertisement call* rates) from the central nervous system, a powerful peripheral limitation would prevent the female larynx from producing rapid trills. Whether the patterns of activity generated by the male and female CNS differ is a current focus of research.

When male *Xenopus* answer a female, the fast portions of their calls are highly amplitude-modulated: each successive click is louder than the preceding one. Amplitude modulation is also apparent in the *vox in vitro* preparation of the male larynx; this pattern of amplitude modulation cannot be evoked by nerve stimulation in the female larynx (figure 1.6). Potentiation of the electromyogram is associated with

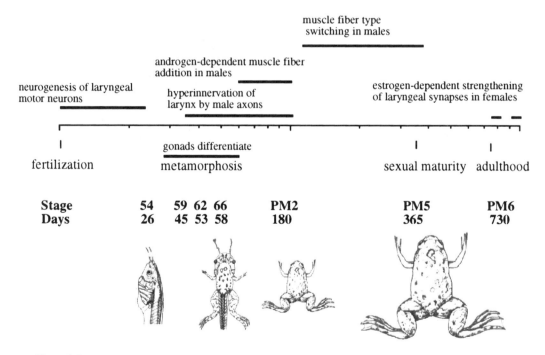

Figure 1.6
Sexual differentiation of neural and muscular effectors for vocal behavior in *X. laevis*. The period from fertilization (0 days) to adulthood (~730 days) is shown using a logarithmic scale. Stages of tadpole development correspond to the Normal Table of Nieuwkoop and Faber (1956); postmetamorphic stages correspond to the masculinization stages of Tobias et al. 1991b.

properties of the synapse between laryngeal motor neurons and laryngeal muscle fibers. As the clicks produced by the male larynx become louder, the EMG becomes progressively larger, indicating the successive recruitment of muscle fibers throughout the fast portion of the trill.

Intracellular recordings from laryngeal muscle fibers reveal that most fibers in males produce only a subthreshold excitatory potential to a single shock delivered to the laryngeal nerve (Tobias and Kelley 1988). These subthreshold potentials become progressively larger during trains of nerve activity (i.e., they facilitate) until the threshold for muscle-fiber action potential production is reached and the fiber contracts. The progressive recruitment of laryngeal muscle fibers during trains of nerve activity could be due to facilitation of the weak synapse of males if fibers have somewhat different thresholds for action potential production. In contrast, female laryngeal synapses are strong; single shocks to the laryngeal nerve produces suprathreshold postsynaptic potentials that result reliably in muscle fiber contraction (Tobias and Kelley 1988). The laryngeal neuromuscular synapse thus uses sex differences in synaptic efficacy to produce sex-typical features of the vocal repertoire.

What is the locus of sex differences in synaptic efficacy in the vocal system? A quantal analysis of synaptic transmission at the vocal synapse suggests that the locus is presynaptic: adult males release less neurotransmitter per nerve impulse than females (Tobias et al 1995). This conclusion derives from an examination of the quantal contents of the laryngeal synapse of adults. Under the same ionic conditions, the quantal content at male synapses was depressed relative to female synapses. We saw no evidence of a sex difference in the postsynaptic receptor: miniature endplate potential amplitudes and rise times were the same and the structure of the active zone could not be distinguished using ultrastructural methods (freeze fracture and transmission electron microscopy). Somewhat to our surprise, the sex difference in quantal content is not accompanied by a sex difference in the ability of the synapse to facilitate in response to repeated nerve stimulation (Ruel et al. 1998).

Gonadal Hormones and Their Targets

Sexually differentiated vocal behaviors in *Xenopus laevis* reflect the actions of gonadal steroids on target tissues. The major gonadal steroids in *X. laevis* are the androgens, testosterone and dihydrotestosterone (Kang et al. 1995), the estrogens, primarily estradiol 17b (Wright et al. 1983), and the progestins such as progesterone (Baulieu et al. 1978). The receptors for these steroids are ligand-activated transcription factors that belong to a large family of nuclear receptors (reviewed in Thornton and Kelley 1998). The hormones are secreted by the gonads and carried through the bloodstream to specific tissues where they are retained within the nuclei of target cells. The expression of a specific steroid hormone receptor thus marks a cell population whose pattern of gene expression (and thus development and physiology) can be directly influenced by exposure to that hormone.

A remarkable feature of the vocal system in *X. laevis* is that expression of these receptor proteins marks the vocal circuit in the central nervous system as well as the vocal organ itself. Using radioactively tagged ligands, the locations for sex-steroid receptors have been mapped in the *X. laevis* nervous system (Kelley et al. 1975; Morrell et al. 1975; Kelley 1980; Roy et al. 1986). Androgen-concentrating neurons are found within most of the CNS nuclei implicated in the generation of song including N. IX–X, Ri, and DTAM (see figure 1.4). The highest level of expression of the AR gene is in N. IX–X, including the laryngeal motor neurons (Perez and Kelley 1996) which form the final common path for vocal production.

Androgen receptors are not, however, confined to the brain. Biochemical studies reveal the presence of high affinity, high specificity androgen-binding in the larynx of adults and juveniles (Segil et al. 1987; Kelley et al. 1989). Levels of androgen-receptor gene expression are highest in juvenile larynges, probably because proliferating myoblasts and chondroblasts express high levels of the β androgen receptor isoform (see below; Fischer et al. 1993, 1995).

In males, androgens are required for the production of *advertisement calls*; castrated males stop singing within a few weeks after gonadectomy, and androgens, testosterone and dihydrotestosterone, restore song (Wetzel and Kelley 1983). As described above, both the vocal organ and neurons in vocal nuclei of the CNS express androgen; where does androgen act to activate male calling? Since the isolated larynx of adult castrated males can produce the mating call (Watson and Kelley 1992), it is likely that androgen activates central vocal neuroeffectors. Our current evidence thus suggests that androgens are required during adulthood for the generation of the *advertisement call* pattern by the central nervous system.

Cellular and Molecular Analyses of Sexual Differentiation in Vocal Neuroeffectors

Developmental Actions of Steroid Hormones; Muscle and Motor Neurons

The earliest signs of sexual differentiation in the laryngeal system can be discerned at tadpole stage 59 when the axons of vocal motor neurons in males are more numerous than those of females (figure 1.6; Kelley and Dennison 1990). Antiandrogen blocks this hyperinnervation and androgen promotes hyperinnervation, suggesting that hormonal regulation of the sexually differentiated vocal system begins during late tadpole stages (Robertson et al. 1994). The masculinization of the larynx starts after metamorphosis is complete and finishes approximately 6 months later; the acquisition of male-typical cell numbers and cell types requires gonadal androgen (reviewed in Kelley 1996). The sexual differentiation of synaptic efficacy begins in adulthood, after the female is reproductively mature (>2 years postmetamorphosis; Tobias et al. 1998).

When the *Xenopus* androgen receptors were cloned (He et al. 1990; Fischer et al. 1993), the vocal organ of juvenile *Xenopus* was found to express extremely high levels of the androgen-receptor gene, among the highest in any vertebrate. Expression of the androgen-receptor gene peaks in the developing larynx and falls as the organ matures, suggesting that the receptor plays a role in the androgen-regulated development of the vocal organ (Kelley et al. 1989; Fischer et al. 1995). Two mRNA isoforms were recognized, an α isoform that is constituitively expressed in all laryngeal cells and a β isoform that is expressed in stem cells, both myoblasts and chondroblasts. We have hypothesized that expression of the β isoform is required for the mitogenic action of androgen on laryngeal stem cells (Fischer et al. 1993).

Because both the central and peripheral components of the vocal system express androgen receptor, distinguishing the site of action of hormone effects is complicated by their synaptic interconnections. Some insight is afforded by examining effects of hormone treatment in animals in which the laryngeal nerve has been severed on one side. Using hormone-treated juveniles subject to unilateral axotomy we have shown that androgen control of muscle fiber type does not require innervation but androgen-induced muscle fiber number increases do require innervation (Tobias et al. 1993). For the laryngeal motor nucleus, we have shown that androgen rescues neurons from axotomy-induced cell death; rescue is accompanied by increased expression of the AR gene and maintenance of calbindin (a calcium buffering protein) expression (Perez and Kelley 1996, 1997). Thus androgen can act on motor neurons without a connection to androgen-sensitive muscle and on muscle deprived of innervation from androgen sensitive motor neurons. It is likely, however, that many developmental and physiological regulatory mechanisms involve reciprocal signaling between synaptically connected, androgen target, nerve and muscle partners.

The Sexually Differentiated Vocal Synapse

The weak, facilitating laryngeal synapses of a male allow him to produce the amplitude-modulated trills he uses to answer females; these weak synapses are associated with low quantal contents (Tobias et al. 1995). To determine when the sex difference in quantal content first arises we examined synaptic strength in juveniles. At six months after the end of metamorphosis (stage PM2 of Tobias et al. 1991a), quantal content is low in both sexes (Tobias and Kelley 1995); synaptic efficacy in females increases abruptly at 26 months after the end of metamorphosis (figure 1.6; Tobias et al. 1998). Males thus retain subthreshold synapses, a juvenile feature which adult females lose as they become fully mature.

How does the vocal synapse become sexually differentiated? We considered two possible scenarios; first that male synapses are maintained in a subthreshold state under the influence of gonadal androgen, and second that a subthreshold synapse is the developmental "default state" and female synapses become suprathreshold for action potential production under the influence of ovarian estrogen. Our evidence to date supports the second hypothesis: treatment with estrogen increases quantal content at the laryngeal synapse of juveniles. Neither androgen treatment nor castration has major effects on quantal content (Tobias and Kelley 1995). Some evidence that estrogen secretion is the endogenous factor in control of synaptic efficacy comes from the observation that high quantal content in developing females accompanies maturation of the reproductive tract and the sustained production of high levels of estradiol; adult females lose their strong sysapses if ovariectomized (Tobias et al. 1998).

How and where estrogen acts to increase synaptic efficacy is unknown. The ultimate effect must be on the laryngeal motor neuron since we cannot detect postsynaptic differences in adults (Tobias et al. 1995). Laryngeal motor neurons do not, however, accumulate radioactive estrogen in their cell nuclei (Morrell et al. 1975). One possibility is that laryngeal muscle fibers produce a retrograde signal in response to estrogen, which strengthens the female synapse. Preliminary support for this possibility is generated by the ability to detect expression of the estrogen-receptor gene in laryngeal muscle using reverse transcription polymerase chain reactions and ribonuclease protection assays (Wu et al. 1997). If a classic nuclear receptor mechanism is ruled out, it is still possible that estrogen acts on synaptic membranes via an as yet undescribed receptor mechanism, perhaps one coupled to increases in calcium influx. Alternatively, estrogen might change the characteristics or pattern of the expression of synaptic vesicle associated proteins to increase their sensitivity to calcium influx or may regulate channel open times.

Critical and Sensitive Periods for Androgen Action on Vocal Behaviors

A powerful idea, used to good effect by Peter Marler in his early studies of song learning in birds, is that of the critical or sensitive period, a time during which a specific influence such as hearing the song of another male can permanently influence a behavior produced when the animal is fully adult (reviewed in Marler 1990). This framework has also been used by Eric Knudsen in his studies of the alignment of auditory and visual receptive fields in the owl midbrain. He distinguishes sensitive periods, times during which an experience normally acts to produce a particular behavioral result, from critical periods, times in which this same experience can "rescue" a deprived animal (reviewed in Knudsen and Brainard 1995).

Many developmental actions of steroid hormones are also confined to limited periods (reviewed in Kelley 1992). The literature on sexual differentiation has historically focused on hormonal control of masculinization because the early stages of female-typical development can proceed in the absence of the gonads (the "default" program). Males can be demasculinized by castration, and gonadectomized juveniles of both sexes can be masculinized by hormone treatment at specific times; "rescue" experiments thus typically consist of masculinizing a behavior in a female or a gonadectomized male. Because of the permanence of many developmental actions of steroid hormones, their actions have been described as "organizational"; in contrast, the reversible effects of hormones on adult animals have been termed "activational" (Phoenix et al. 1959).

Are there critical or sensitive periods for hormone action on the developing song system in *Xenopus*? Our early experiments suggested that androgen action was confined to early stages of development. Castrated adult males will produce *advertisement calls* if given an implant of testosterone or dihydrotestosterone while ovariectomized adult females will not, even if androgen-treated for several years (Hannigan and Kelley 1986; Watson and Kelley 1992); perhaps androgen must be present earlier in development to masculinize the female's vocal system. However, if female *X. laevis* receive a testicular transplant (instead of an androgen implant) and sufficient time is allowed for masculinization (>10 months), they will produce a recognizable *advertisement call* (Watson and Kelley 1992). The earlier the testicular transplant is performed during juvenile development, the closer in acoustic quality the song produced by the female is to a male *advertisement call*. Even adult females after ovariectomy and testis transplant, however, can produce an *advertisement call* recognizable by alternating fast and slow trills. We can conclude from these studies that provision of androgen does not recreate the endocrine stimulation provided by a transplanted testis; androgens may be necessary but not sufficient for masculinizing the behavioral phenotype. Females retain, even into adulthood, the capacity to respond to testicular secretions with masculinization; the critical period for testicular rescue of the masculine behavioral phenotype extends into adulthood.

Cellular and Molecular Underpinnings of Critical and Sensitive Periods; Cell Type

The vocal systems of adult male and female *Xenopus* differ in cell type, and differences in behavior can be related to these differences in the neuroeffector unit. For example, the rapid trills of mate-calling require an entirely fast twitch muscle. Slow twitch muscle tetanizes during rapid activity; during development males do not begin to produce mate calls until the last slow twitch fibers convert to fast (Tobias et al. 1991a). This sexually differentiated muscle fiber-type composition reflects a developmental program that, in males, requires gonadal androgen secretion. At the end of metamorphosis, most muscle fibers are slow twitch in both sexes and thus resemble the pattern seen in adult females (Tobias et al. 1991a). For the next six months, males add muscle fibers at a rapid rate and females more slowly (Marin et al. 1990); despite fiber addition, the predominantly slow fiber type pattern of the newly metamorphosed juvenile is preserved during this period. When fiber numbers have attained a near adult complement, the laryngeal muscles of males start to convert from slow to fast twitch until an entirely fast twitch complement is achieved 6 to 9 months later (Tobias et al. 1991a).

From this evidence we conclude that the rapid trills of male *advertisement calling* are subserved by an entirely fast twitch vocal muscle that results from an androgen-driven developmental program. Other muscles do not change their complement of fiber types in response to androgen. How then is sexual differentiation of fiber type confined to the larynx? We believe that the answer lies in the expression of an unusual myosin-heavy chain gene, LM or laryngeal myosin (Catz et al. 1992). Using a probe containing the 3' coding and noncoding sequences, we detect expression of LM in all laryngeal muscle fibers of adult males and some laryngeal fibers in females—all of these are fast fibers. No other muscle fiber of the adult has yet been shown to express LM. It is likely that expression of the LM gene contributes to the sexually differentiated contractile properties of adult laryngeal muscle.

During development, the LM gene is expressed first at the end of metamorphosis in both sexes; expression is then maintained and enhanced in males but not females (Catz et al. 1995; Edwards et al. 1999). The maintenance of LM expression requires gonadal androgen secretion; castration at the end of metamorphosis blocks LM expression in male larynges, and androgen treatment increases expression in female larynges (Catz et al. 1995). What opens the sensitive period for androgen effects on LM expression? In amino acid sequence, LM is most similar to embryonic myosins (Catz et al. 1992) but ribonuclease protection assays indicate that the LM gene is not expressed in the larynx until metamorphosis is complete (Edwards et al. 1999). From this point on, LM expression can be regulated by exposure to androgen.

Recent evidence suggests that the pituitary hormone, prolactin, opens the sensitive period for androgen-regulation of LM expression (Edwards and Kelley 1997). How long the potential for androgen-regulation of LM persists without exposure to prolactin (the length of the critical period) is not known.

Another example of a sex difference in cell type with a clear behavioral consequence is the strength of the laryngeal synapse. The weak, facilitating synapses of males strengthen with use and can recruit successively larger populations of muscle fibers to contract, thus producing an amplitude modulated call. Synapses start out subthreshold in both sexes and become strong in females as a consequence of exposure to estrogen (see above). Juvenile synapses in both sexes strengthen in response to estrogen and adult female synapses weaken when the ovary, an estrogen source, is removed (Tobias and Kelley 1995; Tobias et al. 1998). Strengthening the laryngeal synapse in females usually occurs late in development, >2 years after metamorphosis is complete. The presynaptic terminal of the laryngeal motor neuron probably retains the capacity to regulate neurotransmitter release in response to estrogen into adulthood, and the effects of estrogen are reversible. Estrogen-regulation of synaptic efficacy thus displays neither a sensitive nor a critical period and exemplifies a purely activational affect of the hormone.

Cellular and Molecular Underpinnings of Critical and Sensitive Periods; Cell Number

One difference between androgen-treated adult females that do not *advertisement call* and testis-transplanted females that do is that in the former the number of laryngeal motor neurons and muscle fibers remain female-like, whereas in the latter cell numbers are masculinized (Watson et al. 1993). The association between cell number and behavioral masculinization is not confined to *Xenopus laevis*. Another example is provided by the birdsong system in which telencephalic vocal control nuclei are typically larger in males than in females due to sex differences in number and size of neurons (Nottebohm and Arnold 1976). In the rat, the number and size of motor neurons in the SNB nucleus, which controls copulatory reflexes (Sachs 1982), is also greater in males (Breedlove and Arnold 1980). How do the greater numbers of cells in males contribute to behavioral performance? For motor neurons, one might argue that a greater number in males is required to direct a greater male muscle mass (size matching) or produce more finely graded muscle contractions (fine tuning). In *X. laevis* the greater numbers of laryngeal muscle fibers and motor neurons might permit males to produce relatively subtle acoustic features, such as amplitude modulation. Another possibility is that the larger numbers permit males to call for extended periods of time; if not all motor neurons or fibers are active simultaneously, inactive cells have increased opportunities for recovery during prolonged periods of activity.

Neither of these ideas is supported by the limited experimental evidence: in females with testis transplants neither amplitude modulation nor the amount of time calling correlate with cell numbers (Watson and Kelley 1992; Watson et al. 1993). An alternative is that androgen-regulation of target cell numbers is important for establishing the synaptic connectivity of motor neurons (Kelley 1988); the larger numbers of cells present in adult males may simply be a residual effect of the developmental program that establishes sex differences in synaptic connectivity.

The greater number of laryngeal muscle fibers of adult male *Xenopus* is due to an androgen-driven myogenic program (Sassoon and Kelley 1986). After metamorphosis is complete, males begin adding muscle fibers at an average rate of ~150/day until the adult complement is attained 6 months later. Castration halts but does not reverse muscle fiber addition (Marin et al. 1990). Adult females maintain a reserve population of myogenic cells that permit the addition of new muscle fibers in response to testicular secretions. The survival and continued responsiveness of these myoblasts presumably accounts for the increased number of muscle fibers induced in adult females by a testicular transplant (Watson et al. 1993); muscle fiber addition can thus be said to have an extended critical period.

What opens the sensitive period for muscle fiber addition? Exogenous androgen does not induce growth of laryngeal muscle until metamorphosis is initiated at late tadpole stages (Robertson and Kelley 1996); the secretion of thyroxine is required for androgen-induced cell proliferation in the larynx (Cohen and Kelley 1996). Like LM expression, then, the sensitive period for androgen action is opened by another hormone: prolactin from the pituitary for LM and thyroxine from the thyroid for proliferation.

In the birdsong and rat SNB systems, the greater number of neurons in males is attributable to androgen rescue from cell death during development. This mechanism also accounts for sex differences in laryngeal motor neuron number in *Xenopus* (Kay et al. 1999). Androgen treatment does not induce tritiated thymidine labeling in neurons of N. IX–X in either adults or juveniles (Segil et al. 1987; Perez and Kelley 1996), suggesting that neurogenesis cannot account for increased number. All of the laryngeal motor neurons present in adulthood are generated during early tadpole life (Gorlick and Kelley 1987); number peaks in males during late tadpole stages and then declines until adult values are reached 6 months after the end of metamorphosis (Kelley and Dennison 1990; Perez and Kelley 1996). If both neurogenesis and ontogenetic cell death are complete at juvenile stages, what accounts for the ability of testicular transplants to increase laryngeal motor-neuron axon numbers at later stages (Watson et al. 1993)? The most intriguing possibility is that androgen can respecify interneurons within the CNS to redirect their axons to the periphery and innervate newly formed laryngeal muscle fibers.

The Acoustic Worlds of Males and Females

We are beginning to understand how vocalizations in *X. laevis* are produced, but we know much less about how calls are perceived. Part of the difficulty in this area is that bioassays for perception have been either unavailable or unreliable. For example, Picker established that the male mating call attracts females (Picker 1980); broadcasts of taped male calls induced females to swim to the speaker with a characteristic behavioral approach pattern (Picker 1983). Even after hormone priming (with HCG to induce ovulation, separation of pairs in amplexus immediately prior to testing), less than a third of his females responded to the broadcast calls in any way, perhaps because females are only attracted to male calls at a particular stage in ovulation/oviposition. We have obtained similar results. The low frequency of female responsiveness in laboratory playback experiments has impeded investigation of several issues including the behavioral significance of amplitude modulation, although preliminary results suggested that amplitude-modulated calls were more attractive to females than calls from which amplitude modulation had been removed (Tobias et al. 1991).

A significant advance in this area has come from the discovery of *rapping*, a call made by ovipositing females. Males respond to a tape of *rapping* in a manner indistinguishable from the response to a *rapping* female (Tobias et al. 1998). The response includes rapid orienting movements to the sound source, production of repeated answer calls, short latency-positive phonotaxis, and (more rarely) attempted amplexus with the speaker. Under laboratory conditions, provided that the male is vocalizing spontaneously, he will approach the sound source. The enhanced reliability of this response permits analysis of the salient acoustic feature of *rapping*. In particular, we can determine what cues the male uses to distinguish *rapping* from *ticking*, vocalizations that differ reliably only in duration and loudness. Given the strong selective pressure for males to locate a rare ovipositing female, it is even possible that *rapping* and *ticking* are perceived categorically, another favorite idea of Peter Marler's. This theory can be tested systematically by varying temporal and loudness parameters (morphing *rapping* into *ticking* and vice versa) and observing whether and for how long the male answers or remains silent, orients and approaches, or avoids.

We have focused most of our attention on *advertisement calling, rapping*, and *ticking*, but it is becoming increasingly clear that the vocal repertoire of *Xenopus laevis* is much more complex. What determines which male sings on a given night? Why do males *growl* and *chirp*? What is the function of the *amplectant call*? An elaborate vocal repertoire suggests a more subtle use of signaling than generally acknowledged, and there may be many ways in which individual frogs communicate during the African night.

References

Altman, J. S. and Dawes, E. A. (1983) A cobalt study of medullary sensory projections from lateral line nerves, associated cutaneous nerves, and the VIIIth nerve in adult *Xenopus*. *J. Comp. Neurol* 213:310–326.

Andersson, M. (1994) *Sexual Selection*. Princeton, NJ: Princeton University Press.

Balinsky, B. I. (1969) The reproductive ecology of amphibians of the Transvaal highveld. *Zool. Afr.*: 4:37–93.

Baulieu, E.-E., Godeau, F., Scoderet, M., and Schodert-Slatkine, S. (1978) Steroid-induced meiotic division in *Xenopus laevis* oocytes: Surface and calcium. *Nature* 275:593–598.

Birkhofer, M., Bleckmann, H., and Gorner, P. (1994) Sensory activity in the telencephalon of the clawed toad, *Xenopus laevis. Eur. J. Morphol.* 32:262–266.

Breedlove, S. M. and Arnold, A. P. (1980) Hormone accumulation in a sexually dimorphic motor nucleus of the rat spinal cord. *Science* 210:564–566.

Catz, D., Fischer, L., and Kelley, D. B. (1995) Androgen regulation of a laryngeal-specific myosin heavy chain isoform whose expression is sexually differentiated. *Dev. Biol.* 171:448–457.

Catz, D., Fischer, L., Tobias, M., Moschella, T., and Kelley, D. (1992) Sexually dimorphic expression of a laryngeal-specific, androgen-regulated myosin heavy chain gene during *Xenopus laevis* development. *Dev. Biol.* 154:366–376.

Cohen, M. and Kelley, D. (1996) Androgen-induced proliferation in the developing larynx of *Xenopus laevis* is regulated by thyroid hormone. *Dev. Biol.* 178:113–123.

Darwin, C. (1871) *The Descent of Man and Selection in Relation to Sex.* London: J. Murray.

Edwards, C. J., Yamamoto, K., Kikuyama, S., and Kelley, D. B. (1999) Prolactin opens the sensitive period for androgen regulation of a larynx-specific myosin heavy chain gene. *J. Neurobiol.*, in press.

Elepfant, A., Ringeis, A., and Fischer, W. (1995) Calling and territoriality in the clawed frog, *Xenopus laevis*. In *Nervous Systems and Behaviour,* ed. by M. Burrows, T. Matheson, P. Newland, and H. Schuppe. Stuttgart: Georg Thieme Verlag.

Elephandt, A. (1996) Underwater acoustics and hearing in the clawed frog, *Xenopus*. In *The Biology of* Xenopus, ed. by R. Tinsley and H. Kobel, pp. 177–193. Oxford: Oxford University Press.

Farabaugh, S. (1982) The ecological and social significance of duetting. In *Acoustic Communication in Birds*, D. E. Kroodsme and E. H. Miller volume 2, pp. 85–124. New York: Academic Press.

Fischer, L. and Kelley, D. B. (1991) Androgen receptor expression and sexual differentiation of effectors for courtship song in *Xenopus laevis. Seminars in the Neurosciences* 3:469–480.

Fischer, L., Catz, D., and Kelley, D. B. (1993) An androgen receptor mRNA isoform associated with hormone-inducible cell proliferation. *Proc. Natl. Acad. Sci.* 90:8254–8258.

Fischer, L., Catz, D., and Kelley, D. B. (1995) Androgen-directed development of the *Xenopus laevis* larynx: Control of androgen receptor expression and tissue differentiation. *Dev. Biol.* 170:115–126.

Graf, J.-D. (1996) Molecular approaches to the phylogeny of *Xenopus*. In *The Biology of* Xenopus, ed. by R. Tinsley and H. Kobel, pp. 143–176. Oxford: Oxford University Press.

Gorlick, D. and Kelley, D. B. (1987). Neurogenesis in the vocalization pathway of *Xenopus laevis. J. Comp. Neurol.* 254:614–627.

Hannigan, P. and Kelley, D. B. (1986) Androgen-induced alterations in vocalizations of female *Xenopus laevis*: Modifiability and constraints. *J. Comp. Physiol.* A 158:17–28.

He, W.-W., Fischer, L., Sun, S., Bilhartz, D., Zhu, X., Young, C., Kelley, D. B., and Tindall, D. (1990) Molecular cloning of androgen receptor from divergent species with the PCR technique: Complete cDNA sequence of the mouse androgen receptor and isolation of cDNA probes from dog, guinea pig and frog. *Biochem. Biophys. Res. Comm.* 171:697–704.

Hutchison, J. B. (1964) Investigations on the neural control of clasping and feeding in *Xenopus laevis* (Daudin). *Behaviour* 24:47–66.

Hutchison, J. and Poynton, J. (1963). A Neurological study of the clasp reflex in *Xenopus laevis* (Daudin). *Behaviour* 22:41–63.

Kalk, M. (1960) Climate and breeding in *Xenopus laevis*. *S. Afr. J. Sci.* 56:271–276.

Kang, L., Marin, M., and Kelley, D. (1995) Androgen biosynthesis and secretion in developing *Xenopus laevis*. *Gen. Comp. Endocrinol.* 100:293–330.

Kay, J. N., Hannigan, P., and Kelley, D. B. (1999) Trophic effects of androgen: Development and hormonal regulation of neuron number in a sexually dimorphic vocal motor nucleus. *J. Neurobiol.*, in press.

Kelley, D. (1980) Auditory and vocal nuclei of frog brain concentrate sexhormones. *Science* 207:553–555.

Kelley, D. (1981) Locations of androgen-concentrating cells in the brain of *Xenopus laevis*: Autoradiography with 3H-dihydrotestosterone. *J. Comp. Neurol.* 199:221 131.

Kelley, D. B. (1982) Hormone control of female sex behavior in South African clawed frogs, *Xenopus laevis*. *Horm. Behav.* 1:158–174.

Kelley, D. B. (1988) Sexually dimorphic behavior. *Ann. Rev. Neurosci.* 11:225–251.

Kelley, D. B. (1992) Opening and closing a hormone-regulated period for the development of courtship song. *Annals of the New York Academy of Sciences* 662:178–188.

Kelley, D. B. (1996) Sexual differentiation in *Xenopus laevis*. In *The Biology of* Xenopus, ed. by R.Tinsley and H. Kobel, pp. 143–176. Oxford: Oxford University Press.

Kelley, D. B. and Dennison, J. (1990) The vocal motor neurons of *Xenopus laevis*: Development of sex differences in axon number. *J. Neurobiol.* 21.869–882.

Kelley, D., Fenstemaker, S., Hannigan, P., and Shih, S. (1988) The sexually dimorphic laryngeal motor neurons of *Xenopus laevis*. A Quantitative Golgi study. *J. Neurobiol.* 19:413 429.

Kelley, D. B., Morrell, J. I., and Pfaff, D. W. (1975) Autoradiographic localization of hormone-concentrating cells in the brain of an amphibian, *Xenopus laevis*. *J. Comp. Neurol.* 164:63–78.

Kelley, D. B. and Pfaff, D. W. (1976) Hormone effects on male sex behavior in adult South African clawed frogs, *Xenopus laevis*. *Hormones and Behavior* 7:159–182.

Kelley, D., Sassoon, D., Segil, N., and Scudder, M. (1989) Development and hormone regulation of androgen receptor levels in the sexually dimorphic larynx of *Xenopus laevis*. *Dev. Biol.* 131:111–118.

Kelley, D. B., Weintraub, A. S., and Bockman, R. S. (1987) Oviductal prostaglandin synthesis and female sexual receptivity in *Xenopus laevis*. In *Advances in Prostaglandin, Thromboxane and Leukotriene Research*, Vol. 17B, ed. by B. Samuelsson, R. Paoletti, and P. Ramwell, pp. 1133–1135. New York: Raven Press.

Knudsen, E. I. and Brainard, M. S. (1995) Creating a unified representation of visual and auditory space in the brain. *Ann. Rev. Neurosci.* 18:19–43.

Marin, M., Tobias, M., and Kelley, D. (1990) Hormone-sensitive stages in the sexual differentiation of laryngeal muscle fiber number in *Xenopus laevis*. *Development* 110:703–771.

Marler, P. (1990) Song learning: The Interface between behaviour and neuroethology. *Phil. Trans. Roy. Soc. Lond.* 329:109–114.

Morrell, J. I., Kelley, D. B., and Pfaff, D. W. (1975) Autoradiographic localization of hormone-concentrating cells in the brain of an amphibian, *Xenopus laevis*. *J. Comp. Neurol.* 164:63–78.

Mudry, K. M. and Capranica, R. R. (1987) Correlation between auditory evoked responses in the thalamus and species-specific call characteristics. *J. Comp. Physiol.* A160:477–489.

Nieukoop, P. D. and Faber, J. (1956) *Normal Table of* Xenopus laevis *(Daudin)*. Amsterdam: North Holland Publishing Company.

Nottebohm, F. and Arnold, A. P. (1976) Sexual dimorphism in vocal control areas of the songbird brain. *Science* 194:211–213.

Paton, J., Kelley, D., Sejnowski, T., and Yodlowski, M. (1982) Mapping the auditory CNS of *Xenopus laevis* with 2 -deoxyglucose autoradiography. *Brain Res.* 249:15–22.

Pérez, J. and Kelley, D. (1996) Trophic effects of androgen: Receptor expression and the survival of laryngeal motor neurons after axotomy. *J. Neurosci.* 16:6625–6633.

Pérez, J. and Kelley, D. B. (1997) Androgen mitigates axotomy-induced decreases in calbindin expression in motoneurons. *J. Neurosci.* 17:7396–7403.

Phoenix, C., Goy, R., Gerall, A., and Young., W. (1959) Organizing action of prenatally administered testosterone propionate on the tissues mediating mating behavior in the female guinea pig. *Endocrinol.* 65:369–382.

Picker, M. (1980) *Xenopus laevis* (Anura:Pipidae) mating systems—A preliminary synthesis with some data on the female phonoresponse. *S. Afr. J. Zool.* 15:150–158.

Picker, M. D. (1983) Hormonal induction of the aquatic phonotactic response of *Xenopus*. *Behaviour* 86:74–90.

Ridewood, W. (1898) On the structure and development of the hyobranchial skeleton and larynx in *Xenopus* and *Pipa*; with remarks on the affinities of the aglossa. *Linn. Soc. J. Zool.* 26:53–128.

Robertson, J. and Kelley, D. B. (1996) Thyroid hormone controls the onset of androgen sensitivity in the developing larynx of *Xenopus laevis*. *Dev. Biol.* 178:15–101.

Robertson, J., Watson, J., and Kelley, D. B. (1994) Androgen directs sexual differentiation of laryngeal innervation in developing *Xenopus laevis*. *J. Neurobiol.* 25:1625–1636.

Roy, E., Wilson, M. A., and Kelley, D. B. (1986) Estrogen-induced progestin receptors in the brain and pituitary of the South African clawed frog, *Xenopus laevis*. *Neuroendo.* 42:51–56.

Ruel, T., Kelley, D., and Tobias, M. (1998) Facilitation at the sexually differentiated laryngeal synapse of *Xenopus laevis*. *J. Comp. Physiol.* 182:35–42.

Russell, W. (1954) Experimental studies of the reproductive behavior of *Xenopus laevis*. I. The control mechanisms for clasping and unclasping, and the specificity of hormone action. *Behaviour* 7:113–188.

Sachs, B. D. (1982) Role of striated penile muscles in penile reflexes, copulation, and induction of pregnancy in the rat. *Journal of Reproduction and Fertility* 66:433–443.

Sassoon, D. and Kelley, D. (1986) The sexually dimorphic larynx of *Xenopus laevis*: Development and androgen regulation. *Am. J. Anat.* 177:457–472.

Sassoon, D., Gray, G., and Kelley, D. (1987) Androgen regulation of muscle fiber type in the sexually dimorphic larynx of *Xenopus laevis*. *J. Neurosci.* 7:3198–3206.

Segil, N., Silverman, L., and Kelley, D. B. (1987) Androgen-binding levels in a sexually dimorphic muscle of *Xenopus laevis*. *Gen. Comp. Endocrinol.* 66:95–101.

Simpson, H., Tobias, M., and Kelley, D. B. (1986) Origin and identification of fibers in the cranial nerve IX–X complex of *Xenopus laevis*: Lucifer Yellow backfills in vitro. *J. Comp. Neurol.* 244:430–444.

Taylor, J. and Boyd, S. (1991) Thyrotropin-releasing hormone facilitates display of reproductive behavior and locomotor behavior in an amphibian. *Horm. Behav.* 25:128–136.

Thornton, J. and Kelley, D. B. (1998) Evolution of the androgen receptor: Structure-function implications. *BioEssays* 23:860–869.

Tinsley, R. C., Loumont, C., and Kobel, H. R. (1996) Geographical distribution and ecology. In *The Biology of* Xenopus, ed. by R. Tinsley and H. Kobel, pp. 143–176. Oxford: Oxford University Press.

Tinsley, R. C. and McCoid, M. J. (1996) Feral populations of *Xenopus* outside Africa. In *The Biology of* Xenopus, ed. by R. Tinsley and H. Kobel, pp. 143–176. Oxford: Oxford University Press.

Tobias, M., Bivens, R., Nowicki, S., and Kelley, D. B. (1991) Amplitude modulation is an attractive feature of *X. laevis* song. *Soc. Neurosci. Abstr.* 17:1403.

Tobias, M. and Kelley, D. B. (1987) Vocalizations of a sexually dimorphic isolated larynx: Peripheral constraints on behavioral expression. *J. Neurosci.* 7:3191–3197.

Tobias, M. and Kelley, D. B. (1988) Electrophysiology and dye coupling are sexually dimorphic characteristics of individual laryngeal muscle fibers in *Xenopus laevis*. *J. Neurosci.* 8:2422–2429.

Tobias, M. and Kelley, D. B. (1995) Sexual differentiation and endocrine regulation of the laryngeal synapse in *Xenopus laevis*. *J. Neurobiol.* 28:515–526.

Tobias, M., Kelley, D. B., and Ellisman, M. (1995) A sex difference in synaptic efficacy at the laryngeal neuromuscular junction of *Xenopus laevis*. *J. Neurosci.* 15:1660–1668.

Tobias, M., Marin, M., and Kelley, D. B. (1991a) Development of functional sex differences in the larynx of *Xenopus laevis*. *Dev. Biol.* 147: 251–259.

Tobias, M., Marin, M., and Kelley, D. B. (1991b) Temporal constraints on androgen directed laryngeal masculinization in *Xenopus laevis*. *Dev. Biol.* 147:260–270.

Tobias, M., Marin, M., and Kelley, D. B. (1993) The roles of sex, innervation and androgen in laryngeal muscle of *Xenopus laevis*. *J. Neurosci.* 13:324–333.

Tobias, M. L., Tomasson, J., and Kelly, D. B. (1998) Attaining and maintaining strong vocal synapses in female *Xenopus laevis*. *J. Neurobiol.* 37:441–448.

Tobias, M., Viswanathan, S., and Kelley, D. B. (1998) Rapping, a female receptive call, initiates male/female duets in the South African clawed frog. *Proc. Natl. Acad. Sci.* 95:1870–1875.

Trueb, L. (1996) Historical constraints and morphological novelties in the evolution of the skeletal system of pipid frogs (Anura:Pipidae). In *The Biology of* Xenopus, ed. by R. Tinsley and H. Kobel, pp. 143–176. Oxford: Oxford University Press.

Vigny, C. (1979) The mating calls of 12 species and sub-species of the genus *Xenopus* (Amphibia: Anura). *J. Zool. Lonf.* 188:103–123.

Watson, J. and Kelley, D. B. (1989) Development of sex differences in dendritic length in *Xenopus laevis* larngeal motor neurons. *Soc. Neurosci. Abstr.* 15:579.

Watson, J. and Kelley, D. (1992) Testicular masculinization of vocal behavior in juvenile female *Xenopus laevis*: Prolonged sensitive period reveals component features of behavioral development. *J. Comp. Physiol.* 171:343–350.

Watson, J., Robertson, J., Sachdev, U., and Kelley, D. (1993) Laryngeal muscle and motor neuron plasticity in *Xenopus laevis*: Analysis of a sensitive period for testicular masculinization of a neuromuscular system. *J. Neurobiol.* 24:1615–1625.

Weintraub, A., Kelley, D., and Bockman, R. S. (1985) Prostaglandin E2 induces receptive behaviors in female *Xenopus laevis*. *Horm. Behav.* 19:386–399.

Wells, K. (1977) The social behavior of anuran amphibians. *Anim. Behav.* 25:666–693.

Wetzel, D. and Kelley, D. (1983) Androgen and gonadotropin control of the mate calls of male South African clawed frogs, *Xenopus laevis*. *Horm. Behav.* 17:388–404.

Wetzel, D., Haerter, U., and Kelley, D. (1985) A Proposed efferent pathway for mate calling in South African clawed frogs, *Xenopus laevis*: Tracing afferents to laryngeal motor neurons with HRP-WGA. *J. Comp. Physiol.* A 157:749–761.

Wever, G. E. (1985) *The Amphibian Ear*. Princeton, NJ: Princeton University Press.

Wright, C., Wright, S., and Knowland, J. (1983) Partial purification of estradiol receptor from *Xenopus laevis* liver and levels of receptor expression in relation to estradiol concentration. *EMBO J.* 2:973–977.

Wu, K.-H., Kelley, D. B., and Tobias, M. L. (1997) Estrogen receptor in laryngeal muscle of *Xenopus laevis*. *Abstr. Soc. Neurosci.* 23:797.

Yager, D. (1992) A Unique sound production system in the pipid anuran *Xenopus borealis*. *Zool. J. of the Linnean Society* 104:351–375.

2 The Motor Basis of Vocal Performance in Songbirds

Roderick A. Suthers

One of the striking attributes of oscine birdsong, suborder Passeres, is its acoustic diversity. The role that this extreme variety in tempo, frequency range, structure, and repertoire size has in vocal communication (Searcy 1986; Searcy and Brenowitz 1988; Read and Weary 1992; Searcy 1992; Hauser 1996) and its basis in the mechanisms of song production (Gaunt 1983; Konishi 1985; Gaunt 1987; Nowicki and Marler 1988; Vicario 1991; Konishi 1994; Brenowitz and Kroodsma 1996; Nottebohm 1996; Suthers and Goller 1998) are important issues in understanding the acoustic behavior of this exceptional group. Ironically, the oscine vocal organ, the syrinx, is as noteworthy for its absence of morphological diversity as the song it produces is for its presence. The basic plan of the syrinx is surprisingly similar in all oscines and the modest variation that exists in this group (King 1989) does not prepare us for the variety of their vocal skills. How is it that, using essentially the same peripheral vocal apparatus, different songbirds vary so widely in their vocal ability?

The peripheral vocal system has evolved with the ears and brain to transform the electrical signals of the nervous system into acoustic signals for vocal communication. If we are to appreciate its vital role in this process we must understand how this transformation takes place. In this chapter I adopt a comparative perspective to examine the relationship between different motor strategies and vocal performance in songbirds. By exploiting, in different ways, the acoustic flexibility made possible by the two independent and laterally specialized sound sources contained in their syrinx, songbirds have increased and diversified their vocal skills. Recent information on the production mechanisms underlying this acoustic diversity provides new insights into the evolutionary choices associated with different song properties and allows a more accurate assessment of the motor constraints on song structure.

A variety of different techniques have been employed to investigate the peripheral mechanisms responsible for song production (see reviews by Brackenbury 1973; Gaunt et al. 1973; Gaunt and Gaunt 1985b; Gaunt 1987; Brackenbury 1989). Approaches to this subject have included inferences about vocal mechanisms based on syringeal anatomy and acoustic properties of song (e.g., Greenewalt 1968), analysis of song deficits after surgical intervention (e.g., Nottebohm 1971; Nowicki and Capranica 1986b; McCasland 1987; Hartley and Suthers 1990), measurement of various physiological parameters during other kinds of vocalizations from restrained birds (e.g., Gaunt et al. 1973; Gaunt and Gaunt 1985a; Gaunt 1986) and mathematical modeling (e.g., Fletcher 1988; Fletcher 1989).

More recently it has also been possible to directly monitor respiratory and motor events during spontaneous song from behaving birds with both sides of their syrinx

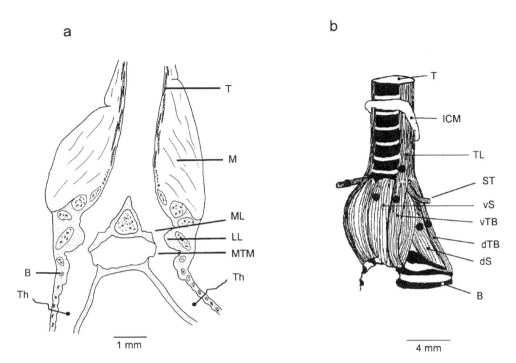

Figure 2.1
The oscine syrinx is a bipartite structure containing two sound sources. (a) Frontal section through a brown thrasher syrinx. Th, position of microbead thermistor to measure rate of airflow through each side of syrinx. See Suthers (1990) and Suthers et al. (1994) for detailed methods and surgical procedures. (b) Ventrolateral external view of a thrasher syrinx depicting syringeal muscles. Black dots indicate for one side the approximate location where bipolar wire electrodes were placed. Abbreviations: T, trachea; M, syringeal muscle; ML, medial labium; LL, lateral labium; MTM, medial tympaniform membrane; B, bronchus; ICM, membrane of the interclavicular air sac; TL, m. tracheolateralis; ST, m. sternotrachealis; vS, m. syringealis ventralis; vTB, m. tracheobronchialis ventralis; dTB, m. tracheobronchialis dorsalis; dS, m. syringealis dorsalis. (Modified from Goller and Suthers 1996a. © American Physiological Society, reproduced with permission.)

functionally intact. This is accomplished by inserting a microbead thermistor into each primary bronchus (figure 2.1a) to record the rate of respiratory airflow. These thermistors also monitor the ipsilaterally generated sound, up to about 4kHz, by detecting flow oscillations associated with the vibrating labia. Concurrent measures of respiratory pressure, obtained with a miniature piezoresistive pressure transducer attached to a cannula in a cranial thoracic air sac, permit the direction of airflow to be determined. Changes in the syringeal aperture, or resistance to airflow, can be calculated from flow and pressure. The activity of various syringeal or respiratory muscles can be determined from their electromyograms (EMG), which are recorded with a pair of very fine wires inserted into the muscle (Suthers. 1990; Suthers et al. 1994; Goller and Suthers 1995a). Small wires carrying these physiological signals are attached to a miniature electrical connector on a backpack worn by the bird. Other flexible wires rise from the backpack through the top of the cage and transmit these data to recording instruments, leaving the subject free to move about its cage.

These various experimental approaches have substantially increased our understanding of how song is produced. They reveal some aspects of song production that appear to be shared by all species studied, despite the diverse properties of their songs, as well as other mechanisms that differ according to the type of song.

Song Production in the Bipartite Syrinx: Basic Mechanisms

Independent Sound Generators in Left and Right Sides of the Syrinx

Oscine songbirds have a tracheobronchial syrinx, formed of modified cartilages at the confluence of the bronchi and trachea and suspended in the interclavicular air sac. The arrangement of this bipartite vocal organ, which contains a separate set of sound generators at the cranial end of each bronchus (figure 2.1; King 1989), gives additional versatility to the ways song can be produced and has far-reaching ramifications for our understanding of song diversity.

The structures in each bronchus that produce sound have been widely assumed to be the medial tympaniform membranes (Miskimen 1951; Greenewalt 1968), but recent endoscopic observations of the syrinx during spontaneous vocalization by the common crow (*Corvus brachyrhynchos*) and vocalizations induced by brain stimulation in northern cardinals (*Cardinalis cardinalis*) and brown thrashers (*Toxostoma rufum*) (Goller and Larsen 1997) suggest that sound is produced instead by vibration of the medial and lateral labia on each side of the syrinx (figures 2.1a and 2.2). Prior to sound production, these labia are adducted into the syringeal lumen where they meet to form a narrow slit. During vocalization, air is forced though this slit in an expiratory direction and both labia can be seen to vibrate, probably driven by Bernoulli forces. Goller and Larsen further showed that bilateral destruction of the medial tympaniform membranes has only a modest effect on song production.

Sound generation on each side of the syrinx is controlled by the ipsilateral members of several bilaterally paired syringeal muscles (figure 2.1b). The motor neurons innervating these muscles are located in the ipsilateral hypoglossal nucleus, where their activity is controlled by the efferent output of the brain's system of song control nuclei (e.g., Brenowitz and Kroodsma 1996; Yu et al. 1996; Wild 1997).

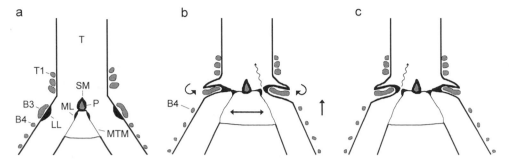

Figure 2.2
Schematic ventral view of the songbird syrinx in quiet respiratory (a) and phonatory positions (b, c). In preparation for phonation the syrinx moves rostrad and the lateral and medial labia are drawn into the lumen through rotation of bronchial cartilages mediated by contraction of syringeal muscles (arrows). Unilateral phonation is achieved by full closure of one side of the syrinx (right in b, left in c) whereas on the contralateral side the labia vibrate and generate sound. Abbreviations: T, trachea; T1, first tracheal cartilage; B3, B4, third and fourth bronchial cartilage, SM, semilunar membrane; P, pessulus; ML, medial labium; LL, lateral labium; MTM, medial tympaniform membrane. (Modified after Suthers and Goller 1997.)

Ventral Syringeal Muscles Control the Fundamental Frequency

The two sides of the brain can deliver different motor programs to the left and right sides of the syrinx, giving each side an ability to generate sound independently (Suthers 1997). The possibility that the two sides of the syrinx contribute different frequency components to song was noted more than a century ago (see Greenewalt 1968). Greenewalt (1968) and Stein (1968) were, however, the first to undertake a more rigorous, systematic analysis of birdsong, providing strong circumstantial evidence for two acoustical sources presumed to arise from the left and right sides of the syrinx. Syllables of this type, that contain temporally overlapping or concurrent components that are not harmonically related, are referred to as "two-voice" syllables. Two-voice syllables are common features in the songs of a number of species (figure 2.3).

The fundamental frequency of song elements generated on each side of the syrinx is regulated independently by the large ipsilateral ventral syringeal muscles. These muscles insert onto a bronchial cartilage and control the fundamental frequency on the ipsilateral side, presumably by varying the tension of the vibratory sound-generating structures. In singing brown thrashers, the fundamental frequency generated on each side of the syrinx has a positive exponential correlation with the EMG of the ipsilateral ventral syringeal muscle (figs. 2.1 and 2.4; Goller and Suthers 1995b; Goller and Suthers 1996a).

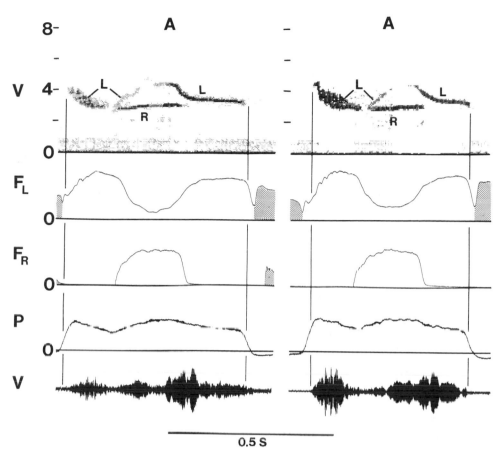

Figure 2.3
Example of a brown thrasher syllable with a prominent two-voice component. These two presentations were separated by 38 syllables of different types, indicating a high degree of acoustic and motor stereotypy. Each syllable type is characterized by a distinctive pattern of bilateral airflow and subsyringeal air sac pressure. Air sac pressure (P) is positive during vocalization. Zero line equals ambient pressure. Oscillogram of the vocalization (V) at bottom is also shown spectrographically at top. Sound frequency in kHz. The rate of air flow through the left (F_L) and right (F_R) sides of the syrinx show that the beginning and end of the syllable is generated primarily on the left side but that the right side an almost constant frequency element (R) during the middle of the syllable at the same time the left side is generating a sinusoidal frequency modulation (L). Horizontal lines equal zero airflow; stippled areas equal inspiration; vertical lines mark beginning and end of syllable. (From Suthers, Goller, and Hartley 1996 © John Wiley and Sons Inc., reproduced by permission.)

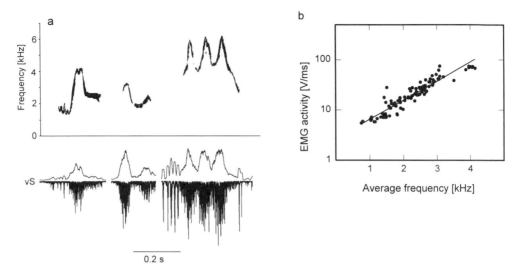

Figure 2.4
Role of ventral syringeal muscles in the control of sound frequency by brown thrashers. (a) Amplitude of EMG activity is positively correlated with frequency modulation of sounds produced on the ipsilateral side. (b) Amplitude of EMG activity is exponentially correlated with the fundamental frequency of ipsilaterally generated sounds. EMG activity was averaged over segments of syllables having a relatively constant frequency. vS, EMG of M. syringealis ventralis. See fig. 2.2 for explanation. (From Goller and Suthers 1996a. © American Physiological Society, reproduced by permission.)

The need to accurately produce the often complex spectral patterns of song places rigorous demands on the bird's ability to control the frequency of each song element. The exact frequency of certain notes or syllables is an important aspect of vocal communication in some species. Male black-capped chickadees (*Parus atricapillus*), for example, control the frequency change precisely within and between the two "fee bee" notes of their advertising song. Female chickadees are sexually less responsive to male advertising songs in which these frequency relationships have been experimentally altered, suggesting that accurate frequency control during the production of these notes is important in sexual communication (Weisman and Ratcliffe 1989; Weisman et al. 1990; Weisman and Ratcliffe 1992; Ratcliffe and Otter 1996). The whistled "fee bee" notes of the chickadee contrast with the wideband "dee" syllables. The latter contain a stack of different frequency components, which Nowicki and Capranica (1986a) concluded arise from nonlinear interactions between the two sides of the syrinx. This kind of bilateral interaction has not yet been found in other birdsong.

Dorsal Syringeal Muscles Turn Sound Production On and Off

The complexity of song is further increased by the songbird's ability to control which side(s) of the syrinx produce sound at any instant. A note may be generated only on one side of the syrinx, or on both sides, or sound production can be switched from one side to the other. Lateral switches of this kind can occur either between syllables or even during the course of a single syllable. In all of these instances, the timing (or gating) of sound generation in each half-syrinx is regulated by the valving action of the dorsal syringeal muscles, *M. syringealis dorsalis* and *M. tracheobronchialis dorsalis* (figure 2.1b). These muscles adduct the medial and lateral labia against the opening force of the elevated subsyringeal air pressure and the antagonistic syringeal abductors. Weak or incomplete adduction of the labia allows air to flow between them and induce vibration, which generates sound; full adduction silences the ipsilateral side of the syrinx by preventing airflow (figure 2.2; Suthers 1990; Suthers et al. 1994; Goller and Suthers 1995b; Goller and Suthers 1996b; Goller and Larsen 1997).

This neuromuscular gating of phonation has been studied most carefully in brown thrashers. EMG recordings from each of the six syringeal muscles in this species show that these dorsal muscles are the only ones that are consistently activated when the ipsilateral syrinx is being adducted (figure 2.5; Goller and Suthers 1995b; Goller and Suthers 1996b). By controlling the contractile force of these dorsal muscles, the bird can switch ipsilateral airflow, and therefore phonation, on or off and determine whether the left, right, or both sides of the syrinx produce sound.

Different species vary in the extent to which each side of their syrinx contributes to song. This lateralization of song production arises from the motor programs sent to the dorsal muscles that gate syringeal airflow. It is of particular interest that motor nerves to the ventral syringeal muscles, which regulate fundamental frequency, and to other syringeal muscles involved primarily with the regulation of acoustic or phonetic[1] structure continue their activity during song regardless of whether the ipsilateral syringeal valve is open or closed. Song lateralization and lateral dominance (in which one side of the syrinx produces most of the song) are thus controlled by these dorsal muscles. They regulate the aperture of the labial valve on each side of the syrinx and determine whether the ongoing phonetic motor programs arriving at the other syringeal muscles can generate sound (Goller and Suthers 1995b; Goller and Suthers 1996b; Suthers 1997).

Respiratory Adjustments for Singing

Respiratory muscles move air through the syrinx, which then converts some of this fluid energy into acoustic energy. Both sides of the syrinx are exposed to similar

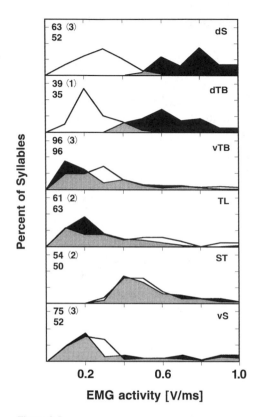

Figure 2.5
Frequency distributions of the normalized amplitude of EMG activity in syringeal muscles of brown thrashers during full adduction while the contralateral side generates sound (black area) and during ipsilaterally produced syllables (white area). The overlapping area of the two distributions is shaded. The difference in distributions is highly significant for dS and dTB ($p < 0.001$), marginal for TL ($p < 0.05$) and not significant for all other muscles ($p > 0.05$). In each panel the number of syllables measured during adduction (upper number) and phonation (lower number) is indicated, together with the number of individuals contributing to data sets for each muscle (parentheses). See fig. 2.1 for names and location of muscles (Reprinted from Goller and Suthers, "Implications for lateralization of birdsong from unilateral gating of bilateral motor patterns," *Nature* **373**: 63–66. © 1995 Macmillan Magazines Limited. Reproduced by permission.)

respiratory pressures (Brackenbury 1971), since air can flow between various laterally paired air sacs via connections across the midline or through the interclavicular air sac (McLelland 1989).

Singing requires that special motor patterns be sent to the respiratory muscles, as well as to those of the syrinx. There are significant changes in both respiratory pattern and pressure during song. Expiratory pressure increases by an order of magnitude, or more, above that during normal quiet respiration (Hartley and Suthers 1989; Suthers et al. 1994). The overall temporal pattern of song is set by the respiratory rhythm, which typically increases in rate and complexity. The temporal fine structure of song within the framework of the respiratory rhythm is further regulated by the dorsal syringeal muscles that control the timing of airflow, and hence the precise timing of notes on each side of the syrinx within each expiration.

Many birds sing continuously at a rapid tempo for long periods of time without pausing for a normal inspiration. For example, a canary (*Serinus canaria*), which has a respiratory rate between about 1.5 and 2 breaths per second while resting silently on its perch, can sing continously for 30s or more at syllable repetition rates that commonly reach 15/s and sometimes exceed 30/s (e.g., Hartley and Suthers 1989). Calder (1970) showed that the thorax of canaries expands briefly between each syllable and suggested that these expansions represent very short inspirations or "minibreaths" that make it possible for the bird to sing songs of this length. Gaunt (1973) suggested an alternative respiratory mechanism by which canaries may simply exhale pulses of air to produce each sound, instead of inhaling air between syllables. Subsequent measures of tracheal airflow in singing canaries (Hartley and Suthers 1989) showed that both minibreaths and pulsatile expiration are used, depending on the tempo of the song (see below).

The respiratory rhythm that accompanies song is produced by alternating contraction of the expiratory and inspiratory muscles. In canaries (Hartley 1990), brown thrashers (Goller and Suthers 1995a), brown-headed cowbirds (*Molothrus ater*), and zebra finches (*Taeniopygia guttata*; Wild et al. 1998), for example, the abdominal expiratory muscles are electrically active during the production of each syllable. This EMG activity varies during the course of each syllable, contributing to changes in its amplitude and other acoustic properties (Hartley 1990). At the end of each syllable the respiratory muscles generate a negative subsyringeal pressure for inspiration during the minibreath (Hartley and Suthers 1989; Goller and Suthers 1996b; Wild et al. 1998). EMG recordings from thoracic inspiratory muscles in singing cowbirds and zebra finches show that they contract with each minibreath (Wild et al. 1998). In birds that sing at a high tempo, the cyclical pattern of activity in these two muscle groups is repeated many times per second.

Singing requires a delicate, complex interplay between the activity of syringeal and respiratory muscles. The timing, magnitude, and sign of respiratory muscle activity must be accurately coordinated with that of syringeal muscles that gate sound production, modulate the fundamental frequency, and open the syrinx for each inspiration. Recently discovered connections between the song control nuclei and the respiratory system of certain finches (Vicario 1993; Wild 1993a; Wild 1993b) may provide the pathway for coordinating the activity of these two muscle groups, but very little is known about how the brain accomplishes the daunting task of generating and integrating appropriate motor programs for diverse respiratory and syringeal muscles.

Lateral Specializations of Syringeal Function

Although the two sides of the syrinx act independently, they are not necessarily equal in their ability to produce various acoustic features of song. Lateralized acoustic specializations that increase the versatility of the oscine syrinx have been found in all oscines in which syringeal function during song has been carefully studied. In some species there are clear differences in the dimensions (personal observation) or mass of the two sides of the syrinx (Luine et al. 1980), whereas in other species such differences, if present, are more subtle.

Left and Right Vocal Registers

The frequency range and spectral complexity of song is increased by lateral differences in the range of frequencies that can be generated by the syrinx. The fundamental of the left syrinx covers a lower frequency range than that of the right in those songbirds studied. In some of these species there is considerable overlap between the two sides. In other species, such as northern cardinals, the amount of overlap is small (table 2.1; Suthers and Goller 1996). The basis of this lateralized spectral difference is not known. It may arise from small differences in the dimensions or physical properties of the structures that generate sound on each side. The right side of the syrinx is slightly smaller in some species (Luine et al. 1980) and so might be expected to have a higher resonant frequency.

Lateralization of Frequency and Amplitude Modulation

In canaries (Nottebohm and Nottebohm 1976), zebra finches (Williams et al. 1992), cowbirds (see figure 2.8; Allan and Suthers 1994), and probably also in mimic thrushes (*Mimidae*; figure 2.6; Suthers et al. 1994) the right syrinx generates more

Table 2.1
Vocal registers of the left and right syrinx.

Species	Left syrinx (kHz)	Right syrinx (kHz)	Source
Northern cardinal[1]	1–4	3–7	(Suthers and Goller 1996)
Brown thrasher			
Unilateral syllables[2]	1.5–1.9	2.8–4.2	(Suthers et al. 1994)
Two voice syllables[3]	—	+0.6–+0.9	
Grey catbird[2]	1.5–2.1	2.7–3.8	(Suthers et al. 1994)
Waterslager canary[4]	1.25–2.40	2.50–4.20	(Nottebohm and Nottebohm 1976)
Brown-headed cowbird			
Introductory notes[5]	0.68	2.16	(Allan and Suthers 1994)
Entire song including whistle[6]	0.2–2.0	1.5–13.0	
Zebra finch[7]	0.515	0.780	(Williams et al. 1992)

1. Frequency range of fundamental
2. Mean minimum and mean maximum value of fundamental
3. Mean minimum and mean maximum frequency increase re left side
4. Median ranges after section of contralateral tracheosyringeal nerve
5. Average mean frequency of introductory notes
6. Frequency range
7. Mean of lowest value of fundamental after section of contalateral tracheosyringeal nerve

frequency-modulated (FM) notes than does the left. In northern cardinals, on the other hand, both sides of the syrinx contribute to the majority of FM syllables, although the left usually produces a larger portion of the syllable than the right side, and of those syllables that include only one vocal register, more are produced by the left than by the right syrinx.

In brown thrashers and gray catbirds (*Dumetella carolinensis*), the right syrinx plays a special role in generating rapid amplitude modulation (AM) that is a prominent acoustic feature of some syllables. Syringeal mechanisms for producing this kind of AM vary in detail, but they typically require rapid, cyclical adduction and abduction of the right syrinx to produce a modulation frequency up to about 100Hz, while the left side is either closed or has a less prominent cyclical fluctuation of its aperture (Suthers 1994; Goller and Suthers 1996a; Suthers et al. 1996). However, not all AM is produced by the syrinx. Relatively low AM rates are associated with changes in respiratory pressure generated by activity of expiratory muscles. Very high modulation rates, often in the range of a few hundred Hz, accompany the "difference tones" that sometimes arise between left and right frequency elements in two-voice syllables (Suthers et al. 1994; Goller and Suthers 1995a; Goller and Suthers 1996a; Suthers and Goller 1998).

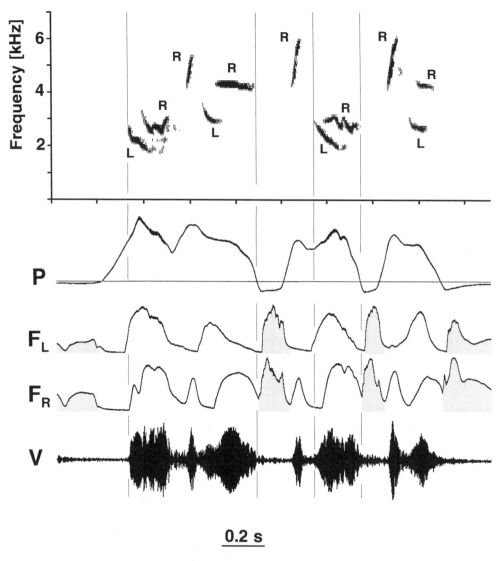

Figure 2.6
Segment of brown thrasher song showing four two-voice syllables with independent frequency modulation
of the left and right side contributions. These are separated from each other by shorter upward sweeping
syllables produced by airflow through the right syrinx while the left side is closed, and therefore silent.
Note how vocal production switches between sides of the syrinx with the vocal register of the right side
being higher than that of the left. R and L in spectrogram indicates contributions from right and left side
of syrinx; inspiratory airflow (minibreaths) is stippled. Other abbreviations as in fig. 2.2. (From Suthers
et al. 1994. © John Wiley and Sons Inc. Reproduced by permission.)

Syringeal Lateralization of Inspiration

Some songbirds exhibit asymmetries in respiratory ventilation during song such that minibreaths between song syllables are inhaled predominantly through one side of the syrinx. This is particularly prominent in waterslager canaries, which produce most of their song with the left syrinx (Nottebohm and Nottebohm 1976) while the right syrinx is closed (see below). During the minibreath between each syllable, the left side of the syrinx remains partially adducted or may even close completely while the right side is fully abducted to provide a low resistance pathway for inspiratory air (figure 2.7; Suthers 1992). In this species, both phonation and inspiration are lateralized, but to opposite sides of the syrinx. In cowbirds (Allan and Suthers 1994) and cardinals, the rate of airflow through the right side of the syrinx during a minibreath is also often greater than that through the left side, raising the possibility that inspiration is also lateralized to some extent in these species.

At least in waterslager canaries, lateralization of inspiration may provide a degree of separation between the conflicting requirements of phonatory versus inspiratory motor patterns. Especially at high syllable repetition rates, it may be advantageous not to abduct the phonatory side out of its sound-producing configuration, therefore avoiding the necessity of reconfiguring it at the end of each minibreath, which might limit syllable repetition rate or phonetic precision. This can be avoided by assigning the silent contralateral side a primary role in inspiration (Suthers 1992; Suthers 1997). It remains to be seen if this hypothesis can be applied to other species.

Patterns of Song Lateralization: Exploiting the Bipartite Syrinx to Enhance Vocal Performance

Although the respiratory and syringeal mechanisms of song production have been studied in only a few species, these birds have been selected in part because their distinctively different songs reflect the temporal and spectral diversity that is such a prominent feature of birdsong. Each of these groups has evolved specialized motor strategies, superimposed on shared principles of song production described above, which enable them to take advantage of their duplex syrinx in different ways to achieve their particular brand of "vocal virtuosity"—be it very high syllable repetition rates, extreme spectral complexity, the precision-switching of sound production from side to side, or some other acoustic feat. As more species are studied, new strategies will doubtless be discovered, but the range of vocal performance encompassed by those already investigated provides a new perspective on the relationship between song production, vocal performance, and the evolution of song diversity.

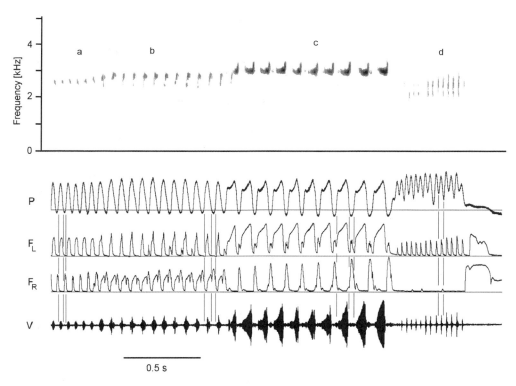

Figure 2.7
Representative segment of canary song containing 4 phrases, each composed of repetitions of a different syllable type. Each syllable type is characterized by a distinct pattern of airflow through each side of the syrinx and subsyringeal air sac pressure. Minibreaths are used in the first 3 phrases. The fourth phrase is a trill produced by pulsatile expiration through the left syrinx while air sac pressure remains positive. Phrases a, c, and d are produced in the left side of the syrinx. Phrase b is unusual in that expiration starts on the left side but switches sides in midexpiration to produce the syllable on the right. The minibreath is still on the right side. Note the lateralization of minibreaths to the right syrinx. Direction of airflow is indicated by air sac pressure. For each syllable type, the first and second vertical lines indicate expiration and the second and third lines indicate inspiration. Symbols as in legend of fig. 2.2. (From Suthers and Goller 1997. © Plenum Press.)

Independent Bilateral Phonation: Brown Thrasher and Gray Catbird

As befits their position in the family *Mimidae*, the songs of brown thrashers and gray catbirds are noteworthy for their variability. Both can sing continuously for many minutes at a relatively slow tempo of about 2 or 3 syllables per second. Due to the diversity of their song, the syllable repertoire of these birds has only been estimated. Catbirds may have repertoires of a few hundred syllables (Thompson and Jane 1969; Boughey and Thompson 1976; Lohr 1989), whereas brown thrashers probably have over a thousand syllables in their repertoire (Kroodsma and Parker 1977; Boughey and Thompson 1981). Each syllable is phonetically distinct, in terms of its morphology, from those that closely precede or follow it, with the exception of single immediate repetitions of certain syllables to form a "couplet." Couplets are much more common in the songs of thrashers than in those of catbirds (Boughey and Thompson 1976; Suthers et al. 1996). The songs of both species include a wide range of frequencies with most of the acoustic energy between about 1 and 7kHz.

Studies of syringeal and respiratory motor function in spontaneously singing catbirds and thrashers show that both produce song in a similar manner. Neither side of the syrinx has a clearly dominant role in phonation. Instead, both the left and right syrinx make about equal overall contributions to song (Suthers and Hartley 1990; Suthers et al. 1994; Suthers et al. 1996), with sound often produced simultaneously on both sides or being switched from one side to another even within a single syllable (figure 2.6). Brief inspirations between syllables provide adequate oxygen and replenish the volume of respiratory air, enabling the bird to sing continuously for many minutes.

This flexibility in using the left and right syrinx for song production enables these mimids to combine sounds produced on the two sides of the syrinx in various ways that can significantly increase the spectral complexity of the syllables in mimid song. Two-voice syllables, with independently modulated fundamentals that are not harmonically related, are common in the songs of brown thrashers and gray catbirds (figures 2.3 and 2.6). Difference tones are created by acoustic interaction between the two syringeal voices (Suthers et al. 1994). Phonetic complexity is also increased by the ability of the dorsal syringeal muscles to separately determine the timing of phonation on each side, so that the spectral components contributed by each side may follow different temporal patterns within the syllable (Suthers and Hartley 1990; Suthers et al. 1994; Suthers et al. 1996).

Lateralized acoustic specializations of the syrinx, described above, further increase the phonetic diversity in mimid song. The use of both left and right vocal registers increases the range of frequencies. Acoustic elements generated on the right side of the syrinx are usually higher in frequency and may have more FM than those generated on the left side (table 1; Suthers et al. 1994). Mimid songs also contain segments with prominent rapid AM, in which one side of the syrinx modulates the output of the other side (Suthers et al. 1994; Goller and Suthers 1996a).

The relatively long duration and deliberate pacing of syllables in mimid song is well suited for displaying the particular kind of vocal prowess made possible by independent bilateral phonation. Long syllables allow the singer to develop time-varying spectral and temporal patterns by using two voices, inserting an AM component and demonstrating fine bilateral motor coordination while switching repeatedly between sides. The phonetic complexity of mimid song does not come without a price, however (table 2.2). Bilateral phonation is expensive in its use of respiratory air, since expiratory air flows through both sides of the syrinx during song production (Suthers and Goller 1998).

Unilateral Dominance: Waterslager Canary

The characteristics of canary song are in many ways opposite those of mimic thrushes. Although canary song types vary somewhat between different domesticated strains, which have acquired inbred genetic mechanisms for learning their strain-specific songs (Mundinger 1995), the tempo is markedly faster than that of catbirds

Table 2.2
Patterns of song lateralization: Motor implications for vocal performance.

Independent Bilateral Phonation: Brown thrasher and gray catbird.

Advantages:	*Disadvantages:*
Two independent voices increase spectral and phonetic complexity.	Expensive in use of air supply. Best suited for a low syllable repetition rate.

Unilateral Dominance: Waterslager canary.

Advantages:	*Disadvantages:*
Conserves air, favoring shorter minibreaths and longer phrases with pulsatile expiration. Separation of phonatory and inspiratory motor patterns to opposite sides of syrinx. Both of these may facilitate higher syllable repetition rates.	Use of one voice limits frequency range and certain kinds of spectral and temporal complexity. Minibreath may be smaller than tracheal deadspace.

Alternating Lateralization: Brown-headed cowbird.

Advantages:	*Disadvantages:*
Enhances spectral contrast between notes. Efficient use of air supply. Extended frequency range for overall song.	Two-voice complexity limited to note overlap.

Sequential Lateralization: Northern cardinal

Advantages:	*Disadvantages:*
Extended frequency range for continuous FM sweeps. Conserves air supply.	Lacks spectral complexity of two voices.

or thrashers. The vocal differences between canaries and mimic thrushes are reflected in their different syringeal-respiratory mechanisms of song production. Studies of the physiological mechanisms of song production in the Belgian waterslager strain reveal motor mechanisms optimized for high syllable-repetition rates, which at times exceed 30/s, and the ability to sustain a rapid tempo for longer periods of time. Among canaries, waterslager song is distinctive for the presence of notes having an unusually low sound frequency and the general absence of high frequency sounds. There is little sound energy above about 4kHz. Waterslager song is composed of several phrases, each consisting of a number of repetitions of a given syllable type (figure 2.7). Song duration varies, but not uncommonly it exceeds 30s without a pause for a normal inspiration. An adult male canary may have a repertoire of two or three dozen different syllable types, several of which may be sung in successive phrases to produce a song (Nottebohm et al. 1976; Nottebohm and Nottebohm 1978; Hartley and Suthers 1990).

Waterslager canaries exhibit a strong unilateral dominance of song production in which the left syrinx produces about 90% of the song repertoire (Nottebohm and Nottebohm 1976). Simultaneous sound production in the left and right syrinx to generate two-voice syllables is rare. During phonation, the silent (typically right) side of the syrinx is closed to airflow. As soon as the syllable is finished the silent side opens for a very brief inspiratory minibreath before the syllable is repeated. During this minibreath the side (typically left) that produced the syllable may remain partially open or may close, but is not abducted to maximize inspiratory airflow (see above; figure 2.7; Suthers 1992; Suthers 1997; Suthers and Goller 1998).

Direct measurements of respiratory airflow during song (Hartley and Suthers 1989; Suthers 1997; Suthers and Goller 1998) show that singing canaries use either of two different respiratory patterns, depending on the syllable repetition rate (figure 2.7). At syllable repetition rates below about 30/s, canaries insert a minibreath between each syllable. This small inspiration prevents them from running out of air for sound production and perhaps enables them to sing longer songs (Hartley and Suthers 1989). Each of these minibreaths approximately replaces the volume of air exhaled to produce the previous syllable. The volume of each minibreath is thus correlated with the duration of the syllable, being about 250µL for long syllables compared to about 70µL for short syllables.

In addition to maintaining the supply of air for sound production, minibreaths probably also replace at least some of the oxygen used while singing. But the extent to which they do this may depend on syllable repetition rate, or more precisely, on the volume of the minibreath relative to that of the tracheal "deadspace," which in a waterslager canary is about 90µL. At low syllable-repetition rates, the volume of the minibreaths is several times the deadspace so they should help to maintain respiratory gas exchange. However, at high syllable-repetition rates, minibreaths are smaller than the tracheal deadspace. Even inspirations having a volume less than the deadspace might still assist in replenishing oxygen if the respiratory rate is high and there is turbulent mixing of tracheal and pulmonary air (Bech et al. 1988). Although minibreaths may delay the development of hypoxia during long songs in canaries, changes in respiratory ventilation following song suggest that canaries accumulate an oxygen debt while singing. Immediately after a song lasting 25s, for example, the respiratory rate increased and tidal volume was more than twice its value during resting silent respiration or during respiration immediately before a song (Hartley and Suthers 1989).

At syllable repetition rates greater than about 30/s, the interval between syllables is apparently too short for an inspiration, so canaries switch to pulsatile expiration in which the expiratory muscles maintain a continuous positive pressure and each syllable is generated by using syringeal muscles to rapidly open and close the phonating side of the syrinx—producing sound with puffs of expiratory air (figure 2.7). Song phrases produced with pulsatile expiration are accompanied by a net loss of respiratory air and without the possibility of replenishing its oxygen. It is not surprising that, though these phrases have the highest syllable-repetition rates, they are short in duration (Hartley and Suthers 1989).

Unilateral sound production in combination with minibreaths conserves respiratory air and facilitates high syllable-repetition rates with longer uninterrupted periods of singing. Female canaries, presented with six different song phrases of equal length, gave copulation solicitation displays most frequently to phrases with high syllable-repetition rates, regardless of the order in which the phrases were presented (Vallet and Kreutzer 1995). Perhaps such phrases indicate something about the male's fitness through his ability to tolerate periods of reduced pulmonary ventilation or to coordinate very rapid, rhythmic motor patterns on each side of his syrinx (Suthers and Goller 1998).

The disadvantages of unilateral dominance include a limitation in the frequency range of song, since most syllables are restricted to the vocal range of one side of the syrinx, and (with rare exceptions) the absence of spectral complexity or other features contributed by two-voice syllables (table 2.2).

Alternating Lateralization: Brown-headed Cowbird

Adult male brown-headed cowbirds have a repertoire of several song types consisting of two or three clusters of notes followed by a higher frequency whistle (King et al. 1980; Dufty 1985; West and King 1986). Each note cluster lasts about 0.2s, and the duration of the entire song is about a second. Cowbird song is typically produced during four expirations separated from each other by a short inspiration (figure 2.8; Allan and Suthers 1994). An introductory note cluster is sometimes produced during each of the first three expirations, but often the first expiration is silent and the song contains only two note clusters. The notes within each cluster increase progressively in frequency and intensity. The first note of each cluster is generated on the left side of the syrinx at a low, almost constant frequency. Successive notes in the cluster alternate between the two sides of the syrinx. Left-side notes in these note clusters have frequencies between about 200 and 2,000Hz while most right-side notes are between 1,500 and 6,000Hz (table 2.1). Right notes also have more FM. The last expiration generates the high-frequency, high-intensity final whistle on the right side of the syrinx, which, due to its higher vocal register, substantially expands the frequency range of the song from a high of about 6kHz during note clusters to about 13kHz during the whistle (figure 2.8). The right syrinx of the cowbird thus has a remarkable frequency range covering more than three octaves from about 1.5–13kHz.

Cowbirds utilize the two sides of their syrinx in different ways in different portions of their song (Allan and Suthers 1994). Alternating unilateral song production during the note clusters enhances the spectral contrast between successive notes, which may partially overlap in time to produce some two-voice notes (e.g., figure 2.8, third note cluster) before the right side alone generates the final whistle. Each brown-headed cowbird song-type thus contains a stereotypical sequence of left-right switches, emphasized by their spectral contrast, and which build in pitch and intensity to a final complex whistle from the right syrinx. This motor pattern takes advantage of the bipartite syrinx to gain a wide frequency range while enhancing spectral contrast between notes and conserving respiratory air (table 2.2).

Sequential Lateralization: Northern Cardinal

Northern cardinals have taken advantage of the two sound sources in their syrinx in yet another way. A male cardinal's song repertoire usually consists of about six to ten different syllable types, one or more of which are repeated in phrases to produce a song. A single song may contain from one to several syllable types. Minibreaths occur between syllables unless the repetition rate exceeds about 16/s, in which case a pattern of pulsatile expiration is used. Songs are relatively short and often do not last more than several seconds (Suthers and Goller 1996). Most syllables are composed of upward or downward frequency sweeps over a broad range of frequencies between about 1–7kHz (figure 2.9; Lemon 1965; Lemon 1966; Lemon and Herzog 1969; Lemon and Chatfield 1971).

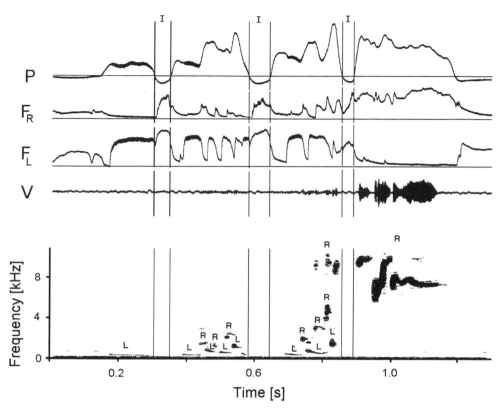

Figure 2.8
Songs of the brown headed cowbird are produced during four expirations separated by minibreaths (I). The first three expirations each produce a cluster of notes that increase gradually in frequency and intensity, beginning with a left side note and alternating sides while the frequency increases in a staggered manner. In contrast to right side notes, most left side notes are lower in frequency and lack prominent frequency modulation. Some two-voice components accompany temporal overlap of left and right sounds. The final whistle during the last expiration is produced on the only on the right side. Note clusters are of a much lower intensity than the final whistle and are barely detectable in the oscillographic trace.

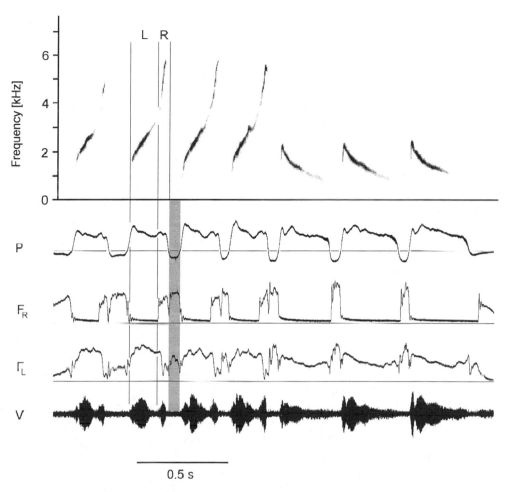

Figure 2.9
Portion of northern cardinal song showing two syllable types organized into separate phrases. The first four syllables sweep upward from about 1.5 to nearly 6kHz. Patterns of left and right syringeal airflow show that the first portion of each syllable, up to about 3.5kHz, is generated by the left side of the syrinx, which then closes as the right side opens to produce the higher portion of the frequency sweep. This sequence is reversed for downward sweeping syllables that start at a high frequency (not shown). The last three syllables do not exceed 3kHz and are produced entirely on the left side with the right syrinx closed.

To achieve this bandwidth, cardinals exploit the different vocal registers of their left and right syrinx. Frequencies below about 3.5 or 4.0kHz are generated by the left syrinx. Frequencies above this are generated by the right syrinx. Broadband FM syllables are produced by sequential contributions from each side of the syrinx (figure 2.9), with a left-right sequence for upward sweeping syllables and a right-left sequence for downward sweeping ones (Suthers and Goller 1996; Suthers 1997; Suthers and Goller 1998). The switch from one side to the other in the middle of a frequency sweep is often so smoothly coordinated that it is not detectable in a sound spectrograph. A few syllable-types only contain frequencies in one vocal register and are produced entirely on one side of the syrinx.

Through precise motor coordination between the left and right sound generators, northern cardinals have evolved a pattern of sequential unilateral phonation, which takes advantage of the lateral specialization of the duplex syrinx for different frequency ranges to maximize the bandwidth of the FM syllables while conserving the available air (table 2.2).

Conclusion

Despite its general morphological similarity throughout most oscines, the duplex nature of the tracheobronchial syrinx gives songbirds additional possibilities for flexible motor control and endows them with the ability to produce a wide range of vocal effects. Independent motor control of two separate sound sources in the bipartite syrinx is an important advance in the evolution of song complexity. The number of species studied is still small, but it is already clear that songbirds have evolved a variety of ways to exploit the acoustic potential of their double vocal organ. A functional consequence of this exploitation is the production of acoustically rich and varied song-types. Most oscine song probably includes substantial contributions from both sides of the syrinx, with the timing and coordination between sides precisely controlled to achieve particular acoustic effects. The strong unilateral dominance present in waterslager canaries may represent a relatively rare example of extreme song lateralization that reflects the inbreeding to which this strain has been subjected (Suthers 1997).

The adoption of a particular motor strategy can be thought of as an evolutionary choice favoring the development of certain types of vocal performance at the cost of limiting other vocal abilities that require conflicting motor routines (Suthers and Goller 1998). It remains for future research to identify the manner in which various perceptual, respiratory, and motor needs or constraints have shaped the diversity of oscine song. Little is known about the factors that determine which motor strategy a species or taxon adopts. Are species-specific motor strategies immutable or can they be modified by, for example, tutoring young birds with the song of another species? Comparative studies of song production and perception can provide a perspective from which to view more clearly the evolution of song diversity and its biological significance.

Acknowledgments

The author thanks Drs. F. Goller, M. Hauser, and M. Konishi for comments that improved the manuscript. Much of the research by the author and his colleagues reported here was supported by grants from NIH and NSF.

Note

1. The term "phonetic" as used in this paper refers to the time-varying pattern of frequency components that comprise a song syllable, i.e., the "syllable morphology" of the vocal output.

References

Allan, S. E. and Suthers, R. A. (1994) Lateralization and motor stereotypy of song production in the brown-headed cowbird. *J. Neurobiol.* 25:1154–1166.

Bech, C., Johansen, K., and Nicol, S. (1988) Gas exchange during high-frequency ventilation in the pigeon (*Columba livia*). *Acta Physiol. Scand.* 132:217–221.

Boughey, M. J. and Thompson, N. S. (1976) Species specificity and individual variation in the songs of the brown thrasher (*Toxostoma rufum*) and catbird (*Dumetella carolinensis*). *Behavior* 57:64–90.

Boughey, M. J. and Thompson, N. S. (1981) Song variety in the brown thrasher (*Toxostoma rufum*). *Z. Tierpsychol.* 56:47–58.

Brackenbury, J. H. (1971) Airflow dynamics in the avian lung as determined by direct and indirect methods. *Respir. Physiol.* 13:319–329.

Brackenbury, J. H. (1973) Respiratory mechanics in the bird. *Comp. Biochem. Physiol.* 44A:599–611.

Brackenbury, J. H. (1989) Functions of the syrinx and the control of sound production. In *Form and Function in Birds*, ed. by A. S. King and J. McLelland, pp. 193–220. London: Academic.

Brenowitz, E. A. and Kroodsma, D. E. (1996) The neuroethology of birdsong. In *Ecology and Evolution of Acoustic Communication in Birds*, ed. by D. E. Kroodsma and E. H. Miller, pp. 283–304. Ithaca: Comstock.

Calder, W. A. (1970) Respiration during song in the canary (*Serinus canaria*). *Comp. Biochem. Physiol.* 32:251–258.

Dufty, Jr., Alfred M. (1985) Song sharing in the brown-headed cowbird (*Molothrus ater*). *Z. Tierpsychol.* 69:177–190.

Fletcher, N. H. (1988) Bird song—a quantitative acoustic model. *J. Theor. Biol.* 135:455–481.

Fletcher, N. H. (1989) Acoustics of bird song—some unresolved problems. *Comments Theoretical Biology* 1:237–251.

Gaunt, A. S. (1973) Models of syringeal mechanisms. *Amer. Zool.* 13:1227–1247.

Gaunt, A. S. (1983) An hypothesis concerning the relationship of syringeal structure to vocal abilities. *Auk* 100:853–862.

Gaunt, A. S. (1986) Interaction of syringeal structure and airflow in avian phonation. In *Acta XIX Internationalis Congressus Ornithologici*, ed. by H. Ouillet, pp. 915–924. Ottowa: University of ottawa Press.

Gaunt, A. S. (1987) Phonation. In: Seller, T. J. (ed) *Bird Respiration*, Vol. 1, ed. by T. J. Seller, pp. 71–94. Boca Raton: CRC.

Gaunt, A. S. and Gaunt, S. L. L. (1985a) Electromyographic studies of the syrinx in parrots (*Aves, Psittacidae*). *Zoomorph.* 105:1–11.

Gaunt, A. S. and Gaunt, S. L. L. (1985b) Syringeal structure and avian phonation. In Johnston, R. F. (ed) *Current Ornithology*, Vol. 2, ed. by R. F. Johnston, pp. 213–245. New York: Plenum Press.

Gaunt, A. S., Stein, R. C., and Gaunt, S. L. L. (1973) Pressure and air flow during distress calls of the starling, *Sturnus vulgaris* (*Aves; Passeriformes*). *J. Exp. Zool.* 183:241–262.

Goller, F. and Larsen, O. N. (1997) A New mechanism of sound generation in songbirds. *Proc. Nat. Acad. Sci. USA* 94:14787–14791.

Goller, F. and Suthers, R. A. (1995a) Contributions of expiratory muscles to song production in brown thrashers. In *Nervous Systems and Behaviour: Proc. 4th Int. Cong. Neuroethology*, ed by M. Burrows, T. Matheson, P. Newland, and H. Schuppe, Georg pp. 334. Stuttgart: Thieme Verlag.

Goller, F. and Suthers, R. A. (1995b) Implications for lateralization of bird song from unilateral gating of bilateral motor patterns. *Nature* 373:63–66.

Goller, F. and Suthers, R. A. (1996a) Role of syringeal muscles in controlling the phonology of bird song. *J. Neurophysiol.* 76:287–300.

Goller, F. and Suthers, R. A. (1996b) Role of syringeal muscles in gating airflow and sound production in singing brown thrashers. *J. Neurophysiol.* 75:867–876.

Greenewalt, C. H. (1968) *Bird Song: Acoustics and Physiology.* Washington, DC: Smithsonian Institution Press.

Hartley, R. S. (1990) Expiratory muscle activity during song production in the canary. *Respir. Physiol.* 81:177–187.

Hartley, R. S. and Suthers, R. .A. (1989) Airflow and pressure during canary song: Evidence for minibreaths. *J. Comp. Physiol.* A 165:15–26.

Hartley, R. S. and Suthers, R. A. (1990) Lateralization of syringeal function during song production in the canary. *J. Neurobiol.* 21:1236–1248.

Hauser, M. D. (1996) *The Evolution of Communication.* Cambridge, MA: MIT Press.

King, A. P., West, M. J., and Eastzer, D. H. (1980) Song structure and song development as potential contributors to reproductive isolation in cowbirds (*Molothrus ater*). *J. Comp. Physiol. Psychol.* 94:1028–1039.

King, A. S. (1989) Functional anatomy of the syrinx. In *Form and Function in Birds*, ed. by A. S. King and J. McLelland, pp. 105–192. London: Academic.

Konishi, M. (1985) Birdsong: From behavior to neuron. In Cowan WM (ed) Annual Review of Neuroscience, Vol. 8, ed. by W. M. Cowan, pp. 125–170. Palo Alto: Annual Reviews, Inc.

Konishi, M. (1994) Pattern generation in birdsong. *Current Opinion in Neurobiology* 4:827–831.

Kroodsma, D. E. and Parker, L. D. (1977) Vocal virtuosity in the brown thrasher. *Auk* 94:783–785.

Lemon, R. E. (1965) The song repertoires of cardinals (*Richmondena cardinalis*) at London, Ontario. *Can. J. Zool.* 43:559–569.

Lemon, R. E. (1966) Geographic variation in the song of cardinals. *Can J. Zool.* 44:413–428.

Lemon, R. E. and Chatfield, C. (1971) Organization of song in cardinals. *Anim. Behav.* 19:1–17.

Lemon, R. E. and Herzog, A. (1969) The vocal behavior of cardinals and pyrrhuloxias in Texas. *Condor* 71:1–15.

Lohr, B. S. (1989) *The Organization of Song Elements in the Gray Catbird.* Milwaukee, Wl: University of Wisconsin—Milwaukee Press.

Luine, V., Nottebohm, F., Harding, C., and McEwen, B. S. (1980) Androgen affects cholinergic enzymes in syringeal motor neurons and muscle. *Brain Res.* 192:89–107.

McCasland, J. S. (1987) Neuronal control of bird song production. *J. Neurosci.* 7:23–39.

McLelland, J. (1989) Anatomy of the lungs and air sacs. In King AS, McLelland J (eds) Form and Function in Birds, Vol. 4, ed. by A. S. King and J. McLellard, pp. 221–279. New York: Academic Press.

Miskimen, M. (1951) Sound production in passerine birds. *Auk* 68:493–504.

Mundinger, P. C. (1995) Behaviour-genetic analysis of canary song: Inter-strain differences in sensory learning and epigenetic rules. *Anim. Behav.* 50:1491–1511.

Nottebohm, F. (1971) Neural lateralization of vocal control in a passerine bird, I: Song. *J. Exp. Zool.* 177:229–262.

Nottebohm, F. (1996) A White canary on Mount Acropolis. *J. Comp. Physiol.* A179:149–156.

Nottebohm, F. and Nottebohm, M. E. (1976) Left hypoglossal dominance in the control of canary and white-crowned sparrow song. *J. Comp. Physiol.* 108:171–192.

Nottebohm, F. and Nottebohm, M. E. (1978) Relationship between song repertoire and age in the canary, *Serinus canarius. Z. Tierpsychol.* 46:298–305.

Nottebohm, F., Stokes, T., and Leonard, C. M. (1976) Central control of song in the canary, *Serinus canarius. Comp. Neurol.* 165:457–486.

Nowicki, S. and Capranica, R. R. (1986a) Bilateral syringeal coupling during phonation of a songbird. *J. Neurosci.* 6:3595–3610.

Nowicki, S. and Capranica, R. R. (1986b) Bilateral syringeal interaction in vocal production of an oscine bird sound. *Science* 231:1297–1299.

Nowicki, S. and Marler, P. (1988) How do birds sing? *Music Percep.* 5:391–426.

Ratcliffe, L. and Otter, K. (1996) Sex differences in song recognition. In *Ecology and Evolution of Acoustic Communication in Birds,* ed. by D. E. Kroodsma and E. H. Miller, pp. 339–355. Ithaca: Cornell University Press.

Read, A. F. and Weary, D. M. (1992) The Evolution of bird song: Comparative analyses. *Phil. Trans. R. Soc. Lond.* B338:165–187.

Searcy, W. A. (1986) Sexual selection and the evolution of song. *Ann. Rev. Ecol. Syst.* 17:507–533.

Searcy, W. A. (1992) Song repertoire and mate choice in birds. *Am. Zool.* 32:71–80.

Searcy, W. A. and Brenowitz, E. A. (1988) Sexual differences in species recognition of avian song. *Nature* 332:152–154.

Stein, R. C. (1968) Modulation in bird sound. *Auk* 94:229–243.

Suthers, R. A. (1990) Contributions to birdsong from the left and right sides of the intact syrinx. *Nature* 347:473–477.

Suthers, R. A. (1992) Lateralization of sound production and motor action on the left and right sides of the syrinx during bird song. *14th Inter. Cong. Acoustics* I:1–5.

Suthers, R. A. (1994) Variable asymmetry and resonance in the avian vocal tract: a structural basis for individually distinct vocalizations. *J. Comp. Physiol.* A175:457–466.

Suthers, R. A. (1997) Peripheral control and lateralization of birdsong. *J. Neurobiol.* 33:632–652.

Suthers, R. A. and Goller, F. (1996) Respiratory and syringeal dynamics of song production in northern cardinals. In *Nervous Systems and Behaviour: Proc. 4th Int. Cong. Neuroethology*, ed. by M. Burrows, T. Matheson, P. Newland, and H. Schuppe, p. 333. Stuttgart: Georg Thieme Verlag.

Suthers, R. A. and Goller, F. (1998) Motor correlates of vocal diversity in songbirds. In *Current Ornithology*, Vol. 14, ed. by V. Nolan, Jr., E. Ketterson, and C. F. Thompson, pp. 235–288. New York: Plenum Press.

Suthers, R. A., Goller, F., and Hartley, R. S. (1994) Motor dynamics of song production by mimic thrushes. *J. Neurobiol.* 25:917–936.

Suthers, R. A., Goller, F., and Hartley, R. S. (1996) Motor stereotypy and diversity in songs of mimic thrushes. *J. Neurobiol.* 30:231–245.

Suthers, R. A. and Hartley, R. S. (1990) Effect of unilateral denervation on the acoustic output from each side of the syrinx in singing mimic thrushes. *Society for Neurosci. Abst.* 16:1249.

Thompson, W. L. and Jane, P. L. (1969) An analysis of catbird song. *Jack-Pine Warbler* 47:115–125.

Vallet, E. and Kreutzer, M. (1995) Female canaries are sexually responsive to special song phrases. *Anim. Behav.* 49:1603–1610.

Vicario, D. S. (1991) Neural mechanisms of vocal production in songbirds. *Cur. Op. in Neurobiol.* 1:595–600.

Vicario, D. S. (1993) A new brain stem pathway for vocal control in the zebra finch song system. *NeuroReport* 4:983–986.

Weisman, R. G. and Ratcliffe, L. M. (1989) Absolute and relative pitch processing in Black-capped Chickadees, *Parus atricapillus. Anim. Behav.* 38:685–692.

Weisman, R. G. and Ratcliffe, L. M. (1992) The perception of pitch constancy in bird song. In *Cognitive Aspects of Stimulus Control*, ed. by W. K. Honig and J. G. Fetterman, pp. 243–261. Hillsdale, NJ: Erlbaum.

Weisman, R. G., Ratcliffe, L., Johnsrude, I., and Hurly, T. A. (1990) Absolute and relative pitch production in the song of the black-capped chickadee. *Condor* 92:118–124.

West, M. J. and King, A. P. (1986) Song repertoire development in male cowbirds (*Molothrus ater*): Its relation to female assessment of song potency. *J. Comp. Psych.* 100:296–303.

Wild, J. M. (1993a) The avian nucleus retroambigualis: A nucleus for breathing, singing and calling. *Brain Res.* 606:119–124.

Wild, J. M. (1993b) Descending projections of the songbird nucleus *Robustus Archistriatalis. J. Comp. Neurol.* 338:225–241.

Wild, J. M. (1997) Neural pathways for the control of birdsong production. *J. Neurobiol.* 33:653–670.

Wild, J. M., Goller, F., and Suthers, R. A. (1998) Inspiratory muscle activity during bird song. *J. Neurobiol.* 36:441–453.

Williams, H., Crane, L. A., Hale, T. K., Esposito, M. A. and Nottebohm, F. (1992) Right-side dominance for song control in the Zebra Finch. *J. Neurobiol.* 23:1006–1020.

Yu, A. C., Dave, A. S., and Margoliash, D. (1996) Temporal hierarchical control of singing in birds. *Science* 273:1871–1875.

3 The Anatomy and Timing of Vocal Learning in Birds

Fernando Nottebohm

W. H. Thorpe conducted the first detailed laboratory study of vocal learning in a songbird, the chaffinch (*Fringilla coelebs*). He showed that hand-reared chaffinches imitated conspecific songs that had been played over a loudspeaker during the first year of their lives. Isolated birds that were not exposed to such models during this time developed much simpler, aberrant songs. Moreover, isolates did not correct their song when exposed, as adults, to the song of wild chaffinches. Thorpe (1958, 1961) concluded that there was a "sensitive period" for song learning, and that in chaffinches it occurred only once and lasted from the juvenile stage up to the time of sexual maturity. More recent work emphasizes that young chaffinches may be particularly sensitive to models presented during their first summer and the following spring (Slater and Ince 1982; Thielcke and Krome 1989, 1991).

Thorpe (1961) noted that in the chaffinch "The onset of the period of maximum sensitivity for song-learning can be delayed by experimental techniques such as crowding and light-control, and can be correspondingly extended into the late summer, but once over it cannot—so far as we know—be renewed." The manipulations Thorpe mentions would have affected the levels of gonadal hormones. It was later shown that castration can delay the end of the sensitive period for song learning in the chaffinch (Nottebohm 1969). These early experiments suggested that termination of the sensitive period was not an age-dependent phenomenon, but followed the acquisition of stable adult song at whatever age this occurred.

The sensitive period for song-learning should be treated as a hypothesis. The work of Baptista and Petrinovich (1984) illustrates this need for caution. Their research showed that young birds that were no longer receptive to recorded song—*sensu* imitation—would, nonetheless, imitate a live model presented in a social context. Observations of captive individuals seldom cover all the natural contingencies that might affect the outcome of a learning opportunity. In addition, "sensitive periods" that may occur under laboratory conditions do not necessarily occur in nature. Ideally, one should gather lots of data on the onset and termination of song learning in individually marked free-ranging individuals. Subsequently, laboratory experiments would help define the mechanisms involved.

The hypothesis of a sensitive period for song learning has close affinity with the sensitive period hypothesis that others have postulated for social and sexual imprinting. In all these cases the hypothesis holds that learning occurs more readily during a particular stage of development, and with greater difficulty or not at all at a later time.

The Two-Step Model of Vocal Learning

Studies on the neurobiology of song learning in birds started in the mid-1960s, when
Konishi (1965) produced the first detailed description of the effects of deafening on
song development in an oscine songbird. Marler and Tamura (1964) had shown that
hand-reared white-crowned sparrows (*Zonotrichia leucophrys*) imitated conspecific
song models presented during the first 50 days after hatching, but did not imitate
models heard later (cf. Marler 1970). The imitation was mastered as the bird
approached sexual maturity; no further song changes occurred thereafter. Konishi
(1965) showed that when adult white-crowned sparrows were deafened after they
had mastered their song, this song was maintained with little change for a period of
up to two years. However, early deafening blocked song imitation and the birds
developed a very aberrant song. Of particular interest was the observation that
young white-crowned sparrows deafened soon after exposure to conspecific song
developed a song no different from that of white-crowned sparrows deafened before
exposure to such a model. Konishi (1965) concluded that auditory experience did not
act directly on song motor programs. Instead, he suggested, song learning consists in
two steps: first, a model is acquired as an auditory memory; and second, the young
bird alters its vocal output until the auditory feedback generated matches the
remembered model (figure 3.1). He concluded, too, that once the motor skill has
been mastered it can be maintained without auditory feedback.

Konishi's (1965) two-step model of song learning influenced thinking about sensitive periods. Clearly, there could be two critical periods, the first determining when a
song was acquired as an auditory memory, the second determining when a song was
learned as a motor skill. Each of these two learning events could be controlled by a
separate and different "mechanism," and the onset and termination of these two
sensitive periods could result from separate and different variables.

By the mid-1960s, the sensitive period for song learning had been studied in some
detail in three songbirds: the chaffinch (Thorpe 1958), the white-crowned sparrow
(Marler 1970), and the zebra finch (*Taeniopygia guttata*) (Immelman 1969). In each
case it was discovered that there is an early period when the auditory model is
acquired, and a later period when it is converted into a motor imitation. However,
auditory and motor learning often overlap, and this interfered with identification of
the variables that governed each of the two learning processes. Later studies, particularly those on swamp sparrows (*Melospiza georgiana*) (Marler and Peters 1982),
have shown that in some species the periods for model acquisition and model imitation can be separated by as much as 200 days. Such species should provide good

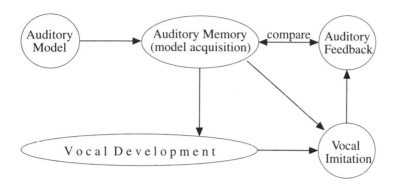

Figure 3.1
Schematic representation of the events contemplated by the two-step model of vocal learning. During *step 1*, exposure to an Auditory Model leads to the formation of an Auditory Memory. During *step 2*, vocal output is modified until the auditory feedback it generates matches the model. Attempts at model matching can start during juvenile vocal development, as indicated by the arrow from "Auditory Memory" to "Vocal Development." The emerging motor program, here labeled "Vocal Imitation," must be informed about the goodness of the match between auditory feedback and auditory memory, and that is why this diagram includes an arrow between "Auditory Memory" and "Vocal Imitation." When the match is accomplished, the motor program for the Vocal Imitation is in place. However, this may not be the end of learning because, as discussed in the text, maintenance of the learned motor program still requires access to auditory feedback.

material for identifying factors that determine the timing of these two kinds of learning. The relation between these two sensitive periods is illustrated in figure 3.2.

Age-limited and Open-ended Learners

It seems likely that all oscine songbirds acquire their song, and some calls, by reference to auditory information, that is, they are vocal learners (Kroodsma 1982). However, the timing of this event differs between species, and it can be placed in either of two main categories: (1) In some species, vocal learning occurs only during the juvenile stage and up to the time of sexual maturity. Well-known examples are the chaffinch (Thorpe 1958), white-crowned sparrow (Marler and Tamura 1964; Marler 1970), zebra finch (Immelman, 1969), swamp sparrow (Marler and Peters 1982, 1988), song sparrow, *Melospiza melodia* (Marler and Peters 1987), and marsh wren, *Cistothorus palustris* (Kroodsma and Pickert 1980). These birds are sometimes referred to as "age-limited" learners. However, as mentioned for the chaffinch, hormonal changes and experience, not age, may bring vocal learning to an end. (2) In other songbirds, vocal learning also occurs first during the juvenile stage, but in addition the song repertoire is modified and expanded in adulthood. Examples are

A. Zebra Finch

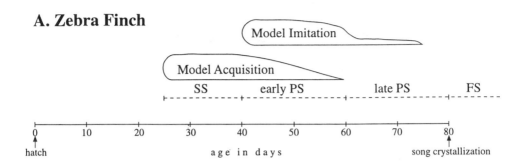

B. Swamp Sparrow

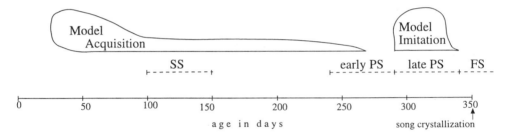

Figure 3.2
Diagrammatic representation of the temporal relation between model acquisition and model imitation in two "age-limited" learners, the zebra finch and swamp sparrow. (A) Model acquisition in aviary reared male zebra finches starts during the subsong (SS) stage, before the birds make any attempts at model imitation, and continues during early plastic song (PS), when other models are already being imitated. Improvements in the imitation of models acquired earlier continues during late plastic song, but at this time no new models are imitated (for refs., see text). (B) Model acquisition in swamp sparrows is particularly effective between post-hatching days 26 and 47, when 57% of model learning occurs. By day 85, 71% of model acquisition is completed, but some birds imitate models first heard as late as at 250–300 days of age. First identifiable imitations occur when swamp sparrows are close to 300 days old (Marler and Peters 1982, 1988; Marler et al. 1987). The horizontal axis shows age in days, starting at hatching.

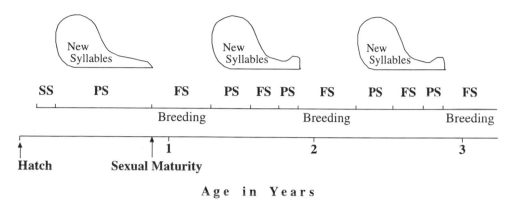

SS   PS   FS   PS   FS PS   FS   PS   FS PS   FS

          Breeding   Breeding   Breeding

↑   ↑ 1   2   3
Hatch   Sexual Maturity

A g e   i n   Y e a r s

Figure 3.3
Young male canaries go through the subsong (SS) and plastic song (PS) stages of song development before they reach sexual maturity which, depending on when the bird was hatched, occurs at 7–12 months of age; at sexual maturity the birds sing stable full song (FS). Most of the song syllables sung at sexual maturity are already recognizable at 4 months of age. After then, many new syllables appear each year during the summer and early fall, when adult male canaries revert to plastic song, with a smaller secondary peak of additions in late winter and early spring. Canaries are "open-ended" learners (Nottebohm and Nottebohm 1978; Nottebohm et al. 1986).

the red-winged blackbird, *Agelaius phoeniceus* (Marler et al. 1972; Yasukawa et al. 1980), the starling, *Sturnus vulgaris* (Böhner et al. 1990), and the canary, *Serinus canaria* (Nottebohm and Nottebohm 1978). Birds belonging to the latter category have been called "open-ended" learners (figure 3.3). However, the term "open-ended" should not be taken to mean that new songs are equally likely to be acquired throughout the bird's life, but just that such learning continues to be possible. Comparisons between age limited and open-ended learners may yield insights into the factors that make it possible for song learning to occur in adulthood.

Processes of song learning and retention may differ between the above two groups and between species within one of these groups. A chaffinch or white-crowned sparrow—both age-limited learners—retains its learned song after deafening in adulthood (Konishi 1965; Nottebohm 1968; Konishi and Nottebohm 1969), but a canary—an open-ended learner—"forgets" its learned song after deafening in adulthood (Nottebohm et al. 1976). Is this an important difference between age-limited and open-ended learners? Perhaps not. Deafening also interferes with song retention in the adult zebra finch (Nordeen and Nordeen 1992), one of the best-studied age-limited learners. There may not be a single, invariant neurobiology of song learning and song remembering that applies to all songbirds, and there may not be a single, unified explanation for the sensitive period for vocal learning. Despite these caveats, it seems likely that brain pathways for the acquisition and production of learned vocalization are very similar among songbirds. Before I describe these pathways and their ontogeny, I will review song development in one of the most widely studied species, the zebra finch.

Song Development in the Zebra Finch

Subsong in the zebra finch starts as "quiet bursts of sound of variable structure that are produced at irregular intervals" (Arnold 1975). According to Immelmann (1969), the sounds of subsong "develop continuously from the begging calls of the young." Strong similarities between food-begging calls and subsong have also been noticed in the chaffinch (Nottebohm 1972).

Zebra finch subsong has been observed as early as day 18, though it may take hours of observation to witness these events, and virtually all males may have sung by day 28 (Böhner and Cate, unpublished data), a period during which young zebra finches still beg for food. By day 40, "some song elements may be recognized which are remotely similar to each other and may faintly resemble elements in the bird's final song" (Arnold 1975). This more structured song is called "plastic song." During early plastic song, the sounds produced are still highly variable. This variability is gradually reduced until, by day 60, "almost all of the elements of the final song are present and may be given in sequences which are like those of the final song" (Slater et al. 1988). The "stable song" of adult male zebra finches is in place by day 80, when these birds are sexually mature and capable of reproduction (Immelmann 1969). However, some variability may normally persist beyond that time, and possibly for a few weeks (Morrison and Nottebohm 1993).

Different Brain Pathways for Production of Learned and Unlearned Vocalizations

Immelmann's description of the emergence of learned song from presumably unlearned food-begging calls is of interest because the motor pathways that control song production in male zebra finches—and probably in other songbirds—can be thought of as consisting of two modules (figure 3.4), and their ontogeny differs in important ways: module 1 consists of a *brainstem pathway* that, by itself, produces unlearned sounds; in evolutionary terms, this is an old pathway, and it develops early in ontogeny. Module 2 consists of a *caudal forebrain pathway* responsible for the production of learned sounds (Simpson and Vicario 1990); this pathway, found only in vocal learners (Nottebohm 1980a), develops late in ontogeny, at the very time when song is first acquired. When module 2 is present, it controls and modifies

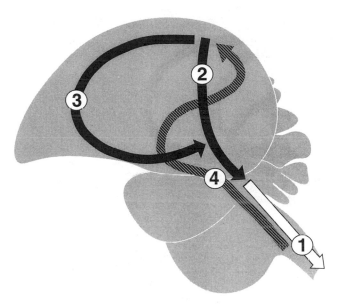

Figure 3.4
Diagrammatic sketch of the songbird brain showing four pathways, refered to in the text as "modules," involved in the acquisition and production of learned song. *Module 1* consists of brain stem nuclei that control the vocal tract and respiratory muscles involved in call and song production; this pathway suffices for the production of unlearned calls (Simpson and Vicario 1990). *Module 2* consists of telencephalic nuclei necessary for the production of learned calls and song (Nottebohm et al. 1976; Simpson and Vicario 1990). *Module 3* consists of telencephalic and thalamic nuclei necessary for song learning, but not necessary for the production of learned song (Bottjer et al. 1984; Sohrabji et al. 1990; Scharff and Nottebohm 1991). *Module 4* consists of brain stem and telencephalic nuclei that are part of the ascending auditory pathway shown in more detail in figure 3.7.

the performance of module 1. A schematic drawing of these relations is shown in figure 3.4.

The Relations between Pathways for the Production and Acquisition of Learned Song

The caudal forebrain pathway for song production is well developed in adult male zebra finches, which learn their song and some calls, but poorly developed in adult female zebra finches, which produce only unlearned calls (Nottebohm and Arnold 1976; Konishi and Akutagawa 1985). The anatomy and connectivity of song-system pathways are very similar in canaries and zebra finches and so may be similar in most oscine songbirds. The posterior forebrain motor pathway for the production of learned song is closely linked to an *anterior forebrain pathway* (module 3 in figure

3.4) that is necessary for the acquisition of learned song. I will now describe what is known about modules 2 and 1—in that order—and will then describe the relations between modules 2 and 3. A schematic representation of the relations between nuclei in these three modules is shown in figure 3.5.

The posterior forebrain pathway for the production of learned song consists of two nuclei, the high vocal center (HVC) and its only known efferent target, the robust nucleus of the archistriatum (RA). HVC receives input from four sources: (1) from nucleus Uvaeformis of the thalamus (Uva); (2) from nucleus interface of the neostriatum (NIf), which also receives input from Uva; (3) from the medial magnocellular nucleus of the anterior neostriatum (mMAN); and (4) from a "shelf" of neostriatal tissue that underlies HVC and that is part of the classical ascending auditory pathway (Nottebohm et al. 1976; Kelley and Nottebohm 1979; Katz and Gurney 1981; Nottebohm et al. 1982; Bottjer et al. 1989; Vates et al. 1996).

RA has five known efferent projections: (1) to the tracheosyringeal part of the hypoglossal nucleus (nXIIts), which has the motor neurons that innervate the muscles of the trachea and syrinx; (2) to lateral medullary respiratory centers, including nucleus ambiguus; (3) to nucleus dorsalis medialis (DM) of the intercollicular complex, which in turn projects to nXIIts and to medullary nuclei of the respiratory system; (4) to the medial part of the dorsolateral thalamic nucleus (DLM); and (5) to the posterior portion of the dorsomedial thalamic nucleus (DMP) (Nottebohm et al. 1976; Wild and Arends 1987; Vicario 1991; Wild 1993a,b; Vates et al. 1997). The fact that RA innervates several nuclei involved with respiration makes sense since the sounds of song are produced during expiration (Greenewalt 1968; Paton and Manogue 1982) and the patterning of expiratory pulses provides much of the temporal pattern of song (Suthers 1990).

It is not known whether activity in Uva leads all other events in song production, but we know that electrical stimulation of either the right or left Uva of zebra finch males can produce a bilateral cascade of responses in the song motor pathway, ending with activation of the nXIIts motorneurons (S. Okuhata, pers. comm.). Lesions in HVC, RA, nXIIts, and Uva have been shown to disrupt the production of learned song (Nottebohm et al. 1976; Simpson and Vicario 1990; Williams and Vicario 1993). Uva may respond, too, to auditory and proprioceptive feedback engendered by song production (Okuhata and Nottebohm 1992). Since Uva lesions in adult zebra finch males result in repetitions of a same song syllable before the bird moves on to the next one ("stammering"), this little nucleus seems to convey to HVC information necessary for normal pattern expression (Williams and Vicario 1993).

We can think of module 3, the anterior forebrain pathway, as the other pathway that connects HVC to RA. In this pathway HVC projects to Area X of lobus parol-

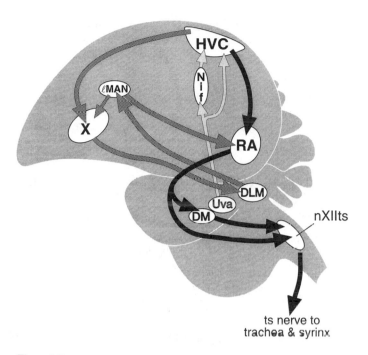

Figure 3.5
Schematic diagram of the relation between some of the brain nuclei known to be involved with the production or just the acquisition of learned song. In terms of the modules shown in figure 3.4, HVC and RA correspond to *module 2*, DM and nXIIts to *module 1*, and Area X, DLM and lMAN to *module 3*. We do not know which part of the brain is first in deciding whether to sing or not to sing, but input from NIf could play such a role (McCasland and Konishi 1981), while input from Uva seems important for the serial delivery of song components (Williams and Vicario 1993). Black arrows: descending motor pathway; light gray arrows, ascending motor control.; medium gray arrows, *module 3*. All connections shown here are ipsilateral and pathways on both sides of the brain are very similar. Abbreviations: HVC, high vocal center; RA, robust nucleus of the archistriatum; DM, nucleus dorsalis medialis of the intercollicular complex; nXIIts, tracheosyringeal part of the hypoglossal nucleus; Uva, nucleus uvaeformis of the thalamus; NIf, nucleus interface; X, Area X of lobus parolfactorius; DLM, medial portion of the dorsolateral thalamic nucleus; lMAN, lateral part of the magnocellular nucleus of the anterior neostriatum (see text for refs.).

factorius and Area X projects to the thalamic nucleus DLM; DLM projects to the lateral magnocellular nucleus of the anterior neostriatum (lMAN), and lMAN projects both to RA and back to Area X (Nottebohm et al. 1982; Okuhata and Saito 1987; Bottjer et al. 1989; Nixdorf-Bergweiler et al. 1995; Vates and Nottebohm 1995). What is particularly interesting about this circuit is that lesions placed in lMAN (Bottjer et al. 1984; Morrison and Nottebohm 1993), DLM (Halsema and Bottjer 1992), or Area X (Sohrabji et al. 1990; Scharff and Nottebohm 1991) interfere with the development of learned song. Notice that HVC and RA are part of both the circuits for production (module 2) and acquisition (module 3) of learned song.

Nucleus RA deserves special attention because it broadcasts to the brainstem the instructions for production of learned song. It may also appraise other telencephalic nuclei about the substance of these instructions. The latter effect could occur via either of two pathways (figure 3.6). RA sends an ipsilateral projection to the posterior portion of the dorsomedial thalamic nucleus (DMP), which projects back to the ipsilateral and contralateral mMAN. Since mMAN is one of the inputs to HVC, there is in place a bilateral feedback loop from each RA to HVC. There is also a weaker projection from each RA to the ipsilateral thalamic nucleus DLM, which as we saw above projects to lMAN as part of module 3.

Because of these relations, there are in the songbird brain at least four feedback loops (figure 3.6) that, without counting auditory feedback, could carry information germaine to the acquisition and production of song patterns. These loops are: (1) Area X to DLM to lMAN to Area X; (2) HVC to RA to DMP to mMAN to HVC; (3) RA to DLM to lMAN to RA; and (4) HVC to RA to medullary nuclei involved with phonation and then from one or more of these medullary nuclei and/or from the peripheral structures they innervate travelling back to Uva (S. Okuhata, pers. comm.) and from there to HVC (Okuhata and Nottebohm 1992; Vicario 1993; S. Okuhata, pers. comm.). Loops (1) and (3) include anterior pathway relays (lMAN and Area X) that are not necessary for the production of learned song; these loops, therefore, are not likely to be involved in the short-term patterning of song. However, loop (4) may be necessary for this moment-to-moment patterning, as suggested by the effect of lesions to nucleus Uva. Loops (1), (2), (3), and (4) may well play a role in song acquisition.

Auditory Input to Nucleus HVC

An account of the brain pathways for song acquisition would be incomplete without module 4 (figure 3.4), the ascending auditory pathway. A partial and schematic representation of this pathway is included as figure 3.7, which shows connections from

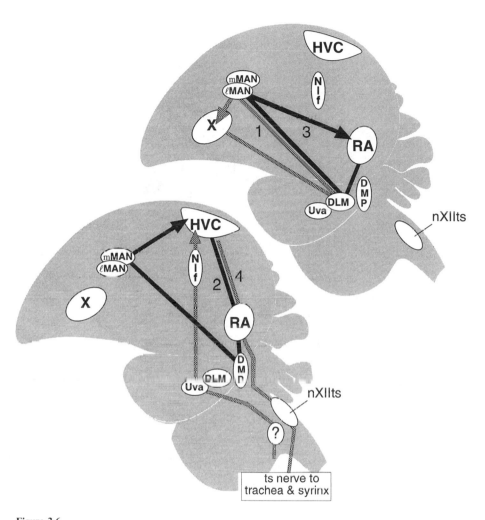

Figure 3.6
The song system's feedback loops are shown in two separate schematic diagrams. This was done to avoid clutter. *Loop 1*, also shown in figure 3.5, links Area X to DLM to lMAN and back to Area X. *Loop 2* links HVC to RA to DMP to mMAN and back to HVC. *Loop 3* links RA to DLM to lMAN and back to RA. *Loop 4* links HVC to RA to nXIIts and other medullary nuclei, such as n. Ambiguus (not shown), thought to be involved with phonation (Vicario 1993); peripheral feedback that accompanies singing is thought to reach Uva (Okuhata and Nottebohm 1992) and Uva projects back to HVC, directly and via NIf. The exact source of the peripheral feedback remains unknown, hence the question mark in the diagram.

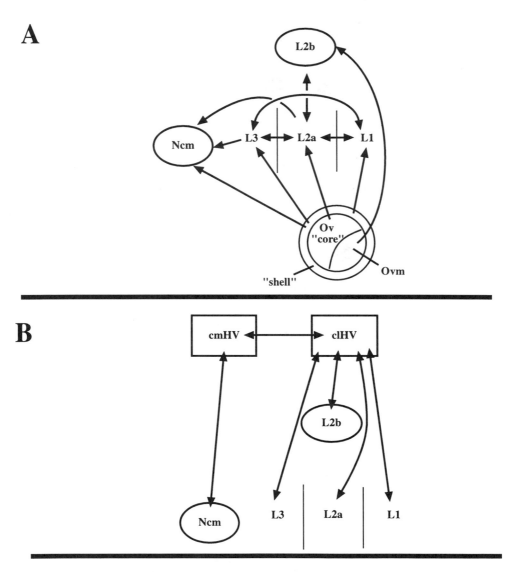

Figure 3.7
Schematic diagram of the ascending auditory pathway, starting from the thalamic ovoidalis (Ov) complex and ending in the "Shelf" under HVC and the "Cup" adjacent to RA. Ov and its surrounding "shell" project to five subdivisions (L1, L2a, L2b, L3 and Ncm) of caudal neostriatum that are probably homologous to the primary auditory cortex of mammals. Notice, however, that only one of these five regions, L2a, receives a direct projection from the Ov "core," while another one, L2b, receives input from the ventromedial part of the ovoidalis complex (Ovm), suggesting a parcellation of the auditory inputs entering the neostriatum. The caudomedial and caudolateral hyperstriatum ventrale (cmHV and clHV) represent a still higher, perhaps polymodal, tier of auditory processing. The Shelf and Cup may antedate the

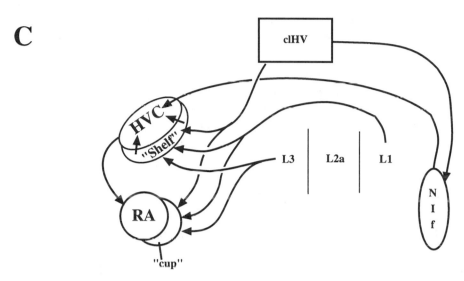

Figure 3.7 (continued)
existence of a song system, for in addition to providing input to HVC, the Shelf also projects to the Cup, which in turn innervates the shell that surrounds the Ov core. It is not known whether the shell and core parts of Ov are interconnected, but even in the absence of this information it is clear that the projection from Shelf to Cup back to Ov constitutes a descending "cortico-thalamic" auditory pathway with the potential to regulate ascending auditory input. So, much as the song system has its feedback loops, so too we find feedback loops in the auditory system (Vates et al. 1996; Mello et al. 1998).

the thalamic ovoidalis complex up to HVC. We do not know, yet, where in this pathway reside the auditory memories that are eventually imitated, but it is tempting to suppose that the higher reaches of this pathway, such as the caudomedial neostriatum (Ncm), the caudomedial and caudolateral hyperstriatum ventrale (cmHV and clHV), and the neostriatal Shelf under HVC play a role in the storage of this memory.

Much of the "classical" ascending auditory pathway shown in figure 3.7 converges, eventually, via the nucleus interphase (NIf) and via the Shelf onto HVC proper. To this extent, one can think of HVC as one more auditory relay, and we know that from there auditory information reaches other song system nuclei (Williams 1989), down to the very motor neurons that innervate the syrinx (Williams and Nottebohm 1985). More on this topic will be discussed under the heading "The Establishment of a Relation between Perception and Production."

Because of its connectivity, HVC can be thought of as a member of modules 2, 3, and 4, and in evolutionary time, HVC may have emerged as an auditory nucleus that specialized in intraspecific communication. As we learn more about the homologues of modules 2, 3, and 4 in other groups of birds, it will be interesting to see if a neo-striatal relay with access to vocal output occurs in birds that do not show vocal learning.

The Shelf under HVC gives rise, too, to a descending auditory pathway that innervates archistriatal tissue closely apposed to RA called the RA "Cup." There are no known connections between RA and the Cup, but Cup neurons project down to thalamic auditory relays (Mello et al. 1998). This descending pathway (not shown in figure 3.7) could play a role in screening auditory inputs and thus affect the perception of vocal signals as well as song-learning.

Growth and Regression of Song Circuits Accompany Vocal Development

Several of the telencephalic nuclei that participate in the production and acquisition of learned song are small in nestlings, before the onset of song development, and their volume (Nottebohm 1980a; Bottjer et al. 1985), cell number (Alvarez-Buylla et al. 1988; Kirn and DeVoogd 1989; Nordeen and Nordeen 1988a), cell size (Konishi and Akutagawa 1985; Bottjer et al. 1986), and connections (Konishi and Akutagawa 1985) grow during the subsequent weeks or months. As a result of these changes, many components of the circuits for the acquisition and production of learned song are formed and connected during the very period when song first develops.

It seems reasonable to infer that the timing and sequential order of song development—food-begging calls, subsong, plastic song, and song crystallization—result, at least in part, from the timing and order in which these anatomical changes occur. For example, projections from HVC to RA (figure 3.5) are sparse or absent in 15-day-old male Zebra finches, are partly formed by day 25, and have reached much of RA by day 35 (Konishi and Akutagawa 1985). The total number of synapses that HVC neurons form on RA cells increases between days 25 and 53, and it remains stable thereafter (Hermann and Arnold 1991a). The first appearance of subsong and plastic song may depend on the increasing control that HVC exerts over RA. Stages of song development that depend on the establishment of higher levels of control could not occur earlier. If song learning, as a motor skill, can only occur during times when new HVC-to-RA connections are established, then times of formation of these connections could define the sensitive period for song learning. This rationale could extend to connections between other late developing components of the song system.

In other parts of the song system, connections are in place before the sensitive period for song learning commences. For example, the projection from lMAN to RA (figure 3.5), which is important for song learning (Bottjer et al. 1984), can already be backfilled by post-hatching day 20 in male zebra finches and, contrary to other claims (Bottjer and Sengelaub 1989; Korsia and Bottjer 1989), the number of RA-projecting lMAN neurons in it remains constant between day 20 and adulthood (Morrison 1991; Nordeen et al. 1992). It is not known whether some or all of lMAN's projecting fibers present on day 20 have formed synapses on RA cells at that time. However, it is known that the number of lMAN synapses formed on RA neurons decreases between days 25 and 53 and stays constant thereafter (Herrmann and Arnold 1991a).

The possibility of a correlation between a reduction in the number of lMAN inputs to RA and the end of the sensitive period for song learning is suggested by another observation. Juvenile male zebra finches in plastic song that receive bilateral lesions of lMAN produce a much simpler and more stereotyped song one day after the lesion than immediately before the operation (Scharff and Nottebohm 1991). lMAN endings in RA may produce during the juvenile stage a substance that maintains the plasticity of RA song-motor circuits. As long as this substance is present in sufficient amounts, song may remain variable and thus capable of modification by learning. A drop in the release of this substance would bring the sensitive period for song learning to an end; such a drop would follow lMAN lesions or could result from a reduction in the number of lMAN synapses in RA. Thus, whereas an increase in the number of HVC endings in RA would create the possibility for ever finer control of the learned vocal output, a decrease in the number of lMAN synapses in RA would reduce the plasticity in RA circuits necessary for vocal learning. These two processes could, by themselves, determine the onset, progression, and end of the sensitive period for song learning.

Even though the number of lMAN neurons that project to the male zebra finch RA remains constant between days 20 and adulthood, the volume of lMAN shrinks significantly during this period (Bottjer et al. 1985; Morrison 1991; Nordeen et al. 1992). This shrinkage is accompanied by an increased packing density of the RA-projecting cells. I will argue later (under the heading "Auditory, Motor, or Social Experience?") that the reduction in lMAN volume does not prevent a bird from imitating new models (Morrison 1991).

lMAN receives input from the dorsolateral nucleus of the anterior thalamus (DLM), which in turn receives input from Area X (figure 3.5). The projection from DLM reaches lMAN and a shell of tissue that surrounds lMAN. The overall size of the projection to the shell around lMAN peaks at day 35 after hatching in male zebra finches and subsequently regresses (Johnson and Bottjer 1992). The timing of these changes suggests that they could be related to the changing ability of a juvenile zebra finch to engage in song learning.

In sum, changes in the connections between some nuclei of the song system may explain why song acquisition, as a motor skill, occurs in some species only during a particular developmental age. However, we do not know whether these changes in connectivity are age-, hormone-, or experience-dependent, and all three variables could interact. In open-ended learners, the extent of lMAN's innervation of RA may not change between the juvenile and adult stage, or it may show seasonal changes at times when vocal learning occurs. This issue has not been studied. Finally, we have no data on the timing of neurogenesis and the development of connectivity in the classical ascending auditory pathways (module 4 in figure 3.4). When such data become available, they may explain the timing of model acquisition. As suggested for the formation of motor song memories, the acquisition of auditory memories may also be particularly effective and lasting if the sound stimuli are encountered when auditory connections are first formed.

Anatomical Changes in the Adult Song System and Their Relation to Vocal Learning

Marked anatomical changes may continue to occur in the adult song system of some species. Such changes were first reported in canaries, with the suggestion that they were related to the seasonal occurrence of song learning. The HVC of adult male canaries was found to be twice as large in the spring (April), when these birds are in stable song, as it is in late summer (mid-September), at the end of their moult, when song is unstable and the birds are in the process of acquiring a new song repertoire (Nottebohm 1981). The brain sections used to make these observations were stained with Cresyl violet, a Nissl stain. Subsequently, it was suggested that this was not a reliable way to visualize the boundaries of HVC because the darkness of the stain was proportional to the level of protein synthesis and this could change seasonally (Gahr 1990). However, another study that used backfills from RA corroborated the original observation, noticing that HVC was significantly smaller in early fall (first week of October) than in early summer or late fall (Nottebohm et al. 1994). Two other studies using Nissl stains, have also reported photoperiod-related changes in the size of HVC. In both cases HVC was considerably larger in birds in breeding condition than in those that were not in breeding condition. Unlike canaries, the birds involved in the latter two studies—the orange bishop (*Euplectes franciscanus*) and the rufous-sided towhee (*Pipilo erythrophthalmus*)—do not modify their song in adulthood (Arai et al. 1989; Brenowitz et al. 1991). Other song-system nuclei, such as RA and Area X, have also been reported to show seasonal changes in volume (Arai et al. 1989; Brenowitz et al. 1991; Kirn et al. 1989; Nottebohm 1981).

Despite uncertainty about the significance of seasonal volume changes in nuclei of the adult song system, the phenomenon itself is probably real. The weight of the entire brain of adult canaries and red-winged blackbirds is greater in the spring than in the fall (Kirn et al. 1989; Nottebohm 1981). Seasonal changes in brain weight have also been reported in mammals (Weiler 1992), suggesting that this is not just an avian peculiarity.

How Does Vocal Learning Take Place?

The two-step model of vocal learning (Konishi 1965) proposes that model acquisition must precede model imitation (figure 3.1). An auditory memory for a song model is established, presumably, by repeated exposure to that same song. As the details of this memory are acquired, the circuits that hold them should respond to playbacks of this song in a selective and predictable manner, that is, learning becomes recognition. It will be important to discover when and where in the young songbird brain the first selective responses to a song model appear. The next step, converting the model to an imitation, brings us back to HVC.

Because of its position at the origin of modules 2 and 3 (figure 3.4) and its apparent status as end-recipient of information conveyed by the ascending auditory pathway (figure 3.5), HVC would seem well positioned to alter vocal output until it matches a learned model. To play this role, however, HVC or some other part of the brain should be able to compare the auditory feedback from sounds produced with the auditory memory of the model. Mismatches between model and feedback should produce an "error signal" that is forwarded to motor nuclei that can help correct the error upon subsequent renderings of the same song. If learned vocal programs are stored in HVC (as suggested by Vu et al. 1994, and Yu and Margoliash 1996), or partly, at least, also in RA (as suggested by Vicario and Simpson 1995), or in both these nuclei and associated pathways, then the "error signal" should reach these nuclei and pathways. However, there is no evidence that HVC is responsive to sound while the bird is singing (McCasland and Konishi 1981) and so it may not receive auditory feedback from the sounds it produces.

Do NMDA Receptors Play a Role in Song Learning?

Lesions of nuclei such as Area X, DLM, and lMAN affect vocal learning but not the maintenance of learned song (Bottjer et al. 1984; Halsema and Bottjer 1992; Sohrabji et al. 1990; Scharff and Nottebohm 1991). The connections that lMAN forms in RA have attracted considerable attention because glutamate released by lMAN endings activates NMDA glutamate receptors in RA cells (Kubota and Saito 1991; Mooney and Konishi 1991; Mooney 1992). Activation of NMDA receptors has been linked to processes of circuit plasticity, including long-term potentiation and learning (Constantine-Paton 1990; Udin and Scherer 1990; Lipton and Kater 1989). Therefore, lMAN's proven role in song learning (Bottjer et al. 1984; Morrison and Nottebohm 1993) and the presence of NMDA receptors in the synapses that lMAN forms in RA have fostered speculation that this part of the song circuit is particularly important for learning. It was mentioned earlier that lMAN innervation of RA is important for maintaining circuit plasticity in RA (Scharff and Nottebohm 1991). It is conceivable that a same pathway from lMAN to RA, mediated by NMDA receptors, regulates circuit plasticity and conveys information necessary for song learning.

A relation between RA's NMDA receptors and learning is supported by the observation that the number of these receptors is much greater in 30-day-old male zebra finches at the beginning of song learning than in adulthood (Aamodt et al. 1992). However, activation of these receptors by lMAN stimulation persists in adulthood (Kubota and Saito 1991), and one must wonder what role these receptors play at that time.

Does Hearing Have a Direct Effect on Some Song-system Neurons?

Circuits used for the acquisition and production of learned song receive auditory inputs and develop late in ontogeny. Auditory inputs reaching some of these circuits could have a direct and selective effect on the genesis and survival of cells and connections in these circuits. If so, then auditory stimulation could bias the development of vocal circuits. In this manner, some "vocal learning" could occur in the absence of vocal rehearsal. Deafness after tutoring with a conspecific model could reverse the effect of tutoring by causing the demise of cells and connections that depended on auditory stimulation, yielding the results described by Konishi (1965). There is as yet no evidence that supports this alternative model of vocal learning, yet it seems worth testing. If the effect suggested here occurs, it would add to the complexity of the two-step model of vocal learning.

The Establishment of a Relation between Perception and Production

It has been suggested that some brain pathways and processes are used both for song production and song perception (Williams and Nottebohm 1985; review in Nottebohm et al. 1990). They might also be used for model acquisition and model imitation. Let us look at the facts. Several—possibly all—of the song system's late developing nuclei—HVC, RA, Area X—and their connecting pathways—for example, DLM and lMAN—respond to sound in general (Katz and Gurney 1981; Williams 1989) and discriminate between playbacks of different songs (Margoliash 1983; Williams and Nottebohm 1985). These same pathways respond best to playbacks of the bird's own song (Doupe and Konishi 1991; Margoliash 1986; Margoliash and Konishi 1985; Vicario and Yohay 1993). The latter observation is intriguing. However, does selective responsiveness to a bird's own song tell us something important about the mechanisms of vocal learning, or does it tell us about perceptual changes that result from vocal learning?

Selective HVC responses to playbacks of a bird's own song could result from an overlap of auditory and motor maps in HVC, such that circuits that produce a sound also respond selectively to playbacks of that sound. This overlap could develop during vocal learning, when the bird first encounters the auditory consequences of its vocal output. Once such an overlap is established, sounds similar to the bird's own song would trigger the activation of a well rehearsed HVC circuit normally used in song production. Sounds that differed from the bird's own song would yield weaker responses. If auditory processing in HVC plays a role in perception, then sounds that share properties with the bird's own song are likely to have a privileged perceptual status (Margoliash and Konishi 1985).

Volman (1993) tested HVC's responsiveness to song playbacks during various stages of song development. She recorded auditory responses from the HVC of white-crowned sparrows before the plastic song stage of song development, during plastic song, and in adulthood. Responses to sound in the HVC of the juveniles that were not yet in plastic song tended to be inhibitory or weak and inconsistent. By contrast, clear auditory responses were recorded in almost any electrode penetration in the HVC of birds in plastic song stage or in adults. Recordings from the HVC of 8–10-month-old juveniles in plastic song showed that the best responses were obtained to playbacks of the bird's own plastic song; next in effectiveness were playbacks of the song that had been used to tutor these birds. Since white-crowned sparrows memorize song models they hear during the first 2–3 months of life (Marler 1970; Baptista and Petrinovich 1984), the late appearance of model responses in HVC suggests that model-selective auditory responses in HVC are not necessary for model acquisition. Similar work by Doupe and Solis (1997) on zebra finches shows that the relative selectivity of the auditory responses of neurons in Area X and lMAN reflects the level of organization shown at that time by the bird's own song. Both examples suggest that guidance for song acquisition must rely heavily on auditory information stored outside the song system.

The previous arguments suggest that the particularly strong responses of HVC neurons to a bird's own learned song result from learning, but may not play a role in learning. Deafening an adult canary or zebra finch results in the gradual disassembling of learned song (Nottebohm et al. 1976; Nordeen and Nordeen 1992). In these cases, song feedback is, apparently, necessary for maintaining the learned pattern. Intriguingly, though, we do not yet know of a way whereby this could occur in HVC. HVC neurons that normally respond to playbacks of the bird's own song do not respond to sound during adult song production and for a period of a few seconds after a song ends (McCasland and Konishi 1981). It is not known whether this inhibition of HVC auditory responses during singing occurs also when the bird is learning its song. Auditory input to the HVC and other song-system nuclei of young and adult songbirds may generate trophic factors that are necessary for the survival of some cells in these nuclei and for the maintenance of existing connections. The levels of such trophic factors may be reduced by deafening. Thus deafness-induced song changes could result from: (1) the loss of song feedback as a source of information that the bird needs to maintain or constantly relearn its song; or (2) from a non-specific atrophy of vocal pathways that depend on activity levels induced by auditory stimulation (see the section on BDNF-mediated neuronal survival).

Despite the uncertainties raised by the previous paragraph, it seems likely that the number and nature of auditory connections in HVC changes during the months of song development, but a causal link between such changes and vocal learning has not been established.

Neurons that respond selectively to playbacks of conspecific song are found not just in HVC, but also in several other nuclei of the song system, down to the level of nXIIts (e.g., Doupe and Konishi 1991; Vicario and Yohay 1993; Williams and Nottebohm 1985) and the muscles of the syrinx (D. S. Vicario, unpub. data). The awake bird whose vocal pathways respond in this manner remains, nonetheless, silent. These responses could influence communication. Much as smiling can make a person relax and scowling conjures anger, activation of the song system may induce in male songbirds physiological changes that best prepare the individual for territorial defense. An aggressive response may be particularly strong when a male bird hears close imitations of its own song, which would most likely come from young apprentices starting to claim an adjacent territory. If song is a form of aggression, a close imitation may best find its way into the victim's brain and emotions. The strong HVC responses secured by playbacks of a bird's own song result from song learning, but their main function may be communication, not learning.

In support of this perceptual role of song system nuclei, lesions of Area X in adult male zebra finches interfere with the discrimination of conspecific songs, and this effect is particularly acute when one of two songs to be discriminated is the bird's own (Scharff et al. 1998).

Acquisition of Auditory Song Memories Is Not Limited by the Sensitive Period for Song Learning

Although acquisition and imitation of a song model and perception of conspecific song may share common pathways, the end of the sensitive period for song learning does not terminate the ability to acquire new song memories. Adult male zebra finches do not modify their song in adulthood, yet they can discriminate between different songs they first hear in adulthood and respond differently to them even when the differences are very subtle (Nottebohm et al. 1990; Cynx and Nottebohm 1992). Adult female zebra finches do not sing, yet they show preferences for the song of their father and their mate (Miller 1979a,b), and they can also discriminate between the songs of strangers (Cynx and Nottebohm 1992). Thus the acquisition of song memories does not require a special developmental state or a male song system.

Observations of free-ranging songbirds of both sexes also indicate that these birds acquire long-term perceptual memories of the songs of other conspecifics in adulthood, as described for male hooded warblers (*Wilsonia citrina*) (Godard 1991), female dunnocks (*Prunella modularis*) (Wiley et al. 1991), and stripe-backed wrens of both sexes (*Campylorhynchus nuchalis*) (Wiley and Wiley 1977). This allows mates and territory owners to discriminate between familiar and unfamiliar songs and respond accordingly. Thus three facts are evident: (1) The memories of songs imitated are acquired during a sensitive period; (2) Male songbirds continue to memorize new songs well after the end of the sensitive period for song learning and use these memories to discriminate between individuals (e.g., Stoddard et al. 1992); and (3) Female songbirds can do this too, even when they themselves do not sing and, as in the case of the female zebra finch, have a very rudimentary song system. However, a caveat is in order: the memories of songs that are imitated and of those that are not may be acquired differently. Auditory inputs that will be imitated may modify not just the ascending auditory pathways, but may, in addition, act directly on the developing song system.

Laterality as a Developmental Variable

The development of the song system or of the afferents it receives may differ between the two halves of the brain. This would be yet another parallel between song learning and imprinting. The reasons for suggesting this possibility follow.

Many of the sounds produced by nestling and fledgling songbirds have a jangling quality that results from the simultaneous presence of two different fundamental frequencies generated, presumably, by two sound sources, one in each syringeal half (Greenewalt 1968). As song development advances, one of the sound sources tends to be silenced so that, for example, adult chaffinches, canaries, and white-crowned sparrows produce most of their learned song with the sound source in their left syringeal half (Nottebohm 1971, 1972; Nottebohm and Nottebohm 1976), under the dominant control of the ipsilateral song-control pathways (Nottebohm 1977).

Denervation of the left syringeal half in adult chaffinches produces lasting song deficits (Nottebohm 1971). The same operation in adult canaries also produces marked deficits, but over a period of months these canaries, but not chaffinches, shift control to the normally subordinate side and its ipsilateral control pathways (Nottebohm 1977). Thus, the plasticity that allows an adult canary to acquire new songs may underlie its ability to shift dominant sides. Age-limited and open-ended learners may differ not just in their ability to imitate new models in adulthood, but also in their ability to reverse dominance in adulthood.

It is useful to consider parallels with the human situation. Speech in most humans is a left-hemisphere skill, underlaid by brain anatomical asymmetries. Speech lateralization is thought to be part of a broad array of functional differences between the two hemispheres (review in Nottebohm 1979). If this were also the case in songbirds, then reversal of lateralization for song control in adulthood implies a remarkable degree of central functional plasticity. We have begun to investigate the scope of functional asymmetries in the brain of the zebra finch.

Zebra finches, unlike chaffinches and canaries, produce most of the components of song with their right hypoglossal and right syringeal half. Their right HVC plays a dominant role in the temporal organization of song (Williams et al. 1992). In addition, lateralization affects the way in which songs are discriminated. This was shown by interrupting the ascending auditory pathway at the level of the thalamic auditory relay, nucleus ovoidalis. Each nucleus ovoidalis projects only to relays in the ipsilateral telencephalon (Field L), which in turn send auditory information to HVC (Kelley and Nottebohm 1979; Katz and Gurney 1981; Vates et al. 1996). Unilateral lesions of nucleus ovoidalis allowed us to ask adult male zebra finches to discriminate between sounds using just right-hemishere or left-hemisphere auditory pathways. The birds had to produce an operant response, hopping on a perch, when they heard one of two songs and were then rewarded with food. The left hemisphere of birds tested in this manner was superior at discriminating between the playbacks of the bird's own song and that of another zebra finch; the right hemisphere was better at discriminating between two copies of a same song that differed only in the presence or absence of a particular harmonic (Cynx et al. 1992). If processes of song acquisition incorporate right/left asymmetries in the way in which sounds are heard, discriminated, and imitated, then brain properties associated with the occurrence and termination of the sensitive period may also have different representations in each hemisphere.

Song Learning in Young and Adult Canaries

The relation between neurogenesis and song learning, to be reviewed in the next section, has been studied in some detail in canaries, so it is appropriate that we review here this species' timetable for song learning. Male canaries kept under a natural photoperiod start to develop their song at about 40 days after hatching. The subsong stage lasts roughly from day 40 to day 60. By day 60 one can already recognize distinct song syllable types, and some of these syllables will be retained as part of the bird's adult song. The plastic song stage lasts approximately from day 60 until the advent of sexual maturity, which normally occurs sometime in the seventh or eighth month of life. Most of the song syllables present at sexual maturity are produced already, albeit in a variable form, by day 120 after hatching. By about day 240 the structure of song syllables is stable and remains so for the entire duration of that breeding season (Nottebohm et al. 1986).

New song syllables can appear in adult canary song any month of the year (Nottebohm et al. 1986). However, such influxes are particularly marked in late summer/early fall (August–September–October), with a secondary, smaller peak in late winter (February–March), right before the onset of the breeding season (Nottebohm et al. 1987) (figure 3.3).

The Relation of Neurogenesis and Neuronal Replacement to Song Learning

Approximately 1% of the RA-projecting HVC neurons of a one-year-old male canary is formed before hatching (Alvarez-Buylla et al. 1988). The remainder of these cells is formed after hatching and during the entire period when song is first developed (Alvarez-Buylla et al. 1988, 1992). A similar situation occurs in male zebra finches (Nordeen and Nordeen 1988a). Thus new connections between HVC and RA are made at the time song is learned. One could infer from this that we are dealing just with a process of net growth, but the real situation is more complicated.

Four-month-old canaries have already an adult number of HVC neurons, yet HVC neurogenesis continues at that time as briskly as during the preceding months.

Thus a process of neuronal replacement is well under way by 4 months of age and perhaps even earlier, well before canaries reach sexual maturity and produce stable adult song (Alvarez-Buylla et al. 1992). Since most of the HVC neurons born after hatching project to RA, there is a gradual increase in the strength of this projection during song development. The establishment and growth of this pathway during the first 4 months may enable the acquisition of the bird's syllable repertoire; the subsequent addition of new neurons to this pathway may help achieve syllable stereotypy.

HVC neurogenesis occurs at comparable rates in 4- and 8-month-old male canaries (cf. Alvarez-Buylla et al. 1988 and 1992); no samples have been taken between these two ages. The neurogenesis that occurs at 4 months could be related to song development, but probably not the one at 8 months. Moreover, the rates of HVC neurogenesis are higher in adult female canaries than in adult males (F. Nottebohm unpub. data), even though females rarely sing and their song is simpler. HVC neurogenesis is perhaps related not just to song acquisition.

Nonetheless, one can also find correlations between neurogenesis and song learning. New neurons are added at a relatively low rate to the HVC of 12-month-old canaries in stable song, but the rates climb sharply by the end of the summer, at 16–17 months of age (Alvarez-Buylla et al. 1990), when canaries are once more in plastic song and show a peak in new syllable acquisition (Nottebohm et al. 1986). There is a correlation, too, between the higher rates of HVC neurogenesis seen in adult canaries, which are capable of modifying their song, and the much lower rates seen in adult male zebra finches, which do not modify their song. In addition, whereas 56% of all neurons produced in adult canary HVC project to RA, only 23% of all neurons produced in adult zebra finch HVC do so (Alvarez-Buylla et al. 1990). Perhaps a brisk turnover of RA-projecting neurons is important for a constant retooling of adult song.

The above observations can be summarized as follows: addition of new HVC neurons occurs in male canaries immediately before and during periods of song change. However, addition can also occur when song is relatively stable (e.g., at 8 months of age), and in females, which sing little. Interpretation: HVC is involved not only with song learning as a motor skill, but also with song perception. If so, then the production and turnover of HVC neurons seen at any particular time may be related to motor and perceptual learning, or just to perceptual learning. It could serve other unsuspected roles, as well.

Neurogenesis also occurs in Area X of juvenile male zebra finches and canaries (Nordeen and Nordeen 1988b; Alvarez-Buylla unpubl. data) and in adult canaries (F. Nottebohm unpubl. data). In addition, post-hatching neurogenesis has been reported in the nucleus RA of nestling and juvenile zebra finches (Kirn and

DeVoogd 1989), and its possible significance for song learning should receive careful attention. Neurogenesis is not known to occur after hatching in other nuclei of the song system.

Replaceable Neurons as Units of Learning and Forgetting

A causal relation between the timing of learning and the timing of neurogenesis could result from properties of neuronal growth and differentiation. New neurons have uncommitted, growing neurites, ready to form new synapses and modify existing circuits. Neurite growth and synaptogenesis may be shaped by the activity of cells that the new neurons approach or contact. If this activity is driven by auditory or motor events, then the connections formed by the new neurons would be biased by ongoing experience. In addition, cellular mechanisms for long-term learning may be akin to processes of cell differentiation. Once a cell is part of a circuit, experiences that lead to long-term learning may induce changes in gene expression that are difficult to reverse. Because of this possible similarity between long-term memory formation and irreversible cell differentiation, in the extreme situation some neurons may be able to acquire persistent memories only once. In this case, the whole neuron —not the synapse—is the unit of long-term memory. Replacement of these learned neurons by freshly minted ones—with consequent forgetting—may be necessary to restore full learning flexibility to the circuits involved. This need may be particularly acute when brains are small, memory loads are large, and life spans are long, as is the case in many songbirds.

RA-projecting HVC neurons added to the adult male canary HVC in late summer and early fall live for at least 8 months. They would be appropriate repositories for new songs learned at that time and retained until the following breeding season (Kirn et al. 1991). Similar neurons born in late spring have shorter half-lives (Kirn and Nottebohm 1993), and the information held by many of these spring born neurons must be correspondingly shorter lived. Approaches are now becoming available for the selective induction and blockage of cell death, so it might soon be possible to evaluate critically the relevance of neuronal death and neuronal replacement to the acquisition and maintenance of learned song.

The Influence of Steroid Hormones on the Development of the Song System

Song is predominantly a male behavior in many oscine songbirds, and in them the song system is better developed in males than in females. An extreme example of this phenomenon is found in zebra finches (Nottebohm and Arnold 1976). The establishment of this behavioral and anatomical dimorphism seems to result from early hormonal influences that have a lasting "organizational" effect (Gurney and Konishi 1980). If hormones can influence the development of the song system, then they may also influence the timing of song learning. Let us explore such a model. It revolves around three steroid hormones: testosterone (T) and its two metabolites 17B-estradiol (E2) and 5a-dihydrotestosterone (DHT). The enzyme aromatase is responsible for converting T into E2. DHT and E2 are not interconvertible among themselves. Therefore, their effects must be mediated, presumably, by different mechanisms.

The hormonal influences on the development of the zebra finch nucleus RA have been described in some detail. The number and size of RA neurons is considerably greater in males than in females. DHT and E2 administered at hatching masculinize, respectively, the number and size of the female RA neurons (Gurney 1981; Schlinger and Arnold 1991a).

Some of the early hormonal effects can bring about changes that influence developmental events that occur later. For example, E2 treatment of newly hatched female zebra finches affects HVC's ability to incorporate neurons born later in ontogeny (Nordeen and Nordeen 1989), and this early effect also determines whether or not the HVC neurons will innervate RA (Konishi 1985). In both cases, the primary effect may be that of E2 on RA neurons.

If E2 and DHT are to affect the sexually dimorphic development of the song system, then the hormonal profile of young male and female zebra finches should differ during the period after hatching when the male or female fate of the song system becomes established. However, there is no evidence of such a difference for DHT (Adkins-Regan et al. 1990; Hutchison et al. 1984), and the situation for E2 is unclear. An early surge in the plasma E2 levels of males was reported by one study (Hutchison et al. 1984), but two other studies (Adkins-Regan et al. 1990; Schlinger and Arnold 1992a) failed to confirm this result. If there is an E2 effect, it would be expected to interact with the timetable of a developing song system. This expectation is met: the earlier the start of E2 treatment, the more marked the anatomical and behavioral masculinization (Konishi and Akutagawa 1988; Pohl-Apel and Sossinka 1984; Simpson and Vicario 1991).

E2 could exert its effects on the developing female zebra finch brain by acting directly on various posttranscriptional cell processes, but perhaps posttranscriptional influences would not have a permanent organizational effects. E2 could also exert its effects by binding to a specific receptor that then carried the hormone and its receptor into the nucleus, where they would affect genomic transcription. A search for E2 receptors in the song system of juvenile female zebra finches was conducted between post-hatching days 20 and 50. Nucleus HVC was the only member of the song system to have cells with E2 receptors. The number of these cells declined sharply after day 40 (Gahr and Konishi 1988). Since other nuclei of the song system can be masculinized by early systemic E2 treatment, Gahr and Konishi (1988) concluded that the action of E2 on these other nuclei must be indirect, via HVC. There is some evidence for this suggestion from a study that used HVC lesions. E2's masculinizing influence on RA and Area X of juvenile female zebra finches did not occur if HVC was removed before onset of E2 treatment; however, E2's masculinizing effect on lMAN still occurred in such birds and presumably was not mediated by HVC (Herrmann and Arnold 1991b).

Though there is strong evidence that early administration of E2 and DHT to female songbirds masculinizes their song system and singing behavior, there is as yet no clear mechanism for how this occurs under natural conditions. Plasma T, E2, and DHT levels and brain aromatase levels are remarkably similar in male and female zebra finches during the first two weeks after hatching (Schlinger and Arnold 1992a). Moreover, E2 receptors are present in the HVC of juvenile female zebra finches (Gahr and Konishi 1988). As a result, it is not clear what keeps female zebra finches from showing male-like development of their song system. Once one is aware of this puzzle, one is inclined to be cautious in modeling how steroid hormones interact with the various stages of song development. Schlinger and Arnold (1992b) have evidence that the brain, not the gonads, of adult male zebra finches produces the majority, or perhaps even all of the E2 present in the plasma. If E2 is produced by the brain and E2 regulates learning (see next section), then what regulates the brain's pathways for E2 production? Clearly, local differences in the presence of aromatase, the enzyme that converts T to E2, could, at any time, have a profound effect on the development and performance of E2-sensitive circuits. Thus there are still many uncertainties, and, for now, we know of no clear mechanism by which sex steroids affect the development and plasticity of song circuits.

Despite these uncertainties, it seems very likely that E2 and aromatase play an important role in the post-hatching masculinization of the song system. And yet, aromatase inhibitor injected into genetically female chicken eggs during the first 7 days after laying masculinizes development, so that the adults look like roosters and have active testis (Elbrecht and Smith 1992).

The Role of Steroid Hormones in Song Acquisition and Production

Newly hatched zebra finch females treated with E2 have the motivation and capacity as adults to produce male-like song, and even to imitate models presented to them as juveniles. However, most of these birds sing little, and their song is usually variable and poorly structured and the imitations are not very good. If such females receive T in adulthood, they sing more and the structure of their song syllables and order of syllable delivery tend to be more stereotyped (Simpson and Vicario 1991).

However, much as a late rise in T levels leads to increased song production and to song stereotypy, so that a bird better expresses what it has learned, an earlier rise in T levels may promote premature stereotypy and thus interfere with song development and song learning. Male zebra finches that receive supplementary doses of T during the first 95 days of life develop abnormally simple songs. A significant reduction in the number of song syllables also occurs when T-treatment is restricted to the time between post-hatching days 20–40, but not if it occurs after then (Korsia and Bottjer 1991). Unfortunately, this study did not include data on vocal imitation, and so we do not know if the high T levels used had a specific effect on a bird's ability to imitate a model.

Adult female canaries that sing little, or sing only very variable songs, sing more and produce a more stereotyped song under the influence of T (Nottebohm, unpub. data). T treatment of adult females also results in a larger HVC and RA (Nottebohm 1980b). This effect can be obtained in intact females and in females ovariectomized soon after hatching. Early ovariectomized female canaries do not sing as adults. In them, dendrites of RA type IV cells (which project to nXIIts) are shorter than in intact controls. However, physiological doses of T given in adulthood induce the ovariectomized birds to sing, and dendritic lengths in their RA type IV cells become similar to those found in adult males (DeVoogd and Nottebohm 1981). The T-induced increase in dendritic length is accompanied by a doubling in the number of synapses in RA (DeVoogd et al. 1985). In this experiment, T brought about morphological and behavioral changes reminiscent of the organizational effects induced by early E2 treatment in female zebra finches.

The hormone-induced masculinization of the song system of adult female canaries may be a hallmark of open-ended learners. Adult exposure to T in previously untreated female zebra finches does not induce them to sing, nor does such a treatment alter the anatomy of their song system (Arnold 1980; Gurney and Konishi 1980; Simpson and Vicario 1991).

Ironically, with so much evidence pointing to a role for gonadal hormones in ontogeny, early castration nonetheless seems to have little effect on song ontogeny and model imitation. Male zebra finches castrated 9–17 days after hatching develop normal song and show normal learning, though their song develops over a somewhat longer period of time (Arnold 1975). The situation is somewhat different in canaries. Male canaries castrated as juveniles also develop song normally, yet fall silent at the time when juvenile plastic song gives way to adult stereotyped song (Nottebohm 1980b). Thus use of song as a reproductive tool is under testosterone control, but song development is not.

Several longitudinal studies have related naturally occurring hormone levels to song development and learning in songbirds. The first of these shows that the T and DHT plasma levels of juvenile male and female canaries are comparable, but that the E2 levels tend to be considerably higher in males than in females. Thus the gradually increasing stereotypy that occurs in the song of juvenile canaries may be influenced by the modest differences in T levels that occur, or by the larger differences in plasma E2 levels, or it may result just from singing practice—or a combination of these factors (Weichel et al. 1986). These same authors noticed, too, that males castrated as juveniles did not improve their vocal quality beyond plastic song.

Another detailed longitudinal study was done with song sparrows and swamp sparrows. Early castrates of both species start their subsong one month later than intacts. Their subsong and plastic song stages are otherwise similar to those of intacts, yet these birds fail to develop stable adult song. The plasma T levels of the castrates were too low for detection, yet these birds had normal or above normal E2 levels. Clearly in this case neither E2 nor the substrate for E2 production could be of testicular origin. When these castrates were treated as adults with physiological levels of T, they imitated in a stereotyped manner songs they had heard as castrate juveniles during the normal sensitive period for model acquisition (Marler et al. 1988; see also Marler et al. 1987).

These longitudinal studies of first-year birds might encourage one to believe that E2 is necessary for vocal learning. This inference, however, is not supported by the adult hormonal profiles of open-ended learners such as the canary and starling. There is no obvious relation between times of year when plasma E2 levels are high (or low) and the times when adult male canaries revert to plastic song and introduce new syllable types into their song; however, periods of song modification coincide with periods when plasma T levels are relatively low (Nottebohm et al. 1987). Adult starlings, which apparently show undetectable levels of E2 throughout the year (Dawson 1983), continue to add new song types to their song repertoire (Böhner et al. 1990; Eens et al. 1992). Thus, if E2 plays a special role in the actual process of song learning, this role may be restricted to the juvenile period and not extend into adulthood.

To sum up, observations of canaries, swamp sparrows, and song sparrows suggest, but do not prove, that E2 plays a role in juvenile vocal learning. A test of this hypothesis would be to produce a condition in which E2 is not present during either the model acquisition or model imitation stages of song learning. It might be possible to do such an experiment with swamp sparrows, in which these two stages can be clearly separated (Marler and Peters 1982; figure 3.2). In addition, the observations reviewed suggest that T is not necessary for song learning or song production, but that it is necessary for high singing rates and for the production of stereotyped adult song. Perhaps as a result of this relation between T and song stereotypy, high levels of T interfere with vocal learning. Song stereotypy and high singing rates advertise a male's reproductive condition, social dominance, territorial ownership, and fighting readiness. At that time the broadcasting of these messages takes precedence over vocal learning.

Experience Affects the End of the Sensitive Period

A very limited amount of song exposure is sufficient for song imitation to occur. As an example, male nightingales imitate in their first spring songs they heard only 20 times as fledglings (Hultsh and Todt 1989). However, earlier song exposure need not preempt the imitation of models presented later. As in other aspects of the development of song learning, some of the best data on this topic come from work done with zebra finches.

Immelman's (1969) studies of the sensitive period for song learning used cross-fostering experiments, in which pairs of Bengalese finches, *Lonchura striata*, reared zebra finches. Immelman took 80- to 90-day-old zebra finch males that had imitated their foster father's song. He placed these birds in an aviary with 10–20 colony-reared adult male zebra finches. He reported that

Despite the constant acoustic contact with conspecific males possessing a normal song, the experimental birds did not supplement their song phrases further to any great extent. Only a few very minor alterations could be detected in some of the birds. This means that once the song phrase of a bird is fully developed, basic alterations are apparently no longer possible. This applied even to birds which, because they had been raised by another species, did not yet possess the species-specific song, and which afterwards had opportunity to listen to conspecific males. The song phrase seems to be irreversibly fixed once it has been fully developed.   (Immelman 1969, pp. 67–67)

Immelman (1969) noticed, too, that if males were separated from their foster parents at earlier times, learning was less perfect. Males isolated after post-hatching days 38–66 "developed a song which consisted of song elements only of the foster father, but which was not identical in the sequence of elements or in the total length of the song phrase." Males that had been isolated even earlier, before post-hatching day 40, "developed a song containing some very marked song elements of the foster father but differing in almost all other characters (length, number and sequence of elements, etc.).'' Immelman concluded that whereas song elements can be acquired early—even before the young male starts to produce its own juvenile song—imitation of syllable sequence and tempo requires a more protracted exposure (Immelman 1969, pp. 65–66).

Immelman's early pioneering work did not look at the possibility that the sounds of conspecific song and the visual stimuli that usually accompany them—as different from the corresponding stimuli from a foster father of a different species—may induce earlier, faster, or more complete memorization of all features of a model. Many years later, Böhner (1990) noted that the accuracy with which young male zebra finches copy their father's song is equally good regardless of whether they had been separated from their father at post-hatching days 35 or 100. This observation suggests that an auditory memory acquired before day 35 can have all the detail needed to assure a close imitation of the model. However, in another study, male zebra finches isolated from their parents at day 35 and kept in monosexual groups of 6–10 individuals of the same age developed atypical songs (Eales 1985). Böhner (1990), commenting on this work, suggests that Eales's (1985) results may have stemmed from using fathers with atypical songs. Another possibility is that birds placed with nonsib male companions at the age of 35 days are not really in auditory or social isolation but interact in complex ways among themselves, a situation that is far removed from auditory isolation. Unless proven wrong, Böhner's (1990) finding stands: full details of a conspecific song model can be acquired before day 35, and therefore the sensitive period for model acquisition must start before that time, though the exact beginning remains undefined.

In another, related experiment, Eales (1985) removed young males from their parents at three different ages, at 35, 50, and 65 days. On removal from their parents, the young zebra finches were housed with another adult male. Birds given a new tutor at 35 days learned their song from this second male. Males given a new tutor at 50 days of age learned part of their song from their father and part from the new tutor. Those given a new tutor at 65 days showed no evidence of imitating its song but developed songs based entirely on those of their fathers. By that time, most if not all of the syllables that will appear in adult song are already in place, albeit in a variable manner (Tchernichovski and Nottebohm 1998). By 65 days of age, a young male and its song system may already be too committed to the imitation of a model heard earlier to find it easy, necessary, or desirable to change course.

It has been customary to discuss the success of model imitation only in terms of information conveyance—information received, remembered, and imitated. However, exposure to a model for varying amounts of time could affect the brain in more complex ways: for example, it could affect the production of hormones or of trophic factors that affect neurogenesis, neuronal survival, synaptogenesis, or other processes that affect the maintenance or growth of circuits. By acting in these ways, the absence or presence of song models, the quality of the songs used, and the nature of the attendant social interactions could all affect—hasten or delay—the development of song pathways. So, when zebra finch males isolated from their parents at day 35 and kept in groups with other juvenile males sing, as adults, songs that are atypical (Eales 1985), one possibility is that the song circuits of these birds remain arrested at an immature and still plastic state. Another possibility is that keeping a male zebra finch as an isolate—by itself or in groups of monosexual juveniles—affects the rate of sexual maturation; at 90 days of age, a bird kept under such conditions may not be an adult. This could explain why, in Eales (1985) experiment, exposure of isolates to live conspecific tutors at 6 months of age could still induce changes leading to a species-typical pattern. It is important to note that Eales (1985, p. 1298) herself did recognize that the end of the sensitive period could be delayed in these indirect ways. Thus the results of experiments with zebra finches (see also Eales 1987a,b; Clayton 1988) confirm, but with much greater detail, what had been reported earlier for the chaffinch (Nottebohm 1969), namely, that the end of the sensitive period is determined not by age, but by hormones or experience, or an interplay of these two.

Auditory, Motor, or Social Experience?

Further insight into the factors responsible for the occurrence of delayed song learning in zebra finches is found in a study by Morrison and Nottebohm (1993), in which male zebra finches were raised under either of two conditions. Some birds were raised in soundproof chambers by their mother and held after independence (day 32), singly, in a soundproof chamber. From there on these birds could not see nor hear other conspecifics, a situation that was maintained until day 120. These birds are referred to as "soundproof chamber isolates." Another group of juveniles was raised in an aviary. In this case, upon reaching independence, each of these birds was housed singly in a cage from which it could hear, but not see, other juvenile and aviary-reared adult conspecifics; these birds were kept in this condition, called "visual isolation," until day 90. Isolates in either group developed fairly stable adult songs, though this parameter was not quantified. However, the phonology of song syllables differed between the two groups. Only the soundproof chamber isolates included in their song abnormal syllable types; the syllables of the visual isolates were much like those of colony-reared birds. At the end of isolation, each isolate was caged with an adult male zebra finch tutor and was kept with it for the next 4–5 months. Birds in both groups copied syllables from their tutors—2.7 syllables per soundproof chamber isolate, 4.4 syllables per visual isolate. These results suggest that production of a fairly stable adult song composed of atypical or normal-sounding syllable types does not, by itself, bring an end to the sensitive period for song learning (Morrison and Nottebohm 1993).

The size of lMAN is reduced significantly between day 25 and day 50, and it has been suggested that this change could affect vocal learning (Bottjer and Sengelaub 1989). This possibility was tested using the same birds and experimental protocol described in the previous paragraph. Neither the volume of lMAN nor the number of lMAN neurons projecting to RA were significantly affected by rearing the young male zebra finches in soundproof chamber isolation or in visual isolation, as compared to colony-reared males. Moreover, the number of RA-projecting neurons in the lMAN of all three groups was the same at 25 days and in adulthood (Morrison 1991). These two features of lMAN anatomy do not seem to be influenced by learning, nor are they likely to determine when song learning comes to an end.

A minimum amount of social interaction with live conspecific models—with consequent hormonal changes?—may be necessary for the sensitive period for song learning to come to an end. An important role for social stimulation in song learning is not uncommon among oscine songbirds. In many species, song tutoring is particularly effective when combined with social interaction, as provided by a live tutor (Baptista and Petrinovich 1984; Kroodsma and Pickert 1984; Payne 1981; Thielcke 1970; Waser and Marler 1977). One cannot help but wonder what would be the consequences of allowing a male juvenile zebra finch to interact socially with a mute adult conspecific male. Might the hormonal sequelae of such an interaction influence the termination of the sensitive period for song learning, or is the coincident exposure to an auditory model necessary for this?

The results of delayed song learning in zebra finches show that new song syllables can be added after the bird has already acquired a well-defined adult song. However, other observations suggest that motor song learning may restrict, to some extent, the nature of further vocal learning. Thus canaries that continue to modify their song in adulthood do so mainly by gradually changing existing syllables. This process is particularly active during the late summer and early fall, when stable adult song gives way to plastic song (Nottebohm et al. 1986). Birds that learn to produce new sounds in adulthood may favor sounds that can be easily derived from others already present in their repertoire. The mastery of a set of sounds may determine the range of imitations that is still possible.

The sensitive period for song learning may not come to an end unless a bird can hear its own vocalizations. Birds deafened before they reach stable adult song produce as adults unstable song (Konishi 1965; Nottebohm 1968; Konishi and Nottebohm 1969). Otherwise, their vocal ontogeny goes through stages—for example, subsong and plastic song—comparable to those of intact birds. However, the deaf birds develop aberrant sounds—the more so the earlier the deafening (Nottebohm 1968)—and even when deafened late in their vocal ontogeny, the resulting song is never as stereotyped as that of intacts (Nottebohm 1972). Since these birds cannot imitate models, we do not know if their sensitive period for song learning has ended. This issue could be tested by muting or deafening birds in a reversible manner. Unfortunately, there is as yet no satisfactory way to do this. If stages in the development of the song system determine the nature of the song a bird will produce— subsong, plastic song, stable adult song—then a bird first able to hear itself in adulthood may not be able to start its vocal ontogeny with subsong, and that, by itself, could hinder vocal learning.

The experiment (Marler et al. 1973) that explored these issues used 100dB of white noise to mask a young canary's hearing of its own song. This noise was stopped when the birds were 40 or 200 days old. The effects on song were more marked in the individuals that remained in noise for the longer time; these birds produced songs with only 2–6 syllable types, a number comparable to that of chronically deafened canaries. However, these birds improved their song during the months after the noise was stopped, and the number of syllables they produced rose, suggesting the birds now had access to auditory feedback. This approach has not been followed in other work because the high levels of noise used also induced partial deafness, a condition that persisted even a year later (Marler et al. 1973). The inference was that in these canaries, as in other vertebrates, the high levels of noise induced the death of hair cells in the cochlea, and perhaps other changes in central auditory pathways. We now know that hair cells can be replaced in adult birds (Ryals and Rubel 1988), and so it may be worthwhile to persevere with this approach, perhaps finding levels of white noise and durations of treatment that, while interfering with the birds' hearing of its own song, will nonetheless not induce permanent loss of hearing sensitivity.

Some of the Mechanisms for Song Imitation Seem to Be Similar in Young and Adults

A subset of the zebra finch isolates described in the first paragraph of the previous section received bilateral lesions of nucleus lMAN immediately before the onset of adult tutoring. These birds retained the songs they had developed, as would be the case following lesion of lMAN in adult colony reared male zebra finches. However, the lMAN lesioned isolates were unable to imitate any of the syllables produced by their tutors. Apparently, the acquisition of new syllables during delayed adult learning requires, as in juveniles (Bottjer et al. 1984; Scharff and Nottebohm 1991), an intact nucleus lMAN (Morrison and Nottebohm 1993).

Fraternal Inhibition of Song Learning

Many of the experiments testing the variables that control song learning have featured juvenile males housed singly, either by themselves and exposed to song broadcast over a speaker, or in the company of a live tutor. The natural situation is often more complex, as exemplified by young male cowbirds (*Molothrus bonariensis*), in whom song learning is influenced by subtle responses that females give to their song (King and West 1983). Another example comes from song development in family-reared male zebra finches. In this study (Tchernichovski and Nottebohm 1998), the father, mother, and all members of a clutch were housed together from hatching until sexual maturity. Under these conditions the accuracy of song imitation, defined as percentage of father's syllables produced in a recognizable manner, ranged from 100% to 20% The best imitations occurred in single male clutches (the number of sisters did not matter). When more than one brother was present (range 2–5) then the last-hatched birds—that is, the youngest—produced the best imitations. Interestingly, last-hatched birds were also the ones that were most likely to lead in the process of song development, in that their song was first to include all the syllables that would be present in their adult song. The mechanisms behind these effects, which were robust, remain unclear. What is clear, though, is that even as there are conditions that favor learning, there are others that, though offering seemingly similar access to models, discourage learning. Moreover, though male zebra finches reared in auditory isolation improvise a multiparted, complex song (e.g., Price 1979), those reared with a live model do virtually no improvisation even when, because of fraternal inhibition, they end up producing an absurdly stunted song. Though this experiment did not pretend to replicate the conditions in nature, it suggests some rules that may guide song development in zebra finches. One rule is that a live model blocks improvisation; the second rule may be that completeness of song imitation is determined by model abundance; too much of it, as when several siblings and their father rehearse the same song, may hinder imitation. This latter effect may explain why zebra finches reared in a colony often imitate syllables from more than one model, achieving in this way a more unique song (Williams 1990).

Mechanisms for Song Maintenance Differ between Age-dependent and Open-ended Learners

We know that intact hearing is necessary for the maintenance of adult zebra finch song (Nordeen and Nordeen 1992), and we know that neurons in the lMAN of adult male zebra finches respond selectively to playbacks of a bird's own song (Doupe and Konishi 1991). Yet the auditory pathways that male zebra finches use for song maintenance and acquisition seem to differ: lMAN is necessary for auditorily guided song acquisition—whether by juveniles or adults—but not for adult auditorily guided song maintenance. The situation is different in canaries, which need both intact hearing and an intact lMAN to maintain their learned song repertoire (Nottebohm et al. 1990). The importance of lMAN for song maintenance may be a feature that distinguishes open-ended from age-dependent learners. Open-ended learners such as the canary may be constantly relearning their song, and in them the relation between lMAN and RA may remain much as in juveniles. Understanding the different status of the lMAN-RA connection in adult canaries and zebra finches may help explain why the acquisition of a novel song pattern occurs only during a sensitive period in the zebra finch, but throughout adult life in the canary.

Hearing Song Induces Changes in Gene Expression

We have seen that song exposure influences song development and song discrimination. These effects are mediated, presumably, by cells that are part of circuits. Lasting effects on these cells are, one supposes, brought about by changes in gene expression. Immediate early genes are particularly interesting in this context, because they regulate the expression of other genes. Though effects of experience on immediate early gene expression were expected, they came as a surprise when first described (Mello et al. 1992). The observation is that the expression of an immediate early gene, called ZENK, is induced or upregulated in parts of the auditory pathways, and in particular in the caudomedial neostriatum (Ncm) (figure 3.7), when songbirds are exposed to playbacks of conspecific song. This response can be measured by quantifying the amount of messenger RNA specific for this gene that is produced. The effect is much smaller when using playbacks of the song of another species.

The ZENK response in Ncm can also distinguish between different songs of the same species. Thus, if zebra finches are exposed to the same song repeatedly over a period of an hour, by the end of that hour the ZENK mRNA produced earlier has disappeared and no new ZENK mRNA is produced in response to new playbacks of this song. However, if at that time the bird is presented with a different conspecific song, then the full ZENK response reappears. Thus the molecular response to a novel song stimulus is modified by learning (Mello et al. 1995; cf. Jarvis et al. 1995). The different intensity of the ZENK response given to novel and familiar sounds may be related to a drop in the electrophysiological responses of Ncm neurons as a particular song is heard again and again. This process of electrophysiological habituation is stimulus-specific and can be prevented by local injection of a protein synthesis blocker such as cycloheximide (Chew et al. 1995). Taken together, these observations suggest that a genomic response to novel song mediates changes in protein synthesis that underlie the establishment of a song-specific memory.

Playbacks of conspecific song also induce ZENK expression in the neostriatal Shelf under HVC and in the Cup of tissue adjacent to antero-ventral RA (Mello and Clayton 1994; figure 3.7). The Cup receives input from the Shelf under HVC and is part of a feedback circuit linking auditory neostriatum to auditory thalamus and midbrain (Vates et al. 1996; Mello et al. 1998). Because of their relation to auditory and song control circuits, the Shelf and the Cup are strategically placed to (1) monitor and perhaps filter the sounds that reach the song system and (2) selectively attend to incoming sounds. The interplay of anatomical, neurophysiological, and molecular approaches represented in this section should work well for understanding processes of model acquisition during the sensitive period for song learning.

Song Production also Induces Changes in Gene Expression

The changes in gene expression described in the previous section are restricted to auditory relays. Interestingly, increases in ZENK expression are also seen in song system nuclei, but in this case, when the bird sings and the increase in ZENK expression in these nuclei are proportional to the amount of singing. This effect is clear in motor nuclei such as HVC and RA. Surprisingly, it is most marked in Area X, which is not thought to be necessary for the production of stable adult song. In all cases, the magnitude of the effect is comparable in hearing and deaf birds, leading to the inference that it results from the act of singing. This motor-driven gene expression was found in both juvenile and adult zebra finches (Jarvis and Nottebohm 1997). We do not know whether the practice of singing is necessary to maintain the patterns of learned song, though we do know that hearing is (Nordeen and Nordeen 1992). If adult zebra finches are aware of little "errors" they might make every time they sing, then the act of singing would be part of a constant learning process—even if in this case learning is not the acquisition of new information. The reason to believe that motor-driven ZENK expression in a nucleus such as Area X is related to learning is that it occurs when males produce undirected song, but not when they direct their song at females (Jarvis et al. 1998). Undirected song may be a form of rehearsal, but directed song is a form of courtship; in the latter case the bird's attention may be not so much on its own song, but on the female being courted.

BDNF-Mediated Neuronal Survival

Pathway use, as in hearing and singing, can induce the production of trophic substances that in turn determine neuronal survival. An example of the latter has been described in adult male canaries. Brain-derived neurotrophic substance (BDNF) is produced in the HVC of these birds and is necessary for the survival of newly recruited neurons (Rasika et al. 1999). BDNF levels in HVC are relatively low in adult male canaries prevented from singing, but they rise as the birds sing and in a manner directly related to the amount of singing (Li et al. 1997). Taken together, these observations suggest that the act of singing can, through regulation of BDNF levels, determine neuronal survival.

In principle, this system is an action-dependent mechanism that can regulate the survival of subsets of cells and of the memories they hold. This mechanism of memory maintenance, based on selective survival of neurons, is different from a practice-dependent correction of errors based on an increase or decrease in the effectiveness or number of synapses linking subsets of neurons. Both these mechanisms could be at work in the HVC of adult birds, and both could determine the persistence of learned song memories.

There is no direct evidence that singing regulates the survival of HVC neurons, and there is no direct evidence that ZENK or BDNF are necessary for the maintenance of auditory or motor song memories. All the same, it is hard not to be excited by these first examples of genomic responses that are driven by selective experience and that occur in parts of the brain that are involved with the perception and production of a learned skill. Clearly, the molecular approach to mechanisms of song encoding and decoding has come of age. These first examples (see also Kimpo and Doupe 1997; Jin and Clayton 1997) will surely embolden others to search for molecular evidence of how song learning—auditory memories, motor memories—changes cells and pathways in both transient and permanent ways. It should be possible, eventually, to use the song system and the complex skills it masters to describe the molecular machinery that makes for long-term perceptual and motor memories and that determines the end of a sensitive period for learning.

Overview

I have argued that stages in the development of the pathways for the acquisition and production of learned song determine the kinds of sounds—food-begging calls, sub-song, plastic song, stable song—a young bird produces as it grows and matures. I have argued, too, that these pathways should not be thought of as exclusively motor, but as partaking of motor and perceptual roles—the encoding and decoding of signals used in communication.

Song is first learned as an auditory-motor integration during the very time when the circuits that handle this behavior are established. This is a time when neurons are born, axons and dendrites grow, and synapses are formed and discarded. The plasticity inherent in these processes seems ideal for the incorporation of experiential influences and the acquisition of a new behavior. The completion of growth and advent of hormonal changes—for example, a rise in testosterone—seem to bring this plasticity to an end, thus signaling the end of the sensitive period for song learning.

New episodes of growth, as they normally occur in nuclei such as HVC, that show neurogenesis and neuronal replacement in adulthood, may be necessary, though by themselves perhaps not sufficient, for new episodes of song learning.

Though the scenario described is, in broad strokes, probably correct, we cannot yet say how each of the developmental changes that occurs in each of the song nuclei studied in detail—HVC, RA, Area X, DLM, lMAN—relates to vocal learning. This is not a 3-cell system, as studied in *Aplysia*, and so testing for the roles played by specific nuclei, specific cells, specific synapses, specific transmitters, specific trophic substances, specific receptors, and specific genes will be much harder. This complexity should make us cautious, but it should not discourage us. The study of the brain pathways for vocal learning has already played a seminal role in our understanding of nervous systems—sensitive periods, laterality, sexual dimorphism, sexual differentiation, adult neurogenesis, adult neuronal replacement, gene induction, neuronal survival—and this role can only expand. The song system continues to be the premier system for studying how the acquisition and maintenance of a complex learned skill depends on specific circuitry, on specific kinds of plasticity and on specific genes. And so, while this review is little more than a traveler's diary of research conducted and witnessed during the last third of this century, it brings together much of what we know about the conditions that affect, or may affect, the timing of vocal learning in birds.

Summary of Specific Variables that May Affect Vocal Learning in Birds

The following specific variables may affect the timing of vocal learning in oscine songbirds:

1. Timing of changes in the auditory pathway that allow for the acquisition of a fine grain memory of the auditory model.

2. Timing of neurogenesis of RA-projecting cells in HVC.

3. Timing of HVC's innervation of RA.

4. Timing of the contraction of DLM projections that end on the shell of tissue around lMAN.

5. Timing of the reduction in the number of lMAN synapses in RA.

6. Timing of changes in the number of NMDA glutamate receptors in RA.

7. Temporal profile of E2 levels in nuclei of the song system.

8. Timing of increases in circulating T levels.

9. Timing of formation of specific auditory connections in HVC.

Other variables that may affect the timing—and extent—of vocal learning, but whose neural and endocrine underpinnings remain unknown, are order of birth, the social context in which learning occurs (e.g., live models, number of male siblings that interact during learning), and number of times a model song is heard.

A separate list could probably be drawn for factors that regulate the maintenance of learned song, but this list would be shorter for it is a topic that has received little attention. The half-life of synapses, neuronal turnover, and the role of trophic substances such as BDNF would be on this latter list.

It seems unlikely that a single master switch regulates all the variables that affect the acquisition or maintenance of learned song. The challenge is to identify key variables and decide which of them affect learning by virtue of making it possible, and which are integral to the processes of memory acquisition, persistence, and retrieval. As we better understand long-term memory, and in particular how it is maintained, we may come to realize to what extent remembering and learning are incompatible with each other.

Acknowledgment

Dear Peter, it was my incredible good luck to have you as my mentor. My memories of all the years—from 1962 to 1988—that I spent close to you are laden with nostalgia. They were the best. It was a time when the study of behavior held the key to understanding life and the human mind. That is how I felt then. I still do. You showed us the way.

You established an approach and a method for studying the ontogeny, the physical nature, and the information content of animal signals that is applicable to all animals and that is at the heart of the comparative study of animal communication. This chapter is about a part of that project, the timing of vocal learning, a topic to which you contributed so much. It is not as elegant as your studies, but it gets at some of the little pieces.

I do not have enough words to thank you for all you did for me. I have never regarded another scientist more highly, nor have I encountered a lovelier integration of brilliance, character, and kindness.

References

Aamodt, S. M., Nordeen, E. J., and Nordeen, K. W. (1992) MK801 binding declines steadily with age in a nucleus involved in avian song learning. *Abs. Soc. Neurosci.* 18:528.

Adkins-Regan, E., Abdelnabi, M., Mobarak, M., and Ottinger, M. A. (1990) Sex steroid levels in developing and adult male and female zebra finches (*Poephila guttata*). *Gen. Comp. Endocrinol.* 78:93–109.

Alvarez Buylla, A., Kirn, J. R., and Nottebohm, F. (1990) Birth of projection neurons in adult avian brain may be related to perceptual or motor learning. *Science* 249:1444–1446.

Alvarez-Buylla, A., Ling, C.-Y., and Nottebohm, F. (1992) High vocal center growth and its relation to neurogenesis, neuronal replacement, and song acquisition in juvenile canaries. *J. Neurobiol.* 23:396–406.

Alvarez-Buylla, A., Theelen, M., and Nottebohm, F. (1988) Birth of projection neurons in the higher vocal center of the canary forebrain before, during, and after song learning. *Proc. Nat. Acad. Sci.* (USA) 85:8722–8726.

Arai, O., Taniguchi, I., and Saito, N. (1989) Correlation between the size of song control nuclei and plumage color change in orange bishop birds. *Neurosci. Let.* 98:144–148.

Arnold, A. P. (1975) The effects of castration on song development in zebra finches (*Poephila guttata*). *J. Exp. Zool.* 191:261–277.

Arnold, A. P. (1980) Effects of androgens on volumes of sexually dimoprhic brain regions in the zebra finch. *Brain Res.* 185:441–444.

Baptista, L. F. and Petrinovich, L. (1984) Social interaction, sensitive phases, and the song template hypothesis in the white-crowned sparrow. *Anim. Behav.* 32:172–181.

Böhner, J. (1990) Early acquisition of song in the zebra finch (*Taeniopygia guttata*). *Anim. Behav.* 39:369–374.

Böhner, J., Chaiken, M. L., Ball, G. F., and Marler, P. (1990) Song acquisition in photosensitive and photorefractory male European starlings. *Horm. & Behav.* 24:582–594.

Bottjer, S. W., Glaessner, S. L., and Arnold, A. P. (1985) Ontogeny of brain nuclei controlling song learning and behavior in zebra finches. *J. Neurosci.* 5:1556–1562.

Bottjer, S. W., Halsema, K. A., Brown, S. A., and Miesner, E. A. (1989) Axonal connections of a forebrain nucleus involved with vocal learning in zebra finches. *J. Comp. Neurol.* 279:312–326.

Bottjer, S. W., Miesner, E. A., and Arnold, A. P. (1984) Forebrain lesions disrupt development but not maintenance of song in passerine birds. *Science* 224:901–903.

Bottjer, S. W., Miesner, E. A., and Arnold, A. P. (1986) Changes in neuronal number, density, and size account for increases in volume of song-control nuclei during song development in zebra finches. *Neurosci. Letters* 67:263–268.

Bottjer, S. W. and Sengelaub, D. R. (1989) Cell death during development of a forebrain nucleus involved with vocal learning in zebra finches. *J. Neurobiol.* 20:609–618.

Brenowitz, E. A., Nalls, B., Wingfield, J. C., and Kroodsma, D. E. (1991) Seasonal changes in avian song nuclei without seasonal changes in song repertoire. *J. Neurosci.* 11:1367–1374.

Chew, S. J., Mello, C., Nottebohm, F., Jarvis, E., and Vicario, D. S. (1995) Decrements in auditory responses to a repeated conspecific song are long-lasting and require two periods of protein synthesis in the songbird forebrain. *Proc. Natl. Acad. Sci.* (USA) 92:3406–3410.

Clayton, N. S. (1988) Song learning and mate choice in estrildid finches raised by two species. *Anim. Behav.* 36:1589–1600.

Constantine-Paton, M. (1990) NMDA receptor as a mediator of activity-dependent synaptogenesis in the developing brain. *Cold Spring Harbor Symp. Quant. Biol.* 55:431–443.

Cynx, J. and Nottebohm, F. (1992) Role of gender, season, and familiarity in discrimination of conspecific song by zebra finches (*Taenipygia guttata*). *Proc. Natl. Acad. Sci.* (USA) 89:1368–1371.

Cynx, J., Williams, H., and Nottebohm, F. (1992) Hemispheric differences in avian song discrimination. *Proc. Natl. Acad. Sci.* (USA) 89:1372–1375.

Dawson, A. (1983) Plasma gonadal steroid levels in wild starlings, *Sturnus vulgaris*, during the annual cycle and in relation to the stages of breeding. *Gen. Comp. Endocrinol.* 49:286–294.

Devoogd, T. J. and Nottebohm, F. (1981) Gonadal hormones induce dendritic growth in the adult brain. *Science* 214:202–204.

Devoogd, T. J., Nixdorf, B., and Nottebohm, F. (1985) Synaptogenesis and changes in synaptic morphology related to acquisition of a new behavior. *Brain Res.* 329:304–308.

Doupe, A. J. and Konishi, M. (1991) Song-selective auditory circuits in the vocal control system of the zebra finch. *Proc. Natl. Acad. Sci.* (USA) 88:11339–11343.

Doupe, A. J. and Solis, M. M. (1997) Song- and order-selective neurons develop in the songbird anterior forebrain during vocal learning. *J. Neurobiol.* 33:694–709.

Eales, L. A. (1985) Song learning in zebra finches: Some effects of song model availability on what is learnt and when. *Anim. Behav.* 33:1293–1300.

Eales, L. A. (1987a) Song learning in female-raised zebra finches: Another look at the sensitive phase. *Anim. Behav.* 35:1356–1365.

Eales, L. A. (1987b) Do cross-fostered zebra finches still tend to select a conspecific song tutor to learn from? *Anim. Behav.* 35:1347–1355.

Eens, M., Pinxten, R., and Verheyen, R. F. (1992) Song learning in captive European starlings, *Sturnus vulgaris*. *Anim. Behav.* 44:1131–1143.

Elbrecht, A. and Smith, R. G. (1992) Aromatase enzyme activity and sex determination in chickens. *Science* 255:467–470.

Gahr, M. (1990) Delineation of a brain nucleus: comparisons of cytochemical, hodological, and cytoarchitectural views of the song control nucleus HVC of the adult canary. *J. Comp. Neurol.* 294:30–36.

Gahr, M. and Konishi, M. (1988) Developmental changes in estrogen-sensitive neurons in the forebrain of the zebra finch. *Proc. Natl. Acad. Sci.* (USA) 85:7380–7383.

Godard, R. (1991) Long-term memory of individual neighbours in a migratory songbird. *Nature* 350:228–229.

Greenewalt, C. H. (1968) *Bird Song: Acoustics and Physiology*. Washington, D.C.: Smithsonian Inst. Press.

Gurney, M. E. (1981) Hormonal control of cell form and number in the zebra finch song system. *J. Neurosci.* 1:658–673.

Gurney, M. E. and Konishi, M. (1980) Hormone-induced sexual differentiation of brain and behavior in zebra finches. *Science* 208:1380–1383.

Halsema, K. A. and Bottjer, S. W. (1992) Chemical lesions of a thalamic nucleus disrupt song development in male zebra finches. *Abs. Soc. Neurosci.* 18:529.

Hermann, K. and Arnold, A. P. (1991a) The Development of afferent projections to the robust archistriatal nucleus in male zebra finches: A Quantitative electron microscopic study. *J. Neurosci.* 11:2063–2074.

Hermann, K. and Arnold, A. P. (1991b) Lesions of HVC block the developmental masculinizing effects of estradiol in the female zebra finch song system. *J. Neurobiol.* 22:29–39.

Hultsch, H. and Todt, D. (1989) Song acquisition and acquisition constraints in nightingales, *Luscinia megarhynchos. Naturwissenschaften* 76:83–85.

Hutchison, J. B., Wingfield, J. C., and Hutchison, R. E. (1984) Sex differences in plasma concentrations of steroids during the sensitive period for brain differentiation in the zebra finch. *J. Endocrinol.* 103:363–369.

Immelman, K. (1969) Song development in the zebra finch and other estrildid finches. In *Bird Vocalizations*, ed. by R. A. Hinde, p. 61. London and New York: Cambridge University Press.

Jarvis, E. D., Mello, C. V., and Nottebohm, F. (1995) Associative learning and stimulus novelty influence the song-induced expression of an immediate early gene in the canary forebrain. *Learning and Memory* 2:62–80.

Jarvis, E. D. and Nottebohm, F. (1997) Motor-driven gene expression. *Proc. Natl. Acad. Sci.* (USA) 94:4097–4102

Jarvis, E. D., Scharff, C., Grossman, R., Ramos, J. A., and Nottebohm, F. (1998) For whom the bird sings: Context-dependent gene expression. *Neuron* 21:775–788.

Jin, H. and Clayton, D. F. (1997) Localized changes in immediate-early gene regulation during sensory and motor learning in zebra finches. *Neuron* 19:1049–1059.

Johnson, F. and Bottjer, S. W. (1992) Growth and regression of thalamic efferents in the song-control system of male zebra finches. *J. Comp. Neurol.* 326:442–450.

Katz, L. C. and Gurney, M. E. (1981) Auditory responses in the zebra finch's motor system for song. *Brain Res.* 221:192–197.

Kelley, D. B. and Nottebohm, F. (1979) Projections of a telencephalic auditory nucleus—field L—in the canary. *J. Comp. Neurol.* 183:455–470.

Kimpo, R. R. and Doupe, A. J. (1997) FOS is induced by singing in distinct neuronal populations in a motor network. *Neuron* 18:315–325.

King, A. P. and West, M. J. (1983) Epigenesis of cowbird song: A joint endeavour of males and females. *Nature* 305:704–706.

Kirn, J. R., Alvarez-Buylla, A., and Nottebohm, F. (1991) Production and survival of projection neurons in a forebrain vocal center of adult male canaries. *J. Neurosci.* 11:1756–1762.

Kirn, J. R., Clower, R. P., Kroodsma, D., and Devoogd, T. J. (1989) Song-related brain regions in the red-winged blackbird are affected by sex and season but not repertoire size. *J. Neurobiol.* 20:139–163.

Kirn, J. R. and Devoogd, T. J. (1989) Genesis and death of vocal control neurons during sexual differentiation in the zebra finch. *J. Neurosci.* 9:3176–3187.

Kirn, J. R. and Nottebohm, F. (1993) Direct evidence for loss and replacement of projection neurons in adult canary brain. *J. Neurosci.* 13:1654–1663.

Konishi, M. (1965) The role of auditory feedback in the control of vocalization in the white-crowned sparrow. *Z. Tierpsychol.* 22:770–783.

Konishi, M. (1985) Birdsong: From behavior to neuron. *Ann. Rev. Neurosci.* 8:125–170.

Konishi, M. and Akutagawa, E. (1985) Neuronal growth, atrophy, and death in a sexually dimorphic song nucleus in the zebra finch brain. *Nature* 315:145–147.

Konishi, M. and Akutagawa, E. (1988) A Critical period for estrogen action on neurons of the song control system in the zebra finch. *Proc. Natl. Acad. Sci.* (USA) 85:7006–7007.

Konishi, M. and Nottebohm, F. (1969) Experimental studies in the ontogeny of avian vocalizations. In *Bird Vocalizations*, ed. by R. A. Hinde, p. 29. London and New York: Cambridge University Press.

Korsia, A. and Bottjer, S. W. (1989) Developmental changes in the cellular composition of a brain nucleus involved with song learning in zebra finches. *Neuron* 3:451–460.

Korsia, A. and Bottjer, S. W. (1991) Chronic testosterone treatment impairs vocal learning in male zebra finches during a restricted period of development. *J. Neurosci.* 11:2362–2371.

Kroodsma, D. E. (1982) Learning and the ontogeny of sound signals in birds. In *Acoustic Communication in Birds*, ed. by D. E. Kroodsma and E. H. Miller, pp. 21–23. New York: Academic Press.

Kroodsma, D. E. and Pickert, R. (1980) Environmentally dependent sensitive periods for avian vocal learning. *Nature* 288:477–479.

Kroodsma, D. E. and Pickert, R. (1984) Sensitive phases for song learning: Effects of social interaction and individual variation. *Anim. Behav.* 32:389–394.

Kubota, M. and Saito, N. (1991) NMDA receptors participate differentially in two different synaptic inputs in neurons of the zebra finch robust nucleus of the archistriatum in vitro. *Neurosci. Lett.* 125:107–109.

Li, X.-C., Jarvis, E., and Nottebohm, F. (1997) Singing-regulated expression of brain-derived neurotrophic factor in the high vocal center of the songbird's brain. *Soc. Neurosci. Abs.* 23:1330–1331.

Lipton, S. A. and Kater, S. B. (1989) Neurotransmitter regulation of neuronal outgrowth, plasticity, and survival. *Trends Neurosci.* 12:265–270.

Margoliash, D. (1983) Acoustic parameters underlying the responses of song-specific neurons in the white-crowned sparrow. *J. Neurosci.* 3:1039–1057.

Margoliash, D. (1986) A preference for autogenous song by auditory neurons in a song system nucleus of the white-crowned sparrow. *J. Neurosci.* 6:1643–1661.

Margoliash, D. and Fortune, E. S. (1992) Temporal and harmonic combination-sensitive neurons in the zebra finch's HVC. *J. Neurosci.* 12:4309–4326.

Margoliash, D. and Konishi, M. (1985) Auditory representation of autogenous song in the song system of white-crowned sparrows. *Proc. Natl. Acad. Sci.* (USA) 82:5997–6000.

Marler, P. (1970) A Comparative approach to vocal learning: Song learning in white-crowned sparrows. *J. Comp. Physiol. Psychol.* 71:1–25.

Marler, P., Konishi, M., Lutjen, A., and Waser, M. S. (1973) Effects of continuous noise on avian hearing and vocal development. *Proc. Natl. Acad. Sci.* (USA) 70:1393–1396.

Marler, P., Mundinger, P., Waser, M. S., and Lutjen, A. (1972) Effects of acoustical stimulation and deprivation on song development in red-winged blackbirds (*Agelaius phoeniceus*). *Anim. Behav.* 20:586–606.

Marler, P. and Peters, S. (1981) Sparrows learn adult song and more from memory. *Science* 213:780–782.

Marler, P. and Peters, S. (1982) Long-term storage of learned birdsongs prior to production. *Anim. Behav.* 30:479–482.

Marler, P. and Peters, S. (1987) A Sensitive period for song acquisition in the song sparrow, *Melospiza melodia*: A Case of age-limited learning. *Ethology* 76:89–100.

Marler, P. and Peters, S. (1988) Sensitive periods for song acquisition from tape recordings and live tutors in the swamp sparrow, *Melospiza georgiana*. Ethology 77:76–84.

Marler, P., Peters, S., Ball, G. F., Duffy, A. M., and Wingfield, J. C. (1988) The Role of sex steroids in the acquisition and production of birdsong. *Nature* 336:770–772.

Marler, P., Peters, S., and Wingfield, J. C. (1987) Correlations between song acquisition, song production, and plasma levels of testosterone and estradiol in sparrows. *J. Neurobiol.* 18:531–548.

Marler, P. and Tamura, M. (1964) Culturally transmitted patterns of vocal behaviour in sparrows. *Science* 146:1483–1486.

McCasland. J. S. and Konishi, M. (1981) Interaction between auditory and motor activities in an avian song control nucleus. *Proc. Natl. Acad. Sci.* (USA) 78:7815–7819.

Mello, C. V. and Clayton, D. F. (1994) Song-induced ZENK gene expression in auditory pathways of songbird brain and its relation to the song control system. *J. Neurosci.* 14:6652–6666.

Mello, C. V., Nottebohm, F., and Clayton, D. F. (1995) Repeated exposure to one song leads to a rapid and persistent decline in an immediate early gene's response to that song in zebra finch telencephalon. *J. Neurosci.* 15:6919–6925.

Mello, C. V., Vates, G. E., Okuhata, S., and Nottebohm, F. (1998) Descending auditory pathways in the adult male zebra finch (*Taeniopygia guttata*). *J. Comp. Neurol.* 395:137–160.

Mello, C. V., Vicario, D. S., and Clayton, D. F. (1992) Song presentation induces gene expression in the songbird forebrain. *Proc. Natl. Acad. Sci.* (USA).

Miller, D. B. (1979) The acoustic basis of mate recognition by female zebra finches (*Taeniopygia guttata*). *Anim. Behav.* 27:376–380.

Miller, D. B. (1979) Long-term recognition of father's song by female zebra finches. *Nature* 280:389–391.

Mooney, R. and Konishi, M. (1991) Two distinct inputs to an avian song nucleus activate different glutamate receptor subtypes on individual neurons. *Proc. Natl. Acad. Sci.* (USA) 88:4075–4079.

Mooney, R. (1992) Synaptic basis for developmental plasticity in a birdsong nucleus. *J. Neurosci.* 12:2464–2477.

Morrison, R. G. (1991) Neural correlates of sensitive periods for song learning in zebra finches. Ph.D. diss., The Rockefeller University.

Morrison, R. G. and Nottebohm, F. (1993) Role of a telencephalic nucleus in the delayed song learning of socially isolated zebra finches. *J. Neurobiol.* 24:1045–1064.

Nixdorf-Bergweiler, B. E., Lips, M. B., and Heinemann, U. (1995) Electrophysiological and morphological evidence for a new projection of lMAN neurones to Area X. *NeuroReport* 6:1729–1732.

Nordeen, E. J., Grace, A., Burek, M. J., and Nordeen, K. W. (1992) Sex-dependent loss of projection neurons involved in avian song learning. *J. Neurobiol.* 23:671–679.

Nordeen, K. W. and Nordeen, E. J. (1988a) Projection neurons within a vocal motor pathway are born during song learning in zebra finches. *Nature* 334:149–151.

Nordeen, E. J. and Nordeen, K. W. (1988b) Sex and regional differences in the incorporation of neurons born during song learning in zebra finches. *J. Neurosci.* 8:2869–2874.

Nordeen, E. J. and Nordeen, K. W. (1989) Estrogen stimulates the incorporation of new neurons into avian song nuclei during adolescence. *Dev. Brain Res.* 49:27–32.

Nordeen, K. W. and Nordeen, E. J. (1992) Auditory feedback is necessary for the maintenance of stereotyped song in adult zebra finches. *Behav. Neural Biol.* 57:58–66.

Nottebohm, F. (1968) Auditory experience and song development in the chaffinch, *Fringilla coelebs*. *Ibis* 110:549–568.

Nottebohm, F. (1969) The "critical period" for song learning. *Ibis* 111:386–387.

Nottebohm, F. (1971) Neural lateralization of vocal control in a passerine bird. I. Song. *J. Exp. Zool.* 177:229–261.

Nottebohm, F. (1972) Neural lateralization of vocal control in a passerine bird. II. Subsong, calls, and a theory of vocal learning. *J. Exp. Zool.* 179:35–49.

Nottebohm, F. (1977) Asymmetries in neural control of vocalization in the canary. In *Lateralization in the Nervous System*, ed. by S. Harnad, R. W. Doty, L. Goldstein, J. Jaynes, and G. Krauthamer, pp. 23–44. New York: Academic Press.

Nottebohm, F. (1979) Origins and mechanisms in the establishment of cerebral dominance. In *Handbook of Behavioral Neurobiology*, ed. by M.S. Gazzaniga, vol. 2, pp. 295–344. New York: Plenum Press.

Nottebohm, F. (1980a) Brain pathways for vocal learning in birds: A review of the first 10 years. *Prog. Psychobiol. Physiol. Psychol.* 9:85–124.

Nottebohm, F. (1980b) Testosterone triggers growth of brain vocal control nuclei in adult female canaries. *Brain Res.* 192:89–107.

Nottebohm, F. (1981) A brain for all seasons: Cyclical anatomical changes in song control nuclei of the canary brain. *Science* 214:1368–1370.

Nottebohm, F., Alvarez-Buylla, A., Cynx, J., Kirn, J., Ling, C.-Y., Nottebohm, M. E., Suter, R., Tolles, A., and Williams, H. (1990) Song learning in birds: The relation between perception and production. *Phil. Trans. R. Soc. Lond.* B 329:115–124.

Nottebohm, F. and Arnold, A. P. (1976) Sexual dimorphism in vocal control areas of the songbird brain. *Science* 194:211–213.

Nottebohm, F., Kelley, D. B., and Paton, J. A. (1982) Connections of vocal control nuclei in the canary telencephalon. *J. Comp. Neurol.* 207:344–357.

Nottebohm, F. and Nottebohm, M. E. (1976) Left hypoglossal dominance in the control of canary and white-crowned sparrow song. *J. Comp. Physiol.* A 108:171–192.

Nottebohm, F. and Nottebohm, M. E. (1978) Relationship between song repertoire and age in the canary, *Serinus canaria*. *Z. Tierpsychol.* 46:298–305.

Nottebohm, F., Nottebohm, M. E., and Crane, L. A. (1986) Developmental and seasonal changes in canary song and their relation to changes in the anatomy of song-control nuclei. *Behav. Neur. Bio.* 46:445–471.

Nottebohm, F., Nottebohm, M. E., Crane, L. A., and Wingfield, J. C. (1987) Seasonal changes in gonadal hormone levels of adult male canaries and their relation to song. *Behav. Neur. Biol.* 47:197–211.

Nottebohm, F., O'Loughlin, B., Gould, K., Yohay, K., and Alvarez-Buylla, A. (1994) The life span of new neurons in a song control nucleus of the adult canary brain depends on time of year when these cells are born. *Proc. Natl. Acad. Sci.* (USA) 91:7849–7853.

Nottebohm, F., Stokes, T. M., and Leonard, C. M. (1976) Central control of song in the canary, *Serinus canaria*. *J. Comp. Neurol.* 165:457–486.

Okuhata, S. and Nottebohm, F. (1992) Nucleus Uva might be part of a feedback circuit for song processing. *Abs. Soc. Neurosci.* 18:527.

Okuhata, S. and Saito, N. (1987) Synaptic connections of thalamo-cerebral vocal nuclei of the canary. *Brain Res. Bull.* 18:35–44.

Paton, J. A. and Manogue, K. R. (1982) Bilateral interactions within the vocal control pathway of birds: Two evolutionary alternatives. *J. Comp. Neurol.* 212:329–335.

Payne, R. B. (1981) Song learning and social interaction in indigo buntings. *Anim. Behav.* 29:688–697.

Pohl-Apel, G. and Sossinka, R. (1984) Hormonal determination of song capacity in females of the zebra finch: Critical phase of treatment. *Z. Tierpsychol.* 64:330–336.

Price, P. H. (1979) Developmental determinants of structure in zebra finch song. *J. Comp. Physiol. Psych.* 93:260–277.

Rasika, S., Alvarez-Buylla, A., and Nottebohm, F. (1999) BDNF mediates the effects of testosterone on the survival of new neurons in an adult brain. *Neuron* 22:53–62.

Ryals, B. M. and Rubel, E. W. (1988) Hair cell regeneration after acoustic trauma in adult Coturnix quail. *Science* 240:1774–1776.

Sassoon, D. and Kelley, D. (1986) The sexually dimorphic larynx of *Xenopus laevis*: Development and androgen regulation. *Am. J. Anat.* 177:457–472.

Scharff, C. and Nottebohm, F. (1991) A comparative study of the behavioral deficits following lesions of various parts of the zebra finch song system: Implications for vocal learning. *J. Neurosci.* 11:2896–2913.

Scharff, C., Nottebohm, F., and Cynx, J. (1998) Conspecific and heterospecific song discrimination in male zebra finches with lesions in the anterior forebrain pathway. *J. Neurobiol.* 36:81–90.

Schlinger, B. A. and Arnold, A. P. (1991a) Androgen effects on the development of the zebra finch song system. *Brain Res.* 561:99–105.

Schlinger, B. A. and Arnold, A. P. (1991b) Brain is the major site of estrogen synthesis in a male songbird. *Proc. Natl. Acad. Sci.* (USA) 88:4191–4194.

Schlinger, B. A. and Arnold, A. P. (1992a) Plasma sex steroids and tissue aromatization in hatchling zebra finches: Implications for the sexual differentiation of singing behavior. *Endocrinol.* 130:289–299.

Schlinger, B. A. and Arnold, A. P. (1992b) Circulating estrogens in a male songbird originate in the brain. *Proc. Natl. Acad. Sci.* (USA) 89:7650–7653.

Simpson, H. B. and Vicario, D. S. (1990) Brain pathways for learned and unlearned vocalization differ in zebra finches. *J. Neurosci.* 10:1541–1556.

Simpson, H. B. and Vicario, D. S. (1991) Early estrogen treatment of female zebra finches masculinizes the brain pathway for learned vocalizations. *J. Neurobiol.* 22:777–793.

Slater, P. J. B., Eales, L. A., and Clayton, N. S. (1988) Song learning in zebra finches (*Taeniopygia guttata*): Progress and prospects. In: *Advances in the Study of Behaviour*, ed. by J. Rosenblatt, C. Beer, M. C. Busnel, and P. J. B. Slater, vol. 18., pp. 1–32. San Diego: Academic.

Slater, P. J. B. and Ince, S. A. (1982) Song development in chaffinches: What is learnt and when? *Ibis* 124:21–26.

Sohrabji, F., Nordeen, E. J., and Nordeen, K. W. (1990) Selective impairment of song learning following lesions of a forebrain nucleus in the juvenile zebra finch. *Behav. Neural Biol.* 53:51–63.

Stoddard, P. K., Beecher, M. D., Loesche, P., and Campbell, S. E. (1992) Memory does not constrain individual recognition in a bird with song repertoires. *Behaviour* 122:274–287.

Suthers, R. (1990) Contributions to birdsong from the left and right sides of the intact syrinx. *Nature* 347:473–477.

Tchernichovski, O. and Nottebohm, F. (1998) Social inhibition of song imitation among sibling male zebra finches. *Proc. Natl. Acad. Sci.* (USA) 95:8951–8956.

Thielcke, G. (1970) Lernen von Gesang als möglicher Schrittmacher der Evolution. *Z. Zool. syst. Evolutionsforsch.* 8:309–320.

Thielcke, G. and Krome, M. (1989) Experimente über sensible Phasen und Gesangsvariabilität beim Buchfinken (*Fringilla coelebs*). *J. Orn.* 130:435–453.

Thielcke, G. and Krome, M. (1991) Chaffinches, *Fringilla coelebs*, do not learn song during autumn and early winter. *Bioacoustics* 3:207–212.

Thorpe, W. H. (1958) The learning of song patterns by birds, with especial reference to the song of the chaffinch, *Fringilla coelebs*. *Ibis* 100:535–570.

Thorpe, W. H. (1961) *Bird-Song*. Cambridge Monographs in Experimental Biology, no. 12. Cambridge: Cambridge University Press.

Udin, S. B. and Scherer, W. J. (1990) Restoration of the plasticity of binocular maps by NMDA after the critical period in Xenopus. *Science* 249:669–672.

Vates, G. E. and Nottebohm, F. (1995) Feedback circuitry within a song-learning pathway. *Proc. Natl. Acad. Sci.* (USA) 92:5139–5143.

Vates, G. E., Broome, B. M., Mello, C. V., and Nottebohm, F. (1996) Auditory pathways of caudal telencephalon and their relation to the song systems of adult male zebra finches (*Taeniopygia guttata*). *J. Comp. Neurol.* 366:613–642.

Vates, G. E., Vicario, D. S., and Nottebohm, F. (1997) Reafferent thalamo-"cortical" loops in the song system of oscine songbirds. *J. Comp. Neurol.* 380:275–290.

Vicario, D. S. (1991) Organization of the zebra finch song control system. II. Functional organization of outputs from nucleus *Robustus archistriatalis.*

Vicario, D. S. (1993) A new brain stem pathway for vocal control in the zebra finch song system. *Neuro-Report* 4:983–986.

Vicario, D. and Yohay, K. (1993) Song selective auditory input to a forebrain vocal control nucleus in the zebra finch. *J. Neurobiol.* 24:488–505.

Vicario, D. and Simpson, H. B. (1995) Electrical stimulation in forebrain nuclei elicits learned vocal patterns in songbird. *J. Neurophysiol.* 73:2602–2607.

Volman, S. F. (1993) Development of neural selectivity for birdsong during vocal learning. *J. Neurosci.* 13:4737–4747.

Vu, E. T., Mazurek, M. E., and Kuo, Y. C. (1994) Identification of a forebrain motor programming network for the learned song of zebra finches. *J. Neurosci.* 14:6924–6934.

Waser, M. S. and Marler, P. (1977) Song learning in canaries. *J. Comp. Physiol. Psychol.* 91:1–7.

Watson, J., Robertson, J., Sachdev, U., and Kelley, D. (1993) Laryngeal muscle and motor neuron plasticity in *Xenopus laevis*: Analysis of a sensitive period for testicular masculinization of a neuromuscular system. *J. Neurobiol.* 24:1615–1625.

Weichel, K., Schwager, P., Heid, P., Güttinger, H. R., and Pesch, A. (1986) Sex differences in plasma steroid concentrations and singing behaviour during ontogeny in canaries (*Serinus canaria*). *Ethology* 73:281–294.

Weiler, E. (1992) Seasonal changes in adult mammalian brain weight. *Naturwissenschaften* 79:474–476.

Wild, J. M. (1993a) The avian nucleus retroambigulais: A nucleus for breathing, singing, and calling. *Brain Res.* 606:119–124.

Wild, J. M. (1993b) Descending projections of the songbird nucleus *Robustus archistriatalis*. *J. Comp. Neurol.* 338:225–241.

Wild, J. A. and Arends, J. J. A. (1987) A respiratory-vocal pathway in the brainstem of the pigeon. *Brain Res.* 407:191–194.

Wiley, R. H., Tatchwell, B. J., and Davies, N. B. (1991) Recognition of individual males' songs by female dunnocks: A mechanism increasing the number of copulatory partners and reproductive success. *Ethology* 88:145–153.

Wiley, R. H. and Wiley, M. S. (1977) Recognition of neighbors' duets by stripe-backed wrens *Campylorhynchus nuchalis*. *Behaviour* 62:10–34.

Williams, H. (1989) Multiple representations and auditory-motor interactions in the avian song system. *Ann. N.Y. Acad. Sci.* 563:148–164.

Williams, H. (1990) Models for song learning in the zebra finch: fathers or others? *Anim. Behav.* 39:745–757.

Williams, H. and Nottebohm, F. (1985) Auditory responses in avian vocal motor neurons: A motor theory for song perception in birds. *Science* 229:279–282.

Williams, H., Crane, L. A., Hale, T. K., Esposito, M. A., and Nottebohm, F. (1992) Right-side dominance for song control in the zebra finch. *J. Neurobiol.* 23:1006–1020.

Williams, H. and Vicario, D. S. (1993) Temporal patterning of song production: Participation of nucleus uvaeformis of the thalamus. *J. Neurobiol.* 24:903–912.

Yasukawa, K., Blank, J. L., and Patterson, C. B. (1980) Song repertoires and sexual selection in the red-winged blackbird. *Behav. Ecol. Sociobiol.* 7:233–238.

Yu, A. C. and Margoliash, D. (1996) Temporal hierarchical control of singing in birds. *Science* 273:1871–1875.

4 The Dance Language of Honeybees: Recent Findings and Problems

Axel Michelsen

Successful forager honeybees (*Apis mellifera*) are able to recruit other bees to a food source. For centuries, it was believed that foragers lead the recruits to the food. Since the pioneering work of Karl von Frisch (review 1967) it has been known that bees are recruited by odors and by dances, and that several components of the "waggle" dance are correlated with the direction of and distance to food (or resin, water, or a new nest site). It has not been known, however, which of these components are perceived as signals by the follower bees, or how the follower bees detect the movements of the dancing bee in the darkness of the hive.

The dance language of these bees is an exception to the general rule that animals do not, on the whole, communicate about remote events, but rather about immediate events connected with the actor and its surroundings (like readiness to mate or the approach of a predator). Furthermore, in the dance language an abstract code is used to transmit an impressive amount of information.

In the waggle dance, the dancer moves in a straight line (the wagging run) and circles back, alternating between a left and a right return path so that the entire dance path takes on a figure-eight shape (figure 4.1). On a vertical comb, the direction of the wagging run relative to gravity indicates the direction to the food relative to the sun's azimuth in the field. The velocity of the dance (and the number of figure eights per unit of time) depends on the distance to the food source. A few follower bees keep close contact with the dancer, and these bees may be recruited to visit the food.

The waggle dance is named for the wagging run, in which the dancer wags her body from side to side 15 times per second and emits 280Hz sounds by vibrating her wings. Recent high-speed video analysis shows that the term "run" is misleading (Tautz et al. 1996). Although the body moves continuously forward, the legs have firm contact with the comb most of the time. At least one of the legs moves forward only once, and the entire waggle run is thus achieved in a single stride. The firm contact with the comb allows the dancer to perform very intense wagging. The movement of the body during wagging is similar to that of a pendulum fixed in front of the head. The excursion of the tip of the abdomen may be 8mm (peak-peak) during vigorous dancing, and the body may rotate around its length axis. It is tempting, then, to rename the wagging run "rock and swing," but such a name is hardly appropriate in scientific texts.

The main part of this review deals with two problems, which are probably interconnected: How can the follower bees perceive the message carried by the dance in

Figure 4.1
The waggle dance. The dancer waggles and emits sounds at the middle of the "8" and then returns, alternating between a left and a right path. Four follower bees observe the dance. In a real situation many other bees would be close to the dancer. (From von Frisch 1967. © Springer-Verlag.)

the darkness of the hive? And which of the many components of the dance do the follower bees perceive as signals (i.e., which components transmit the information)? I will also discuss the sensory mechanisms involved. I conclude from this discussion that further studies are needed of the behaviour, the physics of the potential signals, and the biophysics of the sense organs that may be involved.

How Do the Follower Bees Sense the Dance?

Despite the huge body of work by von Frisch and his colleagues, we do not yet understand how dance followers detect the dancer's movements in the darkness of the hive. Von Frisch (1967) suggested two possible mechanisms: (1) the dance sounds might travel as substrate-borne vibrations through the wax comb from the dancer to the follower bees; and (2) the followers might touch the dancer. The discovery that a three-dimensional field of intense air currents exists around the dancer (Michelsen et al. 1987) suggested a third strategy: (3) the follower bees might keep a small distance to the dancer and estimate her dance by means of receptor organs sensitive to such air currents. In the following, I shall briefly examine the evidence for each of these proposed strategies.

Vibrations

Substrate-borne, 200–500Hz vibration signals are well known in honeybees. The queens may emit toots and quacks when the colony is preparing for swarming, and follower bees attending dances may emit stop signals (earlier called "begging signals"). These signals are transmitted through the comb as bending waves with fairly large (0.1–1μm) displacement amplitudes perpendicular to the surface. From physical and behavioral studies, we know that the power required for the generation of these signals in the combs corresponds roughly to the likely power output of the flight muscles. A reasonable quantitative agreement also exists between the behavioral threshold, signal strength, degree of attenuation with distance, and observed communication distance (Michelsen et al. 1986a,b).

Although the hypothesis put forward by von Frisch thus is in accordance with the realities of physics, measurements with laser vibrometry of vibrations perpendicular to the surface of the comb closest to dancing bees did not disclose any 280Hz vibrations synchronized to the dance sounds (Michelsen et al. 1986a). Combs are complicated structures, however, and this preliminary study did not rule out the possible involvement of other modes of 280Hz vibration or a transmission of 15Hz vibrations caused by wagging movements.

Recently, interest in a possible transmission of vibrations has revived. It was discovered that forager bees dancing on open, empty combs recruit three times as many nest mates to feeding sites as those that dance on capped brood combs (Tautz 1996). Tautz noted that foragers prefer to dance on open cells, and he speculated that the mechanical properties of relevance for the generation and transmission of vibrations from the dancer might differ in the two kinds of dance floor. He also argued that the relatively low rate of recruitment achieved by robot dancers (see below) could be due to their lack of contact with the comb.

At present, data on the physics and energy requirements are available only for bending waves that involve the entire comb. Tautz and his colleagues have offered the following suggestions regarding the vibration of the comb. The rims of the wax cells may constitute a web, which is only loosely connected to the thinner walls carrying it. Vibrations may spread within this web with little or no involvement of the rest of the comb. The one-strided nature of the waggle run should maximize a transmission of vibrations into the rim web. Furthermore, the side-to-side wagging movements of the dancer are likely to cause vibrations in the plane of the comb face rather than perpendicular to this plane (Sandeman et al. 1996; Tautz et al. 1996).

However, the experimental evidence is limited to the finding that vibrations spread when artificially induced in the rim web, and attempts to measure such vibrations close to dancing bees have failed. Obviously, these ideas need further support from hard data. As for the different recruitments observed on the two kinds of dance floor, high-speed video recordings suggest that the bees may find it difficult to obtain a firm grasp with their feet when wagging on capped cells. The low recruitments could thus be the result of the bees dancing on a slippery floor (Kristin Rohrseitz, personal communication).

A few words need to be said about the receptor organs involved. The receptor for 200–500Hz bending waves is the subgenual organ. Situated in the legs just below the bee's "knee," the subgenual organ monitors the oscillations of fluid in an internal blood channel in the length axis of the leg. This process can be seen with stroboscopic light, and the physics of the reception is now well understood (Kilpinen and Storm 1997; Storm and Kilpinen 1998). We also understand the transmission of vibrations from the substrate to the sense organ (Rohrseitz and Kilpinen 1997). A reasonable agreement exists between the threshold of the sense organ, the transmission gain, and the behavioral threshold.

The reception of the 200–500Hz signals thus rests on a firm basis of understanding, but this is not the case for the receptors of the proposed low-frequency vibrations, which are outside the frequency range of the subgenual organs. Electrophysiological recordings from the leg nerve in the femur of isolated legs have revealed action potentials from receptors that monitor an extension of the tibia. These receptors also respond to 2µm displacements of the substrate at 15Hz (Sandeman et al. 1996). The relevance of these findings for the dance language remains to be demonstrated.

Even if dancers generate vibrations, it is hard to imagine that such vibrations could provide the follower bees with specific information about the distance to and direction of the target. In addition, that dance communication also occurs on combless swarm clusters demonstrates that substrate vibrations cannot play any essential role.

Touching

The suggestion that the follower bees receive information simply by touching the dancer has been much debated. Studies using normal film records of dancing bees and their surroundings suggested that at any time less than 25% of the surrounding bees were sufficiently close to be able to touch the dancer (Michelsen et al. 1987). However, not all of the bees surrounding a dancer are active followers trying to detect the dancer's movements, and the percentage of active followers able to touch the dancer could not be determined with this method. A later video study focusing on the active followers did indeed report a higher percentage of touching (Božič and Valentinčič 1991).

High-speed video provides much better resolution than traditional video. Using 200 frames/second, one has 13 pictures per waggle instead of 1–2, and it is then possible to see that most follower bees touch the dancer with one or both antennae during each waggle (Rohrseitz and Tautz 1999). However, the interpretation of these exciting findings is not simple. Especially, it is not known whether (and to which extent) the follower bees receive specific information about the direction and distance to the food source by touching the dancer. It may be argued that touching is not likely to be a good strategy for obtaining precise information about the position of the dancer, because the antennae are likely to be hit by the very violent wagging excursions of the dancer's body. The most obvious information to be obtained from touching is whether the follower bee is facing the dancer's abdomen laterally or from behind. In the former case, the two antennae touch the dancer simultaneously, in the latter case alternately. However, the same information could also be obtained from the low-frequency air oscillations caused by the wagging movements.

Oscillating Air Currents

Measurements of the acoustic near field of dancing honeybees have suggested a third strategy (Michelsen et al. 1987). The emission of sound from dancing honeybees was discovered independently by Esch (1961) and Wenner (1962). The sounds cannot be heard by a human at a normal observation distance, but they can be recorded with a microphone close to the dancer. When measured at a distance of 1–2cm from the dancer, the dance sounds are shown to have pressure amplitudes around 0.1Pa (74dB SPL). However, in the near field close to a sound emitter, the sound pressure may be appreciably higher.

The sound pressure measured with miniature probe microphones at the surfaces of the wings is about 1Pa (94dB SPL). In addition, pressure gradients up to 1Pa/mm around the edges of the wings cause the air particles to oscillate with velocities (peak-peak) up to 1m/s (figure 4.2). Intense air particle oscillations are a normal characteristic of acoustic near fields, and they are particularly prominent close to acoustic dipoles like vibrating free plates (wings), where the air currents may have

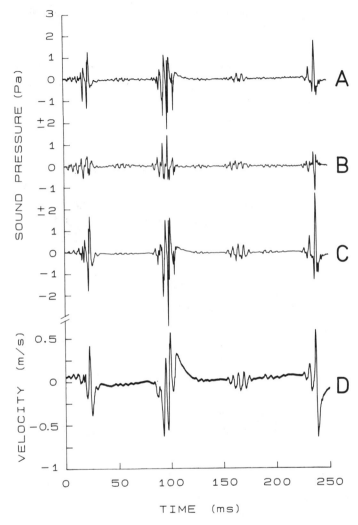

Figure 4.2
Time records of sound pressures measured simultaneously above (A) and below (B) the plane of the wings. C is their difference Δp. D is the air velocity, calculated from C. The measurements were performed with the tips of two probe microphones 2mm apart and close to the edge of the wings of a dancing honeybee. (From Michelsen et al. 1987. © Springer-Verlag.)

complex spatial patterns. The pressure gradients and airflows decrease with the third power of the distance from the dancer, and the zone of intense airflow exists only close to the dancer's wings (that is, close to the abdomen; figure 4.3).

These observations and the fact that most follower bees place their heads in the zone of intense airflows led us to propose that the follower bees might extract the required information about direction and distance by detecting the airflows produced by the dancer. Further measurements have shown that an extremely complicated three-dimensional field of oscillating airflows surrounds the dancer.

The wagging movements of the dancer have two effects on the air currents. First, they cause a 15Hz amplitude modulation of the 280Hz airflow generated by the wings (since the amplitude of this airflow depends on the distance to the source [figure 4.3], and the distance between the dancer and its followers oscillates during wagging). Second, airflows are also generated by the wagging movements (figure 4.4). The lateral component of the wagging airflows may also have velocity amplitudes up to 1m/s (peak-peak), but the physical nature of the wagging airflows differs from that of the wing-generated airflows (by being determined mainly by incompressible fluid mechanics and not by the laws of acoustics). The wagging air currents are only partly laminar.

The frequency composition of the airflows surrounding the dancing bees is complicated. The wing vibrations generate mainly 280Hz air oscillations, but the wagging airflows carry several harmonic components in addition to the fundamental 15Hz component. It is interesting that the spectrum of the wagging airflow behind the dancer is very different from that lateral to the dancer. There is some evidence that the bees have to spend some time behind the dancer in order to obtain the dance information (Judd 1995), and bees attracted to follow a dance tend to approach the lateral side of the dancer and gradually move caudally. One may speculate that they are guided in part by the gradients in the wagging airflows. Furthermore, the 15Hz amplitude modulation of the 280Hz wing vibration airflows is also experienced differently by follower bees lateral to the dancer and observers behind the dancer (see Michelsen et al. 1987). However, touching could lead to the same result.

The Sensory Perception of Oscillating Airflows

The Johnston's organs in the antennae are the likely, but not necessarily the only, receiver systems for the oscillating airflows generated by dancing bees. Johnston's organ is located in the second segment (the pedicel) of the antenna, and it is sensitive to vibrations of the rest of the antenna (the flagellum) relative to the pedicel. It con-

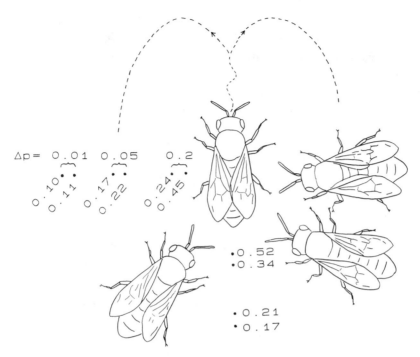

Figure 4.3
Average maximum sound pressures (in Pa) measured in two directions radially away from a dancing bee. Pairs of dots (bracketed to the left of the dancer) show the location of the two microphone probes, which were 1.5mm apart. Note that the pressure difference Δp decreases rapidly with distance from the dancer. A Δp of 0.2Pa over a distance of 1.5mm corresponds roughly to an air velocity of 0.1m/s (peak-peak). (From Michelsen et al. 1987. © Springer-Verlag.)

sists of an array of about 40 scolopidian units arranged in a collar-like fashion. Each unit contains 5–12 scolopidia, and each scolopidium comprises three sensory cells (WenQi Wu, personal communication). A total of about one thousand sense cells thus report the relative position of the base of the flagellum to the brain.

The mechanics of the antenna was investigated by Heran (1959), who reported that the displacement amplitude of the antennal flagellum is at a maximum at about 240–280Hz when the head of a bee is glued to the end of a vibrating rod. (This maximum is often referred to as a "resonance," but the maximum disappears when the vibration amplitude is plotted as a velocity rather than as a displacement; it is therefore not a resonance in a physical sense.) Heran also found that the threshold of Johnston's organ corresponds to a displacement of the antennal tip of about 1μm (but his data show much scatter). In these experiments, the tip of the antenna was moved sinusoidally. Obviously, the forces acting on the antennae during Heran's

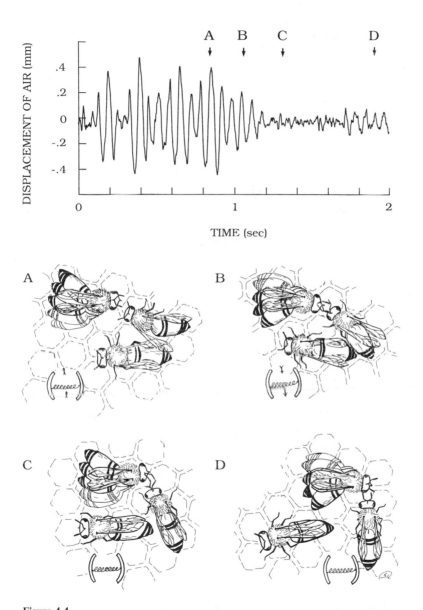

Figure 4.4
The 15Hz air flow caused by the wagging movement can be recorded with a small anemometer. The signal can be detected at a distance of 2cm, if no obstacles are present between the dancer and the anemometer. The body of a bee causes a substantial reduction of the signal (compare the signal with the positions of the transducer and the bees in a–d). (From Michelsen 1992.)

experiments were very different from those acting on an antenna in the near field of a dancing bee.

Following the proposal of the air current hypothesis, the zoologists Wolfgang Kirchner and William Towne and their students began a series of studies on the sensory basis for air current detection. They found that honeybees conditioned to respond to artificially generated oscillating airflows had fairly constant thresholds (indicated as velocity) in the frequency range of 10–400Hz (Kirchner et al. 1991); that the vibrations of the antennal tip faithfully followed the oscillating air currents, and that the amplitude of vibration was about 1% of the amplitude of the air current stimulus over a wide frequency range (Kirchner 1994); that free mobility of the joint between the pedicel and the flagellum was crucial for the behavioral response to oscillating air currents (Dreller and Kirchner 1993a); and that the bees could make a crude frequency discrimination when presented with oscillating air currents of widely different frequencies (20, 100, and 325Hz) in behavioral tests (Kirchner et al. 1991; Towne 1995). Furthermore, a nice quantitative agreement seemed to exist between the thresholds found in these studies (100–300mm/s peak-peak), the 1% relationship between air currents and flagellar vibration, and the thresholds determined by Heran (1959).

A popular article reviewing this work concluded that most problems connected with the dance language had now been solved (Kirchner and Towne 1994). This may be true, but a number of loose ends are apparent. The most serious problem is the level of the thresholds observed. In our 1987 study, the position of the pair of probe microphones relative to the dancing bee was monitored with normal-speed video only, so we could never be quite sure about the exact distance and orientation of the bees during the recordings of sound pulses. We therefore chose to indicate the *maximum* values observed for the measured pressure gradients and calculated air currents. Such maximum values are, of course, not average or typical values.

One of my students has mapped the 280Hz sound field around dancing bees at various distances from the surface of the comb, making use of all pressure amplitudes measured at each position (Jensen 1993). From these data and some computation, she described the average pressure distribution and field of airflows. The values obtained in this manner are on average a factor of 5 below the maximum values reported in our 1987 study.

Furthermore, in agreement with the physical predictions, the largest values were obtained for air currents flowing in the dorsal-ventral direction, perpendicular to the plane of the wings (figure 4.2). This is not the direction of airflow likely to tell a follower bee in which direction the dancer is moving. The air currents radial and parallel to the bee's body are more likely vehicles for the information about direction, and close to the body of the dancer the amplitudes of these air currents are typically a factor of 5 below those measured perpendicular to the wings (compare figures 4.2 and 4.3).

In their summary, Kirchner et al. (1991) wrote: "The hearing threshold is 100–300mm/s peak-to-peak velocity and is roughly constant over the range of detectable frequencies. The amplitude of the signals emitted in the dance language is 5–10 times higher, so we can conclude that bees can easily detect the dance sounds." The maximum value for the air currents perpendicular to the plane of the wings in our study was indeed 1.4m/s (peak-peak), thus the "5–10 times" difference. However, the word "easily" does not seem appropriate, given the differences between the amplitudes of the various air currents and the difference between maximum and average values.

So, the air-current hypothesis is in serious trouble. The threshold values reported by Kirchner et al. are insufficient to allow the follower bees to pick up air currents that carry significant information signaled through the dance. Despite the word "easily," Kirchner et al. (1991) seemed aware that the thresholds were too high to fit the hypothesis; they offered the explanation that since the learning performance of the bees in their study was poorer than in experiments pairing odor, color, or visual patterns with sucrose rewards, the bees seemed relatively unprepared to associate food with "sounds" (oscillating airflows). The thresholds might thus be considerably lower in situations to which oscillating airflows "belong." These speculative ideas are not very helpful, however.

Should we then reject the air-current hypothesis? It was my idea, but I have no sentimental feelings about discarding it. However, a logical explanation for the quantitative misfit of signal strength and receiver threshold may perhaps be found by considering the physical nature of the air currents used in the studies by Kirchner, Towne, and their coworkers. They connected a tube of 11mm internal diameter to a loudspeaker and assumed the oscillating airflows at some distance from the open end to be laminar and fairly homogeneous across the end of the tube. However, this was probably not the case.

Experimental and theoretical work (summarized by Nitsche and Krasny 1994) have shown that ring-shaped vortices are formed at the edge when air (or fluid) is forced to flow in or out of a circular tube. In fact, two vortices (similar to those that can be made by cigar smokers) with opposite directions of rotation are formed during each cycle and travel away from the opening of the tube. Furthermore, experimental studies in my laboratory (Storm 1995) have shown that the relationship between the voltage to the loudspeaker and the air velocity at some distance from the opening can be highly nonlinear. The magnitude of the airflow also critically depends on the exact location relative to the tube.

In most of the experiments by Kirchner, Towne, and their coworkers, pairs of probe microphones were used for calibrating the airflows. This technique is well suited when the airflow is driven by a local pressure gradient (for example, at 280Hz close to a dancing bee), but it is not suited when the airflow is due to inertia (for example, at low frequencies or close to an open tube). In other experiments, a large (8 × 6mm) pressure gradient microphone was used (Towne 1995), although such a large device is likely to distort the field. Obviously, these methods were not suited for a proper calibration, and the nonlinear nature of the flows may have added uncertainty to the results. Further uncertainty may have resulted from variations in the position of the bees antennae within the inhomogeneous flow fields.

Thus it may be too early to reject the air-current hypothesis. A redetermination of the behavioral thresholds is needed in homogeneous and properly calibrated fields with laminar and linear flows. These properties can be controlled by means of laser anemometry. The studies of frequency discrimination assumed equal loudness at the frequencies studied. Here again, the results may be in error, and the studies should be repeated.

A reinvestigation of the properties of the Johnson's organ is needed in order to determine its threshold, dynamic range, and ability for temporal coding when the antennae are subjected to controlled air oscillations. The possible involvement of mechanoreceptive hairs on the front of the bee's head has been dismissed by means of a single experiment involving only 20 bees (Dreller and Kirchner 1993b). Again, a repetition is in order.

A Mechanical Model of a Dancing Bee

Tomorrow it looks as if we should be overhearing the conversation of bees, and the day after tomorrow joining in it. We may be able to tell our bees to fertilize those apple trees five minutes fly to the south-east; Mr Johnson's tree over the wall can wait! To do this we should presumably need a model bee to make the right movements, and perhaps the right noise and smell. It would probably not be a paying proposition, but there is no reason to regard it as an impossible one.
—J. B. S. Haldane, The future of biology (1927)

Since 1957, several unsuccessful attempts have been made to recruit bees by means of mechanical models of dancing bees (for references, see Michelsen et al. 1992). The first models did not emit sounds, but later models (e.g., wax-coated microphones or paralysed bees) both wagged and emitted sounds. In all cases, the bees showed great interest in the models, but the models did not elicit recruitment. Our model (figure 4.5) differs from the previous ones principally by producing airflows similar to those observed close to dancing bees, and this model does recruit a number of bees to the locations indicated by its dances.

Figure 4.5
The mechanical model surrounded by follower bees during the performance of a wagging run. (From Michelsen et al. 1992. © Springer Verlag.)

Our model was made of brass and covered with a thin layer of beeswax. It had the same length as a worker honeybee, but was somewhat broader. The wings were simulated by a single piece of razor blade, which was vibrated by an electromagnetic driver. A stepper motor rotated the model and caused it to waggle during the wagging runs. Other motors moved the model in a figure-eight path. During brief pauses, a second stepper motor pumped "food samples" (scented sugar water) through a tiny plastic tube terminating near the "head" of the model.

All the motors and drivers were interfaced to and controlled by a computer, and all the dance components could be changed through the software. This made it possible to vary the individual dance components independently and to create dances different from the normal waggle dance. At three-minute intervals the computer calculated the sun's azimuth and adjusted the direction of the wagging run to compensate for the (apparent) movement of the sun. The model was deployed on the lower comb close to the entrance of a two-comb observation hive. The sugar water and the wax coating of the model were given a faint scent not familiar to the bees.

Baits were placed at various locations in the field. In the bait, a piece of filter paper with 20μl of pure floral oil placed below a metal mesh was renewed once every hour. At each location an observer noted the number of honeybees approaching the bait and showing the behavior typical of a bee searching for a scented target. The bees did not receive food at the baits (thus we were sure to avoid dances by returning bees).

In the experiments on the transfer of distance information, seven baits were placed at various distances in the direction indicated by the model. In the normal dances (figure 4.6A) we selected dance parameters that instructed the bees to fly for either a short distance (250m) or a long distance (1500m). When using the manipulated dances, we gave the bees conflicting information about whether to fly for a short or a ong distance. In the experiments on direction, eight baits were placed in different directions 370m from the hive. Again, normal dances provided the bees with one direction, and manipulated dances indicated two potentially conflicting directions.

The experiments demonstrated that the follower bees are able to perceive information regarding both distance and direction from the wagging dances performed by the model bee. Furthermore, the bees were recruited not only by imitations of normal wagging dances, but also by some manipulated dances in which components of the dance were changed or shifted to other parts of the dance path.

The transfer of information about direction is shown in figure 4.7. Two experiments with normal dances were performed on consecutive days with the same wind direction, but with the target directions differing by 90°. Approximately 80% of the approaching bees were observed in the direction indicated by the model. This accuracy is similar to that obtained in experiments with live dancers. The number of approaches observed at the seven other baits is in agreement with the numbers observed at a similar distance in control experiments, in which the bees were fed scented sugar water from a motionless model bee.

The results obtained for the transfer of information about distance were less clear. Most bees searched close to the hive when the bees had been "told" to fly 250m with normal dances. A higher percentage of the approaching bees were observed far from the hive when the model indicated a distance of 1500m, but again most bees searched close to the hive. Nevertheless, the distributions of observed approaches at the baits changed significantly when the bees were "told" to fly to another distance.

Obviously, one or more cues for distance were lacking in the model's behavior. It has been found that the wing vibration frequency decreases with distance (Spangler 1991). It is possible, therefore, that the follower bees in our experiments interpreted the constant frequency of the wing vibrations (280Hz) to indicate a fairly short distance, and that they became confused when the model indicated a distance of 1500m

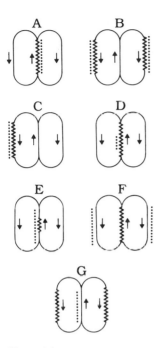

Figure 4.6
Six dance patterns tested in the experiments with the model dancing bee. Wagging and sound emission by the vibrating wing are indicated by a zigzag line and by a series of dots, respectively. (A) A normal wagging dance. (B) and (C) Dances with two and one displaced wagging runs, respectively. The wagging run(s) and the dance path indicate opposite directions. (D) Wagging of long duration combined with sound emission of short duration. (E) The opposite of (D). (F) A dance with wagging during the wagging run and sound emission during a part of the return run. (G) The opposite of (F). (From Michelsen et al. 1992. © Springer-Verlag.)

by the velocity of its dance. Further studies are obviously needed to resolve this problem.

The experiments with manipulated dances included a pair of dances designed to determine whether the bees obtain information about distance from the duration of the wagging run or from the duration of the return run. In one type of dance, the duration of the wagging run corresponded to 250m, whereas the duration of the return run corresponded to 1500m. Another type of dance had the opposite design: the duration of the wagging run signaled 1500m and the return run 250m. In both cases, the bees followed the instructions given by the wagging run and ignored the duration of the return run.

The wagging run thus appeared to be the "master component" for conveying information about distance. That it also indicates direction was demonstrated by

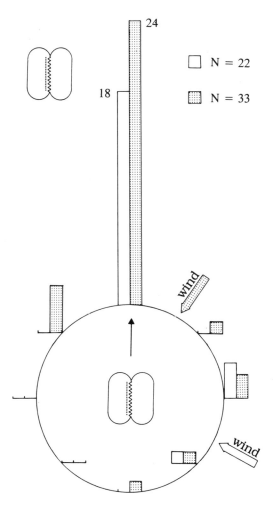

Figure 4.7
Two experiments with normal wagging dances testing the transfer of directional information on two consecutive days. The direction indicated by the model is shown with an arrow. The directions indicated by the model on each day are drawn as though they both pointed in the same direction, even though different directions were actually used on the two days. The number of bees approaching each of eight baits located 370m from the hive are indicated. The direction of the wind is indicated for each experiment. (From Michelsen et al. 1992. © Springer-Verlag.)

means of dance pattern C in figure 4.6, where the wagging run is displaced to one of the return runs. The bees were now provided with conflicting information about direction: the figure-eight dance path pointed in one direction and the wagging run in the opposite direction. We observed approximately one half of the bees in the direction indicated by the wagging run, and we found less than one tenth of the bees in the direction indicated by the figure-eight dance path.

In contrast, dance figure B (figure 4.6) did not recruit any bees. The follower bees were obviously unable to predict where the next wagging run would be taking place. They were attracted by the wagging runs, but generally arrived too late to be able to follow the run. They then remained on the spot, apparently waiting for the next wagging run—only to find out that it now occurred some distance away. They then ran to the place of action, arrived too late, and so on. One may speculate that the stereotyped figure-eight dance path may help the bees to orientate themselves relative to the dancer so that they are in a favorable position for observing the next wagging run.

During a normal wagging run the dancer both wags its body and emits sounds by vibrating its wings. In preliminary experiments (Michelsen et al. 1989), we found that both wagging and sound are necessary for the recruitment of the follower bees. We had expected that these components might have somewhat different roles in the transfer of information. For example, the distance might be signaled by the duration of one of them, and the other component might attract or motivate the bees.

This expectation was not supported by the results of several experiments, in which the wagging and the wing vibration were partly or totally separated (dance patterns D–G in figure 4.6). D and E were designed to test the roles of sound and wagging in the transfer of information about distance. One of these components was present during the entire wagging run (the duration of which corresponded to a distance of 1500m). The duration of the other component was reduced to one-third (which happened to correspond to a distance of 250m). The results showed that although only one component was present during the entire wagging run, the bees still used the duration of the entire wagging run for estimating the distance to the target.

We then completely separated the wagging and sound components (F and G) and tested the transfer of directional information. Much to our surprise, in both cases the bees were recruited to the direction of the return run! The scatter was very large, and in some tests the bees were not recruited at all, but the trend was clear (and significant).

The results of the experiments with dance patterns D–G thus did not support the notion of different roles for the sound and wagging components. In contrast, these dance components seemed to be fairly redundant. Signal redundancy is known to make communication systems more tolerant to transmission errors (see MacKay

1972). Of course, the signal redundancy demonstrated here does not rule out the possibility that the sound and wagging may have additional and separate signal functions.

The number of bees recruited by our model was generally smaller than that observed with live dancers. Given the crude nature of our model, it is perhaps not surprising that it induces only moderate recruitment. Nevertheless, many applications would become easier if the model could be improved. Live dancers are known to have a thoracic surface temperature above 40°C, that is 5–6°C above that of most other bees in the hive (Stabentheiner et al. 1990). We have tested a model with built-in heating elements. Unfortunately, it provoked fierce attacks by the bees each time its temperature exceeded 34°C. The reason for this is not known. Here again, further work is required.

Further Aspects

Our results with the mechanical model confirm that, as suggested by Karl von Frisch, the abstract information carried by the wagging dances is communicated to recruits, which, once in the field, narrow their search by means of odors. According to the odor theory of Wenner and his colleagues (review, Wenner and Wells 1990), the recruitment to specific sites should be due only to odor cues left in the field or carried by foragers. Such (hypothetical) cues were absent in our experiments, where the "forager" (the model) had not been in the field before dancing. In experiments like those shown in figure 4.7, the searching pattern of the recruits changed in accordance with the instructions received from the model and was independent of the direction of the wind, contrary to the expectations of the Wenner theory.

Waggle dances are not the only dances that carry information about the location of food. In the round dance, the dancer circles one or more times in one direction, then turns and circles in the opposite direction, and so on. Von Frisch (1967) interpreted round dances as recruiting signals for food sources within 50–100m distance from the hive. He further assumed that round dances do not contain any information about the location of food sources, but this assumption was not correct. The round dances do indeed contain short wagging runs, the average directions of which correlate well with the directions to food already at a distance of 1m (Kirchner et al. 1988). The scatter is enormous, however, and it is doubtful that the information is available to the follower bees (Jensen et al. 1997). Further research is needed, especially of the often-postulated ability of bees to form averages of somewhat conflicting instructions on where to go. Unfortunately, the present construction of the model bee does not allow us to mimic round dances, so this problem will require work on living dancers.

In this chapter, I have concentrated on the behavior, signals, and possible sensory mechanisms of bees. The three hypothesis on how follower bees perceive the communication dances all suffer from a number of problems. The guesses about the receptor organs involved also have to be substantiated. Even when we reach a reasonable understanding of these questions, the central nervous processing of all this complicated information still remains as a major challenge. It seems fair to conclude that we are still confused, but at a slightly higher level.

Acknowledgment

The Centre for Sound Communication is financed by the Danish National Research Foundation. Most of this review describes the results of a close cooperation between our group and that of Professor Martin Lindauer, Würzburg University. The work was generously financed by the Danish Science Research Council, the Carlsberg Foundation, the Akademie der Wissenschaften und der Literatur (Mainz), the Humboldt Stiftung, and the Stiftung Volkswagenwerk. I am most grateful to Kristin Rohrseitz for access to data from her thesis work. The comments on the manuscript received from Marc Hauser and Fred C. Dyer have been much appreciated.

References

Božič, J. and Valentinčič, T. (1991) Attendants and followers of honeybee waggle dances. *J. Apicult. Res.* 30:125–131.

Dreller, C. and Kirchner, W. H. (1993a) Hearing in honeybees: Localization of the auditory sense organ. *J. Comp. Physiol.* A 173:275–279.

Dreller, C. and Kirchner, W. H. (1993b) How bees perceive the information of the dance language. *Naturwiss.* 80:319–321.

Esch, H. (1961) Über die Schallerzeugung beim Werbetanz der Honigbiene. *Z. vergl. Physiol.* 45:1–11.

Haldane, J. B. S. (1927) The future of biology; In *Possible Worlds and Other Essays*. London: Chatto and Windus. (Also included in *On Being the Right Size and Other Essays*, ed. by John Maynard Smith, Oxford: Oxford University Press, 1985).

Heran, H. (1959) Wahrnehmung und Regelung der Fluggeschwindigkeit bei *Apis mellifera. L. Z. vergl. Physiol.* 42:103–163.

Jensen, L. B. (1993) Air currents around dancing honeybees. Master's thesis, Odense University. (In Danish.)

Jensen, I. L., Michelsen, A. and Lindauer, M. (1997) On the directional indications in the round dances of honeybees. *Naturwissenschaften* 84:452–454.

Judd, T. M. (1995) The waggle dance of the honey bee: Which bees following a dancer successfully acquire the information? *J. Insect Behav.* 8:343–354.

Kilpinen, O. and Storm, J. (1997) Biophysics of the subgenual organ of the honeybee, *Apis mellifera. J. Comp. Physiol.* A 181:309–318.

Kirchner, W. H. (1994) Hearing in honeybees: The mechanical response of the bee's antenna to near field sound. *J. Comp. Physiol.* A 175:261–265.

Kirchner, W. H., Lindauer, M., and Michelsen, A. (1988) Honeybee dance communication: Acoustical indication of direction in round dances. *Naturwiss.* 75:629–630.

Kirchner, W. H., Dreller, C., and Towne, W. F. (1991) Hearing in honeybees: Operant conditioning and spontaneous reactions to airborne sound. *J. Comp. Physiol.* A 168:85–89.

Kirchner, W. H. and Towne, W. F. (1994) The sensory basis of the honeybee's dance language. *Scient. Amer.* June 1994:52–59.

MacKay, D. M. (1972) Formal analysis of communicative processes. In *Non-verbal communication*, ed. by R. A. Hinde, pp. 3–25. Cambridge: Cambridge University Press.

Michelsen, A. (1992) Dance language, signals, and social life of honeybees. Copenhagen: Munksgaard. (In Danish.)

Michelsen, A., Kirchner, W. H., and Lindauer, M. (1986a) Sound and vibrational signals in the dance language of the honeybee, *Apis mellifera. Behav. Ecol. Sociobiol.* 18:207–212.

Michelsen, A., Kirchner, W. H., Andersen, B. B., and Lindauer, M. (1986b) The tooting and quacking vibration signals of honeybee queens: A quantitative analysis. *J. Comp. Physiol.* A 158:605–611.

Michelsen, A., Towne, W. F., Kirchner, W. H., and Kryger, P. (1987) The acoustic near field of a dancing honeybee. *J. Comp. Physiol.* A 161:633–643.

Michelsen, A., Andersen, B. B., Kirchner, W. H., and Lindauer, M. (1989) Honeybees can be recruited by means of a mechanical model of a dancing bee. *Naturwiss.* 76:277–280.

Michelsen, A., Andersen, B. B., Storm, J., Kirchner, W. H., and Lindauer, M. (1992) How honeybees perceive communication dances, studied by means of a mechanical model. *Behav. Ecol. Sociobiol.* 30:143–150.

Nitsche, M. and Krasny, R. (1994) A numerical study of vortex ring formation at the edge of a circular tube. *J. Fluid Mech.* 276:139–161.

Rohrseitz, K. and Kilpinen, O. (1997) Vibration transmission characteristics of the legs of freely standing honeybees. *Zoology* 100:80–84.

Rohrseitz, K., Tautz, J. (1999) Honeybee dance communication: Information transfer through antennal contacts? *J. Comp. Physiol. A* (in press).

Sandeman, D. C., Tautz, J., and Lindauer, M. (1996). Transmission of vibration across honeycombs and its detection by bee leg receptors. *J. Exp. Biol.* 199:2585–2594.

Spangler, H. G. (1991) Do honeybees encode distance information into the wing vibrations of the waggle dance? *J. Insect Behav.* 4:15–20.

Stabentheiner, A., Hagmüller, K., and Kovac, H. (1990) Thermisches Verhalten von Honigbienen im Schwänzeltanz. *Verh. Dtsch. Zool. Ges.* 83:624.

Storm, J. (1995) Measurements of the air flow field in front of a pipette tip. Report, Institute of Biology, Odense University.

Storm, J. and Kilpinen, O. (1998) Modelling the subgenual organ of the honeybee, *Apis mellifera. Biol. Cybern.* 78:175–182.

Tautz, J. (1996) Honeybee waggle dance: Recruitment success depends on the nature of the dance floor. *J. Exp. Biol.* 199:1375–1381.

Tautz, J., Rohrseitz, K., and Sandeman, D. C. (1996) One-strided waggle dance in bees. *Nature* 382:32.

Towne, W. F. (1995) Frequency discrimination in the hearing of honey bees (*Hymenoptera: Apidae*). *J. Insect Behav.* 8:281–286.

von Frisch, K. (1967) *The Dance Language and Orientation of Bees*. Cambridge, MA: Harvard University Press.

Wenner, A. M. (1962) Sound production during the waggle dance of the honeybee. *Anim Behav.* 10:79–95.

Wenner, A. M. and Wells, P. H. (1990) *Anatomy of a Controversy: The Question of "Language" among Bees*. New York: Columbia University Press.

5 Processing Species-specific Calls by Combination-sensitive Neurons in an Echolocating Bat

Jagmeet S. Kanwal

Many animal species have evolved complex societies whose members co-exist and interact on the basis of an established social organization. The evolutionary stability of such societies hinges on the development of species-specific communication schemes. Communication among conspecifics allows fulfillment of sociobiological functions such as mating, predator avoidance, feeding, etc. These interactions sometimes require rapid communication over long distances. The auditory system is ideal for such forms of communication since sound signals can be rapidly produced and transmitted over long distances.

Many species of frogs, birds, primates, and bats are useful models for learning about behavioral and neurophysiological mechanisms of auditory communication. Auditory communication plays an especially important role in the life of micro-chiropteran bats, which live in the darkness of caves and roost in large colonies. The auditory system of bats has been extensively studied by several groups of neuro-physiologists in order to understand echolocation behavior (Grinnell 1963; Suga 1965; Suga et al. 1983; Cassiday et al. 1994). By comparison, until recently, the neuro-physiology of the communication system was largely ignored. In addition to emitting echolocation pulses, bats also emit a complex repertoire of communication sounds or "calls" that rival in variety and complexity of spectral structure those emitted by the most vocal primate species (Sutton 1979; Fenton 1985). A few species, for example, *Myotis lucifugus* (Fenton 1977), *Carollia perspicallata* (Porter 1979b), *Megaderma lyra* (Leippert 1994), and *Pteronotus parnellii* (Kanwal et al. 1994a), employ a large repertoire of vocalizations for social communication. In *Megaderma* and *Carollia*, we know a fair amount about how calls are structured and what they may mean, but we know virtually nothing about their neurophysiological processing. In other species (e.g., *Pteronotus*), we have information on how these sounds are physically structured, but we understand little about the behavioral meaning and the functional roles of these sounds (Kanwal et al. 1994a).

This chapter will briefly review the physical structure of calls in mustached bats and describe some recent findings on the cortical processing of these sounds. At present, virtually no information is available on the specialized processing of these sounds at subcortical levels. Before discussing call processing in bats, a historical perspective on processing of species-specific sounds in other animals including humans can help to clarify the significance of some of the recent advances in this field, for example, the role of combination-sensitive neurons in call processing—the main theme of this chapter.

Cortical Processing of Species-specific Communication Sounds: Historical Perspective

Speech-sound Processing in Humans

Extensive psychophysical and clinical studies of humans have provided insights into the neural organization of speech perception and communication. Thus it is well known that the discrimination of speech sounds involves specialized areas of the auditory cortex (e.g., Wernicke's area and the Angular gyrus). In the case of speech, phonemes constitute the acoustic unit of perception. Psychophysical studies suggest that listeners distinguish between phonemes on the basis of acoustic characteristics, including formant distribution, the rate of formant transitions and voice-onset times (VOT's) (reviews: Pickett 1980; Lieberman and Blumstein 1988). At the neurophysiological level, phoneme discriminations may be mediated by neural filters tuned to some of these complex characteristics (e.g., F1 and F2; Ohl and Scheich 1997). The filter properties of such neurons may be created or modified by language exposure and experience, as in the case of neurons in the anterior forebrain pathway of songbirds (see Doupe and Solis, this volume). Psychophysical evidence both supports and contradicts these assertions, depending on the phoneme in question.

The response specificities of speech-processing neurons are probably more directly related to the acoustic structure of speech sounds than to the manner of their articulation. The spectral features of a particular phoneme, however, may vary with the speaker and with phoneme order (Liberman et al. 1967). Nevertheless, certain acoustic features tend to accompany a given phoneme, independent of the variations in its usage (Cole and Scott 1974; Blumstein and Stevens 1981). Although individual features of speech sounds may be ambiguous, sets of features processed in parallel by the auditory system may reduce ambiguity. In humans, these questions are difficult to address at the single unit level (but see Creutzfeldt et al. 1989; Weber and Ojemann 1995; and Schwartz et al. 1996). Hence the need to conduct neurophysiological studies of communication sound processing in animals.

Call Processing in Animals

Most early studies of the response of cortical auditory units in mammals, aside from those on bats, were carried out on squirrel monkeys (Winter et al. 1966). Both Winter and Funkenstein (1973) and Newman and Wollberg (1973a,b) sought evidence for feature extraction by presenting twelve well-characterized vocalizations. They observed that a unit's response to a pure tone was not a reliable predictor of a response to a natural call, even when the predominant spectral energy of the call fell within that unit's excitatory response range. In 7% of the cases in Winter and Funkenstein's experiments, the units responded to vocalizations but not to any other stimulus tested. Interestingly, Newman and Wollberg (1973a,b) found that a majority (89%) of cortical neurons responded to more than half of the vocal stimuli, whereas 41% of those in the study of Winter and Funkenstein were responsive to only one call. In general, these studies suggested that some units in the auditory cortex of the squirrel monkey discharge more powerfully to natural calls than to pure tones, but the neural mechanisms underlying these results were not resolved.

In a study of the cat, 17% of the units in the auditory cortex responded to complex sounds but not to any of the pure tones used, while 32% of units responded to complex sounds in ways that were not predictable from their response patterns to pure tones (Sovijarvi 1975). This lack of correspondence between pure tone and complex sound responses has been questioned by subsequent research (Glass and Wollberg 1983; Yeshurun et al. 1985; Pelleg-Toiba and Wollberg 1989, 1991). The method of testing for pure-tone responsiveness, however, was very restricted in the intensity domain. Since the total frequency response area to pure tones for each unit was unavailable, it was not possible to relate response patterns to complex sounds. Therefore, in the cat as well as in primates, the apparent selectivity of cell responses could result simply from the limited selection set of acoustic stimuli that were tested. In the end, because of the failure to perform systematic studies, important neural specializations and mechanisms that could explain the results were once again not discovered.

In birds, neurons were once considered to be "call-specialized" merely because they respond selectively to calls (Scheich et al. 1979). This type of selectivity reported in the auditory midbrain and telencephalic Field L (the analog of cortical AI) of the guinea fowl (Scheich et al. 1977, 1979), mynah bird (Langner et al. 1981), and starling (Leppelsack and Vogt 1976) was explained on the basis of a spectral overlap between the excitatory frequency response areas of neurons and the frequency components of certain calls to which they responded. Claims of "call-specialized" neurons based on complex neural filter properties, however, must show facilitation of the response to combinations of a discrete subset of stimulus components or parameters. "Call-specialized" neurons of this type have been found in the auditory system in frogs and songbirds (Fuzessery and Feng 1983; Margoliash and Fortune 1992; Lewicki 1996; Doupe 1997). In these neurons, the isolated call components produce little or no response, but when presented together they elicit clear facilitation. In songbirds, highly specific temporal combinations of sound elements are necessary for maximum excitation of "song-specific" units in several nuclei of the anterior forebrain (white-crowned sparrow: Margoliash 1983, 1986; zebra finch:

Doupe and Konishi 1991, Margoliash and Fortune 1992, Lewicki 1996, Doupe 1997). Responses of these "song-specific" neurons are affected strongly by experimental manipulations of temporal characteristics of the stimulus sequence. The auditory forebrain neurons respond strongly to the bird's own song while songs of conspecifics usually elicit weak excitation (Doupe 1997; Solis and Doupe 1997; see chap. 2, this volume). Recent improved studies of primates have also shown that neurons within localized regions of the auditory cortex respond selectively to species-specific calls (Rauschecker et al. 1995; Wang et al. 1995) and their response may be facilitated by combinations of call components (Tian and Rauschecker 1996; Rauschecker 1997).

These examples, drawn from very different systems, illustrate how neural specialization can be based on facilitation of the response to combinations of call components. Neurons exhibiting such specializations are also referred to as "combination-sensitive" neurons and were first described for processing echolocation signals in bats (Suga et al. 1978). The results of studies described below show that such specialized neurons are also involved in call processing in bats. I will now focus our attention on the structure of calls and their neural processing in the mustached bat.

Acoustic Structure of Calls in Bats

The communication calls of bats that have been studied to date include all three basic types of sound elements, that is, constant frequency (CF) sounds, frequency modulated (FM) sounds, and noise bursts (NB). In the mustached bat, FM-calls have been classified on the basis of the geometrical patterns of frequency modulations seen in their sound spectrograms (Kanwal et al. 1994a). FM sounds are the most common and may be subclassified into those that are predominantly modulated downward (DFM), those that are predominantly modulated upward (UFM), and those that are modulated both upward and downward. In some cases, especially CF sounds, the duration of the sound is also used as a descriptor in the naming scheme. The distinctions between short and long sounds and CF and FM sounds are based on statistical analyses of the natural variation in the sounds. The descriptors are added either as an abbreviated prefix or suffix to the abbreviation describing the overall pattern of the spectrogram for each of the three basic types of sounds, that is, CF, FM, and NB.

On the basis of a hierarchical clustering scheme, mustached-bat calls are considered to consist of simple syllables and complex syllables or "composites" (fig. 5.1). Simple syllables and composites may be emitted either independently or in conjunction with other sounds. However, certain sound elements that are never emitted in isolation but only as components of composites are labeled as "subsyllables." When the same simple syllable is emitted repeatedly in a single stream of vocalization, it is referred to as a "syllable-train." Composites are rarely produced in this fashion but may be emitted together with other types of composites or simple syllables.

The frequency modulation patterns within syllables in the mustached bats' calls are similar to those observed in the calls of several other bat species. Several syllables, for example, "descending rippled FM," "fixed Sinusoidal FM," "rectangular broadband NB," and "gliding downward FM-long quasi CF," when tape-recorded and played back at slow speeds, also show spectral equivalance to the calls of many nonbat species (Boinski 1991; Hauser 1996a). Some syllables such as "checked downward FM" are also found as notes in the song of birds and the humpback whale (Marler and Pickert 1984; Payne and McVay 1971).

Call syllables show a large degree of inherent variation in the structure of their spectrograms so that different syllable types tend to intergrade if defined only on the basis of any one parameter. An effective separation can be achieved, however, if syllables are defined on the basis of multiple parameters. Some of these parameters co-vary and may play an important role in constraining the perception of sounds under adverse signal-to-noise conditions. This variation presumably contains important information such as the identity of the emitter and the behavioral context in which a syllable variant is emitted. Interestingly, not all syllables show the same degree of overall variation. Some of the tightly clustered syllables, for example, the "bent downward FM" and "descending rippled FM," may correspond to warning or alarm calls, where it is critical to avoid ambiguity in the message and where the identity of the emitter is unimportant. Behavioral studies are necessary to test this hypothesis.

In contrast to the simple repeating sounds of frogs and toads (Wells and Schwartz 1984) and the stereotypic song sequences of some birds (Marler and Pickert 1984), mustached bats emit a variety of simple syllables and composites as defined on the basis of statistical analyses of acoustic structure. Figure 5.2 shows a multidimensionally scaled configuration of the parameterized call data (Kanwal et al. 1994a). Syllables with different types of the basic sound elements are the most widely separated in this configuration. Interestingly, echolocation pulses, which may be considered as composites containing two components (CF and FM), are placed in the center of the plot. Our studies show that the acoustic structure of mustached-bat calls is the most elaborate among animals, excluding whales and some species of mimicking birds, for example, mockingbirds and parrots that can mimic virtually any sound with frequencies within their hearing and vocalization range. Only a few

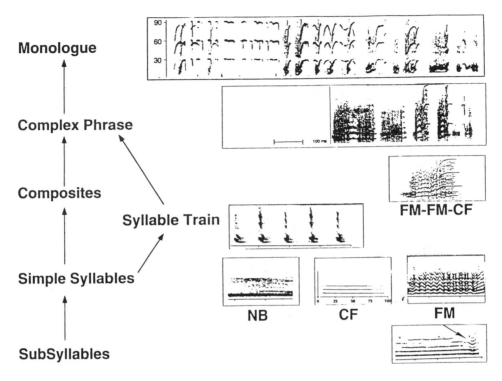

Figure 5.1
Classification and structural syntax in sounds emitted by mustached bats. The segment labeled as a complex phrase is emitted by a single bat as determined from simultaneously obtained audio-video recordings.

primate species, including squirrel monkeys, tamarins, vervets, and macaques, produce a large repertoire of vocalizations that are both distinct and meaningful on the basis of their acoustic structure or the behavioral context in which they may be emitted (Sutton 1979). The parametric boundaries of the natural variants presumably encode important information such as the identity of the emitter and the behavioral context in which a syllable variant is emitted (Hauser 1991; Hauser and Marler 1993; Hauser 1996b).

Bats may combine independently emitted simple syllables to produce composites. Of the 342 disyllabic combinations in composites possible in theory, however, less than 15 have been found to occur (Kanwal et al. 1994a). Therefore, one may ask what are the rules for making composites? Several syntactical rules can be formulated from our knowledge of the bat's repertoire of calls. Rules for these types of combinations in calls of primates have been referred to as "phoneticlike" syntax

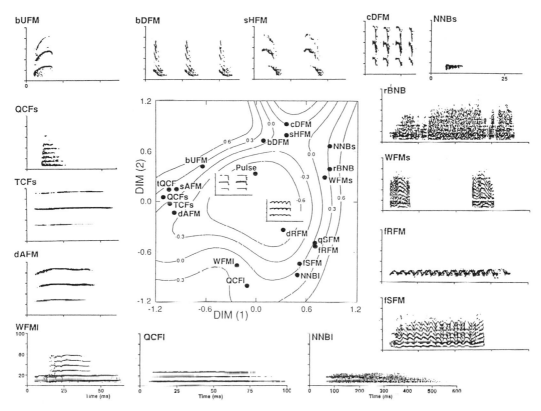

Figure 5.2
The center plot shows a three-dimensional MDS configuration of syllable types and echolocation pulses obtained from average values of 9 parameters, with no missing values. The third dimension is represented by a contour plot. Spectrograms for several different syllable types are shown around the perimeter of the MDS plot. All spectrograms around the perimeter of the MDS plot are drawn to the same scale as WFMl, except for those with their own time scale. Spectrograms for the echolocation pulse and dRFM (not to scale) are placed at the center of the contour plot. Note the separation of CF and CF-like syllables from FM syllables (Kanwal et al. 1994).

(Marler 1977; Snowdon 1982) and in birdsong as "syllabic syntax" (Marler and Peters 1989), although in the latter case, short silent intervals are included within a syllable. For example, some of the rules of syntax in mustached bat calls are: (i) simple syllables are not conjoined in a random fashion for creating composites; (ii) the order of simple syllables in a composite is not reversible; and (iii) a maximum of three simple syllables may be combined to form a composite. From our recordings of the call vocalizations, only 11 of the 19 simple syllables are used to construct composites (for further details, see Kanwal et al. 1994a).

The duration of a simple syllable may be significantly altered when it is combined within a composite since the duration of a composite is constrained by the lung volume and respiratory rate of the animal (Suthers and Fattu 1973). Mustached bats breathe at a rate of approximately 150 breaths/minute. This means that the maximum duration of an expiration phase is less than 200ms. The syntax for forming composites may be further constrained either by mechanisms of sound production or other rules of construction and perception of the message. These mechanisms cannot be identified without functional-anatomical and behavioral studies of sound communication. Such studies in mustached bats have barely begun, although the behavioral context in which some call types, for example, the "rectangular broadband NB", are emitted is known (Gupta et al. 1998). In addition, recent studies show that different subspecies of mustached bats use different dialects, which opens the possibility to examine neural plasticity and audiovocal learning during development in this species (Dietz et al. 1998).

Functional Organization of the Auditory Cortex

The auditory system of the mustached bat is highly specialized for processing echolocation signals. Studies on the echolocating system of the mustached bat have already provided insights into the neural processing of a special class of complex sounds. A brief summary of this is essential for a meaningful description of call processing in bats.

During echolocation, mustached bats emit sounds consisting of the fundamental tone and three harmonics. These are labeled as H_1–H_4, where the fundamental and each harmonic has a constant frequency component (CF_1–CF_4) and a downward-sweeping frequency modulated component (FM_1-FM_4) (figure 5.3a). The CF components are harmonics of an approximately 30kHz fundamental. The flying bat hears both its own pulse and the returning echo, which is Doppler-shifted upward in frequency, and which may show a partial temporal overlap with the pulse. The

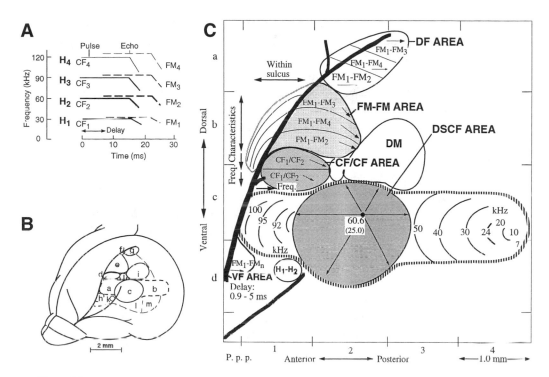

Figure 5.3
Functional organization of the auditory cortex of the mustached bat. (A) Schematized sonogram showing the components of the biosonar pulse and Doppler-shifted echo. (B) Dorsolateral view of the left cerebral hemisphere. The auditory cortex consists of several areas (a-m). Areas a, b, c (A1a, A1p, and DSCF, respectively, of the primary auditory cortex); areas d, e, f, g, represent CF/CF FM-FM, DIF and DF areas, and h, i, j, and k represent VF, DM, H1-H2, and TE areas. Areas c through k are specialized for the systematic representation of echolocation information, whereas the functionality of l and m is unclear. Neurons within areas c, d and e also show specializations for processing communication sounds. Branches of the medial cerebral artery are shown by the branching lines. The longest branch is on the sulcus or fossa. (C) Enlarged view of the auditory cortex shown in B. Combination-sensitivity of neurons and mapped representations within the primary auditory cortex, DSCF, FM-FM, CF/CF, DF, and VF areas are indicated by conventional abbreviations and lines/arrows, respectively (adapted from Suga 1984).

auditory periphery is exquisitely sensitive to the CF_2 echo (near 61kHz) but is relatively insensitive to the bat's emitted CF_2 pulse (near 59kHz); hence masking of the echo by the pulse is minimal. From the cochlea, the signals are processed multiple times in parallel and/or sequentially beginning at the cochlear nucleus and proceeding to the lateral lemniscus, medial geniculate body, and finally to the auditory and frontal cortex.

The auditory cortex contains neurons tuned to combinations of pulse H_1 and echo H_2–H_4. The Doppler-shifted constant frequency (DSCF) area is the largest portion of the primary auditory cortex (A1) and contains frequency-versus-amplitude coordinates for mapping the CF_2 component of the echo from a target (Suga and Manabe 1978) (figures 5.3b and 5.3c). This region occupies nearly 30% of the primary auditory cortex and contains a magnified representation of a narrow range of frequencies between 60.6 and 62.3kHz (when the bat's resting frequency is 61kHz).

In the CF/CF area, neurons tuned to CF combinations (e.g., pulse CF_1 and echo CF_2 or CF_3) are sensitive to the amount of Doppler shift between pulse and echo, and thus they can process relative velocity (Suga et al. 1983). The CF/CF area is functionally organized into columns such that each column of neurons responds best to a particular combination of frequencies and best combinations of frequencies vary in a regular way along the surface of the cortex. Other cortical neurons tuned to FM combinations (e.g., pulse FM_1 and echo FM_2) are selective for certain echo delays, and thus they can process target range (O'Neill and Suga 1982; Suga et al. 1983). The combination-sensitivity of CF/CF and FM-FM neurons is manifested in the facilitation of the response when both components are present. This facilitation, like that described in the leopard frog and white-crowned sparrow, encompasses both spectral (CF/CF neurons) and temporal (FM-FM neurons) domains. Moreover, CF/CF and FM-FM neurons are segregated and organized in the cortex to form maps corresponding to target range and velocity, respectively, on the cortical surface (figure 5.3c).

Specialized Call Processing in the Auditory Cortex

As explained earlier in this chapter, mustached bats use a complex repertoire of calls with a hierarchical structure resembling phonological syntax. Also, the auditory cortex is well organized for processing echolocation signals. I now address the physiological properties of cortical neurons for processing calls. It is curious whether (i) the same cortical areas and cortical neurons that process echolocation signals also process calls and (ii) call-processing neurons show combination-sensitivity as discussed above, that is, can their responsiveness be explained on the basis of overlap between the frequency spectrum of call components and frequency tuning of a neuron?

The first step in the analysis of neural specializations for call processing is to dissect out a preferred call in the frequency and time domains according to the neuronal filter characteristics (tuning curve). Studies based on this paradigm have shown that neurons in the DSCF area are sensitive primarily to variations in calls in the frequency domain and those in the FM-FM area are sensitive to variations primarily in the time domain. The response properties including combination-sensitivity of neurons to calls in these two cortical areas are described below.

Frequency Domain Processing

In studies of the cortical processing of calls in the mustached bat, fourteen of the nineteen observed syllables are energy-matched (on the basis of root-mean-square values) and presented at a rate of 1/s (figure 5.4a). This call series consists of seven call variants (in the frequency domain) for each syllable tested and is presented at several stimulus levels (figure 5.4b and 5.4c). A neuron's responses to the most effective pair of frequencies or call components is quantified by PSTHs (PSTH = peristimulus-time histogram). The neuron's response to each of the syllables is measured as the number of spikes minus spontaneous activity, typically in a 10ms window around the peak response. The "best call" is determined by summing the neuron's responses over several intensity levels. Subsequent testing of the neuron's response selectivities is carried out using the best call variant at its best amplitude (figure 5.4d). The best call (simple syllable or composite) and its individual components (A and B) are presented separately (200 trials each, repetition rate = 1/s) to determine the neuron's response magnitude and facilitation ratio, that is, the response to the original syllable divided by the sum of the responses to the individual parts (figure 5.5). Spectral facilitation is indicated if the response to the entire syllable is >120% of the sum of the responses to the individual components (Esser et al. 1997).

The variation in call preference that emerges across a neural population is related to the match between the dominant frequencies in the calls and the shapes of the excitatory, facilitatory, and inhibitory responses areas of a neuron (see figures 5.4 and 5.5). Data obtained from neurons in the DSCF area illustrate three important points (figure 5.5). First, the neural response to calls is comparable and sometimes may be better than that obtained to tones or pairs of tones. Second, selective, high-magnitude responses to calls are based primarily on spectral facilitation. Thus, when call components that fall within the excitatory response areas are extracted and presented separately, the neuron shows clear facilitation with a response that is better than the sum of the responses to each component alone.

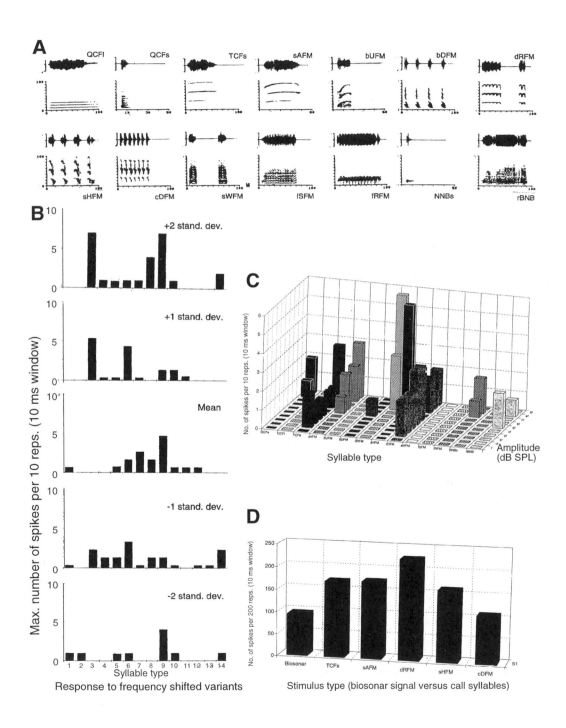

Response to frequency shifted variants

Stimulus type (biosonar signal versus call syllables)

Finally, a combination of bandpass-filtered call components may elicit a larger response magnitude than the whole natural call because of the absence of acoustic energy in the inhibitory areas. Hence responses to calls can be greatly influenced by the organization of the inhibitory frequency response areas. Thus a DSCF neuron does not respond well to the "bent upward FM" syllable if the facilitatory call components are reversed (figure 5.5b and 5.5d). This is explained by the asymmetrical inhibitory areas surrounding the excitatory response areas in the 61kHz region. In short, recent studies show that for DSCF neurons, call responses can be generally explained on the basis of the shape of a neuron's facilitatory and inhibitory frequency response areas.

Time-domain Processing

Figures 5.6a and 5.6b show examples of a "delay scan" and delay tuning for one neuron located in the DSCF area and another in the FM-FM area, respectively. Neurons sensitive to time-domain processing of calls are rare in the DSCF area. In contrast, in the FM-FM area, more than half of the neurons studied (56%, n = 23 of 41) show facilitative interactions between spectral and temporal components of complex syllables or composites as well as to pairs and trains of simple syllables (Ohlemiller et al. 1996).

Temporal facilitation is indicated if the response to the entire syllable is >120% of the sum of responses to the iso- or heterosyllabic parts. For analysis in the time domain, the silent interval between the two syllables is gradually increased from 0ms through a range such that the naturally occuring interval falls approximately in the middle. Also, the first syllable is presented by itself in the beginning and the second one is presented by itself at the end of the scan (figure 5.6a). This type of scan tests for both the tuning of the neuron to various silent intervals as well as the magnitude of facilitation of a combination-sensitive neuron.

Figure 5.4
(A) A sequence of 14 simple syllables to show the different geometric patterns of their spectrograms. (B) Histograms showing peak responses of a DSCF neuron to frequency shifted syllable variants (bin size = 10ms). Each syllable was presented at 3 intensities (responses shown are at 55 ± 5dB SPL) and the responses are summed over all intensities to determine the best variant of a syllable type. Syllables numbered 1–14 are in the same sequence (left to right) as shown in (A). Note that shifting a syllable in the frequency domain can greatly alter a neuron's responsiveness to it. (C). A 3-D plot to show the effect of amplitude on the responses to best syllable variants for each syllable type presented at intervals of 10dB SPL. (D) Comparison of peak responses at best amplitudes for best syllable variants with that for the essential components in a biosonar (pulse-echo) stimulus. All responses shown above were obtained from the same neuron and summed over 10 repetitions (except in 4D where 200 repititions were used) after subtracting the level of spontaneous activity.

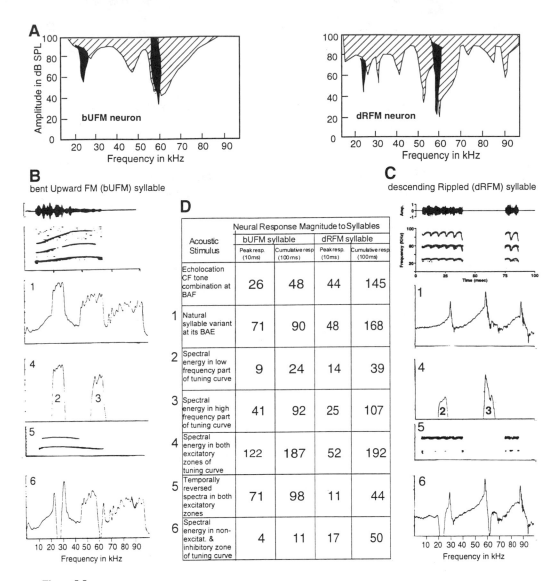

Figure 5.5

(A) Examples of facilitatory (filled) and inhibitory (hatched) tuning curves for two neurons in the DSCF area. The facilitatory tuning of both DSCF neurons is uncommonly broad. (B) Modifications of a bUFM syllable in the frequency and time domains. Amplitude envelop (top), spectrogram (middle), and power spectrum (B1) of bUFM. "B2-B4": Power spectra showing the extracted frequency components in the simple syllable. The power spectra extracted were based on the width of the excitatory tuning at 10dB above threshold. Multiple digital filtering approximated a roll off of about 80dB per octave. B6: Power spectrum of the remaining nonexcitatory, including inhibitory, components in the syllable. (C) Amplitude envelop (top), spectrogram (middle), and power spectrum of dRFM. (2 to 6) Power spectra of the dRFM syllable before and after making similar modifications as for the bUFM syllable. (D) Table of peak and total response magnitudes of DSCF neurons to the syllable components shown in (B) and (C). Responses (number of spikes summed for 50 reps.) to syllables and syllable components are comparable and sometimes better than the best response to a CF/CF or an FM-CF combination characteristic of the minimal components in an echolocation signal.

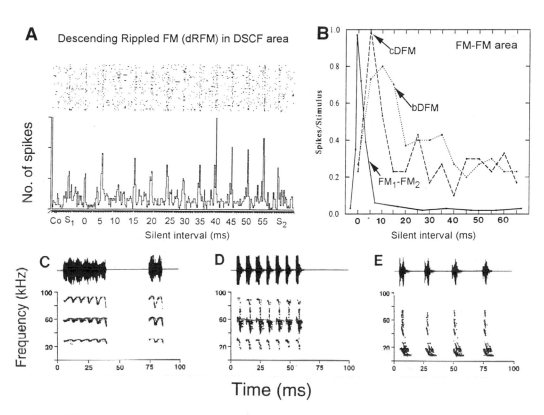

Figure 5.6
(A) Raster plot and PSTH for the response of a DSCF neuron when the silent interval for two dRFM syllables shown in (C) was varied from 0–55ms (Co = control, S_1 = first syllable alone, S_2 = second syllable alone). Responses shown are at a resolution of 50ms. The neuron shows facilitation to a best interval of 40ms, which is close to the typical natural delay between two dRFM syllables (see fig. 5.7G). (B) Tuning curves for intersyllable intervals ranging from 0–70ms for a FM-FM neuron. Note that the same neuron shows different temporal tuning to cDFM and bDFM syllables (shown in D and E, respectively) as well as to an appropriate pulse-echo delay (adapted from Ohlemiller et al. 1994).

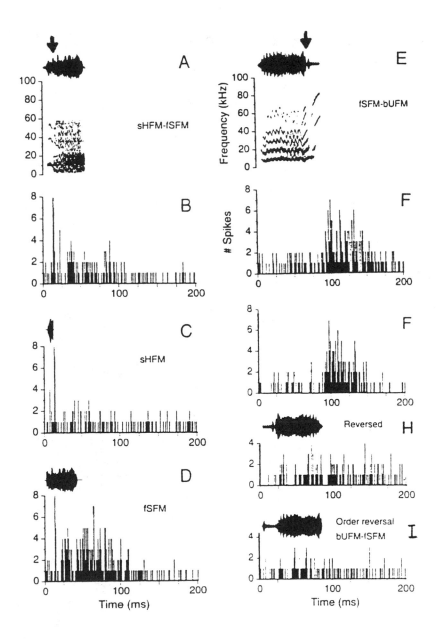

If a silent interval is artificially introduced within a composite, the response to the two syllables declines in a graded fashion in a time-domain-sensitive neuron. Accordingly, to examine the effect of temporal order on the neuron's response selectivity, the original composite (AB) is also played backward and in reverse order (BA). The responses to these manipulations can be then compared with the neuron's response to the original composite (Ohlemiller et al. 1994).

The observations that neuronal responses to composites are highly vulnerable to (i) reversal of order of syllables within a natural composite, to (ii) introducing a silent period between the syllables, and to (iii) playing the stimulus in reverse provide independent lines of evidence at the single-unit level that "phonological" syntax in calls is processed by neurons in the mammalian nonprimary auditory cortex (Esser et al. 1997). These findings, together with evidence of structural syntax in the calls themselves and the occurrence of both facilitative and suppressive intersyllable interactions, clearly point to the importance of syntax for acoustic communication in bats.

Temporal combination-sensitivity of FM-FM neurons for composites is found to coexist with spectral combination-sensitivity. Figure 5.7 shows two neurons that are sensitive to the temporal combination of simple syllables. The first neuron (figures 5.7a–d) does not respond as well to the whole composite as to the second syllable alone. This neuron's response to the whole composite is suppressed by the first syllable in the composite. The response of the neuron shown in figures 5.7e–i is facilitated by the correct temporal combination of the two syllables in the composite. Thus this neuron does not respond well to the reversed composite (figure 5.7h), or to the syllables presented in the reversed temporal order (figure 5.7i). For maximum excitation, equivalent to the response to the original composite, this neuron requires the correct time structure as well as a specific combination of spectral bands that overlap with the neuron's FM_1-FM_n subtype (i.e., FM_1-FM_3).

Figure 5.7
PSTHs showing response suppression because of temporal interactions in a normal (A through D) and modified (E through H) syllables in a composite. The boundary between two syllables is indicated by an arrow. Temporal suppression in A was indicated by a response ratio of 44% when the response to the whole composite is compared to the summed response to individual components. (A) Oscillogram and spectrogram of the sHFM-fSFM composite, the best composite for this unit (FM_1-FM_2, BD = 5.3ms). (B) PSTH of unit's response to original composite (sHFM-fSFM). (C) PSTH of unit's response to the first syllable (sHFM). (D) PSTH shows unit's strongest response was to the second syllable (fSFM). (E) Oscillogram and spectrogram of a fSFM-bUFM composite, the best composite for this unit (FM_1-FM_3, BD = 6.4ms). (F) PSTH showing response to the original fSFM-bUFM composite. (G) PSTH shows unit's robust response to minimal spectral elements of composite fSFM-bUFM necessary to excite this unit to a level equivalent to the original. The first syllable was low-pass filtered at 35kHz; and the second syllable was high-pass filtered at 65kHz. (H) PSTH shows unit's weak response to the reversed composite. (I) PSTH shows unit's weak response to the reversed order of syllables in the fSFM-bUFM composite. Arrows at top indicate junction point of the two syllables in a composite (adapted from Esser et al. 1977).

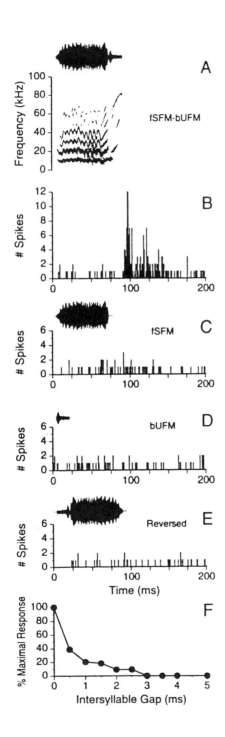

Another example of neuronal specificity for precise temporal features of the acoustic stimulus is shown by the responses of another neuron, in which introduction of a silent period ≥ 0.5ms between both syllables of the composite fSFM-bUFM (figures 5.8a and 5.8f), results in a progressive decline in the neuronal response. At intersyllable silent intervals of ≥ 3ms, this unit completely ceases to respond (figure 5.8f). Reversing the order of syllables also results in the loss of a facilitated response (compare figure 5.8b with 5.8h). Responses to the reversed composite call are nearly always reduced as compared with responses to the corresponding original composite. For instance, this neuron shows temporal facilitation for composite fSFM-bUFM (figures 5.8a and 5.8b) but barely responds to the individual components when presented separately (figures 5.8c and 5.8d) or even to the entire composite played in reverse (figure 5.8e). Approximately 20% of all neurons recorded exhibit this type of behavior.

The recent discovery of combination-sensitive neurons in the auditory cortex of the rhesus monkey confirms the evolutionarily ubiquitous presence of such neurons within the auditory system (Tian and Rauschecker 1996; Rauschecker 1997). In rhesus monkeys, these neurons are present in the posterior portion of the superior temporal gyrus, where a large proportion of neurons are either FM-selective or tuned to certain bandwidths present in monkey calls (Rauschecker et al. 1995). Furthermore, the behavioral context in which many of the rhesus monkey calls are emitted is generally understood (Hauser and Marler 1993; Hauser 1996b). This opens the exciting possibility to study neural processing of semantics as well as syntax in the brain of nonhuman primates (see chapter 8, this volume).

Future Directions

As reviewed above, a number of studies have identified varying degrees of neural selectivity and specializations to species-specific calls in birds, frogs, cats, monkeys, and humans. Thus complex neural filters with nonlinear interactions may represent a general strategy for processing calls in different animals. Studies conducted so far on

Figure 5.8
(A) Oscillogram and spectrogram of the "fSFM-bUFM" composite—the best composite for this unit (FM$_1$-FM$_3$, BD = 8.1ms). The boundary between two syllables is indicated by an arrow. (B) PSTH shows unit's robust response to the original composite (fSFM-bUFM; response ratio = 1108%). (C) The unit almost failed to respond to the first syllable (fSFM). (D) Unit nearly failed to respond to the second syllable (bUFM). (E) No response to playback of the reversed composite. (F) Unit's response decreased dramatically and eventually ceased when a silent period of 0.5ms was inserted between the two components of this composite (adapted from Esser et al. 1977).

birds, bats, and primates represent merely a starting point for understanding the neural processing and perception of complex sounds, including speech sounds. Many questions remain unanswered and many more have yet to be formulated before we can fully comprehend how calls are processed and perceived.

For a complete understanding of call processing, further research is needed at both the subcellular and cognitive or perceptual levels. Studies at the cellular and subcellular level can delineate the sequence of events leading to nonlinear responses as identified by intracellular responses (Lewicki and Konishi 1995, Lewicki 1996) and whole-cell patch clamp recordings, respectively. An example of the latter is the finding of duration-sensitive neurons in the inferior colliculus in the big brown bat (Casseday et al. 1994). Similarly, at the molecular level, discrimination of meaningful complex sounds and audiovocal learning may be based on hyperpolarization receptor mechanisms (Schmidt and Perkel 1998) and second messenger systems acting as molecular coincidence detectors (Anholt 1994).

Other important issues in the neural processing of complex acoustic stimuli such as calls relate to (i) the nature of the neural representation of the stimulus in the cortex; (ii) the spatial organization of neurons that process calls; and (iii) the way in which this neural representation enables an animal to identify the stimulus as a specific call from a particular individual in a recognizable emotional state. Extensive studies on the mustached bat's cortex show the presence of several maps (e.g., for echo-delay, velocity, etc.) for processing echolocation signals. Are calls also mapped in specific areas within the auditory cortex? If so, which acoustic features are mapped, and are maps of one feature orthogonal to maps of other features? The data available in echolocating bats at present suggest that maps may not be important because of the discrete variations between different calls (Kanwal et al. 1994a; Kanwal 1998). Rather, multidimensional representational schemes with calls having similar acoustic features represented within small neuronal clusters may be the rule (Kanwal et al. 1994b). Such local rather than global "maplike" organization of echo delay neurons has recently been described in the auditory cortex of the big brown bat, *Eptesicus fuscus* (Dear et al. 1993). A distributed and redundant representation of song/calls/language is also present in the HVc of the zebra finch (Sutter and Margoliash 1994; Margoliash 1997), where combination-sensitivity has been demonstrated, and in marmosets (Wang et al. 1995) and humans (Modayur et al. 1997), where combination-sensitivity has not yet been demonstrated.

Clearly, knowing the neural mechanisms alone is not sufficient to fully explain perception. Perceptual schemes must involve the activity of populations of neurons and interactions between them. To study these, single-cell electrophysiological techniques are inadequate. However, several new techniques appear promising. Optical recording and functional magnetic resonance imaging, where one can train animals on a cognitive task and image spatiotemporal patterns of neural activations in the cortex, may provide answers to cognition-related questions, for example, those related to categorical perception, or to the representational meaning of alarm calls, etc. Multisite electrical recordings is another way in which the activity of large populations of neurons can be tracked with precision. In combination with telemetry, these techniques can directly address many neuroethological questions related to auditory communication in bats and other animals in which the audiovocal system is critical for survival.

Abbreviations of Syllable Names

bDFM: bent downarrow FM
bUFM: bent upward FM
cDFM: checked downward FM
dAFM: double arched FM
dRFM: descending rippled FM
fRFM: fixed rippled FM
fSFM: fixed sinusoidal FM
gDFM: gliding downward FM
qSFM: quasi sinusoidal FM
QCFs: short, quasi CF
QCFl: long, quasi CF
NNBs: short, narrowband NB
NNBl: long, narrowband NB
rBNB: rectangular broadband NB
sAFM: single arched FM
sHFM: single humped FM
TCFs: short, true CF
tQCF: trapezoidal quasi-CF
WFMs: short, wrinkled FM
WFMl: long, wrinkled FM

Acknowledgments

Supported in part by a NIH grant DC02054 to J.S.K. and a DOD grant DAMD17-93-V-3018 to GICCS. I wish to thank an anonymous reviewer and Dr. M. Hauser for their useful comments and suggestions for improving this manuscript.

References

Anholt, R. R. H. (1994) Signal integration in the nervous system: Adenylate cyclases as molecular con-icidence detectors. *Trends in Neuroscience* 17:37–41.

Blumstein, S. E. and Stevens, K. N. (1981) Phonetic features and acoustic invariance in speech. *Cognition* 10:25–32.

Boinski, S. (1991) The coordination of spatial position: A field study of the vocal behavior of adult female squirrel monkeys. *Anim. Behav.* 41:89–102.

Casseday, J. H., Ehrlich, D., and Covey, E. (1994) Neural tuning for sound duration: Role of inhibitory mechanisms in the inferior colliculus. *Science* 264(5160):847–850.

Cole, R. A. and Scott, B. (1974) Towards a theory of speech perception. *Psychol. Rev.* 81:348–374.

Creutzfeldt, O., Ojemann, G., and Lettich, E. (1989) Neuronal acticity in the human lateral temporal lobe. I. Responses to speech. *Exp. Brain Res.* 77:451–475.

Dear, S. P., Fritz, J., Haresign, T., Ferragamo, M., and Simmons, J. A. (1993) Tonotopic and functional organization in the auditory cortex of the big brown bat, *Eptesicus fuscus. J. Neurophysiol.* 70:1987–2009.

Dietz, N., Peng, J., and Kanwal, J. S. (1998) Call variation in two subspecies of mustached bats, *Pteronotus parnellii:* Do bats have dialects? *Assoc. Res. Otolaryngol. Abstrt.*, no. 563.

Doupe, A. J. (1997) Song- and order-selective neurons in the songbird anterior forebrain during vocal development. *J. Neurosci.* 17:1147–1167.

Doupe, A. J. and Konishi, M. (1991) Song-selective auditory circuits in the vocal control system of the zebra finch. *Proc. Natl. Acad. Sci.* (USA) 88:11339–11343.

Doupe, A. J. and Solis, M. M. (1997) Song- and order-selective neurons develop in the songbird anterior forebrain during vocal learning. *J. Neurobiol.* 33(5):694–709.

Ehret, G. and Bernecker, C. (1986) Low-frequency sound communication by mouse pups (*Mus musculus*): Wriggling calls release maternal behavior. *Anim. Behav.* 34:821–830.

Esser, K.-H., Condon, C. J., Suga, N., and Kanwal, J. S. (1997) Syntax processing by auditory cortical neurons in the FM-FM area of the mustached bat, *Pteronotus parnellii. Proc. Natl. Acad. Sci.* (USA) 94:14019–14024.

Fenton, M. B. (1977) Variations in the social calls of little brown bats (*Myotis lucifugus*). *Can. J. Zool.* 55:1151–1157.

Fenton, M. B. (1985) *Communication in the Chiroptera.* Bloomington, IN: Indiana University Press.

Fitzpatrick, D. C., Kanwal, J. S., Butman, J., and Suga, N. (1993) Combination-sensitive neurons in the primary auditory cortex of the mustached bat. *J. Neurosci.* 320:509–520.

Fuzessery, Z. M. and Feng, A. S. (1983) Mating call selectivity in the thalamus of the leopard frog, (*Rana ppipiens*): Single and multiunit analyses. *J. Comp. Physiol.* 150:333–344.

Glass, I. and Wollberg, Z. (1983) Responses of cells in the auditory cortex of awake squirrel monkeys to normal and reversed species-specific vocalizations. *Hear. Res.* 9:27–33.

Grinnell, A. D. (1963) The neurophysiology of audition in bats: Intensity and frequency prameters. *J. Physiol.* (London) 167:38–66.

Gupta, P., Dietz, N., and Kanwal, J. S. (1998) Vocal communication and stereotypic social behavior patterns in the mustached bat, *Pteronotus parnellii. Assoc. Res. Otolaryngol. Abstrt.*, no. 562.

Hauser, M. D. (1991) Sources of acuostic variation in rhesus macaque vocalizations. *Ethology* 89:29–46.

Hauser, M. D. (1996a) *The Evolution of Communication.* Cambridge, MA: MIT Press.

Hauser, M. D. (1996b) Vocal communication in macaques: Causes of variation. In *Evolutionary Ecology and Behaviour of Macaques*, ed. by J. Fa and D. Lindburg, pp. 551–577. Cambridge: Cambridge University Press.

Hauser, M. D. and Marler, P. (1993) Food-associated calls in rhesus macaques (*Macaca mulatta*). I. Socioecological factors influencing call production. *Behav. Ecol.* 4:194–205.

Kanwal, J. S. (1998) Charting speech with bats without requiring maps. *Behav. Brain Sci.* 21: 272–273.

Kanwal, J. S., Matsumura, S., Ohlemiller, K., and Suga, N. (1994a) Acoustic elements and syntax in communication sounds emitted by mustached bats. *J. Acoust. Soc. Am.* 96:1229–1254.

Kanwal, J. S., Ohlemiller, K. K., and Suga, N. (1994b) Distributed, multidimensional representation of communication sounds in the auditory cortex of the mustached bat. *Assoc. Res. Otolaryngol. Abstrt.*, no. 368.

Kuhl, P. (1986) Theoretical contributions of tests on animals to the special-mechanisms debate in speech. *Exp. Biol.* 45:233–265.

Langner, G., Bonke, D., and Scheich, H. (1981) Neuronal discrimination of natural and synthetic vowels in field L of trained mynah birds. *Exp. Brain Res.* 43:11 24.

Leippert, D. (1994) Social behavior on the wing in the false vampire, *Megaderma lyra. Ethology* 98:111–127.

Leppelsack, H. J. and Vogt, M. (1976) Responses of auditory neurons in the forebrain of a songbird to stimulation with species-specific sounds. *J. Comp. Physiol.* 107:263–274.

Lewicki, M. S. (1996) Intracellular characterization of song-specific neurons in the zebra finch auditory forebrain. *J. Neurosci*, 16.5854–5863.

Lewicki, M. S. and Konishi, M. (1995) Mechanisms underlying the sensitivity of songbird forebrain neurons to temporal order. *Proc. Natl. Acad. Sci.* (USA) 92:5582–5586.

Liberman, A. M., Cooper, F. S., Shankweiler, P. D., and Studdert-Kennedy, M. (1967) Perception of the speech code. *Psychol. Rev.* 74:431–461.

Lieberman, P. and Blumstein, S. E. (1988) *Speech Physiology, Speech Perception, and Acoustic-Phonetics.* New York: Cambridge University Press.

Manabe, T., Suga, N., and Ostwald, J. (1978) Aural representation in the Doppler-shifted CF-processing area of the auditory cortex of the mustache bat. *Science* 200:339–342.

Margoliash, D. (1983) Acoustic parameters underlying the responses of song-specific neurons in the white-crowned sparrow. *J. Neurosci*, 3:1039–1057.

Margoliash, D. (1986) Preference for autogenous song by auditory neurons in a song system nucleus of the white-crowned sparrow. *J. Neurosci.* 6:1643–1661.

Margoliash, D. (1997) Distributed time-domain representations in the birdsong system. *Neuron* 19(5):963–966.

Margoliash, D. and Fortune, E. S. (1992) Temporal and harmonic combination-sensitive neurons in the zebra finch's HVc. *J. Neurosci.* 12:4309–4326.

Marler, P. (1977) The structure of animal communication sounds. In *Recognition of complex acoustic signals*, ed. by T. H. Bullock, pp. 17–35. Berlin: Dahlem Konferenzen.

Marler, P. and Peters, S. (1989) Species differences in auditory responsiveness in early vocal learning In *The Comparative Psychology of Audition*, ed. by R. J. Dooling, and S. H. Hulse, pp. 243–273. Hillsdale, NJ: Lawrence Erlbaum.

Marler, P. and Pickert, R. (1984) Species-universal microstructure in the learned song of the swamp swallow, *Melospiza georgiana*. *Anim. Behav.* 32:673–689.

Modayur, B., Prothero, J., Ojemann, G., Maravilla, K., and Brinkley, J. (1997) Visualization-based mapping of language function in the brain. *Neuroimage* 6:245–258.

Newman, J. D. and Wollberg, Z. (1973a) Responses of single neurons in the auditory cortex of squirrel monkeys to variants of a single call type. *Exp. Neurol.* 40:821–824.

Newman, J. D. and Wollberg, Z. (1973b) Multiple coding of species-specific vocalizations in the auditory cortex of squirrel monkeys. *Brain Res.* 54:287–304.

Nyu, A. C. and Margoliash, D. (1996) Temporal hierarchical control of singing in birds. *Science* 273:1871–1875.

Ohl, F. W. and Scheich, H. (1997) Orderly cortical representation of vowels based on format interaction. *Proceed. Natl. Acad. Sci.* (USA) 94:9440–9444.

Ohlemiller, K. K., Kanwal, J. S., Butman, J., and Suga, N. (1994) Stimulus design for auditory neuroethology: Synethesis and manipulation of complex communication sounds. *Auditory Neurosci.* 1:19–37.

Ohlemiller, K. K., Kanwal, J. S., and Suga, N. (1996) Facilitative responses to species-specific calls in cortical FM-FM neurons of the mustached bat. *NeuroReport* 7:1749–1755.

O'Neill, W. E. and Suga, N. (1982) Encoding of target-range information and its representation in the auditory cortex of the mustached bat. *J. Neurosci.* 2:225–255.

Payne, R. S. and McVay, S. (1971) Songs of humpback whales. *Science* 173:585–597.

Pelleg-Toiba, R. and Wollberg, Z. (1989) Tuning properties of auditory cortex cells in awake squirrel monkeys. *Exp. Brain Res.* 74:353–364.

Pelleg-Toiba, R. and Wollberg, Z. (1991) Discrimination of communication calls in the squirrel monkey: "Call detectors" or "cell ensembles"? *J. Basic Clin. Physiol. Pharmacol.* 2(4):257–272.

Pickett, J. M. (1980) *The Sounds of Speech Communication.* Baltimore, MD: University Park Press.

Porter, F. L. (1979) Social behavior and acoustic communication in the bat, *Carollia perspicillata* (*Chiroptera: phyllostomatidae*). Ph.D. dissertation, Washington University.

Rauschecker, J. P. (1997) Processing of complex sounds in the auditory cortex of cat, monkey, and man. *Acta. Otolaryngol.* (Stockh); suppl. 532:34–38.

Rauschecker, J. P., Tian, B., and Hauser, M. (1995) Processing of complex sounds in the macaque nonprimary auditory cortex. *Science* 268:111–114.

Scheich, H., Langner, G., and Bonke, D. (1979) Responsiveness of units in the auditory neostriatum of the guinea fowl (*Numida meleagris*) to species-specific calls and synthetic stimuli. *J. Comp. Physiol.* 132:257–276.

Scheich, H., Langner, G., and Koch, R. (1977) Coding of narrow-band and wide-band vocalizations in the auditory midbrain nucleus (MLD) of the guinea fowl, (*Numida meleagris*). *J. Comp. Physiol.* 117:245–265.

Schmidt, M. F., and Perkel, D. J. (1998) Slow synaptic inhibition in nucleus HVc of the adult zebra finch. *J. Neurosci.* 18:895–904.

Schwartz, T. H., Ojemann, G. A., Haglund, M. M., and Lettich, E. (1996) Cerebral lateralization of neuronal activity during naming, reading, and line-matching. *Cogn. Brain Res.* 4(4):263–273.

Snowdon, C. T. (1982) Linguistic and psycholinguistic approaches to primate communication. In *Primate communication*, ed. by C. T. Snowdon, C. H. Brown, and M. R. Petersen, pp. 212–238. Cambridge: Cambridge University Press.

Solis, M. M. and Doupe, A. J. (1997) Anterior forebrain neurons develop selectivity by an intermediate stage of birdsong learning. *J. Neurosci.* 17:6447–6462.

Sovijarvi, A. R. A (1975) Detection of temporally and spatially complex acoustic signals by cells in cat's primary cortex. *Acta. Physiol. Scand. Suppl.* 396:47.

Suga, N. (1965) Functional properties of auditory neurons in the cortex of echolocating bats. *J. Physiol.* (London) 181:671–700.

Suga, N., O'Neill, W. E., Kujirai, K., and Manabe, T. (1983) Specialization of "combination-sensitive" neurons for processing of complex biosonar signals in the auditory cortex of the mustached bat. *J. Neurophysiol.* 49:1573–1626.

Suga, N., O'Neill, W. E., and Manabe, T. (1978) Cortical neurons sensitive to combinations of information-bearing elements of biosonar signal in the mustache bat. *Science* 200:778–781.

Sussman, H. M. (1989) Neural coding of relational invariance in speech: Human language analogs to the barn owl. *Psychological Review* 96:631–642.

Sussman, H. M., Frutcher, D., Hibert, J., and Sirosh, J. (1998) Linear correlates in the speech signal: The orderly output constraint. *Behav. Brain Sci.* 21(2):241–259.

Suthers, R. A. and Fattu, J. M. (1973) Mechanisms of sound production by echolocating bats. *Amer. Zool.* 13:1215–1226.

Sutter, M. L. and Margoliash, D. (1994) Global synchronous sponse ot autogenous sing in zebra finch Hvc. *J. Neurophysiol.* 72:2105–2123.

Sutton, D. (1979) Mechanisms underlying vocal control in nonhuman primates. In *Neurobiology of Social Communication in Primates*, ed. by H. Steklis and M. Raleigh, pp. 45–68. New York: Academic Press.

Tian, B. and Rauschecker, J. P. (1996) Rsponses to complex sounds in the lateral belt areas of auditory cortex in awake rhesus monkeys. *Soc. for Neurosci. Abstrt.*, no. 6375.

Wang, X., Merzenich, M. M., Beitel, R., and Schreiner, C. E. (1995) Representation of a species-specific vocalization in the primary auditory cortex of the common marmoset: Temporal and spectral characteristics. *J. Neurophysiol.* 74:685–706.

Weber, P. B. and Ojemann, G. A. (1995) Neuronal recordings in human lateral temporal lobe during verbal paired associate learning. *NeuroReport* 6(4):685–689.

Wells, K. D. and Schwartz, W. J. (1984) Vocal communication in a neotropical treefrog, *Hyla ebraccata*: Advertisement calls. *Anim. Behav.* 32:405–420.

Winter, P. and Funkenstein, H. H. (1973) The effect of species-specific vocalization on the discharge of auditory cortical cells in the awake squirrel monkey (*Saimiri sciureus*). *Exp. Brain Res.* 18: 489–504.

Winter, P., Ploog, D. and Latta, J. (1966) Vocal repertoire of the squirrel monkey (*Samiri sciureus*). *Exp. Brain Res.* 18:489–504.

Yeshurun, Y., Wollberg, Z., Dyn, N. and Allon, N. (1985) Identification of MGB cells by Volterra kernels. I. Prediction of responses to species specific vocalizations. *Biol. Cybern.* 51(6):383–390.

6 A Cellular Basis for Reading Minds from Faces and Actions

David I. Perrett

The theme of this chapter is that high-level visual processing puts both human and nonhuman primates in a position to understand the emotions of other animals and the purpose of their behavior. We recognize the emotions of others by identifying their facial expressions. Similarly, we recognize the purpose of behavioral actions by identifying the component movements and the goal of those movements. This statement is incomplete, however, because part of the recognition involves matching up the sight of the behavior and expressions of others with our own actions and emotions. Through this matching we reap the social benefits of the skills and experience of others. Thus visual recognition includes both the analysis of the visual image and the associations between what we see, what we feel, and what we do. Recognition does not stop at the definition of edges, features, or faces but is performed in a functional context whereby the information revealed helps to guide our actions and shape our survival.

Note that the intended use of the phrases "understanding others" and "reading their minds" is more behavioristic than mentalistic. Behaviorism describes the formation of learned associations between stimuli and responses without recourse or reference to intervening mental events or conscious awareness. It is a moot point as to whether an individual needs to empathize with the feelings of a second individual in order to behave in a way that benefits from the feelings the other. On the other hand, possessing the capacity to recognize the symptoms of feelings in others both offers behavioral benefits and provides the potential for empathy (Brothers 1989).

The main focus of this chapter is the response properties of single cells in the temporal cortex of macaque monkeys. These show how visual information is used to detect and differentiate particular expressions and goal-directed actions. The chapter is organized into sections that consider how processing of particular types of action and expression are elaborated in other brain systems. In tracking down the elaboration of recognition, the discussion includes neurophysiological, neuropsychological, behavioral, and functional imaging studies.

In the macaque monkey, one brain region has been implicated as a focus for the perceptual processing of the visual appearance of the face and body. Within the temporal lobe, the cortex in the anterior section of the superior temporal sulcus (STS) contains a variety of anatomical subregions and a number of distinct cell populations that may contribute to the visual recognition and understanding of actions (Perrett and Emery 1994). In one region (the anterior superior temporal polysensory area, STPa, Felleman and Van Essen 1991) within the upper bank of the

STS, there are several types of neurons relevant to understanding actions. One type of cell encodes the visual appearance of the face and body while they are static *or* in motion (Gross et al. 1972; Perrett et al. 1984, 1985a, 1990a, 1992; Wachsmuth et al. 1994). A second type codes particular face and body movements but is unresponsive to static images or still frames of the face and body (Bruce et al. 1981; Perrett et al. 1985b, 1990b,c; Oram and Perrett 1994a,b, 1996; Oram et al. submitted). A third type of cell in the temporal lobe codes face and body movement as goal-directed actions. This type of cell responds only to particular body movements made in relation to particular objects or positions in space (e.g., a hand reaching for an object, but not to the hand movements alone). This type of cell occurs throughout the STS but is most frequently found in the lower bank of the sulcus, particularly in area TEa (Seltzer and Pandya 1978; Perrett et al. 1989, 1990c,d; Oram et al. submitted). A further type of cell codes any movement that is not a predictable consequence of the monkey's own actions (Perrett et al. 1990d; Hietanen and Perrett 1993a,b, 1996a,b).

Body Posture

Cells that are selectively responsive to visual information about the form of static or moving animal bodies show generalization, in that they respond to the sight of monkeys, humans, and other mammals. Studying them could therefore contribute to understanding the posture and actions of conspecifics and other animals. Sub-populations of these cells are selectively responsive to the sight of particular parts of the body, including the eyes, mouth, whole head, fingers, hand, arms, legs, torso, and whole body. The majority of the cells are sensitive to the perspective view and orientation of body components (Wachsmuth et al. 1994; Ashbridge et al. 1999). (Note here that view and orientation are distinguished because changes in perspective view lead to changes in the visibility of surface details and components of an object whereas changes in orientation do not.) For example, particular cells respond only to the palm side of the hand pointing upward, other cells respond only to the open hand with fingers splayed, other cells respond only to the leg bent at the knee and pointing to left of the observing subject, and yet other cells respond only to the eyes or face pointing up (Gross et al. 1972; Tanaka et al. 1991; Tanaka 1993; Carey et al. 1997; Perrett et al. 1985a, 1990a, 1992).

Sensitivity to the orientation and perspective view of the head and body enables the cells to code specific postures that are components of novel actions (for example, those associated with newly acquired food processing skills; Byrne and Byrne 1991, 1993; Byrne 1995) or some particular social signals (e.g., threat postures in which the head is lowered, the jaw is lowered, and eyebrows are raised; Hinde and Rowell 1961). The cells also specify how the posture of another individual is oriented with respect to the observer. Without such specification, interactions between individuals would be impossible. When one individual presents an arm for grooming, a social partner must perceive the position, orientation, and distance of the arm in order to begin grooming it.

It is not typically thought that the visual processing of static form underlies the comprehension of actions. This, however, overlooks the ability of individuals to understand momentary postures during an action sequence and to infer how an action was performed. The performance of dexterous manual tasks (e.g., tying a knot or performing a magic trick with sleight of hand) can easily be specified as a series of static pictures, each demonstrating particular subgoals or stages in the action sequence.

Direction of Attention

The initial coding of body components in a view- and orientation-specific manner does not prevent subsequent encoding that generalizes for the same posture across different views. Generalization across view can be achieved by combining the outputs of a number of view-specific cells, each sensitive to the same posture seen from a specific vantage point (Perrett et al 1992).

Figure 6.1 illustrates the responses of two types of cell. The first part of figure 6.1 illustrates the responses of a cell type selective for one component head view and orientation, whereas the second part of figure 6.1 illustrates the responses of a cell type that appears to integrate information from different head views and orientations to code posture at a more conceptual level. This cell in figure 6.1 (a) responds to the left profile view facing down but is unresponsive to the face view head down (not shown) or the right profile head down. The cell in figure 6.1 (b) responds to the head-up posture. The cell is responsive both to the front view and to the profile view of the face, but only when these head views display a head-up posture. The responses of this cell illustrate the convergence of information and may be signaling "attention up."

Note that to code postures that might signify attention down or attention up, the visual system needs to discriminate between different orientations of the same head view (e.g., left profile head down vs. left profile head level). Hence it is not surprising that coding of body parts takes place (at least initially) in an orientation- and view-specific manner. Invariance across viewing circumstance, which can include partial

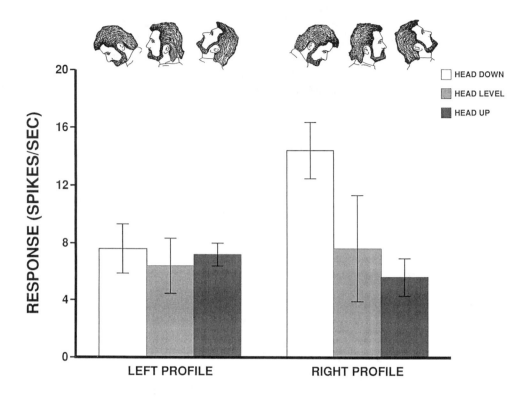

Figure 6.1
(a) The responses of one cell selective for head view and orientation. The mean (± 1 S.E., n = 5) response to left and right profile head in different orientations is illustrated together with a representation of the stimuli. Response to the left profile view facing down was greater than response to profile head views and orientations. The cell was also unresponsive to the face view head down (not shown). (b) The responses of one cell selective for multiple head views and orientations consistent with "attention up." The cell responses (mean ± 1 S.E., n = 5) to the face and profile views of the head were greater for the head up posture than the head level posture.

occlusion or change in perspective, can be achieved by combining the outputs of cells sensitive to particular body components from different views and orientations. The extensive and sophisticated coding of attention direction is indicative of its importance for primate social interaction. Observing threatening gestures and recognizing them as threats is insufficient; knowing whether the gesture is being made in your direction is a crucial determinate of an appropriate response (Perrett and Mistlin 1990; Perrett et al. 1989; Walsh and Perrett 1994).

The outputs of cells coding components of the face and body from one view and orientation appear to be combined hierarchically so that a collection of components

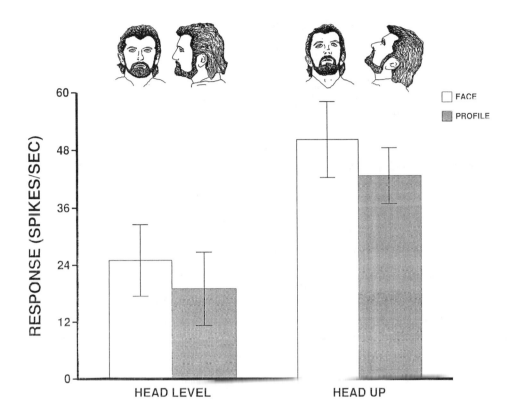

Figure 6.1 (continued)

can specify a particular meaningful posture or action (Perrett et al. 1994, 1995). Evidence for hierarchical combination of signals is limited but is apparent in increased response latency of cells higher up given putative hierarchies (Perrett et al. 1992). Cells higher up in one hierarchy combine outputs from three cell types, one sensitive only to eye direction, a second sensitive to head direction, and a third coding body direction. Thus higher-level cells can respond to the eyes pointing left, or the face pointing left, or the body pointing left (Perrett et al. 1985a, 1992; Wachsmuth et al. 1994). Such a convergence of visual information can signal a conceptually unified action, such as "animal attending left." Note that the response to multiple components allows coding of actions when particular body regions are obscured from sight. The cells may code the face direction if the eyes are obscured by shadow or occluded from sight and may code the body direction if the head is occluded from sight.

The responses to individual body components by the cells that code meaningful actions (such as "attending left") usually have a hierarchy of importance, with the eyes being more important than the head and the head in turn being more important than the body. For example, if the eyes are visible and aimed not left but at the viewer, this can prevent cells from responding to the rest of the face pointing left. Similarly, if the head is pointing at the viewer, this can prevent response to the left profile view of the body (Perrett et al. 1992; Perrett 1996). This hierarchy of importance, coupled with the independent sensitivity to the eyes, face, and body cues, means that the cells can signal direction of attention under differing viewing conditions (where the eyes or face are occluded from sight). Moreover, the cells appear to respond on the basis of the best evidence available, since the eyes may be more informative than the face and the face more informative than the body (see below).

The direction of eye gaze, head and body posture, and the direction of an individual's movements in relation to objects may provide a "window into the mind" of others. These cues can help assess where another individual is attending and why he is performing particular actions. Human infants, in the first year of life, follow the direction of gaze of their mother (Butterworth and Jarrett 1991). This "joint attention" appears crucial to social development in humans and is impaired in cases of autism (Baron-Cohen 1994; Leekam et al. 1997). The capacity to follow gaze is manifest in the chimpanzee (Povinelli and Preuss 1995), but the evolutionary origins of gaze following and shared attention and their underlying neural mechanisms are unknown. Following gaze is a necessary but not a sufficient condition for joint attention. For the latter, there may need to be the additional requirement that two individuals share the knowledge that each is following the gaze of the other (Perrett and Emery 1994; Emery et al. 1997).

Despite the neurophysiological findings of cellular sensitivity to attention direction in macaque monkeys, behavioral evidence for gaze following in Old World monkeys has so far been lacking. Indeed, Anderson et al. (1996) report that rhesus macaques cannot be trained to follow human gaze to locate hidden food. To investigate this discrepancy, we measured eye movements of macaque monkey subjects during presentation of films displaying a conspecific directing attention toward a "target" object and ignoring an identical "distracter" object. Results show that a subject shown the films makes more frequent inspections of the target than the distracter. Thus rhesus macaques do spontaneously utilize the direction of attention of conspecifics to orient their own attention (Emery et al. 1997).

When an observing monkey sees a stimulus monkey attending in one direction, the observer modifies the direction of its own gaze to inspect the region of space that the stimulus monkey is attending to, even if there is no target object present in that space (Emery et al. 1997). Thus it appears that monkeys search out what others are attending to. Further studies with static slides of stimulus monkeys show that the direction of head and gaze is more salient in capturing attention than body orientation (Lorincz et al. in prep). Thus the priority of information at the cellular level (eyes + head > body) parallels the priority of information at the behavioral level.

Under some circumstances (partial occlusion), information from body posture is also predictive of where others are attending. Following head and gaze direction rather than body direction is, however, more likely to result in the observer locating an object that interests both others and the observer. The higher levels of visual processing are evidently sensitive to these contingencies and greater priority is given to the visual cues that are the most predictive.

Linking the Perception of Expressions to Emotions

Particular populations of cells in the temporal cortex are selective for certain facial expressions (Perrett et al. 1984; Perrett and Mistlin 1990; Hasselmo et al. 1989). Some cells code angry or threatening expressions, others code frightened grimaces. For macaque monkeys, threats include a rounded open mouth with the teeth not displayed, the head lowered, vertical contraction of the skin of the forehead (equivalent to raising of eyebrows for humans), and direct eye contact (Hinde and Rowell 1961; Hauser 1996). Individual cells code expressions through the conjoint sensitivity to these multiple facial cues. Indeed, without combined sensitivity to several facial cues, expressions would be ambiguous. For example, an open mouth could signify a threat or it could signify that an individual is eating. This cellular coding can provide the basis for recognizing expressions and comprehending the emotions of others.

In humans, the ability to recognize particular emotional expressions can be selectively disrupted by neuropathological conditions. One of the major output connections from the cortex of the STS is to the amygdala (Aggelton et al. 1980). The amygdala has long been regarded as vital to the processing of emotionally relevant stimuli. Faces are one form of emotionally salient stimuli, and it is perhaps not surprising that lesions to the amygdala produce a variety of impairments in processing facial information, including judgments of gaze direction and the recognition of facial identity (Young et al. 1995). Perhaps the most surprising impairment after lesions to the amygdala is the disruption in understanding the emotions of others. Some patients with amygdala lesions show a disproportional impairment in the recognition of fear in the faces of others (Adolphs et al. 1994; Young et al. 1995; Calder et al. 1996). Amygdala lesions also impair comprehension of auditory cues to fear in the voices of other individuals (Scott et al. 1997).

From the neuropsychological cases, the brain structures implicated in the selective impairment in perception of fear are not clear, since patients with extensive pathology in the region of the amygdala and intact perception of fear expressions have also been reported (Hamann et al. 1996). To investigate the brain systems responsible for the analysis of fear, Morris et al. (1996) used positron emission tomography (PET) to measure the cerebral activation to the sight of happy and fearful facial expressions in normal human subjects. Activity in the amygdala increased with increasing expression of fear and decreased with increasing expression of happiness in the facial stimuli (though see Breiter et al. 1996). This indicates that the amygdala is indeed involved in the analysis of fear expressions. The variability in impairment in the ability to recognize fear following neurological damage to the amygdala requires additional explanation, perhaps in terms of age of acquisition of damage or effects on emotional conditioning (see below).

Unexpectedly, the study of Morris et al. (1996; see also Phillips et al. 1997) revealed that modulation of activity in relation to the amplitude of fear and happy expressions was lateralized predominantly to the left amygdala. The reasons for such lateralization are not clear but they are not without precedent. Left-right cerebral asymmetries occur in the production of speech and spontaneous facial expressions; asymmetries also occur in the perception of facial cues to speech, emotional expression, age, sex, attractiveness, and identity (Burt and Perrett 1997). Within these asymmetries it is usually the right hemisphere that appears predominantly engaged in face perception and the analysis of expression, although there are suggestions that negative and positive emotions engage different cerebral hemispheres. The presence of asymmetries in facial emotional processing are universal, but the differences in the direction of processing asymmetries between functional imaging and neuropsychological studies remains unexplained.

In general, one of the functions of the amygdala appears to lie in linking sensory stimuli to particular emotional responses such as fear (Aggelton 1993). Indeed, the amygdala has been implicated in the formation of conditioned fear responses to auditory stimuli (Le Doux 1995). The neuroanatomy and latency of cell responses are both consistent with a flow of visual information about the face from the temporal cortex to the amygdala. The interplay between the amygdala and temporal cortex in the analysis of emotional visual stimuli remains speculative. Within the amygdala, the particular visual configurations of faces arriving from the temporal cortex may come to be associated with negative emotional states (particularly fear).

This association may feed back to the cortex to consolidate the visual sensitivity of the particular cell groups in the temporal cortex that are sending information to the amygdala. Thus long-term visual representations of important stimuli get laid down within the cortex. The limbic system remains responsible in the formation of new emotional associations and the link between what is seen and the feeling or knowledge of fear, but the cortex comes to hold the look-up table of important visual patterns (e.g., expressions).

Visual analysis of the emotions of others allows vicarious learning: an animal can acquire a fearful response to potentially dangerous objects through associating the sight of objects with the expression of fear in others (Mineka et al. 1984). Through first-order classical conditioning, an infant might come to associate the sight of the fearful expression of a parent with its own startle response (unconditioned response) to a loud noise (unconditioned stimulus). This could easily happen if a loud noise startles both the infant and its parent. After such conditioning, if the infant subsequently witnesses an adult showing fear responses to snakes or wasps, then the infant may acquire the fear response to wasps or snakes through second-order conditioning without the negative experience of being stung or bitten. The infant simply has to witness the parent's fearful face in conjunction with the sight of a wasp or snake.

Note here that a second essential part of the "kit" for such vicarious leaning is proper comprehension of the attention direction of others. The infant needs to attend to the object that is causing the parent to exhibit fear. In any environment there will be many objects in the field of view but following the parent's attention direction (using head or gaze direction, or more subtle body posture cues) allows the infant to experience the object causing the parent's fear.

As reviewed above, the temporal cortex provides two sources of information that are vital in this context. First, many of the cells are sensitive to the direction of attention as specified by the gaze direction, head view and orientation, and body posture. Second, particular cells are sensitive to the facial posture, mouth configuration, and expression (Perrett and Mistlin 1990). The temporal cortex can thus provide a description of facial expressions from which an individual can learn to associate with emotional responses. The emotional associations need not be restricted to facial expressions. The temporal cortex can provide a visual specification of a wealth of gestures that can be associated with the personal experience of positive or negative emotions.

Since the work of Adolphs et al. (1994) suggested that the recognition of fear expression can be selectively disrupted, neuropsychologists have been open to the possibility that selective deficits might occur in the perception of other emotions. Recent studies reveal that recognition of a second emotion can be selectively disrupted. Patients with Huntington's disease exhibit a disproportionate impairment in the perception of disgust (Sprengelmeyer et al. 1996, 1997).

Again, selective impairment in recognition of disgust might seem unlikely, but consideration of learning experience coupled with the constraints of some innate motor patterns provides a plausible basis for the impairment. Retching and vomiting may well be "fixed action patterns" in the sense of the ethological term, in that they are motor patterns that are stereotypic in form across individuals and may not need learning. Such reflexive motor responses presumably have distinct neural circuitry. If so, through similar arguments to those above, it may not be surprising that such motor control systems can be associatively linked to particular sensory stimuli through classical conditioning. First- and second-order conditioning may link poisonous gustatory and unpleasant olfactory stimuli to retching. Indeed, particular stimuli may elicit retching or revulsion as an unconditioned reflex, or there may be innate constraints on learning such that the subject is more "prepared" to learn the association of retching for some stimuli. Further conditioning can associate visual stimuli (such as the sight of vomit or the sight of someone else vomiting or about to vomit) to the personal feeling of disgust and revulsion. It is relevant in this context that the sight of disgust expressions activates the anterior insular cortex, a brain site that probably also processes bad smells and bad tastes (Phillips et al. 1997). Such associations again offer the potential for vicarious learning. Once the sight of others' facial expressions of disgust is associated with the personal experience of the disgust, then conditioned aversion to particular foods can be developed without the individual having to be poisoned by these items. These accounts of vicarious learning from the expressions of disgust and fear are fairly extreme examples. One can imagine similar processes operating on a more subtle scale. The sight of a slightly disapproving expression on a familiar face of a respected individual could easily shape evaluations and emotional disposition to events, the behavior of others, and even our own actions.

The visual analysis of expressions in the temporal lobe provides a window into the feelings of others. Links between the visual appearance of expression and systems engaged in particular patterns of emotional response are an inevitable consequence of learning. Even if the emotions of others are not realized in an empathic sense, there is no doubt that the emotional reactions of others have profound effects on our own learning and attitudes.

Body Movements

A further type of cell in the STS is selectively responsive to particular types of body movement and remains inactive to static images of the body. The function of such cells may lie in their capacity to provide descriptions of how bodies are moving. From this information it is possible, with subsequent processing, to work out what individuals are doing in terms of meaningful "goal-directed" actions (see below). The cells also provide a basis for guiding social interactions. Social contact involves numerous actions and reactions: one individual extends an arm, and a second individual may flinch or may accept this as a grooming gesture. To react, each individual must first recognize the nature of the movements of the other.

Cells that respond to body movement combine information about the form of body components with information about the type of movement they are executing (Oram and Perrett 1994a,b, 1996; Oram et al. submitted). As with the coding of static form, different cell types are selective for the movement of particular body components. Different subpopulations of cells code the sight of movements of the eyes, mouth, whole head, torso, legs, arms and fingers, or whole hands (Perrett et al. 1985b, 1990c, 1994, 1995; Mistlin and Perrett 1990; Oram et al. submitted). Again, movements of components are specified relative to the viewer, such that some cells respond to the head rotation from right profile to facing the viewer and others to the opposite direction. Other populations code rotations of the head in the vertical plane (i.e., head lifting up or bowing down).

In the STS, cellular coding of the type of motion appears to be segregated as to whether the movement involves translation (linear displacement) or rotation. One cell type responds to translation but not rotation, and a second population responds to rotation but not translation. Rotation appears to be specified in polar coordinates (with six subpopulations of cells separately coding rotation up, down, toward, and away from the viewer, rotating clockwise and anticlockwise in the image plane). The direction of translation appears to be specified with respect to Cartesian axes. Again, six subpopulations code translation up, down, left, right, toward, and away (Perrett et al. 1985b, 1990c; Oram et al. 1993). Since tuning for direction in each of the twelve subpopulations is relatively broad, any movement of rigid bodies can be fully specified by reference to how much the object translated up, how much it translated left, how much it rotated up, etc. The tuning of the cells, therefore, covers all the degrees of freedom for motion of a rigid body. In this way, the STPa cells can specify any direction of motion of a rigid object or an articulation of a rigid component of the object. Note that rigid motion is distinguished from motion in which a single component distorts with shearing or bending forces. The complex articulation of the body during natural movement can usually be broken down into a series of discrete rigid motions as the limbs move relative to the torso, etc. (see Johanasson 1973, Oram and Perrett 1994a,b; Perrett et al. 1990b,c).

The components of movements appear to be combined to produce descriptions of coherent whole-body actions such as walking (Perrett et al. 1985b, 1989, 1990b), crouching (Perrett et al. 1984), climbing (Brothers and Ring 1993), and turning (Oram and Perrett 1994a; Oram et al. submitted). The combination of information about the movement of different body parts appears to proceed in an exactly analogous way to that described for cells responsive to static postures. That is, cells responsive to whole body movements code specific directions of motion (e.g., left profile body view walking left) and may respond to several body components moving left (e.g., head alone, torso and arms alone, or legs alone). This convergence again allows the specification of simple whole-body actions even when parts of the body are obscured from sight. Figure 6.2 illustrates the responses of one cell that is selective for the sight of the body approaching yet which generalizes the response to multiple parts of the body (when other parts are occluded from view).

For a few cells, the direction of movement is specified relative to the body performing the action (e.g., an arm moved to a position in front of the chest independent of the observer's perspective view; Perrett et al. 1990c). For a cell of this type that is tuned to a particular body posture or movement of the experimenter, the relative position of the monkey and the experimenter is largely irrelevant to the cell response. Thus for cells responding to the upper torso bowing over, or a foot extending away from the body, cells coding in an object-centered manner will respond to the bowing or the foot extension when the body motion is seen from the profile, from the front, or from the back. Such object-centered sensitivity to one body movement across a variety of perspectives can be established by pooling the outputs of multiple cells, each selective for the same type of body movement seen from a different view.

The cells described in the previous sections fall into two distinct types: those that respond selectively to particular static facial or body postures and those that respond selectively to particular facial and body movements. Understanding actions in order to reproduce them would require the ability to model both static postures and the trajectories to move between them (Kimura and Archibald 1974).

The actions of others can be understood on the basis of motion cues alone. This is revealed through the use of biological motion displays. In these displays, lights are attached to points of limb articulation of an actor. The movement of these lights is sufficient to allow observers to recognize actions (Johansson 1973). The analysis of

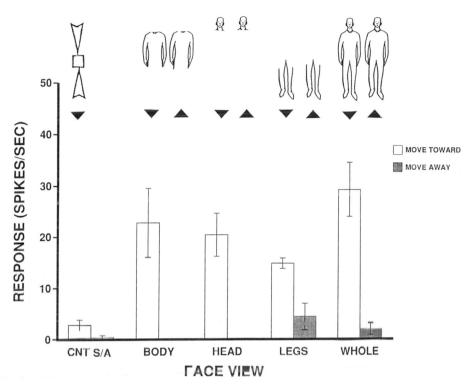

Figure 6.2
The responses (mean ±1 S.E., n = 5) of one cell selective for the sight of multiple components of the body approaching. The upper part of the figure illustrates symbolic depictions of stimuli (control and body parts) in different directions of motion. The cell was directionally selective, responding more to approaching movement to than movement away. The cell was also sensitive to stimulus form, responding more to each body part approaching than to body sized control stimuli approaching (CNT) or spontaneous activity (SA).

body movements in the temporal cortex can proceed using the same reduced point-light displays. About 25% of the cells selective for body movements continue to respond to biological motion displays (Perrett et al. 1990b,c; Oram and Perrett 1994a). PET studies of brain activity in humans indicate that the sight of biological motion displays of a human walking activates areas within the anterior portions of the superior temporal sulcus and the amygdala (Bonda et al. 1996). Recent fMRI recordings also indicate selective involvement of the superior temporal sulcus in the human brain as a site for the visual analysis of movements of the face (Puce et al. 1998).

In the macaque monkey and in humans, there are two major cortical streams of visual information processing. One runs ventrally from the occipital cortex to the temporal cortex and is thought to be responsible for the perception of visual form. A second pathway runs dorsally from the occipital cortex toward the parietal cortex. This second pathway is thought to be responsible for the visual control of actions. The cortex of superior temporal sulcus (containing the cells that are the focus of this chapter) lies between these two pathways and appears to integrate information from both streams (Felleman and Van Essen 1991; Young 1992).

In the macaque, motion information arrives on cells coding body movements in the anterior portions of the STS through a different route to that conveying static information (Oram and Perrett 1996). Motion information appears to arrive at anterior STS cells on average at 100ms post-stimulus-onset and 20ms before information about form. It is often assumed that motion information reaches anterior portions of the STS from projections from the specialized motion-processing regions in posterior and dorsal portions of the STS (areas MT/V5 and MST, Felleman and Van Essen 1991; Young 1992). This may not be the only route, however. Patient LM suffers from akinetopsia (visual movement agnosia) resulting from bilateral brain lesions in the occipito-temporal region. LM's symptoms are enigmatic. Although LM has difficulty seeing any movement >8 degrees per second, LM can understand actions of others even when performed in "biological motion" displays (McLeod et al. 1996). Since the posterior parietal areas including area V5/MT and MST are presumed damaged in LM, one interpretation of her intact comprehension of actions defined by biological motion is that the temporal cortex may receive motion information through routes other than the dorsal cortical areas.

Goal-directed Actions

The coding described above can be understood by sole reference to the movements of a body within the visual image. Actions, however, are more than simple movements; they can involve goal-directed behavior. To understand actions it is necessary to realize the purpose of the movement. Inanimate objects may move, but by definition only animate objects complete actions with goals and purpose.

There is one way that visual information can be used not only to classify the details of the movement but also to specify the goal-directed nature of the movement. This can be achieved by relating body movements to other aspects of the visual environment. Movement coding becomes action coding when visual events are specified in such a way as to clarify both the nature of the movements (of the agent performing the motion) and how these movements relate to their goal, which may be the viewer, an object, another individual, or a place in the environment. This type of coding provides a basis for imitating the actions of others and for understanding the purpose of their behavior or communicative signals.

This type of coding is apparent in several groups of cells within the STS. Some cells code whole body movements such as walking, but only when the movement is directed to reach a particular position in the environment (Perrett et al. 1990b,c). The most extensively studied cells that can be described as coding actions are those in the ventral bank of the STS (area TEa) that are selectively responsive to hand actions (Perrett et al. 1989, 1990c,d). Different subpopulations of these cells show selectivity for specific hand-object interactions, such as reaching for, retrieving, manipulating, picking, tearing, and holding (Perrett et al. 1989).

The responses of such cells are elicited when both the appropriate hand movements and the appropriate movements of the object acted upon are visible. Hand movements alone miming an action without an object fail to elicit a response. Studies of cells sensitive to the act of object manipulation reveal that the relation between hand and object movements can be specified even more exactingly. Cells responsive to object manipulation did not respond to the sight of the appropriate hand movements combined with object movements when the hand and object were spatially separated by a few centimeters (Perrett et al. 1989). In this way, the cells were sensitive to the causal relation between the agent performing the action and the object acted upon; the cells responded to causally related actions and not to hand-object movements that were not causally related.

The cells generalized across several different instances of the same action, including the sight of the action from different perspectives, at different distances or speeds, or even performed on different objects. The majority of cells responded well to the sight of the optimal hand actions performed by a human or another monkey, although the exact visual characteristics of what constitutes a hand remain to be specified. One interesting finding is that these cells respond to the sight of the monkey's own hands performing the action (Perrett et al. 1989). The cells would respond to videotapes of actions performed by the monkey and to the direct sight of the monkey's hands performing the action in real time. This equivalence between the sight of the monkey's own hand performing an action and the sight of other hands performing the same action may well be essential for imitation or shaping one's own actions to match those witnessed (see below).

Linking the Sight of Actions to the Production of Actions

Neural activity in a variety of areas in the frontal lobe is associated with the execution of motor acts. Recently it has become apparent that visual information about motor acts is also encoded in particular premotor areas. Neuronal responses to the sight of hand actions identical to those described in the STS have been found in area F5 of premotor cortex (di Pellegrino et al. 1992; see also Tanila et al. 1992). Some F5 cells respond to the sight of particular hand actions (e.g., grasping, picking, or reaching) made by the experimenter. The same cells respond to the equivalent actions performed by the monkey in the light or dark. Such prefrontal cells thus code both the motor components of hand actions (independent of vision) and the visual appearance of the hand actions. The critical difference between the coding of actions in the frontal and temporal areas is that the frontal cortex appears to code the "general concept" of an action. The frontal cells are activated during the execution of an action (e.g., grasping). The frontal cells are also activated by the sight of an action performed by another (i.e., the experimenter grasping an object). The cells respond to the sight of an object that can form the goal of an action (i.e., an object that is to be grasped). Moreover, following the presentation of an object that the monkey must act upon after a short delay, the cells remain responsive during the delay even in the dark; presumably, this is while the monkey holds in mind the upcoming action that must be performed at the end of the delay. By contrast, the cells in the temporal cortex code only the visual form of the action when performed by the monkey or another. It is quite likely that the visual analysis of actions is performed initially in the temporal cortex and that the visual selectivity for actions in premotor areas depends on input from the action-coding cells in temporal cortex.

The cells in the prefrontal cortex respond selectively both to the performance of a specific action by the monkey and to the sight of the same specific action performed by another. With this dual capacity one neural system can enable the motor performance of an action to be matched to an action witnessed visually. Such a matching capacity can support the visual imitation of simple familiar actions.

The "monkey see, monkey do" prefrontal cells share some of the features of visual selectivity of STS units described above. Neurons in both areas show sensitivity to interactions between the agent performing the action (the hand) and the object or goal of the action. Neither group of cells responds to the sight of the objects alone, which might afford particular actions (tearing, picking, etc.), nor do the cells respond to the sight of appropriate hand movements pantomiming the action in the absence of the objects. Di Pellegrino et al. (1992) argue that the existence of such cells in the premotor cortex provides some evidence for the theory that substrates of perception and action overlap, at least to some extent.

Functional imaging techniques have begun to be used to examine the neural substrates of movement production, perception, and imagery. Decety et al. (1994)

examined brain activity during motor perception and imagery in the same human subjects. Activation patterns associated with watching a computer graphic "hand" move to pick up objects were compared with the activation patterns associated with imagining hand movements needed to pick up static objects. Decety et al. report that the motor imagery task produces greater activation of brain regions associated with movement production than regions associated with visual analysis of motion (see also Parsons et al. 1995). Recent studies indicate that witnessing real hand movements activates the human brain in the premotor cortex and in the left superior temporal sulcus—areas that are presumably homologous to those described in the brain of the macaque monkey (Rizzolatti et al. 1996; Grafton et al. 1996). Thus the populations of visual neurons in the temporal cortex of the macaque monkey reviewed here appear to have homologues in the human brain. Functional imaging studies appear to show that the sight of actions produces changes in the same prefrontal areas that are involved in control of the execution of corresponding actions. Recent studies of humans instructed to watch action sequences with a view to reproducing them indicate that premotor areas are activated by the sight of familiar actions but not by novel, meaningless actions that also must be remembered and imitated (J. Decety, personal communication 1998).

The premotor cortex has been implicated in tasks requiring visual memory but is rarely connected to any perceptual function per se. The experimental investigation of Fadiga et al. (1995) suggests, however, that perception and action share some neural substrates. They stimulated the motor cortex of subjects while they watched actions, such as grasping and drawing, and in comparable control conditions (i.e., looking at the objects that were grasped). The evoked potentials recorded in the hand muscles that resulted following magnetic stimulation were larger in the two conditions where the subjects observed the experimenter making movements. The authors conclude that there is a system that "matches" observations of actions and their execution (Fadiga et al. 1995).

There are several reasons that the neural substrates for action production and action perception could be largely shared. For example, the capacity to copy elaborate manual skills necessary for food processing would seem to confer an advantage by obviating the need for learning by trial and error in situations that may be painful (e.g., a gorilla processing stinging nettles' leaves, Byrne and Byrne 1991, 1993) or dangerous (e.g., chimpanzees catching and eating scorpions). Although it is clear that great apes and even parrots do show evidence for the capacity to imitate actions demonstrated visually by humans (Custance et al. 1995), most reviews conclude that there is little or no good behavioral evidence from observational studies or laboratory experiments that monkeys imitate or comprehend the goals of others (Galef

1988; Visalberghi and Fragaszy 1990; Whiten and Ham 1992; Byrne 1995; but see Bugnyar and Huber 1997). Many instances of so-called imitative behavior made by nonhuman animals can be dismissed as simple instances of "response facilitation" or "stimulus enhancement" with trial-and-error learning (Heyes 1997).

Nevertheless, the physiological recordings from the frontal and temporal neo-cortex provide perhaps the most convincing evidence that there are brain processes in monkey species that can provide a detailed understanding of the actions of con-specifics, and that the sight of these actions can be matched to the motor commands for the individual to reproduce the actions that it sees (Perrett and Emery 1994). The same apparatus may well support imitation of a series of novel actions to produce a specific goal.

Comprehension of Actions after Brain Damage

There have been patients with disturbed execution of movements who can use tools and pantomime movements to verbal command but who have great difficulty in copying and/or recognizing movements or gestures demonstrated visually by the examiner (De Renzi et al. 1980, 1982; Heilman et al. 1982; McDonald ct al. 1994; Rothi et al. 1986, 1991; Varney and Damasio 1987). The problems of these patients are therefore not restricted to motor production, for they appear to have problems in understanding visual presentations of others' actions. The disruption can extend beyond comprehending the dynamic aspects of actions. Some apraxic patients cannot reproduce static limb and hand postures demonstrated by the experimenter (Goldenberg 1995; Goldenberg and Hagmann 1997). It is possible to interpret many of the selective comprehension deficits in apraxia as arising from the disconnection of particular types of visual coding in the temporal lobe for static body posture, body movements, and meaningful actions from the brain systems responsible for action production or elaboration (Carey et al. 1997).

In most cases where visual recognition of an action is impaired (action agnosia) or where visual information cannot access motor planning directly (i.e., a patient can name an action but cannot reproduce it), damage includes the left parietal cortex and typically the inferior parietal lobule. This region of the human brain may not have a directly equivalent structure in the brain of the monkey, but the superior temporal sulcus contains cortex that might, on anatomical and functional grounds, be considered as a homologue of parietal cortex (Petrides and Iversen 1978, 1979; Jones and Burton 1976; Seltzer and Pandya 1978). Certainly from anatomical grounds we know that in the monkey the STS is intimately connected with parietal cortex (Harries and Perrett 1991; Seltzer and Pandya 1978, 1984; Walsh and Perrett 1994; Cusick et al. 1995). Indeed, the STS has been described as one of two brain regions where information from dorsal and ventral streams of cortical visual processing converges (Felleman and Van Essen 1991; Young 1992; Oram and Perrett 1996). As mentioned earlier, recent fMRI recordings indicate that the cortex of the superior temporal sulcus in the human brain is engaged in the analysis of face, hand, and body movements (Puce et al. 1998; Rizzolatti et al. 1996; Bonda et al. 1996). Both studies indicate a closer homology between the human and the macaque cortex.

Visual coding in the temporal lobe is not restricted to meaningful, goal-directed actions but includes arbitrary postures and movements. Indeed, the visual coding of component movements may be analogous to the coding of phonemes in language comprehension. These movements may acquire significance when we learn about new actions. Single postures and multiple sequences of movements can then take on meaning, becoming nonarbitrary; in the same way, one string of phonemes can have a vast variety of meanings.

The effect of left hemisphere lesions on language production in our species has often been attributed to the serial nature of speaking, which requires rapid and accurate sequencing of arbitrary vocal actions. Speech is not unique in requiring sequential motor processing; many of the manual skills of humans and other primates also require sequential production of complex motor acts, each with its own subgoal (Byrne and Byrne 1991, 1993). It is now clear from recordings in the supplementary motor cortex of the rhesus macaque that the production of sequences of arbitrary manual movements is coded at the single-unit level (Tanji and Shima 1994; Halsband et al. 1994; Tanji 1996). It is not difficult to think of an analogous hierarchical coding process in the comprehension of actions. Recognition of sequences could enable the imitation of whole programs of actions rather than the copying of a single act (Byrne 1995). For humans or nonhuman primates, learning may establish cell populations selectively activated by the sight of specific sequences of postures and actions of one or perhaps several individuals. In this way, the temporal cortex could support an understanding of complex social activities.

Consequences of Self-produced Actions

The above descriptions review cells selective for body postures and body movements. A different type of cell in area STPa codes movement more generally and responds to type of movement independent of form. These cells may respond to movement left whether the moving item is a body or an object and will respond to objects that are small or large, dark or light (Bruce et al. 1981; Oram et al. 1993). Superficially, this last group of cells appears the least likely to contribute to an understanding of others' actions, but this conclusion overlooks one important property of the cells: their ability to respond selectively to unexpected movements. Unexpected motions arise almost exclusively from other animals. The cells remain silent when the monkey itself creates movement in the world as a direct consequence of its own actions. For example, the cells respond to the sight of an object moved by an experimenter but do not respond when the same object is moved by the monkey itself (Hietanen and Perrett 1993b, 1996a). This property appears quite common within the STS cell populations and has been found in the processing of somatosensory information (Mistlin and Perrett 1990).

The critical variable for these cells seems to be the distinction between a "self-generated" and "generated by others" dimension of the stimuli, rather than the attention such stimuli generated by others might arouse. This is partly evident in the lack of habituation to visual and tactile events under the control of the experimenter (Mistlin and Perrett 1990; Hietanen and Perrett 1993b). The cells fire over and over again in response to actions repeated by the experimenter. Repeated actions of others even when executed in a rhythmic (predictable) manner do not habituate. It is interesting in this context that several authors have noted the importance of identifying movements that are self-propelled for constructing an understanding of intentionality in children (for review, see Baron-Cohen 1994).

The properties of such cells may contribute to monitoring the consequences of the monkey's own actions (Mistlin and Perrett 1990; Hietanen and Perrett 1993a,b, 1996a,b). The cells are sensitive to experience and lock on to new consequences of actions. In one experiment, a monkey was trained to move a grating by rotating a striped drum (with a video image of the drum projected onto a screen with a fixation spot located at the center). This mechanical arrangement allowed the experimenter and the monkey to produce equivalent grating movements. When the subject rotated the drum, many of the STPa-movement-sensitive cells remained silent; when the experimenter rotated the same drum at comparable speeds, these cells responded.

In this situation, the monkey's actions and the changes in the world were correlated. After a period of training, the nervous system registered the correlation in such a way that the changes in the world no longer activated the STPa neurons.

Impairment in monitoring the visual consequences of actions has yet to be documented in detail, but there are indications that insight into particular pathologies may be gained from studying cases of the disturbance of such monitoring abilities. Predicting the consequences of one's own movements is critical for the accurate execution and correction of actions, as well as veridical perception of the world. Disturbance of such mechanisms could lead to a false attribution of movement. The observations of Grüsser and Landis (1991) on the disturbance of motion perception in patient LM are relevant here. They report that "when walking across the garden or along the street, she reported that she had the impression that the objects in her extra-personal space were moving up and down." These disturbances seem to reflect difficulty in discriminating visual-image motion originating from external sources from motion resulting from the patient's own locomotor activity (Grüsser and Landis 1991).

Realization of the distinction between external and self-generated changes in the world may be important more generally for the psychological health of the individual. Frith (1992) has argued that schizophrenic individuals suffer hallucinations, in part because they fail to attribute the production of stimuli to themselves. Thus a schizophrenic may hear voices because they wrongly attribute self-produced subvocal speech to others. More generally, schizophrenic patients may be impaired in understanding the behavior of others particularly in terms of how the behavior of others relates to the patient's own behavior (see Penn et al. 1997).

It is interesting to speculate on the development of the STS system that discriminates unpredictable sensory events from events consistent with the expectations of one's own actions. In social interactions, specific acts of one individual have a high probability of triggering retaliatory or reciprocal acts in a second individual. Motor plans for a threat lunge are likely to produce a retreating motion of the threatened individual. Predicting where the other will be after a threat is essential for pressing home an attack or completing an intended defense. Predicting the behavior of others is equally important for affiliative interactions. The didactic arrangement of behavior can build in complexity, provided social partners know what to expect from each other. Sensing the relationship between what one does and the consequent changes in the world is one thing, but realizing how one's own actions affect the behavior of others opens up a whole spectrum of social understanding. Others can be seen as not only autonomous entities but also as reactive social partners. Such perceptions will rely on the visual apparatus such as that described earlier for recognizing postures, gestures, and actions, as well as the apparatus for making predictions as to what others are likely to do (and therefore what we expect to see them do) as a consequence of our own behavior. The rudiments of this last ability can be seen in the sensitivity of STS cells to expectations about simple visual changes that are self-produced.

Summary

This chapter has focused on the properties of populations of cells in the temporal cortex that contribute to the visual recognition of postures and actions of the face and body. Collectively these cells can provide a window into the minds of others. They can, in principle, support an understanding of what other individuals are attending to, what they feel emotionally, what aspects of the environment cause them to feel the way they do, how they are acting and interacting, and the intended goals of their actions. Of course, an observer may not explicitly realize the feelings and plans of others; nonetheless, the visual specification provided by the temporal cortex allows the observer to capitalize on the minds and behavior of others and react in the most appropriate way. Provided the visual system can specify what others are doing, one need not understand intentions or be able to "mind-read" (Baron-Cohen 1994) in order to come up with appropriate behavioral reactions. It is clear from neurophysiology and neuropsychology that the neural substrates for producing emotions and actions are intimately linked with the neural machinery responsible for perceiving emotions and actions. In conclusion, the extensive visual analysis of body movements in the temporal cortex forms the foundation for understanding, reproducing, and reciprocating the expressions and complex gestures that underlie the social life of human and nonhuman primates.

References

Adolphs, R., Tranel, D., Damasio, H., and Damasio, A. (1994) Impaired recognition of emotion in facial expressions following bilateral damage to the human amygdala. *Nature* 372:669–672.

Aggelton, J. P. (1993) The contribution of the amygdala to normal and abnormal emotional states. *TINS* 16:328–333.

Aggelton, J. P., Burton, M. J., and Passingham, R. E. (1980) Cortical and subcortical afferents to the amygdala of the rhesus monkey (*Macaca mulatta*). *Brain Res.* 190:347–368.

Anderson, J. R., Montant, M., and Schmitt, D. (1996) Rhesus monkeys fail to use gaze direction as an experimenter-given cue in an object-choice task. 37:47–55.

Ashbridge, E., Perrett, D. I., and Oram, M. W. (1999) Effect of image rotation and size change on object recognition: Responses of single units in the macaque monkey temporal cortex. *Cog. Neuropsych.* (in press).

Baron-Cohen, S. (1994) How to build a baby that reads minds: Cognitive mechanisms in mindreading. *Curr. Psych. Cogn.* 13:513–552.

Bonda, E., Petrides, M., Ostry, D., and Evans, A. (1996) Specific involvement of human parietal cortex in the perception of biological motion. *J. Neurosci.* 16:3737–3744.

Breiter, H. C., Etcoff, N. L., Whalen, P. J., Kennedy, W. A., Rauch, S. L., Buckner, R. L., Strauss, M. M., Hyman, S. E., and Rosen, B. R. (1996) Response and habituation of the human amygdala during visual processing of facial expression. *Neuron* 17:875–887.

Brothers, L. (1989) A biological perspective on empathy. *Am. J. Psych.* 146:10–19.

Brothers, L. and Ring, B. (1993) Mesial temporal neurons in the macaque monkey with responses selective for aspects of social stimuli. *Beh. Brain Res.* 57:53–61.

Bruce, C. J., Desimone, R., and Gross, C. G. (1981) Visual properties of neurons in a polysensory area in superior temporal sulcus of the macaque. *J. Neurophys.* 46:369–384.

Bugnyar, T. and Huber, L. (1997) Push or pull: An experimental study on imitation in marmosets. *Anim. Behav.* 54:817–831.

Burt, M. and Perrett, D. I. (1997) Perceptual asymmetries in judgments of facial attractiveness, age, gender, speech, and expression. *Neuropsychol.* 35:685–693.

Butterworth, G. and Jarrett, N. (1991) What minds have in common is space: Spatial mechanisms serving joint visual attention in infancy. *Brit. J. Dev. Psychol.* 9:55–72.

Byrne, R. W. (1995) *The Thinking Ape: Evolutionary Origins of Intelligence.* Oxford: Oxford University Press.

Byrne, R. W. and Byrne, J. M. E. (1991) Complex leaf-gathering skills of mountain gorillas (*Gorilla g. beringei*): Variability and standardization. *Cortex* 27:521–546.

Byrne, R. W. and Byrne, J. M. E. (1993) Hand preferences in the skilled gathering tasks of mountain gorillas (*Gorilla g. beringei*). *Am. J. Primatol.* 31:241–261.

Calder, A. J., Young, A. W., Rowland, D., Perrett, D. I., Hodges, J. R., and Etcoff, N. L. (1996) Facial emotion recognition after bilateral amygdala damage: Differentially severe impairment of fear. *Cog. Neuropsych.* 13:699–745.

Carey, D. P., Perrett, D. I., and Oram, M. W. (1997) Recognizing, understanding, and reproducing action. In *Handbook of Neuropsychology* (F. Boller and J. Grafman, series eds.) vol 11, *Action and Cognition* ed. by M. Jeannerod, pp. 111–129. Amsterdam: Elsevier.

Cusick, C. G., Seltzer, B., Cola, M., and Griggs, E. (1995) The myloarchitectonics and corticocortical terminations within the superior temporal sulcus of the monkey. Evidence for subdivisions of superior temporal polysensory cortex. *J. Comp. Neurol.* 260:513–535.

Custance, D. M., Whiten, A., and Bard, K. A. (1995) Can young chimpanzees (*Pan troglodytes*) imitate arbitrary actions? Hayes and Hayes (1952) revisited. *Behaviour* 132:837–859.

Decety, J., Perani, D., Jeannerod, M., Bettinardi, V., Tadary, B., Woods R., Mazziotta, J. C., and Fazio, F. (1994) Mapping motor representations with positron emission tomography. *Nature;* 371:600–602.

De Renzi, E., Pieczuro, A., and Vignolo, L. A. (1980) Ideational apraxia: A quantitative study. *Neuropsychol.* 6:41–52.

De Renzi, E., Faglioni, P., and Sorgato, P. (1982) Modality-specific and supramodal mechanisms of apraxia. *Brain* 105:301–312.

di Pellegrino, G., Fadiga, L., Fogassi, V., Gallese, V., and Rizzolatti, G. (1992) Understanding motor events: A neurophysiological study. *Exp. Brain Res.* 91:176–180.

Emery, N. J., Lorincz, E. N., Perrett, D. I., Oram M. W., and Baker, C. I. (1997) Gaze following and joint attention in rhesus monkeys (*Macaca mulatta*). *J. Comp. Psych.* 111:1–8.

Fadiga, L., Fogassi, L., Pavesi, G., and Rizzolatti, G. (1995) Motor facilitation during action observation—A magnetic stimulation study. *J. Neurophys.* 73:2608–2611.

Felleman, D. J. and Van Essen, D. C. (1991) Distributed hierarchical processing in the primate cerebral cortex. *Cerebral Cortex* 1:1–47.

Frith, C. D. (1992) *The Cognitive Neuropsychology of Schizophrenia.* Hillsdale, NJ: Lawrence Erlbaum.

Galef, B. G. (1988) Imitation in animals: Field and laboratory analysis. In *Social learning: Psychological and biological perspectives*, ed. by T. Zentall and B. G. Galef, pp. 1–28. Hillsdale, NJ: Lawrence Earlbaum Assoc.

Goldenberg, G. (1995) Imitating gestures and manipulating a mannequin—The representation of the human body in ideomotor apraxia. *Neuropsychol.* 33:63–72.

Goldenberg, G. and Hagmann, S. (1997) The meaning of meaningless gestures: A study of visuo-imitative apraxia. *Neuropsychol.* 35:333–341.

Grafton, S. T., Arbib, M. A., Fagdiga, L., and Rizzolatti, G. (1996) Localization of grasp representations in humans by positron-emission tomography. 2. Observation compared with imagination. *Exp. Brain Res.* 112:103–111.

Gross, C. G., Rocha-Miranda, C. E., and Bender, D. B. (1972) Visual properties of neurons in infero-temporal cortex of the monkey. *J. Neurophys.* 35:96–111.

Grüsser, O.-J. and Landis, T. (1991) Visual agnosias and other disturbances of visual perception and cognition. In *Vision and visual dysfunction*, vol 12, ed. by J. Cronly-Dillon. London: CRC Press.

Halsband, U., Matsuzaka, Y., and Tanji, J. (1994) Neuronal-activity in the primate supplementary, pre-supplementary, and pre-motor cortex during externally and internally instructed sequential movements. *Neurosci. Res.* 20:149–155.

Hamann, S. B., Stefanacci, L., Squire, L. R., Adolphs, R., Tranel, D., Damasio, H., and Damasio, A. (1996) Recognizing facial emotion. *Nature* 379:497.

Harries, M. H. and Perrett, D. I. (1991) Modular organization of face processing in temporal cortex: Physiological evidence and possible anatomical correlates. *J. Cog. Neurosci.* 3:9–24.

Hasselmo, M. E., Rolls, E. T., and Baylis, G. C. (1989) The role of expression and identity in the face-selective responses of neurons in the temporal visual cortex of the monkey. *Behav. Brain Res.* 32:203–218.

Hauser, M. D. (1996) *The Evolution of Communication.* Cambridge, MA: MIT Press.

Heilman, K. J., Rothi, L. J. G., and Valenstein, E. (1982) Two forms of ideomotor apraxia. *Neurology* 32:342–346.

Heyes, C. M. (1997) Theory of mind in non-human primates. *Behav. Brain Sci.* 21:101–148.

Hietanen, J. K. and Perrett, D. I. (1993a) Motion sensitive cells in the macaque superior temporal polysensory area. I. Lack of response to the sight of the monkey's own hand. *Exp. Brain Res.* 93:117–128.

Hietanen, J. K. and Perrett, D. I. (1993b) The role of expectation in visual and tactile processing within temporal cortex. In *Brain Mechanisms for Perception and Memory: From Neuron to Behaviour*, ed. by T. Ono, L. Squire, M. Raichle, D. I. Perrett, and M. Fukuda, pp. 83–103. Oxford: Oxford University Press.

Hietanen, J. K. and Perrett, D. I. (1996a) A comparison of visual responses to object- and ego-motion in the macaque superior temporal polysensory area. *Exp. Brain Res.* 108:341–345.

Hietanen, J. K. and Perrett, D. I. (1996b) Motion sensitive cells in the macaque superior temporal polysensory area: Response discrimination between self- and externally generated pattern motion. *Behav. Brain Res.* 76:155–167.

Hinde, R. A. and Rowell, T. E. (1961) Communication by postures and facial expressions in the rhesus monkey (*Macaca mulatta*). *Proc. Zool. Soc.* (London) 138:1–21.

Johansson, G. (1973) Visual perception of biological motion and a model for its analysis. *Percep. Psychophys.* 14:201–211.

Jones, E. G. and Burton, H. (1976) Areal differences in the laminar distribution of thalamic afferents in cortical fields of the insular, parietal, and temporal regions of primates. *J. Neurol.* 168:197–248.

Kimura, D. and Archibald, Y. (1974) Motor functions of the left hemisphere. *Brain* 97:337–350.

Leekam, S., Baron-Cohen, S., Perrett, D. I., Milders, M., and Brown, S. (1997) Eye-direction detection: A dissociation between geometric and joint attention skills in autism. *Br. J. Develop. Psych.* 15:77–95.

Le Doux, J. E. (1995) Emotion: Clues from the brain. *Ann. Rev. Psych.* 46:209–235.

McDonald, S., Tate, R. L., and Rigby, J. (1994) Error types in ideomotor apraxia: A qualitative analysis. *Brain Cog.* 25:250–270.

McLeod, P., Dittrich, W., Driver, J., Perrett, D. I., and Zihl, J. (1996) Preserved and impaired detection of structure from motion in a "motion-blind" patient. *Vis. Cog.* 3:363–391.

Mineka, S., Davidson, M., Cook, M., and Keir, R. (1984) Observational conditioning of snake fear in rhesus monkeys. *J. Ab. Psych.* 93:355–372.

Mistlin, A. J. and Perrett, D. I. (1990) Visual and somatosensory processing in the macaque temporal cortex: The role of "expectation." *Exp. Brain Res.* 82:437–450.

Morris, J. S., Frith, C. D., Perrett, D. I., Rowland, D., Young, A. W., Calder, A. J., and Dolan, R. J. (1996) A neural response within human amygdala differentiates between fearful and happy facial expressions. *Nature* 383:812–815.

Oram, M. W. and Perrett, D. I. (1994a) Responses of anterior superior temporal polysensory (STPa) neurons to "biological motion" stimuli. *J. Cog. Neurosci.* 6:99–116.

Oram, M. W. and Perrett, D. I. (1994b) Neural processing of biological motion in the macaque temporal cortex. In *Computational Vision Based on Neurobiology: SPIE Proceedings*, vol. 2054, ed. by T. B. Lawton, pp. 155–165.

Oram, M. W. and Perrett, D. I. (1996) Integration of form and motion in the anterior superior temporal polysensory area (STPa) of the macaque monkey. *J. Neurophys.* 76:109–1297.

Oram, M. W., Perrett, D. I., and Hietanen, J. K. (1993) Directional tuning of motion sensitive cells in the anterior superior temporal polysensory area (STPa) of the macaque. *Exp. Brain Res.* 97:274–294.

Oram, M. W., Perrett, D. I., Wachsmuth, E., and Emery, N. J. (submitted) Coding of limb, body-articulation, and whole body motion in the anterior superior temporal polysensory area (STPa) of the macaque monkey.

Parsons, L. M., Fox, P. T., Downs, J. H., Glass, T., Hirsch, T. B., Martin, C. C., Jerabek, P. A., and Lancaster, J. L. (1995) Use of implicit motor imagery for visual shape discrimination as revealed by PET. *Nature* 375:54–58.

Penn, D. L., Corrigan, P. W., Bentall, R. P., Racenstein, J. M., and Newman, L. (1997) Social cognition in schizophrenia. *Psych. Bull.* 121:114–132.

Perrett, D. I. (1996) View-dependent coding in the ventral stream and its consequences for recognition. In *Vision and Movement Mechanisms in the Cerebral Cortex*, ed. by R. Caminiti, K.-P. Hoffmann, F. Lacquaniti, and J. Altman, pp. 142–151. Strasbourg: HFSP.

Perrett, D. I. and Emery, N. J. (1994) Understanding the intentions of others from visual signals: Neurophysiological evidence. *Curr. Psych. Cog.* 13:683–694.

Perrett, D. I., Harries, M. H., Bevan, R., Thomas, S., Benson, P. J., Mistlin, A. J., Chitty, A. J., Hietanen, J. K., and Ortega, J. E. (1989) Frameworks of analysis for the neural representation of animate objects and actions. *J. Exp. Biol.* 146:87–114.

Perrett, D. I., Harries, M. H., Mistlin, A. J., Hietanen, J. K., Benson, P. J., Bevan, R., Thomas, S., Ortega, J., Oram, M. W., and Brierly, K. (1990a) Social signals analysed at the single cell level: Someone's looking at me, something touched me, something moved. *Int. J. Comp. Psych.* 4:25–50.

Perrett, D. I., Harries, M. H., Benson, P. J., Chitty, A. J., and Mistlin, A. J. (1990b) Retrieval of structure from rigid and biological motion; an analysis of the visual response of neurons in the macaque temporal cortex. In *AI and the Eye*, ed. by T. Troscianko and A. Blake, pp. 181–201. Chichester: J. Wiley.

Perrett, D. I., Harries, M. H., Chitty, A. J., and Mistlin, A. J. (1990c) Three stages in the classification of body movements by visual neurons. In *Images and Understanding*, ed. by H. B. Barlow, C. Blakemore, and M. Weston-Smith, pp. 94–108. Cambridge: Cambridge University Press.

Perrett, D. I., Hietanen, J. K., Oram, M. W., and Benson P. J. (1992) Organization and functions of cells responsive to faces in the temporal cortex. *Phil. Trans. Roy. Soc. Lond.* 335:23–30.

Perrett, D. I. and Mistlin, A. J. (1990) Perception of facial attributes. In *Comparative Perception*, volume 2: *Complex Signals*, ed. by W. C. Stebbins, and M. A. Berkley, pp. 187–215. New York: John Wiley.

Perrett, D. I., Mistlin, A. J., Harries, M. H., and Chitty, A. J. (1990d) Understanding the visual appearance and consequences of hand actions. In *Vision and Action: The Control of Grasping*, ed. by M. Goodale, pp. 163–180. Stanford, CT: Ablex Pub.

Perrett, D. I., Oram, M. W., Wachsmuth, E., and Emery, N. J. (1995) Understanding the behavior and "minds" of others from their facial and body signals: Studies of visual processing within the temporal cortex. In *Emotion, Memory, and Behaviour: Studies on Human and Non-Human Primates*, ed. by T. Nakajima and T. Ono, Taniguchi Symposia on Brain Sciences 18, pp. 155–167. Tokyo: Japan Scientific Societies Press.

Perrett, D. I., Oram, M. W., and Wachsmuth, E. (1994) Understanding minds and expression from facial signals: Studies at the brain cell level. In *Proceedings of the 2nd IEEE International Workshop on Robot and Human Communication*, suppl. pp. 3–12.

Perrett, D. I., Smith, P. A. J., Potter, D. D., Mistlin, A. J., Head, A. S., Milner, A. D., and Jeeves, M. A. (1984) Neurons responsive to faces in the temporal cortex: Studies of functional organization, sensitivity to identity, and relation to perception. *Hum. Neurobiol.* 3:197–208.

Perrett, D. I., Smith, P. A. J., Potter, D. D., Mistlin, A. J., Head, A. S., Milner, A. D., and Jeeves, M. A. (1985a) Visual cells in the temporal cortex sensitive to face view and gaze direction. *Proc. Roy. Soc. Lond.* B 223:293–317.

Perrett, D. I., Smith, P. A. J., Mistlin, A. J., Chitty, A. J., Head, A. S., Potter, D. D., Broennimann, R., Milner, A. D., and Jeeves, M. A. (1985b) Visual analysis of body movements by neurons in the temporal cortex of the macaque monkey: A preliminary report. *Behav. Brain Res.* 16:153–170.

Petrides, M. and Iversen, S. D. (1978) The effect of selective anterior and posterior association cortex lesions in the monkey on performance of a visual-auditory compound discrimination test. *Neuropsychol.* 16:527–537.

Petrides, M. and Iversen, S. D. (1979) Restricted posterior parietal lesions in the rhesus monkey and the performance on visuospatial tasks. *Brain Res.* 161:63–77.

Phillips, M. L., Young, A. W., Senior, C., Brammer, M., Andrew, C., Calder, A. J., Bullmore, E. T., Perrett, D. I., Rowland, D., Williams, S. C. R., Gray, J. A., and David, A. S. (1997) A specific neural substrate for perceiving facial expressions of disgust. *Nature* 389:495–498.

Povinelli, D. J. and Preuss, T. M. (1995) Theory of mind: Evolutionary history of a cognitive specialization. *TINS* 18:418–424.

Puce, A., Allison, T., Bentin, S., Gore, J. C., and McCarthy, G. (1998) Temporal cortex activation in humans viewing eye and mouth movements. *J. Neurosci.* 18:2188–2199.

Rizzolatti, G., Fadiga, L., Matelli, M., Bettinardi, V., Paulesu, G., Perani, D., and Fazio, F. (1996) Localization of grasp representations in humans by PET. 1. Observation vs. execution. *Exp. Brain Res.* 111:246–253.

Rothi, L. J. G., Mack, L., and Heilman, K. M. (1986) Pantomime agnosia. *J. Neurol. Neurosurg. Psych.* 49:451–454.

Rothi, L. J. G., Ocipa, C., and Heilman, K. M. (1991) A cognitive neuropsychological model of limb praxis. *Cog. Neuropsych.* 8:443–458.

Scott, S. K., Young, A. W., Calder, A. J., Hellawell, D. J., Aggleton, J. P., and Johnson, M. (1997) Impaired auditory recognition of fear and anger following bilateral amygdala lesions. *Nature* 385:254–257.

Seltzer, B. and Pandya, D. N. (1978) Afferent cortical connections and architectonics of the superior temporal sulcus and surrounding cortex in the rhesus monkey. *Brain Res.* 149:1–24.

Seltzer, B. and Pandya, D. N. (1984) Further observations on parieto-temporal connections in the rhesus monkey. *Exp. Brain Res.* 55:301–312.

Sprengelmeyer, R., Young, A. W., Karnat, A., Calder, A. J., Lange, H., Homberg, V., Perrett, D. I., and Rowland, D. (1996) Perception of faces and emotions: Loss of disgust in Huntington's disease. *Brain* 119:1647–1665.

Sprengelmeyer, R., Young, A. W., Calder, A. J., Karnat, A., Rowland, D., Perrett, D. I., Homberg, V., and Lange, H. (1997) Recognition of facial expressions of basic emotions in Huntington's disease. *Cog. Neuropsych.* 14:839–879.

Tanji, J. (1996) Involvement of motor areas in medial frontal cortex of primates in sequencing of multiple movements. *In Vision and Movement Mechanisms in the Cerebral Cortex*, ed. by R. Caminiti, K.-P. Hoffmann, F. Lacquaniti, and J. Altman, pp. 63–70. Strasbourg: HFSP.

Tanji, J. and Shima, K. (1994) Role of supplementary motor cells in planning several movements ahead. *Nature* 371:413–416.

Tanaka, K. (1993) Neuronal mechanisms of object recognition. *Science* 262:685–688.

Tanaka, K., Saito, H., Fukada, Y., and Moriya, M. (1991) Coding visual images of objects in the inferotemporal cortex of the macaque monkey. *J. Neurophys.* 66:170–189.

Tanila, H., Carlson, S., Linnnankoski, I., Lindroos, F., and Kahila, H. (1992) Functional properties of dorsolateral prefrontal cortical neurons in awake monkey. *Behav. Brain Res.* 47:169–180.

Visalberghi, E. and Fragaszy, D. (1990) Do monkeys ape? In *"Language" and Intelligence in Monkeys and Apes*, ed. by S. T. Parker, and K. R. Gibson, pp. 247–273. Cambridge: Cambridge University Press.

Varney, N. R. and Damasio, H. (1987) Locus of lesion in impaired pantomime recognition. *Cortex* 23:699–703.

Wachsmuth, E., Oram, M. W., and Perrett, D. I. (1994) Recognition of objects and their component parts: Responses of single units in the temporal cortex of the macaque. *Cereb. Cortex* 5:509–522.

Walsh, V. and Perrett, D. I. (1994) Visual attention in the occipitotemporal processing stream of the macaque. *Cog. Neuropsych* 11:243–263.

Whiten, A. and Ham, R. (1992) On the nature and evolution of imitation in the animal kingdom: Reappraisal of a century of Research. In *Advances in the Study of Behaviour*, vol. 21, ed. by P. J. B. Slater, J. S. Rosenblatt, C. Beer, and M. Miliski, pp. 239–283. New York: Academic Press.

Young, A. W., Aggelton, J. P., Hellawell, D. J., Johnson. M., Broks, P., and Hanley, J. R. (1995) Face processing impairments after amygdalectomy. *Brain* 118:15–24.

Young, M. P. (1992) Objective analysis of the topological organization of the primate cortical visual system. *Nature* 358:152–155.

7 Neural Systems for Recognizing Emotions in Humans

Ralph Adolphs

An understanding of human emotion requires explication at the levels of neurobiology, cognitive psychology, and social psychology. While there is a rich literature on emotion from studies in social psychology and anthropology, neurobiological studies of the relation between brain and emotion are still in their infancy. There are several consequences of this state of affairs: little is known about the neural underpinnings of emotion; the recent neurobiological studies are of necessity limited in scope; and it is not immediately apparent how the conceptual framework that has been used to study emotion in psychology will translate into the conceptual framework used to study emotion in cognitive neuroscience. In fact, some have argued for the eliminativist position that "emotion" as understood in the vocabulary of psychology may not have *any* useful correlate in the vocabulary of the neurosciences (Brothers 1997).

Although the above is intended as a disclaimer of sorts, I do believe that the most constructive approach is to see how much progress can be made in understanding emotion from within cognitive neuroscience. Links to folk-, cognitive-, and social-psychological concepts can be made once the neurobiological studies have attained a level of maturity. With these general caveats in mind, I will discuss neurobiological approaches to one particular aspect of emotion. The framework for thinking about emotion borrows much from work in animals and seeks a continuity with animal studies that is grounded in an evolutionary approach to emotion. In consequence, I will focus on the emotion that has received the most attention in animal studies: fear. By doing so I certainly do not mean to suggest that all emotions share the same neural machinery, nor do I mean to suggest that it is not fruitful to study other specific emotions such as sadness, anger, happiness, let alone love, jealousy, and embarrassment. Rather, given the early stage of our understanding of the neural systems involved in emotion, I think that the particular (and, to be sure, very limited) examples of processing emotions on which I will concentrate will be useful starting points for understanding the great diversity and complexity of emotion in general.

The topic of emotion subsumes several distinct types of processes, which can be operationalized in different ways. Three useful domains in which emotion can be studied are (1) knowledge about emotion, (2) experience of emotion, and (3) expression of emotion. Although all three domains likely share some cognitive processes and some neural structures, they are nevertheless distinct.

My colleagues and I at the University of Iowa have focused on the first domain, the knowledge of emotions. This could also be called evaluation, or recognition, of emotions. The experiments that fall under this heading typically involve presenting subjects with auditory and/or visual stimuli, such as people's voices or photographs of people's faces, and asking the subject what they know about the emotion signaled by the stimulus. We are thus interested in the retrieval of knowledge about an emotion, on the basis of a stimulus that denotes or signals the emotion.

Knowledge of Emotion

The question of this chapter, then, concerns the cluster of knowledge that normally constitutes the concept of a given emotion and investigates how the encoding or the retrieval of such knowledge depends on neural structures. When we speak of "happiness" or "fear," we are using a verbal label as shorthand for a cluster of phenomena (experiences, behaviors, reactions, body states, etc.) that are pieces of knowledge and that together comprise a normal concept of happiness or fear. When we attempt to assess the recognition of emotions in subjects, the particular tasks we use aim to engage the subject in retrieving such knowledge components.

The retrieval of conceptual knowledge is perhaps most easily understood with regard to lexical stimuli, such as words. In such an experiment, a subject reads or hears a word denoting an emotion, for example, the word "anger," and is then asked to retrieve knowledge regarding the emotion denoted by the word "anger." One could ask, for instance, if this is a pleasant or an unpleasant emotion, if anger is more similar to disgust than it is to happiness, if anger is arousing or relaxing, and so on. All these items of knowledge are components of the concept of the emotion "anger." One could do the same experiment without using the lexical label, and instead show subjects a facial expression of anger, asking the same questions of the expression as one might ask about the label.

The Lesion Method

Below, I will present data that link knowledge retrieval about certain emotions to specific neuroanatomical structures in the human brain. The lesion method is one method that yields such data, on the basis of correlations between brain damage to specific structures and impairments on specific tasks (see Damasio and Damasio 1989 for an overview). In a typical experiment, task performances are compared between a group of subjects with damage to a particular brain structure hypothesized to be important in performing the task ("target subjects"), and a group of subjects with no brain damage ("normal controls") or with brain damage outside the target structure ("brain-damaged controls"). Impaired task performances (relative to the control subjects) that correlate with damage to a target structure are interpreted as evidence that the target structure is normally (i.e., in healthy brains) involved in performing the task. Such correlations are the only way to apply the lesion method in humans, because it is not possible to manipulate the lesion experimentally as a variable, as is done with animals. Whereas one can compare the same animal's performance before and after an experimental lesion, one must compare human patients with lesions to human patients without lesions (i.e., one must use between-subject comparisons rather than within-subject comparisons). This approach makes it especially important to consider other differences between the group with lesions and the group without that could affect task performance. Typically, we attempt to control for this possibility by ensuring that subjects in both groups are similar in relevant respects (such as IQ and age, for instance).

A prerequisite for the lesion method to yield useful data is, of course, that cognitive functions must be anatomically regionalized or localized, at least to some degree. The degree to which such localization must occur is both macroscopic and systems-oriented. All that is required is that, at the level of large-scale neural systems (i.e., at a rather macroscopic level), there are regions of the brain that participate (as one among many components) preferentially in some processes. Needless to say, no task makes use of only a single neural component, and many tasks can be performed with different sets of neural structures, depending on the strategy that the subject uses in the task.

Depending on the demands of the task, damage to a particular structure may compromise the system to an extent sufficient to result in impairments. Again, such impairments must be interpreted against the background of other factors that may contribute to task performance. It is quite conceivable, for instance, that an identical lesion in two subjects of different IQ might result in impaired task performance in the subject with lower IQ, but not in the one with higher IQ.

Ecological Relevance

Lexical and prosodic verbal stimuli, and visual stimuli such as facial expressions, gestures, and body posture can all communicate socially relevant information in natural settings. There is no doubt that something is being communicated by these signals, but it has been debated what precisely it is that is being communicated. The debate has been most vociferous with regard to one of the most commonly used experimental stimuli: human facial expressions. This phrase already illustrates the controversy: are smiles, and frowns actually expressing emotions? Or are they social signals that can be used for a variety of purposes in social communication? The former view has been traditional, but recent treatments have argued for the latter (see Fridlund 1994 and Russell and Fernandez-Dols 1997 for reviews of the debate).

However, the debate about whether to treat facial expressions as read-outs of emotions or as social signals is most pertinent with regard to the *expression* of emotions, not to their *recognition*. It may well be that smiles, for example, are not always elicited by happiness, but rather serve a more complex social role (submissiveness, agreement, etc., depending on the context in which the smile is expressed). Nonetheless, a static photograph of a smiling person, devoid of other context, can denote happiness, in much the same way that the lexical label "happy" can do so. That this is so is borne out by the data: when normal subjects are shown prototypical facial expressions of certain emotions, there is high agreement as to which emotion is denoted by the facial expression (Ekman and Friesen 1976), and this performance is quite stable across the adult lifespan (Moreno et al. 1993). Of course, such an experiment leaves out much of the complexity of the real world (there is no context, the expressions are strong and prototypical, we are not told anything else about the person whose face we are seeing, and so on). But by leaving out this complexity, prototypical facial expressions can be used to reliably elicit the retrieval of knowledge about an emotion. It is for this reason that our research has emphasized facial expressions as stimuli.

Theoretical Framework

There are two components to our approach to the study of emotion: a theory about how emotions are classified, and a theory about the neuroanatomical underpinnings of emotion.

The conceptual structure of emotions, particularly their categorization into a small number of basic types and the relation of these basic types to one another, has been a matter of considerable interest and controversy (Damasio 1994; Ekman 1972; Ekman 1992; Fridlund 1994; Izard 1992; Johnson-Laird and Oatley 1992; Oster et al. 1989; Russell 1980). It has been argued that a small number of emotions are basic or primary, in the sense that they are psychological categories that appear to be recognized cross-culturally and appear to rely on neural systems whose function may have a large innate component, and whose operation can be understood in an evolutionary framework (Damasio 1994; Ekman 1972; Ekman 1992; Izard 1992; Johnson-Laird and Oatley 1992). With regard to facial expressions of emotion, data from normal subjects suggest that there are six basic emotional expressions: happiness, surprise, fear, anger, disgust, and sadness (Ekman 1972; Ekman and Friesen 1976). However, these six categories are fuzzy (without clearly demarcated boundaries) and show some overlap (facial expressions can be members of more than one category; Russell 1980; Russell and Bullock 1985; Russell and Bullock 1986). The conceptual structure of emotions may thus bear some similarity to the conceptual structure of colors (Berlin and Kay 1991). As with primary colors, there are basic emotions, and, like colors, an emotion can be intermediate between other emotions.

The six basic emotional expressions are recognized easily by normal subjects, and they are recognized consistently across very different cultures (Ekman 1972; Ekman 1973; Ekman 1992). There is even evidence that rather complex and subtle facial expressions (other than those of basic emotions) are interpreted similarly across different cultures, and already early in life (Baron-Cohen et al. 1996). However, others have argued against this, and claimed that the interpretation and conceptualization of emotions, even basic emotions, can be culturally quite idiosyncratic (Russell 1994). While this debate continues, the most parsimonious reading of the literature would suggest that both views are correct (cf. Hauser 1996): the attribution of emotions to facial expressions is influenced both by innate factors that exert their effect across different cultures, and by culture-specific factors that are learned. No doubt culture-specific learning will help shape and fine-tune emotion categories whose rough bounds, and whose learnability, are in large part innate. Facial expression, like other aspects of communication, is likely guided by innate predispositions to assimilate culturally learnable features, what Peter Marler has called an "instinct to learn" (Marler 1989; Marler and Terrace 1984).

A good example of how an emotion concept can be fleshed out during development is illustrated by the case of disgust. All infants make a stereotyped face of disgust (as will most mammals) when they have ingested an unpalatable food (readers with infants can easily observe the response to sour lemon, for example). The facial response is derived from expulsion of and aversion to the item. In adulthood, both the lexical term, "disgust," and the facial expression are applied more broadly, to include responses to other people whom one finds aversive (the adjective "distasteful" illustrates how the concept is applied to both food and people; cf. Rozin 1996). Thus a basic emotional expression can be applied by adults, metaphorically, to a large variety of situations. Although the circumstances under which an emotional expression may be elicited can be complex and can depend on the subject's culture, a basic core set of emotional reactions are likely shared across different cultures.

Each of the six basic emotions is distinct at the level of concept, experience, and expression, but psychological studies have also examined the possibility that these emotions might share certain aspects. There is evidence from cognitive psychological studies that valence (pleasantness/unpleasantness) and arousal are two orthogonal factors that may capture the entire spectrum of basic emotions (Russell 1980; Russell and Bullock 1985; Russell et al. 1989), findings that have recently been corroborated by psychophysiological data (Johnsen et al. 1995; Lang et al. 1993). Data from normal subjects show that emotions, as depicted both in facial expressions and in verbal labels, can be represented on a two-dimensional grid with valence and arousal as orthogonal axes. Such a representation makes sense intuitively, but one need not conclude that emotions can be analyzed completely in terms of their valence and arousal. I favor a more pragmatic view and treat valence and arousal simply as two attributes of emotions that are useful for interpreting performances on many tasks.

Our hypotheses regarding the neuroanatomical substrates of emotion have come out of evolutionary considerations of the function of emotion. Emotions may have evolved as a necessary consequence of decoupling stimuli from reflexive responses (cf. Scherer 1984). As more complex organisms interposed additional processing machinery between perception and action, emotions arose in order to predispose the organism to act, without necessarily precipitating the action immediately (features that suggest why it would be important to evolve communication signals that have emotions as their topic). Two fundamental properties of emotions are thus that they are dispositional, and that they are of adaptive value to the organism (Damasio 1994; Damasio 1995; Frijda 1986; Lazarus 1991). Extending ideas first espoused by the psychologist William James over a century ago (James 1884), recent theories emphasize that emotion pertains to the well-being and survival of the organism. This view has been developed in substantial detail by Antonio Damasio (it is beyond the scope of this chapter to discuss this framework in detail; the interested reader is referred to Damasio 1994, 1995). Damasio proposes that an emotion consists in a collective change in body and brain states, in response to the evaluation of a particular event or entity (or in response to the memory of a particular event or entity). These state changes produce, respectively, somatic changes (including motor behavior, facial expression, autonomic changes, and endocrine changes) and changes in the processing mode of neural systems (changes in the way the brain processes information).

Thus emotion concerns the continual changes of body and brain states that occur in an organism as it interacts with its environment. Importantly, this view goes well beyond William James's view, in stressing that emotion is much more than bodily responses. Additionally, emotions pertain to global information-processing modes of the brain, and to neural representations of body states. Damasio's framework for thinking about emotion suggests specific neuroanatomical hypotheses. The neural structures involved in processing emotions include those structures that represent body states, and those structures that link perception of external stimuli to body states. This includes structures such as the somatosensory cortices, and structures such as the ventral frontal cortex and amygdala, respectively.

The Amygdala

Arguably, the brain structure that has received the most attention with regard to its role in emotion is the amygdala (see Aggleton 1992a and LeDoux 1996 for reviews). The amygdala is a collection of nuclei in the anterior mesial temporal lobe that receives highly processed sensory information from all modalities (with the exception of relatively direct olfactory input from the olfactory bulb), and which have extensive, reciprocal connections with a large number of other brain structures whose function can be modulated by emotion. Thus the amygdala has massive connections, both directly and via the thalamus, with the ventromedial frontal cortices, which are known to play a key role in planning and decision making. The amygdala connects with hippocampus, basal ganglia, and basal forebrain, structures that participate in various aspects of memory and attention. And, of course, the amygdala projects to structures, such as the hypothalamus, that are involved in controlling homeostasis, visceral, and neuroendocrine output. Consequently, the amygdala is situated so as to link information about external stimuli conveyed by sensory cortices, with modulation of decision making, memory, attention, and somatic, visceral, and endocrine processes that all will be influenced by the emotional significance of the external stimulus that is being processed.

Insights into the function of the amygdala date back to the early experiments of Kluver and Bucy, who found that in the laboratory, bilateral ablation of the monkey amygdala in addition to large sectors of adjacent temporal lobe resulted in a constellation of impairments in social and emotional functioning that is best described as an agnosia for the social and emotional meanings conveyed by external stimuli (Kluver and Bucy 1939). Subsequent studies in monkeys have shown that damage confined to the amygdala results in a more restricted set of impairments, which varies depending on the species and on whether the behavior is assessed in the laboratory or in the wild (Amaral et al. 1997; Kling and Brothers 1992; Meunier et al. 1996; Weiskrantz 1956; Zola-Morgan et al. 1991). The most consistent finding is that the animals are more placid and tend to approach stimuli that normal monkeys would avoid. Depending on the species and the circumstances, this can render the amygdalectomized monkeys the objects of unusual friendliness or unusual aggressiveness by other monkeys. In broad terms, similar results have been reported following lesions of the amygdala in a variety of animals and in humans (Aggleton 1992b; Blanchard and Blanchard 1972; Davis 1992b; Jacobson 1986; Kling and Brothers 1992; Lee et al. 1988; Narabayashi 1972; Rosvold et al. 1954). However, the results from humans are by no means homogeneous, and several cases of bilateral amygdala damage have been reported without the placidity found in studies with animals (Markowitsch et al. 1994; Tranel and Hyman 1990). We have conjectured that, following amygdala damage, impairments in many aspects of overt social behavior might be less severe in humans than they are in monkeys or rats, because humans possess special compensatory mechanisms (Adolphs et al. 1995). Most notably, humans possess an enormous store of declarative knowledge that relies on language; it is thus conceivable that humans with amygdala damage could behave relatively normally because they have declarative knowledge of what constitutes normal social behavior. This option is not available to other animals, whose behavior thus may be relatively more impaired.

Studies in which the amygdala was stimulated electrically have shown that experiences or behaviors of fear and anger can be elicited by such stimulation (Chapman et al. 1954; Gloor et al. 1982; Halgren et al. 1978; Heath et al. 1955). However, the conclusion that the amygdala plays an important role in the conscious experience of emotions is not presently warranted, since a number of studies using functional imaging have failed to find activation of the amygdala during the experience of emotions, specifically of aversion and fear (Fredrikson et al. 1995; Cahill et al. 1996), nor is there any evidence that subjects with amygdala lesions are unable to experience fear (cf. Adolphs et al. 1997a).

Neurophysiological recording of neurons in the amygdala has shown that neuronal reponses are modulated by the affective significance of sensory stimuli (Muramoto et al. 1993; Nishijo et al. 1988). Responses selective for faces have also been reported in the primate amygdala (Rolls 1992; Nakamura et al. 1992), and responses selective for gender, identity, and expression of faces have been found in the human amygdala (Fried et al. 1997). We have obtained recent preliminary data from single-unit recordings of amygdala neurons in human patients with chronically implanted electrodes. In these studies, subjects were shown emotional movie clips, and modulations in the firing rates of amygdala neurons were observed (Mirsky et al. 1997).

There is evidence from lesion studies in rats that the amygdala is required for the acquisition of conditioned behavioral responses to stimuli that have been previously paired with an intrinsically aversive event, a paradigm called "fear conditioning"

(Davis 1992a; LeDoux et al. 1990). In both rats (Hatfield et al. 1996) and monkeys (Gaffan 1992) the amygdala is involved also in associating stimuli with reward. Animal studies have suggested that the amygdala is involved specifically in behaviors and responses associated with high arousal and stress (Davis 1992b; Goldstein et al. 1996; Kesner 1992). In addition to its role in the expression of emotional behaviors, the amygdala thus appears to play a specific role in one type of associative memory: the acquisition of information associated with emotional arousal, an interpretation that is corroborated by recent data from our laboratory described below.

The Amygdala's Role in Conditioning

The amygdala is necessary for some conditioned responses in both animals and humans. While animal studies have shown that specific nuclei within the amygdala are responsible for the acquisition and expression of conditioned fear (Gewirtz and Davis 1997; LeDoux et al. 1990; LeDoux et al. 1988) and that different amygdala nuclei may mediate different types of fear response (Killcross et al. 1997), human studies have addressed the amygdala as a whole. This comparatively coarse level of resolution has been necessitated by the inability to introduce experimental lesions in humans.

We have studied a patient (subject SM) with selective bilateral damage to the amygdala (Nahm et al. 1993; Tranel and Hyman 1990). Subject SM is a 32-year-old woman who suffers from a rare genetic disease, Urbach Wiethe disease, which likely resulted in damage to the amygdala in childhood or infancy, possibly at birth. Detailed analysis of data from MR scans confirmed complete bilateral lesion of the amygdala, with some minor damage to the adjacent left anterior entorhinal cortex; all other structures were spared (figure 7.1b). These findings were corroborated by functional imaging: a resting 18-F deoxyglucose PET study showed essentially no glucose uptake by the tissue of the amygdala (figure 7.1c).

In one study, we tested SM's ability to acquire conditioned autonomic responses to stimuli that had been paired with an aversive startle stimulus. This experiment was similar to fear-conditioning experiments in animals (Davis 1992a; LeDoux 1993). To summarize briefly: subjects were presented with a startling and aversive loud auditory stimulus, which reliably evoked skin-conductance responses in both normal subjects and in SM. This startle stimulus was paired with slides of a certain color: blue slides were occasionally accompanied by the startle stimulus, whereas slides of other colors were not. In this experiment, normal subjects soon acquired conditioned autonomic responses: the presentation of a blue slide alone (without the startle stimulus) now evoked conditioned skin-conductance changes. We found that these conditioned autonomic responses were independent of the acquisition

A.

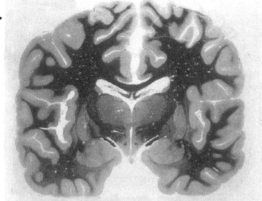

B.

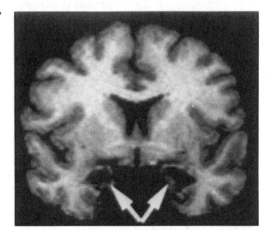

C.

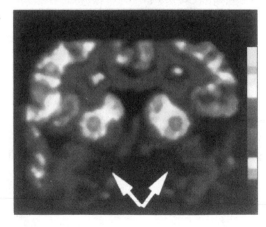

of declarative knowledge, since amnesic subjects also acquired conditioned skin-conductance responses, even though they did not declaratively remember which slides were paired with the startle stimulus. Subject SM, who has bilateral amygdala damage, did not acquire conditioned skin-conductance responses on this task, but she was able to recall the declarative fact that the startle stimulus had been paired with the blue slides (Bechara et al. 1995). Some of these findings have been replicated in subjects with unilateral amygdala damage (LaBar et al. 1995). These studies suggest that in humans, as in animals, the amygdala plays a key role in acquiring conditioned responses to stimuli that have been paired with aversive stimuli in the past.

It should be noted that the amygdala appears not to be required for learning all such nondeclarative kinds of knowledge. In an experiment with an amnesiac patient who had complete bilateral amygdala damage, it was found that the patient could acquire preferences with regard to other people: he would develop a positive bias toward people who had been kind to him in the past, and a negative bias toward those who had not, even though he could not declaratively recall having seen any of the people before (Tranel and Damasio 1993). This experiment shows that the amygdala is not essential to learning all types of emotional response.

The Amygdala's Role in Recognizing Emotional Facial Expressions

We also examined SM's ability to recognize facial expressions of emotion. The subject showed a particularly prominent impairment in recognition of fear in facial expressions (Adolphs et al. 1994; Adolphs et al. 1995), as well as an impairment in

Figure 7.1
The brain of subject SM, who has selective bilateral amygdala lesions as a result of a rare heritable disease. Extensive investigations with this subject have shown that the lesion is stable and chronic (there has been no evidence of any progression in the last decade), and that SM's neuropsychological profile is also stable (her scores on all neuropsychological tasks, including those on which she is impaired, have remained essentially unchanged over the course of more than a decade). This patient is thus an especially valuable research subject on whom hypotheses regarding the functions of the human amygdala can be tested. Results from SM can now be compared with the results obtained from additional subjects with amygdala lesions studied by other groups, and with results from functional imaging of the amygdala. (A) Post-mortem coronal section of a normal human brain showing the amygdala. The section has been stained such that white matter (myelin) is stained black, and cell bodies (grey matter and nuclei) are white. (B) MRI coronal section of SM's brain, showing complete and selective bilateral amygdala lesions (arrows). (C) 18-fluorodeoxyglucose PET image of SM's brain. SM was awake, resting, with eyes closed during the scan. The shadings represent the amount of glucose uptake in different brain regions (black indicates very little or no glucose uptake). SM's amygdala showed no glucose uptake (arrows), confirming that her structural lesion is also a functional lesion (there is no, or very little, metabolically active brain tissue in the amygdala). Hypometabolism of the amygdala, together with structural lesions seen on MR, has been reported in other patients with the same disease (Markowitsch et al. 1994), and is consistent with post-mortem findings that such patients have a calcified, atrophic amygdala.

recognizing the similarity between facial expressions of different emotions (Adolphs et al. 1994). These results could not be accounted for by visuoperceptual impairments, since SM performed normally on a large number of visuoperceptual tasks, including the ability to discriminate between unfamiliar faces (Tranel and Hyman 1990), the ability to recognize people's identities from their faces (Adolphs et al. 1994), and the ability to discriminate between subtly different expressions on the same face.

Additional studies with subject SM have revealed that the impairment extends to the retrieval of various components of conceptual knowledge regarding emotions. She was unable to draw facial expressions of fear from memory (Adolphs et al. 1995) and also showed impaired conceptual knowledge of emotions when given verbal stimuli, such as words or stories denoting emotions; again, the impairment was most striking with regard to fear.

It is not obvious how to characterize SM's impaired performance of the above tasks. Interpretations that clearly *cannot* be made are to conclude that she has no fear, or that she does not know what fear is. None of these statements would be warranted by the data, and they are likely false. The impairment is more specific, and it appears to consist in a gap in some components of knowledge of the emotion signaled by external sensory stimuli. This suggests a role for the amygdala not in the storage of knowledge about fear, or in the experience of fear, but rather in linking external sensory (and perhaps especially social) stimuli to systems from which knowledge about fear can be retrieved. The amygdala may thus connect percepts of sensory stimuli, on the one hand, with a variety of neural systems involved in response to and knowledge of such stimuli, on the other.

The Amygdala's Role in Acquisition of Declarative Knowledge

The above interpretation suggests that it may be that the amygdala plays a role in the acquisition, or encoding, of knowledge about certain aspects of emotion, rather than in the storage or retrieval of such knowledge. This interpretation is supported by several recent findings. We tested two subjects on the same task previously administered to SM. These subjects had sustained complete bilateral amygdala damage, but unlike SM, whose amygdala damage was acquired early in life, these two had acquired their damage in adulthood, and were entirely normal up to that point in time. We found that the two subjects with adult-onset amygdala damage were not impaired in their ability to recognize fear (or any other emotion) in facial expressions (Hamann et al. 1996), which led to the proposal that perhaps SM was impaired in recognizing fear because she never acquired normal knowledge about fear in the first place (Adolphs et al. 1996a; Phelps and Anderson 1997). Some lesion studies are at odds with this interpretation (Calder et al. 1996; Young et al. 1995; Young et al. 1996), but several other studies using both the lesion method and functional imaging support it.

Two functional-imaging studies (Breiter et al. 1996; Morris et al. 1996) found increased amygdala activation when subjects were shown facial expressions of fear, either passively (Breiter et al. 1996), or while performing an unrelated task (Morris et al. 1996). Although neither study asked subjects to *retrieve* knowledge, during the scan session they would have been *acquiring* knowledge about the stimuli (for instance, they would be able to recognize many of the stimuli later, or they would be able to recall what emotions they saw during the scan session). An explicit role for the amygdala in the acquisition of declarative knowledge regarding emotionally arousing and unpleasant stimuli was found by a different imaging study (Cahill et al. 1996), which reported that amygdala activation that occurred at the same time arousing, unpleasant emotional stimuli (movies) were encoded into memory correlated significantly with how accurately the stimuli could subsequently be recalled; the authors argued that the amygdala is activated during the encoding of emotionally arousing material into declarative long-term memory.

The hypothesis that the amygdala is important for the ability to acquire knowledge associated with emotional stimuli and situations makes specific predictions. First, amygdala damage should impair the ability to acquire new knowledge about highly emotional material on anterograde learning tasks. Second, damage to the amygdala early in life should lead to impaired encoding of knowledge associated with emotional arousal during development. Third, there should be neural structures other than the amygdala from which knowledge about emotions can be retrieved, if appropriately triggered. All three of these predictions have been tested in our laboratory.

In a recent study (Adolphs et al. 1997a; Kinsey and Adolphs 1997), we showed subjects a series of 12 slides accompanied by a narrative. Together, the slides and narrative formed a story that contained both emotionally neutral material, and emotionally arousing, unpleasant material. Memory for the stimuli was assessed 24 hours later. Normal and brain-damaged control subjects showed profiles on the task very similar to those published for normal controls from other studies. Previous studies with normal subjects found a reliable profile, wherein subjects remembered best those slides that they found the most emotionally arousing (Burke et al. 1992; Cahill and McGaugh 1995; Heuer and Reisberg 1990).

Two subjects with bilateral amygdala damage showed a selective impairment in memory for the emotional but not for the neutral material (Adolphs et al. 1997a; Kinsey and Adolphs 1997). Data from one of the subjects with bilateral amygdala damage (subject SM) are shown in figure 7.2. SM showed a normal memory profile,

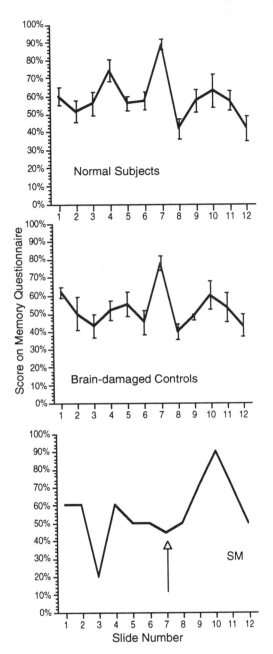

Figure 7.2
Declarative memory for emotional stimuli is impaired in subject SM. Subjects were shown 12 slides that told a short story; parts of the story were relatively neutral, and parts were highly emotional. The most emotionally arousing slide was slide 7, showing the reattached legs of a car-crash victim. Subjects' memory for the material was assessed 24 hours later with a multiple-choice questionnaire that asked 9–10 questions about each slide. SM did not show the normal enhancement of memory for emotionally arousing material (arrows). Memory scores are shown from: (*top*) 7 normal controls similar to SM on age, education, and IQ (means ± SEM); (*middle*) 6 brain-damaged controls; (*bottom*) subject SM. Chance performance is at 25%. From Adolphs et al. 1997a. © Cold Spring Harbor Laboratory Press, 1997.

except on the most emotionally arousing slide. Her performance suggests that bilateral amygdala damage impairs the normal facilitation of memory when the subject matter is emotional. The finding is consistent with a previous report, using the same task, that also suggested bilateral amygdala damage impaired emotional memory (Cahill et al. 1995).

A second set of studies from our laboratory examined five subjects who had bilateral amygdala damage (Adolphs et al. 1997b). Three of these subjects had sustained bilateral damage to the amygdala early in life, whereas two of the subjects had sustained bilateral amygdala damage in adulthood. We found that the subjects with early-onset amygdala damage showed a similar profile of impaired knowledge regarding emotions: they were impaired in judging the arousal signaled by stimuli denoting unpleasant emotions and consistently attributed abnormally low arousal to unpleasant emotions. The impairment was evident with regard to visual stimuli of facial expressions and auditory lexical stimuli (words or stories denoting emotions). For example, subjects with early-onset amygdala damage rated very angry and afraid faces as being less aroused than neutral faces, and they stated that angry and afraid people would typically feel rather relaxed and sleepy. By contrast, the two subjects with adult-onset amygdala damage were not impaired on the same tasks. All subjects rated the valence (pleasantness or unpleasantness) of the stimuli normally. Both this study and the earlier one described above support the hypothesis that the human amygdala is important early in life for the acquisition, during development, of certain components of the conceptual knowledge store about emotions, but that it may not be necessary for the retrieval of such knowledge, once acquired, in adulthood.

Right Hemisphere Cortices

Clinical and experimental studies have suggested that the right hemisphere is preferentially involved in processing emotion in humans. Lesions in the right temporal and parietal cortices have been shown to impair emotional experience and arousal (Heller 1993) and to impair imagery for emotion (Blonder et al. 1991; Bowers et al. 1991). It has been proposed that the right hemisphere contains modules for nonverbal affective computation (Bowers et al. 1993), which may have evolved to subserve aspects of social cognition (Borod 1993).

Much recent work has focused on the recognition of emotion signaled by human facial expressions. Selective impairments in recognizing facial expressions, with sparing of the ability to recognize identity, can occur following right temporoparietal lesions (Bowers et al. 1985). Specific anomia for emotional facial expressions has been reported following right middle temporal gyrus lesions (Rapcsak et al. 1993;

Rapcsak et al. 1989). The evidence that the right temporoparietal cortex is important in processing emotional facial expressions is corroborated by data from PET imaging (Gur et al. 1994) and neuronal recording (Ojemann et al. 1992) in humans. Additionally, anthropological analyses of the depiction of faces in art and painting support the idea that the right hemisphere is specialized to process the emotional and social signals that faces can signal (Grusser 1984). Again, however, the extent to which performance on tasks that attempt to assess emotion recognition depends on the right hemisphere will depend on the particular demands the task makes and on the strategies the subject is using (cf. Stone et al. 1996).

A prediction of the hypothesis that the human amygdala is critical for the acquisition of knowledge regarding emotion is that structures other than the amygdala play a key role in the storage and retrieval of such knowledge. On this view, the amygdala's contribution to memory is in some ways analogous to that of the hippocampal formation: both structures are important during acquisition and/or consolidation but are no longer essential once the knowledge has been acquired. The storage and retrieval of knowledge is presumed to rely on neocortical sectors.

We developed new methods of analyzing neuroanatomical data in order to visualize brain regions that might be most responsible for impaired task performances. We tested the ability to retrieve knowledge of emotions depicted in facial expressions of a large group of brain-damaged subjects with lesions in right hemisphere. Although the precise location and extent of each lesion differed among subjects, many subjects' lesions overlapped. We wanted to know if damage to a particular sector might correlate best with impaired task performance and might hence be most crucial for retrieving knowledge about emotions. To obtain such information, we mapped each subject's lesion onto a common reference brain and analyzed their overlaps. A detailed analysis of the lesions visible on the cortical surface revealed that sectors in right parietal cortex, when lesioned, reliably impaired the retrieval of knowledge about emotions depicted in facial expressions (Adolphs et al. 1996a). A recent study extended these methods to a three-dimensional analysis of the overlaps of lesions that correlated with the most impaired performances. The analysis showed that volumetric overlaps of lesions in the right primary somatosensory cortex, possibly including S-II, insula, and the anterior supramarginal gyrus as well as underlying white matter, most reliably correlated with impaired recognition of emotional facial expressions (Adolphs et al. 1996b). The results of this analysis are shown in figure 7.3.

The task we used required subjects to judge all the different emotions expressed by a face stimulus. For example, subjects might see an angry face, and would be asked

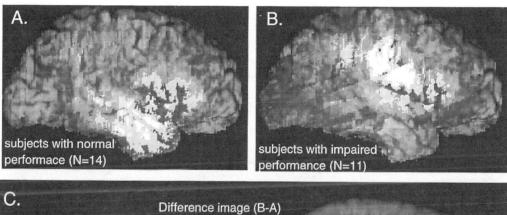

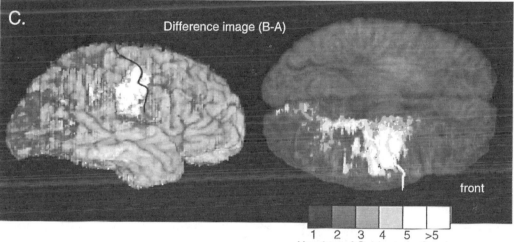

Figure 7.3
The right somatosensory cortices are an important component of the neural systems whereby subjects retrieve knowledge of the emotion signaled by facial expressions. We asked 25 subjects with focal right cortical lesions to rate facial expressions of emotion, and compared their ratings with those given by 15 normal controls. Data were mapped onto a normal reference brain, using a technique called MAP-3. Briefly, each subject's lesion was mapped onto the corresponding spatial location in the normal reference brain, and color was used to encode the number of lesions from different subjects that overlapped at a given volumetric location. All computations were done using the software BRAINVOX (Frank, Damasio, and Grabowski 1997) on Silicon Graphics workstations. (A) Lesions of all subjects who were normal in rating facial expressions of emotion. (B) Lesions of all subjects who were impaired in rating facial expressions of emotion. (C) Subtraction image (B-A), showing the difference in the lesion overlaps between all impaired subjects and all normal subjects. The central sulcus is indicated (black at left; white at right) for reference. The subtraction revealed a focal, 3-dimensional, region which, when damaged, always correlated with impaired task performance. We thus infer that lesions that include this "hot-spot" region result in impairments due to damage to this specific region. Lateral (left) and dorsal (right) views of the brain that have been rendered partly transparent show that this region, damage to which appeared to be most responsible for impaired recognition of emotional facial expressions (especially fear), comprised the face representation of primary somatosensory cortex (SI), some of SII, possibly some insula and supramarginal gyrus, as well as considerable white matter which may serve to connect visual cortical regions with somatosensory cortical regions. Data are from Adolphs et al. 1996b.

to judge how much happiness, surprise, fear, anger, disgust, and sadness the face expressed. The correlation of performance on this task with somatosensory cortex damage may relate to which strategy the subjects use in this difficult task. When a subject is shown a facial expression of anger, for example, and asked to rate the intensity of fear or surprise signaled by that expression, this is not a question to which there is an automatic, ready-made answer. Instead, the subject will in all likelihood adopt a strategy akin to asking, "what would I feel like, how much fear or surprise would I feel, if I were making that facial expression?" To answer this question, one must be able to access knowledge about the experience and the expression of the emotion (this need not be done deliberately, but rather could be occuring at an automatic and covert level). I believe that this scenario is in fact engendered by the tasks we used, and that it is what accounts for the otherwise rather surprising finding that somatosensory cortices (including the face representation of right primary somatosensory cortex) are necessary to perform normally on this visual task.

Data from nonhuman primates suggest that they may share with humans similar hemispheric specialization for processing emotion (Hamilton and Vermeire 1988; Hauser 1993; Morris and Hopkins 1993; see also the chapters by Hauser, Perrett, and Kanwal in this volume). The question arises as to why the processing of emotion, much like the processing of language, should be notably lateralized. One recent idea begins with the fact that both language and emotion serve an important role in communication. As such, there is a premium on processing speed. In the case of language, this has been clear for some time: both the comprehension and production of language require neural processing with high temporal acuity. This point has been driven home by the recent finding that subtle and general impairments in processing very rapid signals can result in a relatively severe and specific impairment in language: some forms of developmental dyslexia are due to abnormal neural processing of rapid signals and may be ameliorated when auditory signals are slowed (Merzenich et al. 1996). In the case of emotion, ecological considerations similarly suggest that signals need to be processed rapidly: responding to facial expressions of fear or anger in social situations puts a premium on speed. One would therefore expect the design of the neural systems that process language and facial expression to show evidence of architectural constraints that reflect processing speed. Hemispheric lateralization is one such feature. The compact spatial arrangement of all neural components required to process language, or facial expression, in one hemisphere would enable rapid processing. Intrahemispheric delay, on the other hand, would introduce an unacceptable lag. This constraint would be expected to be all the more acute the larger the brain, and one would expect lateralization to be especially prominent in human brains, where spatial proximity of processing components are a major factor in processing speed (Ringo et al. 1994).

Finally, it is important to point out that different aspects of "processing emotion" (a term whose vagueness indicates the heterogeneous set of processes that it subsumes) may rely on different hemispheres. There is considerable evidence for a right hemispheric specialization especially for retrieval of knowledge about emotion, but both hemispheres appear to be important in the experience of emotion. Recent data indicate that the sets of emotional experience that are subserved by mechanisms located in the right hemisphere are different from those subserved by mechanisms in the left hemisphere. The data that support this view have tended to show that negative emotions rely preferentially on right hemisphere processes, whereas positive emotions rely preferentially on left hemisphere processes (Brockmeier and Ulrich 1993; Christianson et al. 1995; Davidson and Fox 1982; Davidson 1992; Gainotti et al. 1993; Sackheim et al. 1982; Silberman and Weingartner, 1986).

What Is Special about Emotion and Communication?

Other chapters in this volume discuss communication in a variety of systems, from birds to frogs to primates. The present chapter has dealt with the recognition of stimuli that signal emotions in humans. The reader may wonder what distinguishes emotion, or social communication, from other behaviors and stimuli. Is recognition of emotion or other social signals special in some way? Is the expression of emotion or of other social signals special? The answer is that both the recognition and expression of social signals are special in that they both depend on one another. There is every reason to believe that the expression and the recognition of social signals, including those that signal emotions, have coevolved. To take one example: the human smile is meaningless to most other animals; to many nonhuman primates it will instead be interpreted as a threat gesture. There is thus nothing inherently "happy" about the smile. For a smile to signal anything, there must be special recognition systems in the individuals who are seeing the smile, and these systems must have coevolved with expressions of smiles in order to recognize them as smiles.

The recognition, experience, and expression of emotion are all closely linked. The operationally useful division of emotion into these three domains belies the fact that they all interact. Several lines of evidence bear this out. Perhaps expectedly, the experience and expression of emotion are highly correlated (Rosenberg and Ekman 1994), although, as noted above, the degree of correlation depends on the circumstances under which the emotion is expressed (Fridlund 1994). It has been reported that facial expressions (Adelman and Zajonc 1989) and somatovisceral reponses (Cacioppo et al. 1992) directly cause changes in emotional experience and in brain activity (Ekman and Davidson 1993). Viewing facial expressions causes systematic changes in one's own facial expression (Dimberg 1982) and emotional experience (Schneider et al. 1994), and voluntary expressions affect autonomic state and emotional experience (Levenson et al. 1990). A more complete understanding of emotion will need to acknowledge the rich interdependence of the conscious experience of emotion, the expression of emotion as social signals, and knowledge retrieval. In real life, all three types of process overlap in time and in the extent to which they draw upon various neural systems.

Acknowledgments

I would like to thank my colleagues at the University of Iowa for their extensive help and involvement in all stages of the studies reported in this chapter: Antonio and Hanna Damasio, Daniel Tranel, and Antoine Bechara. My thinking about human emotion and social behavior were shaped substantially by what I learned from my mentors, Mark Konishi and Antonio Damasio. The studies reported here were supported by a Life Sciences Research Foundation Fellowship to R.A., and a Program Project Grant from NINDS to Antonio Damasio.

References

Adelman, P. K. and Zajonc, R. B. (1989) Facial efference and the experience of emotion. *Ann. Rev. Psychol.* 40:249–280.

Adolphs, R., Cahill, L., Schul, R., and Babinsky, R. (1997a) Impaired declarative memory for emotional material following bilateral amygdala damage in humans. *Learn. Mem.* 4:291–300.

Adolphs, R., Damasio, H., Tranel, D., and Damasio, A. R. (1996a) Cortical systems for the recognition of emotion in facial expressions. *J. Neurosci.* 16:7678–7687.

Adolphs, R., Damasio, H., Tranel, D., Frank, R., and Damasio, A. R. (1996b) The right second somatosensory cortex (S-II) is required to recognize emotional facial expressions in humans. *Soc. Neurosci. Abstr.* 22:1854.

Adolphs, R., Lee, G. P., Tranel, D., and Damasio, A. R. (1997b) Bilateral damage to the human amygdala early in life impairs knowledge of emotional arousal. *Soc. Neurosci. Abstr.* 23:1582.

Adolphs, R., Tranel, D., Damasio, H., and Damasio, A. (1994) Impaired recognition of emotion in facial expressions following bilateral damage to the human amygdala. *Nature* 372:669–672.

Adolphs, R., Tranel, D., Damasio, H., and Damasio, A. R. (1995) Fear and the human amygdala. *J. Neurosci.* 15:5879–5892.

Aggleton, J. P., (ed.) (1992a) *The Amygdala: Neurobiological Aspects of Emotion, Memory, and Mental Dysfunction.* New York: John Wiley and Sons.

Aggleton, J. P. (1992b) The functional effects of amygdala lesions in humans: a comparison with findings from monkeys. In *The Amygdala: Neurobiological Aspects of Emotion, Memory, and Mental Dysfunction*, ed. by J. P. Aggleton, pp. 485–504. New York: John Wiley and Sons.

Amaral, D. G., Capitanio J. P., Machado, C. J., Mason, W. A., and Mendoza, S. P. (1997) The role of the amygdaloid complex in rhesus monkey social behavior. *Soc. Neurosci. Abstr.* 23:570.

Baron-Cohen, S., Riviere, A., Fukushima, M., French, D., Hadwin, J., Cross, P., Bryant, C., and Sotillo, M. (1996) Reading the mind in the face: A cross-cultural and developmental study. *Vis. Cog.* 3:39–60.

Bechara, A., Tranel, D., Damasio, H., Adolphs, R., Rockland, C., Damasio, A. R. (1995) Double dissociation of conditioning and declarative knowledge relative to the amygdala and hippocampus in humans. *Science* 269:1115–1118.

Berlin, B. and Kay, P. (1991) *Basic Color Terms: Their Universality and Evolution.* Berkeley, CA: University of California Press.

Blanchard, D. C. and Blanchard, R. J. (1972) Innate and conditioned reactions to threat in rats with amygdaloid lesions. *J. Comp. Physiol. Psychol.* 81:281–290.

Blonder, L. X., Bowers, D., and Heilman, K. (1991) The role of the right hemisphere in emotional communication. *Brain* 114:1115–1127.

Borod, J. C. (1993) Cerebral mechanisms underlying facial, prosodic, and lexical emotional expression: A review of neuropsychological studies and methodological issues. *Neuropsych.* 7:445–463.

Bowers, D., Bauer, R. M., Coslett, H. B., and Heilman, K. M. (1985) Processing of faces by patients with unilateral hemisphere lesions. *Brain Cog.* 4:258–272.

Bowers, D., Bauer, R. M., and Heilman, K. M. (1993) The nonverbal affect lexicon: Theoretical perspectives from neuropsychological studies of affect perception. *Neuropsych.* 7:433–444.

Bowers, D., Blonder, L. X., Feinberg, T., and Heilman, K. M. (1991) Differential impact of right and left hemisphere lesions on facial emotion and object imagery. *Brain* 114:2593–2609.

Breiter, H. C., Etcoff, N. L., Whalen, P. J., Kennedy, N. A., Rauch, S. L., Buckner, R. L., Strauss, M. M., Hyman, S. E., Rosen, B. R. (1996) Response and habituation of the human amygdala during visual processing of facial expression. *Neuron* 17:875–887.

Brockmeier, B. and Ulrich, G. (1993) Asymmetries of expressive facial movements during experimentally induced positive vs. negative mood states: A video-analytical study. *Cog. Emotion* 7:393–406.

Brothers, L. (1997) *Friday's Footprint.* New York: Oxford University Press.

Burke, A., Heuer, F., and Reisberg, D. (1992) Remembering emotional events. *Mem. Cog.* 20:277–290.

Cacioppo, J. T., Berntson, G. G., Klein, D. J. (1992) What is an emotion? The role of somatovisceral afference, with special emphasis on somatovisceral "illusions." In *Emotion and Social Behavior,* ed. by M. S. Clark, pp. 63–98. Newbury Park, CA: Sage Publications.

Cahill, L., Babinsky, R., Markowitsch, H. J., and McGaugh, J. L. (1995) The amygdala and emotional memory. *Nature* 377:295–296.

Cahill, L., Haier, R. J., Fallon, J., Alkire, M. T., Tang, C., Keator, D., Wu, J., and McGaugh, J. L. (1996) Amygdala activity at encoding correlated with long-term, free recall of emotional information. *PNAS* 93:8016–8021.

Cahill, L. and McGaugh, J. L. (1995) A novel demonstration of enhanced memory associated with emotional arousal. *Consc. Cog.* 4:410–421.

Calder, A. J., Young, A. W., Rowland, D., Perrett, D. I., Hodges, J. R., and Etcoff, N. L. (1996) Facial emotion recognition after bilateral amygdala damage: Differentially severe impairment of fear. *Cog. Neuropsych.* 13:699–745.

Chapman, W. P., Schroeder, H. R., Geyer, G., Brazier, M. A. B., Fager, C., Poppen, J. L., Solomon, H. C., and Yakovlev, P. I. (1954) Physiological evidence concerning importance of the amygdaloid nuclear region in the integration of circulatory function and emotion in man. *Science* 120:949–950.

Christianson, S.-A., Saisa, J., and Silfvenius, H. (1995) The right hemisphere recognizes the bad guys. *Cog. Emotion* 9:309–324.

Damasio, A. R. (1994) *Descartes' Error: Emotion, Reason, and the Human Brain.* New York: Grosset/Putnam.

Damasio, A. R. (1995) Toward a neurobiology of emotion and feeling: Operational concepts and hypotheses. *The Neuroscientist* 1:19–25.

Damasio, H. and Damasio, A. R. (1989) *Lesion Analysis in Neuropsychology*. New York: Oxford University Press.

Davidson, R. and Fox, N. (1982) Asymmetrical brain activity discriminates between positive and negative affective stimuli in 10-month-old infants. *Science* 218:1235–1237.

Davidson, R. J. (1992) Anterior cerebral asymmetry and the nature of emotion. *Brain Cog.* 6:245–268.

Davis, M. (1992a) The role of the amygdala in conditioned fear. In *The Amygdala: Neurobiological Aspects of Emotion, Memory, and Mental Dysfunction*, ed by J. P. Aggleton, pp. 255–306. New York: John Wiley and Sons.

Davis, M. (1992b) The role of the amygdala in fear and anxiety. *Ann. Rev. Neurosci* 15:353–375.

Dimberg, U. (1982) Facial reactions to facial expressions. *Psychophys.* 19:643–647.

Ekman, P. (1972) Universals and cultural differences in facial expressions of emotion. In *Nebraska Symposium on Motivation*, 1971, ed. by J. Cole, pp. 207–283. Lincoln, NE: University of Nebraska Press.

Ekman, P. (1973) *Darwin and Facial Expression: A Century of Research in Review*. New York: Academic Press.

Ekman, P. (1992) An argument for basic emotions. *Cog. Emotion* 6:169–200.

Ekman, P. and Davidson, R. J. (1993) Voluntary smiling changes regional brain activity. *Psych. Sci.* 4:342–345.

Ekman, P. and Friesen, W. (1976) *Pictures of Facial Affect*. Palo Alto, CA: Consulting Psychologists Press.

Fredrikson, M., Wik, G., Annas, P., Ericson, K., and Stone-Elander, S. (1995) Functional neuroanatomy of visually elicited simple phobic fear: additional data and theoretical analysis. *Psychophys.* 32:43–48.

Fridlund, A. J. (1994) *Human Facial Expression*. New York: Academic Press.

Fried, I., MacDonald, K. A., and Wilson, C. L. (1997) Single neuron activity in human hippocampus and amygdala during recognition of faces and objects. *Neuron* 18:753–765.

Frijda, N. H. (1986) *The Emotions*. New York: Cambridge University Press.

Gaffan, D. (1992) Amygdala and the memory of reward. In *The Amygdala: Neurobiological Aspects of Emotion, Memory, and Mental Dysfunction*, ed. by J. P. Aggleton, pp. 471–484. New York: John Wiley and Sons.

Gainotti, G., Caltagirone, C., and Zoccolotti, P. (1993) Left/right and cortical/subcortical dichotomies in the neuropsychological study of human emotions. *Cog. Emotion* 7:71–94.

Gewirtz, J. C. and Davis, M. (1997) Second-order fear conditioning prevented by blocking NMDA receptors in amygdala. *Nature* 388:471–474.

Gloor, P., Olivier, A., Quesney, L. F., Andermann, F., and Horowitz, S. (1982) The role of the limbic system in experiential phenomena of temporal lobe epilepsy. *Ann. Neurol.* 12:129–144.

Goldstein, L. E., Rasmusson, A. M., Bunney, B. S., and Roth, R. H. (1996) Role of the amygdala in the coordination of behavioral, neuroendocrine, and prefrontal cortical monoamine responses to psychological stress in the rat. *J. Neurosci.* 16:4787–4798.

Grusser, O.-J. (1984) Face recognition within the reach of neurobiology and beyond it. *Hum. Neurobio.* 3:183–190.

Gur, R. C., Skolnick, B. E., and Gur, R. E. (1994) Effects of emotional discrimination tasks on cerebral blood flow: Regional activation and its relation to performance. *Brain Cog.* 25:271–286.

Halgren, E., Walter, R. D., Cherlow, D. G., and Crandall, P. H. (1978) Mental phenomena evoked by electrical stimulation of the human hippocampal formation and amygdala. *Brain* 101:83–117.

Hamann, S. B., Stefanacci, L., Squire, L. R., Adolphs, R., Tranel, D., Damasio, H., and Damasio, A. (1996) Recognizing facial emotion. *Nature* 379:497.

Hamilton, C. R. and Vermeire, B. A. (1988) Complementary hemispheric specialization in monkeys. *Science* 242:1691–1694.

Hatfield, T., Han, J.-S., Conley, M., Gallagher, M., and Holland, P. (1996) Neurotoxic lesions of baso-lateral, but not central, amygdala interfere with Pavlovian second-order conditioning and reinforcer de-valuation effects. *J. Neurosci.* 16:5256–5265.

Hauser, M. D. (1993) Right hemisphere dominance for the production of facial expression in monkeys. *Science* 261:475–477.

Hauser, M. D. (1996) *The Evolution of Communication.* Cambridge, MA: MIT Press.

Heath, R. G., Russell, R. M., and Mickle, W. A. (1955) Stimulation of the amygdaloid nucleus in a schizophrenic patient. *Am. J. Psychiat.* 111:862–863.

Heller, W. (1993) Neuropsychological mechanisms of individual differences in emotion, personality, and arousal. *Neuropsychol.* 7:476–489.

Heuer, F. and Reisberg, D. (1990) Vivid memories of emotional events: The accuracy of remembered minutiae. *Mem. Cog.* 18:496–506.

Izard, C. E. (1992) Basic emotions, relations among emotions, and emotion-cognition relations. *Psychol. Rev.* 99:561–565.

Jacobson, R. (1986) Disorders of facial recognition, social behavior and affect after combined bilateral amygdalotomy and subcaudate tractotomy—A clinical and experimental study. *Psych. Med.* 16:439–450.

James, W. (1884) What is an emotion? *Mind* 9:188–205.

Johnsen, B. H., Thayer, J. F., and Hugdahl, K. (1995) Affective judgment of the Ekman faces: A dimen-sional approach. *J. Psychophys.* 9:193–202.

Johnson-Laird, P. N. and Oatley, K. (1992) Basic emotions, rationality, and folk theory. *Cog. Emotion* 6:201–223.

Kesner, R. P. (1992) Learning and memory in rats with an emphasis on the role of the amygdala. In *The Amygdala: Neurobiological Aspects of Emotion, Memory, and Mental Dysfunction,* ed. by J. P. Aggleton, pp. 379–400. New York: John Wiley and Sons.

Killcross, S., Robbins, T. W., and Everitt, B. J. (1997) Different types of fear-conditioned behavior medi-ated by separate nuclei within the amygdala. *Nature* 388:377–380.

Kinsey, K. and Adolphs, R. (1997) Impaired declarative memory for emotional stimuli following damage to the human amygdala. *Soc. Neurosci. Abstr.* 23:1582.

Kling, A. S. and Brothers, L. A. (1992) The amygdala and social behavior. In *The Amygdala: Neuro-biological Aspects of Emotion, Memory, and Mental Dysfunction,* ed. by J. P. Aggleton, pp. 353–378. New York: Wiley.

Kluver, H. and Bucy, P. C. (1939) Preliminary analysis of functions of the temporal lobes in monkeys. *Arch. Neurol. Psychiatry* 42:979–997.

LaBar, K. S., LeDoux, J. E., Spencer, D. D., and Phelps, E. A. (1995) Impaired fear conditioning follow-ing unilateral temporal lobectomy in humans. *J. Neurosci.* 15:6846–6855.

Lang, P. J., Bradley, M. M., Cuthbert, B. N., and Patrick, C. J. (1993) Emotion and psychopathology: A startle probe analysis. In *Experimental Personality and Psychopathology Research,* ed. by L. J. Chapman, J. P. Chapman, and D. C. Fowles, pp. 163–199. New York: Spring Publishing Co.

Lazarus, R. S. (1991) *Emotion and Adaptation.* New York: Oxford University Press.

LeDoux, J. (1996) *The Emotional Brain.* New York: Simon and Schuster.

LeDoux, J. E. (1993) Emotional memory systems in the brain. *Beh. Brain Res.* 58:69–79.

LeDoux, J. E., Cicchetti, P., Xagoraris, A., and Romanski, L. M. (1990) The lateral amygdaloid nucleus: Sensory interface of the amygdala in fear conditioning. *J. Neurosci.* 10:1062–1069.

LeDoux, J. E., Iwata, J., Cicchetti, P., and Reis, D. J. (1988) Different projections of the central amygda-loid nucleus mediate autonomic and behavioral correlates of conditioned fear. *J. Neurosci.* 8:2517–2529.

Lee, G. P., Arena, J. G., Meador, K. J., Smith, J. R., Loring, D. W., and Flanigin, H. F. (1988) Changes in autonomic responsiveness following bilateral amygdalotomy in humans. *Neuropsychophys. Neuropsych. Behav. Neurol.* 1:119–129.

Levenson, R. W., Ekman, P., and Friesen, W. V. (1990) Voluntary facial action generates emotion-specific autonomic nervous system activity. *Psychophys.* 27:363–384.

Markowitsch, H. J., Calabrese, P., Wuerker, M., Durwen, H. F., Kessler, J., Babinsky, R., Brechtelsbauer, D., Heuser, L., and Gehlen, W. (1994) The amygdala's contribution to memory—a study on two patients with Urbach-Wiethe disease. *NeuroReport* 5:1349–1352.

Marler, P. (1989) Learning by instinct: Birdsong. *American Speech-Language Association* 89:75–79.

Marler, P. and Terrace, H. (1984) *The Biology of Learning.* Berlin: Springer Verlag.

Merzenich, M. M., Jenkins, W. M., Johnston, P., Schreiner, C., Miller, S. L., and Tallal, P. (1996) Temporal processing deficits of language-learning impaired children ameliorated by training. *Science* 271:77–80.

Meunier, M., Bachevalier, J., Murray, E. A., Malkova, L., and Mishkin, M. (1996) Effects of aspiration vs. neurotoxic lesions of the amygdala on emotional reactivity in rhesus monkeys. *Soc. Neurosci. Abstr.* 22:1867.

Mirsky, R., Adolphs, R., Volkov, I., Bechara, A., Damasio, H., and Howard, M. A. (1997) Single-unit neuronal activity in human amygdala and ventral frontal cortex recorded during emotional experience. *Soc. Neurosci. Abstr.* 23:1318.

Moreno, C., Borod, J. C., Welkowitz, J., and Alpert, M. (1993) The perception of facial emotion across the adult life span. *Developmental Neuropsychology* 9:305–314.

Morris, J. S., Frith, C. D., Perrett, D. I., Rowland, D., Young, A. W., Calder, A. J., and Dolan, R. J. (1996), A. differential neural response in the human amygdala to fearful and happy facial expressions. *Nature* 383:812–815.

Morris, R. D. and Hopkins, W. D. (1993) Perception of human chimeric faces by chimpanzees: Evidence for a right hemisphere advantage. *Brain Cog.* 21:111–122.

Muramoto, K., Ono, T., Nishijo, H., and Fukuda, M. (1993) Rat amygdaloid neuron responses during auditory discrimination. *J. Neurosci.* 52:621–636.

Nahm, F. K. D., Tranel, D., Damasio, H., and Damasio, A. R. (1993) Cross-modal associations and the human amygdala. *Neuropsychol.* 31:727–744.

Nakamura, K., Mikami, A., and Kubota, K. (1992) Activity of single neurons in the monkey amygdala during performance of a visual discrimination task. *J. Neuropsychophys.* 7:1447–1463.

Narabayashi, H. (1972) Stereotaxic amygdalotomy. In *The Neurobiology of the Amygdala*, ed. by B. E. Eleftheriou, pp. 459–483. New York: Plenum.

Nishijo, H., Ono, T., and Nishino, H. (1988) Single neuron responses in amygdala of alert monkey during complex sensory stimulation with affective significance. *J. Neurosci.* 8:3570–3583.

Ojemann, J. G., Ojemann, G. A., and Lettich, E. (1992) Neuronal activity related to faces and matching in human right nondominant temporal cortex. *Brain* 115:1–13.

Oster, H., Daily, L., and Goldenthal, P. (1989) Processing facial affect. In *Handbook of Research on Face Processing*, ed. by A. W. Young and H., D. Ellis, pp. 107–186. Amsterdam: Elsevier Science Publishers.

Phelps, E. A. and Anderson, A. K. (1997) What does the amygdala do? *Curr. Biol.* 7:R311–R314.

Rapcsak, S. Z., Comer, J. F., and Rubens, A. B. (1993) Anomia for facial expressions: Neuropsychological mechanisms and anatomical correlates. *Brain Lang.* 45:233–252.

Rapcsak, S. Z., Kaszniak, A. W., and Rubens, A. B. (1989) Anomia for facial expressions: Evidence for a category specific visual-verbal disconnection syndrome. *Neuropsychol.* 27:1031–1041.

Ringo, J. L., Doty, R. W., Demeter, S., and Simard, P. Y. (1994) Time is of the essence: A conjecture that hemispheric specialization arises from interhemispheric conduction delay. *Cerebral Cortex* 4:331–343.

Rolls, E. T. (1992) Neurophysiology and functions of the primate amygdala. In *The Amygdala: Neurobiological Aspects of Emotion, Memory, and Mental Dysfunction*, ed. by J. P. Aggleton, pp. 143–167. New York: John Wiley and Sons.

Rosenberg, E. L. and Ekman, P. (1994) Coherence between expressive and experiential systems in emotion. *Cog. Emotion* 8:201–230.

Rosvold, H. E., Mirsky, A. F., and Pribram, K. (1954) Influence of amygdalectomy on social behavior in monkeys. *J. Comp. Physiol. Psychol.* 47:173–178.

Rozin, P. (1996) Towards a psychology of food and eating: From motivation to module to marker, morality, meaning, and metaphor. *Current Directions in Psychological Science* 5:18–24.

Russell, J. A. (1980) A circumplex model of affect. *J. Pers. Soc. Psych.* 39:1161–1178.

Russell, J. A. (1994) Is there universal recognition of emotion from facial expression? A review of the cross-cultural studies. In *Human Facial Expression* ed. by A. J. Fridlund, pp. 194–265. San Diego, CA: Academic Press.

Russell, J. A. and Bullock, M. (1985) Multidimensional scaling of emotional facial expressions: similarity from preschoolers to adults. *J. Pers. Soc. Psych.* 48:1290–1298.

Russell, J. A. and Bullock, M. (1986) Fuzzy concepts and the perception of emotion in facial expressions. *Soc. Cog.* 4:309–341.

Russell, J. A. and Fernandez-Dols, J. M., eds. (1997) *The Psychology of Facial Expression*, Cambridge: Cambridge University Press.

Russell, J. A., Weiss, A., and Mendelsohn, G. A. (1989) Affect grid: A single-item scale of pleasure and arousal. *J. Pers. Soc. Psych.* 57:493–502.

Sackheim, H. A., Greenberg, M. S., Weiman, A. L., Gur, R. C., Hungerbuhler, J. P., and Geschwind, N. (1982) Hemispheric asymmetry in the expression of positive and negative emotions: Neurologic evidence. *Arch. Neurol.* 39:210–218.

Scherer, K. (1984) On the nature and function of emotion: A component process approach. In *Approaches to Emotion*, ed. by K. R. Scherer and P. Ekman, Hillsdale, NJ: Lowrence Erlbaum.

Schneider, F., Gur, R. C., Gur, R. E., and Muenz, L. R. (1994) Standardized mood induction with happy and sad facial expressions. *Psych. Res.* 51:19–31.

Silberman, E. K. and Weingartner, H. (1986) Hemispheric lateralization of functions related to emotion. *Brain Cog.* 5:322–353.

Stone, V. E., Nisenson, L., Eliassen, J. C., and Gazzaniga, M. S. (1996) Left hemisphere representations of emotional facial expressions. *Neuropsychologia* 34:23–29.

Tranel, D. and Damasio, A. R. (1993) The covert learning of affective valence does not require structures in hippocampal system or amygdala. *J. Cog. Neurosci.* 5:79–88.

Tranel, D. and Hyman, B. T. (1990) Neuropsychological correlates of bilateral amygdala damage. *Archives of Neurology* 47:349–355.

Weiskrantz, L. (1956) Behavioral changes associated with ablation of the amygdaloid complex in monkeys. *J. Comp. Physiol. Psychol.* 49:381–391.

Young, A. W., Aggleton J. P., Hellawell, D. J., Johnson, M., Broks, P., and Hanley, J. R. (1995) Face processing impairments after amygdalotomy. *Brain* 118:15–24.

Young, A. W., Hellawell, D. J., Van de Wal, C., and Johnson, M. (1996) Facial expression processing after amygdalotomy. *Neuropsychol.* 34:31–39.

Zola-Morgan, S., Squire, L. R., Alvarez-Royo, P., and Clower, R. P. (1991) Independence of memory functions and emotional behavior: Separate contributions of the hippocampal formation and the amygdala. *Hippocampus* 1:207–220.

8 The Neuroendocrine Basis of Seasonal Changes in Vocal Behavior Among Songbirds

Gregory F. Ball

Seasonal Reproduction, Photoperiodism, and Song Behavior in Birds

One of the most conspicuous and well-known features of the natural history of temperate-zone birds is that there are reliable changes over the course of the year in physiology and behavior. Behavioral changes are among the most prominent and obvious changes that occur. In particular, the onset of courtship behavior among birds is an excellent predictor of the arrival of spring. Vocalizations represent a particularly salient aspect of courtship. Among songbirds (members of the suborder passeres or "oscines"), males in many temperate-zone species typically initiate singing more frequently in the late winter and early spring (see, e.g., Cox 1944; Slagsvold 1977). These songs are often produced from a prominent perch, at a high amplitude, and at a high rate of production making them obvious to even the most uninterested observer. In this chapter, I will discuss the endocrine and neural mechanisms associated with seasonal changes in songbird behavior. Although it is well known that many aspects of physiology change seasonally, the discovery by Nottebohm (1981) that there are prominent seasonal changes in the morphology of the song control system in canaries (*Serinus canaria*) surprised many neuroscientists and is still one of the few clear examples of such a marked brain plasticity in an adult vertebrate. The mechanistic control of these seasonal changes in the brain, and the explication of their behavioral significance, has emerged as an area of active interest in the field of avian vocal communication. Questions addressed by these studies are of fundamental significance to the fields of neuroendocrinology and behavioral neuroscience. I will first review basic information about the environmental control of seasonal changes in brain and behavior and then I will discuss the focus of current research and future prospects for new research questions.

Seasonal Changes in Song Behavior

Anecdotal observations collected in the 1700s (see, e.g., White 1789) suggested that songbirds sing at a higher rate in the spring. Only recently, however, has this phenomenon been properly documented. This review provides a selective overview of seasonal changes in brain and song behavior among oscine songbirds.

The current literature suggests five general trends. (1) It is common among temperate-zone male songbirds to sing at higher rates in the spring as compared with other seasons (e.g., Cox 1944; Slagsvold 1977). These seasonal differences in male song are positively correlated with seasonal increases and decreases in reproductive physiology such as gonadal size and hormone secretion in the plasma (Wingfield and Farner 1993). Female song, when it occurs in temperate-zone species, is often produced at a lower rate than male song, and it may not be so closely associated with the spring (Nottebohm 1975). (2) The highest rates of male song output are often associated with the egg-laying period of the female and/or the female's fertile period (e.g., Catchpole 1973; Logan 1983). (3) Among temperate-zone birds there is interspecific variability in the degree to which maximal rates of singing are observed outside the breeding period. For example, robins (*Erithacus rubecula*) living in northern Europe sing at relatively high rates throughout the year (Hoelzel 1986), pausing only in July (Cox 1944). In contrast, most songbird species living sympatrically with robins sing very little in the fall (Cox 1944). (4) The quality as well as the rate of output of song may also change seasonally in some species (Cox 1944). This pattern is possibly related to the occurrence of age-independent (or "open-ended"—see Marler 1987) learning, in that adults are able to acquire new songs throughout the year. Changes in song repertoires have been observed in such age-independent learners as the European starling (*Sturnus vulgaris*; Eens 1997) and the canary (Nottebohm et al. 1986), in which the number of song types and other measures of song complexity may change. However, seasonal changes in song stereotypy have been described in age-limited learners such as the white-crowned sparrow (*Zonotrichia leucophrys*, Smith et al. 1995) and the song sparrow (*Melospiza melodia*, Smith et al. 1997b). (5) The pattern of song production over the course of the year appears to be quite different among tropical birds as compared with temperate-zone species just discussed (Morton 1996). Sex differences in song are much less pronounced and song is produced at a relatively steady rate in many species, perhaps because of year-round territoriality (Morton 1996). Seasonal cycles in hormone secretion are also more muted in some tropical species as compared with temperate zone species (e.g., Levin and Wingfield 1992).

Photoperiodism and Seasonal Breeding in Songbirds

Striking seasonal differences in song behavior among temperate-zone species are but one component of marked seasonal variation in reproductive activity in general. Birds, like many vertebrate taxa, do not maintain the ability to reproduce at all times of the year. Rather reproduction is timed to coincide with the environmental requirements for the successful generation of progeny (Baker 1938; Perrins 1970), and many of the physiological systems that mediate reproduction are only fully developed and active during the breeding season. The environmental factors that birds and other animals utilize to time breeding successfully are referred to as proximate cues (Baker 1938). Proximate cues include stimuli that provide information for predicting the future amelioration of the environment in the spring, which facilitates successful reproduction (Farner and Lewis 1971; Wingfield and Farner 1980). Proximate cues should be distinguished from ultimate cues, which involve the factors that directly limit reproductive success (e.g., food availability and the occurrence of predators).

The prediction process involves an interaction between proximate environmental cues (Wingfield 1980, 1983; Farner 1986; Hahn et al. 1998). One type of cue can be thought of as providing "initial predictive information" (Wingfield 1980, 1983; Farner 1986). These types of cues help to time the initiation and cessation of breeding. The best-known example of this sort of cue is the annual change in photoperiod that appears to either directly "drive" annual changes in gonadal activity in many species or act as a *Zeitgeber* to entrain endogenous rhythms that appear to be circannual in some species (e.g., Follett 1984; Gwinner 1986). Other cues supplement or modify these photoperiodic cues and can speed up or slow down the reproductive cycle (Wingfield 1980, 1983; Farner 1986; Ball 1993; see also the chapter by Wingfield et al. in this volume). Many seasonally breeding birds and mammals experience annual cycles in which the responsiveness of their reproductive system to photoperiod changes. In the winter and spring among temperate-zone avian species a long day above a particular threshold will greatly stimulate many aspects of reproductive physiology. The exact increase in day-length that will be effective in a given population of birds varies among species, as well as within species, depending on their latitude or past photoperiodic experience (see, e.g., Silverin et al. 1993). However, if this threshold is exceeded, the birds will be photostimulated. Photostimulation induces a physiological cascade that includes increases in gonadotropin secretion, gonadal growth, and a range of hormone-dependent reproductive processes, including behavior (Nicholls et al. 1988; Wilson and Donham 1988; Sharp 1996). This state of responsiveness to long day-lengths in birds is known as photosensitivity. However, temperate zone birds gradually loose this neuroendocrine responsiveness to these stimulatory day-lengths over time so that at other times of the year the same day-length is ineffective in eliciting changes in reproductive physiology (for reviews, see Wingfield and Farner 1980; Farner et al. 1983; Nicholls et al. 1988; Wilson and Donham 1988). This state of nonresponsiveness in birds is known as photorefractoriness.

Detailed studies of several songbird species, such as the canary, the European starling, the white-crowned sparrow (*Zonotrichia leucophrys*), the American tree sparrow (*Spizella arborea*), and the Great tit (*Parus major*), have revealed that long days induce both accelerated gonadal growth and the onset of photorefractoriness

(Farner et al. 1983; Nicholls et al. 1988; Wilson and Donham 1988; Silverin 1994). Such a dual response appears to have evolved because a simpler mechanism—for example, one that worked by stimulating breeding when the photoperiod was longer than a given threshold and inhibiting breeding when it was shorter than a particular threshold—would not necessarily have corresponded to the actual period of time when conditions are most conducive for breeding. Photorefractoriness ensures that temperate-zone seasonal breeders stop breeding at an appropriate time consistent with the attainment of successful reproduction.

The stimulatory effects of long day-lengths on reproduction are well documented among birds. This has contributed to the widespread assumption that seasonally breeding birds should be viewed as long day breeders. However, the discovery that short days dissipate photorefractoriness and that the dissipation of this photo-refractory state is an essential prelude for birds to exhibit an endocrine response to an environmental cue of any sort (i.e., a photoperiodic or some other supplementary cue) has led to the notion that one should think of birds as being "switched on" by short days and "switched off" by long days (Nicholls et al. 1988; Sharp 1996). Based on this view of avian breeding cycles, short days normally experienced in the fall grad-ually dissipate a general inhibitory state (i.e., photorefractoriness) and allow a bird to respond to a variety of different cues, including increases in photoperiod, court-ship interactions, changes in temperature, weather, food availability, and so on. In highly photoperiodic species, long days greatly stimulate gonadal growth and related phenomena but also set in motion the gradual acquisition of the regressed gonadal state (i.e., photorefractoriness). This photorefractory state involves an interruption of signals from the brain that can regulate the endocrine system so that environmental cues are no longer able to stimulate the endocrine system. As we will see, the gradual onset of the photorefractory state also involves more general changes in the respon-siveness of the brain to endogenous and exogenous stimuli, which are important to our understanding of the mechanisms controlling seasonal changes in song behavior.

It has become clear that seasonal breeding, especially among songbirds, involves more than just dramatic changes in the functioning of the peripheral endocrine sys-tem. It also involves marked changes in the brain. One such change involves the neuronal system containing the neuropeptide gonadotropin-releasing hormone (GnRH), a neuropeptide that is key to controlling reproduction via the regulation of gonadotropin secretion. There are two forms of this peptide in birds, referred to as chicken GnRH-I (cGnRH-I) and chicken GnRH-II (cGnRH-II). The cGnRH-I form is critical to reproduction, and it is only this form that will be discussed in this review (see Ball and Hahn 1997 for a discussion). Seasonal changes in the regulation of this peptide are an important reason that signals from the brain to the endocrine system are interrupted at the onset of photorefractoriness (Parry et al. 1997; see Ball and Hahn 1997 for a review). Other dramatic changes also occur in the telencephalic song control nuclei. I will first briefly review the occurrence and significance of seasonal changes in the GnRH system, and then I will turn to seasonal changes in the song control system.

Seasonal Changes in Gonadotropin-releasing Hormone Neuronal Systems in the Avian Brain and Their Relation to Species Variation in the Environmental Regulation of Breeding Cycles

All of the songbird species discussed thus far exhibit a photoperiodic response, whereby individuals become absolutely photorefractory to the stimulatory effects of long days (Farner et al. 1983; Nicholls et al. 1988; Wilson and Donham 1988). That is, they either will regress the gonads spontaneously without any decline in photoperiod, cease to be able to grow the gonads even on long days, or both (Nicholls et al. 1988). There are other patterns of the photoperiodic response. For example, some species exhibit a response known as relative photorefractoriness (Robinson and Follett 1982; Follett 1984). This response differs from absolute photorefractoriness phenomenologically in that relative photorefractory individuals remain reproductively active for as long as long days persist. In addition, after gonadal regression after the experience of short day-lengths, relatively photorefractory birds can be restimulated with very long days. They simply require longer days to maintain or reinstate reproductive competence when photorefractory than would be sufficient when maximally photosensitive at the beginning of the breeding season. To date, the only species known to display only this form of photorefractoriness without also becoming absolutely photorefractory is the Japanese quail (*Coturnix japonica*). There may be other examples (e.g., crossbills [*Loxia*], discussed below), and many other species may also be relatively photorefractory prior to becoming absolutely photorefractory, or during dissipation of absolute photorefractoriness (see, e.g., Hamner 1968).

In contrast with species that become absolutely photorefractory, Japanese quail show no decline in hypothalamic GnRH when relatively photorefractory (Foster et al. 1988). They also show no change in hypothalamic GnRH content when photostimulated (Creighton and Follett 1987). In fact, male quail transferred to short days after months of long day stimulation actually show an *increase* in hypothalamic GnRH, as if GnRH production continues but secretion ceases and consequently the peptide accumulates in the brain (Foster et al. 1988). These findings suggest that there may be a difference between the neuroendocrine mechanisms underlying the two forms of photorefractoriness. Because quail are the only birds yet studied that

are known definitively to exhibit relative photorefractoriness, this idea requires
further exploration.

There are other songbird species that may become only relatively photorefractory
and thus may be useful for studies of seasonal GnRH plasticity. For example, red
crossbills (*Loxia curvirostra*) show some of the features typical of quail that characterize relative photorefractoriness. They remain in reproductive condition during
protracted exposure to long days (i.e., at least 225 days on 16L:8D; Hahn 1995).
In addition, their gonads regress as day-length declines in autumn. Importantly,
during this time, days are still longer than those sufficient to stimulate gonadal
development in spring (Hahn 1995). Comparisons of seasonal plasticity in the
GnRH system of these and other species that may become only relatively photorefractory may help to reveal the relationship between patterns of GnRH change
and different types of photoperiodic responses. Crossbills are an example of a species
that exhibit very flexible breeding cycles in that at times they seem to breed almost
independently of photoperiod. They do, however, continue to exhibit photoperiodic
responses. Species that seem to breed in response to the experience of a specific
environmental cue besides photoperiod (such as rainfall) are often referred to as
opportunistic breeders. It is sometimes thought that most tropical species are of this
type, given that photoperiodic changes are minimal in the tropics. Nonetheless,
avian populations in the tropics still exhibit periodic breeding. There is evidence that
some species can measure the very small changes in photoperiod that occur in the
tropics (e.g., Gwinner and Dittami 1985; Hau et al. 1998), and it is also possible that
periodic breeding is in response to some other cue such as rainfall (see Murton and
Westwood 1977).

Studies of the neuroendocrine regulation of GnRH thus suggest that relative photorefractoriness and absolute photorefractoriness may differ with respect to changes
in the GnRH system. Specifically, the synthesis of GnRH appears to be inhibited
during absolute photorefractoriness, but not during relative photorefractoriness. This
difference, if generally true, is of substantial significance to the potential a species
may have for temporal reproductive flexibility. Individuals that maintain active neuroendocrine transduction systems (i.e., GnRH cells containing GnRH) may retain at
all times of the year the capacity for rapid stimulation by environmental cues, even if
relative photorefractoriness has greatly reduced the net hypothalamic drive due to
photoperiod. In contrast, individuals that have switched off GnRH production may
be unresponsive to all manner of cues (Ball 1993; Ball, Besmer et al. 1994). In other
words, species that become absolutely photorefractory would display breeding seasons that are more rigidly timed, with little capacity to adjust breeding duration
flexibly in contrast with species that become only relatively photorefractory.

One of the most commonly studied songbird species in relation to the neural and hormonal mechanisms mediating song learning and production is the zebra finch (*Taeniopygia guttata*, Zann 1996). This species is a native to xeric regions of Australia and has long been claimed to be an opportunistic breeder because its breeding seems to be initiated primarily in response to changes in rainfall (Immelmann 1971). Recent studies suggest that there is no difference in the hypothalamic content of GnRH in gonadally active zebra finches who have unlimited supplies of water as compared with water-restricted finches with regressed gonads (Salvi and Ball 1997). Thus zebra finches do not seem to vary brain content GnRH as a function of their reproductive condition, but in all probability the release of this neuropeptide in the portal vessel system varies as a function of reproductive state. The maintenance of high brain content of GnRH when they are gonadally regressed may be part of the physiological mechanism that allows this species to breed with such flexibility. These contrasting styles in the physiological regulation of breeding should be kept in mind when considering the mechanisms regulating the control of vocal behavior.

The Songbird Vocal Control System

Brief Description of the Neural Circuit Mediating Birdsong Learning, Perception, and Production

Studies of canaries, zebra finches, and a few other songbird species have revealed a well-defined vocal control circuit that includes a group of interconnected, cytoarchitecturally distinct nuclei (see, e.g., Nottebohm et al. 1976; Nottebohm et al. 1982; Bottjer et al. 1989; see also chapters by Doupe and Nottebohm in this volume). Comparative studies of songbirds, and other avian taxa, clearly indicate that many aspects of this circuit represent neural specializations that are unique to the songbird suborder and are associated with the evolution of vocal learning and production in this group of birds (Ulinski and Margoliash 1990; Brenowitz 1991a; Kroodsma and Konishi 1991; Ball 1994). This circuit includes motor nuclei that are involved in song production and nuclei that also exhibit auditory characteristics that are presumably involved in the auditory feedback necessary for vocal learning and perception (Vates et al. 1996; for reviews see Konishi 1989 and Nottebohm 1993). The motor pathway that is necessary for the production of song in adult birds (Nottebohm et al. 1976; Nottebohm 1993) includes a series of nuclei in the telencephalon, mesencephalon, and the brainstem that control the neural output to the vocal production organ, the syrinx. This pathway is illustrated in figure 8.1. It includes a projection from the nucleus hyperstriatum ventrale, pars caudale (HVc, a nucleus now known to be in

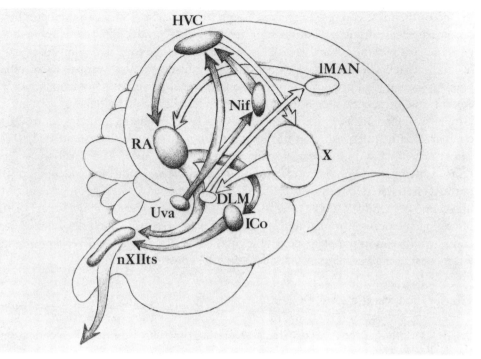

Figure 8.1

Diagram of the of the vocal control system in the song bird brain presented in the sagittal plane. This system has been studied in the most detail in zebra finches (*Taeniopygia guttata*) and canaries (*Serinus canaria*), but it has been described, at least in part, in over a dozen songbird species. The neural pathway mediating the motor production of song consists of the darkly shaded pathway in the figure. In particular, HVc and RA are critical forebrain nuclei that mediate vocal production; lesions to these areas prevent birds from producing all learned vocalizations such as their song. HVc and RA are also connected to one another by a more circuitous pathway that is illustrated by the lightly shaded pathway. This pathway is responsive to auditory stimuli and is needed for the learning of song. (HVc = high vocal center; X = Area X; lMAN = lateral part of the magnocellular nucleus of the anterior neostriatum; RA = robust nucleus of the archistriatum; DLM = the medial part of the dorsolateral nucleus of the anterior thalamus; Nif = Nucleus interface of the neostriatum; Uva = nucleus uvaeformis; ICo = intercollicular complex; nXIIts = tracheosyringeal division of the hypoglossal nucleus.)

the neostriatum and therefore also referred to as the High Vocal Center) to the nucleus robustus archistriatalis (RA) that in turn projects to both the nucleus inter-collicularis (ICo) and the tracheosyringeal division of the XIIth cranial nerve (nXIIts). Efferent projections from motor neurons in this brainstem nucleus inner-vate the vocal production organ, the syrinx. There are other projections made by RA that are not illustrated in the figure for the sake of simplicity. For example, ICo and RA innervate the nucleus retroambigualis and nucleus ambiguus; these are brain-stem structures that coordinate song production with respiration (Wild 1993; Wild 1997; Vicario 1993). RA also sends an ipsilateral projection to the posterior portion of the dorsomedial thalamus (DMP). This nucleus in turn projects to the medial portion of MAN (mMAN) and this area projects back to HVc (Vates et al. 1997; Foster et al. 1997). This latter loop constitutes a feedback pathway within the song system.

As illustrated in figure 8.1, neural impulses from HVc also reach RA through a route more circuitous than that of the motor pathway (Okuhata and Saito 1987; Bottjer et al. 1989). This anterior forebrain pathway consists of a projection from HVc to area X of the lobus parolfactorius (LPO) that in turn projects to the medial portion of the dorsolateral nucleus of the anterior thalamus (DLM). DLM projects to the lateral portion of the nucleus magnocellularis of the anterior neostriatum (lMAN) that in turn projects to RA. The connection from DLM to lMAN to RA actually contains two topographically organized parallel projection pathways (John-son et al. 1995). One portion of DLM projects to the shell of lMAN while another projects to the core of lMAN. The shell and core regions of lMAN project differ-entially to RA or to an adjacent region of the dorsal archistriatum. In adult zebra finches, all of the song control nuclei in this rostral forebrain pathway contain cells that display auditory properties in that they respond to the presentation of species-specific song (Doupe and Konishi 1991). However, these responses appear to be dependent in many cases on the birds being anesthetized (Margoliash 1997). Audi-tory information is conveyed to the song system via connections between the tele-ncephalic auditory area, Field L, and areas adjacent to HVc and RA (Kelley and Nottebohm 1979; Fortune and Margoliash 1995; Vates et al. 1996).

The anterior forebrain pathway has been implicated in the process of song learn-ing. For example, lesions of nuclei in the forebrain pathway of juvenile zebra finches (especially area X and lMAN) before stereotyped species song has been learned and crystallized result in song abnormalities, such as lack of note stereotypy and abnor-mal song length (Bottjer et al. 1984; Sohrabji et al. 1990; Scharff and Nottebohm 1991). Similar lesions, administered after the development of stereotyped song, have no effect on song production in adult male zebra finches. However, neurons in nuclei such as area X within this pathway are active during song production, suggesting that the anterior forebrain circuit may play a larger role in motor production than previously thought (Margoliash 1997).

Many of the forebrain nuclei in the oscine vocal control circuit (e.g., HVc, RA, and MAN) are not recognizable in non-oscines (Ball 1994; Brenowitz 1991a; Kroodsma and Konishi 1991). However, midbrain and medullary components of the circuit (i.e., ICo and nXIIts) are clearly recognizable in all birds that have been investigated to date (Ball 1994; Brenowitz 1991a; Kroodsma and Konishi 1991). Although interesting species variation in the ICo complex has been reported, Puelles et al. (1994) have argued that a basic organization of this complex is similar across avian species. When investigating species variation in the distribution of various markers of neurochemical function in the vocal control system, species differences are also more prominent in forebrain areas than in the midbrain and the brainstem.

Sex Steroid Hormone Receptors in the Song Control Circuit

An important feature of the song control circuit relevant to any discussion of seasonal changes in song behavior and the associated brain areas concerns the distribution of receptors for sex steroid hormones. Selected nuclei in the brains of songbird species, as is the case for all vertebrates, contain cells that possess receptors for gonadal steroid hormones such as the androgens and the estrogens. In general, the distribution of androgen and estrogen receptors in the septal-preoptic area, various nuclei in the hypothalamus, and in the midbrain corresponds to the common pattern that has been described previously in all vertebrate classes (e.g., Martinez-Vargas et al. 1976; Pfaff 1976). In addition to the receptors in these brain areas that seem to be present in all bird species, songbirds possess androgen and estrogen receptors in brain regions that are part of the song control circuit (e.g., Arnold et al. 1976; Gahr et al. 1993; Balthazart et al. 1992). In particular, the telencephalic nuclei HVc, RA, and MAN all appear to contain androgen receptors, based on studies of zebra finches and canaries (Arnold et al. 1976; Balthazart et al. 1992), and in many species, including the canary, HVc contains receptors for estrogens (Gahr et al. 1993). Studies of nonsongbird species such as members of the order *Galliformes* or *Columbiformes* and even studies of suboscines do not reveal the presence of sex steroid receptors in forebrain areas similar to those observed in many songbird species (e.g., Watson and Adkins-Regan 1989; Balthazart et al. 1992; Gahr et al. 1993). Thus part of the neural specialization associated with vocal learning in songbirds seems to be the presence of receptors for sex steroid hormones within certain song control nuclei (Ball 1994). The possible reasons that over the course of evolution the nuclei in the telencephalic part of the vocal control circuit acquired steroid-sensitive neurons is not completely understood. However, there are marked sex differences in many aspects of song behavior and in the vocal control circuit (Arnold 1992; Ball, Casto, and Bernard 1994; Brenowitz 1997). Steroid hormones are often involved in the activation of sexually dimorphic behaviors (Kelley 1988). There are sex differences in both the relative proportion and absolute number of androgen-accumulating cells in lIVc and lMAN of zebra finches (Arnold and Saltiel 1979). Sex differences in the total number of steroid-sensitive neurons in the song control regions has been related to sex differences in the ability to produce complex song (Brenowitz et al. 1996). Though many of these sex differences in the song control system appear to develop independently of gonadal sex-steroid secretion (Balthazart and Ball 1995; Arnold 1997), song is often used in the context of reproduction. It is necessary for successful reproduction that song behavior be activated in coordination with other reproductive behaviors such as courtship displays and copulatory behavior (Nottebohm 1980). It is very common among vertebrate species for sex-steroid hormones to serve as the chemical communication system coordinating reproductive physiology with reproductive behavior (see, e.g., Nelson 1995).

Seasonal and Photoperiodic Studies of Morphological Plasticity in the Songbird Vocal Control System

Seasonal Changes in the Vocal Control System of Adult Songbirds

The coincidence between seasonal changes in song behavior and seasonal changes in the morphology of the vocal control system was first described in canaries by Nottebohm (1981). Males housed in a laboratory in New York State on a naturally cycling photoperiod (latitude approximately 42° N) were collected either in the spring (in April while photostimulated and on long days) when song output was high or in the fall (in September while photorefractory and on short days) when song output was low. The measurement of the boundaries of HVc and RA based on Nissl-stained sections collected from the canaries revealed that the nuclei were 99% and 77% larger in volume, respectively, in the spring birds than in the fall birds. There was no significant difference in the volume of other brain nuclei not involved in song behavior whose boundaries were measured. This pioneering investigation was followed by a series of subsequent studies over the next 15 years.

Photoperiodic Manipulations of the Song Control System   Most studies of "seasonal" changes in the morphology of the song control system have investigated captive birds maintained on artificial photoperiodic regimes that are thought to mimic many of the physiological changes that occur seasonally in the field. As discussed pre-viously, however, photoperiod is initially the key predictive cue that governs sea-sonal changes in the physiology of temperate-zone songbirds. Other supplementary cues such as the social and physical context can then enhance or retard the progres-sion of seasonal changes in reproductive physiology (Wingfield 1980, 1983; Ball 1993; Hahn et al. 1998). Therefore, studies that utilize photoperiodic manipulations to mimic seasonal variation in physiology and behavior must be interpreted with this in mind. Photoperiodic manipulations with captive birds do, however, allow one to attain a relatively high level of experimental control; furthermore, such manipula-tions often induce changes in the volume of song control nuclei similar to those first observed by Nottebohm in canaries. For example, captive, hand-reared, male red-winged blackbirds (*Agelaius phoeniceus*) maintained on a photoperiod of 15L:9D were compared with those maintained on a photoperiod of 9.5L:14.5D. The males on long days had volumes of HVc, RA, and area X that were 20% to 30% larger than those of the birds maintained on short days (Kirn et al. 1989). Studies of cap-tive orange bishop birds (*Euplectes franciscanus*; Arai et al. 1989) housed on artificial photoperiods, whose brains were collected while the males were in either a breeding or a nonbreeding condition also revealed significant differences in the volumes of HVc and RA. Similar photoperiodic differences in the volume of song nuclei such as HVc, RA, and area X have been obtained in studies with captive male Eastern tow-hees (*Pipilo erythrophthalmus*; Brenowitz et al. 1991) and Gambel's white-crowned sparrow (*Zonotrichia leucophrys gambelii*; Smith et al. 1995, 1997a) that were main-tained on either long, springlike photoperiods or short, fall-like photoperiods.

A photoperiodic manipulation of male European starlings (*Sturnus vulgaris*) also revealed significant differences in the volume of HVc, but in this case photosensitive males were placed either on a photoperiod of 11L:13D or on a photoperiod of 16:8D (Bernard and Ball 1995a). In this case, the birds on the *shorter* photoperiod exhibited a larger volume of HVc than the birds on the longer photoperiod. This is because starlings placed on a photoperiod of 11L:13D photoperiod grow their gonads at a slow, steady rate but do not become photorefractory (the photoperiodic threshold for the induction of photorefractoriness is 12L:12D). Starlings maintained on 16L:8D exhibit rapid gonadal growth followed by photorefractoriness involving gonadal regression, plumage molt, and a decrease in the availability of reproductive hormones including the gonadal sex-steroids (Nicholls et al. 1988). Brains from the males maintained on 16L:8D were collected after the birds had become photo-refractory and had regressed reproductive systems, while the birds maintained on 11L:13D are essentially "locked" into a state of increased reproductive activity that is associated with increases in the volume of the song control nuclei.

There is a large literature investigating the parametric relationship between quantitative variation in the amount of photostimulation (i.e., the length of the day and the number of long days experienced) and quantitative changes in reproductive dependent variables such as gonad size or hormone secretion (Farner and Follett 1979; Nicholls et al. 1988; Wilson and Donham 1988). However, it is only recently that the success of experimental approaches involved in understanding seasonal responses in reproductive physiology have been applied to the song control system. Most studies of the relationship between photoperiodic variation and the song control system have only compared birds kept in different photoperiods for at least four to six weeks (e.g., Smith et al. 1995; Smith et al. 1997c). Recently, studies conducted on American tree sparrows (a high arctic breeder) have determined how quickly the song control nuclei increase in response to photostimulation. The surprising finding is that three weeks of photostimulation were sufficient to induce changes in the volume of HVc, RA, and area X (Bernard et al. 1997). Another study found that even one week of photostimulation could significantly increase the volume of HVc and area X (Ball et al. 1996a). These studies raise interesting questions concerning the physiological mechanisms that can mediate such rapid changes in song system morphology.

Field Studies of Seasonal Changes   Another approach to the study of seasonal changes in the song control system utilizes the original design of Nottebohm (1981). Birds are collected at different times of the year, and thus they can be observed while experiencing natural variation in photoperiod. For example, studies of captive canaries sampled either in spring or fall revealed seasonal changes in the volume of RA (DeVoogd et al. 1985). In many other studies, however, wild birds have been collected in the field at different times of the year and the volume of their song nuclei volumes have been measured (e.g., Kirn et al. 1989; Bernard and Ball 1995b; Smith 1996; Smith et al. 1997b). This research strategy has the advantage of investigating changes in birds that have experienced the full range of environmental stimuli associated with the seasonal response. There is the disadvantage, however, that certain uncontrolled variables may influence one's ability to detect seasonal changes in the morphology of song nuclei. These include such factors as variability in age and variability in the progression of the breeding season phenology, so that it is difficult in some cases to know exactly when to collect birds to ensure that they are in different physiological states. It is perhaps for some of these reasons that there has been more variability from the results of field studies than of laboratory studies and that there are a few inconsistencies between the two types of approach.

Investigations of field-caught Eastern towhees detected dramatic differences in the volume of song control nuclei HVc, RA, and area X between short-day, presumably photosensitive males caught in late December–January and photostimulated males caught in spring (March–May; Smith 1996). HVc, for example, was found to be 188% larger in spring males than in winter males (Smith 1996). This difference between groups was greater in magnitude than the difference in HVc volume of 68% reported by the previous laboratory study comparing towhees held on long days versus short days (Brenowitz et al. 1991). Such a difference in magnitude is what one would have expected based on comparisons of various aspects of reproductive physiology measured in either field or laboratory studies; in some species, certain variables such as plasma levels of steroid hormones are far lower in captive animals than in field-caught animals (Wingfield and Farner 1980). Such differences in endocrine physiology between field-caught and laboratory-housed birds are often interpreted as resulting from the fact that wild birds encounter more environmental stimuli that enhance reproductive physiology (Wingfield and Farner 1980). The idea that field-caught birds are somehow more enhanced physiologically than laboratory-house birds, however, does not appear to explain the difference in the size of the song control nuclei in field- versus laboratory-housed towhees. The greater differences in volume observed between the spring and fall field-caught birds as compared with the laboratory-housed birds maintained either for long or short photoperiods was due to the fact that the wild towhees collected in the winter exhibited much smaller volumes of the song control nuclei than did the captive birds maintained for a short photoperiod. It was not the case that the spring-caught birds attained volumes much larger than did the captive birds housed on long days. This suggests that the wild birds collected in the winter experienced inhibitory stimuli not present in the laboratory, rather than that the laboratory-housed birds on long days were deprived of some enhancing stimulus that the wild birds collected in the spring experienced.

A field study of the Nuttal's subspecies of the white-crowned sparrow (*Z. l. nuttali*) also helped illuminate laboratory findings (Brenowitz et al. 1998). An early study that utilized photoperiodic manipulations of this resident white-crowned subspecies failed to detect differences in the volume of HVc and RA when the birds were maintained on long-day as compared with short-day photoperiods (Baker et al. 1984). Recently, however, wild male Nuttal's white-crowned sparrows were collected in both the spring and in the fall. The birds collected in the spring had volumes of HVc, RA, and area X that were significantly larger than the fall-caught birds (Brenowitz et al. 1998). These data suggest that the failure to detect photoperiodic differences in the previous study may have been due to the lack of sufficient supplementary stimulation in the laboratory setting to mimic what happens in the field. Other field studies of wild songbirds have also detected seasonal differences in the volume of various song control nuclei. A study of dark-eyed juncos (*Junco hyemalis*) in Alaska detected a decline between 30% and 40% in the volumes of HVc and area X in adult non-breeding males collected in the October as compared with breeding males collected in June (Gulledge and Deviche 1997). Wild male song sparrows were collected at four times of the year in western Washington State (early and late spring as well as early and late fall), and significant differences were found in the volumes of HVc and RA, with the spring birds tending to have brain areas larger than that of the birds collected in the fall (Smith et al. 1997b).

Other cases studies of field-caught birds have failed to detect the differences in volume of song control nuclei that had been observed in laboratory situations. For example, comparisons of laboratory-reared male red-winged blackbirds held on photoperiods of either 15L:9D or 9.5L:14.5D revealed volumes of HVc and area X significantly larger in the long-day birds than in the short-day birds (Kirn et al. 1989). However, wild males collected in either May or October did not have significant differences in the volume of song control nuclei such as HVc, RA, and area X, though the brainstem motor nucleus nXII that innervates the syrinx was significantly larger in the spring birds than in the fall birds (Kirn et al. 1989). In this study, detailed physiological data were not collected, so it is hard to know exactly what the condition the birds were in when collected. One of the most thorough field studies involved the collection of wild male and female starlings during every month for an entire year in Maryland (Bernard and Ball 1995b). Though the birds exhibited a clear annual cycle in reproductive activity (i.e., gonad size and hormone levels), significant differences in the volumes of HVc and RA were not detected. These were found to be the largest in April but such increases in volume were not significantly different from those measured during other months of the year (Bernard and Ball 1995b). The social context and singing behavior of these birds was unknown. Perhaps seasonal changes in the song control system only occur in association with certain changes in song behavior that the birds caught in this study did not experience.

What Exactly Is Changing When the Vocal Control Nuclei Exhibit Seasonal Changes in Volume?

Thus far, discussion of seasonal changes in the song control system has focused on variation in the volume of particular nuclei. Studies of volume require that one be able to utilize unambiguous boundaries of a brain nucleus. Though the nuclei in the song control system are cytoarchitecturally distinct, there has been some disagreement over how to define the border of a nucleus. Furthermore, changes in nuclear volume, though indicative of substantial neuroplasticity, constitute a rather gross measure of brain activity and raise several questions concerning the cellular basis of the observed change in volume. Such information is critical for an understanding of the significance of an observed change in volume. I will consider both of these issues below.

How Should One Define the Boundary of a Song Control Nucleus, and Does It Matter?
The initial investigations of seasonal changes in the song system employed standard histological methods (i.e., Nissl stains) to explore changes in the song nuclei (Notte-bohm 1981). Most of the vocal control nuclei are cytoarchitectonically distinct, and the boundaries of the nuclei in Nissl-stained material are generally unambiguous, especially when compared with nuclei in other parts of the avian brain such as the hypothalamus. The presence of these sharp nuclear boundaries has been identified as one of the advantages of studying the song control system (Arnold 1990). However, a study by Gahr (1990) used additional criteria to delineate the boundaries of HVc in male canaries and to investigate seasonal changes in volume. Although Gahr repli-cated the seasonal change in Nissl-stained material, no seasonal variation was found when the volume of HVc was measured using the distribution of cells immunore-active for the estrogen receptor. This study also utilized the distribution of cells projecting from HVc to area X (identified by injecting a retrograde tracer in area X) as a basis for defining nuclear boundaries and found no seasonal changes in volume. Subsequent studies in canaries were somewhat equivocal. One study also found that HVc volume in male canaries as defined by the distribution of RA-projecting neu-rons did not change over the course of the year (Kirn et al. 1991), but another study did find that when the boundaries of HVc were defined in this way, canaries col-lected in October had a smaller volume than birds collected in November, January, or July (Nottebohm et al. 1994). In both of these studies, however, Nissl-defined boundaries were not investigated, so one does not know if changes in the boundaries of HVc based on Nissl criteria actually occurred.

These studies raise general questions concerning the significance and appropriate-ness of using Nissl-defined boundaries to infer functional changes in the song control system related to season or even to assess variation in the song system in general within a species, such as the occurrence of sex differences in nuclear volume. Like all methods, Nissl stains are limited in the information they provide. These stains darken those parts of a cell that are highly basophilic, such as free ribosomes and ribosomes bound to the rough endoplasmic reticula (Raine 1989). Because ribo-somes are important organelles in the cascade of events involved in protein synthesis, it is likely that Nissl stains are good indicators of relative cellular activity (Raine 1989). That is, cells that stain more darkly are presumably more active than cells that stain less darkly. In the case of the song system, many of the nuclei in the circuit are remarkably distinct in Nissl-stained material. The darkness, and in some cases, the size and/or density of cells within the various song nuclei are often used to define the boundaries of the nuclei and hence their volumes. It is these Nissl-defined boundaries that are observed to change seasonally. Therefore it is important to be reminded that cell activity and other measures of underlying structure need not always co-vary. Also, Nissl preparations appear to work best in identifying the cell bodies of neurons. They do not allow one to identify glial cells easily, because these cells contain too few ribosomes to accumulate substantial amounts of the Nissl dye (Nauta and Feirtag 1986).

Following the studies by Gahr (1990) and Kirn et al. (1991), three different laboratories have compared and assessed the boundaries of HVc and other song nuclei based on multiple criteria for boundary definition. For example, results from Nissl-stained material have been contrasted with results from neurotransmitter and hormone receptor autoradiography (Johnson and Bottjer 1993; Ball, Casto, and Bernard 1994; Bernard and Ball 1995a), peptide and hormone receptor immunohistochemistry (Ball et al. 1995a; Ball et al. 1995b; Soma et al. 1997), tract-tracing methods (Johnson and Bottjer 1993; Smith et al. 1997a), and enzyme stains (Smith et al. 1997a). These studies have investigated males and females (Bernard et al. 1993; Ball, Casto, and Bernard 1994; Ball et al. 1995a,b) as well as male birds in different hormonal (Johnson and Bottjer 1993), photoperiodic (Bernard and Ball 1995a; Smith et al. 1997a), and seasonal (Soma et al. 1997) conditions. Evidence points to a congruence between all these different neurohistological techniques. The following review is restricted to those studies that are most relevant to seasonal changes in the song control system. It is important to appreciate, however, that when multiple measures of a nuclear boundary are utilized, they are more apt to be in agreement rather than in disagreement (see Gahr 1997a,b; Ball and Balthazart 1997; Bottjer and Johnson 1997; Brenowitz and Smith 1997 for discussion of these issues).

As previously discussed, Bernard and Ball (1995a) performed photoperiodic manipulations to place male European starlings into different physiological conditions. They also used two different histological markers, a Nissl stain and the high density of α_2-adrenergic receptors in HVc and other song control nuclei as determined by autoradiography, which allows one to delineate the boundaries of the nuclei. Photosensitive male starlings were placed on 11L:13D or 16L:8D photoperiods for at least 5 months. Birds on 11L:13D have recrudesced gonads and high levels of circulating testosterone in the plasma. In contrast, starlings maintained on 16L:8D initially show marked gonadal growth. However, after about 6–8 weeks the birds are photorefractory (i.e., the gonads are regressed and testosterone falls to undetectable levels). The volume of the HVc was 44% larger in the 11L:13D than in

16L:8D birds in Nissl-stained tissue. The density of α_2-adrenergic receptors as determined by *in vitro* receptor autoradiography with [^{3}H] p-amino-clonidine (PAC) is higher in HVc than in the surrounding neostriatum, clearly delineating the boundaries of the nucleus (see figure 8.2). Bernard and Ball (1995a) reconstructed the volume of HVc using PAC autoradiography on adjacent sections. The results were identical to those from the Nissl-stained tissue. Thus two histochemical markers indicate a photoperiodic difference in the HVc volume of male starlings. Part of what changes seasonally in HVc in starlings involves the noradrenergic projection to this nucleus.

Gambel's white-crowned sparrows were maintained on either 8L:16D or 20L:4D and the boundaries of HVc were compared using three different histochemical markers (Smith et al. 1997a). The Nissl-defined boundaries of HVc were compared with the boundaries based on staining for acetylcholinesterase and the distribution of neurons that project to area X. As had been previously reported by these authors for this species, the volume of HVc based on Nissl-stained sections was significantly larger in the birds maintained on long days than in the birds maintained on short days. A nearly identical difference in HVc volume between the long-day birds and the short-day birds was observed when the volume of HVc was calculated using the high density of acetylcholinesterase staining or the distribution of neurons projecting from HVc to area X. Thus in this study multiple markers of the boundaries of HVc were in full agreement.

A study by Johnson and Bottjer (1993) examined the correspondence between the boundaries of HVc in castrated male canaries given different hormone treatments, as defined by Nissl stain, projection neurons to RA and area X, and in vivo autoradiography for androgen receptors. As will be reviewed, the manipulation of testosterone can lead to changes in nuclear volumes similar to that which has been observed when birds are collected at different times of the year. Johnson and Bottjer (1993) found that HVc volume in Nissl-stained tissue is significantly larger in testosterone-treated birds than in birds given a combination of an anti-androgen, flutamide, and an aromatase inhibitor, 1,4,6-androstratriene-3,17-dione. Volumes were also reconstructed for two animals in each group from retrograde labeling of HVc from RA and area X. The volumes as defined by Nissl-stained tissue and RA-projection neurons corresponded closely, but area X-projection neurons indicated a larger HVc volume in all cases. This difference appears to result from the labeling of a group of cells located medial to Nissl-defined HVc.

What Is the Cellular Basis of the Observed Changes in Volume?   The surprising discovery of seasonal changes in the volume of specific nuclei in the adult brain raises a number of important questions concerning the cellular basis of this phenomenon.

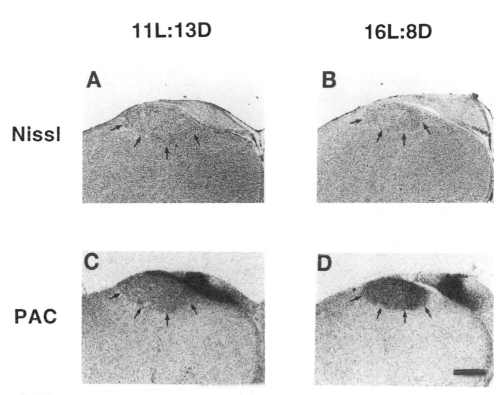

11L:13D   **16L:8D**

Figure 8.2
The top panels show photomicrographs of Nissl-stained coronal sections containing HVc in male starlings housed on 11L:13D (A) or 16L:8D (B) photoperiods. The distribution of α_2-adrenergic receptors in HVc in sections adjacent to those pictured in panels A and B are presented in the autoradiograms pictured in panels C (11L:13D) and D (16L:8D). The autoradiographic images were generated by incubating sections with the α_2-adrenergic receptor agonist, [^{3}H] p-amino clonidine (PAC). The high density of receptors in HVc relative to the surrounding neostriatum allows for clear delineation of the boundaries of HVc. Note the close correspondence between the boundaries of HVc as defined by the Nissl stain and the distribution of α_2-adrenergic receptors. Scale bar = 1mm. Taken from Bernard and Ball 1995a.

One class of questions has already been addressed. If one uses various indicators of the cell phenotype to measure the boundaries of a nucleus, one does detect changes in volume in most cases. However, even if it is clear that a seasonal change in the volume of a brain nucleus involves changes in multiple aspects of the cell phenotype, one still needs to establish what types of morphological changes are occurring in these cells. There are two important classes of questions about cellular changes that one can address. The first class of questions concerns what cell types are changing, that is, neurons, glia, or both? The second type of question concerns what happens to the cell type(s) that change: are there changes in cell number, cell size, cell shape, other aspects of cell morphology (such as the organelles or the chemical phenotype of the cell), or some combination of these changes? Most studies have concentrated on changes in neurons or presumed neurons.

One of the first questions addressed in the literature was whether seasonal changes in the brain involves actual changes in cell number. For brain nuclei to wax and wane seasonally based on changes in cell number would require that adult neurogenesis occur in the songbird brain. This is exactly what Goldman and Nottebohm (1983) investigated. They injected [^{3}H] thymidine (a precursor of DNA formation that allows one to identify newly dividing cells) into adult male and female canaries. Unexpectedly, they found that new neurons are born in the ventricular zone and migrate to brain areas throughout the forebrain including song control nuclei such as HVc. This finding was unexpected because it was previously thought that in homeothermic vertebrates, new neurons are not produced in adulthood. Adult neurogenesis in the avian brain is not specific to the song system nor is it specific to songbirds (Nottebohm 1989; Ling et al. 1997). However, there is interesting inter- and intraspecific variation in neurogenesis within HVc. For example, new neurons that project from HVc to RA are incorporated at a higher rate in canaries, which continue to learn new songs throughout their lives (and show seasonal changes in the volume of their song control nuclei), than in zebra finches, which are age-limited learners (Nordeen and Nordeen 1988; Alvarez-Buylla, Kirn, and Nottebohm 1990). Also, the incorporation of new projecting neurons in canaries changes over the course of the season, peaking in October and March (Alvarez-Buylla, Kirn, and Nottebohm 1990; Kirn et al. 1994). Furthermore, the survival time of new neurons varies seasonally, with most neurons born in May dying four months later, whereas neurons born in October live at least for four months (and perhaps much longer, though the limit of life has not been measured yet).

Seasonal changes in cell number have been reported in HVc of towhees (Brenowitz et al. 1991), white-crowned sparrows (Smith et al. 1995), and song sparrows (Smith et al. 1997b), with lower numbers being reported in the fall than in the spring.

Thus a component of the seasonal change in the volume of HVc may involve seasonal differences in the number of neurons, owing in part to the differential survival or migration of neurons born in May as compared with the fall. Changes in neuron number have not been detected in RA, though studies of white-crowned sparrows (Smith et al. 1995) and song sparrows (Smith et al. 1997b) have detected changes in somal size and cell spacing associated with a seasonal change in volume. Again in this case cells tend to be smaller and more densely packed in the fall than in the spring. These data suggest, as one might expect, that the cellular basis of a seasonal change in brain nucleus volume may vary among the different song control nuclei.

In addition to these seasonal changes in cell size and cell number, seasonal changes in synaptic and dendritic morphology have also been identified (DeVoogd et al. 1985; Clower et al. 1989; Hill and DeVoogd 1991). In female canaries, short fall photoperiods are associated with reductions in the size of pre- and postsynaptic profiles in RA and in the number of transmitter vesicles per synapse (DeVoogd et al. 1985). A similar reduction in the number of synaptic vesicles in nXIIts was observed in female canaries collected in the fall as compared with female canaries collected in the spring (Clower et al. 1989). Dendritic fields in RA and the density of dendritic spines for neurons in RA were also found to be smaller in male red-winged blackbirds maintained on short days than in those maintained on long days (Hill and DeVoogd 1991).

Thus changes in the volume of song control nuclei provide markers for the occurrence of neuroplasticity at the cellular level. Boundaries of brain nuclei based on cells expressing specific cellular phenotypes do change seasonally. These changes in the song control nuclei can also involve changes in cell number, cell size, and aspects of synaptic and dendritic morphology. However, important questions at the cellular level still remain unanswered.

What Don't We Know and What Should Be Done in the Future? Recent work on steroid hormone effects on brain functioning has suggested that glial cells may be an important target of steroid hormones (Garcia-Segura et al. 1996). Studies of the importance of changes in glia during the development of the song control system have been initiated (Nordeen and Nordeen 1996). Changes in glia may be an important part of the mechanism mediating seasonal neuroplasticity in the song control system and should be investigated.

A second area of ignorance concerns the consequences of seasonal changes in the song control system for synaptic physiology. In vitro slice preparations have been developed for use in the zebra finch song system that have been very effective in elucidating the synaptic mechanisms underlying song learning (see, e.g., Mooney and

Konishi 1991; Mooney 1992). If such approaches could be adapted to canaries or other photoperiodic species, the synaptic properties of the HVc and lMAN inputs to RA could be compared in birds in different seasonal conditions. This could provide invaluable insight into the cellular consequences of these seasonal changes in song control nucleus volume.

Is Testosterone the Primary Endogenous Factor Mediating Seasonal Changes in the Vocal Control System?

A major endogenous factor responsible for seasonal changes in song behavior and the song control system is seasonal variation in plasma levels of testosterone, a sex-steroid hormone that coordinates many aspects of reproductive physiology and behavior in wild birds (Wingfield and Farner 1993). However, many aspects of the action of testosterone remain to be elucidated. For example, the effectiveness of testosterone may vary as a function of the time of year due to variation in the sensitivity of the brain to the steroid. Also, the target of testosterone action may not always be the song control system itself; the steroid could, for example, be acting transsynaptically. Finally, many physiological systems change seasonally. In addition to the hypothalamo-hypophyseal-gonadal axis, seasonal variation in other systems could also be involved in the regulation of seasonal changes in song behavior and the song control system.

Evidence Supporting the Role of Testosterone in Regulating Seasonal Changes in the Song Control System   As alluded to previously, a preponderance of evidence suggests that seasonal fluctuations in plasma concentrations of the gonadal sex-steroid hormone testosterone are the primary endogenous signal mediating seasonal changes in volume and other aspects of the song control nuclei. Several different kinds of studies support the contention that testosterone is a potent regulator of the size of HVc in canaries and is the main factor regulating seasonal changes in the vocal control system of canaries, the species in which seasonal changes in the vocal control nuclei were first discovered. First, laboratory studies on canaries indicate that the song nuclei are large when testosterone titers are high and smaller when testosterone titers are low (Nottebohm et al. 1986, 1987). Second, castration of males at ages of 5–10 days leads to decreased song output and a decrease in HVc and RA volume (Nottebohm 1980). Also, Johnson and Bottjer (1993) castrated adult male canaries and provided testosterone replacement to some of these males. They found that HVc volume was significantly larger in testosterone-treated birds than in birds given a combination of an anti-androgen, flutamide, and an aromatase inhibitor, 1,4,6-androstratriene-3,17-dione. Third, testosterone administration to female canaries, which ordinarily do not sing, not only causes the birds to sing, but also increases the size of the song nuclei (Nottebohm 1980). Fourth, as mentioned above, several song control nuclei have cells that concentrate both androgenic and estrogenic steroids (e.g., Balthazart et al. 1992; Gahr et al. 1993). Fifth, a recent study by Ball et al. (1996b) on male canaries has found that castration attenuates the photoperiodic stimulation of increases in the volume of vocal control nuclei. In this study, the effects of castration on the photoperiodic induction of volume increases in HVc, RA, and area X were investigated in male canaries. Nuclear boundaries were defined based on Nissl-staining characteristics or based on immunoreactivity for the enzyme tyrosine hydroxylase (TH-ir). Photosensitive male canaries (N = 12) were held on short days (7L:17D) and 7 males castrated and 5 sham-castrated. The males were then transferred to long days (16L:8D), and after 6 weeks they were perfused and their brains dissected. Sections were collected throughout the forebrain and alternate sections were either Nissl-stained or stained for TH with an immunocytochemistry procedure. The volume of HVc, RA, and area X as reconstructed based on the Nissl-stained sections was substantially smaller in the castrated males than in the intact males. This difference in HVc was also apparent when one defined the boundaries of HVc based on the dense plexus of TH-ir fibers. Additionally, castration induced an apparent anatomical reorganization of the TH innervation of HVc. TH-ir fibers were more or less randomly distributed in the HVc of intact birds, but they formed dense, basket-like ring structures around a limited number of cells in the HVc of castrates. These data suggest that testosterone is required for the spring increase in song control nucleus volume and that the noradrenergic input to HVc as defined by TH-ir changes seasonally in a testosterone-dependent fashion.

Studies of other species also suggest that testosterone is one of the primary endogenous factors regulating seasonal changes in song system morphology, though the amount of evidence supporting this varies among the different studies. Endogenous testosterone concentrations have been assessed simultaneously with the measurement of variation in the song control nuclei in several songbirds species besides canaries; these species include white-crowned sparrows, song sparrows, eastern towhees, and dark-eyed juncos (Smith et al. 1995; Smith 1996; Smith et al. 1997b; Gulledge and Deviche 1997). In these studies, blood samples were collected from birds either in different photoperiodic conditions in captivity or at different times of the year in wild birds in the field. In all these studies, there is a clear positive correlation between high levels of testosterone in the plasma and large volumes in the song control system. In many species, exogenous testosterone needs to be given to laboratory-housed birds to mimic plasma levels of testosterone measured under field conditions (Wingfield and Farner 1980). Laboratory-housed birds do not experience the full complement of environmental cues that can stimulate androgen secretion (Wingfield and Farner 1980). Such supplementary treatments with testosterone in laboratory-housed white-crowned sparrows have resulted in enhancements in the size of nuclei in the song control system (Smith et al. 1995). Castration of dark-eyed juncos during the breeding season leads to decreases in the volumes of area X and HVc relative to intact males in similar conditions, and castrates treated with testosterone have volumes similar to intact males (Gulledge and Deviche 1997). These data suggest that testosterone is necessary for the maintenance of large volumes of the song control nuclei during the breeding season.

Is Testosterone Equally Effective at All Times of the Year?   Seasonal changes in plasma hormone levels are accompanied in many cases by seasonal changes in the responsiveness of the tissue target to the steroid hormone. Such changes may constrain the ability of steroids to induce a biological response. Therefore, testosterone may not be equally effective in inducing changes in song behavior and in the song control system at all times of the year. Studies of estrogen-induced nest building in canaries, for example, were among the first to identify seasonal changes in the effectiveness of sex-steroid hormones (Steel and Hinde 1972; see Hinde and Steel 1978 for a review). The same dose of estradiol that activates intense nest-building in birds housed during a springlike photoperiod is ineffective when administered to photorefractory birds held for a winterlike day length (Steel and Hinde 1972). Similar seasonal alterations in steroid-sensitive processes have been observed in a large number of seasonally breeding vertebrate species (see Turek and Van Cauter 1994 for a review).

Studies of canaries have also revealed seasonal changes in the effectiveness of testosterone in stimulating song production and changes in song system morphology. Female canaries implanted with testosterone during springlike photoperiods exhibited higher rates of singing and a greater magnitude of changes in synaptic morphology in nucleus RA than females treated with a similar dose of testosterone maintained on short days characteristic of fall (DeVoogd et al. 1985). Photorefractoriness attenuates the stimulatory effects of testosterone on the volumes of song control nuclei in European starlings (Bernard and Ball 1997). One group of long-day photorefractory males (16L:8D) was exposed to exogenous testosterone, and two groups of short-day photosensitive birds (8L:16D) were implanted with either testosterone or blank (control) capsules. After eight weeks, testosterone levels were elevated in both groups of testosterone-implanted birds and were not elevated in control animals. HVc volumes were larger in testosterone-implanted photosensitive birds than in both testosterone-implanted photorefractory and control photosensitive males, which did not differ (see figure 8.3).

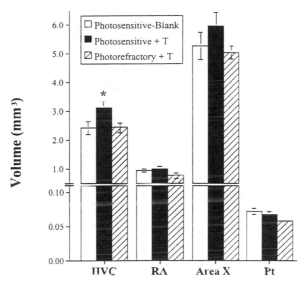

Figure 8.3
Frequency histograms showing the mean (plus standard error) volumes of HVc, RA, area X, and Pt (nucleus pretectalis) in short-day photosensitive, testosterone-treated short-day photosensitive and testosterone-treated long-day photorefractory male starlings. An asterisk indicates a statistically significant difference from the other groups at $p < 0.05$. Note the break in the ordinate to facilitate observation of the measures for Pt. Taken from Bernard and Ball (1997).

These results suggest that photorefractoriness renders the song nuclei of starlings less sensitive to stimulatory effects of testosterone. Plasticity in the starling song system appears to require the coordination of the appropriate hormonal milieu with a permissive photoperiodic condition. In a related study, song nuclei volumes were compared in intact and castrated male European starlings in different photoperiodic conditions (Ball and Bernard 1997). Surprisingly, there were no significant differences in volumes between any of the treatment groups; however, the photostimulated groups appeared to develop photorefractoriness after only four weeks of long-day exposure, making interpretation of the results difficult. Nonetheless, one group of putatively photorefractory birds was implanted with testosterone capsules and had high plasma T levels. Despite four weeks of exogenous T exposure, these birds did not have enlarged song control nuclei. These data suggest that photorefractoriness may attenuate the effects of T on song nuclei volumes in this species.

Is There Evidence That Changes in Day-length Can Influence Seasonal Changes in the Song Control System Independent of the Action of Testosterone? Many studies suggest that changes in day-length have effects on seasonal variation in song behavior and brain morphology that are independent of the actions of testosterone. For example, song rates increased when testosterone-treated male song sparrows on a short day were transferred to a long-day photoperiod (Nowicki and Ball 1989), even though the dose of testosterone did not change. Work on male American tree sparrows provides some of the strongest evidence that there are testosterone-independent mechanisms associated with long-day exposure that affect song control nuclei volumes (Bernard et al. 1997). Intact and castrated adult males were placed into one of three photoperiodic conditions: short-day photosensitive, long-day photostimulated, and long-day photorefractory. The volumes of three song nuclei (HVc, RA, and area X of the parolfactory lobe) were significantly larger in animals housed on long days than on short days, regardless of photoperiodic condition or gonadal state. This is especially noteworthy in the case of the castrated photostimulated birds and both groups of photorefractory birds, because these animals do not have detectable levels of circulating testosterone (see, e.g., Wilson 1986). Thus long-day exposure affected song nuclei volumes in a testosterone-independent fashion. However, the intact photostimulated birds had the largest nuclei of all the groups, suggesting that photoperiod has both testosterone-dependent and testosterone-independent effects on song control nuclei volumes in tree sparrows (see figure 8.4). A similar study was con-

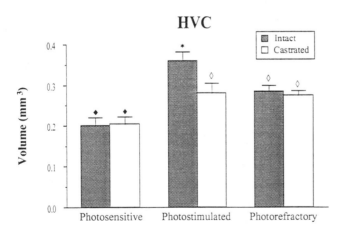

Photoperiodic Condition

Figure 8.4
Bar graphs showing the mean volume (plus standard error) of HVc in intact (shaded) and castrated (white) male American tree sparrows in different photoperiodic conditions. Bars with different symbols differ significantly. Taken from Bernard et al. (1997).

ducted on Gambel's white-crowned sparrows (Smith et al. 1997c). It was found that long-day photoperiods exerted small but significant effects on the volume of HVc and the size of neurons in RA in castrated males in comparison with the much larger effects that occurred in castrated males that received exogenous testosterone. These data suggest that testosterone is the primary factor mediating seasonal changes in the morphology of the song control system but that photoperiod may also act via mechanisms independent of steroid hormone levels.

A study of the photoperiodic regulation of neuron death in adult canaries reached a similar conclusion. A change in photoperiod from 14.5L:9.5D to 8L:16D for only two weeks resulted in a dramatic increase in cell death in male canaries as compared with males maintained on the 14.5L:9.5D photoperiod (Kirn and Schwabl 1997). This increase occurred even though there was no apparent change in plasma levels of testosterone (Kirn and Schwabl 1997). The higher rate of cell death in short-day birds was associated with a statistically nonsignificant decrease in the volume of HVc.

What Do We Not Know and What Should Be Done in the Future?   All the studies reviewed above suggest that (1) the sensitivity of the brain to the action of testosterone action is dynamic, and one needs to take this into account to understand the effects of testosterone on seasonal changes in song and the song control system; and (2) hormone systems other than the gonadal sex-steroids may be involved in the regulation of seasonal changes in the song control system.

Possible Mechanisms Mediating Seasonal Changes in Responsiveness to Steroids
The mechanisms mediating these seasonal differences in the responsiveness to testosterone have not yet been elucidated; however, photoperiodic differences in steroid hormone receptors or in steroid metabolism are obvious candidates. Photoperiodic changes in the mRNA for steroid receptors in the song control nuclei have recently been described in canaries (Gahr and Metzdorf 1997), though a previous study suggested that the distribution of estrogen-receptor-containing cells in HVc does not change seasonally in canaries (Gahr 1990). Testosterone is known to regulate androgen-receptor distribution (Brenowitz and Arnold 1990; Johnson and Bottjer 1993) as well as androgen-receptor mRNA levels (Nastiuk and Clayton 1995). Therefore, it is possible that seasonal changes in steroid hormone concentrations influence seasonal changes in the sensitivity of the brain to steroids.

Both androgenic and estrogenic metabolites of testosterone appear to be necessary for the full expression of song (e.g., Harding et al. 1983, 1988). Therefore, changes in testosterone-metabolizing enzymes such as aromatase and 5α- and 5β-reductase may play a role in changes in testosterone sensitivity induced by changes in photoperiod. All of these enzymes have been localized in song control nuclei in zebra finches (Vockel et al. 1990). In starlings, 5β-reductase activity is enhanced in the hypothalamus and the hyperstriatum of photorefractory males in July relative to breeding birds in May (Bottoni and Massa 1981). This may account, in part, for the reduced sensitivity of HVc to testosterone in photorefractory males. The 5β-reduced androgens are regarded as biologically inactive (Balthazart 1989); therefore, increased 5β-reductase activity may act as an inactivation pathway for testosterone in the song system (as well as other parts of the brain).

It is not known if steroid receptors or the activity of steroid metabolizing enzymes can change seasonally independently of seasonal changes in the plasma levels of steroids. Characterization of photoperiodic effects on steroid receptor concentration, distribution, and synthesis as well as photoperiodic effects of steroid metabolism will provide useful information regarding possible receptor-mediated mechanisms of photoperiodic changes in steroid sensitivity.

The Possible Importance of Transsynaptic Effects of Steroid Hormones   One plausible hypothesis for seasonal variation in steroid hormone effectiveness is that afferent inputs such as those provided by noradrenergic system to steroid-sensitive areas such as the song control nuclei could play a significant role in the regulation of the effectiveness of steroid hormone action. A general concept emerging in the study of hormones and behavior is that steroids may regulate brain morphology both directly and indirectly. In a direct action, steroids act on cells in the brain area of interest; an indirect action (transsynaptically) involves action on cells at a distant brain site that then project to the site of interest and modify neural activity (Beyer and Feder 1987; Balthazart and Ball 1995). This mode of action is well illustrated by studies of sex steroid feedback on the GnRH system. Sex steroids are known to exert negative feedback on GnRH immunoreactive cells, but these neurons do not contain receptors for sex-steroid hormones. Rather, the effects of steroids on these neurons are mediated by changes in the activity of peptidergic (e.g., opioids), catecholaminergic (e.g., norepinephrine), and amino-acid transmitter inputs to the GnRH cells (see, e.g., Barraclough and Wise 1982; Kalra et al. 1997). During the development of the song system, it has been suggested that steroid hormones may influence the development of area X (an area not thought to contain steroid receptors) by acting through HVc (a target for androgens as well as estrogens in many species). Thus seasonal effects of steroids on the morphology of the song control system could be activated by the direct action of sex-steroid hormones on a song control nucleus, or they could exert their effect via a transsynaptic mechanism within nuclei in the song control circuit. Therefore, steroid effects on some nuclei in the vocal control system (such as area X) could be mediated by steroids acting at other target nuclei in the song control system that project to this brain area. Another possibility is that steroid hormones act on nuclei elsewhere in the brain (i.e., the brainstem) that project to the song control nuclei and affect the song control system throuh these pathways. These transsynaptic mechanisms could be acting independently of any hormone effects on the song system, or they could be the intermediary of hormone effects on the song system (i.e., hormones act on the afferent input directly, and then changes in this input modify the morphology of the song control system), or the afferent input could be acting synergistically with direct hormone effects on the vocal control system.

A related idea is that afferent input into a steroid-sensitive area can modify the effectiveness of sex-steroid hormone action (Blaustein et al. 1995). The best evidence for transsynaptic regulation of the steroid-sensitive neural substrate has been collected for noradrenergic inputs to the hypothalamus in rats (Blaustein ct al. 1995). Previous work has shown that catecholamines and in particular norepinephrine can change both the concentration of estrogen receptors (see, e.g., Blaustein et al. 1995) and the activity of steroid-metabolizing enzymes such as aromatase (see Balthazart and Ball 1992 for a review). The importance of afferent inputs in the mediation of steroid action on brain and behavior has received the most attention in relation to the organizational actions of sex steroids during the perinatal period in birds and mammals (Beyer and Feder 1987; Balthazart and Ball 1995). Afferent inputs may also mediate certain aspects of steroid-induced changes in adult brains and behavior, but this mechanism of steroid hormone action in adults remains relatively unexplored. There is already evidence in songbirds that photoperiod can influence afferent noradrenergic inputs into the song control system (Bernard and Ball 1995a) and that the manipulation of circulating testosterone levels by castration and replacement influences the rates of monoaminergic turnover in the vocal control system (Barclay and Harding 1990). An attractive but unexplored hypothesis is that seasonal variation in catecholaminergic afferent input into the song control system is an important factor regulating seasonal changes in the morphology of the vocal control system.

Other Hormone Systems That May Be Important   Several physiological changes occur in response to long days, including the absolute levels as well as the patterns of secretion of other hormones. Of particular interest are changes in melatonin and thyroid hormones. The pineal hormone melatonin may affect the song nuclei. Although circulating melatonin has not been measured in tree sparrows, patterns of melatonin secretion in both birds and mammals are tightly linked to photoperiod in that the duration of the melatonin peak closely parallels the length of the dark phase of the light/dark cycle (see, e.g., Dawson and King 1994; Goldman and Nelson 1993; Kumar and Follett 1993). If the same pattern holds for tree sparrows, birds on 20L:4D, whether photostimulated or photorefractory, would experience similar short-duration peaks in melatonin secretion relative to the longer melatonin peak in photosensitive birds on 8L:16D. Thus, despite other differences between photostimulated and photorefractory animals, the length of melatonin exposure would be similar and, therefore, could account for the nearly identical volume measures in castrated photostimulated birds and in intact and castrated photorefractory birds. Melatonin binding sites have been described in the song nuclei of several species, including house sparrows (*Passer domesticus*) and zebra finches (Gahr and Kosar 1996; Whitfield-Rucker and Cassone 1996); therefore, melatonin may act directly on the song nuclei to have its effects. A recent study in castrated male European starlings does suggest that implants of melatonin can attenuate long-day induced stimulation of HVc volume (Bentley and Ball 1998).

Thyroid hormones represent another physiological variable that may influence song system morphology. There is clear evidence that the thyroid, via the secretion of thyroxine into the blood, is involved in the transition from photosensitivity to photorefractoriness (see, e.g., Wilson and Reinert 1993; see Nicholls et al. 1988 for a review). In European starlings, the evidence indicates that long days elevate plasma levels of thyroxine (Bentley et al. 1997). Although the function of this elevation is unknown at present, it does not appear necessary for the onset of photorefractoriness (Bentley et al. 1997). Thyroid hormone receptors are known to occur in avian brain (Haidar et al. 1993), and the thyroid gland plays an important role in neural development in vertebrates (see, e.g., Lu and Brown 1984).

What Is the Functional Significance of These Seasonal Changes in Volume?

As reviewed previously there are dramatic changes in song behavior across the breeding cycle in songbirds. The functional significance of these seasonal changes in the song control system may seem obvious at first. Birds sing far more in the spring, when the nuclei in the song control system are large, than they do in the fall, when these nuclei are small. However, these changes are not "all or none," in that some singing goes on at all times of the year. In addition to changes in song performance, there are changes in the quality of the song produced. The first theory concerning the functional significance of the song control system addressed the issue of seasonal differences in song quality, in particular the complexity of song. Nottebohm (1981) hypothesized that seasonal changes in the song control system would be restricted to species that are age-independent learners (birds that continue to learn new songs in adulthood), such as canaries, and that the changes would be associated with the acquisition of new auditory memories. It is now clear, though, that species with age-limited learning also exhibit such changes (see, e.g., Brenowitz et al. 1991). Further, although there is a positive correlation between the complexity of the song repertoire and the size of song control nuclei in many songbird species (DeVoogd et al. 1993), a study in marsh wrens has shown that learning a more complex song is not necessarily associated with a larger volume of HVc and other song control nuclei (Brenowitz et al. 1995).

More recent studies have investigated whether there are seasonal changes in motor performance aspects of song correlated with seasonal changes in the song control system rather than with seasonal variation in learned differences in song complexity. Studies of seasonal changes in the song system of white-crowned sparrows (Smith et al. 1995) and song sparrows (Smith et al. 1997b) show that such variations are more clearly associated with changes in song stereotypy rather than with measures of song complexity. The song sparrow study is particularly illuminating. This species exhibits well-documented variability among males in the number of song types. Despite this potential for variability in song type production, males singing in the fall produced the same number of song types as they did in the spring (Smith et al. 1997b). However, there were significant changes in song performance as measured by trill rate and note stereotypy (Smith et al. 1997b). These authors note that there were also substantial changes in song rate between the two seasons that were not assessed quantitatively. However, they point out that in other studies of white-crowned sparrows they observed substantial differences in song rate without significant differences in the song control system, indicating that changes in song rate can occur in the absence of changes in the song control system (Smith et al. 1995). Thus, these authors argue, change in stereotypy rather than song rate represents the key behavioral change correlated with variation in the song control nuclei.

What Should Be Done in the Future?   Measures of song performance other than those assessed to date should be carefully measured in birds in different seasonal states and correlated with seasonal changes in the song control system. For example, studies of different morphs of the white-throated sparrows (*Zonotrichia albicollis*) that sing at different rates have found positive correlations between the size of area X and lateral and medial MAN and song rate (DeVoogd et al. 1995). Though this variation among morphs is probably genetically based, perhaps changes in song rate are another performance variable affected by seasonal changes in the song control system. European starlings exhibit increases in their repertoire size as they age. Older birds also exhibit larger volumes of HVc and RA than yearling birds (Bernard et al.

1996). Among older birds, however, the most significant correlation with variation in the size of HVc is not repertoire size but rather the average song bout length produced by the male (Bernard et al. 1996). Therefore, the length of a given song bout is a performance variable worth investigating in birds at different times of the year. One does, however, need to be sensitive to species differences in song behavior. Song bout length may be a more relevant variable in species such as starlings, which produce long complex songs, rather than species such as white-crowned sparrows, which produce relatively short and discrete song types.

Finally, the song system is involved in the perception of species-typical song as well as its production (Brenowitz 1991b). Studies of zebra finches (Cynx and Nottebohm 1992) and European starlings (Calhoun et al. 1993) have suggested that photoperiod can influence song perception, though there are always questions about whether the motivation to perform a task has changed rather than the perceptual ability. The morphology of the song control system was not measured in these studies. Could seasonal changes in the song system influence certain aspects of song perception? It seems unlikely that peripheral sensitivity to sound would change, but could there be biases in processing by the central nervous that are more apparent at one season than another? There are some hints from studies on other taxa that suggest that these questions are worth pursuing. For example, photoperiod has been shown to attenuate responses of the immediate early gene c-fos to the experience of conspecific urine that induces estrus in prairie voles (*Microtus orchrogaster*; Moffatt et al. 1995). Prairie voles on short days require more urine to be brought into estrus than do voles on long days, and the fos response in the olfactory bulb and the amygdala to urine is attenuated in the short-day animals. The functional basis of this difference is thought to be related to the fact that successful breeding, though possible, is generally much more difficult during the short days of winter than the long days of spring (Nelson 1987; Bronson and Heideman 1994). Fall breeding among temperate-zone songbirds, though rare, does occur on occasion (see, e.g., Payne 1969). This is not really surprising now that we know that the hypothalamo-gonadal axis is "switched on" in the fall. Enhanced supplementary cues can therefore stimulate fall breeding when the conditions are right (Hahn et al. 1998). However, fall breeding is usually associated with poor reproductive success (Payne 1969). Could seasonal changes in the song control system attenuate perceptual responses by the central nervous system to song? It is a hypothesis that is worth investigating. Songbirds show a robust induction of the immediate early gene ZENK to the experience of conspecific song (Mello et al. 1992). The investigation of seasonal changes in this response is one obvious initial study to conduct.

Acknowledgments

I thank Peter Marler for the inspiration he has provided me over the years. Marc Hauser and Mark Konishi provided very helpful editorial assistance. I thank Eliot Brenowitz for a critical review of the manuscript and George Bentley and Jacques Balthazart for discussion and comments on an early version of the chapter. My research on seasonal reproduction in birds is supported by grants from the NSF and the NIH (IBN 951425; NS 35467).

References

Alvarez-Buylla, A., Kirn, J. R., and Nottebohm, F. (1990) Birth of projection neurons in adult avian brain may be related to perceptual or motor learning. *Science* 249:1444–1446.

Arai, A., Taniguchi, I., and Saito, N. (1989) Correlation between the size of song control nuclei and plumage color change in orange bishop birds. *Neurosci. Lett.* 98:144–148.

Arnold, A. P. (1990) The passerine song system as a model in neuroendocrine research. *J. Exp. Zool. Supp.* 4:22–30.

Arnold, A. P. (1992) Developmental plasticity in neural circuits controlling birdsong: Sexual differentiation and the neural basis of learning. *J. Neurobiol.* 23:1506–1528.

Arnold, A. P. (1997) Sexual differentiation in the zebra finch song system: Positive evidence, negative evidence, null hypotheses, and a paradigm shift. *J. Neurobiol.* 33:572–584.

Arnold, A. P., Nottebohm, F., and Pfaff, D. W. (1976) Hormone-concentrating cells in vocal control areas of the brain of the zebra finch (*Poephila guttata*). *J. Comp. Neurol.* 165:487–512.

Arnold, A. P. and Saltiel, A. (1979) Sexual difference in pattern of hormone accumulation in the brain of a songbird. *Science* 204:702–705.

Baker, J. R. (1938) The evolution of breeding seasons In *Evolution: Essays on Aspects of Evolutionary Biology*, ed. by G. D. DeBeer, pp. 161–177. Oxford: Clarendon Press.

Baker, M. C., Bottjer, S. W., and Arnold, A. P. (1984) Sexual dimorphism and lack of seasonal changes in vocal control regions of white-crowned sparrows. *Brain Res.* 295:85–89.

Ball, G. F. (1993) The neural integration of environmental information by seasonally breeding birds. *Am. Zool.* 33:185–199.

Ball, G. F. (1994) Neurochemical specializations associated with vocal learning and production in songbirds and budgerigars. *Brain Behav. Evol.* 44:234–246.

Ball, G. F. and Balthazart, J. (1997) Letter to the editor. *Trends Neurosci.* 20:344.

Ball, G. F. and Bernard, D. J. (1997) Photoperiodic and endocrine regulation of seasonal plasticity in the vocal control system of European starlings. In *Perspectives in Avian Endocrinology*, ed. by S. Harvey and R. Etches, pp. 133–147. Bristol: J. Endocrinology Ltd.

Ball, G. F. and Hahn, T. P. (1997) GnRH neuronal systems in birds and their relation to the control of seasonal reproduction. In *GnRH Neurons. Gene to Behavior*, ed. by I. S. Parhar and Y. Sakuma, pp. 325–342. Tokyo: Brain Shuppan Publishers.

Ball, G. F., Besmer, H. R., Li, Q., and Ottinger, M. A. (1994) Effects of social stimuli on gonadal growth and brain content of cGnRH-I in female starlings on different photoperiods. *Soc. Neurosci. Abstr.* 20:159.

Ball, G. F., Casto, J. M., and Bernard, D. J. (1994) Sex differences in the volume of avian song control nuclei: Comparative studies and the issue of brain nucleus delineation. *Psychoneuroendocrinology* 19:485–504.

Ball, G. F., Absil, P., and Balthazart, J. (1995a) Peptidergic delineations of nucleus interface reveal a sex difference in volume. *NeuroReport* 6:957–960.

Ball, G. F., Absil, P., and Balthazart, J. (1995b) Assessment of volumetric sex differences in the song control nuclei HVC and RA in zebra finches (*Taeniopygia guttata*) by immunocytochemistry for met-enkephalin and vasoactive intestinal polypeptide. *Brain Res.* 699:83–96.

Ball, G. F., Bernard, D. J., and Wilson, F. E. (1996a) Rapid effects of photoperiod on the volume of song control nuclei in American tree sparows. *Soc. Res. Biol. Rhythms* 5:23.

Ball, G. F., Hahn, T. P., Edmonds, E., and Balthazart, J. (1996b) Effects of castration on the volume of song control nuclei and tyrosine hydroxylase immunoreactivity in male canaries. *Soc. Neurosci. Abstr.* 22:1401.

Balthazart, J. (1989) Steroid metabolism and the activation of social behavior. In *Advances in Comparative and Environmental Physiology*, vol. 3, ed. by J. Balthazart, pp. 105–159. Berlin: Springer Verlag.

Balthazart, J. and Ball, G. F. (1992) Is dopamine interacting with aromatase to control sexual behavior in male quail? *Poultry Science Reviews* 4:217–233.

Balthazart, J. and Ball, G. F. (1995) Sexual differentiation of brain and behavior in birds. *Trends Endocrinol. Met.* 6:21–29.

Balthazart, J., Foidart, A., Wilson, E. M., and Ball, G. F. (1992) Immunocytochemical localization of androgen receptors in the male songbird and quail brain. *J. Comp. Neurol.* 317:407–420.

Barraclough, C. A. and Wise, P. M. (1982) The role of catecholamines in the regulation of pituitary luteinizing hormone and follicle stimulating-hormone secretion. *Endo. Rev.* 3:91–119.

Barclay, S. R. and Harding, C. F. (1990) Differential modulation of monoamine levels and turnover rates by estrogen and/or androgen in hypothalamic and vocal control nuclei of male zebra finches. *Brain Res.* 523:251–262.

Bentley, G. E. and Ball, G. F. (1998) Melatonin effects upon seasonal changes in the volumes of song control nuclei in European starlings. *Soc. Neurosci. Abst.* 24:1698.

Bentley, G. E., Goldsmith, A. R., Dawson, A., Glennie, L. M., and Sharp, P. J. (1997) Photorefractoriness in European starlings (*Sturnus vulgaris*) is not dependent upon the long-day induced rise in plasma thyroxine. *Gen. Comp. Endocrinol.* 107:428–438.

Bernard, D. J. and Ball, G. F. (1995a) Two histological markers reveal a similar photoperiodic difference in the volume of the high vocal center in male European starlings. *J. Comp. Neurol.* 360:726–734.

Bernard, D. J. and Ball, G. F. (1995b) Seasonal changes in the volume of song control nuclei in free-living male and female European starlings. *Soc. Neurosci. Abst.* 21:961.

Bernard, D. J. and Ball, G. F. (1997) Photoperiodic condition modulates the effects of testosterone on song control nuclei volumes in male European starlings. *Gen. Comp. Endocrinol.* 105:276–283.

Bernard, D. J., Casto, J. M., and Ball, G. F. (1993) Sexual dimorphism in the volume of song control nuclei in European starlings: Assessment by a Nissl stain and autoradiography for muscarinic cholinergic receptors. *J. Comp. Neurol.* 334:559–570.

Bernard, D. J., Eens, M., and Ball, G. F. (1996) Age- and behavior-related variation in the volume of song control nuclei in male European starlings. *J. Neurobiol.* 30:329–339.

Bernard, D. J., Wilson, F. E., and Ball, G. F. (1997) Testis-dependent and -independent effects of photoperiod on volumes of song control nuclei in American tree sparrows (*Spizella arborea*). *Brain Res.* 760:163–169.

Beyer, C. and Feder, H. H. (1987) Sex steroids and afferent input: Their roles in brain sexual differentiation. *Ann. Rev. Physiol.* 49:349–364.

Blaustein, J. D., Tetel, M. J., and Meredith, J. M. (1995) Neurobiological regulation of hormonal response by progestin and estrogen receptors. In *Neurobiological Effects of Sex Steroid Hormones*, ed. by P. Micevych and R. Hammer, Jr., pp. 324–349. New York: Cambridge University Press.

Bottjer, S. W., Halsema, K. A., Brown, S. A., and Miesner, E. A. (1989) Axonal connections of a forebrain nucleus involved with vocal learning in zebra finches. *J. Comp. Neurol.* 279:312–326.

Bottjer, S. W. and Johnson, F. A. (1997) Letter to the editor. *Trends Neurosci.* 20:344–345.

Bottjer, S. W., Meisner, E. A., and Arnold A. P. (1984) Forebrain lesions disrupt development but not maintenance of song in passerine birds. *Science* 224:901–903.

Bottoni, L. and Massa, R. (1981) Seasonal changes in testosterone metabolism in the pituitary gland and central nervous system of the European starling (*Sturnus vulgaris*). *Gen. Comp. Endocrinol.* 43:532–536.

Brenowitz, E. A. (1991a) Evolution of the vocal control system in the avian brain. *Sem. Neurosci.* 3:399–407.

Brenowitz, E. A. (1991b) Altered perception of species-specific song by female birds after lesions of a forebrain nucleus. *Science* 251:303–305.

Brenowitz, E. A. (1997) Comparative approaches to the avian song system. *J. Neurobiol.* 33:517–531.

Brenowitz, E. A. and Arnold, A. P. (1990) The effects of systemic androgen treatment on androgen accumulation in song control regions of the adult female canary brain. *J. Neurobiol.* 21:837–843.

Brenowitz, E. A., Arnold, A. P., and Loesche, P. (1996) Steroid accumulation in song nuclei of a sexually dimorphic duetting bird, the rufous and white wren. *J. Neurobiol.* 31:235–244.

Brenowitz, E. A., Baptista, L., Lent, K., and Wingfield, J. C. (1998) Seasonal plasticity in the song control system of wild Nutall's white-crowned sparrows. *J. Neurobiol.* 34:69–82.

Brenowitz, E. A., Lent, K., and Kroodsma, D. E. (1995) Brain space for learned song in birds develops independently of song learning. *J. Neurosci.* 15:6281–6286.

Brenowitz, E. A., Nalls, B., Wingfield, J. C., and Kroodsma, D. E. (1991) Seasonal changes in avian song control nuclei without seasonal changes in song repertoire. *J. Neurosci.* 11:1367–1374.

Brenowitz, E. A. and Smith, G. T. (1997) Letter to the editor. *Trends Neurosci.* 20:345.

Bronson, F. and Heideman, P. D. (1994) Seasonal regulation of reproduction in mammals. In *The Physiology of Reproduction*, vol. 2, 2nd ed., ed., by E. Knobil and J. D. Neil, pp. 541–583. New York: Raven Press.

Calhoun, S., Hulse, S. H., Braaten, R. F., Page, S. C., and Nelson, R. J. (1993) Responsiveness to conspecific and alien song by canaries (*Serinus canaria*) and European starling (*Sturnus vulgaris*) as a function of photoperiod. *J. Comp. Psych.* 107:235–241.

Catchpole, C. K. (1973) The functions of advertising song in the Sedge warbler (*Acrocephalus schoenobaenus*) and reed warbler (*A. scirpaceus*). *Behaviour* 46:300–320.

Clower, R. P., Nixdorf, B. E., and DeVoogd, T. J. (1989) Synaptic plasticity in the hypoglossal nucleus of female canaries: Structural correlates of season, hemisphere, and testosterone treatment. *Behav. Neur. Biol.* 52:63–77.

Cox, P. R. (1944) A statistical investigation into bird-song. *British Birds* 38:3–9.

Creighton, J. A. and Follett, B. K. (1987) Changes in gonadotrophin-releasing hormone and LH in Japanese quail during the first few days of photostimulation. *J. Endocrinol.* 113:419–422.

Cynx, J. and Nottebohm, F. (1992) Role of gender, season, and familiarity in discrimination of conspecific song by zebra finches (*Taeniopygia guttata*). *Proc. Natl. Acad. Sci.* (USA) 89:1368–1371.

Dawson, A. and King, V. (1994) Thyroidectomy does not affect the daily or free-running rhythms of plasma melatonin in European starlings. *J. Biol. Rhythms* 9:137–144.

DeVoogd, T. J., Nixdorf, B., and Nottebohm, F. (1985) Synaptogenesis and changes in synaptic morphology related to acquisition of a new behavior. *Brain Res.* 329:304–308.

DeVoogd, T. J., Houtman, A. M., and Falls, J. B. (1995) White-throated sparrow morphs that differ in song production rate also differ in the anatomy of some song-related areas. *J. Neurobiol.* 28:202–213.

DeVoogd, T. J., Krebs, J. R., Healy, S. D., and Purvis, A. (1993). Relations between song repertoire size and the volume of brain nuclei related to song: comparative evolutionary analyses amongst oscine birds. *Proc. R. Soc. Lond.* B 254:75–82.

Doupe, A. J. and Konishi, M. (1991) Song-selective auditory circuits in the vocal control system of the zebra finch. *Proc. Natl. Acad. Sci.* (USA) 88:11339–11343.

Eens, M. (1997) Understanding the complex song of the European starling: An integrated ethological approach. In *Advances in the Study of Behavior*, vol. 26, ed. by P. J. B. Slater, J. S. Rosenblatt, C. T. Snowdon, and M. Milinski, pp. 355–434. San Diego: Academic Press.

Farner, D. S. (1986) Generation and regulation of annual cycles in migratory passerine birds. *American Zoologist* 26:493–501.

Farner, D. S., Donham, R. S., Matt, K. S., Mattocks, Jr., P. W., Moore, M. C., and Wingfield, J. C. (1983) The nature of photorefractoriness. In *Avian Endocrinology: Environmental and Ecological Perspectives*, ed. by S. Mikami, K. Homma, and M. Wada, pp. 149–166. Berlin: Springer-Verlag

Farner, D. S. and Follett, B. K. (1979) Reproductive periodicity in birds. In *Hormones and Evolution*, ed. by E. J. W. Barrington, pp. 829–872. London and New York: Academic Press.

Farner, D. S. and Lewis, R. A. (1971) Photoperiodism and reproductive cycles in birds. *Photophysio.* 6:325–370.

Follett, B. K. (1984) Birds. In *" Marshall's" Physiology of Reproduction*, vol. 1, ed. by G. E. Lamming, pp. 283–350. Edinburgh: Longman Green.

Fortune, E. S. and Margoliash, D. (1995) Parallel pathways and convergence onto HVc and adjacent neostriatum of adult zebra finches (*Taeniopygia guttata*). *J. Comp. Neurol.* 360:413–441.

Foster, R. G., Panzica, G. C., Parry, D. M., and Viglietti-Panzica, C. (1988) Immunocytochemical studies on the LHRH system of the Japanese quail: Influence by photoperiod and aspects of sexual differentiation. *Cell. Tiss. Res.* 253:327–335.

Foster, E. F., Mehta, R. P., and Bottjer, S. W. (1997) Axonal connections of the medial magnocellular nucleus of the anterior neostriatum in zebra finches. *J. Comp. Neurol.* 382:364–381.

Gahr, M. (1990) Delineation of a brain nucleus: Comparisons of cytochemical, hodological, and cytoarchitectural views of the song control nucleus HVc of the adult canary. *J. Comp. Neurol.* 294:30–36.

Gahr, M. (1997a) How should brain nuclei be delineated? Consequences for developmental mechanisms and for correlations of area size, neuron numbers, and functions of brain nuclei. *Trends Neurosci.* 20:58–62.

Gahr, M. (1997b) Reply. *Trends Neurosci.* 20:345–346.

Gahr, M., Güttinger, H.-R., and Kroodsma, D. E. (1993) Estrogen receptors in the avian brain: Survey reveals general distribution and forebrain areas unique to songbirds. *J. Comp. Neurol.* 327:112–122.

Gahr, M. and Kosar, E. (1996) Identification, distribution, and developmental changes of a melatonin binding sites in the song control system of the zebra finch. *J. Comp. Neurol.* 367:308–318.

Gahr, M. and Metzdorf, R. (1997) Distribution and dynamics in the expression of androgen and estrogen receptors in vocal control systems of songbirds. *Brain. Res. Bull.* 44:509–517.

Garcia-Segura, L. M., Chowen, J. A., and Naftolin, F. (1996) Endocrine glia: Roles of glial cells in the brain actions of steroid and thyroid hormones and in the regulation of hormone secretion. *Frontiers Neuroendocrinol.* 17:180–211.

Goldman, B. D. and Nelson, R. J. (1993) Melatonin and seasonality in mammals. In *Melatonin: Biosynthesis, Physiological Effects, and Clinical Application*, ed. by H. S. Yu and R. J. Reiter, pp. 225–252. Boca Raton: CRC Press.

Goldman, S. and Nottebohm, F. (1983) Neuronal production, migration, and differentiation in a vocal control nucleus of the adult female canary brain. *Proc. Nat. Acad. Sci.* (USA) 80:2390–2394.

Gulledge, C. C. and Deviche, P. (1997) Androgen control of vocal control region volumes in a wild migratory songbird (*Junco hyemalis*) is region and possibly age dependent. *J. Neurobiol.* 32:391–402.

Gwinner, E. (1986) *Circannual Rhythms*. Berlin: Springer Verlag.

Gwinner, E. and Dittami, J. (1985) Photoperiodic responses in temperate zone and equatorial stonechats: A contribution to the problem of photoperiodism in torpical organisms. In *The Endocrine System and the Environment*, ed. by B. K. Follett, S. Ishii, and A. Chandola, pp. 279–294. Berlin: Springer Verlag.

Hahn, T. P. (1995) Integration of photoperiodic and food cues to time changes in reproductive physiology by an opportunistic breeder, the red crossbill, *Loxia curvirostra* (*Aves: Carduelinae*). *J. Exp. Zool.* 272:213–226.

Hahn, T. P., Boswell, T., Wingfield, J. C., and Ball, G. F. (1998) Temporal flexibility in avian reproduction: Patterns and mechanisms. In *Current Ornithology*, vol. 14, ed. by V. Nolan Jr., E. Ketterson and C. F. Thompson, pp. 39–80. New York: Plenum Press.

Hamner, W. H. (1968) The photorefractory period of the house finch. *Ecology* 49:211–227.

Haidar, M. A., Dube, S., and Sarkar, P. K. (1983) Thyroid hormone receptors of developing chick brain are predominantly in the neurons. *Biochem. Biophys. Res. Comm.* 112:221–227.

Harding, C. F., Sheridan, K., and Walters, M. J. (1983) Hormonal specificity and activation of sexual behavior in male zebra finches. *Horm. Behav.* 17:111–113.

Harding, C. F., Walters, M. J., Collado, M., and Sheridan, K. (1988) Hormonal specificity and activation of social behavior in male red-winged blackbirds. *Horm. Behav.* 22:402–418.

Hau, M., Wikelski, M., and Wingfield, J. C. (1998) A neotropical forest bird can measure the slight changes in tropical photoperiod. *Proc. Roy. Soc. Lond. B* 265:89–95.

Hill, K. M. and DeVoogd, T. J. (1991) Altered daylength affects dendritic structure in a song-related brain region in red-winged blackbirds. *Behav. Neur. Biol.* 56:240–250.

Hinde, R. A. and Steel, E. (1978) The influence of daylength and male vocalizations on the estrogen-dependent behavior of female canaries and budgerigars, with discussion of data from other species. In *Advances in the Study of Behavior*, vol. 8, ed. by J. S. Rosenblatt, R. A. Hinde, C. G. Beer, and M. C. Busnel, pp. 39–73. New York: Academic Press.

Hoelzel, A. R. (1986) Song characteristics and response to playback of male and female robins, *Erithacus rubecula*. *Ibis* 128:115–127.

Immelmann, K. (1971) Ecological aspects of periodic reproduction. In *Avian Biology*, vol. 1, ed. by D. S. Farner and J. R. King, pp. 341–389. New York: Academic Press.

Johnson, F. and Bottjer, S. W. (1993) Hormone-induced changes in identified cell populations of the higher vocal center in male canaries. *J. Neurobiol.* 24:400–418.

Johnson, F., Sablan, M. M., and Bottjer, S. W. (1995) Topographic organization of a forebrain pathway involved with vocal learning in zebra finches. *J. Comp. Neurol.* 358:260–278.

Kalra, S. P., Horvath, T., Naftolin, F., Xu, B., Pu, S., and Kalra, P. S. (1997) The interactive language of the hypothalamus for the gonadotropin releasing (GnRH) system. *J. Neurendocrinol.* 9:569–576.

Kelley, D. B. (1988) Sexually dimorphic behaviors. *Ann. Rev. Neurosci.* 11:225–251.

Kelley, D. B. and Nottebohm, F. (1979) Projections of a telencephalic auditory nucleus-field L-in the canary. *J. Comp. Neurol.* 183:455–470.

Kirn, J. R., Alvarez-Buylla, A., and Nottebohm, F. (1991) Production and survival of projection neurons in a forebrain vocal center of male adult canaries. *J. Neurosci.* 11:1756–1762.

Kirn, J. R., Clower, R. P., Kroodsma, D. E., and DeVoogd, T. J. (1989) Song-related brain regions in the red-winged blackbird are affected by sex and season but not repertoire size. *J. Neurobiol.* 11:139–163.

Kirn, J. R., O'Loughlin, B., Kasparian, S., and Nottebohm, F. (1994) Cell death and neuronal recruitment in the high vocal center of adult male canaries are temporally related to changes in song. *Proc. Natl. Acad. Sci.* (USA) 91:7844–7848.

Kirn, J. R. and Schwabl, H. (1997) Photoperiod regulation of neuron death in the adult canary. *J. Neurobiol.* 33:223–231.

Konishi, M. (1989) Birdsong for neurobiologists. *Neuron* 3:541–549.

Kroodsma, D. E. and Konishi, M. (1991) A suboscine bird (eastern phoebe *Sayornis phoebe*) develops normal song without auditory feedback. *Anim. Behav.* 42:477–487.

Kumar, V. and Follett, B. K. (1993) The circadian nature of melatonin secretion in Japanese quail (*Coturnix coturnix japonica*). *J. Pineal Res.* 14:192–200.

Levin, R. N. and Wingfield, J. C. (1992) The hormonal control of territorial aggression in tropical birds. *Ornis Scan.* 23:284–291.

Ling, C., Mingxue, Z., Alvarez-Buylla, A., and Cheng, M.-F. (1997) Neurogenesis in juvenile and adult ring doves. *J. Comp. Neurol.* 379:300–312.

Logan, C. A. (1983) Reproductively dependent song cyclicity in mated male mockingbirds (*Mimus polyglotts*). *Auk* 100:404–413.

Lu, E. J. and Brown, W. J. (1984) The developing caudate nucleus in the euthyroid and hypothyroid rat. *J. Comp. Neurol.* 171:261–284.

Marler, P. (1987) Sensitive periods and the roles of specific and general sensory stimulation in birdsong learning. In *Imprinting and Cortical Plasticity*, ed. by J. P. Rauschecker and P. Marler, pp. 99–135. New York: Wiley and Sons.

Margoliash, D. (1997) Functional organization of forebrain pathways for song production and perception. *J. Neurobiol.* 33:671–693.

Martinez-Vargas, M. C., Stumpf, W. E., and Sar, M. (1976) Anatomical distribution of estrogen target cells in the avian CNS: A comparison with the mammalian CNS. *J. Comp. Neurol.* 167:83–104.

Mello, C. V., Vicario, D. S., and Clayton, D. F. (1992). Song presentation induces gene expression in the songbird forebrain. *Proc. Natl. Acad. Sci.* (USA) 89:6818–6822.

Moffatt, C. A., Ball, G. F., and Nelson, R. J. (1995) The effects of photoperiod on olfactory c-fos expression in prairie voles, *Microtus ochrogaster. Brain Res.* 677:82–88.

Mooney, R. (1992) Synaptic basis for developmental plasticity in a birdsong nucleus. *J. Neurosci.* 12:2464–2477.

Mooney, R. and Konishi, M. (1991) Two distinct inputs to an avian song nucleus activate different glutamate receptor subtypes on individual neurons. *Proc. Natl. Acad. Sci.* (USA) 88:4075–4079.

Morton, E. S. (1996) A comparison of vocal behavior among tropical and temperate passerine birds. In *Ecology and Evolution of Acoustic Communication in Birds*, ed. by D. E. Kroodsma and E. H. Miller, pp. 258–268. Ithaca, NY: Cornell University Press.

Murton, R. K. and Westwood, N. J. (1977) *Avian Breeding Cycles.* Oxford: Clarendon Press.

Nauta, W. J. H. and Feirtag, M. (1986) *Fundamental Neuroanatomy.* New York: Freeman and Company.

Nastiuk, K. L. and Clayton, D. F. (1995) The canary androgen receptor mRNA is localized in the song control nuclei of the brain and is rapidly regulated by testosterone. *J. Neurobiol.* 26:213–224.

Nelson, R. J. (1987) Photoperiodic-nonresponsive morphs: A possible variable in microtine population-density fluctuations. *Am. Nat.* 130:350–369.

Nelson, R. J. (1995) *An Introduction to Behavioral Endocrinology.* Sunderland, MA: Sinauer Associates Inc.

Nicholls, T. J., Goldsmith, A. R., and Dawson, A. (1988) Photorefractoriness in birds and comparison with mammals. *Physiol. Rev.* 68:133–176.

Nordeen, K. W. and Nordeen, E. J. (1988) Projection neurons within a vocal motor pathway are born during song learning in zebra finches. *Nature* 334:149–151.

Nordeen, E. J. and Nordeen, K. W. (1996) Sex difference among non-neural cells precedes sexually dimorphic neuron growth and survival in an avian song control nucleus. *J. Neurobiol.* 30:531–542.

Nottebohm, F. (1975) Vocal behavior in birds. In *Avian Biology*, vol. 5, ed. by D. S. Farner and J. R. King, pp. 287–332. New York: Academic Press.

Nottebohm, F. (1980) Brain pathways for vocal learning in birds: A review of the first 10 years. In *Progress in Psychobiology and Physiological Psychology*, vol. 9, ed. by J. M. Sprague and A. N. Epstein, pp. 85–214. New York: Academic Press.

Nottebohm, F. (1981) A brain for all seasons: Cyclical anatomical changes in song-control nuclei of the canary brain. *Science* 214:1368–1370.

Nottebohm, F. (1989) From bird song to neurogenesis. *Scientific American* 260:74–79.

Nottebohm, F. (1993) The search for neural mechanisms that define the sensitive period for song learning in birds. *Netherlands J. Zool.* 43:193–234.

Nottebohm, F., Kelley, D. B., and Paton, J. A. (1982) Connections of vocal control nuclei in the canary telencephalon. *J. Comp. Neurol.* 207:344–357.

Nottebohm, F., Nottebohm, M. E., and Crane, L. A. (1986) Developmental and seasonal changes in canary song and their relation to changes in anatomy of song control nuclei. *Behav. Neur. Biol.* 46:445–471.

Nottebohm, F., Nottebohm, M. E., Crane, L. A., and Wingfield, J. C. (1987) Seasonal changes in gonadal hormone levels of adult male canaries and their relation to song. *Behav. Neur. Biol.* 47:197–211.

Nottebohm, F., O'Loughlin, B., Gould, K., Yohay, K., and Alvarez-Buylla, A. (1994) The life span of new neurons in a song control nucleus of the adult canary depends on me of year when these cells are born. *Proc. Natl. Acad. Sci.* (USA) 91:7849–7853.

Nottebohm, F., Stokes, T. M., and Leonard, C. M. (1976) Central control of song in the canary, *Serinus canaria J. Comp. Neurol.* 165:457–486.

Nowicki, S. and Ball, G. F. (1989) Testosterone induction of song in photosensitive and photorefractory male sparrows. *Horm. Behav.* 23:514–525.

Okuhata, S. and Saito, N. (1987) Synaptic connections of thalamo-cerebral vocal control nuclei of the canary. *Brain Res. Bull.* 18:35–44.

Parry, D. M., Goldsmith, A. R., Millar, R. P., and Glennie, L. M. (1997) Immunocytochemical localization of GnRH precursor in the hypothalamus of European starlings during sexual maturation and photorefractoriness. *J. Neuroendocrinol.* 9:235–243.

Payne, R. B. (1969) Breeding seasons and reproductive physiology of tricolored blackbirds and redwinged blackbirds. *Univ. Cal. Pub. Zool.* 90:1–137.

Perrins, C. M. (1970) The timing of birds' breeding seasons. *Ibis* 112:242–255.

Pfaff, D. W. (1976) The neuroanatomy of sex hormone receptors in the vertebrate brain. In *Neuroendocrine Regulation of Fertility*, ed. by T. C. Anand Kumar, pp. 30–45. Basel: Karger.

Puelles, L., Robles, C., Martínez-de-la-Torre, M., and Martínez, S. (1994) New subdivision schema for the avian torus semicircularis: Neurochemical maps in the chick. *J. Comp. Neurol.* 340:98–125.

Raine, C. S. (1989) Neurocellular anatomy In Basic Neurochemistry, 4th ed., ed. by G. J. Siegel and B. W. Agranoff, pp. 3–33. New York: Raven Press.

Robinson, J. E. and Follett, B. K. (1982) Photoperiodism in Japanese quail: The termination of seasonal breeding by photorefractoriness. *Proc. Roy. Soc. Lond.* B 215:95–116.

Salvi, E. and Ball, G. F. (1997) Effects of dehydration on gonadal size and hypothalamic GnRH in zebra finches. *Soc. Neurosci. Abst.* 23:415.

Scharff, C. and Nottebohm, F. (1991) A comparative study of the behavioral deficits following lesions of various parts of the zebra finch song system: Implications for vocal learning. *J. Neurosci.* 11:2896–2913.

Sharp, P. J. (1996) Strategies in avian breeding cycles. *Anim. Reprod. Sci.* 42:505–513.

Silverin, B. (1994) Photoperiodism in male great tits (*Parus major*). *Ethology, Ecology, and Evolution* 6:131–157.

Silverin, B., Massa, R., and Stokkan, K. A. (1993) Photoperiodic adaptation to breeding at different latitudes in great tits. *Gen. Comp. Endocrinol.* 90:14–22.

Slagsvold, T. (1977) Bird song activity in relation to breeding cycle, spring weather, and environmental physiology. *Ornis Scand.* 8:197–222.

Smith, G. T. (1996) Seasonal plasticity in the song nuclei of wild rufous-sided towhees. *Brain Res.* 734:79–85.

Smith, G. T., Brenowitz, E. A., Beecher, M. D., and Wingfield, J. C. (1997b) Seasonal changes in testosterone, neural attributes of song control nuclei, and song structure in wild songbirds. *J. Neurosci.* 17:6001–6010.

Smith, G. T., Brenowitz, E. A., and Wingfield, J. C. (1997a) Seasonal changes in the size of the avian song control nucleus HVC defined by multiple histological markers. *J. Comp. Neurol.* 381:253–261.

Smith, G. T., Brenowitz, E. A., and Wingfield, J. C. (1997c) Roles of photoperiod and testosterone in seasonal plasticity of the avian song control system. *J. Neurobiol.* 32:426–442.

Smith, G. T., Brenowitz, E. A., Wingfield, J. C., and Baptista, L. F. (1995) Seasonal changes in song nuclei and song behavior in Gambel's white-crowned sparrows. *J. Neurobiol.* 28:114–125.

Sohrabji, F., Nordeen, K. W., and Nordeen, E. J. (1990) Selective impairment of song learning following lesions of a forebrain nucleus in the juvenile zebra finch. *Behav. Neural Biol.* 53:51–63.

Soma, K. K., Hartman, V., Brenowitz, E. A., and Wingfield, J. C. (1997) Seasonal plasticity of the avian song nucleus HVc as indicated by androgen receptor immunocytochemistry in a wild songbird. *Soc. Neurosci. Abst.* 23:1328.

Steel, E. and Hinde, R. A. (1972) The influence of photoperiod on oestrogenic induction of nest-building in canaries. *J. Endocrinol.* 55:265–278

Turek, F. and Van Cauter, E. (1994) Rhythms in reproduction. In *The Physiology of Reproduction*, 2nd ed., ed. by E. Knobil, and J. D. Neill, pp. 487–540. New York: Raven Press.

Ulinski, P. S. and Margoliash, D. (1990) Neurobiology of the reptile-bird transition. In *Cerebral Cortex*, vol. 8A, *Comparative Structure and Evolution of Cerebral Cortex*, ed. by E. G. Jones and S. Peters, pt. 1, pp. 217–265. New York: Plenum Press.

Vates, G. E., Broome, B. M., Mello, C. V., and Nottebohm, F. (1996) Auditory pathways of caudal telencephalon and their relation to the song system of adult male zebra finches (*Taeniopygia guttata*). *J. Comp. Neurol.* 366:613–642.

Vates, G. E., Vicario, D. S., and Nottebohm, F. (1997) Reafferent thalamo-"cortical" loops in the song system of oscine songbirds. *J. Comp. Neurol.* 380:275–290.

Vicario, D. S. (1993) A new brain stem pathway for vocal control in the zebra finch song system. *NeuroReport* 4:983–986.

Vockel, A., Prove, E., and Balthazart, J. (1990) Sex- and age-related differences in the activity of testosterone-metabolizing enzymes in microdissected nuclei of the zebra finch brain. *Brain Res.* 511:291–302.

Watson, J. T. and Adkins-Regan, E. (1989) Neuroanatomical localization of sex steroid-concentrating cells in the Japanese quail (*Coturnix japonica*): Autoradiography with [3H]-testosterone, [3H]-estradiol, and [3H]-dihydrotestosterone. *Neuroendocrinol.* 49:51–64.

White, G. (1789) *The Natural History and Antiquities of Selborne.* London: Benjamin White and Son.

Whitfield-Rucker, M. G. and Cassone, V. (1996) Melatonin binding in the house sparrow song control system: Sexual dimorphism and the effect of photoperiod. *Horm. Behav.* 30:528–537.

Wild, J. M. (1993) The avian nucleus retroambigualis: A nucleus for breathing, singing, and calling. *Brain Res.* 606:319–324.

Wild, J. M. (1997) Neural pathways for the control of birdsong production. *J. Neurobiol.* 33:653–670.

Wilson, F. E. (1986) Testosterone sensitivity of the seminal sacs of tree sparrows (*Spizella arborea*) in different reproductive states. *J. Endocrinol.* 109:125–131.

Wilson, F. E. and Donham, R. S. (1988) Daylength and control of seasonal reproduction in male birds. In *Processing of Environmental Information in Vertebrates*, ed. by M. H. Stetson, pp. 101–120. Berlin: Springer-Verlag.

Wilson, F. E. and Reinert, B. D. (1993) The thyroid and photoperiodic control of seasonal reproduction in American tree sparrows (*Spizella arborea*). *J. Comp. Physiol.* B 163:563–573.

Wingfield, J. C. (1980) Fine temporal adjustment of reproductive functions. In *Avian Endocrinology*, ed. by A. Epple and M. H. Stetson, pp. 367–389. New York: Academic Press.

Wingfield, J. C. (1983) Environmental and endocrine control of reproduction: An ecological approach. In *Avian Endocrinology: Environmental and Ecological Perspectives*, ed. by S. I. Mikami, K. Homma, and M. Wada, pp. 265–288. Berlin: Springer-Verlag.

Wingfield, J. C. and Farner, D. S. (1980) Control of seasonal reproduction in temperate-zone birds. *Prog. Reprod. Biol.* 5:62–101.

Wingfield, J. C. and Farner, D. S. (1993) Endocrinology of reproduction in wild species. In *Avian Biology*, vol. 9, ed. by D. S. Farner, J. R. King, and K. C. Parkes, pp. 163–247. London: Academic Press.

Zann, R. A. (1996) *The Zebra Finch: A Synthesis of Field and Laboratory Studies.* Oxford: Oxford University Press.

9 Testosterone, Aggression, and Communication: Ecological Bases of Endocrine Phenomena

John C. Wingfield, Jerry D. Jacobs, Kiran Soma, Donna L. Maney, Kathleen Hunt, Deborah Wisti-Peterson, Simone Meddle, Marilyn Ramenofsky, and Kimberly Sullivan

Agonistic communication between individuals commonly serves to establish dominance and access to food, shelter, mates, nest sites, and other resources. Territorial aggression is a widespread, almost universal form of agonistic behavior that has received considerable investigation at multiple levels, from theory and behavioral ecology to hormone and cell mechanisms. Territorial behavior in wild birds has been a particularly fruitful model to study, because many species are abundant, easily observed, and able to adapt well to captive conditions. It is thus not surprising that a significant fraction of the literature on ultimate and proximate aspects of territorial behavior has focused on the class *Aves* (see, e.g., Konishi et al. 1989).

Agonistic interactions in territorial contexts have marked effects on the life cycles of birds and other vertebrates. For example, social interactions can retard or enhance reproductive development through several sensory modalities, including visual, auditory, tactile, pheromonal, and electrical. Additionally, behavioral interactions regulate the actual onset of breeding (i.e., the onset of ovulatory cycles after the gonads have matured), provide support functions for the reproductive process (e.g., establishment of a territory, pair bond), and influence parent-offspring interactions (see Wingfield and Kenagy 1991; Wingfield et al. 1994). The role of androgens, particularly testosterone, in the regulation of agonistic interactions has been studied extensively, although there remains much controversy and contradiction in the published literature. This may be due in part to differences in experimental approach and the degree to which the subject animals establish dominance relationships prior to experiment (see, e.g., Wingfield et al. 1987). However, additional problems arise when considering hormonal control mechanisms for the same suite of behavior (e.g., territorial aggression) expressed in very different stages of life such as the breeding and nonbreeding seasons (see, e.g., Wingfield 1994; Wingfield et al. 1997a). Behavior exhibited during territorial aggression at different seasons may appear identical, but are the contexts and hormonal bases truly similar?

An organism rarely remains in a constant state throughout its life. It changes morphology, physiology, and behavior patterns that presumably maximize overall fitness in a changing environment. The individual life-history cycle consists of a series of stages, each with a unique combination of morphological, physiological, and behavioral characteristics, and each expressed at a specific time of year. Because different populations have characteristic cycles of life-history stages and even different numbers and types of stages, Jacobs (1996) has applied finite-state machine theory to describe them. This theory is derived from mathematical principles developed to describe computer network systems. Each stage has a set of inputs (i.e., environmental signals) with a fixed set of predictable outputs (morphological, physiological, and behavioral expressions characteristic of that stage). There are also unique networks of internal mechanisms (i.e., neural and neuroendocrine/endocrine systems) that regulate the appropriate output given a certain combination of inputs. This approach allows us to formally describe life-history cycles of individuals and to compare morphology, physiology, and behavioral processes at different stages within an individual as well as between individuals or populations. A typical example is given for the migratory white-crowned sparrow, *Zonotrichia leucophrys*, in figure 9.1. This has been modified from Jacobs (1996) to emphasize components of the animal's life history relevant to communication and aggression. There could be many other substages within each stage. In figure 9.1 there are five major life-history stages, winter (nonbreeding), vernal migration, breeding, prebasic moult, and autumnal mi-

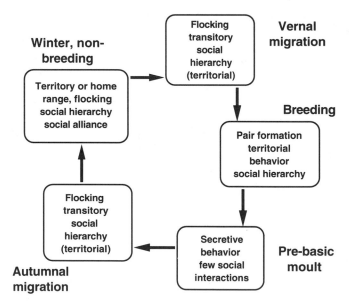

Figure 9.1
Life-history stages in relation to communication and aggression in typical passerines (e.g., white-crowned sparrow and song sparrow, modified from Jacobs 1996). Each stage is represented by a box and within each box is a list of behavioral substages expressed within that stage. Finite-state machine theory (Jacobs 1996) suggests that even though some behaviors are expressed in several life-history stages, their control mechanisms may be different. If this is true, then this model has considerable implications for environmental and endocrine control of behavior in changing environments.

gration. Note that other populations may have more or less major stages. Although each has its own unique set of substages, some behaviors appear to be identical in different life-history stages. For example, many sparrows form flocks on their wintering grounds as well as temporarily during migration. Another example is that some species maintain territories in both the breeding and nonbreeding seasons. Additionally, many behaviors such as singing, and postures associated with threats and fights, are expressed both while in flocks and while alone in territories. These aggressive behaviors thus appear to be common to more than one life-history stage despite very different contexts. Nonetheless, superficially identical substages (i.e., outputs) in different life-history stages may have unique environmental inputs that vary with time of year, social status, and location. It follows that internal mechanisms (i.e., hormonal bases) may also be different (Jacobs 1996). Recent work on territorial aggression in birds during different life-history stages of the annual cycle has been consistent with this view (see, e.g., Wingfield 1994; Wingfield et al. 1997a).

Transition from one life-history stage to the next is a predictable progression in time, usually as an annual cycle. Environmental cues such as the annual change in day length, temperature, and food availability regulate these transitions (Jacobs 1996). Each stage is thus timed to be expressed at a season when that stage will maximize survival. Superimposed on this predictable cycle are unpredictable events including potentially stressful environmental perturbations. This is illustrated in figure 9.2. In this case the progression of life-history stages is the same as in figure 9.1 but is presented in a linear fashion. A facultative life-history stage can be attained from any normal (predictable) life-history stage, and its expression is triggered by many unpredictable environmental cues called "labile perturbation factors" (Jacobs 1996). This stage has also been called the "emergency" life-history stage, particularly when the environmental perturbations are severe and more prolonged (Wingfield et al. 1997b). In relation to communication, and particularly aggression, territorial behavior may be expressed in response to unpredictable intrusions by other conspecifics attempting to take over the territory, or sudden changes in social status (again unpredictable) that may involve agonistic interactions. It is important to note that although some unpredictable events in the environment may be potentially stressful, not all are. These facultative physiological and behavioral responses to unpredictable events are transitory (lasting for seconds or hours, perhaps a few days in extreme cases such as the "emergency" life-history stage), following which the individual returns to the appropriate normal life-history stage (as indicated by the two-way arrows in figure 9.2). Note that the individual would assume the next life-history stage in a predictable sequence if a labile perturbation factor triggers the transitory facultative life-history stage during a change from one normal stage to the next (Jacobs 1996).

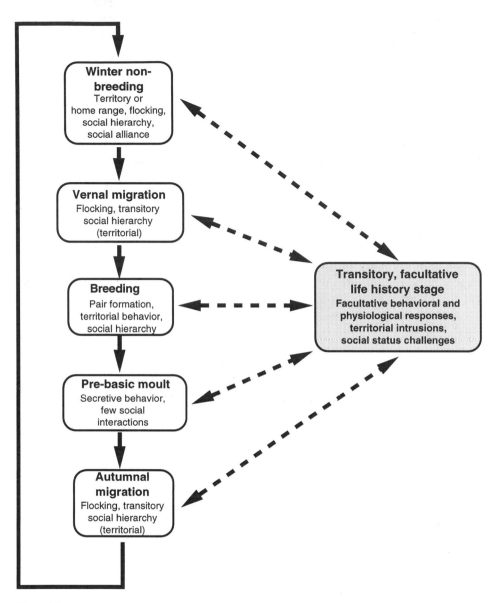

Figure 9.2
Life-history changes in relation to communication and aggression as in figure 9.1 but arranged in a linear fashion to show the transitory, facultative life-history stage and how it can be triggered from any normal, predictable stage in the life-history cycle. Note the list of behavioral substages within each box. Again, finite-state machine theory (Jacobs 1996) suggests that even though apparently similar behaviors may be expressed in the facultative stage, the mechanisms controlling behavior may be different from those in the normal sequence of stages. The facultative stage is transitory, and individuals return to their normal life-history stage once the unpredictable event has passed. This model may provide a useful starting framework from which to understand the complexities of context and type of agonistic behaviors as well as their potential control mechanisms.

From figures 9.1 and 9.2 it is clear that an individual may express similar aggressive behaviors not only from one season to the next (i.e., different, predictable life history stages), but also in response to unpredictable events such as territorial challenges, competition for mates or other partners, and sudden changes in dominance status. These are largely unpredictable events, but the individual must have some way of responding facultatively to such challenges. This complexity of agonistic interactions may also have contributed to the confusion and contradiction in the literature on hormonal control mechanisms. Are these behaviors expressed in different life-history stages truly identical, and if so, are the hormonal control mechanisms the same? Finite-state machine theory predicts that context, environmental inputs, and control mechanisms are different at different stages (Jacobs 1996; Wingfield et al. 1997a). To investigate these possibilities, we will begin in this chapter by focusing on one life-history stage, breeding, and go on to outline the role of androgens such as testosterone in the activation of aggression, and how behavioral interactions may in turn influence androgen secretion. Responses to unpredictable and the transitory facultative life-history stages will also be addressed. Next, we will discuss the instances in life-history cycles in which territorial aggression is expressed in the nonbreeding season and how hormonal control mechanisms may differ. Finally, we will discuss future directions by which mechanisms may be investigated further and then used to determine possible ecological bases of endocrine phenomena related to territorial behavior and communication.

Interrelationships of Testosterone and Aggression in Reproduction

It has long been established that the steroid hormone testosterone has organizational (i.e., during development) and activational effects on territorial aggression (see, e.g., Balthazart 1983; Harding 1983; but see also Arnold et al. 1996). Such territorial aggression includes song, at least in passerines, other postures such as threats and movements of appendages (e.g., tail flicks, wing waves, grass-pulling), vocalizations associated with threat (other than song), attack behavior, and fights. Clearly, this involves an extremely complex suite of behaviors, undoubtedly regulated by diverse regions of the brain. Song control nuclei in the oscine brain have been well studied in many contexts, but other regions of the brain regulating nonsinging territorial behaviors have been less well studied. Although the behavioral actions of testosterone are particularly well known, their nature is also controversial and the loci of action are only incompletely known (see, e.g., Harding 1983). In this section we will outline the controversies inherent to this subject and offer possible testable hypotheses to explain them.

Hypothalamo-pituitary-gonad Axis and Actions of Testosterone

Environmental signals, both physical and social, are received by sensory receptors, and this information is transduced into neuroendocrine secretion of a decapeptide, gonadotropin-releasing hormone (GnRH, figure 9.3; see also Ball 1993; Francis et al. 1993; Wilczynski et al. 1993). This peptide circulates to the anterior pituitary gland where it stimulates secretion of the gonadotropins, particularly luteinizing hormone (LH). LH circulates in the peripheral blood to its target, the gonad, in this case the testis, where its actions are primarily steroidogenic to promote synthesis and release of testosterone (figure 9.3). Testosterone acts within the testis to regulate spermatogenesis and is also transported in the blood circulation to various target tissues to regulate development of accessory sexual organs, some secondary sex characteristics, and song control nuclei in the brain, as well as to activate aggressive behavior and provide a negative feedback signal for GnRH and LH secretion (figure 9.3). This basic scenario is typical of most vertebrates, including birds.

Note that testosterone has multiple actions, and not all of them need be advantageous to the individual (figure 9.4). The processes in the upper right-hand corner of figure 9.4 indicated by thick arrows are central actions including negative feedback signals, activation, and organization of sexual and aggressive behaviors. Biological actions indicated by medium arrows (lower part of figure 9.4) are morphological and related to reproductive function (e.g., spermatogenesis, sexual characters and in some cases muscle hypertrophy for male-male competition over mates and territories). All of these are clearly beneficial for reproductive function. On the other hand, the underlined actions of testosterone indicated in the upper left side of figure 9.4 are deleterious. Increased territorial behavior makes an individual conspicuous, thus increasing potential for predation; the likelihood of injury in fights with conspecific males is heightened; high levels of testosterone interfere with parental care and may suppress the immune system. Oncogenic effects are also possible if testosterone levels are high for prolonged periods, such as long breeding seasons in the tropics. These deleterious effects of testosterone may provide strong selection for mechanisms that turn off testosterone secretion, or at least hold it in check, even during the breeding season itself (see Wingfield et al. 1997a).

Testosterone and Aggression in Reproductive Contexts

Numerous experiments in which the testes (the primary source of testosterone) are removed show a decrease in agonistic behavior, particularly songs and other vocalizations, as well as postures associated with territorial aggression. Transplant of testes into castrated birds, or replacement therapy with testosterone, reinstates these

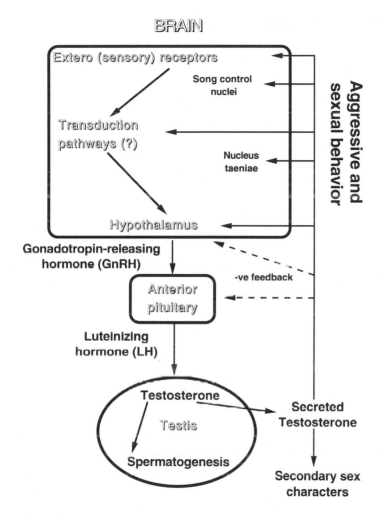

Figure 9.3
Schematic diagram summarizing the environmental, neuroendocrine, and endocrine control mechanisms for testosterone secretion. See text for details and Balthazart 1983; Harding 1983; and Wingfield and Farner 1993 for references.

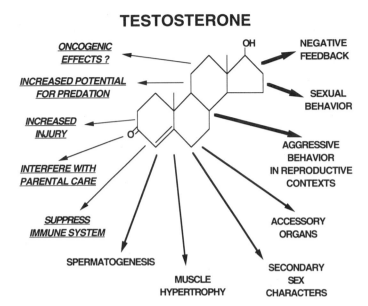

Figure 9.4
Schematic representation of the structure of testosterone and its major known actions. See text for details.
Modified from Wingfield et al. 1997. See also Witschi 1961; Silverin 1980; Balthazart 1983; Gorbman et al.
1983; Harding 1983; Gause and March 1986; Hegner and Wingfield 1987; Wingfield et al. 1987; Marler
and Moore 1988; Dufty 1989; Wingfield 1990; Becker et al. 1992; Ketterson et al. 1992; Nolan et al. 1992;
Wingfield and Farner 1993; DeNardo and Sinervo 1994; March and Scanes 1994; Wingfield et al. 1994;
Nelson 1995; Beletsky et al. 1995; Ketterson et al. 1996; Hillgarth et al. 1997; Hillgarth and Wingfield
1997.

behaviors (see Balthazart 1983 and Harding 1983 for extensive reviews). However,
there are also numerous reports claiming that testosterone is not required for expression of aggression. This is especially true if circulating levels of testosterone are
correlated with aggressive behavior (see Wingfield and Ramenofsky 1985 and Wingfield et al. 1987 for references). It must be emphasized here that there are several
types of aggression (see Moyer 1968), only three of which are strictly associated with
reproduction: breeding territoriality, mate guarding, and parental aggression in
defense of offspring. Aggression may also be expressed in relation to access to food
and shelter during the nonbreeding season, winter territories, and social status. Such
types of aggression may apply equally to other life-history stages as well as the
breeding stage (figure 9.1). Facultative aggression is also expressed against intruders
onto a territory (whether during the breeding season or not) and against predators.
These are applicable to the transitory, facultative life-history stage of figure 9.2.

However, at least in birds, the postures and vocalizations given during agonistic interactions are very similar regardless of context or life-history stage. This suggests that the neural circuits regulating their expression may be similar, but presumably the control mechanisms are different. Only during the breeding stage when testosterone levels are elevated for reproductive function would this hormone provide a useful signal to activate aggression. An increase of testosterone at other times would be an inappropriate signal because of the multiple actions of this hormone on morphology and physiology as well as behavior. A similar argument has also been postulated for the control of sexual behavior (Crews 1984, 1997; Crews and Moore 1986).

The apparent contradictions in the literature linking testosterone and aggression are also explained in part by the "challenge" hypothesis. Simply stated, this asserts that there is an interrelationship of testosterone and aggression in reproductive contexts and especially when social relationships are unstable. Although testosterone and metabolites may activate territorial and mate-guarding aggression so that they are expressed at the appropriate life-history stage (breeding, figure 9.1), aggressive interactions also may actually increase the secretion of testosterone, especially when one male is challenged for his territory by a conspecific (see Wingfield and Ramenofsky 1985; Wingfield et al. 1987, 1990). Experimental evidence supports the hypothesis, and it appears that circulating testosterone levels in males correlate with expressed aggression only when social interrelationships are unstable, such as when a territory is established, when the mate is sexually receptive and males guard their paternity, and when one male is challenged by another male for his territory (Wingfield and Ramenofsky 1985; Wingfield et al. 1987, 1990, 1994). Unfortunately, even this explanation does not account for all of the controversy in the literature, for in many avian species testosterone levels in blood do not change when the male is challenged or exposed to a sexually receptive female.

Closer examination of a number of studies reveals that mating system and breeding strategy may explain some further confusion in the literature on testosterone-aggression interrelationships. It is important here to consult figures 9.3 and 9.4 again and remind ourselves that testosterone has many actions, including some that are potentially deleterious to a breeding male. Most avian species are socially monogamous, with males providing varying degrees of parental care. Experimental manipulation of testosterone levels indicate that prolonged high concentrations interfere with paternal behavior (Silverin 1980; Hegner and Wingfield 1987; Beletsky et al. 1995), as well as result in injury or reduced survival (Dufty 1989; Wingfield 1990; Nolan et al. 1992; Beletsky et al. 1995), suppress the immune system (Gause and March 1986; Hillgarth et al. 1997), and have potential oncogenic effects (figure 9.4).

This "trade-off" of beneficial and deleterious effects of testosterone suggests that there is a strong selection for testosterone levels to decrease in socially monogamous males, especially during the parental phase of breeding, but that mechanisms remain by which testosterone secretion is elevated again if a male is challenged, or the brood lost to a predator and renesting begins. This precise control of testosterone secretion is critical to maximize reproductive success. Therefore we see strong social modulation of testosterone secretion in socially monogamous males. Polygynous males, on the other hand, generally provide little or no parental care, and the constraints of increased testosterone level on paternal behavior are lessened (Wingfield et al. 1990). The strategy here would be for males to undergo marked increases in testosterone secretion at the onset of breeding and maintain them throughout in relation to continuous male-male competition for territories and mates. The other potentially injurious effects of testosterone would still be important (Beletsky et al. 1995), but because male reproductive success is likely to be enhanced in relation to the number of females he can mate with, the deleterious effects of testosterone may be outweighed by increased reproductive success. Thus in polygynous species in which males show no parental behavior, we predict much less modulation of testosterone secretion by social interactions (see, e.g., Wingfield et al. 1990; Beletsky et al. 1995). This may be particularly true for short-lived species that are not likely to survive for more than one breeding season. In longer-lived species with more potential breeding seasons, partial modulation of testosterone secretion by social cues may occur, but it should be less marked than in species that show male parental care.

Finite-state Machine Theory and the Concepts of Behavioral and Physiological States

The challenge hypothesis proposes an interrelationship of testosterone and aggression that raises some fundamental questions. At first it suggests a positive feedback loop: testosterone activates aggression and aggressive interactions result in elevated testosterone secretion. Such loops are inherently unstable and rare in biological systems. It is thought that normal seasonal changes in testosterone levels, stimulated by the increase in photoperiod in spring, activate aggression so that territories can be established. These territories are abandoned and territorial aggression wanes at the end of the breeding season when testosterone levels decline. However, during the breeding season, testosterone secretion can be modulated further, particularly in socially monogamous males that show parental care. In these cases, plasma concentrations of testosterone must decline when males are parental, but not below a level that will sustain reproductive function. If the male is then challenged by an intruding conspecific, then testosterone rises, not to activate aggression (it has already been activated), but to sustain a high level of aggression in the face of an intrusion. High circulating levels of testosterone also promote persistence of aggression both during and immediately after the intrusion (see Wingfield et al. 1990; Wingfield 1994). The stimulus for testosterone secretion is greatly reduced as soon as the male drives the intruder (i.e., the social stimulation) from his territory, or conversely, when the male is defeated and forced off his territory. Thus the interrelationship is transitory and unstable. Nonetheless, problems remain to be explained because this system includes several different phenomena that are potentially difficult to reconcile. Finite-state machine theory may provide a framework by which such contradictions can indeed be explained, or at least provide testable hypotheses to explore these complex interrelationships further.

Testosterone secretion is controlled in a seasonal cycle and is highest during reproduction (i.e., consistent with development and termination of the breeding life-history stage in figure 9.1). Unpredictable social cues such as an intruding male may also elevate testosterone secretion within the breeding life-history stage (i.e., consistent with the transitory facultative life-history stage in figure 9.2). The finite-state machine model predicts that control of territorial aggression in one life-history stage will be different from that in another, that is, if testosterone is involved in both scenarios, then the mechanisms by which it acts should differ (Jacobs 1996). To address this problem we raise the concept of physiological and behavioral states, and the endocrine control mechanisms that regulate them. Each life-history stage—whether predictable or the transitory facultative stage—has a unique repertoire of substages. The combination of substages expressed (output) in relation to environmental conditions (input) at any one time results in a specific state of morphology, physiology, and behavior (Jacobs 1996). Three major state levels have been proposed (Wingfield et al. 1990; lower panel of figure 9.5). Level A represents the basic homeostasis processes required to sustain life in the individual. Level B represents the scale of changes in homeostasis required to maximize fitness at different seasons (i.e., changes in morphology, physiology, and behavior within each life-history stage). We suggest that levels A and B are common to all normal life-history stages and encompass the range of states that can be expressed during the predictable life cycle (figure 9.1). Superimposed on this is level C (lower panel of figure 9.5), which represents the limits of facultative homeostasis changes triggered by unpredictable events in the environment, that is the transitory facultative life-history stage. States within level C are mostly physiological and behavioral because they are too brief for morphological changes to occur. Using the scheme in figure 9.5, it is possible to envision normal, predictable changes in state occurring throughout the life cycle within levels A and B. Adjustments in response to unpredictable perturbations of the environment can be made at level C, which can be reached at any time in the life cycle.

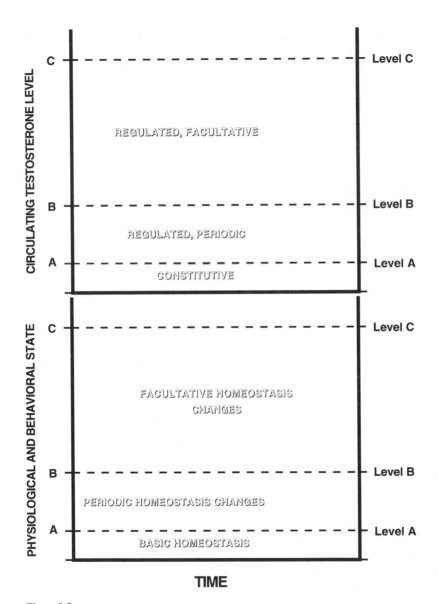

Figure 9.5
The concept of behavioral and physiological state (lower panel) and levels A, B, and C of testosterone secretion. Physiological and behavioral state is a function of the life history substages expressed at any one moment in response to environmental cues (from figure 9.1). Level A represents basic homeostasis required to sustain life. Level B represents the range of behavioral and physiological change required to adjust to changing environmental conditions on a predictable scale (i.e., the normal progression of life-history stages in figure 9.1). Level C encompasses the facultative homeostasis changes required in the face

We can use these state levels to infer three levels of hormone action (Wingfield et al. 1990). Hormonal control mechanisms (upper level of figure 9.5) may change in relation to the physiological and behavioral state level (lower panel of figure 9.5). Different hormones may operate at each level of behavioral and physiological state, but in the case of territorial aggression, testosterone may act at all these levels. Level A (upper panel of figure 9.5) is the seasonal low in plasma levels, perhaps typical of the nonbreeding life-history stages, that is required to maintain negative feedback loops (i.e., it is not a zero level). Level B represents the normal predictable seasonal change in testosterone level required to regulate morphological, physiological, and behavioral changes associated with reproductive function in males. This is likely regulated by changes in photoperiod, etc. Level C represents the facultative changes in testosterone secretion, that is, surges above level B, that are a result of unpredictable social challenges. Thus there are three potential levels of action of testosterone that have distinct effects on behavior and physiology (see also Wingfield et al. 1990).

To put this scheme in the context of an animal in its environment, we can compare different cycles of testosterone levels in song sparrows, *Melospiza melodia* (figure 9.6). This species is an excellent example because it expresses territorial aggression in different life-history stages as well as during the transitory facultative life-history stage (Wingfield 1994). The cycle of testosterone in captive male song sparrows exposed to long day-length (open circles and broken line in figure 9.6) shows a simple peak and declines slowly to a minimum at about day 100 of photostimulation (note the breeding season of this taxon is about 3.5 months). On the other hand, the cycle of testosterone in breeding males in the field shows a dramatically different cycle (solid circles and lines in figure 9.6). Not only are plasma levels of testosterone higher in free-living males, but there are at least two extra peaks not seen in captive, nonbreeding birds. Experiments in the field and laboratory indicate that the surges of testosterone levels in free-living males above those seen in captive birds are a result of behavioral challenges from intruding males, territory establishment (Wingfield

Figure 9.5 (continued)
of unpredictable environmental perturbations whether physical or social. These are equivalent to those seen in figure 9.2. Testosterone levels may change throughout time (life-history cycle) to accommodate these different levels of physiological and behavioral states (upper panel). Level A may be constitutive secretion of testosterone at extremely low levels, but it is still required in the nonbreeding season to maintain negative feedback signals for gonadotropin and GnRH secretion. Level B is the upper limit of a cycle of testosterone during the normal onset of the breeding life-history stage. These levels are sufficient to result in complete reproductive development. Level C is the limit of transitory facultative surges of testosterone in relation to unpredictable events such as challenges. At each level, testosterone may have markedly different actions, although the mechanisms by which this occurs at the target cell level remain largely unknown. Adapted from Wingfield et al. 1990.

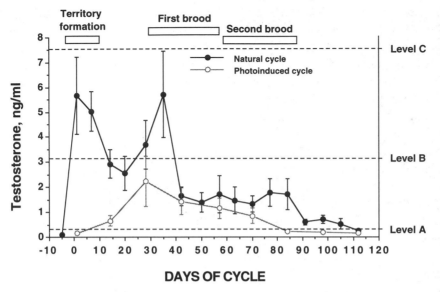

Figure 9.6
Application of physiology and behavioral states (and their respective hormone state levels) to cycles of testosterone in captive but mature male song sparrows, and in free-living males. See legend for figure 9.7 for details of levels A, B, and C. Note how natural patterns of testosterone secretion fit the theoretical patterns. Compiled from Wingfield 1984; Wingfield et al. 1990.

1985), and the presence of sexually mature females (Moore 1983; Wingfield et al. 1989; Wingfield and Goldsmith 1990). Note that testosterone levels drop dramatically during the parental phase (first and second broods in figure 9.6). Referring now to levels of physiological state and hormone levels in figure 9.5, we can propose that the nonbreeding baseline level of testosterone in figure 9.6 represents level A and that the photoperiodically induced rise in testosterone and its subsequent fall occurs within the bounds of level B (figure 9.6). Note that captive male song sparrows exposed to long days show full reproductive development, including complete spermatogenesis, development of all accessory organs and some secondary sex characters, and they express the full repertoire of sexual and aggressive behaviors (e.g., Wingfield et al. 1987, 1990). Thus the transitory surges of testosterone above level B (to level C) in figure 9.6 are not involved in reproductive development per se, but in expression of behavior in the face of intrusions by conspecific males (see, e.g., Wingfield 1985; Wingfield et al. 1990). The pattern of testosterone secretion at levels A and B represents the normal progression of life-history stages (of figure 9.1), whereas the surges above level B to level C represent the transitory facultative life history stage (of figure 9.2). Evidence that the peaks above level B in figure 9.6 are not part of the predictable life-history cycle but are truly facultative is given below.

The challenge hypothesis and the levels of physiological and behavioral state described above allow us to predict the patterns of testosterone secretion in free-living males in relation to their social environment. In figure 9.7a, there is a simple peak of testosterone within level B, which we expect in male song sparrows that are not mated and that receive no social cues from sexually receptive females, and at low density in which male-male encounters are infrequent. Since there are few, or no, social cues to stimulate a surge above level B to level C, then the cycle in these males should resemble those of captive birds in figure 9.6. Testosterone levels are known to be lower in unmated males and at low density in several avian species (see, e.g., Wingfield and Hahn 1994; Wingfield et al. 1994; Beletsky et al. 1995). In figure 9.7b, there is a single surge of testosterone above level B in male song sparrows that have mates and are exposed to the stimulatory social cues of receptive females—but only at the time of ovulation. However, male-male interactions are infrequent because of low density of territories, and thus there are no other stimuli for increased testosterone secretion. Figure 9.7c is the most complex pattern, with three surges of testosterone above level B. In this case, territories are at high densities with frequent stimulatory male-male encounters. All these males are also mated so that they are exposed to sexually receptive females as well. Testosterone profiles are extremely labile in this scenario. Note that testosterone levels surge again during courtship and copulation for a second brood if the first is lost to a predator, that is, if no young are present, then there is no constraint of parental care requiring a low testosterone level (see Wingfield and Goldsmith 1990; Wingfield et al. 1989). Finally, in figure 9.7d, we see a different pattern of testosterone secretion that is entirely due to mate-guarding activities during the first brood and after loss of clutch to a predator (renesting). As this is a low-density territory with few male-male encounters, there is no elevation of testosterone above level B early in the season when territories are established, but there are surges when females are sexually receptive. Many other patterns are possible. One intriguing prediction of these data is that the response of males to sexually receptive females (with a surge in testosterone secretion) is also facultative. Although ovulation (the time of effective sexual receptivity) may be part of the predictable life-history cycle, its actual timing within the breeding season depends on many local factors and on the condition of the female. Thus males must be ready to respond appropriately whenever a female becomes receptive. The testosterone surge triggered by sexual behavior of receptive females may also be dependent upon the presence of other males, which provide potential competition for copulations and thus paternity

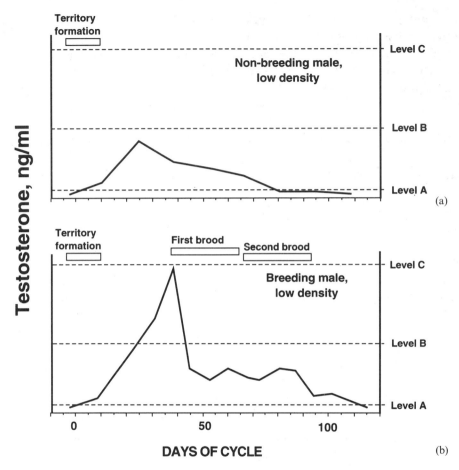

Figure 9.7
Four potential scenarios in the pattern of circulating testosterone levels in the reproductive cycle of the song sparrow, *Melospiza melodia*. Caption (a) represents testosterone cycles in males breeding at low density (few male-male interactions) and unmated (i.e., no social cues from receptive females). Here levels of testosterone stay within levels A and B—the normal life-history stages. Caption (b) includes breeding males at low density in which there are few male-male interactions, but social cues from receptive females are important at least for the first brood. Here there is one surge of testosterone above level B (i.e., triggers the transitory, facultative life-history stage). Caption (c) depicts the pattern of testosterone in males at high density when frequent male-male interactions and the presence of sexually receptive females may result in several peaks of testosterone secretion in the realm of transitory facultative life history stages (level C). Caption (d) shows a pattern that might be expected in a population with low density territories (few male-male interactions) but mated males lost a nest and renested. Here there will be fewer surges of testosterone above level B but more than in captions (a) and (b). See text for further details. These theoretical examples have actual documented examples in free-living male song and white-crowned sparrows (see Wingfield 1984; Wingfield and Farner 1978, 1979; Wingfield and Hahn 1994; Ball and Wingfield 1987; Wingfield and Goldsmith 1990).

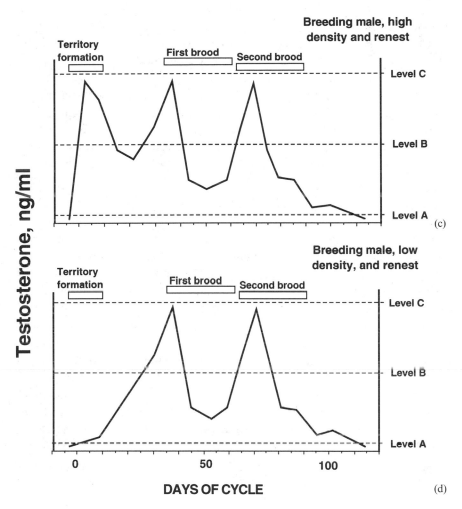

Figure 9.7 (continued)

of the brood. This is an entirely testable hypothesis that may further illuminate hormone-behavior interactions during the life cycle.

These four examples serve to illustrate how finite-state machine theory may provide a framework for explaining individual variation in testosterone secretion and the resulting pattern, which in turn provides bases for determining mechanisms. For example, these variations and the levels of physiological and behavioral state require either different hormones acting at each level or, more interestingly, different actions of the same hormone at each level. Possible mechanisms by which this could occur will be discussed later.

Territorial Aggression in Nonreproductive Contexts

Territorial behavior and aggression associated with dominance status in flocks may be expressed in many life-history stages (figures 9.1 and 9.2). The only exception is the prebasic moult stage, when individuals tend to be secretive and avoid agonistic interactions while growing feathers (which are vulnerable to damage during development). The transitory, facultative life-history stage may be triggered at any time in the predictable life-history cycle (figure 9.2). Does testosterone regulate aggression at these times also? Activation of territorial behavior by elevated circulating testosterone levels would obviously be appropriate in a breeding stage, but would be highly inappropriate in the nonbreeding season because of effects on reproductive physiology and morphology (figures 9.3 and 9.4). Diverse effects of a single hormone such as testosterone pose a number of problems for the regulation of territorial aggression in life-history stages other than breeding. These problems include inappropriate expression of physiological processes and morphology when the hormone is secreted in different life-history stages as well as "costs" in terms of reduced overall fitness such as increased mortality, suppression of the immune system, and other potentially deleterious effects (e.g., figure 9.4, Wingfield et al. 1997a). There is now growing evidence for different mechanisms activating aggression in nonreproductive contexts. Similar evidence has been presented for the control of sexual behavior in vertebrates when the expression of sexual behavior and the production of gametes (spermatogenesis and oocyte development) become dissociated (Crews 1984; Crews and Moore 1986).

Territorial Behavior in the Nonbreeding Season

There are many species of birds and other vertebrates, that are territorial in many life-history stages. Few have been studied in regard to the hormonal control mechanisms at different stages in the life-history cycle. Rufous song sparrows, *Melospiza melodia morphna*, are nonmigratory, remain territorial throughout much of the year, and mate or form an association with another individual on these territories (Wingfield 1994). Circulating levels of testosterone are high throughout the breeding stage, coincident with territorial behavior in a reproductive context. During the prebasic molt (August to September), males remain on their territories but show little aggression even if challenged by a simulated territorial intrusion consisting of a decoy male and broadcast of tape-recorded songs. As expected, plasma levels of testosterone are undetectable (Wingfield and Hahn 1994). In early autumn, just following the moult, male rufous song sparrows once again become territorial, but with no concomitant increase in circulating testosterone levels (Wingfield and Hahn 1994). Castration of free-living male song sparrows in October has no effect on their ability to maintain territories (Wingfield 1994), suggesting that neither circulating testosterone nor other gonadal hormones are essential. Males at this time also fail to respond to females made sexually receptive by experimental implants of estradiol (Wingfield and Monk 1994), suggesting that these males were unable to express any behaviors typical of the breeding stage. Additionally, the reproductive and nonreproductive territories of individual male rufous song sparrows may not always be the same. At one study site in western Washington State, it was found that breeding and nonbreeding territories may overlap extensively, or in part or be separated by up to 100m. Furthermore, many pairs on winter territories were not breeding pairs but had formed territorial alliances (Wingfield and Monk 1992). These data suggest that whereas territorial aggression in the reproductive and nonreproductive stages (see figure 9.1) may be similar in postures and vocalizations, the context may be totally different. Control mechanisms also appear to be different, at least in the breeding and nonbreeding stages.

High levels of testosterone during the breeding season may increase persistence of territorial aggression, especially after a territorial intrusion. In spring, territorial males patrol their territories and sing at a high frequency even after a simulated intrusion has been terminated and the decoy removed. In contrast, removal of a decoy after termination of a simulated territorial intrusion in autumn is followed by immediate cessation of territorial behavior. Implants of testosterone into free-living territorial males in autumn reinstate persistence of territorial aggression compared with controls (Wingfield 1994). It appears that although territorial aggression can be activated in the absence of testosterone in this species, persistence of aggression in the face of a simulated territorial intrusion, or after the intruder has retreated, is indeed testosterone-dependent. Apparently persistence of aggression following an intrusion is important in the breeding stage when reproductive success is in jeopardy, but not during the nonbreeding stage (Wingfield et al. 1997a).

An Apparent Paradox: Autumn "Sexuality"

Field endocrinology investigations allow us to ask questions about *why* there appear to be different hormone mechanisms regulating apparently similar behavioral traits in different life-history stages. They also generate precise hypotheses about determine mechanisms at a more reductionist level, as well as allow us to gain insight into how these diverse patterns evolved. It is clear that territorial aggression and associated agonistic behaviors occur at different life-history stages, but hormonal bases of aggression demonstrated in one stage may not apply in another. Finite-state machine theory has the potential to indicate where mechanisms that underlie the regulation of behavior in various taxa, or within a taxon at different states in the life cycle, may be expected to be similar or different. Autumn sexuality is an interesting case in which sexual behavior is expressed at a time when birds are presumably in the nonbreeding stage. However, in some avian species, autumnal territorial aggression and pair formation are indeed sexual in context because these pairs remain together through the winter and breed the following spring. Plasma levels of testosterone are also high at this time (see Wingfield et al. 1997a). Five avian species in which autumnal territoriality and pair formation are not sexual in context show no such peak in testosterone. All species have the normal spring peak of circulating testosterone at the beginning of the breeding season regardless of autumn sexuality (Wingfield et al. 1997a). These data in the context of finite-state machine theory raise the hypothesis that in species with autumnal peaks of testosterone secretion, the winter nonbreeding stage may be very short in duration and restricted to a short period after the prebasic moult. Thus the breeding stage for these species is much longer, beginning in autumn. In contrast, those species that show territorial behavior and alliances in nonreproductive contexts may have a much longer nonbreeding stage and a correspondingly shorter breeding stage (Wingfield et al. 1997a). These ideas are testable and may explain some contradictions in the literature in which there are claims of variation in reproductive function with season—some apparently overlapping with the nonbreeding season, whereas others clearly show complete temporal separation of breeding and winter nonbreeding seasons.

New Directions

The investigations described thus far indicate how behavioral ecology studies (of how and why animals interact in their natural habitat) can be combined with field endocrinology techniques. We can then follow hormonal changes accompanying patterns of behavior or manipulate endocrine profiles experimentally. These are powerful tools, which shed new light on apparent paradoxes of the multiple expression of similar behavioral traits at different stages in life history without common hormone mechanisms. Experimental manipulations of hormonal state in the field allow us to identify potential common themes, or to indicate where traditional thinking needs to be revised (Wingfield 1994; Wingfield et al. 1987). Comparing closely related taxa that live and breed at high elevations or latitudes with those from more temperate climes that express the same behavioral traits but in different patterns and contexts may reveal the ecological bases of hormone mechanisms and their role in maximizing fitness. Conversely, one could compare species that are not closely related but live in similar habitats and determine if hormone control mechanisms are also similar (convergent evolution) or whether each species uses different mechanisms to solve similar problems (Crews 1997). Controlling for simple phylogenetic differences is particularly important, and these approaches are entirely testable. A theoretical approach using finite-state machine theory and natural history data appears to be predictive of potential hormone mechanisms, but further testing in the laboratory is also needed. Understanding control mechanisms at the receptor and metabolite level is critical for interpreting field data. Any behavioral traits that are expressed in predictable patterns require regulatory mechanisms. Some possible future research directions are discussed below.

Central Actions of Peptides

Typically, hormone secretions activate behavioral traits in three ways (Becker et al. 1992; Nelson 1995; see also Wingfield et al. 1997). Hormones (1) may be secreted in a paracrine fashion and act locally as neurotransmitters or neuromodulators; (2) may be secreted into the blood (i.e., true endocrine) and then enter the CNS; or (3) may act though a combination of effects in which a blood-borne hormone may influence neurotransmitters and neuromodulators, which in turn regulate behavior.

In many vertebrates, particularly in the tropics, territorial aggression may be expressed throughout much of the life cycle, and breeding seasons may span much of the year (see, e.g., Levin and Wingfield 1992; Wingfield et al. 1997). It has been suggested that in these populations many behavioral patterns associated with reproduction and territorial aggression may be independent of hormonal activation (Wingfield 1994). In other words, such behaviors may be "hardwired" and the frequency of expression regulated by paracrine secretions and neurotransmitters within the brain. For example, gonadotropin-releasing hormone (GnRH) has well-known central effects on sexual behavior (see, e.g., Nelson 1995). In passerine birds there are two forms of GnRH, chicken-I and chicken-II (Sherwood et al. 1988). Both forms appear to be equipotent in releasing LH when injected into song sparrows (Wingfield and Farner 1993), but it is generally thought that only chicken-I GnRH is hypophysiotropic. Chicken-II GnRH is expressed in neurons that do not project to the median eminence of the hypothalamus and are not neuroendocrine in function (see, e.g., Maney et al. 1997). Furthermore, central injection (into the third ventricle in the hypothalamus) of both GnRH forms into white-crowned sparrows indicates that chicken-II GnRH promotes sexual behavior and that chicken-I form has separate effects (Maney et al. 1997). Other peptides may also act centrally. Recent evidence in white-crowned sparrows suggests that arginine vasotocin (AVT) administration into the third ventricle of the hypothalamus stimulates vocalizations that could be associated with territorial behavior such as components of song and some aggressive calls (Maney et al. 1997). This line of research may in the future provide a basis for centrally acting peptides that regulate reproductive and territorial behavior even in the absence of peripheral sex steroids.

Development   There is growing evidence that exposure to hormones during development, that is, from sex steroids deposited in egg yolk by the mother, may have marked effects on aggressive behavior when the chick becomes adult (Schwabl 1993, 1996) and independent of circulating sex steroids during the breeding season. It will be intriguing to determine whether surges of sex steroids during development may influence centrally acting peptides such as GnRH forms and AVT in the adult.

Receptors and Hormone Metabolism within Target Cells   There is considerable evidence that some steroid hormones can be metabolized to alternative, biologically active forms within target cells that then bind to different receptors. Testosterone, for example, has four potential fates within cells (see, e.g., Balthazart 1983). First, a direct action of testosterone is possible after binding to a receptor specific for that steroid hormone. Second, there may be aromatization to estradiol-17B which then acts through estrogen receptors. Third, five-α reductase may reduce testosterone to 5a-dihydrotestosterone, which may have its own receptor; and fourth, five-β reductase may reduce testosterone to 5β-dihydrotestosterone, which apparently has little biological effect and thus may be a deactivation shunt. Any of these pathways may be utilized to modify a cell's response to testosterone and regulate seasonal behaviors (see, e.g., Silverin and Deviche, 1991). Aromatization has received considerable attention in both development and during seasonal reproduction in relation to sexual behavior and song in birds. Furthermore, it appears that the brain may be a major site for aromatase activity, which results in significant production of estradiol in some species. The substrate for aromatization can be testosterone itself or any other aromatizable androgen (Schlinger and Arnold 1991). This raises the possibility that temporal or population changes in the cellular distribution of aromatase could significantly alter the responsiveness of a tissue to testosterone. Alternatively, secretion of an aromatizable androgen other than testosterone could reduce morphological, physiological, and behavioral effects of testosterone but still activate estrogen-dependent processes within cells that express aromatase (Schlinger 1994). It has been suggested that in white-crowned sparrows, expression of reproductive behaviors (especially song) in the nonbreeding season may be regulated by estrogens since aromatase activity in the telencephalon is high in autumn and winter (Schlinger et al. 1992). Such studies coupled with analyses of distribution of testosterone receptors will be critical in the future. The avian models cited above may be ideal for these studies, in that they focus on diverse patterns of behavior related to ecological constraints rather than variation due to phylogeny.

Multiple Receptor Types   In addition to having enzymatic effects on testosterone at the target cell, different receptor types may be involved in mediating the responses of a neuron to fluctuating concentrations of testosterone. If hormones act at three different levels (figure 9.5), different receptor types may have evolved that specialize in mediating hormonal effects characteristic of each level. There is growing evidence for this hypothesis. Two types of intracellular receptors have been identified for glucocorticosteroids in mammals (see McEwen et al. 1988 for review). The type I receptor has a high affinity for corticosteroids and may regulate day-to-day actions. This receptor appears to be saturated at intermediate and low levels of corticosterone such as at levels A and B. The type II receptor has a lower affinity for corticosterone and requires higher concentrations of steroid to become saturated. It is tempting to suggest that type II receptors may mediate effects of corticosteroids at level C. Indeed, McEwen et al. (1988) have suggested three possible roles that glucocorticosteroids may play in mammalian nervous systems. First, they may activate neural activity during the diurnal changes in pituitary-adrenal function, which suggests a primary role for the type I receptor. Second, they are important for adaptation of the central nervous system to "stress," suggesting a role for the type II receptor. Third, chronically high levels of glucocorticosteroids lead to loss of neurons, especially in the hippocampus. However, down-regulation of corticosteroid receptors in response to chronic high levels may act as a protective mechanism to reduce deleterious effects such as neuron loss (McEwen et al. 1988). These actions may vary across taxa and with time of year, but the evidence is compelling that at least two types of glucocorticoid receptor could mediate different effects at levels B and C. It remains to be seen whether there are different receptor types for testosterone, especially with differences in affinity that would be conducive to activation at levels A, B, or C.

A characteristic of genomic actions of steroid hormones is that it takes time (at least 30 min., usually hours) for the responses to become apparent. However, some actions of glucocorticosteroids may occur within minutes. In amphibians, evidence exists for a membrane receptor for corticosterone (Orchinik et al. 1991) that may mediate glucocorticosteroid effects much more rapidly. If such membrane receptors for steroid hormones prove to be more widespread, they may play a role in mediating rapid responses to environmental stimuli in many contexts. A combination of membrane and genomic actions of glucocorticosteroids may then mediate different effects at levels A, B, and C. Again, it remains to be seen whether such a receptor might exist for testosterone.

Deactivation of Behavior There is at least preliminary evidence that other hormones may "deactivate" the expression of a specific suite of behavior for restricted periods, for example, stress-induced abandonment of reproduction. Wingfield and Silverin (1986) show that in song sparrows, implants of corticosterone, which deliver a pulse of corticosterone for approximately two days, result in marked suppression of territorial aggression even though plasma levels of testosterone remain within the normal range for that time of year. Furthermore, in the side-blotched lizard, *Uta stansburiana*, implants of testosterone increase size of the home range, but simultaneous implants of corticosterone block this effect (DeNardo and Sinervo 1994). These data suggest that corticosterone may truly deactivate behavior associated with maintaining a home range rather than decrease secretion of testosterone, which then results in a decrease of territorial behavior. Corticosterone has since been shown also to decrease sexual behavior and parental behavior, although whether this is through a direct mechanism or is indirect through suppression of other hormones that have appropriate activational effects remains to be determined (Moore and Zoeller 1985; Wingfield and Silverin 1986). The possibility that other hormones (e.g., endorphins) may deactivate reproductive and associated behaviors for short periods, for example, during molt, is also possible (see, e.g., Maney and Wingfield 1998), but this remains to be determined in the natural habitat. This may prove to be a highly productive area of research, especially given the diverse patterns of behavior within closely related species, which allow us to at least partly separate phylogenetic effects.

Effects of Behavior on Neuroendocrine and Endocrine Secretions A potentially useful tool of investigation is to use seasonal changes and populational differences as natural "gene knockouts" to determine mechanisms. These, in combination with techniques such as immunocytochemistry or in situ hybridization for immediate early gene products, may allow us to identify possible neural pathways. Several years ago, research on oncogenes revealed that protein products of immediate early genes such as c-fos and jun in the nuclei of neurons can be useful indicators of responses to environmental stimuli in mammals (see, e.g., Curran et al. 1990; Sheng and Greenberg 1990). These proteins form complexes that influence transcription of other genes in response to incoming signals (see, e.g., Curran and Franza 1988). They are expressed only briefly (usually for a few hours or less) and thus are excellent signals of neuronal activation in response to neuronal stimulation (by, e.g., environmental cues). Exposure of adult male Japanese quail, *Coturnix japonica*, to a receptive female results in an elevation of c-fos protein immunostaining in the hyperstriatum, nucleus intercollicularis, and hypothalamus (Meddle et al. 1997). Free-living male song sparrows exposed to a simulated territorial intrusion showed higher expression of another immediate early gene, ZENK, in the song control nuclei and auditory regions of the brain (Jarvis et al. 1997). The act of singing also increased expression of ZENK in the higher vocal center and other song control nuclei of male canaries, *Serinus canarius*, and zebra finches, *Taenopygia guttata* (Jarvis and Nottebohm 1997). As these authors point out, visualization of immediate early gene expression will be a useful tool to identify neurons that respond to either physical or social environmental signals.

Conclusions

Given the almost bewildering array of social behaviors exhibited by vertebrates, it is not surprising that the mechanisms by which these behavioral patterns are regulated by hormones, and the effects of behavioral interactions on hormone secretion are equally complex. Nevertheless, field and laboratory experiments, especially comparative studies of closely related taxa that display markedly different patterns of behavior, are beginning to indicate that general underlying themes—possibly mechanisms—do exist. Beginning with finite-state machine theory, we can suggest a framework for describing changes in life-history stages that allows us to rationalize expression of similar behaviors at different times of year and in different contexts. This in turn enables us to take a more reductionist route and explore possible multiple hormone mechanisms in these different stages. Comparative studies on birds reveal that testosterone activates a type of aggression, territorial behavior, in those species that are territorial only during the breeding season. Territoriality at other times appears to be independent of sex-steroid control, at least from gonadal sources. Why are there different control mechanisms? It appears that there are evolutionary "costs" to high levels of circulating testosterone. In males that express parental behavior, high circulating testosterone levels interfere with parental care, resulting in reduced reproductive success. On the other hand, agonistic interactions between males tend to increase testosterone levels. Thus control mechanisms of testosterone secretion must balance the need to compete with other males and provide parental care. Other costs of high concentrations of testosterone include wounding, increased risk of predation, and energetic considerations. Clearly, strong natural selection must exist for individuals that can balance mechanisms that not only turn on testosterone secretion, but also turn it off or control its effects. Using a combination of behavioral ecology, field endocrine techniques, and laboratory investigations, we may be able to explore the ecological bases of endocrine phenomena in much greater depth. One cannot help but imagine that a great deal remains to be discovered using this approach.

Acknowledgments

Much of the work presented herein was initiated while two of the authors (J. Wingfield and M. Ramenofsky) were at the Rockefeller University Field Research Center working with Peter Marler. He had a marked influence on many of the theoretical ideas as well as interpretation of apparently contradictory data. Both of these authors are eternally grateful for the opportunity to work at R.U.F.R.C., and for the ideas, guidance, and unflagging encouragement that Marler gave. Preparation of this manuscript was aided by grants from the National Science Foundation (IBN-9631350 and OPP-9530826) and by a Russell F. Stark University Professorship to JCW. A John Simon Guggenheim Fellowship, a Benjamin Meaker Fellowship (from the University of Bristol), and a grant from the University of Washington, Royalties Research Fund to JCW are also gratefully acknowledged.

References

Arnold, A. P., Wade, J., Grisham, W., Jacobs, E. C., and Campagnoni, A. T. (1996) Sexual differentiation of the brain in birds. *Dev. Neurosci.* 18:124–136.

Ball, G. F. (1993) The neural integration of environmental information in seasonally breeding birds. *Am. Zool.* 33:185–199.

Ball, G. F. and Wingfield, J. C. (1986) Changes in plasma levels of sex steroids in relation to multiple broodedness and nest site density in male starlings. *Physiol. Zool.* 60:191–199.

Balthazart, J. (1983) Hormonal correlates of behavior. In *Avian Biology*, ed. by D. S. Farner, J. R. King, and K. C. Parkes, vol. 7, pp. 221–365. New York: Academic Press.

Becker, J. B., Breedlove, S. M., and Crews, D., eds. (1992) *Behavioral Endocrinology*. Cambridge, MA: MIT Press.

Beletsky, L. D., Gori, D. F., Freeman, S., and Wingfield, J. C. (1995) Testosterone and polygyny in birds. *Current Ornithology* 12:1–41.

Crews, D. (1984) Gamete production, sex hormone secretion, and mating behavior uncoupled. *Horm. Behav.* 18:22–28.

Crews, D. (1997) Species diversity and the evolution of behavioral controlling mechanisms. *Ann. N.Y. Acad. Sci.* 807:1–21.

Crews, D. and Moore, M. C. (1986) Evolution of mechanisms controlling mating behavior. *Science* 231:121–125.

Curran, T., Abate, C., Cohen, D. R., MacGregor, P. F., Rauscher, F. J., Sonnenberg, J. L., Connor, J. A., and Morgan, J. I. (1990) Inducible proto-oncogene transcription factors: Third messengers in the brain? *Cold Spring Harbor Symp. Quant. Biol.* 55:225–234.

Curran, T. and Franza, B. R. (1988) Fos and Jun: The AP-1 connection. *Cell* 55:395–397.

DeNardo, D. F. and Sinervo, B. (1994) Effects of steroid hormone interaction on activity and home range size of male lizards. *Horm. Behav.* 28:273–287.

Dufty, Jr., A. M. (1989) Testosterone and survival: A cost of aggressiveness? *Horm. Behav.* 23:185–193.

Francis, R. C., Soma, K., and Fernald, R. D. (1993) Social regulation of the brain-pituitary-gonadal axis. *Proc. Natl. Acad. Sci.* (USA) 90:7794–7798.

Gause, W. C. and March, J. A. (1986) Effect of testosterone treatments for varying periods on autoimmune development and on specific infiltrating leukocyte populations in the thyroid gland of obese strain chickens. *Clin. Immunol. Immunopathol.* 39:664–478.

Glickman, S. E., Frank, L. G., Holecamp, K. E., Smale, L., and Licht, P. (1993) Costs and benefits of "androgenization" in the female spotted hyena: The natural selection of physiological mechanisms. In *Perspectives in Ethology*, volume 10: *Behavior and Evolution*, ed. by P. P. G. Bateson et al., pp. 87–117. New York: Plenum Press.

Gorbman, A., Dickhoff, W. W., Vigna, S. R., Clark, N. B., and Ralph, C. L. (1983) *Comparative Endocrinology*. New York: John Wiley and Sons.

Harding, C. F. (1983) Hormonal influences on avian aggressive behavior. In *Hormones and Aggressive Behavior*, ed. by B. Svare, pp. 435–467. New York: Plenum Press.

Hegner, R. E. and Wingfield, J. C. (1987) Effects of experimental manipulation of testosterone levels on parental investment and breeding success in male house sparrows. *Auk* 104:462–469.

Hillgarth, N., Ramenofsky, M., and Wingfield, J. C. (1997) Testosterone and sexual selection. *Behav. Ecol.* 8:108–109.

Hillgarth, N. and Wingfield, J. C. (1997) Parasite-mediated sexual selection: Endocrine aspects. In *Host-Parasite Evolution*, ed. by D. H. Clayton and J. Moore, pp. 78–104. Oxford: Oxford University Press.

Jacobs, J. (1996) Regulation of Life History Stages within Individuals in Unpredictable Environments. Ph.D. Thesis, University of Washington.

Jarvis, E. D. and Nottebohm, F. (1997) Motor-driven gene expression. *Proc. Natl. Acad. Sci.* (USA) 94:4097–4102.

Jarvis, E. D., Schwabl, H., Ribeiro, S., and Mello, C. V. (1997) Brain gene regulation by territorial singing behavior in freely ranging songbirds. *NeuroReport* 8:2073–2077.

Ketterson, E. D., Nolan, Jr., V., Wolf, L., Ziegenfus, C. (1992) Testosterone and avian life histories: Effects of experimentally elevated testosterone on behavior and correlates of fitness in the dark-eyed junco (*Junco hyemalis*). *Am. Nat.* 140:980–999.

Ketterson, E. D., Nolan, Jr., V., Cawthorn, M. J., Parker, P. G., and Ziegenfus, C. (1996) Phenotypic engineering: using hormones to explore the mechanistic and functional bases of phenotypic variation in nature. *Ibis* 138:70–86.

Konishi, M., Emlen, S., Ricklefs, R., and Wingfield, J. C. (1989) Contributions of bird studies to biology. *Science* 246:465–472.

Logan, C. A. and Wingfield, J. C. (1990) Autumnal territorial aggression is independent of plasma testosterone in mockingbirds. *Horm. Behav.* 24:568–581.

Levin, R. and Wingfield, J. C. (1992) Control of territorial aggression in tropical birds. *Ornis Scand.* 23:284–291.

McEwen, B., Brinton, R. E., and Sapolsky, R. M. (1988) Glucocorticoid receptors and behavior: Implications for the stress response. *Adv. Exp. Med. Biol.* 245:35–45.

Maney, D. L., Richardson, R. D., and Wingfield, J. C. (1997) Central administration of chicken gonado-tropin-releasing hormone II enhances courtship behavior in a female sparrow. *Horm. Behav.* 32:11–18.

Maney, D., Goode, C. T., and Wingfield, J. C. (1997) Intraventricular infusion of arginine vasotocin induces singing in a female songbird. *J. Neuroendocrinol.* 9:487–491.

Maney, D. and Wingfield, J. C. (1998) Neuroendocrine suppression of female courtship in a wild passerine: Corticotropin-releasing factor and endogenous opioids. *J. Neuroendocrinol.* 10:593–599.

March, J. A. and Scanes, C. G. (1994) Neuroendocrine-immune interactions. *Poultry Sci.* 73:1049–1061.

Marler, C. A. and Moore, M. C. (1988) Evolutionary costs of aggression revealed by testosterone manipulations in free-living male lizards. *Behav. Ecol. Sociobiol.* 23:21–26.

Meddle, S. L., King, V. M., Follett, B. K., Wingfield, J. C., Ramenofsky, M., Foidart, A., and Balthazart, J. (1997) Copulation activates fos-like immunoreactivity in the male quail forebrain. *Behav. Brain Res.* 85:143–159.

Moore, F. L. and Zoeller, R. T. (1985) Stress-induced inhibition of reproduction: Evidence of suppressed secretion of LHRH in an amphibian. *Gen. Comp. Endocrinol.* 60:252–258.

Moore, M. C. (1983) Effect of female sexual displays on the endocrine physiology and behavior of male white-crowned sparrows, *Zonotrichia leucophrys. J. Zool.* (Lond.) 199:137–148.

Moyer, K. E. (1968) Kinds of aggression and their physiological basis. *Commun. Behav. Biol.* 2:65–87.

Nelson, R. J. (1995) *An Introduction to Behavioral Endocrinology.* Sunderland, MA: Sinauer Assoc.

Nolan, Jr., V., Ketterson, E. D., Ziegenfus, C., Cullen, D. P., and Chandler, C. R. (1992) Testosterone and avian life histories: Effects of experimentally elevated testosterone on prebasic molt and survival in male dark-eyed juncos. *Condor* 94:364–370.

Orchinik, M., Murray, T. F., and Moore, F. L. (1991) A corticosteroid receptor in neuronal membranes. *Science* 252:1848–1851.

Schlinger, B. A. (1994) Estrogens to song: Picograms to sonograms. *Horm. Behav.* 28:191–198.

Schlinger, B. A. and Arnold, A. P. (1991) Brain is a major site of estrogen synthesis in a male songbird. *Proc. Natl. Acad. Sci.* (USA) 88:4191–4194.

Schlinger, B. A., Slotow, R. H., and Arnold, A. P. (1992) Plasma estrogens and brain aromatase in winter white-crowned sparrows. *Ornis Scand.* 23:292–297.

Schwabl, H. (1993) Yolk is a source of maternal testosterone for developing birds. *Proc. Natl. Acad. Sci.* (USA): 11446–11450.

Schwabl, H. (1996) Environment modifies the testosterone levels of a female bird and its eggs. *J. Exp. Zool.* 276:157–163.

Schwabl, H. and Kriner, E. (1991) Territorial aggression and song of male European robins (*Erithacus rubecula*) in autumn and spring: Effects of antiandrogen treatment. *Horm. Behav.* 25:180–194.

Sheng, M. and Greenberg, M. E. (1990) The regulation and function of c-fos and other immediate early genes in the nervous system. *Neuron* 4:477–485.

Sherwood, N., Wingfield, J. C., Ball, G. F., and Dufty, Jr., A. M. (1988) Identity of GnRH in passerine birds: Comparison of GnRH in song sparrow (*Melospiza melodia*) and starling (*Sturnus vulgaris*) with 5 vertebrate GnRHs. *Gen. Comp. Endocrinol.* 69:341–351.

Silverin, B. (1980) Effects of long-acting testosterone treatment on free-living pied flycatchers, *Ficedula hypoleuca*, during the breeding period. *Anim. Behav.* 28:906–912.

Silverin, B. and Deviche, P. (1991) Biochemical characterization and seasonal changes in the concentration of testosterone-metabolizing enzymes in the European great tit (*Parus major*) brain. *Gen. Comp. Endocrinol.* 81:146–159.

Wilczynski, W., Allison, J. D., and Marler, C. A. (1993) Sensory pathways linking social and environmental cues to endocrine regions of amphibian forebrains. *Brain Behav. Evol.* 42:252–264.

Wingfield, J. C. (1984) Environmental and endocrine control of reproduction in the song sparrow, *Melospiza melodia.* I. Temporal organization of the breeding cycle. *Gen. Comp. Endocrinol.* 56:406–416.

Wingfield, J. C. (1985) Short-term changes in plasma levels of hormones during establishment and defense of a breeding territory in male song sparrows, *Melospiza melodia*. *Horm. Behav.* 19:174–187.

Wingfield, J. C. (1990) Interrelationship of androgens, aggression, and mating systems. In *Endocrinology of Birds: Molecular to Behavioral*, ed. by M. Wada, S. Ishii, and C. G. Scanes, pp. 187–205. Tokyo: Jap. Sci. Soc. Press; Berlin: Springer-Verlag.

Wingfield, J. C. (1994) Control of territorial aggression in a changing environment. *Psychoneuroendocrinology* 19:709–721.

Wingfield, J. C., Ball, G. F., Dufty, Jr., A. M., Hegner, R. E., and Ramenofsky, M. (1987) Testosterone and aggression in birds: Tests of the "challenge hypothesis." *Am. Sci.* 75:602–608.

Wingfield, J. C. and Farner, D. S. (1978) The endocrinology of a naturally breeding population of the white-crowned sparrow (*Zonotrichia leucophrys pugetensis*). *Physiol. Zool.* 51:188–205.

Wingfield, J. C. and Farner, D. S. (1979) Some endocrine correlates of renesting after loss of clutch or brood in the white-crowned sparrow, *Zonotrichia leucophrys gambelii. Gen. Comp. Endocrinol.* 38:322–331.

Wingfield, J. C. and Farner, D. S. (1993) The endocrinology of wild species. In Avian Biology, ed. by D. S. Farner, J. R. King, and K. S. Parkes, vol. 9, pp. 163–237. New York: Academic Press.

Wingfield, J. C. and Goldsmith, A. R. (1990) Plasma levels of prolactin and gonadal steroids in relation to multiple brooding and renesting in free-living populations of the song sparrow, *Melospiza melodia. Horm. Behav.* 24:89–103.

Wingfield, J. C. and Hahn, T. P. (1994) Testosterone and territorial behavior in sedentary and migratory sparrows. *Anim. Behav.* 47:77–89.

Wingfield, J. C., Hegner, R. E., Dufty, Jr., A. M., and Ball, G. F. (1990) The "challenge hypothesis": Theoretical implications for patterns of testosterone secretion, mating systems, and breeding strategies. *Am. Nat.* 136:829–846.

Wingfield, J. C., Jacobs, and J., Hillgarth, N. (1997a) Ecological constraints and the evolution of hormone-behavior interrelationships. *The Integrative Neurobiology of Affiliation*, ed. by C. S. Carter, I. I. Lederhendler, and B. Kirkpatrick. N. Y. Acad. Sci. 807:22–41.

Wingfield, J. C. and Kenagy, G. J. (1991) Natural regulation of reproductive cycles. In *Vertebrate Endocrinology: Fundamentals and Biomedical Implications*, ed. by M. Schreibman and R. E. Jones, vol. 4, part B, pp. 181–241. New York: Academic Press.

Wingfield, J. C. and Monk, D. (1992) Control and context of year-round territorial aggression in the nonmigratory song sparrow, *Melospiza melodia morphna. Ornis Scand.* 23.298–303.

Wingfield, J. C. and Monk, D. (1994) Behavioral and hormonal responses of male song sparrows to estrogenized females during the non-breeding season. *Horm. Behav.* 28:146–154.

Wingfield, J. C. and Ramenofsky, M. (1985) Hormonal and environmental control of aggression in birds. In *Neurobiology*, ed. by R. Gilles and J. Balthazart, pp. 92–104. Berlin: Springer-Verlag.

Wingfield, J. C., Breuner, C., Jacobs, J., Lynn, S., Maney, D., Ramenofsky, M., and Richardson, R. (1998) Ecological bases of hormone-behavior interactions: The "emergency life history stage." *Amer. Zool.* 38:191–206.

Wingfield, J. C., Ronchi, E., Marler, C., and Goldsmith, A. R. (1989) Interactions of steroids and prolactin during the reproductive cycle of the song sparrow (*Melospiza melodia*). *Physiol. Zool.* 62:11–24.

Wingfield, J. C. and Silverin, B. (1986) Effects of corticosterone on territorial behavior of free-living song sparrows, *Melospiza melodia. Horm. Behav.* 20:405–417.

Wingfield, J. C., Whaling, C. S., and Marler, P. R. (1994) Communication in vertebrate aggression and reproduction: The role of hormones. In *Physiology of Reproduction*, second edition, ed. by E. Knobil and J. D. Neill, pp. 303–342. New York: Raven Press.

Witschi, E. (1961) Sex and secondary sexual characters. In *Biology and Comparative Physiology of Birds*, ed. by A. J. Marshall, vol. 2, pp. 115–168. New York: Academic Press.

II ONTOGENY OF COMMUNICATION

Marc D. Hauser

Development represents a process of change, of losing, gaining, and modifying particular characteristics. Of interest to biologists and psychologists are the mechanisms involved in this transformational process. What factors constrain the potential range of phenotypic variation? What is the initial starting point? How does the organism's genome affect what can be learned? Are there critical periods for learning, and if so, what triggers the opening and closing of these windows of opportunity? How long does the brain remain open to learning? What determines differences between species in how they learn and what they learn? What are the adaptive consequences of particular learning styles?

These are fascinating questions. They are also difficult to answer. The difficulty stems, in part, from our obsession with creating dichotomies, of labeling a character as either innately specified or experientially constructed. And this dichotomy emerges, to some extent, from a desire to set up the scientific study of development in terms of an equation with two input variables: genes + experience = character form/function at time t. This conceptual partitioning of the world in turn mandates a specific experimental approach. In particular, development is studied by manipulating one of the input variables while holding the other constant. Thus, with recent advances in gene knockout procedures, molecular biologists can delete a gene from the organism's genome and then document the phenotypic consequences, or lack thereof. Conversely, particular types of experience can be withheld or augmented in an attempt to determine how the timing and quality of experience influences character development.

As several historical treatises have documented, the two-variable approach to development has led to acrimonious debates in the literature, the famous nature-nurture arguments (Bateson 1991; Elman et al. 1996; Gottlieb 1992; Marler and Terrace 1984; Oyama 1982; Piatelli-Palmarini 1980; Pinker 1994, 1997; Raff 1996). To move beyond such academic wars, many researchers have taken the position that developmental change involves an interaction between genes and the environment; to those well versed in quantitative genetics and the analysis of heritability, the significance of this interaction term will come as no surprise. In contrast to the increasing attention given to gene and experience interactions, there has been less interest in the position that the genome constrains what can be learned and what kinds of experience are attended to and incorporated into the ontogenetic process (Marler 1989; Pinker 1994). This view befits many developmental systems and is a position taken by many of the authors in this section.

One way to think of the problem of development is as a naturalist, taking notes on the patterns of change and then assessing the underlying causes. This leads to a documentation of the range of phenotypic variation, the initial state, and the time course for change. Figure II.1 represents an attempt to characterize a suite of possible ontogenetic trajectories and their underlying causes (see also Gottlieb 1992; Werker 1989). The top two cases represent caricatures of nature and nurture, trajectories that may well lack real-world analogs. Though hypothetical, they represent extremes on the topological landscape of developmental possibilities. The three other conditions are more representative of real-world phenomenon, and they generally map on to the patterns of ontogenetic change depicted by the authors in this section. Thus, in case 3, the character undergoes some modification prior to the onset of experience and then, upon exposure to particularly relevant experience, undergoes substantial change leading to a family of phenotypic trajectories. The end state, or what I have described as the species-typical level, represents a set of possible phenotypes, all of which fall within the range of natural variation. What I envision here is that the genome sets up what is possible, allowing experience to guide the organism to a stylized phenotypic outcome. This pattern, which is reminiscent of Waddington's (1957, 1975) epigenetic landscape, is characteristic of the ontogeny of call usage in several nonhuman primate species (chapter 14). In case 4, experience rapidly takes the character to a normal adult form and, if experience is maintained, preserves the character in this state. If, however, experience is removed, then the character atrophies. A classic example of such maintenance followed by loss is the perception of phonemes in human language acquisition (chapter 15). Prior to the age of 10–12 months, human infants can discriminate all of the critical speech distinctions of the world's languages. This period of global discrimination is immediately followed by significant loss, as the details of the native language environment begin to channel the infant's attention and restrict its discriminatory capacity to distinctions within the local linguistic environment; if the child grows up in a bilingual environment, then it maintains a larger set of discriminations. Case 5 builds in a critical or sensitive period for exposure to character-relevant experiences and attempts to distinguish between cases where experience has an immediate effect on form and function and cases where there is a period of quiescence, with experience integrated into the system at some level, only to be expressed at a later date in its species-typical form. Some aspects of song learning among passerine birds fall under this ontogenetic pattern (chapters 10–13).

The landscape of potential ontogenetic trajectories is certainly broader than what I have sketched. The five cases presented in figure II.1, however, provide a skeletal structure of developmental patterns, one that is given flesh by the authors in this section.

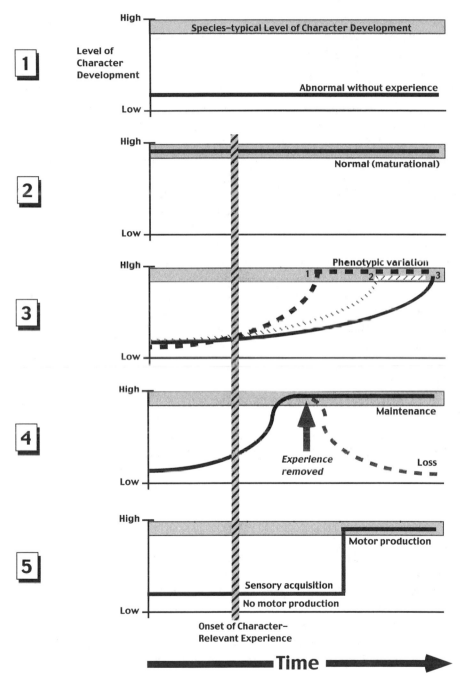

Figure II.1

In the opening chapter (chapter 10), Peter Marler directly attacks the *innate-learned* dichotomy, first laying out some of the historical reasons for such terms, and then arguing that they have severely compromised the kinds of discoveries we have made in the area of vocal communication. To illustrate this point, he returns to some of his own classic work on song development in the passerine songbirds, critically evaluating the early models of acquisition. In particular, Marler argues that songbirds come equipped with innate knowledge of the species-typical song repertoire, neurally encoded song elements such as notes, syllables, and phrasing. This initial knowledge determines *what* the young bird attends to, and *when* it should attend. In contrast with earlier views, then, on this view the function of social and acoustic experience is not to tutor the young bird, but rather to select from the potential range of song variants that could be realized during the course of development. These ideas are not only of great importance to those studying behavioral development, but have significant implications for those working on the neurobiology of memory and learning (chapters 3 and 12), as well as sensory motor coordination (chapter 2).

It is not uncommon to hear people talk about *the bird*, as if there was a prototypical exemplar for the group. If there was ever an antidote to this naive view, it is clearly articulated in Don Kroodsma's chapter (11) on the causes and consequences of variation in avian song structure. Some passerines species acquire one song during a sensitive period of development and then sing this song for the rest of their lives. These are *closed-ended* learners. Other species learn a song during a sensitive period, but then modify their song from season to season. These are the *open-ended* learners. Within each of these groups, there is further variation, with some species showing significant differences in song structure across a broad geographic range, and others showing none at all; for some species, the kind of material learned, as well as the timing of learning, is highly influenced by the social context, whereas other species are only weakly influenced. These patterns of variation serve as important warnings for those who wish to draw parallels between field and laboratory studies, and for those neuroscientists hoping to find a model system on the basis of a single species. Kroodsma's chapter therefore provides us with an elegant cataloging of song variation among the passerines, a dissection of the possible causes and consequences of such variation (see chapter 21), and a programmatic handbook for future work on avian song learning.

In part 1, we learned from the chapters by Nottebohm, Ball, and Suthers that the songbirds, and particularly the males of each species, are equipped with neural circuitry that selectively subserves song production and perception. Most of this work has focused on the nuclei responsible for song production in adult birds, with relatively less work on single neurons and the neural changes that accompany the earliest phases of song acquisition. Alison Doupe and Michele Solis (chapter 12) provide an overview, with much new data, on how neurons in the anterior forebrain of the zebra finch respond to different song classes over the course of development. Paralleling the ontogeny of alarm call usage in vervet monkeys (chapter 14) and the development of speech in humans (chapter 15), young zebra finches begin life with a quite general response to song. Over time, the specificity of the neural response increases. As the period of song crystallization approaches, the neurons become selectively tuned to the bird's own song. In the future, it will be important to compare these data on a closed-ended learner (zebra finch) with an open-ended learner such as the canary, where new songs wax and wane across mating seasons.

The canary has long served as a model species in studies of avian song, and in particular, as a model of the neurobiological substrate subserving song production and perception (chapters 2, 3, and 8). When describing *the canary*, however, we must move cautiously, for there are several genetic strains, artificially bred for either their morphology (e.g., Border, Norwich, and Yorkshire) or for their song (e.g., Roller and Belgian Waterschlager). Paul Mundinger (chapter 13) takes advantage of this artificial selection experiment to explore the behavioral genetics of song and song learning, contrasting strains where song has changed little from the wild type with those where it has changed markedly. Results show clear genetic effects on learning, with some strains (e.g., Border and Border-Roller hybrids) revealing great facility in acquiring the wild-type song, whereas other strains (e.g., pure Roller) fail to acquire such song material. These studies, still in their infancy, set the stage for further analyses into the genetics of song learning, and as discussed by Nottebohm (chapter 3), for assessing how stimulation of the genes for song production may turn on a cascade of neurobiological processes.

Much of the work on vocal development in animals has focused on changes in the acoustic morphology of the signal over time, on characterizing how acoustic experience sculpts call or song structure. In contrast with this component of vocal learning, relatively less effort has been devoted to the ontogeny of call usage and comprehension, that is, to how animals work out the function or meaning of a call and the context for its implementation. Robert Seyfarth and Dorothy Cheney (chapter 14) tackle this empirical gap by reviewing the current literature on nonhuman primate vocal development, using as their conceptual guide many of the most recent discoveries in human language acquisition. In striking contrast with its significance in both songbirds and humans, as well as some bats and marine mammals, acoustic experience plays only a limited role in the ontogeny of nonhuman primate call structure; most monkeys and apes are apparently born with the capacity to produce accurate renditions of the species-typical call, with changes in structure determined by maturational changes in the vocal tract. The fact that nonhuman primates appear to lack the capacity for this kind of vocal learning is paradoxical, with no convincing explanations yet provided. Vocal usage and comprehension, however, present a different story. Here, experience plays an important role. Like the songbirds described by Doupe and Solis, several monkey species are born with a quite general understanding of call function or meaning; they tend to overgeneralize their usage of calls in the same way that a young child might say "doggie" to all four-legged animals. With time, the precise contextual target for a call is refined, with comprehension of call function and meaning preceding call usage. These findings parallel those obtained on human children's acquisition of words.

Most work in linguistics, with its focus on parameter setting, cross-cultural similarities and differences in syntactical structure, and constraints on word order and sentence length, has no bearing on studies of animal communication. One area of research, however, of considerable relevance to studies of animal communication comes from work on how human infants acquire the sound patterns of spoken language. Patricia Kuhl's chapter (15), which concludes this section, provides a state-of-the-art review of this literature, focusing in particular on some of her most recent findings on the perception of speech, an ontogenetic process that involves not only sound, but visual input from the face producing speech sounds. Among the many important results reviewed by Kuhl, perhaps the most important, and certainly the most radical, is that language input alters the structure of the infant's brain, setting up biases with respect to how speech is perceived and organized conceptually. Specifically, although humans are born with a capacity to discriminate sound contrasts from both native and non-native languages, by six months, input from the native language has altered the infant's perceptual world. She now hears her native language in a fundamentally different way than she hears comparable sounds from non-native languages. Within her native language, there are prototypical exemplars—especially good representatives of a phonetic category—that help to anchor a perceptual map of the relevant linguistic distinctions. This map, in turn, serves as a filter, guiding the infant's attention, and ultimately, functioning as an instructional mechanism for acquiring language. Like Marler's theoretical ideas on song learning in birds, Kuhl's conceptual perspective provides a number of important insights into human brain development.

References

Bateson, P. (1991) Are there principles of behavioural development? In *The Development and Integration of Behaviour*, ed. by P. Bateson, pp. 19–40. Cambridge: Cambridge University Press.

Elman, J., Bates, E., Johnson, M., Karmiloff Smith, A., Parisi, J., and Plunkett, J. (1996) *Rethinking Innateness*. Cambridge, MA: MIT Press.

Gottlieb, G. (1992) *Individual Development and Evolution: The Genesis of Novel Behavior*. New York: Oxford University Press.

Marler, P. (1989) Learning by instinct: Birdsong. *American Speech-Language Association* 89:75–79.

Marler, P. and Terrace, H. (1984) *The Biology of Learning*. Berlin: Springer-Verlag.

Oyama, S. (1982) *Ontogeny of Information*. Cambridge: Cambridge University Press.

Piatelli-Palmarini, M. (1980) *Language Learning: The Debate Between Jean Piaget and Noam Chomsky*. Cambridge, MA: Harvard University Press.

Pinker, S. (1994) *The Language Instinct*. New York: William Morrow and Company.

Pinker, S. (1997) *How the Mind Works*. New York: Norton.

Raff, R. A. (1996) *The Shape of Life*. Chicago: The University of Chicago Press.

Waddington, C. H. (1957) *The Strategy of the Genes*. London: Allen and Unwin.

Waddington, C. H. (1975) *Evolution of an Evolutionist*. Ithaca, NY: Cornell University Press.

Werker, J. F. (1989) Becoming a native listener. *American Scientist* 77:54–59.

10 On Innateness: Are Sparrow Songs "Learned" or "Innate"?

Peter Marler

A layperson might be excused for wondering if the nature-nurture debate will ever be resolved to everyone's satisfaction. There is no unanimous agreement on this theme even among serious students of animal behavior. Many still seem to be either unaware of the contemporary revolution in molecular genetics and developmental biology, or reluctant to admit its relevance. No sooner does a biologically satisfactory consensus seem to have emerged than the assertion resurfaces that any invocation of genetic influences on the development of behavior implies complete predestination, eliminating all prospects of mutability and adaptive ontogenetic change. Outdated attitudes such as these are not the only obstacles to scientific progress. There is also a problem with the terminology that many of us use, and that is the issue this paper seeks to address.

Even those of us who are all too aware of the maze of interactive, often probabilistic steps to be taken in the journey from a gene to a complex behavioral trait sometimes still apply, albeit somewhat casually, terms like *innate* and *learned* to a behavior. We use them as useful adjectives that provide an apparently objective and instructive way of classifying behavioral traits. This classificatory usage of pairs of dichotomous terms, like *instinctive* and *acquired*, *learned* and *innate*, or *learned* and *unlearned*, is deeply ingrained, apparently continuing to be useful as a way of distinguishing between categories of behavior with very different ontogenetic histories. It is true that some refrain completely from using the term *innate*, but they still label behaviors as unlearned without any hesitation. I will use data on song development in birds to question the logic behind all of these pairs of terms, if used as antithetical categories for classifying behavior. I believe that they are ultimately a hindrance to progress in the study of behavioral development.

Perhaps the most serious barrier to resolution of the nature-nurture dilemma is the dearth of efforts to manipulate both components in the ontogenetic equation underlying the development of complex behaviors. This is especially true of those behaviors that display the high degree of between-individual variation we associate with learning. If a behavior is classified as *learned*, then the proper focus of research is usually deemed to be the role of experiential variables. Studies of avian song learning have been more tenacious than most in striving to explore the role not only of experience but also of the genome in song learning, although even here, as in so many studies of animal learning, biases sometimes intrude into the very design of the experiments we conduct.

If we approach song learning as a preparation for the study of behavioral plasticity and its physiological basis, it is only natural to stress the role of experience in development at the expense of genetic contributions. Genetic endowment is never completely ignored, just shortchanged. The unique importance of the pan-specific perquisites that all oscine songbirds bring to bear on the task of song learning is acknowledged, at least implicitly. These include the unusually complex and versatile vocal apparatus and the apparently crucial contributions from the song system in the brain, so conspicuously lacking from the brains of nonlearners. But we are more inclined to overlook adaptations of the process of song development at the species level. Adaptive learning mechanisms pertain, both to the general issue of vocal plasticity, and also more narrowly to the particular needs of each species, but we often set these aside, if only because species-specificity seems to limit the generalizability of our research findings. Often we design studies of song learning in such a way that evidence of any special processing that species-specific predispositions might involve is unlikely to be obtained. In doing so we may actually forego the possibility that understanding how species differences arise may in turn yield insights into the basic mechanisms underlying song learning that all songbirds share.

Given the great diversity of the morphology, ecology and behavior of the 4,500 or so oscine songbirds, we should be more prepared than we are for the likelihood that species vary in the song-learning strategies that they have evolved. The nature-nurture issue inevitably arises because species differ in the degree to which they rely solely on cultural transmission to ensure that species and population differences in singing behavior, where they are functionally important, are perpetuated. That there are general principles underlying the process of vocal plasticity can hardly be questioned, but to discover them requires that adequate attention be paid to genetic contributions to the learning process, contributions that bias the outcome of experiments on any particular species. My aim here is to show that species differences in how the task of learning to sing is approached can provide some insight into how we can best deal with the nature-nature question in behavioral development. In this review, at a more general level, I shall focus especially on the role of motor predispositions in vocal ontogeny.

To exemplify the convenience of using *learned* and *innate* casually as a way of classifying mature behavioral phenotypes, I shall use these terms freely in the body of this paper, italicizing them for emphasis. Later I shall reconsider the wisdom of continuing to use them in this fashion.

Learned Birdsongs as Subjects for Ontogenetic Study

Ideal subjects for the study of learning and its physiological basis would be organisms that are experimentally tractable, displaying behavior that is unquestionably *learned*, with behaviors that are complex enough to exemplify the various ways by which a new behavior can be *learned*. Oscine birdsongs come close to this ideal. They are among the most complex of all natural behaviors known to us. Learning plays a fundamental role in their development, and birdsongs are fast becoming one of the most intensely investigated behaviors from the viewpoint of their physiological substrates (Konishi 1985, 1994; Nottebohm 1993; Brenowitz et al. 1977; Doupe and Solis, this volume). Especially valuable if we wish to borrow from the approaches of developmental biology, and distinctive to the context of song development, is the fact that each songbird species seems to go about the process of learning to sing in its own way. The songbird literature abounds with cases of species differences in the rules governing the process of learning to sing. Birds thus provide many opportunities to explore problems of nature and nurture in the development of a complex behavior, especially if we can find ways to exploit the power of the comparative method in explicating the details of behavioral ontogeny in different bird species.

A Definition of "Song"

Birds are the most vocal of all animals. There are 9,000 species and virtually all have a repertoire of up to a dozen distinct calls, squawks, peeps, clucks, buzzes, and whistles that they use to communicate with one another about such things as predators, food, sex, aggression, and the establishment and maintenance of social bonds. Most are simple cries, sometimes given repeatedly, often monosyllabic. Usually, somewhere in the repertoire, there is another pattern of sound that stands out as frequently used, especially loud, longer in duration than calls, often highly patterned, with a variety of acoustically distinct notes. This is the song, often a male prerogative, with many functions, the most obvious of which are signaling occupation of a territory and the establishment and maintenance of sexual bonds. Songs are sometimes seasonal, and sometimes given year-round.

Most calls seem to be *innate*, although there are interesting exceptions, often arising when the functional responsibilities of song appear to be shifting from one part of the vocal repertoire to another (Nicolai 1959; Hughes, Nowicki, and Lohr 1998). In most birds, the song is also *innate*. In only 3 of the 27 orders of birds is there unequivocal evidence of vocal learning. These are the parrots, the hummingbirds, and above all, the subgroup of the very populous perching birds known as the oscine songbirds. Oscines make up the majority of known learner species. Their prowess as songsters is augmented by the two distinctive assets already mentioned, their uniquely complex vocal apparatus, and the specialized network of brain nuclei that constitutes the "song system," lacking from the brains of suboscines, and as far as we know, from the brains of all birds with *innate* songs. The song system appears to provide circuitry that is necessary to sustain the process of vocal learning and production. Interestingly, parrots seem to have achieved a similar end by their own neuroanatomically distinct neural system (Streidter 1994), apparently independently evolved.

On a scale of physical complexity, some learned birdsongs are relatively simple, on a par with those that are *innate*. Other *learned* songs are extraordinarily complex, with individual repertoires of song types numbered in the tens, hundreds, and in a few cases, even in the thousands. These are among the most highly patterned sequences of actions that animals perform naturally; only the songs of whales come close in the degree of complexity that they display.

Birdsongs have another attribute that makes them valuable as subjects for the study of behavioral ontogeny. Whereas many calls are relatively conservative from an evolutionary point of view, with an acoustic structure that is often widely shared across taxa, songs are typically highly species-specific within a given avifauna. As a consequence, birds and bird-watchers alike can always identify a songster as a member of a species quickly and accurately. Even the mimics, such as the mocking-bird and the starling, which construct their songs largely from imitations of the sounds of others, utter them in a distinctive, species-specific temporal pattern. Birds that are close genetic relatives, with many structural and behavioral attributes in common, often sharing call types, nevertheless often have a song that is *learned*, but distinctively different (Marler 1957). Such contrasts imply that the process of song learning follows a distinctive path from bird to bird. Species contrasts in learned songs provide an opportunity, both to explore how different birds come to conduct the process of song development in contrasting ways, and by exposing species differences, to lay bare the essential mechanisms that they have in common.

Learning to Sing

There are three phases in the learning of a song. A bird first memorizes a song that is heard, then stores the memory for a period, sometimes short, sometimes long, and finally begins to sing. If the song includes imitations, these are reproduced from memory, thus providing a classic preparation for the study of learning and its physiological basis. Although the role of learning is clear, contributions of special predispositions to the development of a *learned* song are also evident from the very beginning. During the memorization phase, there are sensory constraints that take the form of learning preferences, typically favoring songs of the bird's own species (see, e.g., Marler and Peters 1989). Several converging lines of evidence, reviewed elsewhere (Marler 1997), indicate the existence of sensory predispositions that permit the discrimination of conspecific (one's own species) songs from heterospecific (other species) songs in young birds, early in the process of song development. They may also facilitate the process of song memorization, which can be extraordinarily rapid and complete. Studies of sensory constraints on song memorization sometimes reveal a degree of *innate* foreknowledge that is remarkably comprehensive, sufficient to have stimulated new ways of thinking about the physiological basis of song memorization (Marler 1997; Whaling et al. 1997).

Predispositions are also manifest in the motor phase of song development. Songbirds reveal a variety of motor predispositions during the production phase of vocal development, when they start to sing. Some involve more or less subtle preferences, revealed only by giving birds a choice. Others involve basic and inviolable restrictions on the sounds that the vocal apparatus can produce. Podos has cleverly demonstrated some of these restrictions both by cross-species comparisons of maximal trill rates (Podos 1997) and experimentally by artificially speeding up the syllable rate of tutor songs presented to young male swamp sparrows as learning stimuli in the laboratory. Beyond a certain point, males continue to imitate syllables, but with what Podos (1996) calls a "broken syntax." They rearrange the rapid-rate note sequences into clusters, and then repeat them at a rate of their own choosing, closer to what is typical for the species. Podos makes a good case that these syntactical rearrangements reflect general physical limitations on how fast a song can be trilled. They impose constraints, not during memorization of song models but at a later stage, when a bird tries to utter imitations of song models it has previously memorized. These motor predispositions appear to be pan-specific. Others that are much more narrowly focused, down to the species level, are species-specific, and these are the special focus of the present review. I will use them to explore first how we arrive at judgments about which songs or aspects of singing behavior are *learned* and which are *innate*, leading me to a reconsideration of the wisdom of classifying behaviors, or components of behavior in this way.

Motor Development of Song in Two Species Raised in the Same Conditions

How tenable is the view that naturally occurring species differences in song are completely dependent on the contrasting circumstances that individuals experience in the wild as they grow to maturity? If species song differences were completely dependent on experience, birds should develop similar songs when raised under the same set of conditions. This prediction would seem to be favored by the fact, known for centuries, that birds can acquire and reproduce the songs of other species, leading them to utter sounds that are sometimes far beyond the normal acoustic repertoire for the species (cf. Konishi 1985). This is true both of natural mimics and also of nonmimics when raised under certain conditions. Innate song differences, on the other hand, should persist in the face of uniform conditions, provided, of course, that those conditions permit normal development. It turns out that experimental studies designed to test these alternatives confirm neither prediction in a clear, unequivocal fashion. Some species song differences disappear under uniform rearing conditions, thus implying learning. But a surprisingly large number persist in one form or another, seemingly indicating innateness (Marler and Sherman 1983, 1985; Marler and Peters 1987, 1988, 1989).

Among the most telling experiments are those Virginia Sherman and I conducted some years ago on two sparrows with very different songs, both members of the genus *Melospiza*, which live together through much of their range. Under natural conditions the swamp sparrow, *M. georgiana*, has a two-second, one-phrase song consisting of a dozen or so repetitions of a multinote syllable. Each male has its own distinctive repertoire of 3 or so syllable types, distinguished by the number and type of notes that form a repeated cluster. The closely related song sparrow, *M. melodia*, has songs that are on average about 20% longer, and more complex. They contain 3 or 4 phrases with acoustically distinct trills alternating with clusters of unrepeated notes or note complexes. An individual song sparrow has a repertoire of up to a dozen song types, 3 or 4 times more than a male swamp sparrow. When reared under identical conditions of individual isolation, some of the species contrasts are preserved. Although this allowed us to reject the hypothesis that all contrasts are culturally determined, there were some fascinating ambiguities.

Fertile eggs of the two species were taken from wild nests, fostered by canaries and raised by hand. Once independent, at about 4 weeks, they were rehoused individually, each in its own chamber, for the first year of life. We compared the songs they developed with natural songs recorded from wild adults near where the birds' parents lived. None of them fell within the normal range. To our ears they seemed to be simpler, and this impression (figure 10.1) was confirmed by measurements from sound spectrograms (table 10.1). Individual song-type repertoires shrank to about half usual size. The number of notes per song and the number of notes in each syllable were reduced. Together with an increase in the duration of notes and of internote intervals, the overall result was a slower tempo. Equally distinctive to our ears but harder to quantify were contrasts in timbre. Isolate songs often had a raspy

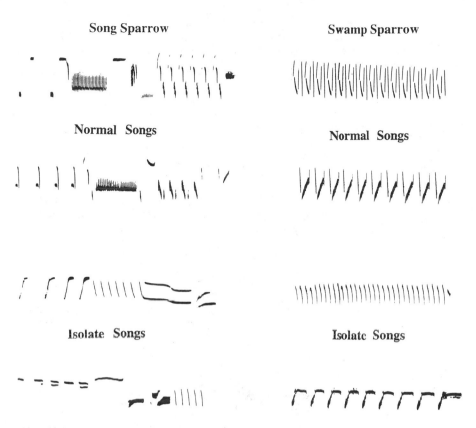

Figure 10.1
Sonograms of four normal sparrow songs (top) and four songs of males raised from the egg without experience of songs of their species. Song sparrows (left) have more complex songs than swamp sparrows (right).

quality, lacking the pure tonality that is so typical of normal songs of these birds and of many other songbirds (Nowicki and Marler 1988; Nowicki et al. 1992). Strikingly, as has been noted in some other species (Kroodsma 1977), songs of both were influenced by isolation in the same way.

Given the abnormalities of isolate song and the fact that normal development can be instated simply by playing recordings of normal song to young males at the appropriate stage of development, we do not hesitate to conclude that learning plays a major role in song development. We are inclined to speak of sparrows as having *learned* songs. But there is another side to this coin. Recall that the strong prediction from the cultural transmission hypothesis for explaining species song differences is

Table 10.1
A comparison of normal and isolate songs of swamp and song sparrows, based on twelve measures. The
> and < signs are inserted between each pair of columns to emphasize that the two species differ in the
same direction in both normal and in isolate song. (From Marler and Sherman 1985.)

	Isolate Songs		Normal Songs	
	Song sparrow (5 birds)	Swamp sparrow (5 birds)	Song sparrow (4 birds)	Swamp sparrow (7 birds)
Repertoire size	5.0 ± 1.0 >	1.6 ± 0.5	10.3 ± 1.5 >	3.0
Song duration (s)	2.898 ± 0.439 >	2.006 ± 0.292	2.573 ± 0.188 >	2.099 ± 0.135
No. of segments	3.5 ± 0.3 >	2.2 ± 0.6	3.9 ± 0.2 >	1.0 ± 0
Notes per song	10.4 ± 2.1 <	19.8 ± 8.3	35.8 ± 8.3 <	45.3 ± 7.5
Note duration (s)	0.232 ± 0.034 >	0.092 ± 0.072	0.047 ± 0.007 >	0.030 ± 0.005
Inter-note interval (s)	0.084 ± 0.025 <	0.044 ± 0.012	0.032 ± 0.005 <	0.019 ± 0.003
Number of trills	1.9 ± 0.3 >	1.7 ± 0.7	2.1 ± 0.1 >	1.0 ± 0
Total no. of trilled syllables	7.6 ± 1.9 <	17.7 ± 8.8	9.3 ± 0.6 <	14.8 ± 1.6
No. of notes in trilled syllables	1.0 ± 0 <	1.5 ± 0.7	2.6 ± 0.4 <	3.1 ± 0.7
No. of syllables in a single trill	3.6 ± 0.8 <	10.7 ± 7.0	4.2 ± 0.1 <	14.8 ± 1.6
No. of note complexes	1.5 ± 0.3 >	0.5 ± 0.3	1.8 ± 0.2 >	0
No. of notes in a note complex	2.1 ± 0.9 >	1.1 ± 0.1	9.7 ± 4.5 >	0

that the two species should develop *similar* songs in isolation. Confronted with
sound spectrograms, we had no trouble in immediately assigning them to the correct
species. Songs of the two species raised under similar conditions of social isolation
are in fact as obviously species-specific as their natural equivalents (figure 10.1).
Measurements confirm that certain species-typical song features persist in isolation
in more or less normal fashion (figure 10.2). In song sparrows, the shared features
between normal and isolate songs include several of the syntactical features that
characterize the more complex temporal patterning of this species. In swamp sparrows, the temporal structure of isolate songs is more variable (table 10.1), reinforcing
other indications that swamp-sparrow song syntax is somewhat less stable than that
of song sparrows, but the general trend is similar. In isolation, one-phrased songs
still prevail (Marler and Sherman 1983).

So what conclusions can we draw about the *innate-learned* dichotomy? If we
restricted our attention to these syntactical features, we might well conclude that
song sparrow song is *innate*, as Mulligan (1966) was inclined to do in his earlier
study of song sparrow song development. But we have already concluded, on the
basis of other data, that sparrow songs are *learned*. So, we have a paradox.
Depending on the aspect of song you consider, song sparrow song can be viewed as
either *learned* or *innate*.

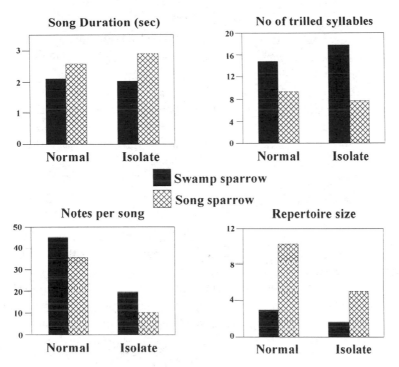

Figure 10.2
Song features that are similar (top) and differ significantly (bottom) in normal and isolate sparrow songs. Small repertoires, a slow tempo and relatively simple note structure are typical characteristics of isolate song. (Data from Marler and Sherman 1985.)

The paradox heightens when we compare the two species more closely. For many students of behavior, innateness is synonymous with immutability. But with song we find that so-called *innate* features are by no means stereotyped and unchangeable. Isolate songs are abnormal, but many of the contrasts between natural swamp- and song-sparrow songs that bird-watchers use to distinguish between them are still present. If we look again at measures of such features as trilled syllables and syllables per trill in isolate songs (figure 10.2), we find that, although they are "abnormal," they differ between species in the same direction as in normal songs (table 10.1), indicating *innateness*. Those who believe that complete stereotypy is a necessary mark of innateness are clearly mistaken.

Consider individual song type repertoires. Recall that, in nature, wild song sparrows have 3 or 4 times as many songs as a swamp sparrow (10–12 versus 2–3 song types). In social isolates, repertoire size is drastically reduced to about half normal size (table 10.1). Yet the species difference persists, with an average of 5 song types per male in isolate song sparrows and between 1 and 2 per male in isolate swamp sparrows. In both species, the reductions in repertoire size in isolates are highly significant. Despite the "abnormalities," the two species differ in the same direction and to the same degree as in the wild. Do we conclude then that repertoire size is *learned* or have we that it is *innate*? Clearly neither conclusion is satisfactory. Perhaps it is more useful to focus on the *difference* in repertoire size between the two species, and to conclude that the difference is *innate*? I will return to this terminological conundrum later.

Do Species Differences Develop without Auditory Feedback?

The contrasts in the patterning of developmental plasticity I have described, in two species raised under similar conditions, serve to identify behavioral traits that are, at some point, subject to different genomic influences. With the right kind of experimental design, such behavioral experiments can provide indications of when during the developmental trajectory these influences take effect, resulting in divergences. However, there are obvious limits to the insights that can be gleaned from purely behavioral studies about the precise nature of the genetic and physiological mechanisms responsible. Nevertheless, there is one other approach that has demonstrated dramatically where in the brain we could begin looking for such mechanisms, by studying the role of auditory feedback.

There are at least two ways in which vocal behavior could be pre-encoded. There could be internalized motor programs, providing endogenously patterned output from the central nervous system to the sound-producing organs; in principle, we can visualize such programs as being species-specific. Alternatively, internalized auditory templates in the brain could encode acoustic specifications to which the voice would be matched during development by auditory feedback (Marler 1964). We know from the pioneering studies of Konishi (1963, 1964, 1965a, 1965b) and Nottebohm (1966, 1968; Konishi and Nottebohm 1969) that auditory feedback does in fact play a major role in the production of *learned* birdsongs.

Although the importance of auditory feedback in development is unquestioned, there are conflicting views on its importance once mature song has been achieved. In open-ended learners such as the canary (Nottebohm et al. 1976), its continuing role is clear, but in closed-ended learners there is disagreement. Chaffinches and white-crowned sparrows deafened as adults retained their songs unchanged for two years (Konishi 1965a; Konishi and Nottebohm 1969) and there are similar reports for zebra finches, at least for the short term (Price 1979; Bottjer and Arnold 1984). But Nordeen and Nordeen (1992) found significant song deterioration in adult-deafened zebra finches after six weeks. In the bengalese finch, another closed-ended learner, adult deafening resulted in abnormal song syntax within 5 days, phonological deterioration within 30–60 days, and an eventual reduction in the number of syllable types (Okanoya and Yamaguchi 1997; cf. Wooley and Rubel 1997)—clear evidence that adults depend on auditory feedback for the maintenance of the structure of crystallized song. Leonardo and Konishi (1998) present evidence that delayed auditory feedback for 1–4 months in adult male zebra finches also results in syntactical changes, prolonged stuttering, and loss of syllable types. These abnormalities gradually disappear over a period of months as males' original song patterns reappear, presumably either by reinstatement of central motor programs, by matching output to auditory templates, or by some combination of the two. The delayed-feedback preparation offers an ideal opportunity to study the maturational dynamics of both song syntax and song phonology, which may be subject to somewhat distinct controls. Syntax and phonology deteriorate after deafening at different rates in bengalese finches (Okanoya and Yamaguchi 1997) and emerge according to somewhat different timetables in normal song development in swamp sparrows, with phonology crystallizing earlier than song syntax (Marler and Peters 1982). A picture is thus beginning to emerge of how birds proceed through the complex process of assembling the complete motor patterns of crystallized song during ontogeny and how they maintain those patterns as adults.

In experiments on the effects of deafening on song development in young chaffinches, *Fringilla coelebs*, Nottebohm (1966, 1968) found that males deafened early, prior to any significant song production, produced what appeared to him to be a virtually structureless song. This suggested that elimination of sensory pathways for auditory feedback early in life, before any song development had started, might erase virtually all species differences in song structure, with the stage of development at which the auditory feedback loop is severed being a critical factor. By deafening male chaffinches at various stages, Nottebohm showed that the further they have progressed towards adult song, the more they retain of the structure achieved prior to deafening. His demonstration that the amount of preoperative singing experience influences the impact of deafening suggested some reinterpretation of previous studies by Konishi that inspired his own work.

Konishi, who previously had pioneered studies of the effects of deafening on song development, found that deafened males of a number of songbird species produced a virtually structureless, anonymous song, anticipating the performance of Nottebohm's early-deafened chaffinches. But other species developed a significant degree of species-specific song structure after deafening, especially the Oregon junco, *Junco oreganus* (Konishi 1964). The song syllables of deaf juncos were abnormal and unstable, but the basic overall form of the song was much like that of wild birds, hinting at the possibility of central motor programming (Konishi and Nottebohm 1969). However, the four male Oregon juncos studied were deafened rather late, at 58 days in one case, and 100 days in three others. Thus they may have had significant singing experience earlier in life with their hearing intact. Similarly, a black-headed grosbeak, *Pheucticus melanocephalus*, that developed a significant degree of species-specific song structure while deaf (Konishi 1965a), was not operated on until about 90 days of age. Konishi and Nottebohm (1969) suggested that earlier deafening of these species, prior to any song production, might have eliminated these species differences in song structure.

One clear requirement for such studies is the need, now obvious, to equate the extent of predeafening song practice that subjects being compared have had. It would also be an advantage if we had a well-defined metric for deciding how degraded a motor pattern must be before it is judged completely structureless. As we have seen, conclusions about *innateness* can be highly dependent on which aspects of song structure are analyzed. One way to bring the issue of the species-specificity of songs of deaf birds into sharper focus is to concentrate especially on those song features displayed in isolate song. Armed with these insights from the Konishi-Nottebohm experiments, Sherman and I decided to reopen these questions, again using sparrows as subjects. We set out to pose the question whether or not any species contrasts are evident in the songs of male sparrows who, from an early age, are deprived of the ability to hear their own voice.

Sparrow Songs Compared without Auditory Feedback

In its strongest form, the Konishi-Nottebohm hypothesis predicts that those species differences in song that develop in social isolation will be erased by early deafening. To test this hypothesis, five male swamp sparrows and two male song sparrows were raised by hand and deafened bilaterally at three weeks of age. At this stage, neither subsong nor any other kind of singing had begun. The prediction was that early deafening would render songs of the two species indistinguishable. The results were unexpected. As in all songbirds subjected to this treatment (Konishi and Nottebohm 1969), most of these early-deafened sparrow songs were highly degraded and exceedingly variable (figure 10.3). But despite the variability, and the rather small sample (6 swamp sparrows: 9 song types; 2 song sparrows: 7 song types), it was

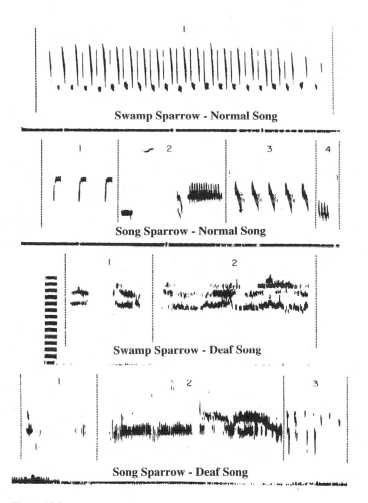

Swamp Sparrow - Normal Song

Song Sparrow - Normal Song

Swamp Sparrow - Deaf Song

Song Sparrow - Deaf Song

Figure 10.3
Sonagrams of four sparrow songs, two normal (top) and two developed by males deafened early in the life (bottom). They illustrate the degradation of note structure that typically develops in birds that cannot hear their own voice. Vertical dotted lines mark the boundaries between song segments, plotted in figure 10.4. (From Marler and Sherman 1983.)

obvious that some species song differences persist after deafness. The results were reminiscent of those Konishi (1964) had found in Oregon juncos.

Normal songs of swamp and song sparrows differ most strikingly in their phrase structure. Hints of this same contrast in phrase structure can still be discerned in deaf birds even when note and syllable structure has been rendered virtually amorphous. Natural song-sparrow song is always multipartite, whereas a swamp-sparrow song consists of a single phrase. Similarly, there is more segmentation of early-deafened song sparrow songs than in the swamp sparrow (figure 10.4). Other species differences that persist despite deafening include shorter, higher-pitched songs in swamp than in song sparrows, and larger individual song repertoires in song than in swamp sparrows. The difference in repertoire size is especially interesting because it develops despite reduction to half normal size, in both species, as in intact isolates. The results confirm Konishi's original finding that aspects of species-specific song structure can develop in some species without auditory feedback (Konishi 1964, 1965a). This result suggests that endogenous, species-specific motor programs play some role in song development in sparrows.

Despite these indications of central motor programs, it is also clear that the role for auditory feedback is a major one. In deaf sparrows, as in other learner species, structure of their individual song notes and syllables is highly abnormal (cf. Konishi and Nottebohm 1969). Their songs are also exceedingly variable, to the extent that the song patterning of the two species begins to overlap, in extreme cases becoming virtually indistinguishable (figure 10.5). However long one searched, it would be impossible to find natural, mature swamp- and song-sparrow songs so similar that their species identity would be uncertain. The results of song recognition tests show that deaf songs do not even qualify as songs to the birds themselves. Playbacks to males on territory and to females in a state of hormonally induced sexual receptivity (Searcy and Marler 1981) reveal a complete loss of functional effectiveness. For both sexes, their own-species, normal songs are potent stimuli. Other-species songs are ineffective, and this is equally true of own-species deaf songs. As might be predicted from their intermediate structure, isolate songs fall somewhere in between (Searcy and Marler 1987).

It appears to be a general rule that in birds with a *learned* song, most organized note structure is virtually eliminated by early deafening (Konishi and Nottebohm 1969), but there are occasional puzzling exceptions. In deaf songs, note durations, spectral structure, and patterns of frequency modulation all vary greatly and unpredictably from bird to bird, from song type to song type, and even from one utterance to the next. Perhaps the most remarkable and perplexing outcome of the Marler and

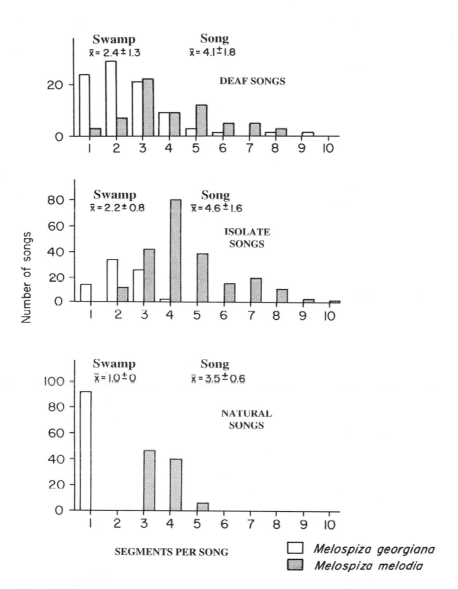

Figure 10.4
A comparison of patterns of segmentation in natural, isolate, and deaf songs of two sparrows. Distinctions between the two species become blurred as you go from the bottom, normal song, to the top of the figure, but even in deaf songs, contrasts are present. (Modified from Marler and Sherman 1983.)

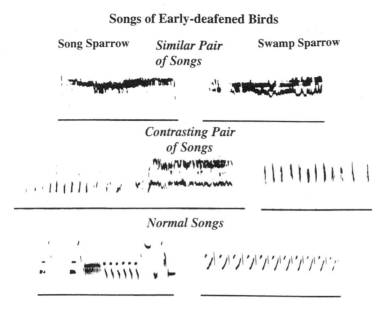

Songs of Early-deafened Birds

Figure 10.5
Pairs of songs of deaf males of two sparrow species selected for minimal and maximal contrast. Two normal songs are presented for comparison. (Modified from Marler and Sherman 1983).

Sherman (1983) study is the extraordinarily wide range of alternative song patterns displayed by different individuals of the same species reared under identical conditions. Some come fairly close to normal and even approximate stable syllabic structure, but others are so degraded that, as already mentioned, almost all species differences are lost. Extreme contrasts may occur even within the repertoire of the same individual, in different song types (figure 10.6). This strange finding suggests that the mechanism underlying emergence of the abnormalities associated with early deafness may wax and wane during development, perhaps at times completely masking whatever potential a bird may otherwise have to produce a degree of normal song structure.

It is conceivable that auditory input is significant, not only for the memorization and production of *learned* songs, but also for the activation of latent central mechanisms that actually encode more information about normal species-specific song structure than is usually evident in the amorphous morphology of deaf songs. This possibility is intriguing because there are indications that dependence of vocal development on auditory feedback is a strong correlate of song learning. In an elegant

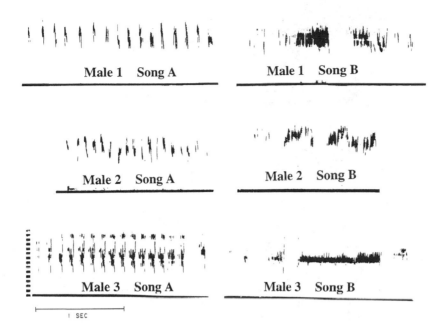

Figure 10.6
Three pairs of songs of deaf male swamp sparrows. Each pair is present in the song repertoire of the same deaf bird. They were chosen to demonstrate that relatively well structured (left, A) and highly degraded song types (right, B) can occur in the same bird. (Modified from Marler and Sherman 1983.)

study, Kroodsma and Konishi (1991) looked at the effects of deafening on song development in a non-oscine passerine, the Eastern Phoebe, a bird with an *innate* song (figure 10.7). They found that song developed in identical fashion in isolation, after deafening, and in the wild. This pattern of song ontogeny is no different in principle from that in other nonlearners such as doves or domestic chickens (Konishi 1963; Nottebohm and Nottebohm 1971). Central motor programs must play a major role in song development in such species. Conceivably the need for generalized, tonic activation of such central programs by auditory feedback was a first step toward vocal learning (cf. Marler 1977). Intensive study of song development in suboscines, focusing especially on species with more complex and variable songs, might reveal intermediate cases, requiring an activational role for auditory feedback but without learning in the traditional sense. If there are such cases, it would be important to determine whether there is anything equivalent to a "song system" in their brains. *Innate* knowledge about song structure could be extensive, but deafness could render the individual incapable of expressing that knowledge by voice.

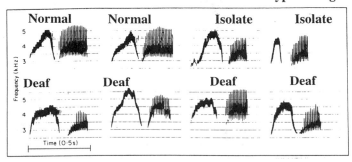

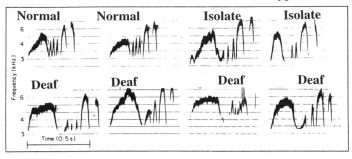

Figure 10.7
Sonograms of samples of the two song types of the Eastern Phoebe, a suboscine, recorded in nature, in isolates, and in deaf males. Song structure develops perfectly normally, not only in isolation, but even in birds deafened soon after hatching, illustrating the condition that probably prevails in most birds. (Modified from Kroodsma and Konishi 1991.)

Are Sparrow Songs "Learned" or "Innate"?

I have intentionally used the terms *learned* and *innate* freely in this paper, drawing attention to them by the use of italics. In doing so, my aim has been to illustrate their utility for purposes of discussion. In considering the differences in brain circuitry in oscine songbirds and suboscines, for example, it seems only natural to come directly to the point by defining songs of one as *learned*, and of the other as *innate*. The terms seem to capture the essence of the radical contrast in developmental strategy of the two taxa, and neuroethologists use them frequently in this way. The *learned-innate* dichotomy provides a way of classifying mature song phenotypes into two types. On the one hand, there are those birds with *learned* songs in which individual experience plays a major developmental role, responsible for the variation that occurs in songs of individuals, populations, and species, and within an individual at difference phases of development. On the other hand, there are those birds with *innate* songs, displaying behavioral phenotypes in which variation at these various levels, from individuals to species, is genetically determined. Use of paired terms in this way, as the basis for a kind of behavioral taxonomy, is so well entrenched in behavioral biology that it is resistant to change. I have shown that they can serve as a convenient shorthand. But the studies I have reviewed also provide some strong arguments against their use in this fashion.

What exactly do we imply when we use the terms *learned* and *innate*? Strictly speaking, when we use the term *learned* we actually refer to a contrast in patterns of development between two groups of subjects with different experiential histories. As I have illustrated, in casual discourse we often set aside explicit reference to the multitude of genomic-environmental interactions that are necessary antecedents to the development of any behavior. We often speak of one set of traits as *learned* and another as *innate*, as I have done repeatedly in this paper, without necessarily acknowledging that what is actually referred to is the developmental basis of the variation that those traits display in a population. We have to ask ourselves, should this more casual usage be condoned, or discouraged?

Consider again the term *learned*. A contrast is implied between the developmental trajectories that individuals follow with and without a particular set of experiences in their personal history. When we use the term more casually, we do not necessarily imply that the entire behavior is *learned* with all of the neural, neuromuscular and somatic events that are its necessary antecedents. Nevertheless there is a tendency to assume that because a behavior has not been labeled as *innate*, the role of, for example, genetically based learning predispositions can be ignored. The literature of behavioral science is full of cases where an undue preoccupation with effects of experience on behavioral development has led to the neglect of the genetic side of the developmental equation, perhaps the cardinal sin of the behaviorist movement of Watson and Skinner. Similarly, the practice of labeling a behavior as *innate* can lead to the neglect of the role of experience in behavioral development. As all students of behavior are aware, arguments about where the emphasis should be placed in discussions of the *innate-learned* dichotomy are notoriously contentious, often becoming so strident that their scientific productivity is questionable (see, e.g., Johnston 1988). Thus one drawback to the *learned-innate* dichotomy is that it tends to polarize our thinking about how a particular behavior develops. Perhaps most importantly, it encourages us to underestimate genetic contributions to the development of *learned* behaviors.

Close scrutiny of patterns of song development reveals other reasons to question the wisdom of a simple classificatory use of *innate* and *learned*. Even used only as labels, the terms are inherently ambiguous. Song-sparrow and swamp-sparrow songs develop abnormally when males are raised without any opportunity to hear their adult species' song. They are significantly simpler than normal, with drastic reductions in the number of notes per song and of notes per syllable (figures 10.1 and 10.2), and with lengthening of the intervals between notes. In both species, most of the distinctive species-specific note structure is lacking in isolate songs. In addition, individual song-type repertoires are reduced to half the size of those found in nature. By all of these criteria, we hardly hesitate to classify these songs as *learned*, especially when we know that to restore normal singing behavior we need only to provide the experience of normal songs at the appropriate time.

But what if we shift the focus to a different set of song features? We have seen that several of the distinctive characteristics by which songs of the two species normally differ are present in isolate song, and a few of them can be discerned even in songs of deaf birds. Obviously, use of the *learned-innate* dichotomy as a way of classifying complete behavioral phenotypes is seriously flawed. It could be argued that the dichotomy still makes sense if, instead of applying it to entire behaviors, we specify the particular components of the behavioral phenotype we have in mind. But even then contradictions arise, as we have seen with song repertoires. Repertoires are abnormally small in isolates of both species, about half normal size. Nevertheless, the relationship between song and swamp sparrow repertoires, the former three or four times larger than the latter, remains unchanged. If we focus on the species difference, repertoire size is *innate*. If we focus on absolute values, repertoire sizes are *learned*.

My own view is that the convention of classifying behaviors or components of behavior typologically as either *learned* or *innate* is not only logically flawed, but actually hinders progress in understanding the principles underlying behavioral development. If, on the other hand, we apply these same terms to behavioral *differences* rather than using them as categorical labels, they become informative in an interesting way. We can picture the development of an individual's behavior as traversing a range of possible trajectories, with series of choice-points recurring at intervals, rather as Waddington (1957) portrayed his "epigenetic landscapes." We can visualize the particular choices that an individual makes between available trajectories during development as being guided either by individualized genomic instructions, by current or past individual experience, or by both, with guidance influencing what to attend to in the environment, as well as affecting more traditional processes of growth and development. Given a multiplicity of such choice-points, we can begin to see how the ontogeny of two species might diverge on the basis of different genomic instructions, as revealed experimentally by raising different subjects with similar experiences.

Perhaps the most significant aspect of the Waddingtonian viewpoint for students of behavioral development is the reminder that a given genome encodes developmental instructions not just for one, but for many alternative phenotypes. Which developmental pathway is chosen depends on a variety of influences, some endogenous and others exogenous, especially in the case of behavior. A temperature change, a pheromone sensed, a social stressor experienced—each has the potential to switch the developing organism from one ontogenetic trajectory to another and to foreclose options that might be chosen in other circumstances.

The potential for varying degrees of what evolutionary biologists call *phenotypic plasticity* (West-Eberhard 1989; Scheiner 1993), with the same genotype giving rise to more than one phenotype in different environmental circumstances, is extremely widespread if not universal. We have only to think of temperature-dependent sex determination in reptiles (Bull 1983), conditional caste determination in social insects (see, e.g., Holldobler and Wilson 1990), socially determined morphological and behavioral polymorphisms in fish, and the lability of vertebrate social systems in the face of varying environmental circumstances (Lott 1991), to say nothing of the multitudes of phenotypic alternatives in plants, for the ubiquity of phenotypic plasticity to be obvious. We take for granted that there are endless examples of alternative life-cycle strategies, diapause phenomena, seasonal brood size adjustments, alternative winged and wingless morphs, all involving genetically based alternative ontogenies that are environmentally triggered.

The triggering environmental stimuli are sometimes few and simple, sometimes many and complex, depending on the *innate* predispositions that the organism brings to bear on a given situation. In ants, Holldobler and Wilson (1990) list at least six factors that determine whether a female *Myrmica* will become a worker or a queen, including larval nutrition, winter chilling, post-hibernation temperature, queen influence, egg size, and queen age. These factors all conspire to determine which choice is made between the two morphological, physiological, and behavioral phenotypes, genetic instructions for which are in place and awaiting activation or suppression.

As West-Eberhard (1989) points out, "it is a mistake to consider phenotypic plasticity a 'nongenetic' phenomenon," as some behaviorists have done. This assertion does not in any way diminish the significance of experience in behavioral development. "It is important to appreciate the deterministic role of the environment, alongside the genes, in the production and evolution of the phenotypic" (West-Eberhard, *loc. cit.*). But to achieve a full understanding of the evolutionary process, neither genetic nor environmental contributions to this interactive process can ever be ignored, a position that becomes self-evident if we approach the nature-nurture problem in developmental terms rather than as an issue of phenotypic typology.

In real life, adult behavior can never be fully predicted from laboratory experiments like those I have described here, based as they are on an unnaturally simplified array of artificially engineered environmental circumstances. In nature, individual differences in genotype and experience always impose their own unique weighting in the ontogenic equation. Our ignorance of the principles of behavioral development is such that we are far from understanding the ontogeny of any complex, *learned* behavior well enough to identify such choice-points. But by focusing our attention not on a typological classification but on ontogenetic contrasts between organisms with different genotypes, we have logic in place to investigate behavioral development in a fashion that acknowledges the importance of both genes and environments while at the same time allowing us to disentangle one from the other. Looking to research prospects in the future, it may not be unreasonable to anticipate that behavioral experimentation will set the stage for progress in the developmental genetics of behavior in much the way that ethology has been a source of neurobiological insights, as embodied in the nascent science of neuroethology. We can look forward to new insights derived both from selective breeding and hybridization experiments (Hinde 1956; Guttinger 1985; Mundinger, this volume), and from application of the methods of modern molecular biology (Clayton 1997).

Perhaps the most compelling message emerging from this review is the inadvisability of treating birdsongs as purely *learned* behaviors. The process of song development is subject to pervasive genetic influences, many of them hidden from view until we take a comparative approach. It is all too easy for a student of learning who focuses on a single species to overlook the many species-specific predispositions that contribute to development, some obvious, and others so subtle that they are only revealed by appropriately designed experiments. To the extent that multiple choices are predictably encountered in nature, as animals learn from experience, it is inevitable that preferential biases in responsiveness to them will evolve, favoring varying degrees of canalization of processes underlying phenotypic plasticity. We can anticipate that genetically based predispositions will prove to be widespread, given the high cost of learning the wrong thing at the wrong time and thus suffering handicaps that may persist for a lifetime. Whatever the behavior under study, it behooves us to bear in mind the likelihood that arrays of distinctive developmental biases will play some role, ranging from those that are broad-based and pan-specific, to some that are more proscribed and species-specific, and to others that reflect individual geno-typic differences.

The primary focus of this review is the motor side of song development, occurring as the culmination of the song learning process. The *learned-innate* dilemma is no less unavoidable when we consider the initial phase of the learning process, when tutor songs are committed to memory, as Susan Peters and I have shown (Marler and Peters 1988, 1989, reviewed in Marler 1997). Experiments on the initial respon-siveness of newly-fledged birds to song stimulation, long before they themselves have done any singing, reveals that some birds possess "*innate* foreknowledge" about the normal song of their species that extends far beyond what can be inferred from the songs they develop in social isolation (Nelson and Marler 1994; Whaling et al. 1995). The evidence is compelling enough to suggest that we may have misinter-preted the nature of the song-learning process (Marler 1997). Building on indications of *innate* knowledge about a bird's own species song, and other lines of evidence, such as the widespread occurrence of species universals in song structure that young birds respond to, but which they fail to develop in isolation, a model of song memo-rization has been proposed. It is based on the idea that songbirds actually inherit much of the information required to generate a normal species-specific vocal reper-toire. According to this model, experience is required for them to realize much of this potential in their own behavior, as though memorization is based not on instruction, which is the usual view, but on selective processing, imposed on a fund of *innate* knowledge that is to some degree unique to each species (Marler and Nelson 1992; Marler 1997). That such a radical theory of song memorization should even be worth entertaining suffices to remind us how unwise it would be to overlook genetic contributions to behavioral development, even when we are dealing with a behavior that is often taken to be a paradigmatic illustration of a natural culturally transmitted behavior. It is already clear that when we finally solve the developmental equation for song learning, genomic and experiential contributions will both prove to be criti-cally important. With birdsong, as with any other kind of behavior, anyone who studies learning should scrutinize genomic contributions as closely as the effects of individual experience, especially as they contribute to the emergence of alternative phenotypes. To fail to do so is to guarantee that the nature-nurture dilemma will never be satisfactorily resolved.

Acknowledgments

I have had the benefit of many thoughtful comments and criticisms from Marc Hauser, Mark Konishi, and Don Kroodsma in preparing this paper. Jill Soha and

Jeni Trevitt helped with the figures and the manuscript. The research was supported by NIH Research Grant number MH 14651.

References

Bottjer, S. W. and Arnold, A. P. (1984) The role of feedback from the vocal organ. I. Maintenance of stereotypical vocalizations by adult zebra finches. *J. Neurosci.* 4:2387–2396.

Brenowitz, E. A., Margoliash, D., and Nordeen, K. W. (eds.) (1997) The neurobiology of birdsong. *J. Neurobiol.* (special issue) 33:495–709.

Bull, J. J. (1983) *Evolution of Sex-Determining Mechanisms.* Menlo Park, CA: Benjamin Cummings.

Clayton, D. F. (1997) The role of gene regulation in song circuit development and song learning. *J. Neurobiol.* 33:549–571.

Guttinger, H. R. (1985) Consequences of domestication on the song structures in the canary. *Behaviour* 94:254–278.

Hinde, R. A. (1956) The behaviour of certain cardueline F1 interspecies hybrids. *Behaviour* 9:202–213.

Holldobler, B. and Wilson, E. O. (1990) *The Ants.* Cambridge, MA: Harvard University Press.

Hughes, M., Nowicki, S., and Lohr, B. (1998) Call learning in black-capped chickadees (*Parus atricapillus*): The role of experience in the development of "chick-a-dee" calls. *Ethology* 104:232–249.

Johnston, T. D. (1988) Developmental explanation and the ontogeny of birdsong: Nature/nurture redux. *Behav. Brain Sci.* 11:617–663.

Konishi, M. (1963) The role of auditory feedback in the vocal behavior of the domestic fowl. *Z. Tierpsychol.* 20:349–367.

Konishi, M. (1964) Effects of deafening on song development in two species of juncos. *Condor* 66:85–102.

Konishi, M. (1965a) The role of auditory feedback in the control of vocalization in the white-crowned sparrow. *Z. Tierpsychol.* 22:770–783.

Konishi, M. (1965b) Effects of deafening on song development in American robins and black-headed grosbeaks. *Z. Tierpsychol.* 22:584–599.

Konishi, M. (1985) Bird song: From behavior to neuron. *Ann. Rev. Neurosci.* 8:125–170.

Konishi, M. (1994) An outline of recent advances in birdsong neurobiology. *Brain Beh. Evol.* 44:279–285.

Konishi, M. and Nottebohm, F. (1969) Experimental studies on the ontogeny of avian vocalizations. In *Bird Vocalizations*, ed. by R. A. Hinde, pp. 29–48. Cambridge: Cambridge University Press.

Kroodsma, D. E. (1977) A re-evaluation of song development in the song sparrow. *Anim. Behav.* 25:390–399.

Kroodsma, D. E. and Konishi, M. (1991) A suboscine bird (Eastern Phoebe, *Sayornis phoebe*) develops normal song without auditory feedback. *Anim. Behav.* 42:477–487.

Leonardo, A. and Konishi, M. (1998) Decrystallization of adult birdsong by perturbation of auditory feedback. *Proceedings of the 5th International Congress of Neuroethology* (San Diego), 314.

Lott, D. F. (1991) *Intraspecific Variation in Social Systems of Wild Vertebrates.* New York: Cambridge University Press.

Marler, P. (1957) Specific distinctiveness in the communication signals of birds. *Behaviour* 11:13–39.

Marler, P. (1964) Inheritance and learning in the development of animal vocalizations. In *Acoustic in Behavior Animals*, ed. by M. C. Busnel, pp. 228–243. Amsterdam: Elsevier.

Marler, P. (1997) Three models of song learning: Evidence from behavior. *J. Neurobiol.* 33:501–516.

Marler, P. and Nelson, D. (1992) Neuroselection and song learning in birds: Species universals in a culturally transmitted behavior. In *Seminars in the Neurosciences*, vol. 4: *Communication: Behavior and Neurobiology*. London: Saunders Scientific Publications, pp. 415–423.

Marler, P. and Peters, S. (1982) Structural changes in song ontogeny in the swamp sparrow *Melospiza georgiana*. *Auk* 99:446–458.

Marler, P. and Peters, S. (1987) A sensitive period for song acquisition in the song sparrow, *Melospiza melodia*: A case of age-limited learning. *Ethology* 76:89–100.

Marler, P. and Peters, S. (1988) The role of song phonology and syntax in vocal learning preferences in the song sparrow, *Melospiza melodia*. *Ethology* 77:125–149.

Marler, P. and Peters, S. (1989) Species differences in auditory responsiveness in early vocal learning. In *The Comparative Psychology of Audition: Perceiving Complex Sounds*, ed. by R. Dooling, and S. Hulse, pp. 243–273. Hillsdale, NJ: Lawrence Erlbaum Assoc.

Marler, P. and Sherman, V. (1983) Song structure without auditory feedback: Emendations of the auditory template hypothesis. *J. Neurosci.* 3:517–531.

Marler, P. and Sherman, V. (1985) Innate differences in singing behaviour of sparrows reared in isolation from adult conspecific song. *Anim. Behav.* 33:57–71.

Mulligan, J. A. (1966) Singing behavior and its development in the song sparrow, *Melospiza melodia*. *Publ. Zool.* 81:1–76.

Nelson, D. A. and Marler, P. (1994) Selection-based learning in bird song development. *Proc. Nat. Acad. Sci.* 91:10498–10501.

Nicolai, J. (1959) Familientradition in der Gesangsentwicklung des Gimpels (*Pyrrhula pyrrhula*). *J. Ornithol.* 100:39–46.

Nordeen, K. W. and Nordeen, E. J. (1992) Auditory feedback is necessary for the maintenance of stereotyped song in adult zebra finches. *Behav. Neural Biol.* 57:58–66.

Nottebohm, F. (1966) The role of sensory feedback in the development of avian vocalizations. PhD. dissertation, University of California, Berkeley.

Nottebohm, F. (1968) Auditory experience and song development in the chaffinch, *Fringilla coelebs*. *Ibis* 110:549–568.

Nottebohm, F. (1993) The search for neural mechanisms that define the sensitive period for song learning in birds. *Neth. J. Zool.* 43:193–234.

Nottebohm, F. and Nottebohm, M. E. (1971) Vocalizations and breeding behaviour of surgically deafened ring doves. *Anim. Behav.* 19:313–327.

Nottebohm, F., Stokes, T. M., and Leonard, C. M. (1976) Central control of song in the canary, *Serinus canarius*. *J. Comp. Neurol.* 165:457–468.

Nowicki, S. (1987) Vocal tract resonances in oscine bird sound production: Evidence from birdsongs in a helium atmosphere. *Nature* 325:53–55.

Nowicki, S. and Marler, P. (1988) How do birds sing? *Music Perception* 5:391–426.

Nowicki, S., Marler, P., Maynard, A., and Peters, S. (1992) Is the tonal quality of birdsong learned? Evidence from song sparrows. *Ethology* 90:225–235.

Nowicki, S., Mitani, J. C., Nelson, D. A., and Marler, P. (1989) The communicative significance of tonality in birdsong: Responses to songs produced in helium. *Bioacoustics* 2:35–46.

Okanoya, K. and Yamaguchi, A. (1997) Adult Bengalese finches (*Lonchura striata var. domestica*) require real-time auditory feedback to produce normal song syntax. *J. Neurobiol.* 33:343–356.

Podos, J. (1996) Motor constraints on vocal development in a songbird. *Anim. Behav.* 51:1061–1070.

Podos, J. (1997) A performance constraint on the evolution of trilled vocalizations in a songbird family (*Passeriformes:emberizidae*). *Evolution* 51:537–551.

Podos, J., Sherer, J. L. K., Peters, S., and Nowicki, S. (1995) Ontogeny of vocal tract movements during song production in the song sparrow. *Anim. Behav.* 50:1287–1296.

Price, P. H. (1979) Developmental determinants of structure in zebra finch song. *J. Comp. Physiol. Psychol.* 93:260–277.

Scheiner, S. M. (1993) Genetics and evolution of phenotypic plasticity. *Ann. Rev. Ecol. Syst.* 24:35–68.

Searcy, W. A. and Marler, P. (1981) A test for responsiveness to song structure and programming in female sparrows. *Science* 213:926–928.

Searcy, W. A. and Marler, P. (1987) Response of sparrows to songs of deaf and isolation- reared males: Further evidence for innate auditory templates. *Dev. Psychobiol.* 20:509–520.

Streidter, G. F. (1994) The vocal control pathways in budgerigars differ from those in songbirds. *J. Comp. Neurol.* 343:35–56.

Waddington, C. H. (1957) *The Strategy of the Genes.* London: Allen and Unwin.

West-Eberhard, M. J. (1989) Phenotypic plasticity and the origins of diversity. *Ann. Rev. Ecol. Syst.* 20:249–278.

Whaling, C. S., Solis, M. M., Doupe, A. J., Soha, J. A., and Marler, P. (1997) Acoustic and neural bases for innate recognition of song. *Proc. Natl. Acad. Sci.* 94:12694–12698.

Wooley, S. M. N. and Rubel, E. W. (1997) Bengalese finches, *Lonchura striata domestica*, depend upon auditory feedback for the maintenance of adult song. *J. Neurosci.* 17:6380–6390.

11 Making Ecological Sense of Song Development by Songbirds

Donald E. Kroodsma

The variety of singing styles and song developmental programs among songbirds is enormous (Kroodsma 1988; Slater 1989). The potential for this diversity undoubtedly arose when songbirds acquired the ability to learn[1] the fine structure of their songs from one another (Marler and Mundinger, 1971; Marler and Pickert, 1984); specialized song centers arose in the forebrain (Nottebohm 1980), and these centers then guided diverse song developmental and adult singing strategies among species (Brenowitz 1991; DeVoogd et al. 1993). Species thus now differ in many ways, such as the extent to which songs are learned, how many songs are learned, how songs are packaged in any singing performance, and so on (Catchpole and Slater 1995; Kroodsma and Miller 1996). Anyone attempting to make sense of this great diversity must be prepared to tease apart these differences in a search for patterns (Kroodsma 1996).

And patterns must exist (Marler 1967). Selection must act in some unifying way over these thousands of species, so that some integrating rules will be uncovered by a careful, perceptive examination of the diversity. Songs, after all, are used to "manage" other individuals for selfish gain, and only two main categories of individuals, females and males, exist in a population. Perhaps some forces on singing behavior and its development are largely intersexual, and others are largely intrasexual. Perhaps close scrutiny will begin to reveal patterns shared by a variety of species, and these patterns then might suggest the common processes that have produced the patterns. We must remember, too, that we have studied so few species, and general patterns may emerge only as we add to our overview of this remarkable songbird lineage.

In this brief essay, I tell of my hopes. They are not blind hopes, I believe, but realistic ones, based on the confidence that the birds are poised to tell us all that they know and do. The hopes began, unknown to me at the time, during a chance encounter with a tape recorder and parabola in 1968. The pulse quickened in 1969 as I discovered Peter Marler's comparative work on sparrow song ontogeny (Marler et al. 1962; Marler and Tamura 1962; Marler 1964; Marler and Tamura 1964; Marler 1967), and especially a year later as I read and reread his 1970 monograph on song development in white-crowned sparrows (*Zonotrichia leucophrys*; Marler 1970). In these and later works (Marler and Mundinger 1971; Marler and Peters 1977; Marler et al. 1980; Marler and Sherman 1985; Marler 1991a,b; Marler and Nelson 1992; Marler et al. 1994) I found what organized a way of thinking that persists today, that species differ often in dramatic ways, and that the drama must make some evolutionary sense. I am especially grateful for the inspiration and guidance from Peter Marler during eight good years at Rockefeller University, from 1972 to 1980.

I use several approaches in trying to make sense of the diverse developmental styles of songbirds. First, I focus on several species, emphasizing the chestnut-sided warbler (*Dendroica pensylvanica*), that use different songs for different purposes (Spector 1992); in these species, the consequences of intra- and intersexual selective forces on vocal behavior should be clearer than in species that use multipurpose songs, in which the outcome of these two selective processes must be a compromise (Byers 1996b). Next, I consider different developmental programs that might be used if selection were to promote geographic uniformity of songs; several means are available to achieve what might be viewed as a common end (Kroodsma 1996). Last, I consider several other ecological factors that might influence singing styles and their development.

Divergent Developmental Programs within Species

Using the comparative approach to understand the evolution of behavior, one typically strives to find closely related organisms that differ in some fundamental way, such as in mating system, communication system, or the like. One then searches for correlations between behavior and ecology, attempting to reconstruct selective forces and evolutionary pathways that have led to the divergent behaviors in different species. For species that use multipurpose songs, this comparative approach has been especially useful (Kroodsma 1977; Catchpole 1980; Catchpole and McGregor 1986). Some species, however, provide a unique opportunity to examine divergent evolutionary pathways within a single species, because males of these species use two song categories, one of which consists largely of intersexual songs and the other of intrasexual songs (see Spector 1992 for review).

The Chestnut-sided Warbler

Male chestnut-sided warblers, like males of several other paruline species, use two strikingly different kinds of songs to accomplish their tasks (Lein 1978; Byers 1995): songs of one category are used primarily with females, those of the other category with males (figure 11.1). This two-tiered communication system is maintained by two strikingly different song-learning programs (Byers and Kroodsma 1992). Songs of the two categories differ in where, from whom, and when they are learned, and perhaps even how much needs to be learned. This species thus provides a good model

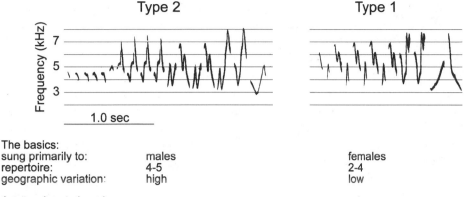

Figure 11.1
The two song categories of the Chestnut-sided Warbler, illustrated by a representative AE (accented-ending, or type 1) and UE (unaccented-ending, or type 2) song, differ in how they are used, in repertoire size, in extent of geographic variation, and in how the songs are acquired.

for understanding how evolution can design distinct learning programs for songs with different functions.

One developmental program produces the familiar "pleased-pleased-pleased-to-meetcha" type 1 song, called the "accented-ending" song because of the emphasis on the end of the song. For simplicity, I will call this the category I song (Spector 1992), or simply the type 1 song. This song form is used by unmated males throughout the day, typically from the treetops, or is used in close association with females; all evidence suggests that this type 1 song is used by males to attract (and perhaps stimulate) females (Byers 1996b).

One feat that the learning program must accomplish is rather remarkable: an almost uniform distribution of several different type 1 songs throughout the geographic range (see figure 3 in Byers 1996a). From Virginia to Massachusetts and from Maine to Wisconsin and Minnesota, five basic type 1 songs occur. Four of these types occur everywhere, but males in Minnesota and Wisconsin seem to have one additional type not found farther east. Each male usually favors one particular type, but extended sampling typically reveals that he is capable of singing two to four of the types. In the Massachusetts population, each of the four song types seems to be distributed randomly among singing males.

Why type 1 songs are geographically invariant can best be surmised from the functions of the songs. These songs are used primarily to address females, so males with conforming type 1 songs must somehow be at a mating advantage over males who do not conform. Females do disperse farther in many songbirds than do males (Dhondt and Huble 1968), and perhaps males maximize their mating opportunities by being able to interact with females who have originated from more distant populations; perhaps ambiguity is reduced, and errors in signal detection minimized (Wiley 1994). Or perhaps females demand from males some standard by which they can all be compared (Zahavi 1980); a highly stereotyped signal would also accomplish such a function. Whatever the reason, it would appear that it is the female who selects for this stereotypy.

A second developmental program must produce the type 2 songs, often called the "unaccented-ending" songs. These songs are used by males especially during the intense singing of the dawn chorus and during male-male interactions at territorial boundaries. The functions of this song appear to be largely intrasexual (Kroodsma et al. 1989; Byers 1996b).

The developmental program for type 2 songs produces a geographic distribution that is markedly different from that of type 1 songs (Byers 1996a). As with type 1 songs, each male has a small repertoire of type 2 songs (median 4 or 5, range 1 to 10), and he favors only one of those type 2 songs in his singing. The others are used more rarely, so that one can never be sure what the actual type 2 repertoire of a male is. Neighboring males share many of the same song types, but a male tends to favor singing the rarely used songs of his neighbors. Although immediate neighbors share their type 2 repertoires, males several territories away typically have another set of type 2 songs, so that minidialects of these type 2 songs occur throughout the range of the species (see figures 1, 2, and 4 in Byers 1996a).

The developmental programs that produce these type 1 and type 2 songs must be markedly different (Byers and Kroodsma 1992). We know that the birds must learn their songs, because isolated males in the laboratory produce abnormal songs. In contrasting these two learning programs, I consider the when, where, and from whom young birds learn their songs, and then I consider what is actually learned.

First, consider when and where. Type 1 songs can be learned anytime and anywhere, because a young male hears the same set of songs at all times and locations throughout his first year of life. The type 1 songs on and near his natal territory will be essentially the same type 1 songs that he hears during dispersal, during spring migration, and after migration on his first breeding territory the next spring. Although these type 1 songs could be learned anytime, we believe that males typically learn them during their hatching year (see Lemon et al. 1994). Nestlings are almost guaranteed early exposure to this song, because adult male warblers often sing their type 1 songs just before, during, or after feeding visits to the nest (Spector 1991). When a male claims his breeding territory the next spring, he is then immediately capable of "advertising" for a female.

The type 2 repertoire cannot be learned just anytime or anywhere. Although each male tends to have at least one unique type 2 song, most songs match the details in songs of neighbors on his breeding territory. The unique songs could be acquired anytime and anywhere, but the songs that match only breeding neighbors must be learned, most likely after migration, when and where the male acquires both his breeding territory and his singing neighbors. If these matching type 2 songs are learned before migration, then the young male must have already settled on a breeding location and learned the songs of the local neighborhood during his hatching year. We do not know when young birds develop a fidelity to a breeding site, but the detailed matching in songs of neighbors suggests to us that the type 2 songs are finalized after migration, when the male begins to breed (Byers and Kroodsma 1992; Lemon et al. 1993). Learning type 2 songs during the hatching year is thus far less important than is learning type 1 songs at that time, because each male can secure his place in the microdialect system of type 2 songs only after migration, when he establishes his breeding territory.

Where and when the young male must learn dictates, to some extent, not only what he learns but also from whom he learns. Consider first what is learned for type 1 songs. These songs are remarkably stereotyped over broad geographic expanses (Byers 1996a), reminiscent of the stereotypy in the nonlearned songs of flycatchers over similar geographic areas (Lanyon 1978; Kroodsma and Konishi 1991). Perhaps significant aspects of the song form of these type 1 songs are already encoded in the brain at hatching; the young male might then need to hear just a few examples of the appropriate type 1 songs before his own songs are able to be "released," or "selected" (Marler and Nelson 1992; see also Marler, this volume). In the laboratory, young males learn these songs from tape recordings more readily than they learn type 2 songs, suggesting that social interactions with live adults is not so crucial for this developmental program. If the "proto-template" for these songs is essentially uniform among chestnut-sided warbler populations, then the young male could "learn" his type 1 songs from any *one* male. In contrast, if males must imitate the entire song from other adults, and significant portions are not already encoded in the genome, then the young male must learn not from just any *one* male but rather from *everyone*. Learning from only one male would perpetuate copy errors from one generation to the next and would destroy the uniformity of songs over space. Learning from everyone, however, a process in which a male "averages" the characteristics of several singing males, would more likely guarantee uniformity over wider expanses of geographic space.

The "from whom" and "what is learned" scenario differs markedly for type 2 songs. The details of the predominant type 2 songs in a male's repertoire must be learned from immediate territorial neighbors wherever the young male settles to breed. Given the immense variety of type 2 songs among these warblers and the variation over geographic space, it is virtually impossible that the diversity of type 2 songs could be somehow encoded at birth, with just a few of those songs being energized by experience. Rather, the form of individual elements and their sequence of delivery must be imitated from immediate, territorial neighbors. In the laboratory, young males seem to require social interactions with singing adults to learn these songs (Byers and Kroodsma 1992), perhaps much as they would learn them on their breeding territories. The local dialects that occur in type 2 songs could be produced by several learning approaches. A male could learn from one particular individual, for example, or he could learn the most common songs in a neighborhood from one or more individuals (Beecher 1996; Beecher et al. 1996).

One especially puzzling feature of the singing of these warblers is the frequency with which certain song forms are used (Lein 1978; Byers 1995). Each male favors one type 1 and one type 2 song, and many other songs are used only rarely. For type 2 songs, it seems that neighbors avoid matching each other, because the common song of one male is typically a rarely used song of his neighbor. Most type 2 songs that are unique to the repertoire of a given male are rarely used; perhaps he learned those songs elsewhere, not on the local breeding territory, and that is why they fall into disuse. Such an explanation does not suffice, however, for songs that are shared with neighbors but are rarely used. Further study is needed to appreciate the significance of these rarely used song forms.

Overall, the chestnut-sided warbler provides a fine model in which to explore ecological approaches to vocal development. Two seemingly independent developmental programs have evolved within this species (Byers and Kroodsma 1992). One program is designed to generate highly stereotyped, largely intersexual signals throughout the geographic range of the species; the second program ensures that neighboring males share details of the songs that they will use to interact with each other (Byers 1995; Byers 1996a). The functions of these two song categories (Byers 1996b) seem to dictate the where, when, from whom, and what of the learning process.

Other Species

Other species also have vocalizations that are specialized for intra- and intersexual use, and some characteristics of their learning programs appear similar to those of the chestnut-sided warbler. Consider first those vocalizations that appear to be largely intersexual. Unmated males repeat these songs all day long, that is, they "advertise," presumably attempting to attract a female. The blue-winged warbler (*Vermivora pinus*) uses its *bee-bzzz* (Gill and Murray 1972), the golden-winged warbler (*Vermivora chrysoptera*) its *beee-bz-bz-bz* (Highsmith 1989), the black-capped chickadee (*Parus atricapillus*) its whistled *hey-sweetie* (Hailman 1989; Hailman and Ficken 1996), and the grasshopper sparrow (*Ammodramus savanarum*) its *pit-tup zeeeeeeeee* (Kroodsma 1996). Just like the type 1 songs of the chestnut-sided warbler, these songs vary little over vast stretches of geographic space. These songs, too, could essentially be learned anywhere, anytime, and from anyone (or, perhaps more accurately, from everyone, depending on exactly what is learned—see above).

The geographic uniformity of the black-capped chickadee's song is especially intriguing, because it could be directly related to migratory habits, irruptive movements of young birds, winter singing of adults, and a learning program that instructs the young male to learn an average song of those that he hears. Throughout most of the North American continent, from the Atlantic to the Pacific, each male sings one song form, the hey-sweetie (figure 11.2). In the laboratory, however, males develop repertoires of 2–4 whistled songs, and birds isolated from one another in different rooms develop their own dialects, too (Shackleton and Ratcliffe 1993; Kroodsma et al. 1995).

These laboratory-reared birds seem to behave much like chickadees in naturally isolated populations (Kroodsma et al. 1999b). On Massachusetts' offshore islands, including Martha's Vineyard, Chappaquiddick, and Nantucket, each male has a repertoire of two or more whistled songs, and dialects occur even on Chappaquiddick, an island only 6km across (see figure 11.2). Chickadees on these islands are resident, we believe, with little mixing among populations and little, if any, immigration from mainland populations; as with other songbirds, dialects in learned songs tend to develop among such resident, isolated populations (Ewert and Kroodsma 1994).

On the mainland of North America, however, migration and irruptive movements, especially of young birds, may help to homogenize the singing behavior of males among locations. As young birds travel, they could readily learn from adults, which sing, especially on warm sunny days, throughout the winter and early spring. A young male that learned the "average song" he encountered throughout his travels would maintain the stereotyped singing of this species over broad geographic areas. Such stereotyped singing does not preclude populations from differentiating genetically, of course, especially if young birds faithfully return to natal populations; chickadees of Newfoundland, for example, appear to be genetically different from

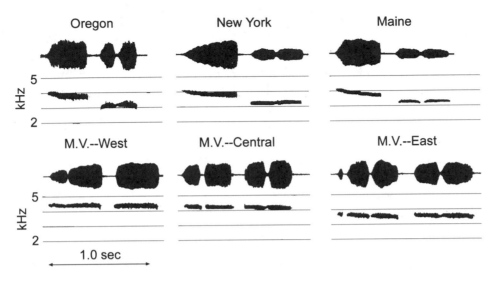

Figure 11.2
For the black-capped chickadee, population movements and isolation seem to affect song stereotypy within both individuals and populations. (Top row) Throughout most of North America, from the Atlantic Ocean to the Pacific Ocean, males sing the highly stereotyped "hey-sweetie," with the first whistle higher than the second (see sonograms), and with an amplitude break in the middle of the second whistle (see corresponding oscillograms); irruptive movements in this mainland population may help to maintain the song conformity. (Bottom row) In some isolated populations, however, such as on Martha's Vineyard and other offshore islands of Massachusetts, individuals can have sizable song repertoires, and dialects occur from population to population. Illustrated here, from left to right, are a "sweetie-hey," a "sweetie-sweetie," and a "sosweetie-sweetie" from western, central, and eastern Martha's Vineyard; all songs are monotonal, i.e., both main whistles are on the same frequency, with dialects identified by the position of the amplitude breaks in the songs. See Kroodsma et al. 1999b.

other North American chickadees (Gill et al. 1993), but they still use the *hey-sweetie*, perhaps maintained in the local populations by the migratory and irruptive movements of young birds.

In sharp contrast to these vocalizations used mostly in intersexual contexts are the vocalizations used in more intrasexual encounters. The type 2 songs of the two warblers vary from place to place (Kroodsma 1981; Highsmith 1989; see also Staicer 1990; Bolsinger 1997), as do the aggressive gargles of the chickadees (Ficken and Weise 1984; Ficken et al. 1987), and the "long, sizzling insect-like tumble of notes" (Peterson 1956, p. 230) of the sparrow (Kroodsma 1996). Interacting, countersinging neighbors thus share the details of these songs only with one another, as if sharing with nonlocal birds were unimportant. It would seem that for both type 1 and type 2 songs, selection has guaranteed that neighboring males share songs, but for type 2 songs, such selection is absent for males from distant locations. Regardless of the selective force(s) involved, these type 2 vocalizations require a different developmental program from that of the type 1 songs; and, like the type 2 songs of the chestnut-sided warbler, the type 2 vocalizations of these other species must also be learned on or near the breeding territory, most likely after postnatal dispersal, and from adult males with whom a young male is likely to interact during the breeding season.

These similar developmental programs appear to have evolved independently in at least three different songbird lineages (warblers, a sparrow, and a chickadee), suggesting that perhaps the selective forces involved are general ones to be found among other songbirds, too (Kroodsma 1996). When the functions of song groups differ, selection can act independently on the learning program for each. But when songs are multipurpose, as with most species, then the single product of potentially disruptive intra- and intersexual selective forces must be a compromise, that is, a song that must satisfy two needs cannot be optimized for both. Perhaps lessons learned from the warblers, sparrow, and chickadee can be applied to other species. In the white-crowned sparrow, perhaps the large dialect areas in songs (Marler and Tamura 1962; Baptista 1975; Baker and Cunningham 1985) have to do especially with females, and the smaller neighborhoods in which males match microdetails of songs with each other (see, e.g., Trainer 1983) is a consequence of intrasexual forces. And with indigo buntings (*Passerina cyanea*), the same song syllables occur throughout the range of the species (for update, see Baker and Boylan 1995), but the arrangements of those syllables vary markedly over both space and time, so that interacting males in a small neighborhood tend to share the same song types (Payne 1996); with a single multipurpose song, perhaps the broad distribution of syllables reflects intersexual selective forces and the microdistribution of the overall song pattern reflects more intrasexual forces.

How to Achieve Low Geographic Variation

Although most bioacousticians have focused on the dialects and high geographic variation found among many songbirds (e.g., see Baker and Cunningham 1985), geographic variation of songs for some other passerines is low. For these species, songs of individuals at one location are no more like one another than they are like those at more distant locations. Exactly what selective forces encourage this low variation is largely unknown, but presumably individuals that conform in some way to the vocal behaviors of others over some larger geographic area have an advantage over individuals who do not conform. Perhaps males can attract a widely dispersing

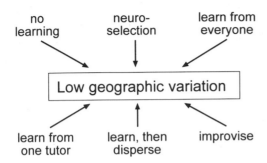

Figure 11.3
Reduced geographic variation in song can be achieved in two basic ways, by either minimizing or maximizing individual variation. All birds over large geographic areas can develop the same song types if no learning is involved (e.g., suboscine flycatchers), if development is guided by neuroselection (Marler and Nelson 1992), or if individuals learn their songs from everyone (thus developing an average song from among the many individuals heard). Alternatively, geographic variation can still be low if individual variation is maximized; individuals can develop highly different songs if they learn from only one tutor, learn at one location and then disperse, or improvise species-typical songs.

female by using a song with which she is more likely to be familiar, and males who conform in their singing are therefore more successful than are males who cannot appeal to females from such a wide geographic area.

In this section, I explore how a variety of developmental processes could be used to achieve low geographic variation (see also Williams and Slater 1991). Some processes minimize individual variation, but others maximize it, and I consider these two broad categories in turn (figure 11.3).

Low Individual Variation (Uniformity of Songs)

Low individual variation and geographic uniformity can be achieved at one extreme by genetically encoded songs, or at the other extreme by a process in which individuals learn average songs within a population. Between these two endpoints of a continuum, intermediate strategies are possible.

1. Genetically Encoded Songs   One of the simplest ways to achieve both low geographic variation and geographic uniformity is to eliminate the learning component. Eastern phoebes (*Sayornis phoebe*), for example, develop normal songs without auditory feedback, which suggests that no song imitation is required for normal development (Kroodsma and Konishi 1991). Other flycatchers, too, such as the alder and willow flycatchers (*Empidonax traillii* and *E. alnorum*), develop normal songs in the laboratory in spite of highly abnormal auditory experiences (Kroodsma 1984). Normal song development thus seems impervious to environmental perturbation. Because the song forms are genetically encoded, each phoebe over a broad geographic region sings essentially the same two song forms. Different songs, in fact, would indicate that the singer is also different genetically, perhaps warranting that the different singers be classified as different species (Isler et al. 1997; Whitney and Pacheco 1997). Evidence from geographic song variation, brain anatomy, and vocal behavior of juvenile birds from several suboscines suggests that this song developmental strategy might be pervasive among suboscines (reviewed in Kroodsma 1988).

2. Neuroselection   Perhaps many features of songs are encoded genetically, but some experience with normal songs is required. It is as if the bird is predisposed and primed to sing a particular song pattern, because that pattern is somehow largely encoded in the brain, but the young bird must first hear that pattern before it can be released (Marler and Nelson 1992). Such a process has been proposed to explain how several songbirds, such as indigo buntings (Payne 1996), can maintain the same song syllables over considerable expanses of their geographic range. Learning is clearly required, because isolated juveniles in the laboratory develop highly abnormal songs (Payne 1981).

3. Learning from Everyone (i.e., from Many Tutors)   At the other end of the continuum, young birds may have tremendous flexibility in what they can sing, but they are for some reason socially constrained to sing the same songs as do others in the population. To achieve uniformity, each male learns not from a single individual (such a practice would perpetuate lineages of copy errors, thereby disrupting the uniformity) but by averaging the characteristics of songs from a large number of singing males, or perhaps (though less likely?) by learning the most common song in the population (e.g., see Beecher 1996). In the absence of the social constraints, such as in the laboratory, the song conformity breaks down, and birds in different singing groups can develop different songs, that is, dialects. If populations from large geographic areas mix during the nonbreeding season, and if singing occurs during those associations, large areas of song uniformity could be maintained relatively easily, as with the black-capped chickadee.

High Individual Variation (No Uniformity of Songs)

Although it seems counterintuitive initially, maximizing individual variation can also result in low geographic variation. Consider three possible processes.

1. Learning from Any *One* Tutor, At the Breeding Location If a young male adopts the song of a particular individual, he will be but one individual in a series of successive generations that sing a particular song. Each generation will add its own wrinkle to the song, and only a few individuals in a population would be expected to share a particular type. With a limited number of sound types available for a species, the song variations would be expected to recur throughout the geographic range of the species.

Perhaps the chipping sparrow (*Spizella passerina*) develops its songs in this manner. During June of 1995, Wan-chun Liu (unpubl. data) banded a nestling chipping sparrow on the campus of the University of Massachusetts, Amherst. By August, this juvenile male had dispersed several km to the north, adjacent to a bachelor male who sang frequently. After migration, the young male returned during the spring of 1996 to the same location in north Amherst, but the adult did not. The young male appeared to have learned the song of this frequent singer during the late summer of 1995. This type of rarely observed event offers a glimpse of how song variability is derived and transmitted within these sparrow populations. Pairs or trios of males might develop similar songs in this way, but many different song forms occur at a given location, and many of these forms recur throughout the geographic range of the species (Borror 1959; Kroodsma 1996).

2. Learning from Anyone or Everyone, then Dispersing Geographic variation would thus be low if a bird learned songs from an individual (or even learned an average song from several local individuals) and then dispersed with those songs to breed at some distant location. Thus both birds and their songs, that is, both the genes and memes, would be dispersed widely, and songs of neighbors would be no more similar to one another than to songs of more distant individuals.

The zebra finch (*Taeniopygia guttata*) is perhaps a good example of this strategy. Young males often imitate the song of a particular individual, such as the father, and then disperse to breed at some distant location. As many as 77% of breeding pairs within a colony were estimated to be immigrants, for example (Zann 1990; Zann and Runciman 1994; Zann 1997).

If strong selection does not exist for neighbors to have similar songs, perhaps precise imitation of songs would not be necessary either, because songs that are improvised, based on some common rule, would suffice. The "cost" or "difficulty" of imitating and improvising a species-typical song is unknown, however. Is one strategy simpler or "cheaper" than the other? If low geographic variation is to be achieved with a small repertoire size, is it simpler to imitate and disperse or to just improvise a species-general kind of song (see item 3, below)? Unfortunately, we know so little about dispersal of young birds, and where they are when they acquire their songs, what they are exposed to, and so on, that it is difficult to know for many species exactly how song development and population movements influence geographic variation in songs.

3.   Improvising   Another way in which low geographic variation can be achieved, especially with large song repertoires, is to improvise the songs (Kroodsma et al. 1997). Like most songbirds, gray catbirds (*Dumetella carolinensis*) can imitate, but laboratory-reared males can also improvise large song repertoires, every bit as large as those of wild birds. If the same improvisation rules are used by catbirds throughout large geographic areas, then individual variation is maximized while geographic variation in songs is minimized. In our surveys of wild catbird song, as obtained from the Library of Natural Sounds at the Cornell Laboratory of Ornithology, we could find no evidence of geographic variation. Our data on song development and geographic variation suggest that song improvisation in this species achieves for each individual a large repertoire of hundreds of song patterns, and that repertoires of neighboring individuals are no more like one another than like repertoires of more distant individuals. With this extreme example, geographic variation is clearly minimized by maximizing individual variation.

Another species that improvises large repertoires of species-typical songs is the North American sedge wren (*Cistothorus platensis*; see Kroodsma et al. 1999a). This developmental strategy has probably coevolved with reduced site-fidelity and opportunistic breeding (see below).

Genes and Memes in Space

Vocal variation is expected, in some way, to be correlated spatially with genetic variation. At one extreme, songs that require no learning and are therefore more or less direct expressions of genes will occur with the genes that express them, and genes and songs will therefore co-vary spatially. Songs of suboscine flycatchers, for example, are a good indication of the overall genetic makeup of the individual.

When songbirds learn their songs, however, the relationship between the distribution of songs and genes is more problematical. The possibility that the striking song dialects of white-crowned sparrows limit dispersal is certainly intriguing and has been the focus of many fascinating studies (e.g., see Baker and Cunningham 1985 and accompanying commentaries). We know, of course, that young birds are able to disperse across dialect boundaries and learn songs at distant sites (Kroodsma 1974; Jenkins 1978; Baptista and Morton 1988), but I do not think that we know the full impact of these boundaries on dispersal.

But what sense can we make of these other songbird species in which songs are learned but their structure varies little over geographic space? Are the genes for controlling those songs less differentiated, too, as in the suboscines? Because songs are used to manage other individuals, we would expect that the distribution of male songs used to manage females, that is, to acquire mating opportunities, would be correlated at some level with the distribution of genes in the species, too. A wide distribution of song forms specialized to attract females, for example, might also suggest a relative genetic uniformity over the same area. Intriguingly, species with low geographic variation in song, such as the gray catbird, chestnut-sided warbler, blue-winged warbler, golden-winged warbler, grasshopper sparrow, and sedge wren, have few if any subspecies listed by the American Ornithologists' Union (1957). This suggests that populations have not differentiated much in these species. With the black-capped chickadee, a large North American population with the *hey-sweetie* song from the Atlantic to the Pacific is also genetically undifferentiated (Gill et al. 1993).

Other Ecological and Social Factors Affecting Development

How a bird sings must be dictated by a variety of ecological and social factors. Such factors might include the proximity of other singers, the probability of counter-singing with the same neighbors throughout life, or mating opportunities with one's own social partner or with the social partners of others. These factors should, in turn, correlate with how songs develop and are used among species. In this section, I consider a few of these possible factors.

Density

The proximity of singing males to one another, that is, density, should make a major difference in both what males sing and how they sing (figure 11.4). A male on an isolated territory, for example, with no immediate competition for his resources (territory or mate), would have little motivation to display intensely. Thus, on coastal islands, Morse (1970) found that male warblers rarely sang their type 2 song, the song used in male-male contests. In higher density warbler populations, however, males countersing intensely across territorial boundaries (e.g., see Wiley 1994). Sedge wrens, too, sing at a leisurely pace when singing alone, repeating each song type many times in succession; when neighboring males also sing, however, rates of singing increase, as do rates of presentation of new song types. The "effective repertoire size," the number of different songs presented per unit time, thus increases during

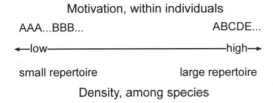

Motivation, within individuals

AAA...BBB...   ABCDE...

←—low————————————————high—→

small repertoire   large repertoire

Density, among species

Figure 11.4
How use and evolution of large song repertoires seem to be affected by individual motivation and by higher intensity of displays at greater population densities. For an individual songbird, the effective song repertoire, i.e., the rate of presentation of new song types, is highest for situations of high motivation. Under low motivation, for example, a male sedge wren repeats one song type (song types indicated by letters A–E) many times before switching to another type, but at higher motivation, successive songs are always different (Kroodsma and Verner 1978). Among *Cistothorus* wren species, selection for large song repertoires seems to occur in dense populations, where males countersing at close range with other males. A sustained high intensity of display in such dense populations seems to select for larger song repertoires.

such encounters (Kroodsma and Verner 1978). During intense dawn singing, eastern towhees (*Pipilo erythrophthalmus*) alternate the different songs in their repertoires, but later in the day males sing with "eventual variety," repeating one song type many times before introducing another (Ewert and Kroodsma 1994). Similarly, during intense courtship and copulation, male red-winged blackbirds (*Agelaius phoeniceus*) deliver their entire song repertoire in a matter of seconds; in contrast, during routine territorial singing, males sing with eventual variety (Searcy and Yasukawa 1990). Thus, among a variety of species, individuals increase the effective repertoire size with the intensity of display.

The repertoire size and how songs are presented should also differ among species in a way that reflects the average display intensity found among those species. Displays of species in which males routinely sing in close proximity might be expected to be more elaborate or intense than displays of species in which intrasexual competition seems reduced. Indeed, evidence from several sources suggests a relationship between song repertoire size and density. Both absolute and effective repertoire sizes among North American wrens appear related to density, for example (Kroodsma 1977). Among *Acrocephalus* warblers, too, the largest repertoires are found in the two species with the smallest territories, that is, the greatest density, not in the socially polygynous species (Catchpole 1980). And among buntings, the reed bunting (*Emberiza schoeniclus*) has the largest song repertoire (Catchpole and McGregor 1986), and it is also found in especially dense populations.

Data from *Cistothorus* wrens strongly support this proposed relationship between repertoire size and density. Sedge and marsh wrens occur in especially high densities

among North American wrens, and these two wrens have among the largest repertoires, too (Kroodsma 1977). The rate of singing and the number of different song
types presented during brief spurts of singing are also directly related to display intensity. Furthermore, western marsh wrens tend to occur more often on smaller territories, and, accordingly, they have larger repertoires than do eastern marsh wrens
(Kroodsma and Verner 1997). Especially convincing is the singing behavior of *Cistothorus meridae*, the Merida wren, in the Venezuelan Andes. Territories are about
100 times the size of a western marsh wren, and neighboring males on adjacent territories countersing only from a considerable distance. Each Merida wren has only
about 20 song types in its repertoire, the smallest song repertoire found among *Cistothorus* wren populations that have been studied throughout North, Central, and
South America. Furthermore, males routinely sing with eventual variety, just as do
North American sedge wrens when they are not interacting with other males
(Kroodsma and Verner 1978).

But just why and how does density affect the evolution of display complexity?
Density is undoubtedly a factor because intensity of display increases with immediate competition. And the competition, of course, must be about mating opportunities, whether the matings occur with one's own or with another's social partner.
Among *Emberiza* sparrows, for example, reed buntings have especially large repertoires and small territories; they also have exceptionally high rates of extrapair
fertilizations (Dixon et al. 1994). Among great reed warblers (*Acrocephalus arundinaceus*), a female chooses to have extrapair copulations with a nearby male who has
a larger repertoire than does her mate (Hasselquist et al. 1996; the data do not,
however, demonstrate that the female chooses on the basis of repertoire size). Additional data on mating patterns among other species are needed before one can test
for a possible relationship between large song repertoires, display intensity, and possible patterns in mating opportunities among males.

Neighborhood Stability and Site-fidelity

Adult singing behaviors and developmental programs could also be affected by the
probability that individual males will interact with the same individuals throughout
their lives. Some populations are resident, for example; a young male may disperse a
few territories from his natal territory, settle in a new neighborhood, learn the songs
there, and remain on that territory for life, interacting only with that same group of
males or their immediate cultural descendents (Jenkins 1978; Beecher et al. 1994). At
the other extreme are nonresident, nomadic species; taking advantage of breeding
opportunities when and where they become available, individuals of these species
might rarely if ever reencounter one another. Songs imitated from one or a few indi

viduals at one site would not match the songs of other interactants at the next site. Between these two extremes, of course, are situations in which stability of territorial neighborhoods might be expected to vary from high to low.

Neighborhood stability seems to promote faithful imitation of song models, so that countersinging males share the same song types. Neighboring males of the resident eastern towhee in Florida and of the spotted towhee (*Pipilo maculatus*) in Oregon, for example, have nearly identical song type repertoires, and their songs change rapidly over space, from one singing neighborhood to the next. In contrast, the migratory male eastern towhees of the Northeast share far fewer songs with their neighbors (Kroodsma 1971; Ewert and Kroodsma 1994).

Two processes could produce a reduced pattern of song sharing in a population. First, males of all locations could imitate songs accurately, but perhaps in some populations males disperse from the site of learning, thereby using songs at one site that had been learned at another. Such dispersal would tend to scramble songs in space, and neighboring males as a result would share fewer songs with one another. Alternatively, because this "expected" dispersal or population mixing is built into the life history of the population, young males might learn less precisely, building into their songs a level of variability (or improvisation) that might help produce a "generalized" song, one that would function well in almost any singing neighborhood. Our laboratory experiments show that New England towhees can imitate from training tapes (Kroodsma and Ewert unpubl. data), but the accuracy does not match the accuracy that we see among free-living resident towhees of Florida or Oregon (Kroodsma 1971; Ewert and Kroodsma 1994). The interpretation of these data is problematic, of course, because any failure of birds to copy precisely in the laboratory could simply be an artifact of laboratory conditions. An improved experimental design for this question would compare relative imitative abilities of resident (Florida) and migratory (New England) eastern towhees under identical conditions in the laboratory.

My working hypothesis with these towhees is that, as the stability of song neighborhoods declines, either selection for precise song imitation is reduced, or selection for some improvisation is increased, or both (figure 11.5). Data from *Cistothorus* wrens are consistent with this working hypothesis. Populations of the sedge wren in North America are unpredictable and site fidelity is low; birds appear to be opportunistic in their breeding attempts, so that males who are neighbors for one breeding attempt are unlikely to be neighbors either later the same year or, especially, the next year (Burns 1982; Bedell 1996). Neighboring males seem to share no more songs with each other than they do with more distant males, and males in the laboratory improvise, rather than imitate, sizable repertoires of good sedge wren songs (Kroodsma

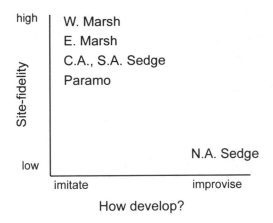

Figure 11.5
How stability of neighborhood singing groups seems to influence how songbirds develop their songs. High site-fidelity seems to promote song imitation among most *Cistothorus* wrens, but low site-fidelity occurs with song improvisation among North American sedge wrens. As stability of singing neighborhoods decreases, so that interacting singers change frequently within or between seasons, selection for strong imitation might be reduced or selection for improvisation increased.

and Verner 1978; Kroodsma et al. 1999a). In contrast, the site fidelity of marsh wrens is much greater, especially in marshes outside of the Great Plains; in some resident populations, males live in stable neighborhoods and interact with the same individuals throughout life (Verner 1965). Marsh wrens are excellent imitators, learning up to 200 songs from other males and using those songs in matched countersinging duels with neighboring territorial males (Verner 1976). In Central and South America, many sedge wren populations are resident, and males of those populations clearly imitate one another and also match each other with identical song types during countersinging (Kroodsma et al. 1999c). Thus, among these *Cistothorus* wrens, song imitation appears correlated with territorial stability, and improvisation appears correlated with instability and opportunistic breeding.

Conclusions

Singing behaviors of songbird species differ greatly, and these differences, in turn, reflect diverse song ontogenies. At first glance, the variety of adult behaviors and their developmental pathways seem too great to comprehend and classify, but the great diversity must be a consequence of common selective forces and compromises between them. Singing is used to manage other individuals, for example, and how many management styles can there be? Surely, once we peel back the outer veneer of species differences we will find common threads and convergent evolutionary patterns among the diverse songbird lineages.

In this essay, I have suggested that species with specialized songs that are used in limited contexts offer unique models for understanding how the forces of selection can both constrain and expand signal variation. Because each song category and its development is molded for a specific purpose, the link between function and signal structure should be especially evident among species. In some of these species with specialized songs, for example, vocalizations used in intrasexual contexts vary widely from place to place, in dialectal fashion; songs used intersexually, to attract females, seem far more stereotyped over broad geographic expanses. An apparent convergence of these behaviors is evident among songbirds of different lineages.

Selection for some behaviors, too, such as reduced geographic variation in song, can be achieved by multiple developmental pathways. Individual variation can be either minimized or maximized. Songs can be directly encoded in the genes, imitated precisely, even improvised or invented, or some combination of these approaches. Among different songbird lineages, a diversity of means in achieving similar ends should not be unexpected.

We should also expect a number of ecological and social factors to affect song in similar ways among songbirds. Effective repertoire sizes (i.e., the extent of an individual's repertoire that is revealed during a brief burst of singing) should increase with motivation within individuals of a given species, just as both effective and absolute repertoire sizes should be greater in species that routinely display in highly competitive, dense populations. Strategies of development, such as whether songs are imitated or improvised, should also be influenced by the probability of interacting with the same individuals throughout life.

Acknowledgments

I thank Sewall Pettingill for putting a parabola and tape recorder in my hands during 1968, John Wiens for encouraging me to study the ecology of grassland birds, and Jerry Verner for his influence with his former postdoctoral advisor, Peter Marler. Thank you, Peter and Judith, for those remarkable years and opportunities at Rockefeller University, and for providing an organizing influence for a lifetime. The following graduate students at the University of Massachusetts have helped form the basis for understanding the behavior of warblers: Jeff Bolsinger, Bruce Byers, Tod Highsmith, Peter Houlihan, David Spector, and Cindy Staicer. And I thank Melissa, my wife, who has been with me since those early days in 1968; her stabilizing influence has been invaluable.

Note

1. Some words play games with us, as Marler (this volume) points out, and the word "learn" is one of those words. Throughout this chapter, I use "learn" in a general sense to refer to how songbirds typically acquire the fine structure of their songs from other birds in their auditory environment. (By a broader definition, one could claim that songbirds also learn from themselves, as they perfect their own songs via auditory feedback.)

References

American Ornithologists' Union (1957) *Check-list of North American Birds*, 5th ed. Washington, D.C.: Am. Ornithol. Union.

Baker, M. C. and Boylan, J. T. (1995) A catalog of song syllables of indigo and lazuli Buntings. *Condor* 97:1028–1040.

Baker, M. C. and Cunningham, M. A. (1985) The biology of bird-song dialects. *Behav. Brain Sci.* 8:85–133.

Baptista, L. F. (1975) Song dialects and demes in sedentary populations of the white-crowned sparrow (*Zonotrichia leucophrys nuttalli*). *Univ. Calif. Publ. Zool.* 105:1–52.

Baptista, L. F. and Morton, M. L. (1988) Song learning in montane white-crowned sparrows: From whom and when. *Anim. Behav.* 36:1753–1764.

Bedell, P. A. (1996) Evidence of dual breeding ranges for the sedge wren in the central Great Plains. *Wilson Bull.* 108:115–122.

Beecher, M. D. (1996) Birdsong learning in the laboratory and field. In *Ecology and Evolution of Acoustic Communication in Birds*, ed. by D. E. Kroodsma and E. H. Miller, pp. 61–78. Ithaca, NY: Cornell University Press.

Beecher, M. D., Campbell, S. E., and Stoddard, P. K. (1994) Correlation of song learning and territory establishment strategies in the song sparrow. *Proc. Natl. Acad. Sci.* (USA) 91:1450–1454.

Beecher, M. D., Stoddard, P. K., Campbell, S. E., and Horning, C. L. (1996) Repertoire matching between neighbouring song sparrows. *Anim. Behav.* 51:917–923.

Bolsinger, J. R. (1997) Patterns of use and variation in the songs of the golden-cheeked warbler (*Dendroica chrysoparia*) Biology. M.A. thesis, University of Massachusetts, Amherst.

Borror, D. J. (1959) Variation in the songs of the rufous-sided towhee. *Wilson Bull.* 71:54–72.

Brenowitz, E. A. (1991) Evolution of the vocal control system in the avian brain. *Semin. Neurosci.* 3:399–407.

Burns, J. T. (1982) Nests, territories, and reproduction of sedge wrens (*Cistothorus platensis*). *Wilson Bull.* 94:338–349.

Byers, B. E. (1995) Song types, repertoires, and song variability in a population of chestnut-sided warblers. *Condor* 97:390–401.

Byers, B. E. (1996a) Geographic variation of song form within and among chestnut-sided warbler populations. *Auk* 113:288–299.

Byers, B. E. (1996b) Messages encoded in the songs of chestnut-sided warblers. *Anim. Behav.* 52:691–705.

Byers, B. E. and Kroodsma, D. E. (1992) Development of two song categories by chestnut-sided warblers. *Anim. Behav.* 44:799–810.

Catchpole, C. K. (1980) Sexual selection and the evolution of complex songs among European warblers of the genus *Acrocephalus*. *Behaviour* 74:149–166.

Catchpole, C. K. and McGregor, P. K. (1986) Sexual selection, song complexity, and plumage dimorphism in European buntings of the genus *Emberiza. Anim. Behav.* 33:1378–1380.

Catchpole, C. K. and Slater, P. J. B. (1995) *Bird song: Biological Themes and Variations.* Cambridge: Cambridge University Press.

DeVoogd, T. J., Krebs, J. R., Healy, S. D., and Purvis, A. (1993) Relations between song repertoire size and the volume of brain nuclei related to song: Comparative evolutionary analyses amongst oscine birds. *Proc. R. Soc. Lond.* B 254:75–82.

Dhondt, A. A. and Huble, J. (1968) Fledging-date and sex in relation to dispersal in young great tits. *Bird Study* 15:127–134.

Dixon, A., Ross, D., O'Malley, S. L. C., and Burke, T. (1994) Paternal investment inversely related to degree of extra-pair paternity in the reed bunting. *Nature* 371:698–702.

Ewert, D. N. and Kroodsma, D. E. (1994) Song sharing and repertoires among migratory and resident rufous-sided towhees. *Condor* 96:190–196.

Ficken, M. S. and Weise, C. M. (1984) A complex call of the black-capped chickadee (*Parus atricapillus*) 1. Microgeographic variation. *Auk* 101:349–360.

Ficken, M. S., Weise, C. M., and Reinartz, J. A. (1987) A complex vocalization of the black-capped chickadee: Repertoires, dominance, and dialects. *Condor* 89:500–509.

Gill, F. B., Mostrom, A. M., and Mack, A. K. (1993) Speciation in North American chickadees: I. Patterns of mtDNA genetic divergence. *Evolution* 47:195–212.

Gill, F. B. and Murray, Jr., B. G. (1972) Song variation in sympatric blue-winged and golden-winged warblers. *Auk* 89:625–643.

Hailman, J. P. (1989) The organization of major vocalizations in the Paridae. *Wilson Bull.* 101:305–343.

Hailman, J. P. and Ficken, M. S. (1996) Comparative analysis of vocal repertoires, with reference to chickadees. In *Ecology and Evolution of Acoustic Communication in Birds*, ed. by D. E. Kroodsma and E. H. Miller, pp. 136–159. Ithaca, NY: Cornell University Press.

Hasselquist, D., Bensch, S., and von Schantz, T. (1996) Correlation between male song repertoire, extra-pair paternity, and offspring survival in the great reed warbler. *Nature* 381:229–232.

Highsmith, R. T. (1989) The singing behavior of golden-winged warblers. *Wilson Bull.* 101:36–50.

Isler, M. L., Isler, P. R., and Whitney, B. M. (1997) Biogeography and systematics of the *Thamnophilus punctatus* (Thamnophilidae) complex. In *Studies in Neotropical Ornithology Honoring Ted Parker*, ed. by J. V. Remsen, Jr., pp. 355–382. Washington, DC: American Ornithologists' Union.

Jenkins, P. F. (1978) Cultural transmission of song patterns and dialect development in a free-living bird population. *Anim. Behav.* 26:50–78.

Kroodsma, D. E. (1971) Song variations and singing behavior in the rufous-sided towhee, *Pipilo erythrophthalmus oregonus. Condor* 73:303–308.

Kroodsma, D. E. (1974) Song learning, dialects, and dispersal in the Bewick's wren. *Z. Tierpsychol.* 35:352–380.

Kroodsma, D. E. (1977) Correlates of song organization among North American wrens. *Am. Nat.* 111:995–1008.

Kroodsma, D. E. (1981) Geographical variation and functions of song types in warblers (Parulidae). *Auk* 98:743–751.

Kroodsma, D. E. (1984) Songs of the Alder Flycatcher (*Empidonax alnorum*) and Willow Flycatcher (*Empidonax traillii*) are innate. *Auk* 101:13–24.

Kroodsma, D. E. (1988) Contrasting styles of song development and their consequences among the Passeriformes. In *Evolution and Learning*, ed. by R. C. Bolles and M. D. Beecher, pp. 157–184. Hillsdale, NJ: Erlbaum Assoc.

Kroodsma, D. E. (1996) Ecology of passerine song development. In *Ecology and Evolution of Acoustic Communication in Birds*, ed. by D. E. Kroodsma and E. H. Miller, pp. 3–19. Ithaca, NY: Cornell University Press.

Kroodsma, D. E., Albano, D. J., Houlihan, P. W., and Wells, J. A. (1995) Song development by black-capped chickadees (*Parus atricapillus*) and Carolina chickadees (*P. carolinensis*). *Auk* 112:29–43.

Kroodsma, D. E., Bedell, P. A., Liu, W.-C., and Goodwin, E. (1999a) The ecology of song improvisation, as illustrated by North American sedge wrens (*Cistothorus platensis*). *Auk* 116:373–386.

Kroodsma, D. E., Bereson, R. C., Byers, B. E., and Minear, E. (1989) Use of song types by the chestnut-sided warbler: Evidence for both intra- and inter-sexual functions. *Can. J. Zool.* 67:447–456.

Kroodsma, D. E., Byers, B. E., Halkin, S. L., Hill, C., Minis, D., Bolsinger, J. R., Dawson, J.-A., Donelan, E., Farrington, J., Gill, F., Houlihan, P., Innes, D., Keller, G., Macaulay, L., Marantz, C. A., Ortiz, J., Stoddard, P. K., and Wilda, K. (1999b) Geographic variation in black-capped chickadee songs and singing behavior. *Auk* 116:387–402.

Kroodsma, D. E., Houlihan, P. W., Fallon, P. A. Wells, J. A. (1997) Song development by grey catbirds. *Anim. Behav.* 54:457–464.

Kroodsma, D. E. and Konishi, M. (1991) A suboscine bird (eastern phoebe, *Sayornis phoebe*) develops normal song without auditory feedback. *Anim. Behav.* 42:477–488.

Kroodsma, D. E. and Miller, E. H. (1996) *Ecology and Evolution of Acoustic Communication in Birds.* Ithaca, NY: Cornell University Press.

Kroodsma, D. E., Sánchez, J., Stemple, D. W., Goodwin, E., DaSilva, M. L., and Uielliard, J. M. E. (1999c) Sedentary lifestyle of neotropical sedge wrens promotes song imitation. *Anim. Behav.* 57:855–863.

Kroodsma, D. E. and Verner, J. (1978) Complex singing behaviors among *Cistothorus* wrens. *Auk* 95:703–716.

Kroodsma, D. E. and Verner, J. (1997) Marsh Wren (*Cistothorus palustris*). In *The Birds of North America*, no. 308, ed. by A. Poole and F. Gill. Philadelphia, PA: The Academy of Natural Sciences; Washington, DC: The American Ornithologists' Union.

Lanyon, W. E. (1978) Revision of the *Myiarchus* flycatchers of South America. *Bull. Am. Mus. Nat. Hist.* 161:427–628.

Lein, M. R. (1978) Song variation in a population of chestnut-sided warblers (*Dendroica pensylvanica*): Its nature and suggested significance. *Can. J. Zool.* 56:1266–1283.

Lemon, R. E., Dobson, C. W., and Clifton, P. G. (1993) Songs of American redstarts (*Setophaga ruticilla*): Sequencing rules and their relationship to repertoire size. *Ethology* 93:198–210.

Lemon, R. E., Perreault, S., and Weary, D. M. (1994) Dual strategies of song development in American redstarts, *Setophaga ruticilla. Anim. Behav.* 47:317–329.

Marler, P. (1964) Inheritance and learning in the development of animal vocalizations. In *Acoustic Behavior of Animals*, ed. by R.-G. Busnel. Amsterdam: Elsevier.

Marler, P. (1967) Comparative study of song development in sparrows. In *Proceedings of the XIV International Ornithological Congress*, ed. by D. W. Snow, pp. 231–244. Oxford: Blackwell Scientific Publications.

Marler, P. (1970) A comparative approach to vocal learning: Song development in white-crowned sparrows. *J. Comp. Physiol. Psychol.* 71:1–25.

Marler, P. (1991a) Differences in behavioural development in closely related species: Birdsong. In *The Development and Integration of Behaviour: Essays in honour of Robert Hinde*, ed. by P. Bateson, pp. 41–70. Cambridge: Cambridge University Press.

Marler, P. (1991b) The instinct for vocal learning: Songbirds. In *Plasticity of Development*, ed. by S. E. Brauth, W. S. Hall, and R. J. Dooling, pp. 107–125. Cambridge, MA: MIT Press.

Marler, P., Kreith, M., and Tamura, M. (1962) Song development in hand-raised Oregon juncos. *Auk* 79:12–30.

Marler, P. and Mundinger, P. (1971) Vocal learning in birds. In *Ontogeny of Vertebrate Behavior*, ed. by H. Moltz, pp. 389–449. New York: Academic Press.

Marler, P. and Nelson, D. (1992) Neuroselection and song learning in birds: Species universals in a culturally transmitted behavior. *Semin. Neurosci.* 4:415–423.

Marler, P., Nelson, D. A., and Palleroni, A. (1994) A comparative approach to vocal learning. II. Intraspecific variation in the learning process. Davis, CA: University of California.

Marler, P. and Peters, S. (1977) Selective vocal learning in a sparrow. *Science* 198:519–521.

Marler, P. and Pickert, R. (1984) Species-universal microstructure in the learned song of the Swamp Sparrow, *Melospiza georgiana. Anim. Behav.* 32:673–689.

Marler, P. and Sherman, V. (1985) Innate differences in singing behaviour of sparrows reared in isolation from adult conspecific song. *Anim. Behav.* 33:57–71.

Marler, P. and Tamura, M. (1962) Song dialects in three populations of the white-crowned sparrow. *Condor* 64:368–377.

Marler, P. and Tamura, M. (1964) Culturally transmitted patterns of vocal behavior in sparrows. *Science* 146:1483–1486.

Marler, P. R., Dooling, R. J., and Zoloth, S. (1980) Comparative perspectives on ethology and behavioral development. In *Comparative Methods in Psychology*, ed. by M. H. Bornstein, pp. 189–230. Hillsdale, NJ: Lawrence Erlbaum Associates.

Morse, D. H. (1970) Territorial and courtship songs of birds. *Nature* (London) 226:659–661.

Nottebohm, F. (1980) Brain pathways for vocal learning in birds: A review of the first 10 years. In *Progress in Psychobiology and Physiological Psychology*, vol. 9, ed. by J. M. S. Sprage and A. N. E. Epstein, pp. 85–124. New York: Academic Press.

Payne, R. B. (1981) Song learning and social interaction in indigo buntings. *Anim. Behav.* 29:688–697.

Payne, R. B. (1996) Song traditions in indigo buntings: Origin, improvisation, dispersal, and extinction in cultural evolution. In *Ecology and Evolution of Acoustic Communication in Birds*, ed. by D. E. Kroodsma and F. H. Miller, pp. 198–200. Ithaca, NY: Cornell University Press.

Peterson, R. T. (1956) *A Field Guide to the Birds.* Boston: Houghton Mifflin Co.

Searcy, W. A. and Yasukawa, K. (1990) Use of the song repertoire in intersexual and intrasexual contexts by male red-winged blackbirds. *Behav. Ecol. Sociobiol.* 27:123–128.

Shackleton, S. A. and Ratcliffe, L. (1993) Development of song in hand-reared black-capped chickadees. *Wilson Bull.* 105:637–644.

Slater, P. J. B. (1989) Bird song learning: Causes and consequences. *Ethol. Ecol. Evol.* 1:19–46.

Spector, D. A. (1991) The singing behavior of yellow warblers. *Behaviour* 117:29–52.

Spector, D. A. (1992) Wood-warbler song systems: A review of paruline singing behaviors. *Current Ornithology* 9:199–238.

Staicer, C. A. (1990) The role of song in the socioecology of a resident tropical wood-warbler: The Adelaide's warbler (*Dendroica adelaidae*) of Puerto Rico Biology. Ph.D. dissertation, University of Massachusetts, Amherst.

Trainer, J. M. (1983) Changes in song dialect distributions and microgeographic variation in song of white-crowned sparrows (*Zonotrichia leucophrys nuttalli*). *Auk* 100:568–583.

Verner, J. (1965) Breeding biology of the long-billed marsh wren. *Condor* 67:6–30.

Verner, J. (1976) Complex song repertoire of male long-billed marsh wrens in eastern Washington. *Living Bird* 14:263–300.

Whitney, B. M. and Pacheco, J. F. (1997) Behavior, vocalizations, and relationships of some *Myrmotherula* antwrens (Thamnophilidae) in eastern Brazil, with comments on the "plain-winged" group. In *Studies in Neotropical Ornithology Honoring Ted Parker*, ed. by J. V. Remsen, Jr., pp. 809–820. Washington, DC: American Ornithologists' Union.

Wiley, H. R. (1994) Errors, exaggeration, and deception in animal communication. In *Behavioral Mechanisms in Evolutionary Ecology*, ed. by L. A. Real, pp. 157–189. Chicago: University of Chicago Press.

Williams, J. M. and Slater, P. J. B. (1991) Simulation studies of song learning in birds. In *Simulation of Adaptive Behavior*, ed. by J. A. Meyer and S. Wilson, pp. 281–287. Cambridge, MA: MIT Press.

Zahavi, A. (1980) Ritualizaton and the evolution of movement signals. *Behaviour* 72:77–81.

Zann, R. (1990) Song and call learning in wild zebra finches in south-east Australia. *Anim. Behav.* 40:818–828.

Zann, R. (1997) Vocal learning in wild and domesticated zebra finches: Signature cues for kin recognition or epiphenomena? In *Social Influences on Vocal Development*, ed. by C. T. Snowdon and M. Hausberger, pp. 85–97. Cambridge: Cambridge University Press.

Zann, R. and Runciman, D. (1994) Survivorship, dispersal, and sex ratios of zebra finches *Taeniopygia guttata* in southeast Australia. *Ibis* 136:136–146.

12 Song- and Order-selective Auditory Responses Emerge in Neurons of the Songbird Anterior Forebrain during Vocal Learning

Allison J. Doupe and Michele M. Solis

Song learning, like speech acquisition, is strongly dependent on auditory experience and feedback (Marler 1970; Konishi 1965). In classic studies on the white-crowned sparrow, Peter Marler and his colleagues showed that this learning occurs in two phases (Marler and Tamura 1964; Marler 1970; figure 12.1a). In the first or "sensory phase" of learning, young birds listen to and memorize their tutor's song. If birds fail to hear a song during this limited ("critical" or "sensitive") period of early ontogeny, they will ultimately produce an abnormal ("isolate") song. This simplified isolate song often contains some features characteristic of the normal song of the species, however, which suggests that some information about song is inherited and then modified by early sensory experience (Marler 1991; Marler, this volume). Songbird researchers continue to investigate to what extent environmental experience of song adds information not previously present (an "instructive" model of learning) and to what extent it acts to select preexisting information in the brain (learning as "selection"; see Marler, this volume; Nelson and Marler 1994).

During the second or "sensorimotor" phase of learning, juveniles begin to sing and gradually come to produce a copy of the song heard earlier, in many cases without ever listening to the original model again (Marler 1970; Marler and Peters 1982). These observations indicate that song learning must involve memorization of the tutor song during the critical period. In another classic experiment, Konishi (1965) demonstrated that if birds are deafened before they start singing, they cannot vocally reproduce the memorized tutor song. This suggests that, during sensorimotor learning, birds compare auditory feedback from their own vocalizations to the internal song model or "template" formed during sensory learning and gradually modify their song to approximate this template. Strikingly, the songs of deaf birds are much more abnormal than those of isolate birds, indicating that even the inherited information present in isolate songs (the "innate" template) requires access to auditory feedback in order to be turned into vocal output.

Both sensory and sensorimotor phases of song learning are thus critically dependent on hearing: interrupting either auditory experience of tutor song or the auditory/vocal experience of the bird's own song (BOS) impairs song learning (Marler 1970; Konishi 1965). The songbird brain must therefore contain mechanisms for auditory learning and recognition and for auditory feedback-guided modification of song. Understanding these mechanisms and how they are shaped by auditory and vocal experience should provide insight into the neural basis of song learning.

a. Song learning in zebra finches

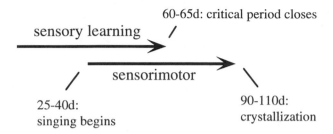

b. Core nuclei of the song system

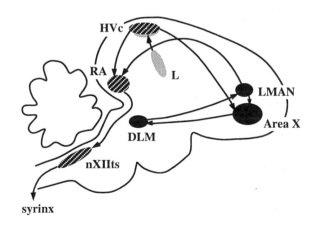

Figure 12.1
(a) The time line of song learning for zebra finches. Unlike more seasonal species, there is clear overlap between sensory learning of the template and sensorimotor learning of song in this species. The beginning of sensory learning is ill defined, but may occur around 10 days post-hatch (Arnold 1975). (b) A simplified schematic of the song system. The cross-hatched nuclei, HVc, RA, and nXIIts, form part of the descending motor pathway for song. The nuclei X, DLM, and LMAN, shown in solid black, form a pathway indirectly connecting HVc to RA and play a special role during song learning. The primary sources of auditory input to the song system are the field L complex (L) and its projections to the "shelf" underlying HVc (stippled areas). A number of other nuclei have been omitted for clarity.

In addition to basic auditory areas of the forebrain, another set of brain regions is potentially involved in processing the important auditory experiences during song learrning. This set of interconnected nuclei, collectively called the song system, is unique to birds that learn their song (figure 12.1b; Nottebohm et al. 1976; Kroodsma and Konishi 1991). The "motor" pathway for song, which includes the nuclei HVc (acronym used as the abbreviation, as proposed in Margoliash and Fortune 1992), RA (robust nucleus of the archistriatum), and nXIIts (tracheosyringeal portion of the hypoglossal nucleus), must be intact throughout life for normal song production (Nottebohm et al. 1976). In contrast, lesion experiments have implicated the anterior forebrain (AF) pathway of the song system as having a particularly critical role during learning. This circuit consists of Area X (X), the medial portion of the dorsolateral nucleus of the thalamus (DLM), and the lateral portion of the magnocellular nucleus of the anterior neostriatum (LMAN; Bottjer at al. 1989; Okuhata and Saito 1987). Lesions of the AF circuit in adult birds have no effect on normal song production (Nottebohm et al. 1976), whereas the same lesions in animals learning their vocalizations lead to highly abnormal song (Bottjer et al. 1984; Nottebohm et al. 1990; Sohrabji et al. 1990; Scharff and Nottebohm 1991). The AF pathway also provides input to the motor pathway, via the projections of LMAN onto RA neurons, consistent with a function of the AF circuit in auditory feedback-guided modification of vocal output.

Because both the AF pathway and auditory experience of the tutor song and BOS are required for a bird to learn song normally, the AF may be one of a number of possible pathways involved in processing the auditory information so crucial to song learning. If so, the AF might contain neurons responsive to sound, particularly song. This review will focus on recent single-unit studies in anesthetized male zebra finches, demonstrating that the AF pathway indeed contains auditory neurons, which change dramatically during learning. In young birds not yet singing or just beginning to sing, these neurons respond equally well to all songs presented to them (Doupe 1997). Then, during the course of vocal development, these cells develop striking spectral and temporal selectivity for BOS (Doupe and Konishi 1991; Doupe 1997; Solis and Doupe 1997). This ontogenetic selectivity is reminiscent of a similar process in human speech learning: infants initially discriminate the phonemes of all languages tested (Eimas et al. 1987), but they quickly come to recognize only the sounds of the language that they are hearing (Werker and Tees 1992; Kuhl et al. 1992).

LMAN and X in Adult Zebra Finches

Adult LMAN Neurons

LMAN neurons in anesthetized adult zebra finches are auditory, responding robustly to complex song stimuli, particularly BOS. Simpler sounds, like broad-band noise or tone bursts, drive these neurons weakly, if at all. These LMAN neurons are extremely song-selective, responding better to BOS than to any other stimulus tested, including the songs of conspecifics (other individuals of the same species; figure 12.2a–c). In fact, LMAN neurons are often inhibited by non-BOS stimuli. Spectral cues are important to these selective responses; for example, specific syllables of conspecific songs and even some tone bursts that resemble portions of BOS elicit phasic responses from some LMAN neurons (figure 12.2c; Doupe 1997). The same neurons show sustained firing over several syllables when BOS is presented, however, indicating responses to more than a single feature of BOS (figure 12.2a).

LMAN neurons are also sensitive to the temporal properties of song, a quality called "order selectivity." Even if all the spectral features of BOS are unchanged, altering the temporal order of these cues dramatically decreases the neural responses (figure 12.2d–f). This happens not only when all the cues are reversed (both the sequence of syllables as well as the temporal order within syllables; figure 2e), but also when the syllables of the song are simply presented in reverse order (figure 12.2f). This reverse-order manipulation preserves the local order within syllables but changes their global context. The weak response to reverse-order stimuli demonstrates that the neural sensitivity to temporal features extends across syllable boundaries.

LMAN neurons also show temporal combination-sensitivity, in which a neuron's response to a combination of syllables is much greater than the sum of responses to the individual syllables (figure 12.3). A similar property has been described for LMAN neurons in experiments using a single complex syllable and its component notes as stimuli (Maekawa and Uno 1996). Combination-sensitivity, which is also found in vocalization-sensitive neurons in bats (O'Neill and Suga 1979; Suga 1990; Kanwal, this volume) and monkeys (Rauschecker et al. 1995), could be very useful for learning vocal sequences.

A surprising feature of LMAN neurons is that all neurons recorded from an individual bird respond to the same features of BOS throughout the nucleus. Within the limits of the small number of cells sampled from each bird (1–11 neurons/bird), there is not an obvious "library" within LMAN, with different neurons tuned to different features of BOS. This result contrasts with a topography for auditory response

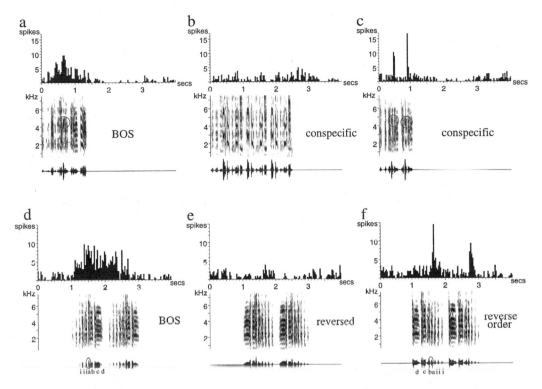

Figure 12.2
Auditory responses of LMAN of adult zebra finches. (a) Response of a single unit to bird's own song (BOS), and (b) and (c) to two different conspecific songs. The conspecific song in (c) elicits a phasic response 60msec after each of two syllables, which contain primarily a loud sound in the 4.5–5kHz frequency range (circled). The BOS (a) also contains a note in that range (circled). (d) Response of a different LMAN unit to BOS, (e) reverse BOS, and (f) reverse order BOS. The BOS played in reverse order, which maintains the order within each syllable while reversing the sequence, elicits a phasic response after each occurrence of syllable "a" (circled). Below each peristimulus time histogram (PSTH) are shown the sonogram (frequency vs. time plot, with energy in each frequency band indicated by the darkness of the signal) and the oscillogram (amplitude waveform) of the song stimulus.

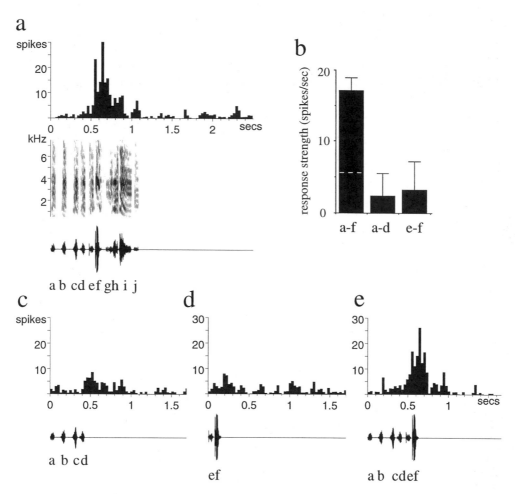

Figure 12.3
A combination-sensitive neuron in adult LMAN. (a) shows the response of the neuron to the entire BOS, whose syllables are indicated with letters below the oscillogram. (b) shows the mean responses to each of the indicated syllable combinations. Neural responses are quantified as a response strength (RS), which is the mean firing rate during the stimulus minus the mean baseline firing rate. Bars are SEM. The dotted white line on the bar on the left indicates the linear sum of the responses to the syllable components of the stimulus. Panels (c)–(e) show the neuron's response to the indicated combinations of syllables.

properties that might have been expected, based on the recently described topography of LMAN projections to RA (Johnson et al. 1995).

The selectivity observed in adult LMAN likely reflects the response properties of neurons in HVc. HVc neurons are the major source of auditory input to LMAN (via X; Katz and Gurney 1981; Doupe, unpublished data), and their responses share many qualities with those of LMAN neurons. HVc neurons have long been known to have strong spectral and temporal selectivity for BOS, temporal and harmonic combination-sensitivity, and to lack topographically organized responses (Margoliash 1983, 1986; Margoliash and Fortune 1992; Margoliash et al. 1994; Sutter and Margoliash 1994; Lewicki and Konishi 1995; Lewicki and Arthur 1996; Volman 1996). Individual neurons in HVc show selectivity equal in degree to that of LMAN neurons, as measured by the relative strength of their responses to BOS versus other songs, and some are also inhibited by non-BOS stimuli. Despite these similarities, HVc responses appear more heterogeneous than those of LMAN. A number of studies (Margoliash 1983; Saito and Maekawa 1993; Lewicki and Arthur 1996) have described HVc neurons that respond well to simple stimuli, or equally to forward and reversed song, while such neurons have not been found in LMAN. Also, average selectivity is slightly greater for LMAN than for HVc (Margoliash and Fortune 1992; Margoliash et al. 1994; Volman 1996; Doupe 1997). The properties of HVc may reflect the fact that HVc actually contains two separate but intermingled populations of projection neurons distinguished by their efferent targets, one projecting to RA and the other to the AF (Katz and Gurney 1981; Gahr 1990; Doupe and Konishi 1991; Kirn et al. 1991; Sohrabji et al. 1993; Vicario and Yohay 1993). These two populations could well differ in their properties, but the selectivity of HVc neurons identified as projecting either to the AF or to RA has not been studied in depth. Thus, fully clarifying the contribution of HVc neurons to AF selectivity will depend on characterizing the selectivity of the X-projecting HVc neurons.

Adult X Neurons

Area X (X) neurons are interposed between HVc and LMAN, and accordingly, share many of the selective properties of neurons in these nuclei. As in LMAN, the majority of X neurons respond strongly to BOS and exhibit song- and order-selectivity (see figs. 12.4d, 12.6, and Doupe 1997). Nonetheless, X neurons also differ somewhat from HVc and LMAN neurons: X neurons are more broadly responsive, firing readily to simple tone bursts and conspecific songs, and they are not inhibited by nonpreferred stimuli. This apparent loss of selectivity of X neurons relative to their inputs may result from their low thresholds, evident by their high spontaneous rates. Alternatively, it is possible that the subset of HVc neurons projecting to the

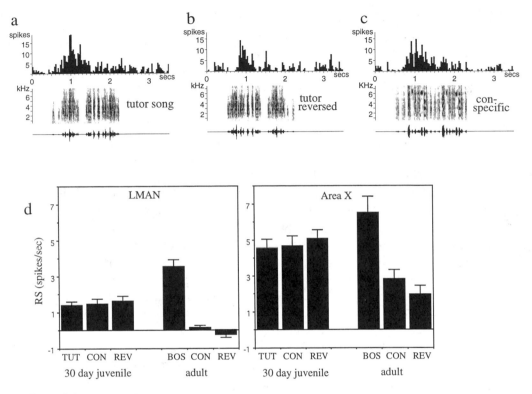

Figure 12.4
Auditory responses of juvenile vs. adult AF neurons. Panels (a)–(c) show the responses of a single LMAN
unit from a 30-day-old juvenile zebra finch. Panel (a) shows the response to the tutor song played forward,
while the next two panels show the similar responses to the tutor song reversed (b), and to a conspecific
song (c). (d) Summary comparison of AF neuron selectivity in 30-day juveniles with that of adults. Left
panel: mean RS of all LMAN neurons to BOS (for adults) or TUT (for juveniles), conspecific song
(CON), and reversed BOS or tutor song (REV) for all neurons recorded in LMAN. Right panel: mean
RS to stimulus types described above for all neurons in Area X. Error bars are SEM.

AF has simpler auditory properties; however, recent results indicate that at least
some of the X-projecting HVc neurons are very song- and order-selective (Lewicki
1996). Because LMAN neurons are more narrowly responsive and more likely to
show inhibition than X neurons, the differences between LMAN and X may be
created by the circuit between these two nuclei, perhaps via inhibitory processing in
X, LMAN, or the intervening thalamic nucleus DLM. In many sensory systems
gradual increases in stimulus selectivity are the result of hierarchical circuits like the
AF pathway (see, e.g., DeYoe and Van Essen 1988; Konishi et al. 1988; Livingstone
and Hubel 1988; Rose et al. 1988). Nonetheless, the differences in selectivity along

the adult AF are slight, and the functional implications of a sequence of highly selective nuclei remain unclear.

Area X has recently been shown to receive a second song system input from recurrent collaterals from LMAN neurons (Nixdorf-Bergweiler et al. 1995; Vates and Nottebohm 1995; figure 12.1a). The functional consequences of these inputs are unknown, however, and are not clarified by any studies to date of X auditory response properties. A study in which LMAN alone was selectively inactivated while the auditory properties of X neurons were recorded would be revealing in this regard.

LMAN and X at an Early Stage of Song Learning: Finches of 30–45 Days of Age

Neurons with the extreme song- and order-selectivity found in the adult AF could be useful for processing auditory information required for song learning. For example, these cells could be the neural implementation of the template. By this hypothesis, such template neurons would be tuned by the tutor song and could provide information, perhaps encoded in the strength of their firing rate, about how well certain vocalizations match the memorized tutor song. Alternatively, AF neurons might not represent the memorized tutor song, but could instead provide information about the current state of BOS, a prerequisite for modifying BOS to match the template. Such neurons would be tuned to the bird's own emerging song. Either way, AF neurons might enable the evaluation of BOS during learning.

To begin to elucidate AF neuron function, these neurons have been recorded in young birds to see if the neurons are auditory, and if so, to see if they share the auditory properties of adult neurons. To examine the influence of tutor song alone on selectivity, the AF nuclei ideally should be characterized after the song memorization of the sensory phase, but before sensorimotor learning. This cannot be done in a straightforward manner in zebra finches, however, whose rapid development is accompanied by an overlap between the two phases of learning (figure 12.1a). Thus young birds partway through sensory learning and just beginning sensorimotor learning (30–45 days old) have been studied. Juvenile 30-day LMAN and X neurons are recorded in the same manner as for adults, except that birds are presented with their tutor song instead of BOS, since they have not yet developed their own song.

AF neurons in birds of 30–45 days of age are auditory, consistent with a role for the AF pathway in learning. However, their auditory properties differ dramatically from those of adult AF neurons (fig. 12.4). Neurons do not prefer tutor song over other conspecific songs, and equal responses are elicited when tutor song is presented in the forward, reverse order, and fully reversed directions. Simple acoustic stimuli such as tone or broadband noise bursts are also much more effective at driving these juvenile neurons than adult neurons. Thus the selectivity observed in adult AF neurons must arise during vocal development. This is also known to be the case for HVc in white-crowned sparrows (Volman 1993).

The emergence of selectivity from previously unselective neurons in the AF is informative in several ways. First, the lack of obvious selectivity of individual AF neurons in young birds for particular conspecific songs argues against a purely selective model of selectivity generation (see Margoliash 1983). In this model, there is a preexisting population of tuned neurons, where each neuron is tuned to different stimuli; with experience, this population is narrowed by the selection of appropriately tuned neurons. In contrast, AF neurons apparently create their auditory selectivity from initially relatively untuned neurons. It remains to be examined whether the AF neurons in juvenile birds respond better to conspecific songs or their component features than to songs of other species. If so, they might encode the innate preference for conspecific song and/or the innate template (see Marler, this volume).

Second, the increase in selectivity of AF neurons during learning appears to result from both a decrease in responsiveness to nonpreferred stimuli (conspecific and reversed songs) and an increase in response to BOS (figure 12.4d). Several cellular events occurring in the AF could subserve this selectivity development. For example, in LMAN, NMDA receptors (Aamodt et al. 1992; Carrillo and Doupe 1995), spine densities (Nixdorf-Bergweiler et al. 1995), synapse number (Nixdorf-Bergweiler 1995), and DLM arborization density (Johnson and Bottjer 1992) all decrease between 35 days and adulthood. Thus an initial reduction of connections could increase the selectivity of a postsynaptic cell, which might then be followed by synaptic strengthening and/or growth of other inputs. A similar sequence occurs during ocular dominance development in the visual cortex (Antonini and Stryker 1993).

Finally, the emergence in originally unselective neurons of extreme selectivity for learned song suggests that the development of this selectivity is an experience-dependent process, as has also been described for neurons in the visual system (see, e.g., Hubel et al. 1977; Shatz 1990; Chapman and Stryker 1993).

LMAN and X at an Intermediate Stage of Song Learning: 60-day-old Finches

To address when auditory selectivity develops, and to begin to identify the experience generating it, individual LMAN and X neurons have been recorded in approximately 60-day-old zebra finches (range 55–65 days). At this age, birds are at an intermediate stage of song development: the critical period for sensory learning is ending, and the sensorimotor phase is underway (figure 12.1a). These birds have probably memorized the tutor song and have been singing plastic song for approximately one month (Immelmann 1969; Eales 1985; Boehner 1990). Although plastic song may have similarities with the tutor song, it is often rambling, has inconsistent syllable morphology, and lacks a stereotyped syllable order. Both BOS (in this case, plastic song) and tutor song are included among the stimuli presented to 60-day birds.

In one month or less, AF neurons have changed considerably from the unselective neurons in 30-day-old birds. Despite the immature quality of plastic song, LMAN and X neurons show significant song selectivity for both BOS and tutor song by 60 days. On average, these neurons respond more to BOS and tutor song than to conspecific and heterospecific songs (figure 12.5a,c). AF neurons also develop order selectivity by 60 days (figure 12.5b,d). These neurons greatly decrease their responses to BOS and tutor song when they are completely reversed. In contrast to adult birds, however, some 60-day neurons do not yet distinguish between forward song and the reverse order manipulation of either BOS or tutor song (figure 12.5b). Thus, such neurons are sensitive to local order within a syllable, but remain insensitive to the global order of syllables within a song. Of those LMAN neurons tested, approximately 40% are similar to the neuron in figure 12.5b, while the rest are more adult-like. Since the two kinds of order selectivity can develop with different time courses, it is possible that they are mediated by different mechanisms. Moreover, this sequence of order selectivity acquisition is analogous to sensory learning in zebra finches: juveniles memorize individual syllables of the tutor song first and memorize their appropriate sequence later (Immelmann 1969).

Although AF neurons have become selective by 60 days, their overall degree of selectivity for BOS is still less than that of adults. To measure a neuron's selectivity, a $d'_{A,B}$ value was employed where

$$d'_{A,B} = 2\frac{(\overline{RS_A} - \overline{RS_B})}{\sqrt{\sigma_A^2 + \sigma_B^2}};$$

$\overline{RS_A}$ and $\overline{RS_B}$ are the mean response strengths (RS; see figure 12.3 legend for definition) to song A and B respectively, and σ^2 is the variance of each mean RS (Green and Swets 1966; Tolhurst et al. 1983). Neurons with greater responses to song A than to song B have values greater than 0, those with greater responses to B than to A have values less than 0, and those responding equally to songs A and B have values around 0. Neurons are considered "selective" for stimulus A over B if their d'_{A-B} value is 0.5 or greater. This d' value corresponds to responses to two stimuli that are

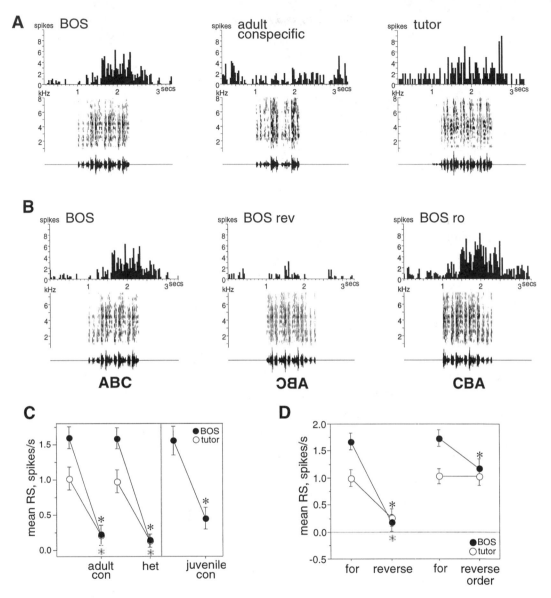

Figure 12.5
Song and order selectivity of LMAN neurons at 60 days. (A) A peristimulus time histogram shows a single LMAN neuron's cumulative responses to multiple trials of song stimuli. This neuron has strong responses to BOS and tutor song and reduced responses to an adult conspecific song. (B) Peristimulus time histograms show a single LMAN neuron's cumulative responses to multiple trials of BOS, reverse BOS ("BOS rev"), and reverse order BOS ("BOS ro"). (C) Paired comparisons are shown of all LMAN neurons' responses to BOS (black) and tutor song (white) with those to adult conspecific, heterospecific, and juvenile conspecific song. (D) shows paired comparisons of responses to BOS and tutor song with responses to reversed and reversed order manipulations of BOS and tutor song. Asterisks indicate significant differences (black for BOS comparisons, white for tutor song comparisons), and bars are SEM.

significantly different from each other by a paired t-test (p = 0.031) when 20 trials of each stimulus are compared; neurons with a d' value of greater than 0.5 also usually had a mean RS to the preferred stimulus that was at least twice as great as that to a nonpreferred stimulus. Distributions of d' values measuring song selectivity (specifically, $d'_{BOS\text{-}ADULT\ CON}$ and $d'_{TUTOR\text{-}ADULT\ CON}$) of individual AF neurons at different ages show that 60-day neurons are more tutor song-selective than those of 30-day birds, but are less BOS-selective than adult neurons (figure 12.6). Similarly, 60-day neurons are intermediate in their degree of order selectivity.

BOS vs. Tutor Song Responses at 60 Days

The function of neural selectivity for song in a bird still learning its vocalizations may be elucidated by identifying the experience responsible for the selectivity. Two possible experiences are BOS and tutor song, both behaviorally salient stimuli to juvenile birds. When responses to BOS and tutor song are compared, individual neurons differ in their preferences for one song over another. Some neurons prefer BOS to tutor song, others prefer tutor song to BOS, and many show no preference, responding equally well to both stimuli (figure 12.7a). A plot of $d'_{BOS\text{-}TUTOR}$ values obtained from LMAN neurons shows the range and distribution of these preferences (figure 12.7b). Although neurons respond significantly to BOS and/or tutor song, 34% of them show no strong preference for either stimulus ($-0.5 < d'_{BOS\text{-}TUTOR} < 0.5$, marked in grey). Importantly, these cells are not simply unselective, because they show song- or order-selectivity (figure 12.7c). X has a distribution of BOS versus tutor song preferences similar to that of LMAN. On average, LMAN responds more to BOS than to tutor song, whereas in X, there is no significant difference between average responses to these two songs.

The heterogeneity of BOS versus tutor song preferences at 60 days does not yield a clear answer to the question of which experience is responsible for selectivity. Nevertheless, several results described above indicate that BOS experience is likely to be important for AF-selectivity. Despite the immature quality of plastic song, many neurons are sensitive to its complex properties: they have significant song and order selectivity for BOS, even when compared to the plastic songs of other juveniles. Also, neurons with strong preferences for BOS over tutor song predominate in both LMAN and X. This is consistent with a study in white-crowned sparrows showing that selectivity in HVc is due to BOS experience (Volman 1993).

On the other hand, at 60 days numerous AF neurons also respond equally to BOS and tutor song, and many also exhibit song- and order-selectivity for tutor song. If BOS experience alone generates the selectivity of AF neurons, these properties could be explained by acoustic similarities between BOS and tutor song. For example, a

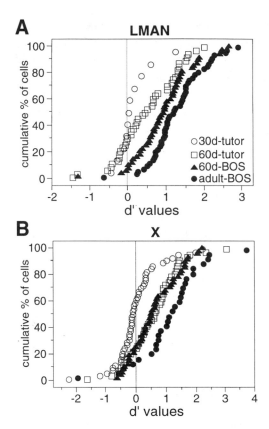

Figure 12.6

A comparison of selectivity at different ages. (A) Cumulative distributions of d′ values obtained from LMAN neurons at three stages of development are shown. For 30-day neurons, $d'_{TUTOR-ADULT\ CON}$ values are shown with open circles. For 60-day neurons, open squares denote $d'_{TUTOR-ADULT\ CON}$ values; black triangles mark $d'_{BOS-ADULT\ CON}$ values. For adult neurons, $d'_{BOS-ADULT\ CON}$ values are shown as solid black circles. (B) Cumulative distributions of d′values of X neurons from three stages of development are shown. Symbols are as in (A).

neuron could actually be tuned by BOS, but because of similarities between BOS and tutor song, it would also respond to tutor song in a selective manner. If this were the case, neurons with equal responses to BOS and tutor song should occur only in birds whose plastic song is very similar to their tutor's song. Similarly, neurons with strong BOS preferences would tend to come from birds with song quite different from their tutors song. Song analysis (see figure 12.8 legend and Solis and Doupe 1997 for details) reveals that neurons with strong preferences for BOS are indeed found in birds with songs most unlike that of their tutor, and BOS preference tends to decrease with increasing similarity of the bird's song to tutor song (figure 12.8a). Nonetheless, not all neurons with equal responses to BOS and tutor song are associated with high similarity to the tutor song: some 60-day neurons respond equally well to two apparently acoustically quite different stimuli (figure 12.8a). Thus an alternative explanation of these neurons is that both BOS and tutor song contribute to their selectivity, and that single neurons are capable of responding to several different sets of acoustic cues.

The correlation between the BOS versus tutor song preference of neurons and similarity between BOS and tutor song suggests that a bird's neural selectivity is related to its particular stage or accuracy of song development. Consistent with this, the $d'_{BOS-TUTOR}$ values of LMAN neurons in individual birds cluster in certain regions of the preference range, rather than spanning the full range of possible values (figure 12.8b). Neither the bird's age (figure 12.8b) nor conditions that may have varied between experiments (anesthesia depth, stimulus duration, experiment duration, neuron location within the nucleus) correlate very well to the neurons' BOS versus tutor song preferences. Clustering of responses in individual birds is also evident in X.

Finally, AF neurons that prefer tutor song over BOS are also inconsistent with an exclusive contribution of BOS experience to selectivity. These neurons are not as numerous as BOS-preferring neurons, however. If tutor song experience confers selectivity to these neurons, then the AF could store information about the tutor song.

Conclusions and Future Directions

Could the Anterior Forebrain Circuit Function as a Template during Learning?

Because AF neurons are required during song learning, have auditory properties, and project to the motor pathway, they are well suited to participate in the evaluation of BOS that is crucial to guiding song learning. Whether song-selective neurons provide information about the current state of BOS or act as template neurons,

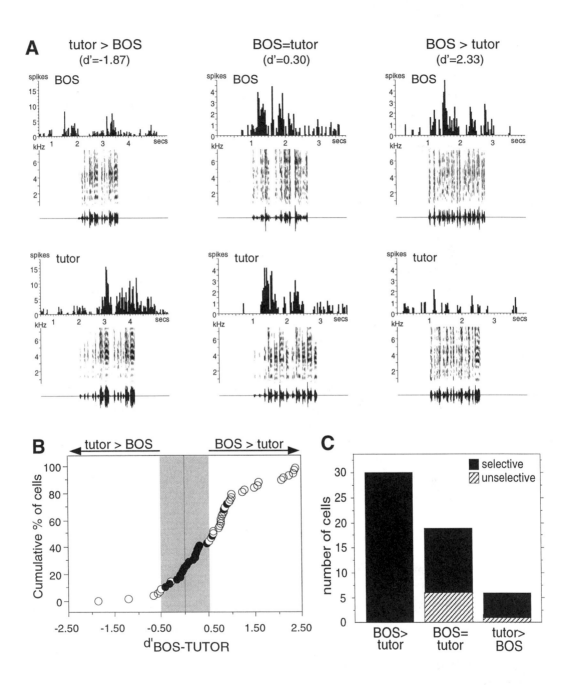

providing information about how well the BOS matches the memorized song, is unclear. The developmental studies discussed here begin to explore AF function, and in particular to investigate whether AF song-selectivity reflects sensory learning of the tutor song, and thus might represent a tutor template.

If tutor song exposure does shape the selectivity of AF neurons, this should be evident at least by the close of the sensory period for learning. In fact, as discussed above, song- and order-selectivity for tutor song emerges in many zebra finch AF neurons by 60 days of age. Such selectivity is consistent with these neurons' encoding the template, although in some birds it could also be due to similarity of the tutor song to BOS. An intriguing feature of the tutor song responses of 60-day zebra finches is that they are primarily found in neurons that also show responses to BOS, even when these two songs do not resemble each other. This result raises the possibility that single AF neurons are shaped both by sensory learning of the tutor and by auditory feedback from the bird's own vocalizations. Along the same lines, template neurons might not necessarily be dedicated exclusively to representation of tutor song, but could reflect other aspects of the bird's sensory experience as well.

Although selectivity for tutor song is apparent at 60 days of age, the lack of selectivity in birds earlier in sensory learning (30–45 days) might imply that the selectivity of AF neurons cannot be associated with acquisition of the tutor song template. This conclusion depends, however, on how much these young birds have memorized, a question that is not yet settled. To determine the age at which the template is encoded, behavioral experiments have isolated birds from their tutors at different ages and studied the resulting songs in adulthood. Two studies have found that the more time birds spend with their tutors prior to isolation, the more their songs resemble that of their tutors (Immelman 1969; Eales 1985). This suggests that the template is gradually acquired. Moreover, birds isolated prior to 40 days of age have little or nothing in common with the tutor, indicating that birds have not yet memo-

Figure 12.7
BOS vs. tutor song preferences of LMAN neurons at 60 days. (A) Pairs of peristimulus time histograms for three different neurons show the range of preferences for BOS vs. tutor song encountered in LMAN. The first pair shows a cell that responds more to the tutor song than to BOS, the second pair is from a neuron that responds equally well to both stimuli, and the third pair is from a cell that responds more to BOS than to its tutor song. The $d'_{BOS-TUTOR}$ value for each pair of responses is indicated. (B) The cumulative distribution of $d'_{BOS-TUTOR}$ values from 56 LMAN neurons is shown. A white circle refers to a neuron whose average response to the preferred stimulus was at least twice as great as that to the nonpreferred stimulus. Grey shading indicates the region of d' values considered unselective. (C) Each 60-day LMAN neuron is classified according to its d' values for different comparisons of selectivity. BOS > tutor neurons have $d'_{BOS-TUTOR} \geq 0.5$, BOS = tutor neurons have $-0.5 < d'_{BOS-TUTOR} < 0.5$, and BOS < tutor neurons have $d'_{BOS-TUTOR} \leq -0.5$. To be counted as selective, a neuron has to have $d' \geq 0.5$ in at least one of the following four selectivity categories: BOS-adult conspecific, tutor-adult conspecific, BOS-reverse BOS, or tutor-reverse tutor. A total of 68% of BOS = tutor neurons in LMAN are selective.

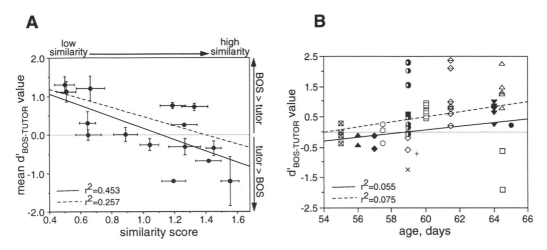

Figure 12.8
Correlations of each bird's neural BOS vs. tutor song preferences in LMAN to its song similarity score
and age. In each graph the linear least squares fit of the mean data (solid line) and of individual cells
(dotted line; this weighs each birds' contribution to the correlation by the number of cells recorded in that
bird) is shown. (A) Each bird's mean $d'_{BOS-TUTOR}$ value from its LMAN neurons is plotted against the
bird's final similarity score; bars are SEM. A value of 0.4 refers to a song with no similarity to the tutor
song, and of 1.6 refers to a song with high similarity to the tutor song. Songs were judged subjectively by
observers familiar with zebra finch song, but blind to the neuronal properties of each experimental bird.
(B) Individual $d'_{BOS-TUTOR}$ values from each bird are plotted against the age of the bird; symbol types refer
to neurons from the same bird.

rized the tutor song by this age. Additional behavioral studies indicate that the bulk
of tutor song memorization happens later, between days 35 and 60–65, after which
the critical period appears to end (Slater et al. 1988). These results may account for
the lack of selectivity for tutor song in AF neurons of birds 30–45 days of age. In
contrast, other studies indicate that tutor song learning does take place before day 35
(Eales 1989; Boehner 1990; Slater and Jones 1995). These observations therefore
predict that the template, and hence tutor song selectivity (if it indeed encodes the
template), should be present by 30–45 days of age. Although these behavioral studies
of song learning differ in their methodological details, the source of the discrepancy
in when the tutor song template is learned is unclear. Nonetheless, the differences
between them highlight the variability in the time course of learning between birds,
and its strong dependence on particular social and environmental conditions. Thus
the best way to settle the issues of (i) when birds have formed the tutor template and
(ii) how this correlates with the properties of the AF would be to determine the
extent of tutor song memorization in individual birds that have also been studied
physiologically. This could be done by recovering birds after characterizing their

neural selectivity at 30–45 days, isolating them from further tutoring, and then analyzing the songs they produce as adults. If AF neurons in birds of 30–45 days of age prove to be unselective like the ones described here, but the same birds go on to sing good copies of the tutor song, then the AF selectivity seen later in learning seems unlikely to reflect tutor song template learning. Ultimately, recording multiple times or even chronically from the AF of individual birds as they progress through the stages of learning will provide the most information about the development of AF selectivity, and about how this relates to behavioral development.

Although the AF shows some tutor selectivity, many neurons in both the AF and HVc are most strongly responsive to BOS, and thus might be shaped by the birds' experience of their own vocalizations (Volman 1993; Margoliash 1983; Solis and Doupe 1997). It is important to point out, however, that neurons with strong BOS selectivity are not necessarily the product of BOS experience, because it is difficult to know exactly what the bird has stored as a template: the only assay of this at present is what the bird eventually sings. For example, if a bird memorizes the tutor song incorrectly, but produces a very good copy of its inaccurate template, then BOS itself might drive template neurons more effectively than the actual tutor song. In this case, birds with songs with low similarity to the tutor would contain BOS-selective neurons, and those with songs with high similarity to the tutor would have more tutor-selective neurons. A similar relationship is indeed observed in 60-day zebra finches (figure 12.8a). To confirm a role of BOS experience in shaping BOS-preferring neurons, it would be informative to study birds experimentally induced to sing abnormal songs during sensorimotor learning. If BOS-preferring neurons existed in such birds, they would be more likely to be the result of BOS experience rather than of storage of a poorly copied tutor song.

One assumption underlying these discussions is that if song-selectivity represents the template, it should be present early in learning. In fact, the narrowness and homogeneity of adult song-selectivity make it in some respects poorly suited to guide song from its earliest, disorganized beginnings to its final form: very immature songs are quite different from the ultimate song produced and would presumably be ineffective at driving adult-like song neurons. Perhaps an evaluation mechanism would be more useful during learning if it were initially very broadly tuned, in order to reinforce the bird's first attempts at song. This learning mechanism should then gradually become more selective, as the bird's song improves, in order to continue guiding the song toward the target. The gradual acquisition of song- and order-selectivity seen in the studies of developing zebra finches might reflect just such a process. It will be crucial, however, to see whether neural selectivity just precedes behavioral improvement during learning or vice versa. Nonetheless, such a narrowing evaluation mechanism still requires some internal representation of the final target of learning. This representation is perhaps a more classical form of the template, and it could be separate from the sensory neurons actively guiding learning. These "final target" template neurons might also be few in number and hence have escaped detection in the studies to date.

These speculations are also a reminder that the brain areas mediating template formation may be different from those where the template is stored or acts. The issues of memory formation, storage, and retrieval have been extensively studied in the medial temporal lobe of primates. The medial temporal lobe is required for the acquisition and temporary storage of declarative knowledge, but a different cortical location is thought to store permanent memory (reviewed in Zola-Morgan and Squire 1993). A similar scheme has been described in an avian neural circuit that is involved in the memory of an avoidance task (Rose 1991). To address directly whether the AF is involved during template formation, a recent study used local blockade of NMDA receptors in LMAN exclusively during tutor song exposure (Basham et al. 1996). The results, which show decreased copying of the tutor song, suggest that LMAN is indeed one area that must be physiologically active during template learning. It remains to be seen whether the essential result of this activity is the acquisition of song- and order-selectivity in LMAN. Strikingly, a previous study involving systemic blockade of NMDA during tutor exposure showed much more impaired tutor copying than the experiments using local infusions into LMAN (Aamodt et al. 1996). Although this difference between local and systemic administration of the antagonists could well reflect nonspecific actions of the systemic drug treatment, it is also consistent with the possibility that the neural representation of tutor song is stored in a distributed manner, dispersed across many brain locations.

Finally, it has often been assumed that a rate code contains the relevant information about a particular song. Responses measured in this way do convey a great deal of information about song, as demonstrated by the selectivity described here. However, information about a song could be also be carried by other codes such as the maximum rate of firing, the temporal patterns of spikes or bursts, or the simultaneous responses of a population of neurons during an auditory stimulus. The optimal stimulus for adult HVc neurons, the BOS played forward, tends to elicit bursts from these neurons, while closely related but less preferred stimuli (such as the BOS played in reverse order) may cause the same number of spikes to fire but do not elicit bursting (Lewicki 1996). Similarly, in the electrosensory lateral line lobe of the electric fish Eigenmannia, bursting of pyramidal cells is correlated best with the occurrence of the particular stimulus feature to which the neurons are tuned (Gabbiani et al. 1996). More detailed analyses of AF neuron responses along these lines could reveal information about the tutor song at a very early age that is not apparent with rate coding.

Thus some evidence is consistent with a role of the AF and of song-selectivity in sensory learning, and as yet no evidence has conclusively ruled out a contribution of the AF to the template. It seems likely, however, that the selectivity of the AF also reflects sensorimotor learning, and it is intriguing that the two facets of song learning may be represented in the properties of single neurons, since numerous units with tutor responses also respond well to BOS. Many of our ideas about how the template is encoded and how it might function are likely to be overly simple, and many crucial experiments, including recording from awake birds while they memorize and practice song, remain to be done.

Future Directions

One of the advantages of the song system for the study of learning is that learning and behavior can be manipulated in order to understand the relationship between the behavioral results of learning and the properties of neurons. For instance, the selectivity for both BOS and tutor song in individual neurons of 60-day birds might reflect the involvement of both songs in shaping AF selectivity. Before accepting this interpretation, however, it must be established that these properties are not due to acoustic similarities between BOS and tutor song. This might be resolved experimentally: birds induced to sing abnormal song by manipulating the syrinx early in development would develop plastic songs extremely different from that of their tutor. If the AF of such birds do not have neurons that respond equally to both stimuli and lack song- and order-selectivity for tutor song, then acoustic similarity between BOS and tutor song is a probable cause of these properties in normal birds. If, however, these properties persist, then it is likely that tutor song can generate AF selectivity independently of the effects of BOS on song neurons. In fact, preliminary studies of birds syringeally denervated as juveniles reveal both neurons tuned to the abnormal BOS as well as neurons equally responsive to BOS and tutor song (Solis and Doupe 1996), further suggesting that both songs are involved in shaping AF selectivity. Another test of whether tutor song can influence AF selectivity could come from studies of muted birds. If juveniles are prevented from vocalizing throughout the sensory phase, then any observed auditory selectivity at 60 days would have to be due to tutor song experience.

Many questions remain about the circuitry leading to AF selectivity, and about how the AF influences the motor pathway. The discrete nuclei of the song system lend themselves well to studies that address these issues. For instance, the selectivity of one nucleus could be characterized while reversibly blocking or stimulating activity in another, or multiple song nuclei could be recorded simultaneously. Behavioral studies that manipulate the activity of the AF and assess the effects on song learning, like those of Basham and colleagues (1996), should also prove very informative. Intracellular investigations of song neurons in acute in vitro brain slices will be useful for revealing their detailed cellular and synaptic properties (Mooney 1992; Livingston and Mooney 1997; Boettiger and Doupe 1998).

It will also be critical to examine the properties of AF neurons in awake birds implanted with chronic electrodes. This will not only allow repeated sequential examination of the AF as the bird learns, but will also reveal how the AF responds to the BOS when it is actually sung by the bird. Preliminary studies already indicate that the AF circuit fires vigorously during singing in adult birds (Hessler and Doupe 1997). This activity precedes song initiation in the way that premotor activity does, suggesting that some of the AF activity during singing may represent an "efference copy" of motor commands from HVc. Moreover, passive presentation of song, as used in studies of anesthetized birds, does not always elicit responses in AF neurons of awake birds. Thus sensory responses in the AF may be present primarily when the bird sings, and could be embedded in motor-related neural activity. To sort out these possibilities, the effects of modifying the bird's motor output or auditory feedback on singing-related AF activity must be determined.

Another unresolved question concerns the role of the AF in adult birds. Recent experiments have shown that whereas deafening of adult birds leads to song deterioration, lesions of the AF in adult finches do not (Nordeen et al. 1992, 1993). These findings have been interpreted to suggest that auditory feedback in adult birds is not mediated by the AF. An alternative interpretation of these results, however, is that just as in juvenile birds (Bottjer et al. 1984; Sohrabji et al. 1990; Scharff and Nottebohm 1991), lesions of the AF block vocal plasticity in adults, even that associated with deterioration. Consistent with this hypothesis is the finding that the changes in song that normally follow deafening of adult birds are largely prevented by a combination of deafening and bilateral AF lesions directed at LMAN (Brainard and Doupe 1997). AF lesions may prevent deterioration of song in a number of (not mutually exclusive) ways. First, AF lesions may interrupt a neural signal (arising from or relayed through the AF) that actively drives changes in the motor pathway of deafened birds. This signal might be auditory or motor or both. Second, AF lesions may eliminate conditions that are permissive for plasticity by removal of neural or trophic inputs to the motor pathway. These possibilities can be investigated in behavioral and physiological experiments. Better understanding of how the AF regulates motor plasticity in the song system in both young and adult birds should yield general insights into the nature of instructive signals for learning and the developmental regulation of plasticity.

Conclusions

AF neurons in adult zebra finches respond selectively to spectrally and temporally complex auditory stimuli. This song- and order-selectivity emerges in initially unselective neurons during the learning of a complex vocal behavior. The selective properties of AF neurons in finches of an intermediate age (60 days) demonstrate that selectivity develops rapidly and is present while learning is still underway. Thus such selectivity could be involved in the process of sensorimotor learning. Finally, investigation of 60-day neurons with both BOS and tutor song stimuli reveals that both types of song experience may influence the properties of single neurons in this circuit. Further studies of the consequences of experience on neural properties within the song system should elucidate possible neural mechanisms of learning.

Acknowledgments

The work reviewed here was supported by the Lucille P. Markey Charitable Trust, the Klingenstein Fund, the McKnight Foundation, the Searle Scholars Program, the Sloan Foundation, NIH grants MH55987 and NS34835 (AJD), and a National Science Foundation Graduate Fellowship (MMS). We thank Virginia Herrera for invaluable editorial help, and Eliot Brenowitz, Charlotte Boettiger, Michael Brainard, Dean Buonomano, Marc Hauser, Mark Konishi, and Daniel Margoliash for helpful comments on the manuscript.

References

Aamodt, S., Kozlowski, M., Nordeen, E., and Nordeen, K. (1992) Distribution and developmental change in [^{3}-II]MK-801 binding within zebra finch song nuclei. *J. Neurobiol.* 23:997–1005.

Aamodt, S., Nordeen, E. J., and Nordeen, K. W. (1996) Blockade of NMDA receptors during song model exposure impairs song development in juvenile zebra finches. *Neurobiol. Learn. Mem.* 65:91–98.

Antonini, A. and Stryker, M. P. (1993) Rapid remodeling of axonal arbors in the visual cortex. *Science* 260(5115):1819–1821.

Arnold, A. (1975) The effects of castration on song development in zebra finches, *Poephila guttata. J. Exp. Zool.* 191:261–278.

Basham, M. E., Nordeen, E. J., and Nordeen, K. W. (1996) Blockade of NMDA receptors in the anterior forebrain impairs sensory acquisition in the zebra finch. *Neurobiol. Learn. Mem.* 66:295–304.

Boehner, J. (1990) Early acquisition of song in the zebra finch, *Taeniopygia guttata. Anim. Behav.* 39:369–374.

Boettiger, C. A. and Doupe, A. J. (1998) Intrinsic and thalamic excitatory inputs onto songbird LMAN neurons differ in their pharmacological and temporal properties. *J. Neurophys.*

Bottjer, S. W., Halsema, K. A., Brown, S. A., and Miesner, E. A. (1989) Axonal connections of a forebrain nucleus involved with vocal learning in zebra finches. *J. Comp. Neurol.* 279:312–326.

Bottjer, S. W., Miesner, E. A., and Arnold, A. P. (1984) Forebrain lesions disrupt development but not maintenance of song in passerine birds. *Science* 224:901–903.

Brainard, M. and Doupe, A. J. (1997) Anterior forebrain in lesions eliminate deafening-induced song deterioration in adult zebra finches. *Soc. Neurosci. Abstracts.* 23:.

Carrillo, G. and Doupe, A. J. (1995) Developmental studies of glutamate receptor and peptide immuno-reactivity in the zebra finch song system. *Soc. Neurosci. Abstr.* 21:960.

Chapman, B. and Stryker, M. P. (1993) Development of orientation selectivity in ferret visual cortex and effects of deprivation. *J. Neurosci.* 13:5251–5262.

DeYoe, E. A. and Van Essen, D. C. (1988) Concurrent processing streams in monkey visual cortex. *Trends in Neurosci.* 11:219–226.

Doupe, A. J. and Konishi, M. (1991) Song-selective auditory circuits in the vocal control system of the zebra finch. *Proc. Natl. Acad. Sci.* (USA) 88:11339–11343.

Doupe, A. J. (1997) Song- and order-selective neurons in the songbird anterior forebrain and their emergence during vocal development. *J. Neurosci.* 17(3):1147–1167.

Eales, L. A. (1985) Song learning in zebra finches: Some effects of song model availability on what is learnt and when. *Anim. Behav.* 33:1293–1300.

Eales, L. A. (1989) The influences of visual and vocal interaction on song learning in zebra finches. *Anim. Behav.* 37:507–508.

Eimas, P. D., Miller, J. L., and Jusczyk, P. W. (1987) On infant speech perception and the acquisition of language. In *Categorical Perception: The Groundwork of Cognition*, ed. by S. Harnad, pp. 161–195. New York: Cambridge University Press.

Gabbiani, F., Metzner, W., Wessel, R., and Koch, C. (1996) From stimulus encoding to feature extraction in weakly electric fish. *Nature* 384:564–567.

Gahr, M. (1990) Delineation of a brain nucleus—comparisons of cytochemical, hodological, and cytoarchitectural views of the song control nucleus HVc of the adult canary. *J. Comp. Neurol.* 249:30–36.

Green, D. M. and Swets, J. A. (1966) *Signal Detection Theory and Psychophysics*. New York: Wiley.

Hessler, N. A. and Doupe, A. J. (1997) Singing-related activity in anterior forebrain nuclei of adult zebra finch. *Soc. Neurosci. Abstracts.* 23:

Hubel, D. H., Wiesel, T. N., and LeVay, S. (1977) Plasticity of ocular dominance columns in monkey striate. *Phil. Trans. Roy. Soc. Lond.* B 278:377–409.

Immelmann, K. (1969) Song development in the zebra finch and other estrildid finches. In *Bird Vocalizations*, ed. by R. A. Hinde, pp. 61–74. Cambridge: Cambridge University Press.

Johnson, F. and Bottjer, S. (1992) Growth and regression of thalamic efferents in the song-control system of male zebra finches. *J. Comp. Neurol.* 326:442–450.

Johnson, F., Sablan, M., and Bottjer, S. W. (1995) Topographic organization of a pathway involved with vocal learning in zebra finches. *J. Comp. Neurol.* 358:268–275.

Katz, L. C. and Gurney, M. E. (1981) Auditory responses in the zebra finch's motor system for song. *Brain Res.* 211:192–197.

Kirn, J. R., Alvarez-Buylla, A., and Nottebohm, F. (1991) Production and survival of projection neurons in a forebrain vocal center of adult male canaries. *J. Neurosci.* 11:1756–1762.

Konishi, M. (1965) The role of auditory feedback in the control of vocalization in the white-crowned sparrow. *Z. Tierpsychol.* 22:770–783.

Konishi, M., Takahashi, T. T., Wagner, H., Sullivan, W. E., and Carr, C. E. (1988) Neurophysiological and anatomical substrates of sound localization in the owl. In *Auditory Function*, ed. by G. M. Edelman, W. E. Gall, and W. M. Cowan, pp. 721–745. New York: Wiley.

Kroodsma, D. E. and Konishi, M. (1991) A suboscine bird (eastern phoebe, *Sayornis phoebe*) develops normal song without auditory feedback. *Anim. Behav.* 42:477–487.

Kuhl, P. K., Williams, K. A., Lacerda, F., Stevens, K. N., and Lindblom, B. (1992) Linguistic experience alters phonetic perception in infants by 6 months of age. *Science* 255:606–608.

Lewicki, M. and Konishi, M. (1995) Mechanisms underlying the sensitivity of songbird forebrain neurons to temporal order. *Proc. Natl. Acad. Sci.* (USA) 92:5582–5586.

Lewicki, M. S. (1996) Intracellular characterization of song-specific neurons in the zebra finch auditory forebrain. *J. Neurosci.* 16:5854–5863.

Lewicki, M. S. and Arthur, B. J. (1996) Hierarchical organization of auditory temporal context sensitivity. *J. Neurosci.* 16:6987–6998.

Livingston, F. S. and Mooney, R. (1997) Development of intrinsic and synaptic properties in a forebrain nucleus essential to avian song learning. *J. Neurosci.* 17:8997–9009.

Livingstone, M. and Hubel, D. (1988) Segregation of form, color, movement, and depth: Anatomy, physiology, and perception. *Science* 240:740–749.

Maekawa, M. and Uno, H. (1996) Difference in selectivity to song note properties between the vocal nuclei of the zebra finch. *Neuroscience Letters* 218(2):123–126.

Margoliash, D. (1983) Acoustic parameters underlying the responses of song-specific neurons in the white-crowned sparrow. *J. Neurosci.* 3:1039–1057.

Margoliash, D. (1986) Preference for autogenous song by auditory neurons in a song system nucleus of the white-crowned sparrow. *J. Neurosci.* 6:1643–1661.

Margoliash, D. and Fortune, E. S. (1992) Temporal and harmonic combination-sensitive neurons in the zebra finch's HVc. *J. Neurosci.* 12:4309–4326.

Margoliash, D., Fortune, E. S., Sutter, M. L., Yu, A. C., Wren-Hardin, B. D., and Dave, A. (1994) Distributed representation in the song system of oscines: Evolutionary implications and functional consequences. *Brain Behav. Evol.* 44:247–264.

Marler, P. (1970) A comparative approach to vocal learning: Song development in white-crowned sparrows. *J. Comp. Physiol. Psychol.* 71:1–25.

Marler, P. (1991) Song-learning behavior: the interface with neuroethology. *Trends Neurosci.* 14:199–206.

Marler, P. and Peters, S. (1982) Long-term storage of learned birdsongs prior to production. *Anim. Behav.* 30:479–482.

Marler, P. and Tamura, M. (1964) Culturally transmitted patterns of vocal behavior in sparrows. *Science* 146:1483–1486.

Mooney, R. (1992) Synaptic basis for developmental plasticity in a birdsong nucleus. *J. Neurosci.* 12:2464–2477.

Nelson, D. A. and Marler, P (1994) Selection-based learning in bird song development. *Proc. Natl. Acad. Sci.* (USA) 91:10948–10501.

Nixdorf-Bergweiler, B. E., Lips, M. B., and Heinemann, U. (1995) Electrophysiological and morphological evidence for a new projection of LMAN-neurones towards Area X. *NeuroReport* 6:1729–1732.

Nixdorf-Bergweiler, B. E., Wallhausser-Franke, E., and DeVoogd, T. J. (1995) Regressive development in neuronal structure during song learning in birds. *J. Neurobiol.* 27(2):204–215.

Nordeen, K. W. and Nordeen, E. J. (1992) Auditory feedback is necessary for the maintenance of stereotyped song in adult zebra finches. *Behav. Neural. Biol.* 57:58–66.

Nordeen, K. W. and Nordeen, E. J. (1993) Long-term maintenance of song in adult zebra finches is not affected by lesions of a forebrain region involved in song learning. *Behavioral and Neural Bio.* 59:79–82.

Nottebohm, F., Alvarez-Buylla, A., Cynx, J., Ling, C. Y., Nottebohm, F., Suter, R., Tolles, A., and Williams, H. (1990) Song learning and birds: The relation between perception and production. *Phil. Trans. R. Soc. Lond.* 329:115–124.

Nottebohm, F., Stokes, T. M., and Leonard, C. M. (1976) Central control of song in the canary, *Serinus canarius*. *J. Comp. Neurol.* 165:457–486.

O'Neill, W. E. and Suga, N. (1979) Target range-sensitive neurons in the auditory cortex of the mustached bat. *Science* 203:69–73.

Okuhata, S. and Saito, N. (1987) Synaptic connections of thalamo-cerebral vocal control nuclei of the canary. *Brain Res. Bull.* 18:35–44.

Rauschecker, J. P., Tian, B., and Hauser, M. (1995) Processing of complex sounds in the macaque non-primary auditory cortex. *Science* 268:111–114.

Rose, G. J., Kawasaki, M., and Heiligenberg, W. (1988) "Recognition units" at the top of a neuronal hierarchy? Prepacemaker neurons in *Eigenmannia* code the sign of frequency differences unambiguously. *J. Comp. Physiol.* 162:759–772.

Rose, S. P. (1991) How chicks make memories: the cellular cascade from c-fos to dendritic remodelling. *Trends. Neurosci.* 14(9):390–397.

Saito, N. and Maekawa, M. (1993) Birdsong: The interface with human language. *Brain and Development* 15:31–39.

Scharff, C. and Nottebohm, F. (1991) A comparative study of the behavioral deficits following lesions of the various parts of the zebra finch song system: Implications for vocal learning. *J. Neurosci.* 11:2896–2913.

Shatz, C. J. (1990) Impulse activity and the patterning of connections during CNS development. *Neuron* 5:745–756.

Slater, P. J., Eales, L. A., and Clayton, N. S. (1988) Song learning in zebra finches (*Taeniopygia guttata*): Progress and prospects. *Adv. in the Study of Beh.* 18:1–33.

Slater, P. J. B. and Jones, A. E. (1995) The timing of song and distance call learning in zebra finches. *Anim. Behav.* 49:548–550.

Sohrabji, F., Nordeen, E. J., and Nordeen, K. W. (1990) Selective impairment of song learning following lesions of a forebrain nucleus in the juvenile zebra finch. *Behav. Neuro. Biol.* 53:51–63.

Sohrabji, F., Nordeen, E. J., and Nordeen, K. W. (1993) Characterization of neurons born and incorporated into a vocal control nucleus during avian song learning. *Brain Res.* 620:335–338.

Solis, M. M. and Doupe, A. J. (1996) Birds' experience of their own songs shapes the auditory selectivity in the anterior forebrain of juvenile zebra finches. *Soc. Neurosci. Abstr.* 22:152.

Solis, M. M. and Doupe, A. J. (1997) Anterior forebrain neurons develop selectivity by an intermediate stage of birdsong learning. *J. Neurosci.* 17:6447–6462.

Suga, N. (1990) Cortical computational maps for auditory imaging. *Neural Networks* 3:3–21.

Sutter, M. L. and Margoliash, D. (1994) Global synchronous response to autogenous song in zebra finch HVc. *J. Neurophysiol.* 72:2105–2123.

Tolhurst, D. J., Movshon, J. A., and Dean, A. F. (1983) The statistical reliability of signals in single neurons in cat and monkey visual cortex. Vision Res. 23(8):775–785.

Vates, G. E. and Nottebohm, F. (1995) Feedback circuitry within a song-learning pathway. *Proc. Natl. Acad. Sci.* (USA) 92:5139–5143.

Vicario, D. S. and Yohay, K. H. (1993) Song-selective auditory input to a forebrain vocal control nucleus in the zebra finch. *J. Neurobiol.* 24:488–505.

Volman, S. F. (1993) Development of neural selectivity for birdsong during vocal learning. *J. Neurosci.* 13:4737–4747.

Volman, S. F. (1996) Quantitative assessment of song-selectivity in the zebra finch "high vocal center." *J. Comp. Physiol.* A 178:849–862.

Werker, J. F. and Tees, R. C. (1992) The organization and reorganization of human speech perception. *Ann. Rev. of Neuroscience* 15:377–402.

Zola-Morgan, S. and Squire, L. R. (1993) Neuroanatomy of memory. *Ann. Rev. of Neuroscience* 16:547–563.

13 Genetics of Canary Song Learning: Innate Mechanisms and Other Neurobiological Considerations

Paul C. Mundinger

Birdsong is a classic example of neural mechanisms underlying a learned communication system. Since Nottebohm's early work on neural lateralization in chaffinches (1971), progress in the field of neurobiology has mushroomed and the basic mechanisms underlying many aspects of singing behavior have been described (reviewed in Catchpole and Slater 1995). This chapter does not review this work (see chapters by Marler and Nottebohm, this volume), nor does it add to these impressive accomplishments by reviewing recent neurobiological advances (see chapters by Nottebohm and by Doupe and Solis, this volume). Rather, it discusses two new genetic studies of song learning. Future neurobiological studies may uncover new mechanisms, or better understand existing ones, by focusing on inbred strains that differ genetically with regard to specific aspects of song learning, production, or development.

The bird used in the genetic studies is the canary, *Serinus canaria*, a species already well studied neurobiologically. However, not all canaries are alike in their song learning and song production behavior. The canary is unique among songbirds in that several genetically different strains were produced by artificial selection. Some strains, like border, Norwich, and Yorkshire canaries are called "type canaries" because they are bred to some morphological type, much like dog and cat breeds. Their songs are apparently little affected by this form of artificial selection, and border canary songs are still rather similar to those of wild canaries (Marler 1959, Güttinger 1985). In contrast, the German roller canary (Harz roller) and the Belgian waterschlager strains were artificially selected for their songs, which are now very different from wild and type canary songs (Güttinger 1985).

Canary song learning is primarily known from Marler's studies of the waterschlager strain (Marler and Waser 1977; Waser and Marler 1977), and the neurobiology of waterschlager song production has been studied intensively by Nottebohm and colleagues (see, e.g., Nottebohm et al. 1976, 1982, 1986; Kelly and Nottebohm 1979; Alvarez-Buylla et al. 1988; Mello et al. 1992; Güttinger 1981).

The waterschlager is also of interest because it is partially deaf (Okanoya and Dooling 1985), and Dooling has recently identified the mechanism involved, namely, cycles of hair cell degeneration and replacement (Gleich et al. 1997). This may be a genetic defect limited to that strain. Other canary strains, specifically roller and American singer canaries (the latter a backcross of roller and border hybrids), have normal hearing comparable with other songbirds (Okanoya and Dooling 1985, 1987).

To my knowledge, roller and border canaries have not otherwise been studied neurobiologically. But these two strains were used in a series of genetic analyses of selective song learning. A recent breeding experiment (Mundinger 1995) showed that marked differences in roller and border song-learning preferences are due to genetic differences between the two strains. However, that study did not say much about the genes involved. The following section summarizes two recent, related breeding experiments that add significant new knowledge about interstrain differences in song learning preferences and production, and the genetic system.

Recent Developments

Interstrain Differences in Learning Wildtype Song

Roller and border canaries are the presumed descendents of wild canaries. The songs of wild canaries are much like those of modern border canaries (Marler 1959; Güttinger 1985), but they sometimes contain a few low-pitched, roller-like tours too (a tour is the same syllable repeated serially; figure 13.1). The presence of high-pitched, border-like syllables and tours together with a small number of low-pitched, roller-like ones in wild canary syllable repertoires is consistent with the hypothesis that the wild canary is the common ancestor of both border and roller canaries.

But domestication has modified these two strains differently. Roller canary songs no longer contain the high-pitched, border-like tours that characterize and dominate wild and type canary songs. Also, modern roller canary tours are longer and generally lower-pitched than their wild canary counterparts (pers. obs.; Güttinger 1985). Given their common ancestry on the one hand, but on the other hand their different

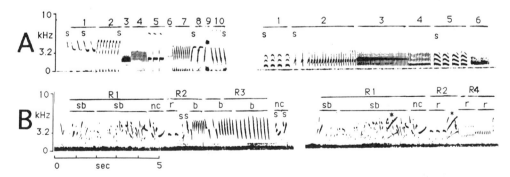

Figure 13.1
Domestic and wild canary songs. (A) border canary (left), and roller canary (right); numbers 1–10 and 1–6 indicate tours, s = selected individual syllables. (B) Two wild canary songs from same dialect, advertising song (left) and courtship song (right). sb = small bit phrases, nc = note complex phrases, r = roller-like phrase, b = border-like phrase, * = alarm call of female canary in background.

domestic histories and different song-learning preferences (Mundinger 1995), one can ask: are there interstrain differences in learning wild canary patterns, and if so, how do they differ?

To answer this question, five border, one roller and border hybrid, and six pure-bred roller canaries (breeding stock for the latter purchased from roller canary breeders belonging to New York or German roller canary societies) were hatched and reared in sound chambers, isolated at the egg stage from adult male song. All young were reared in normal clutches, generally by their biological mother (a foster mother for one clutch), and the parent was removed when the young reached independence (age 24–30 days). At about one month of age the young were group-tutored in small groups with a tape recording 1 hour daily for 40 days (postfledging tutor period, age 30–70 days). The males were then individually isolated in acoustic chambers and were tutored twice more with the same tutor tape for 30 days each (fall tutor period, age 160–190 ± 2 days; prebreeding tutor period, age 210–240 ± 2 days). To see if early tutoring alone was sufficient, tutor experience varied in two instances: the Border male BB43 received only postfledging tutoring, and his sibling BB44 heard only postfledging and fall tutoring.

The tutor tape provided a natural sequence of 46 advertising songs from one wild canary male (a 9 min. sequence), 6 minutes of silence, then a natural bout from a second male of 7 wild canary courtship songs which were repeated 5 times to form a 10 minute sequence. Another 6 minutes of silence followed, making a 31-minute tape loop. The two song bouts were originally recorded on Tenerife, Canary Islands, from two males belonging to the same song dialect, and their songs contained many of the same tours (figure 13.1b). However, the courtship sequence had a high percentage of low-pitched, roller-like tours, and the advertising sequence was primarily composed of the higher-pitched, border-like syllables and tours and only a few roller-like ones. Although 53 different song patterns were on the tape loop, many were structurally similar and could be classified into seven basic song types (see chapter on song variation by Searcy and Nowicki, this volume).

The experiment revealed a marked interstrain difference in learning wild canary song patterns. The border and hybrid canaries readily learned wildtype patterns; the roller canaries exhibited very limited learning from the tutor tape.

All five border canaries and the hybrid learned their tours and syllables from both advertising and courtship models. They primarily acquired the higher-pitched, border-like patterns but each also learned 3 or 4 low-pitched, roller-like ones. From a total of 124 different wild canary syllable patterns, the border male BB42 acquired only 15 (12% of the tutor); his sibling BB41 copied 34 (27%); BB43 (who only received tutoring at age 30–70 days) had 39 (31%); but BB10, BB44 (only tutored at 30–70 and 160–190 days), and the hybrid RB02 acquired, respectively, 70 (56%), 75 (60%), and 76 (61%) different syllable patterns from the tutor. The three smaller syllable repertoires are comparable to domestic canary syllable repertoires, reported as varying between 30–50 syllable types (Güttinger 1985). The three males with repertoires of 70–76 wildtype syllable patterns are more like the syllable repertoires of some wild canaries. For example, a well-sampled (N = 76 songs) wild canary from the Azores had 63 different syllable patterns (pers. obs.). Güttinger (1985), however, reports much larger individual repertoires of 120–180 or more different syllable patterns for several wild canaries recorded in the Canary Islands. The tutor playback loop, with songs from a Canary Island dialect, had 124 different syllables contributed by two birds.

Canary Island syllable repertoires may be especially large because of the distinctive "small-bit" phrases that are sung by the wild canaries there. These phrases are jumbles of small bits of sound (figure 13.1b), and they contribute many patterns to syllable repertoires. One of the two wild canary males whose songs were used in the tutor was very well sampled (46 advertising songs), and 22 of his 91 different syllable patterns (27%) were small-bit syllables. Wild canaries from Madeira and the Azores apparently lack small-bit phrases (pers. obs.), or they are much less common there, and domestic canaries have none. This could, in part, account for their smaller syllable repertoire sizes.

Four of the five border canaries and the hybrid acquired and sang some small-bit phrases in their plastic songs (figure 13.2), and two males retained a few small-bit phrases, sometimes shortened, in their full songs. While still in the plastic song stage, several border males also sang song patterns that were fair to good copies of one or more wild canary whole song patterns (figure 13.2), but as ontogeny progressed, some improvisation and the loss of some syllable or tour patterns resulted in poorer matches at the whole song level. As a result, the border canary full songs resembled normal border canary song patterns except that the constituent syllable and tour patterns were generally copies of wild canary syllables and tours.

In contrast with the rather extensive copying of wild canary sound patterns by some border and hybrid canaries, the six roller canaries showed very limited learning from the tutor, and then in an unexpected direction. I had initially expected that the roller males might selectively learn the low-pitched, roller-like tours that were well represented in the wild canary courtship songs. This expectation was not met. Instead, the roller males developed normal roller song patterns composed of roller-typical syllables and tours that apparently developed independent of their tutor experience. However, two males did include imitations of one low-pitched, wild canary tutor tour in their repertoire of roller tours, and the other four males had a few low-

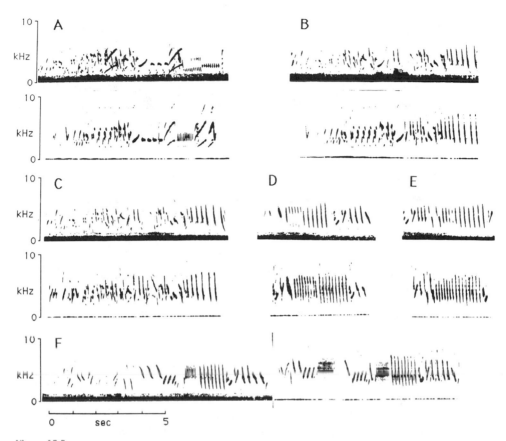

Figure 13.2
Comparisons of six wild canary tutor song patterns (top sonagrams in *A–F*) to plastic song copies by tutored Border canary BB44 (bottom sonagrams in *A–E*, and the two partial copies on right in *F*).

pitched tours that could be interpreted as modified copies of some low-pitched wild canary patterns. But overall, the roller males imitated fewer of these low-pitched, wildtype tours than did the border and hybrid males. This is similar to the results of a recent cross-foster experiment (Mundinger 1995). In that study two roller males, live-tutored by an adult border male, primarily developed many normal roller tours independent of their foster father's tutoring but also sang a few low-pitched, roller-like variants apparently copied in modified form from their border foster father. In contrast, three cross-fostered border canaries copied either four or five low-pitched roller tours from their foster father's songs.

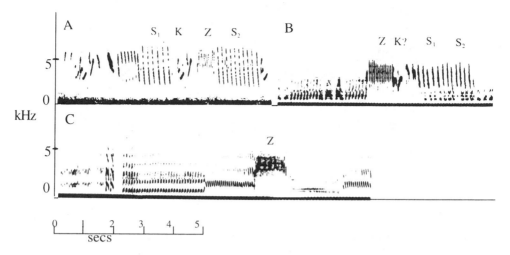

Figure 13.3
Wild canary tour patterns copied by a tutored roller canary (RR-12). (A) Part of a wild canary tutor song with syllable K and tours S_1, Z, and S_2 indicated; (B) Roller plastic song with copies of Z, S_1, S_2 and possibly K. Note two voices when producing $S_1 S_2$, patterns later ontogenetically lost; (C) A full song of RR12. Note the many normal low-pitched roller tours and the unusual (for roller canaries) high-pitched Z tour.

A second, even more unexpected, result was that five of the six roller males did imitate a very few, generally one to three, high-pitched, border-like wild canary patterns. Initially these appeared early in ontogeny (early plastic song stage). In four cases these relatively high-pitched, plastic song patterns were soon lost from the repertoires as song development progressed. However, the fifth male, who had originally imitated three or four border-like wild canary tutor tours (figure 13.3b), retained one of these in his full songs (figure 13.3c). The wild canary patterns preferentially copied by these roller males were primarily sharp down-slur tour patterns, a very prevalent, species-typical pattern (see "border-like" tours in figure 13.1b).

The results of this experiment led to a number of conclusions, some expected, others not. As expected, there are definite interstrain differences in learning wildtype song patterns. When tape-tutored, roller canaries do not imitate entire wild canary song patterns or even a substantial fraction of one. However, they may copy a limited number of low-pitched, roller-like patterns from the tutor, and they may also learn, although not consistently produce, one or a few high-pitched, species-typical down-slur tours. In contrast, border canaries, and apparently interstrain hybrids as well, still have a well-developed capacity to imitate part or all of some of the wild canary songs they are exposed to, including learning some sequences that are structurally and acoustically very different from those found in modern type canary songs (i.e., the acquisition of some small-bit phrases). However, although some border canaries can learn wildtype patterns rather well, there may be substantial individual differences in this ability. For example, three siblings (BB44, BB43, BB10) learned many wild canary patterns ($\bar{X} = 61.3$ syllable types), even though two of these males had limited tutor experience; but two other males (BB41, BB42—also siblings) only learned a fraction of this ($\bar{X} = 21$ syllable types), although they had all three tutorings.

Another conclusion is that the interstrain difference in song learning and production is apparently not due to a syringeal constraint. Suthers reviews the current understanding of song production by the syrinx (see Suthers chapter, this volume). The waterschlager canary is one of the songbirds he discusses in detail. This strain's unusually low-pitched song is highly lateralized, produced primarily or exclusively by the left syringeal half (Nottebohm and Nottebohm 1976). The left half is apparently specialized for producing low frequency sounds in a number of passerine species. Suthers states that the syringeal function of other canary strains has not been studied. This neurobiological analysis needs to be addressed, because the relatively high-pitched syllables sung by border and type canaries suggest that these sounds might be produced on the right, or both sides, instead of the left only. In other words, the syrinx of the wild canary, and of those type canaries with songs not modified by artificial selection, might not be highly lateralized. The waterschlager evidence may be misleading at the species level.

Until the relevant studies are done there is no definitive answer. However, the wild-canary-tutored roller canary RR12 was recorded in plastic song producing two tours simultaneously (figure 13.3b). One was a plastic song version of a low-pitched roller tour, likely produced by the left syrinx. The other was a high-pitched border-like pattern produced by the other syringeal half (the right side?). This recording, and the five roller canaries that did sing a few high-pitched wild canary syllable patterns in plastic song, suggests that the roller syrinx is capable of producing sounds using both syringeal sides. The entire roller syrinx may be potentially functional, but in the course of song development this song-selected strain may have shifted to a highly lateralized song, similar to the waterschlager strain.

For border canaries, the evidence shows that their syrinx is fully capable of producing type and wild canary sound patterns, and the low-pitched patterns of roller canaries too (Mundinger 1995). Thus the syrinx of both strains seems capable of producing the alternative strain's sound patterns.

Backcross Breeding Experiment: Progress Toward Understanding the Genetic System

Another recent study (Mundinger, in prep.) combined a standard backcross breeding experiment with choice tutoring to investigate the genetics of canary song-learning preferences. The sample included 5 roller and 5 border canaries (parental generation); 4 RB and 5 BR reciprocal cross F1 hybrids (RB means roller mother and border father; BR is the reciprocal); and 10 roller-backcrosses and 10 border-backcrosses. All but four of the males were hatched and reared in acoustic chambers, isolated from adult male song. The rearing hens were removed at weaning (age 22–30 days), and all males were individually isolated soon after sexing. The four exceptions (2 RB hybrids, 2 border-backcrosses) hatched in a birdroom in late July, were transferred with their mothers to an isolated room (age 20–24 days), then put in acoustic chambers when weaned (age 23–27 days).

All the males were recorded weekly from August or September until the end of the experiment in March and were untutored until November. Songs produced through October (4–7.5 mo. old) were their innately developed control songs. These control patterns served as a reference to determine if the birds subsequently learned new patterns from the tutor, for they conceivably might have independently developed some tutor-like patterns prior to tutoring. Beginning sometime in November, and again in February, they were choice-tutored for 30 consecutive days, twice daily (an hour in both the A.M. and P.M.). The tutor tape contained 3 type canary songs (originally recorded from a Norwich canary, but called border tutor songs here to simplify description), 2 minutes of silence, and 3 roller canary songs (figure 13.4). This loop was repeated 9 times per tutor session. The first bout (roller or border) to begin a tutor session varied.

Several important results emerged. First, the experimental design included a replication of an earlier genetic analysis (Mundinger 1995). The two studies used entirely different roller and border canary breeding stocks, but obtained similar results: rollers learned only from the roller tutors; borders learned only, or almost only (two males acquired one or two roller tours each), from the border tutor; and all the interstrain hybrids learned from both kinds of tutor songs. Thus differential learning by roller and border canaries under a choice-tutoring regime is a robust phenomenon, and it is readily replicated. In addition to replicating the earlier genetic analysis, this backcross experiment also revealed several important features of the genetic system (see below): (1) it is polygenic; (2) the genes are on several chromosomes; (3) one of these is the sex chromosome; and (4) other genes, apparently including one or more for roller tour learning preferences, are autosomal.

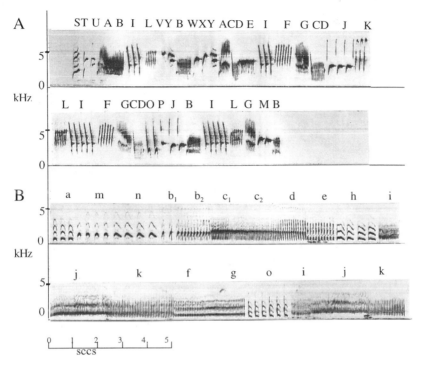

Figure 13.4
Examples of (A) a border tutor song and (B) a roller tutor song used in the choice tutoring experiment. Capital letters $A-Y$ indicate 19 of the 26 different syllable patterns in the border portions of the tutor; lower-case letters $a-o$ (including b_1, b_2, c_1, c_2) indicate 16 of the 17 different roller patterns in the tutor.

The most important data set is summarized in figure 13.5a and b, which compares all 39 males across two parameters: (1) selective song learning, as measured by the maximum number of roller, or border, imitations each male sung over the November–January period; and (2) song production, measured as the average percentage of a male's song output over the November–January period that was roller-like, or border-like.

Figure 13.5a plots each male's roller imitations versus his roller-like production. Figure 13.5b plots each male's border imitations against his border-like production. Border-like production includes all border tutor imitations plus any invented patterns with highest frequency of the fundamental above 3kHz, whereas roller-like singing includes all roller tutor imitations plus any inventions for which the highest frequency of the fundamental is below 3kHz (see figure 13.4). The two plots are

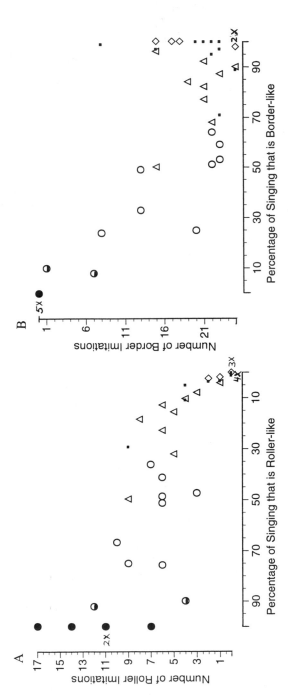

Figure 13.5
Comparison of five genetically different canary lines by their selective learning and song production. (A) Roller-like learning and singing; (B) Border-like learning and singing. ● = 5 roller canaries; ○ = 10 roller canaries; ◖ = 5 roller canaries; ◑ = 10 border-backcrosses; △ = 9 hybrids; ◻ = 10 border-backcrosses; ◇ = 5 border canaries. 2x – 5x = the number of multiple males represented by a single symbol.

complementary and summarize a large amount of singing behavior by 39 individual birds. The graphs show individual variation, and provide evidence for the following:

1. Polygenes Figure 13.5 shows that variation in both parameters (learning and production) is continuous, not discontinuous. Also, the distribution of the hybrids in both graphs is between the parentals. This kind of phenotypic variation supports multifactor inheritance.

2. Genetic Background The males are not distributed randomly across figure 13.5a or 5b. Rather they are clustered according to genetic background. All rollers are in the upper left and borders are in the lower right, with roller-backcrosses, hybrids, and border-backcrosses in predictable locations between the parentals. Genetic background has a marked and readily observed effect on canary song learning and production.

3. Multiple Chromosomes Figure 13.5 reveals greatest individual variation in the backcrosses, especially the roller-backcrosses. One expects greatest individual variation in backcrosses if the polygenes are on multiple chromosomes. The hybrid parent, having one set of roller and border chromosomes, can theoretically meiotically produce an array of gametes that range from a pure haploid roller genome, through many intermediate conditions, to a pure border 1N genome. When backcrossed to a pure roller or pure border canary, the resulting backcross progeny could therefore vary genetically from a pure parental condition to a pure hybrid one. Figure 13.5 shows results like this. roller-backcrosses ranged from two males with song learning or production similar to rollers, through a range of intermediates, to several males expressing typical hybrid song learning or production. The border-backcrosses had a comparable range of variation, from hybrid-like to border-like. This supports the hypothesis that the genes are on multiple chromosomes.

4. Border (Wildtype-like) Learning Preferences are Sex-linked Songbirds like canaries generally have 78–82 chromosomes (2N), most of them microchromosomes (Shields 1982), so locating specific linkage-groups may seem daunting. However, searching for sex-linked traits is an obvious start, and variation in roller-backcross singing can be analyzed for sex-linkage.

In birds, males are the homogametic sex and are ZZ, and females are ZW. A BR mother inherits a W chromosome from her border mother, and gives her sons her roller father's Z. Her sons are Z_rZ_r. Sons of RB hybrid mothers inherit one border Z from her and a roller Z from their roller father. They are Z_bZ_r. Figure 13.5a–b show that the two Z_rZ_r males with a BR hybrid mother (half-filled circles) rank first to second by how roller-like their singing is; those with RB mothers (open circles) rank third to tenth. The difference between the two groups is significant (p = 0.02, Fisher's exact probability test). I conclude from this that border tour learning preferences are sex-linked. (Note: a just completed follow-up study added 7 more BR sons and 1 RB son. Now 9 BR sons rank first to ninth in roller-like singing, while the 9 RB sons rank tenth through eighteenth, and these differences are now highly significant, p = 0.00002.)

These border-tour learning preferences are probably wildtype traits. For example, several border canaries in the wild canary tutoring experiment (above) readily learned and produced wild canary patterns. So the border Z-chromosome may carry wildtype alleles. Exploring this further, table 13.1 examines, in the roller-backcross males, the inheritance of a preference (or capacity) to learn and produce four basic wild canary tour patterns that were represented in the tutor tape: sharp down-slur patterns; up-slurs; vibratos; and tours composed of syllables resembling the border tutor syllable *J*. Culturally acquired variants of these basic categories are found in many wild canary songs (pers. obs.). For example, sharp down-slur patterns were found in all wild canary repertoires sampled in an archipelago-wide survey of the Canary Islands (about 8000 songs and 500 males in the sample, unpublished data). The other three categories appeared less often in the survey, but were encountered repeatedly. The results in Table 13.1 suggest a sex-linked pattern of inheritance for all four of these wildtype categories.

In sum, the high-pitched syllables and tours that characterize wild and type canary songs are preferentially learned (and/or produced) by border, border-backcross, and hybrid canaries because some of the genetic factors involved in the development of mechanisms for learning or producing those patterns apparently are on their border Z-chromosome(s). And it seems that these factors are dominant or codominant as the hybrids are heterozygous and all nine hybrids produced many border imitations ($\bar{X} = 22.55 \pm 3.43$ border syllable patterns out of a possible 26 patterns). Roller canaries may lack all or most of the postulated, functional, wildtype alleles on their Z-chromosomes and, consequently, may not readily learn or produce high-pitched border or wildtype patterns. Roller-backcross males inherit either one or no border Z-chromosome. Those with one border Z acquired many well-formed high-pitched patterns ($\bar{X} = 18 \pm 5.8$, n = 8), but those with no border Z-chromosome learned fewer border tutor patterns ($\bar{X} = 4.5 \pm 2.8$, n = 2) and those they sang lacked some high frequency components (table 13.1).

5. Autosomal Factors   Turning, now, to the 10 border-backcrosses, an autosomal effect was uncovered when the inheritance of a preference to learn and produce roller tour patterns was followed. Modern roller canaries are judged on the basis of how

Table 13.1
Roller-backcrosses learning high-pitched, wildtype syllables.

Roller-Backcross	Mother	Down-slur	Up-slur	Vibrato	J-like
8HR	BR	—	—	B*	J*
11HR	BR	I*N*	F*L E*	R*	—
7HR	RB	I N O	F L E	B	J
1HR	RB	I O	F L E	—	J'
3HR	RB	I O	F L E	A B G	J J'
12HR	RB	I N	F L E	A B G	J
15FR	RB	I N O	F L E	A B G	J
14FR	RB	I N O	F L E	A B G	J
5HR	RB	I N O	F L E	A B G	J
17FR	RB	I N O	F L E	A B G	J

Sex-linked ratios, based on occurance of *well-formed* imitations:

		+ −	ǀ	+ −	+ −
Expected:	for RB sons	0:2	0:2	0.2	0:2
	for BR sons	8:0	8:0	8:0	8:0
Observed:	for RB sons	0:2	1.1	0:2	0:2
	for BR sons	8:0	8:0	7:1	7.1

* modifed, not well-formed (high frequencies missing or shifted lower)
J' = modified copy of tutor pattern J

their tours sound to human judges who are trained to recognize nine tour categories. Not all roller males sing all nine kinds of tours, but all roller males are expected to sing four of them. Three of these roller-defining tour categories are rolls (e.g., c_1, c_2, d, j, k in figure 13.4), hollow bells (e, f, and perhaps b_1, b_2 in figure 13.4), and flutes (a, h, m, n, o in figure 13.4).

Table 13.2 summarizes the learning and subsequent production of these roller tutor tours by border-backcrosses and compares the observed results to expected backcross ratios for a single gene, two allele model. The results were not significantly different from the expected ratios (p = 0.4 to 0.99, Chi square tests). This suggests that one or more major genes may be involved in the inheritance of mechanisms to acquire and/or produce roller-typical tours. If this is correct, then backcrossing $R+$ hybrids (all of whom acquired one or more of these roller-typical tours) to ++ borders (who generally do not learn roller tours) produces a 1 $R+$: 1 ++ ratio, with heterozygotes postulated to learn some roller tours. (This model postulates a dominant or codominant roller mutant allele, with the wildtype allele recessive or codominant.) However, the sample size is small (N = 10 males), and there is much controversy regarding the issue of major genes and behavior traits. So it seems

Table 13.2
Border-backcrosses learning and producing roller-typical patterns.

Border-backcross	Mother	Rolls	Hollow Bells	Flutes
5HB	BR	c_1	b_1	a n
7HB	RB	$c_1 c_2 d$	$b_1 b_2$	a m n o
21HB	RB	d	$b_1 b_2$	n^1
P22	BR	c_1	b_2	—
15HB	BR	c_1	—	—
FB04	Border	—	—	a(m?)
FX07	BR	—	—	—
23HB	BR	—	—	—
8HB	RB	—	—	—
FX05	Border	—	—	—
Ratios for autosomal major gene:				
		+ −	+ −	+ −
Expected		5:5	5:5	5:5
Observed		5:5	4:6	4:6 or (3:7)
p =		0.99	0.4	0.4 or (0.2)

1. syllable appeared only once (may be an error)

prudent at this preliminary stage to conclude only that one or more major gene(s) is suggested by this data. But this analysis does show that the major gene hypothesis is worthy of retesting, and that some of the genes associated with the selective learning of roller-typical patterns are autosomal, not sex-linked. If they, too, were sex-linked, then the sons of BR and RB hybrid mothers would show differences in roller learning preferences, and they do not (table 13.2).

Discussion

Behavior-genetic interpretations are often controversial, especially when the behaviors are alleged to be innate or when specific genes are alleged to affect specific behavioral characters (see critiques by Johnston 1988; Gottlieb 1992). One reason for the controversy is that we know so little about the specific neural mechanisms that link genes to behavioral patterns. Another is that, in the past, the behavior-genetic evidence was missing. Although genetic analyses like those summarized here probably cannot resolve the controversy, they do shed some light on concepts like "innate," and if coupled with neurobiological analysis of the underlying neural mechanisms, a new, deeper understanding of genes and behavior may result.

Innate Preferences and Mechanisms

The term "innate" has different interpretations, some of which may lead to problems. Marler (see his chapter, this volume) shows how difficulties arise when one view in particular is applied. This is the view that innate is the antithesis of learning, and that traits can be classified exclusively as either innate or learned. Most ethologists reject this view and use the term innate in other ways.

Traditionally, ethologists have recognized two meaning of innate, "developmentally innate" and "genetically innate" (Brown 1975). A developmentally innate trait develops normally without social learning. There is substantial empirical support for this concept from social isolation experiments. Also, on this use of the term, there is no innate versus learned dichotomy, because the concept is compatible with some forms of learning. For example, nonsocial learning, such as the self-learning that socially isolated males may experience when they hear their own song production, may be part of the ontogeny of developmentally innate traits (Mundinger 1995).

The genetically innate concept is more problematical as it has a long history of misunderstanding and misinterpretation. "Genetically innate" applies to *differences* in phenotypic traits, not to phenotypic traits themselves (Brown 1975; Marler and Sherman 1985; Marler, this volume). The original canary-breeding experiment (Mundinger 1995) found that (1) "Differences in roller and border canary song learning preferences are due to genetic differences between the strains." When stated that way, most scientists do not misinterpret the message, and it is not very controversial. It is the standard way geneticists describe detecting genes as causal factors. But it can also be restated as (2) "Differences in roller and border canary song learning preferences are genetically innate." This second wording may be unnecessary as statement (1) is adequate and clear. Furthermore, the message of the second statement has been misinterpreted and has led some scientists to erroneously conclude that, used this way, "genetically innate" means "genetically determined." However, the second wording does remind us that genetic heritability is a feature of the innate concept. Innate traits, such as any innate neural mechanisms, have at least two features or criteria: (1) they develop normally in the absence of social learning (i.e., they are developmentally innate); and (2) like other phenotypic traits, they are genetically heritable. As applied to bird songs, or to mechanisms for song learning and production, the first criterion has a good history of empirical support from social isolation experiments. "Developmentally innate" is the meaning most ethologists use or imply when they refer to the innate communication signals (songs, calls, etc.) of animals reared in social isolation.

Empirical evidence for the genetic heritability of behavior, or of neural mechanisms, is more difficult to gather. Nevertheless, the genetic heritability hypothesis is sometimes invoked or inferred even though the genetic evidence is indirect or lacking. For example, in linguistics the innate hypothesis posits that our language capacity is genetically heritable, and some linguists contend that because of this it is subject to organic evolution (Pinker 1994). Although some ingenious linguistic arguments and analyses support the innate hypothesis as applied to language (see, e.g., Chomsky 1975; Bickerton 1984), there is as yet no direct evidence for language genes (see the preface in Rice 1996).

Birdsong learning and development is an interesting animal parallel to human speech learning and development, in part because songbirds culturally learn their communication signals, and in part because the hypothesized mechanism(s) guiding this learning is thought to be genetically heritable and developmentally innate (Marler 1964; Konishi 1965; Marler and Sherman 1983).

Many song development experiments have shown that the songs of intact (i.e., they can hear their voice), socially isolated songbirds are indeed developmentally innate (see, e.g., Thorpe 1958; 1969; Marler 1970; Kroodsma 1984; Marler and Sherman 1985). Presumably, the neural mechanisms underlying those songs are developmentally innate too. But, with the exception of Marler and Sherman's (1985) comparative study of interspecific differences in sparrow songs (reviewed in Marler's chapter, this volume), these developmental studies could say nothing about genetic heritability, because the relevant genetic breeding or comparative experiments were not done.

The canary-breeding and choice-tutoring experiment described in this chapter does provide this evidence. There are now good experimental results showing that differences in the song-learning preferences of roller and border canaries are due to genetic differences between those strains. Furthermore, some of the relevant genes are sex-linked and others are autosomal. These results also support the hypothesis that the underlying neural mechanisms are genetically heritable, and that interstrain differences in these neural mechanisms are due to genetic differences between the strains.

At about 6 months of age, the canaries were exposed to social experience (tutoring) for the first time, and all males subsequently modified their songs by learning and producing a variety of tutor patterns. It took one or two days for some tutor copies (plastic versions) to first appear, a month or more for others (pers. obs.). Presumably, the cultural acquisition of at least the early-appearing tutor patterns was guided by functionally normal, innate neural mechanisms.

Marler (this volume) advises applying "innate" to behavioral *differences*, rather than to behavioral traits, because he sees comparing behavioral differences in genetically different individuals as a method that can both reveal the role of genes and environment in development and also disentangle genes and environment. I agree, and figure 13.5 applies the method. The graphs in figure 13.5 compare differences in the song learning and production of individuals representing five genetically different backgrounds. The comparison shows a clear correlation between different genetic backgrounds and different song development outcomes following exposure to two different tutor songs (social experience). Results from figure 13.5 were used primarily to analyze the genetic side of the song ontogeny question, and this analysis led to the discovery of several new details about the genetic system. Although figure 13.5 does not provide much detail on the process of behavior development itself, the following section, which continues this comparative approach, does focus on some neurobiological outcomes of development.

Combining Genetic and Neurobiological Analyses

The canary has already served as a valuable subject in the neurobiological mapping of the bird brain. But the message of this chapter is that not all canaries are alike genotypically, behaviorally, or neurobiologically. A more powerful tool for future analyses is likely to include comparative studies of genetically different lines. For example, comparing similar neural mechanisms, or neural pathways, in two genetically inbred strains that differ significantly in aspects of sensory learning, song production, or song ontogeny can be done using various canary breeds.

The genetic studies reviewed in this chapter suggest how one might carry out some of these comparative studies. For example, genes for the inheritance of mechanisms for preferentially learning and producing high-pitched, wildtype syllable and tour patterns appear to be sex-linked. Comparing the roller-backcross sons of BR hybrid mothers to those of RB mothers with regard to neural anatomy (e.g., size or organization of brain nuclei like HVC or RA), or the selective responses of song-selective neurons, may lead to discovering differences in specific neural mechanisms underlying heritable, learning preferences.

Another issue is the function of the syrinx, referred to earlier. A study of syringeal laterality in waterschlager, roller, and border canaries may reveal significant differences in unilateral dominance with a waterschlager-border comparison, but perhaps similarities with a waterschlager-roller comparison.

At the molecular level, Mello et al. (1992, 1996) uncovered a molecular genetic response occurring in forebrain neurons. The response is selective as playback of a bird's own song or that of conspecifics initiates a greater level of RNA synthesis by the ZENK or C-jun genes than does hearing alien species songs. This molecular response is thought to function in the processing of auditory input, possibly including memory formation (Mello et al. 1996). As this is a selective response, one might ask if the molecular response is somehow linked to genes of the song learning and development system. Such a link may be discovered through interstrain comparative experiments. Playback of border songs to border and roller canaries conceivably could reveal interstrain differences in ZENK gene activity at the level of RNA synthesis.

Comparative studies have already shed light on the basic question of whether differences in roller and border song learning and/or production is due to central mechanisms or primarily to peripheral effects like partial deafness or to a roller syrinx morphologically incapable of producing high-pitched sounds. Okanoya and Dooling (1985, 1987) compared auditory tuning curves in several strains of canary and other songbirds. Roller and American singer (backcrosses of roller and border hybrids) canaries showed no hearing deficits. The waterschlager strain does show a peripheral hearing deficit (Okanoya and Dooling 1985). This may explain the loudness of that strain's singing, but it is not clear how partial deafness explains its song structure.

Border canaries are large in comparison to roller canaries (border $\bar{X}$ wt. = 35.2 ± 3.1 gm., N = 5 males; roller X wt. = 28.2 ± 4.5 gm., N = 3 males), but this body-size difference does not explain song differences. Wallschlager (1980) quantified a relation between body weight and mean frequency of song for songbirds, with smaller passerine species regularly singing songs with higher mean frequencies than larger songbirds. Border canaries fall in the range of producing songs with mean frequency slightly above 3kHz, which they do (see figure 13.4a). Based on body weight, roller songs are predicted to be slightly higher in mean frequency, but instead song mean frequency is about 1kHz (figure 13.4b). The unusually low-pitched roller song runs counter to a body size related peripheral effect.

A significant difference in nonneural syringeal morphology is a potential cause, but the two genetic studies reviewed in this chapter do not support this view. Tutoring with wild canary songs showed that roller canaries can learn and produce some high-pitched patterns characteristic of the other strain, and that both sides of the roller syrinx are functional on occasion. This, along with the body-size comparison, suggests that the difference in the two strains' songs is not mainly peripheral, but could be due to differences in central mechanisms.

The singing behavior of the roller-backcrosses supports this central mechanism hypothesis. All ten roller-backcrosses learned and reproduced some border imitations, but those with two roller Z-chromosomes produced only a few border imitations, and the high frequency components of these syllables were copied poorly, similar to the production of high-pitched down-slurs imitated by purebred roller canaries tutored with wild canary songs. In contrast, those roller-backcrosses with one border Z-chromosome produced many good border imitations (table 13.1). If roller-backcross syringes are morphologically similar, then the phenotypic difference in behavior between the two backcross groups is most likely due to central mechanism differences.

In summary, the unusual roller song is best explained as due to (1) the loss of the capacity to learn and/or produce high-pitched, border-like patterns that predominate in wild canary songs; and (2) retention and elaboration of the capacity to learn and produce the low-pitched tours that occur naturally in wild canary songs as a minority of the repertoire (compare roller and the roller-like wild canary tours in figure 13.1). The first step in this scenario is supported by the sex-linked results. A modification of the roller Z-chromosome has apparently resulted in the loss, in that strain, of all the relatively high-pitched syllable patterns that predominate in type and wild canary songs. The second step is supported by Güttinger's (1985) comparative analysis of canary song structure in which he found that roller tours are significantly lower in frequency and longer in duration than those of other canary strains. A history of modifying those low-frequency tours by artificial selection, done by roller canary fanciers over several centuries, may have resulted in some minor morphological changes of the roller syrinx (this has yet to be documented), but the primary cause for the unusual roller canary song is more likely due to changes in central mechanisms.

The central mechanism hypothesis, as applied to canaries, considers roller canary tours and at least some of the underlying neural mechanisms of roller canaries as mutant characters. This may have important neurobiological consequences. Recently, mice with point mutations were used to correlate spatial learning deficits with neurophysiological measures at the level of the mutant gene products in hippocampal neurons (see, e.g., Grant et al. 1992; Silva et al. 1992; Tsien et al. 1996). It is certainly conceivable that similar molecular biological analyses will soon be applied to mutant neurons in the song system, neurons that underlie a learned communication system.

References

Alvarez-Buylla, A., Theelen, M., and Nottebohm, F. (1988) Birth of projection neurons in the high vocal center of the canary before, during, and after song learning. *Proc. Nat. Acad. Sci.* 85:8722–8726.

Bickerton, D. (1984) The language bioprogram hypothesis. *Behav. Brain Sci.* 7:173–221.

Brown, J. (1975) *The Evolution of Behavior.* New York: W. W. Norton.

Catchpole, C. K. and Slater, P. J. B. (1995) *Bird Song.* Cambridge: Cambridge University Press.

Chomsky, N. (1975) *Reflections on Language*. New York: Pantheon.

Dooling, R. J. (1982) Auditory perception in birds. In *Acoustic Communication in Birds*, ed. by D. E. Kroodsma and E. H. Miller, pp. 95–130. New York: Academic Press.

Gleich, O., Dooling, R. J., and Presson, J. C. (1997) Evidence for supporting-cell proliferation and hair-cell differentiation in the basilar papilla of adult Belgian waterschalger canaries (*Serinus canaria*). *J. Comp. Neurol.* 377:5–14.

Gottlieb, G. (1992) *Individual Development and Evolution*. New York: Oxford University Press.

Grant, S. G. N., Odell, T. J., Karl, K. A., Stein, P. L., Soriano, P., and Kandel, E. R. (1992) Impaired long term potentiation, spatial learning, and hippocampal development in fyn mutant mice. *Science* 258:1903–1910.

Güttinger, H. R. (1981) Self-differentiation of song organization rules by deaf canaries. *Z. Tierpsychol.* 56:323–340.

Güttinger, H. R. (1985) Consequences of domestication on song structure in the canary. *Behaviour* 94:254–278.

Johnston, T. D. (1988) Developmental explanation and the ontogeny of birdsong: Nature/nurture redux. *Behav. Brain Sci.* 11:617–663.

Kelly, D. B. and Nottebohm, F. (1979) Projections of a telencephalic auditory nucleus—field L—in the canary. *J. Comp. Neurol.* 183:455–470.

Konishi, M. (1965) The role of auditory feedback in the control of vocalization in the white-crowned sparrow. *Z. Tierpsychol.* 22:771–783.

Kroodsma, D. (1984) Songs of the alder flycatcher (*Empidonax alnorum*) and willow flycatcher (*Empidonax traillii*) are innate. *Auk* 101:13–24.

Marler, P. (1959) Developments in the study of animal communication. In *Darwin's Biological Work*, ed. by P. R. Bell, pp. 150–206. New York: John Wiley & Sons.

Marler, P. (1964) Inheritance and learning in the development of animal vocalizations. In *Acoustic Behavior of Animals*, ed. by R. G. Busnel, pp. 228–243. Amsterdam: Elsevier.

Marler, P. (1970) A comparative approach to vocal learning: Song development in white-crowned sparrows. *J. Comp. Physiol. Psychol. Monog.* 71:1–25.

Marler, P. (1976) Sensory templates in species-specific behavior. In *Simpler Networks and Behavior*, ed. by J. C. Fentress, pp. 314–327. Sunderland, MA: Sinauer.

Marler, P. and Sherman, V. (1983) Song structure without auditory feedback: Emendations of the auditory template hypothesis. *J. of Neurosci.* 3:517–531.

Marler, P. and Sherman, V. (1985) Innate differences in singing behavior of sparrows reared in isolation from adult conspecific song. *Anim. Behav.* 33:57–71.

Marler, P. and Waser, M. S. (1977) Role of auditory feedback in canary song development. *J. Comp. & Physiol. Psychol.* 91:8–16.

Mello, C. V., Jarvis, E. D., Denesnko, N., and Rivas, M. (1996) Isolation of song-regulated genes in the brain of songbirds. In *Methods of Molecular Biology*, vol 85, ed. by P. Liang and A. B. Pardee, pp. 205–217. Totowa, NJ: Humana.

Mello, C. V., Vicario, D. S., and Clayton, D. F. (1992) Song presentation induces gene expression in the songbird forebrain. *Proc. Nat. Acad. Sci.* 89:6817–6822.

Mundinger, P. C. (1995) Behaviour-genetic analysis of canary song: Inter-strain differences in sensory learning, and epigenetic rules. *Anim. Behav.* 50:1491–1511.

Nottebohm, F. (1971) Neural lateralization of vocal control in a passerine bird I. Song. *J. Exper. Zool.* 177:229–262.

Nottebohm, F. and Nottebohm, M. (1976) Left hypoglossal dominance in the control of canary and white-crowned sparrow song. *J. Comp. Pysiol.* 108:171–192.

Nottebohm, F., Stokes, T. M., Leonard, C. M. (1976) Central control of song in the canary, *Serinus canarius*. *J. Comp. Neurol.* 165:457–486.

Nottebohm, F., Kelly, D. B., and Paton, J. A. (1982) Connections of vocal control nuclei in the canary telencephalon. *J. Comp. Neurol.* 207:344–357.

Nottebohm, F., Nottebohm, M. E., and Crane, L. (1986) Developmental and seasonal changes in the anatomy of song-control nuclei. *Behav. Neural. Biol.* 46:445–471.

Okanoya, K. and Dooling, R. J. (1985) Colony differences in auditory thresholds in the canary (*Serinus canarius*). *J. Acoust. Soc. Amer.* 78:1170–1175.

Okanoya, K. and Dooling, R. J. (1987) Hearing in passerine and psitticine birds: A comparative study of absolute and masked auditory thresholds. *J. Comp. Psychol.* 101:1–15.

Pinker, S. (1994) *The Language Instinct*. New York: William Morrow & Co.

Rice, M. L. (1996) *Toward a Genetics of Language*. Mahwah: Lawrence Earlbaum Associates.

Shields, G. (1982) Comparative avian cytogenetics: A review. *Condor* 84:45–58.

Silva, A., Payton, R., Wehner, J., and Tonagawa, S. (1992) Impaired spatial learning in alpha calcium calmodulin kinase II mutant mice. *Science* 257:206–211.

Thorpe, W. H. (1958) The learning of song patterns by birds: with special reference to the song of the caffinch (*Fringilla coelebs*). *Ibis* 100:535–570.

Tsien, J. Z., Huerta, P. T., and Tonagawa, S. (1996) The essential role of hippocampal CA1 NMDA receptor dependent synaptic plasticity in spatial memory. *Cell* 87:1327–1338.

Wallschlager, D. (1980) Correlation of song frequency and body weight in passerine birds. *Experientia* 36:412.

Waser, M. S. and Marler, P. (1977) Song learning in canaries. *J. Comp. Physiol. Psychol.* 91:1–7.

14 Production, Usage, and Response in Nonhuman Primate Vocal Development

Robert M. Seyfarth and Dorothy L. Cheney

Over the past thirty-five years, Peter Marler, his students, and colleagues have uncovered striking parallels between the development of speech in human infants and the development of song in birds. Many sparrows, for example, learn their songs more readily during a sensitive period than at other times during development, require practice, and must hear themselves sing for normal song to develop (Marler 1991; Baptista and Petrinovich 1986). These same features characterize both the earliest speech of human infants (see, e.g., Ferguson et al. 1992) and second-language learning, whether spoken or signed, among older individuals (Johnson and Newport 1989). Song production in zebra finches and canaries, like speech production in humans, is under lateralized neural control (Arnold and Bottjer 1985; Nottebohm 1991). Damage to any one of these areas, like damage to Broca's or Wernicke's area in (usually) the left temporal cortex of the human brain (reviewed in Caplan 1987, 1992), produces highly specific deficits in the production or processing of communicative sounds.

As a result of this work, studies of avian song development currently provide the best animal model for research on the mechanisms underlying speech development (Marler 1987). In contrast, although nonhuman primates are our closest living relatives and have often been used as animal models for the study of human social development (see, e.g., Hinde 1984), their vocal communication is generally thought to provide no useful parallels to the development of human speech. This is because, unlike the songs of many birds, the vocalizations of most infant monkeys and apes typically appear fully formed, with the same acoustic features as adults' calls, and seem to undergo relatively little modification in the months and years thereafter (reviewed in Newman and Symmes 1982; Seyfarth 1987; Snowdon 1987, 1988, 1990). It's not that monkeys and apes fail to develop *language*—songbirds don't, either—but that their vocal development seems much more innate and hardwired than the development of either human speech or avian song.

These generalizations, however, are derived exclusively from studies of vocal *production*, which we define here as the delivery of calls with a particular set of acoustic features. By contrast, relatively few studies of either nonhuman primates or birds have focused on two other features of vocal communication: vocal *usage*, defined as the use of particular calls in specific social or ecological circumstances; and the *responses* that animals show to the vocalizations of others. In this paper, we argue that by focusing exclusively on vocal production, comparative studies have highlighted the one area in which human and nonhuman primate vocal development differ most conspicuously and ignored some interesting ways in which they are alike.

To illustrate this point, we review studies of vocal development in vervet monkeys, and we summarize the results of an experiment in which infant rhesus and Japanese macaques were cross-fostered between species. We conclude that in nonhuman primates as in human infants, vocal production, usage, and response develop at different rates and appear to be affected by different social and neurological mechanisms. In both groups, comprehension precedes production; and in both groups, the development of vocal usage includes a period of overgeneralization.

These results allow us to specify more precisely how vocal development in human and nonhuman primates are alike and how they differ. The distinction between production (X vocalizes when he sees a leopard) and response (Y reacts when he hears X's vocalization) is crucial. With regard to vocal production, human and nonhuman primates differ strikingly, because humans, depending on their culture, can learn to produce any of a wide variety of sounds to refer to a particular referent, whereas nonhuman primates are developmentally much more constrained. With regard to responses to vocalizations, however, humans and nonhuman primates are much more alike, because individuals in both groups can learn to associate almost any sound with any external referent.

Vocal Development in Vervet Monkeys

In his doctoral research conducted under Peter Marler's supervision, Tom Struhsaker (1967) described acoustically distinct alarm calls given by East African vervet monkeys (*Cercopithecus aethiops*) to terrestrial carnivores, eagles, and snakes. Each alarm call type, Struhsaker noted, elicited a different, adaptive response from those nearby. When monkeys on the ground heard a leopard alarm call, they ran into trees. Eagle alarm calls caused them to look up into the air or run into a bush, while snake alarm calls caused monkeys to stand on their hind legs and peer into the grass around them. As postdoctoral fellows working with Peter, we were able to demonstrate through playback experiments that these same responses could be elicited by alarm calls alone, even in the absence of actual predators (Seyfarth, Cheney, and Marler 1980).

In addition to their alarm calls, adult vervets grunt to one another in a variety of circumstances. Although these grunts sound very much alike both across contexts and from one individual to the next, field experiments and acoustic analysis have shown that vervets actually produce four different grunt types, each of which elicits a subtly different response from animals nearby (Cheney and Seyfarth 1982; Seyfarth and Cheney 1984b).

Finally, adult vervet monkeys use a distinctive, trilled vocalization called a "wrr" (Cheney and Seyfarth 1988; Hauser 1989) or an "intergroup wrr" (Struhsaker 1967) to signal the presence of another vervet group. Alarm calls, grunts, and wrrs are not the only calls in the vervets' vocal repertoire but they are the vocalizations whose development has been studied in the greatest detail. They are, as a result, the focus of our subsequent sections.

The Development of Vocal Production

To test whether infant vervets (defined as animals younger than 12 months) need "practice" before they can pronounce alarm calls correctly, one would ideally tape-record alarm calls from infants at various ages beginning shortly after birth and examine whether the acoustic properties of these calls become more adult-like over time in ways that could not be explained simply by the maturation of the vocal tract. Such data, however, are difficult to acquire. Young infants rarely give alarm calls, and when they do, their calling is unpredictable and difficult to record on tape. Those alarm calls that have been tape-recorded from infants are acoustically similar to the alarm calls given by adults (Seyfarth and Cheney 1986), which suggests that the production of vervet alarm calls may be largely innate.

Grunts provide a more detailed picture of the development of vocal production because infant vervets begin grunting at high rates from the day they are born. In one respect the production of grunts seems at least partially innate, because the grunts of day-old infants are easily recognizable to human listeners as grunts and not as any of the other calls in the vervets' repertoire. In the fine details of their acoustic features, however, infant grunts differ in many respects from those of adults. Compared with adult grunts, for example, infant grunts are longer, have more acoustic units per call and have longer interunit intervals. As infants grow older, the acoustic features of their grunts gradually come to resemble those of adults (Seyfarth and Cheney 1986). The development of intergroup wrrs is similar to the development of grunts (Hauser 1989).

The Development of Vocal Usage

Vervets in Amboseli, Kenya regularly come into contact with over 150 species of birds and mammals, only some of which pose any danger to them. The monkeys therefore face an intriguing problem in classification: they must learn which species are predators and which are not and, within the former class, which species fall into the categories designated by each of their five different alarm calls. When infant vervets first begin giving alarm calls, they often give alarm calls to harmless species like warthogs, small hawks, or pigeons. The range of species eliciting alarm calls from infants, however, is not entirely random. Infants give leopard alarms only to large, terrestrial animals; eagle alarms to birds or objects, like a falling leaf, that are flying through the air; and snake alarms only to long, snake-like objects (Seyfarth and Cheney 1986). In other words, infants behave as if they are predisposed from birth to divide other species into different classes: predators versus nonpredators and, within the former class, terrestrial carnivores, eagles, and snakes.

This mixture of relatively innate mechanisms and experience in the development of vocal usage is not unique to alarm calls. When infant vervets first begin to grunt, they use many of the acoustically different grunt subtypes found in adult communication. For each of these calls, the relation between grunt type and social situation is imprecise but still not entirely random. Although adults give the "grunt to an animal moving into an open area" only when they themselves or another individual are moving into an open area, infants between one and four months of age use this call as they move into a new area, follow their mothers, or follow a juvenile playmate (Seyfarth and Cheney 1986). Similarly, infant vervets give another type of grunt in a context that can be defined broadly as "distress or the proximity of an unfamiliar conspecific." Over time, this category is further divided to incorporate subtly different grunts for "proximity of a dominant," "proximity of a subordinate," and "proximity of another group." Hauser (1989) describes a similar developmental progression in the vervets' use of intergroup wrrs.

The development of grunts and wrrs illustrates the complex learning that must occur if a young monkey is to begin using vocalizations appropriately. Correct usage requires that an animal distinguish group members from nonmembers and, within the former category, dominant individuals from subordinates. Unlike ground and aerial predators, however, animals in these classes are not grossly different morphologically, and there is considerable evidence that young primates need social experience before they know, for example, which members of their group rank above and below them (see, e.g., Cheney 1977; Berman 1982; Datta 1983).

How, then, do infant vervets develop correct call usage? The most likely answer seems to be through observation and experience. Just as infant monkeys learn their rank by interacting with others and observing interactions in which they are not themselves involved (Berman 1982; Datta 1983; Chapais 1988a,b), so do infants learn which individuals should receive a grunt to a dominant as opposed to a grunt to a subordinate and which should receive an intergroup wrr. In Hauser's (1989) study, infants exposed to higher rates of intergroup encounters (and thus more intergroup wrrs) produced wrrs in the appropriate context at earlier ages than infants who experienced such encounters at lower rates, suggesting that infants do indeed profit from their exposure to adult vocalizations (see also Seyfarth and Cheney 1986).

The Development of Responses to the Calls of Others

Adult vervet monkeys respond differently to different alarm calls. To test whether these responses appear fully developed in infants or are modified during ontogeny, we carried out a series of playback experiments using infants and their mothers as subjects. At monthly intervals, we played to infants aged 3–7 months a leopard alarm call, an eagle alarm call, and a snake alarm call, each originally given by an adult member of their own group. All infants were within 5 meters of their mothers, though not in contact with them, when the alarm calls were played. We divided infants' responses into three categories: (1) run to mother; (2) adult-like responses, defined as the typical responses of juveniles and adults to playbacks of each alarm call type; and (3) "wrong" responses, defined as responses likely to increase the risk of being killed, given the hunting strategy of each predator. For example, since leopards hunt vervets by hiding in bushes and eagles are skilled at taking vervets in trees, running into a bush at the sound of a leopard alarm call or running into a tree at the sound of an eagle alarm call may actually increase an infant's risk of being taken.

Figure 14.1 summarizes the infants' responses. At 3–4 months of age, most infants ran to their mothers. Few showed any adult-like responses. Between 4–6 months of age, running to the mother decreased, and a higher proportion of subjects responded as adults would have under similar circumstances. Many infants, however, also responded in potentially dangerous ways. Among infants over 6 months old, running to the mother was rare, wrong responses declined in frequency, and most infants behaved like adults (Seyfarth and Cheney 1986).

Just as vervets need experience before they can respond appropriately to each others' vocalizations, they require experience before they respond to the calls of other species. For example, vervets in Amboseli are sympatric with a brightly colored songbird, the superb starling (*Spreo superbus*). Like vervets, starlings give acoustically different alarm calls to terrestrial and to avian predators (Cheney and Seyfarth 1990). If adult vervets hear the starling's terrestrial predator alarm call, they often run toward trees; if they hear the starling's avian predator alarm call, they look up in the air (Cheney and Seyfarth 1985). Hauser (1988) noticed that vervet groups living exclusively in dry woodlands hear starling terrestrial predator alarm calls roughly half as often as groups whose territories are closer to swamps. To test whether such differences in exposure affect the age at which infants begin to respond appropriately

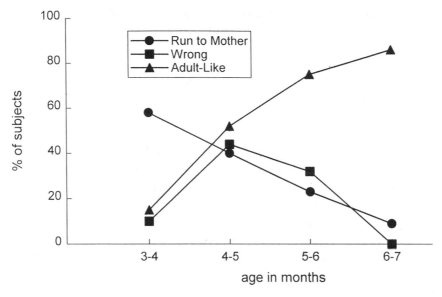

Figure 14.1
The proportion of infant subjects showing different classes of response to playback of alarm calls at different ages. Response classes are defined in the text. Values shown at each age represent mean proportion of subjects. Seven subjects were tested at 3–4 months, for a total of 21 trials; four subjects were retested at 4–5 months (12 trials); and three were retested at 5–6 and 6–7 months (9 trials). For further details see Seyfarth and Cheney 1986.

to starlings' alarm calls, he played starling alarm calls to infants at successively older ages and filmed their responses. Infants living near swamps responded appropriately at significantly earlier ages than did infants inhabiting dry woodlands. Auditory experience seemed to be the crucial variable, since there was no evidence that infants in swamp groups were developmentally more advanced than those living in the woodlands.

Summary

In vervet monkeys, the developmental courses of vocal production, usage, and response are strikingly different. Each component of vocal communication develops at a different rate and is affected by different causal mechanisms. Compared with usage and response, the production of calls appears to be most innate: much of the adult vocal repertoire is recognizable in the calls of even very young infants. In contrast, call usage appears to develop as the result of a mixture of innate mechanisms and experience. Young monkeys seem predisposed from a very early age to use each of their calls in certain broadly defined social or ecological settings, but they require many months before they display the precise relation between call type and social context seen in adult vocalizations. Finally, vervets show no predisposition to respond in particular ways to the different vocalizations of other individuals; instead, their distinctive responses to different call types seem to develop entirely as a result of experience.

Vocal Development in Cross-fostered Macaques

Although field studies of vervet monkeys suggest that the development of vocal production is largely innate, they cannot rule out the possibility that the earliest sounds a monkey makes are influenced by auditory experience, either in the first few weeks after birth or in utero. Moreover, the development of correct call usage and response seems to depend at least partially on an infant's social experience, but it is also possible that social learning is entirely unnecessary; normal development might occur even if adults were absent. Purely observational data do not allow us to specify which cues are necessary and which are sufficient for the emergence of adult-like communication.

Faced with similar observational problems, scientists working on birds have turned to experiments in which individuals are raised in auditory isolation, or reared with tape recorders or live conspecifics as song "tutors." Peter Marler pioneered such experiments, and over the years his work has helped enormously to clarify which components of song production are innate and which depend more upon social and/ or auditory experience (see, e.g., Marler and Sherman 1985). Unfortunately, such tests are difficult to carry out on nonhuman primates. As Harlow's (1958) work was the first to demonstrate, monkeys reared in isolation exhibit many gross social and behavioral abnormalities, including some abnormalities in vocal production (Newman and Symmes 1974). Under such conditions, it is difficult to tell whether abnormal vocal communication results exclusively from an impoverished auditory environment (as seems to be true for birds) or occurs as part of the more general consequences of extreme social deprivation.

In an attempt to overcome the problems created when monkeys are reared in isolation, in 1986 we joined with Michael Owren to begin a study in which infant rhesus (*Macaca mulatta*) and Japanese (*M. fuscata*) macaques were cross-fostered shortly after birth and raised in groups of another species. The goal was to provide infants with a social environment that was almost identical to that of their own species and an acoustic environment that was substantially different from the one they would normally have experienced.

Both Japanese and rhesus macaques use calls (excluding alarm calls) that can be divided into the same general acoustic categories: coos, gruffs, geckers, screams, barks, and creaks (reviewed in Seyfarth and Cheney 1997). Cross-fostered infants would, therefore, physically be capable of producing the same calls as their foster species. However, the frequency with which Japanese and rhesus macaques use each of these six call types differs substantially. Rhesus macaques, for example, tend to use gruffs in the same social contexts that Japanese macaques use coos. As a result, cross-fostered infants would be confronted with social situations in which their own calls would differ markedly from those used by their peers. If these infants adopted their foster species' call types, this would provide evidence of far greater vocal learning than had previously been demonstrated in any nonhuman primate.

The study population consisted of two social groups of each species, housed at the California Regional Primate Research Center. Each of the four groups consisted of a single adult male, four to five adult females, two to five immature offspring, and up to four unrelated immature males. These individuals provided baseline data on the vocal repertoires of adults and on the species-typical course of vocal development in infants and juveniles.

Four infants, two from each species, were fostered from one species to the other during the first week of life. They received normal maternal care, gained weight normally, and were by many behavioral measures fully integrated into their adopted groups (Owren and Dieter 1989; Owren, Seyfarth, and Cheney unpubl. data). To study the development of vocal production and vocal usage, we tape-recorded the calls of all cross-fostered subjects and their normally raised peers during their first two years of life. To study the development of responses to the calls of others, we carried out playback experiments in which cross-fostered and normally raised individuals heard the calls of their mothers and other adult females.

The Development of Vocal Production

We tape-recorded over 3,800 calls from 16 normally raised infants in each of the two species during their first two years and found that over 80% could be classified into one of the six categories described above. The ease with which infants' calls could be sorted into the same categories as those of adults suggests that call production has a substantial innate component. We were, however, particularly interested in the acoustic features of calls produced by cross-fostered infants, since these animals were unable to hear vocalizations from any member of their own species.

Analysis was complicated by the fact that many of the calls given by Japanese and rhesus macaques are acoustically very similar. For example, although the "food coos" produced by rhesus and Japanese macaque infants differed statistically between species and among individuals, they nonetheless showed substantial overlap on every acoustic feature measured (Owren et al. 1992). And while the food coos of adult female rhesus and Japanese macaques were individually distinctive, they showed no species differences.

This extensive overlap between species in the acoustic features of food coos had two unfortunate consequences. First, it meant that cross-fostered subjects had no model for vocal learning that differed substantially from the one they would normally have experienced. Second, similarities in rhesus and Japanese macaque food coos made it difficult for us to determine whether cross-fostered infants adhered to their own species' food coo or modified them to resemble the food coo of their foster species. We turn, then, to research on the developmental of vocal usage, where results were less ambiguous.

The Development of Vocal Usage

Normally raised one- and two-year-old rhesus and Japanese macaques display a striking species difference in call usage. In four well-defined social contexts, Japanese macaques gave coos almost exclusively, while rhesus macaques gave a mixture of coos and gruffs (Owren et al. 1993; Owren and Casale 1994). These species differences provided an excellent opportunity to determine whether cross-fostered infants' call usage was modified as a result of experience. Table 14.1 summarizes the results of a comparison between cross-fostered subjects and (i) normally raised juveniles of their own species, and (ii) normally raised juveniles of their foster species.

Table 14.1
Results of statistical tests comparing the proportion of coos used by cross-fostered (C-F) and normally raised (NR) individuals during their first and second year of life. Reprinted with permission from Owren et al. (1993). $^*p < 0.05$. $^+p < 0.06$.

Year	Context	C-F rhesus macaques tested against:		C-F Japanese macaques tested against:	
		NR rhesus macaques	NR Japanese macaques	NR rhesus macaques	NR Japanese macaques
1	Calm		*	*	
	Cagemate		*	*	
	Play		+	+	
2	Calm	*	+	*	
	Cagemate		*	*	
	Alpha male			+	
	Play	*		*	

Cross-fostered subjects generally adhered to their own rather than their adopted species' call usage. Cross-fostered Japanese macaques rarely used gruffs, even in contexts in which gruffs were commonly given by their foster mothers and other cage-mates. It was not unusual, for example, to see a cross-fostered Japanese macaque giving coos as it played with its rhesus macaque peers, even though the rhesus play-mates were themselves giving gruffs. Cross-fostered rhesus macaques also showed little modification in call usage, though in a few contexts they used coos and gruffs at rates that were intermediate between their own and their foster species (table 14.1).

The lack of modification in the vocal usage of cross-fostered subjects cannot be explained on the basis of species differences in the physiology of sound production, because animals in both species were capable of producing both coos and gruffs. Indeed, the demands placed on cross-fostered subjects to modify their vocal usage were relatively slight: an individual could have acquired its foster species' pattern of vocal usage simply by modifying the rate at which it used calls that were already in its repertoire. On the whole, however, such modifications did not occur.

The cross-fostered animals' failure to modify their vocal usage also cannot be explained as the result of abnormalities in social experience, since by virtually all behavioral measures cross-fostered individuals were fully integrated into their adopted groups. Instead, the evidence from rhesus and Japanese macaques, like the evidence from vervet monkeys, suggests that there is a substantial innate component to the development of vocal usage, and that the development of vocal usage is only partially affected by auditory or social experience.

The Development of Responses to the Calls of Others

Despite their strikingly different use of vocalizations, cross-fostered animals were fully integrated into their adopted social groups. This level of social integration suggests that foster mothers had learned to recognize the calls of their offspring and that cross-fostered infants had learned to identify the calls not only of their mothers but also of groupmates other than their mothers. To test these hypotheses, we conducted playback experiments using as stimuli food coos, coos given in play (called "play coos"), and threat gruffs. Subjects were cross-fostered juveniles, normally raised juveniles, foster mothers, and other adult females. The playback experiments had two aims: to test whether cross-fostered subjects were predisposed to attend preferentially to calls of their own as opposed to those of their foster species; and to determine whether cross-fostered subjects and their mothers had learned to recognize and respond appropriately to each others' vocalizations. The most consistent response to playback was to look in the direction of the speaker.

Responses to Own vs. Adopted Species' Calls Cross-fostered animals' call production and usage were relatively unaffected by auditory experience. If their responses to calls were equally unaffected, they should have reacted more strongly than their foster peers to unfamiliar calls of the cross-fostered animals' own species. To test this hypothesis, each of the four cross-fostered juveniles was played two different food coos given by an unfamiliar juvenile member of its own species. As a control, a normally raised cagemate was played the same calls. Recall that earlier analysis had shown that, despite considerable variation between individuals, the food coos of infant rhesus and Japanese macaques showed a clear species difference (Owren et al. 1992).

There was no difference in the strength with which cross-fostered animals and their normally raised cagemates responded to these playbacks (figure 14.2; Seyfarth and Cheney 1997). There was, as a result, no indication that cross-fostered juveniles had retained a predisposition to attend preferentially to their own rather than their foster species' vocalizations. By contrast, other experiments demonstrated clearly that cross-fostered subjects and their foster mothers had learned to recognize each others' vocalizations. Indeed, if anything, cross-fostered juveniles and their adopted mothers

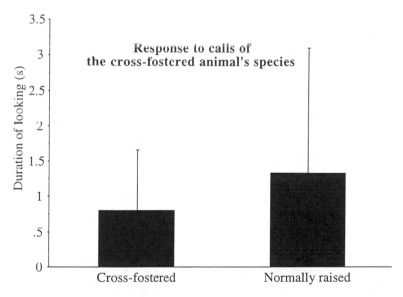

Figure 14.2
Duration of responses shown by cross-fostered (XF) and normally raised (NR) juveniles to playback of food coos given by an unfamiliar member of the cross-fostered animal's own species. Histograms show means and standard deviations.

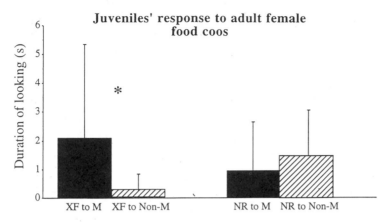

Figure 14.3
Duration of responses shown by cross-fostered (XF) and normally raised (NR) juveniles to playback of food coos given by their mothers and by nonmothers. Legend as in figure 14.2.

responded more strongly to each others' calls than did normally raised juveniles and their mothers.

Responses by Juveniles to Calls of Their Mothers   Cross-fostered juveniles responded more strongly to their mothers' food coos than to the food coos of other adult females, and they also responded more strongly to their mothers' threat gruff (figures 14.3 and 14.4). Normally raised juveniles showed no such bias in response (figures 14.3 and 14.4; Seyfarth and Cheney 1997). The ability of cross-fostered juveniles to distinguish between the threat gruffs of adult females is striking, because the threat gruffs of adult female rhesus and Japanese macaques exhibit a clear species difference (M. J. Owren, unpubl. data). Cross-fostered juveniles therefore learned to recognize individual idiosyncrasies in a call whose acoustic properties differed from the one they would normally have heard.

Responses by Mothers to Calls of Their Offspring   Even more striking was the ability of foster mothers to recognize the calls of their adopted offspring. Unlike other adult females, foster mothers responded more strongly to their adopted offspring's food coos than to the food coos of other juveniles, and, like the mothers of normally raised immatures, foster mothers responded more strongly to their offspring's play calls than to the play calls of other juveniles (figures 14.5 and 14.6; Seyfarth and Cheney 1997). In doing so, however, foster mothers had to learn the individually distinctive features of a call that they would normally not encounter in

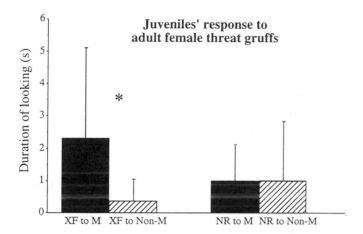

Figure 14.4
Duration of responses shown by cross-fostered (XF) and normally raised (NR) juveniles to playback of threat gruffs given by their mothers and nonmothers. Legend as in figure 14.2.

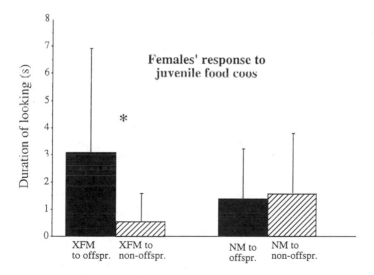

Figure 14.5
Duration of responses shown by the mothers of cross-fostered juveniles (XFM) and the mothers of normally raised juveniles (NM) to playback of food coos given by their offspring and by nonoffspring. Legend as in figure 14.2.

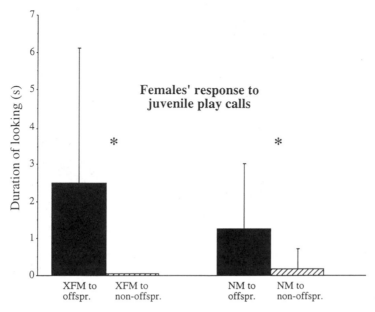

Figure 14.6
Duration of responses shown by the mothers of cross-fostered juveniles (XFM) and the mothers of normally raised juveniles (NM) to playback of play calls given by their offspring and by nonoffspring. Legend as in Fig. 14.2.

these circumstances. Whereas normal rhesus mothers discriminated their offspring's play gruff from the play gruffs of others, foster mothers discriminated their offspring's play *coo* from the play gruffs of others. Similarly, whereas normal Japanese macaque mothers responded more strongly to their offspring's play coo than to the play coos of others, foster mothers responded morestrongly to their offspring's play *gruff* than to the play coos of others. Foster mothers, therefore, learned to recognize their offspring's calls even though they were acoustically different from species-typical calls.

In sum, these experiments provide two sorts of evidence in support of the view that monkeys' responses to the calls of others depend strongly upon experience. First, cross-fostered juvenile macaques show no tendency to respond preferentially to calls of their own as opposed to their adopted species. Second, both juvenile and adult macaques can learn to recognize and respond selectively to individual idiosyncrasies in the calls of animals from another species. At least partly as a result, cross-fostered infants are able to develop bonds with their foster mothers that are as close as the bonds formed between normally raised infants and their mothers.

Summary

Compared with field research on vervet monkeys, cross-fostering experiments use an entirely different technique to study vocal development. Nonetheless, they yield similar results. Just as field observations suggest that vocal production in vervets is largely innate, cross-fostering experiments indicate that the acoustic features of macaque food coos are only slightly altered, if at all, when animals are raised in an auditory environment different from the one they would normally experience. Moreover, just as field observations reveal a predisposition among vervets to use particular vocalizations in specific social or ecological circumstances, cross-fostering experiments show that macaques are strongly predisposed to use particular calls in specific social situations. This predisposition is modified only slightly, if at all, during development. Finally, just as field observations demonstrate that vervets' responses to calls, including the calls of other species, are modified as a result of experience, cross-fostering experiments indicate that macaques, too, can learn to recognize and respond selectively to a wide variety of unfamiliar auditory stimuli.

Comparison with Other Primates

The studies reviewed above suggest that at least three general features characterize the development of vocal communication in nonhuman primates. First, vocal development is the result of three separate processes: the development of production, usage, and response to the calls of others. Second, different causal mechanisms underlie each of these processes. Third, because they are affected by different causal mechanisms, the three components of vocal development emerge in young animals at different rates.

To test the generality of these conclusions, we examined data from 34 studies of 11 other primate species and divided them according to whether they dealt with production, usage, or response. In each case, we considered whether the component(s) of vocal communication under study (1) appeared fully formed at a very early age and subsequently showed little or no change as animals grew older; (2) appeared initially in a form that was different from that of adults but shared some adult-like features, and subsequently showed gradual modification toward the adult pattern as animals grew older; or (3) appeared initially in a form that exhibited few if any adult-like features, and subsequently showed substantial modification toward the adult pattern as individuals grew older. Table 14.2 presents the results of arranging studies in this way.

Table 14.2

	Adult-like, no modification during development	Broadly adult-like, some modification during development	No resemblance to adults, substantial modification during development
Vocal production	Squirrel monkeys: all calls (1–5) Spider monkeys: all vocalizations (6) Cotton-top tamarins: long calls (7) Pygmy marmosets: J-calls (7) Talapoin monkeys: all calls (8) Rhesus macaques: all calls (10, 11) Japanese macaques: all calls (10, 11) Stumptail macaques: chirps, geckers, screams (26) Vervets: alarm calls (13) Gibbons: great calls (25, 29)	Marmosets and tamarins: chirps and long calls (14) Pygmy marmosets: trills (7, 15, 31), chirps (7), J-calls (15) Tamarins: long calls (16) Japanese macaques: food coos (17) Rhesus macaques: "contact calls" (9), food coos (18) Pigtail macaques: screams (17, 18, 36) Vervets: grunts (13), wrrs (30) Chimpanzees: pant-hoots (34) Bonobos: various calls (32)	
Vocal usage		Cotton-top tamarins: long calls (14), alarm calls (33) Cotton-top tamarins: C- and D-chirps (28) Japanese macaques: 'uh' call (27), coos (11) Rhesus macaques: coos, gruffs (11) Pigtail macaques: screams (19, 20) Vervets: alarm calls (12, 13, 21), grunts (13), wrrs (30) Chimpanzees: pant hoots (35)	
Responses to the calls of others			Goeldi's monkeys: alarm calls (22) Japanese macaques: food coos, gruffs (10, 23) Japanese macaques: alarm calls (24) Rhesus macaques: food coos, gruffs (10) Vervets: alarm calls (13)

A classification of 34 studies of vocal development in 14 nonhuman primate species, divided according to whether they dealt with vocal production, usage, or response, and according to whether they found that call development was adult-like at first emergence, with virtually no modification during development, broadly similar to adults at first emergence with some limited modification during development, or exhibited no resemblance to adults at first emergence and showed substantial modification during development.

Vocal Production

Taken together, the data from nonhuman primates provide a strong case for vocal production that is either wholly or in large part genetically fixed at birth. By contrast, vocal production in humans and many songbirds is so labile that the earliest communicative sounds by infants can, and often do, include noises that are seldom given by adults. Avian subsong, for example, often "bears little or no resemblance to natural adult song" and unlike mature song "is often similar across species" (Marler 1990, p. 13). Similarly, although the babbling sounds of human infants "are highly structured and a large proportion are clearly phonetically related to human speech," human infants also produce many communicative sounds that are not obviously early versions of what will later become speech (Oller 1981, p. 85; see also Kent 1981). Some authors (e.g., Kawabe 1973; Takeda 1965, 1966) describe similarly unconstrained babbling in nonhuman primate infants, but at present there is not much quantitative spectrographic data to support such assertions. No monkey or ape has thus far demonstrated as much flexibility in the ontogeny of vocal production as is evident in humans or many songbirds.

Vocal Usage

Comparative research suggests that completely innate vocal usage is unlikely to be found in any animal species. The history of ethology includes many patterns of behavior, like the pecking response of a herring gull chick to the red spot on its mother's beak (Hailman 1969) or the feeding and begging behaviors of ring doves (Lehrman 1972; Klinghammer and Hess 1972), which were originally thought to involve an innate response to one specific, narrowly defined stimulus but which were eventually shown to require at least some learning or experience on the part of young animals (reviewed in Gould 1982). Given the preponderance of such results, it is not surprising that we were unable to find any examples of rigidly fixed, innate vocal usage among nonhuman primates.

Key to references: (1) Winter et al. 1973; (2) Talmadge-Riggs et al. 1972; (3) Lieblich et al. 1980; (4) Symmes et al. 1979; (5) Hertzog, Hopf 1984; (6) Eisenberg 1978; (7) Snowdon 1987; (8) Gautier 1974; (9) Newman, Symmes 1974; (10) Owren et al. 1992; (11) Owren et al. 1993; (12) Seyfarth, Cheney 1980; (13) Seyfarth, cheney 1986; (14) Snowdon et al. 1985; (15) Elowson et al. 1991; (16) Hodun et al. 1981; (17) Green 1975b; (18) Hauser 1992; (19) Gouzoules, Gouzoules 1989a; (20) Gouzoules, Gouzoules 1989b; (21) Brown et al. 1992; (22) Masataka 1983a; (23) Masataka 1985; (24) Masataka 1983b; (25) Brockelman, Schilling 1984; (26) Chevalier-Skolnikoff 1974; (27) Green 1981; (28) Roush, Snowdon 1994; (29) Tenaza 1985; (30) Hauser 1989; (31) Elowson, Snowdon 1994; (32) Hopkins, Savage-Rumbaugh 1991; (33) Heymann 1990; (34) Mitani, Brandt 1994; (35) Pusey 1990; Gouzoules, Gouzoules in press (36).

There are other, more functional reasons that we should not expect primate vocal usage to be fixed and adult-like at first emergence. To begin with, environments change, and animals that use calls to signal about features of their environment must be able to adjust accordingly. Vervet monkeys in Amboseli are preyed upon by only two species of eagle, the crowned eagle and the martial eagle, whose feathers are largely white when seen from below (Seyfarth and Cheney 1980, 1986). In contrast, vervets in Zimbabwe, Botswana, and South Africa are also preyed upon by Verreaux's eagle (*Aquila verreauxi*), whose feathers are largely black (Gargett 1971). The distribution of these raptors, however, is not clear-cut. Martial and crowned eagles can be found in southern Africa, and Verreaux's eagles can be found in the more mountainous areas of eastern Africa. Under these conditions, vervets clearly benefit by using alarm calls that, though closely tied to a particular class of referents (large raptors that are primarily white when seen from below), can nonetheless be modified to include new and physically different exemplars within each class (Marler 1977 makes a similar point with reference to birds).

Many other primate vocalizations are given only to particular individuals, like a frequent grooming partner (Smith et al. 1982), or only to particular individuals in specific circumstances (e.g., to lower-ranking animals during aggression without physical contact; Gouzoules et al. 1984). In such cases, it would obviously be impossible for selection to favor innate vocal usage, since infants require time and experience before they develop close associations and learn who is higher- or lower-ranking than they are.

Given the physiological impossibility of innate vocal usage and the obvious functional advantages of a flexible relation between call and referent (or call and social context), the tendency of young, inexperienced monkeys to use specific calls in particular social contexts is striking. Studies by Snowdon and colleagues on pygmy marmosets (Snowdon 1987; Snowdon, Elowson, and Roush 1997) provide currently the only case in which calls by infants were used in a way that was entirely random with respect to social context and thus showed no relation whatever to adult vocal usage. In contrast, most other primates, when confronted with a novel or unexpected situation, use a call that maintains the existing relation in their repertoire between call type and social context. Captive vervet monkeys living in southern California leave the closed, indoor part of their cages each morning as soon as a technician has opened the door to their outside arena. As they move through this door they give the same vocalization that east African vervets given when moving out onto an open savanna (Seyfarth and Cheney, unpubl. data).

In sum, nonhuman primate infants seem predisposed from birth to use different vocalizations in particular, broadly defined social or ecological circumstances. This partially innate development of vocal usage undoubtedly allows young animals to communicate more effectively with adults than they would if the relation between call type and social context were entirely random. Over time, through a process that is not yet well understood, young animals sharpen the relation between call type and social context. Such gradual development is essential in species where animals give different calls to different individuals, and where infants need time before they can recognize others and learn about their own social position. The development of vocal usage in primates may reflect a compromise between the evolutionary advantages of completely innate and entirely learned communication.

Responses to the Calls of Others

By the time they have reached one year of age, monkeys respond in predictably different ways to the calls of others. Some of these responses depend on the call's acoustic properties: alarm calls elicit flight, screams and grunts elicit vigilance, intergroup calls draw animals to the source of the vocalization. Responses also depend crucially, however, on the identity of the caller. Territorial gibbons (*Hylobates*) and titi monkeys (*Callicebus moloch*) respond more strongly to the calls of a strange male from a border area than to the calls of a neighbor (Mitani 1990; Robinson 1981). Female vervets and macaques respond more strongly to their offspring's scream than to the scream of an unrelated juveniles (Cheney and Seyfarth 1980; Gouzoules et al. 1984). Among vervets, the threat vocalization of an unrelated animal is generally ignored unless that animal has recently groomed with the listener, in which case the listener responds more strongly (Seyfarth and Cheney 1984a). Female baboons (*Papio cynocephalus*) typically ignore grunts from an unrelated animal, but if that individual has recently behaved aggressively toward the listener the grunt acts to reconcile the two animals, restoring their relationship to its earlier condition (Cheney et al. 1995; Cheney and Seyfarth in press).

Nonhuman primates thus live in groups where the most adaptive responses to vocalizations can only emerge after considerable social experience. Young animals must learn who are members of their group and who are not, which individuals are their close associates (generally matrilineal kin) and which are not, where they themselves stand in a dominancehierarchy, and who has interacted with them in a friendly or aggressive way in the recent past. Under these circumstances it is not surprising that natural selection has not favored a fixed, unmodifiable link between hearing a vocalization and responding to it.

The relatively greater developmental flexibility in response to calls as opposed to call production and call usage is perhaps most clearly demonstrated in the study of cross-fostered rhesus and Japanese macaques (see above). These individuals continued to produce their own species' calls and use them in species-typical social contexts, but they showed much greater flexibility in their ability to learn the vocalizations of another species and to recognize the calls of their foster mothers.

Discussion

Production and Perception

Consider a sequence that is typical of many communicative events in group-living animals: one animal responds to a stimulus by giving a vocalization and a second animal reacts to that vocalization with a response. X sees an eagle and gives an eagle alarm; Y hears the alarm call and looks up in the air. The results we review here suggest that although X's calling and Y's response combine to create a smoothly integrated system in the daily lives of adult primates, these two components of communication differ markedly in their development and in the extent to which they can be modified through experience.

As an illustration, consider the following thought experiment. Suppose we used a motorized robot to present vervet monkeys with a novel predator, one they had never seen before. As long as the vervets could escape from the beast by using one of their standard responses—run up a tree, run into a bush, or stand on their hind legs and peer into the grass—all would be well. They would simply use one of their existing alarm calls to signal the appropriate information. As far as the vervets were concerned, the new predator, whatever it looked like, would "be" a leopard if it could be evaded by running up a tree, an eagle if it could be evaded by running into a bush, and so on.

But suppose the monkeys could elude this new predator only by making a novel escape response—say, by burrowing underground. They would then need to invent a new, acoustically different alarm call, and results suggest that this would be extremely difficult. Apparently, nonhuman primates are born with a fairly fixed repertoire of sounds and with a fairly strong predisposition to use specific acoustic signals in particular circumstances. One suspects that many vervets—even many generations of vervets—would die before a new call, signaling a novel escape response, could be incorporated into their repertoire.

Ironically, however, the vervets' problem would be solved if in addition to introducing a robot predator, we also introduced into the vervet group a robot vervet that produced a novel sound—a wailing siren, for example—whenever the new predator appeared; one thing that vervets and other primates *can* do is learn to associate a novel auditory stimulus with a specific sort of danger and perform a specific response. Monkeys in the wild do this, for example, when they learn about the alarm calls of birds, and they do it in captivity when they learn to recognize the voices of their trainers coming down the hall or the jangling of keys that mean they are about to be fed.

In this sense, vervet monkeys and other nonhuman primates seem to live in a world with a kind of half-language: fixed, constrained, and relatively immune to modification by experience when it comes to production, but modifiable, open-ended, and potentially creative when it comes to learning about and responding to the calls of others.

Comparisons with Language Learning

Where, then, does this leave us in our attempt to compare nonhuman primate vocal communication with human language and use the calls of monkeys as apes as model systems for the study of human speech? The answer is not a simple one, but depends upon which feature of communication is under scrutiny.

Clearly, some features of human language are strikingly different from the vocal communication of nonhuman primates. Despite many heroic efforts, there is no evidence that either the natural vocalizations of monkeys and apes or the artificial "languages" taught to chimpanzees possess the kind of generative grammar found in all human languages (Robinson 1981; compare Greenfield and Savage-Rumbaugh 1991 with Pinker 1994).

A similar dichotomous distinction is apparent when we consider certain aspects of vocal production and vocal usage. Human infants and children can produce, voluntarily, an extraordinary variety of sounds, and which sound they link with a particular referent depends entirely upon their auditory and social experience. By contrast, although nonhuman primates can readily learn, through experience, to deliver or withhold vocalizations according to the circumstances, once the eliciting stimulus is known, the acoustic features of the call that is produced by the members of a given species are highly predictable, regardless of the animal's auditory or social experience. In other words, the delivery of calls is voluntary, but the link between a call's acoustic features and its putative referent is highly constrained. This relatively rigid development of vocal production and usage clearly distinguishes nonhuman primate vocal development from that found in certain songbirds—like the catbird, for example—that can learn to imitate almost any other avian species, and it may also distinguish nonhuman primates from the many songbird species that do not normally learn the song of another species but do preferentially learn the dialect of their own species' song to which they were exposed at an early age.

In other respects, however, vocal development in nonhuman primates and human children share some important features. For example, in both groups, vocal production, usage, and response follow different developmental trajectories and become fully adult at different ages. In both groups, comprehension precedes production. These observations prompt us to speculate that different neural mechanisms underlie the development of comprehension and production in both human and nonhuman primates, and that properly focused studies of brain function and communication in monkeys could be used as model systems for research on human language development.

Similarly, in both human and nonhuman primates the development of vocal usage includes a period of "overgeneralization." Children use *dada* to refer to any adult male; infant vervet monkeys give an eagle alarm when they see any flying object. In studies of children's linguistic and cognitive development, considerable debate focuses on whether overgeneralization arises because objects are grouped together based on shared function (all toys [Nelson 1973]), shared features (all round objects [Clark 1973]), or based on some shared resemblance to a prototype that serves as a model for a particular concept (all birds are birds to the extent that they resemble robins [see, e.g., Anglin 1977]). The overgeneralization found in nonhuman primates provides an opportunity to test whether any of these hypotheses applies to a creature that will not eventually develop language.

Finally, results suggest that the development of communication in human and nonhuman primates is most alike in the area of response to signals. Nonhuman primates, like human children, seem capable of forming some kind of association between almost any auditory stimulus and any external referent. This shared, apparently open-ended ability to form sound-meaning associations raises two questions.

First, to what extent does this ability arise because of learning mechanisms common to all organisms? After all, a vervet monkey's ability to form an association between, for example, a starling's eagle alarm and particular avian predators is highly reminiscent of Pavlovian experiments in which rats, pigeons, and even aplysia learn to associate lights or tones with food. One is tempted to conclude that similar processes are at work (Seyfarth and Cheney 1997). But once again, children are clearly different: Pavlovian conditioning might conceivably explain the earliest, one-word stages of vocabulary acquisition, but after their first year, children begin adding to their vocabulary at the extraordinary rate of one new word every two hours, at least through adolescence (Pinker 1994). Pavlovian processes alone are unlikely to explain this sudden surge in vocabulary.

Second, given that both the openness and the developmental course of responses to vocal signals are similar in human and nonhuman primates, can we also conclude that similar *cognitive* processes are involved? Or are the parallels we have uncovered in this feature of communicative development merely superficial resemblances? Do monkeys understand that a particular sound "means" leopard in the same way that a one-year-old understands that a particular word means book, chair, or dessert? The question is complex, and cannot be answered here or anywhere else at the moment. Finding an answer is important, however, because it will have much to say about whether there are any genuine similarities between the cognitive processes that underlie human language development and the ontogeny of primate communication.

Acknowledgments

Research on vervet monkeys was supported by NSF, the Wenner-Gren Foundation, the Harry Frank Guggenheim Foundation, and the Research Foundation of the University of Pennsylvania; research on rhesus and Japanese macaques was supported by NIH and the University of Pennsylvania.

References

Anglin, J. M. (1977) *Word, Object, and Concept Development.* New York: W. W. Norton.

Arnold, A. P. and Bottjer, S. (1985) Cerebral lateralization in birds. In *Cerebral Lateralization in Nonhuman Species*, ed. by S. D. Glick. New York: Academic Press.

Baptista, L. F. and Petrinovich, L. (1986) Song development in the white-crowned sparrow: Social factors and sex differences. *Anim. Behav.* 34:1359–1371.

Berman, C. M. (1982) The ontogeny of social relationships with group companions among free-ranging infant rhesus monkeys. I. Social networks and differentiation. *Anim. Behav.* 30:149–162.

Brockelman, Y. and Schilling, D. (1984) Inheritance of stereotyped gibbon calls. *Nature* 312:634–636.

Brown, M. M., Kreiter, N. A., Maple, J. T., and Sinnott J. M. (1992) Silhouettes elicit alarm calls from captive vervet monkeys (*Cercopithecus aethiops*). *J. Comp. Psych.* 106:350–359.

Caplan, D. (1987) *Neurolinguistics and Linguistic Aphasiology.* Cambridge: Cambridge University Press.

Caplan, D. (1992) *Language: Structure, Processing, and Disorders.* Cambridge, MA: MIT Press.

Chapais, B. (1988a) Experimental matrilineal inheritance of rank in female Japanese macaques. *Anim. Behav.* 36:1025–1037.

Chapais, B. (1988b) Rank maintenance in female Japanese macaques: Experimental evidence for social dependency. *Behaviour* 104:41–59.

Cheney, D. L. (1977) The acquisition of rank and the development of reciprocal alliances among free-ranging immature baboons. *Behav. Ecol. Sociobiol.* 2:303–318.

Cheney, D. L. and Seyfarth, R. M. (1980) Vocal recognition in free-ranging vervet monkeys. *Anim. Behav.* 28:362–367.

Cheney, D. L. and Seyfarth, R. M. (1982) How vervet monkeys perceive their grunts: Field playback experiments. *Anim. Behav.* 30:739–751.

Cheney, D. L. and Seyfarth, R. M. (1985) Social and non-social knowledge in vervet monkeys. In *Animal Intelligence*, ed. by L. Weiskrantz. Oxford: Clarendon Press.

Cheney, D. L. and Seyfarth, R. M. (1988) Assessment of meaning and the detection of unreliable signals by vervet monkeys. *Anim. Behav.* 36:477–486.

Cheney, D. L. and Seyfarth, R. M. (1990) *How Monkeys See the World.* Chicago: University of Chicago Press.

Cheney, D. L. and Seyfarth, R. M. (1997) Reconciliatory grunts by dominant female baboons influence victims' behaviour. *Anim. Behav.* 54, 409–418.

Cheney, D. L., Seyfarth, R. M., and Silk, J. B. (1995) The role of grunts in reconciling opponents and facilitating interactions among adult female baboons. *Anim. Behav.* 50:249–257.

Chevalier-Skolnikoff, S. (1974) The ontogeny of communication in the stumptailed macaque (*Macaca arctoides*). *Cont. Primatol.* 2:1–174.

Clark, E. (1973) What's in a word? On the child's acquisition of semantics in his first language. In *Cognitive Development and the Acquisition of Language*, ed. by T. E. Moore. New York: Academic Press.

Datta, S. (1983) Relative power and the acquisition of rank. In *Primate Social Relationships*, ed. by R. A. Hinde. Oxford: Blackwell Scientific.

Eisenberg, J. F. (1978) Communication mechanisms in New World primates with special reference to vocalizations in the black spider monkey (*Ateles fusciceps robustus*). In *Aggression, Dominance, and Individual Spacing*, ed. by L. Krames, P. Pliner, and T. Alloway. New York: Plenum Press.

Elowson, M. and Snowdon, C. T. (1994) Pygmy marmosets, *Cebuella pygmaea*, modify vocal structure in response to changed social environment. *Anim. Behav.* 47:1267–1277.

Elowson, M., Tannenbaum, P. L., and Snowdon, C. T. (1991) Food associated calls correlate with food preferences in cotton-top tamarins. *Anim. Behav.* 42:931–937.

Ferguson, C., Menn, L., and Stoel-Gammon, C. (1992) *Phonological Development.* Toronto: York Press.

Gargett, V. (1971) Some observations on black eagles in the Matopos, Rhodesia. *Ostrich* (Suppl.) 9:91–124.

Gautier, J. P. (1974) Field and laboratory studies of the vocalizations of talapoin monkeys (*Miopithecus talapoin*). *Behaviour* 51:209–273.

Gould, J. L. (1982) *Ethology: The Mechanisms and Evolution of Behavior.* New York: W. W. Norton.

Gouzoules, H. and Gouzoules, S. (1989a) Design features and developmental modification of pigtail macaque, *Macaca nemestrina*, agonistic screams. *Anim. Behav.* 37:383–401.

Gouzoules, H. and Gouzoules, S. (1989b) Sex differences in the acquisition of communicative competence by pigtail macaques (*Macaca nemestrina*). *Am. J. Primatol.* 19:163–174.

Gouzoules, H. and Gouzoules, S. (1995) Recruitment screams of pigtail monkeys (*Macaca nemestrina*): Ontogenetic perspectives. *Behaviour* 132, 431–450.

Gouzoules, S., Gouzoules, H., and Marler, P. (1984) Rhesus monkey (*Macaca mulatta*) screams: Representational signalling in the recruitment of agonistic aid. *Anim. Behav.* 32:182–193.

Green, S. (1975b) Dialects in Japanese monkeys: Vocal learning and cultural transmission of locale-specific vocal behavior? *Z. Tierpsychol.* 38:304–314.

Green, S. (1981) Sex differences and age gradations in vocalizations of Japanese and lion-tailed monkeys (*Macaca fuscata* and *Macaca silenus*). *Am. Zool.* 21:165–183.

Greenfield, P. M. and Savage-Rumbaugh, E. S. (1991) Imitation, grammatical development, and invention of protogrammar by an ape. In *Biological and Behavioral Determinants of Language Development*, ed. by N. Krasnegor, D. M. Rumbaugh, M. Studdert-Kennedy, and D. Scheifelbusch. Hillsdale, NJ: Lawrence Erlbaum.

Hailman, J. (1969) The ontogeny of an instinct. *Behaviour* (Suppl.) 15:1–159.

Harlow, H. F. (1958) The nature of love. *Am. Psychol.* 13:673–685.

Hauser, M. D. (1988) How infant vervet monkeys learn to recognize starling alarm calls: The role of experience. *Behaviour* 105:187–201.

Hauser, M. D. (1989) Ontogenetic changes in the comprehension and production of vervet monkey (*Cercopithecus aethiops*) vocalizations. *J. Comp. Psych.* 103:149–158.

Hauser, M. D. (1992) Articulatory and social factors influence the acoustic structure of rhesus monkey vocalizations: A learned mode of production? *J. Acoust. Soc. Am.* 91:2175–2179.

Herzog, M. and Hopf, S. (1984) Behavioral responses to species-specific warning calls in infant squirrel monkeys reared in social isolation. *Am. J. Primatol.* 7:99–106.

Heymann, E. W. (1990) Reactions of wild tamarins, *Saguinas mystax* and *Saguinas fuscicollis*, to avian predators. *Int. J. Primatol.* 11:327–337.

Hinde, R. A. (1984) Biological bases of the mother-child relationship. In *Frontiers of Infant Psychiatry*, vol. 2, ed. by J. Call, E. Galensen, and R. L. Tyson. New York: Basic Books.

Hodun, A., Snowdon, C. T., and Soini, P. (1981) Subspecific variation in the long calls of the tamarin, Saguinas fuscicollis. *Z. Tierpsychol.* 57:97–110.

Hopkins, W. D. and Savage-Rumbaugh, E. S. (1991) Vocal communication as a function of differential rearing experiences in *Pan paniscus*: A preliminary report. *Int. J. Primatol.* 12:559–584.

Johnson, J. and Newport, E. (1989) Critical period effects in second language learning: The influence of maturational state on the acquisition of English as a second language. *Cog. Psych.* 21:61–99.

Kawabe, S. (1973) Development of vocalization and behavior of Japanese macaques. In *Behavioral Regulators of Behavior in Primates*, ed. by R. Carpenter. Lewisburg, PA: Associated Universities Press.

Kent, R. D. (1981) Articulatory-acoustic perspectives on speech development. In *Language Behavior in Infancy and Early Childhood*, ed. by R. E. Stark. Amsterdam: Elsevier.

Klinghammer, E. and Hess, E. (1972) Parental feeding in ring doves (*Streptopelia roseogrisea*): Innate or learned? In *Control and Development of Behavior: An Historical Sample from the Pens of Ethologists*, ed. by P. H. Klopfer and J. H. Hailman. New York: Addison-Wesley.

Lehrman, D. (1972) The physiological basis of parental feeding in the ring dove (*Streptopelia risoria*). In *Control and Development of Behavior: An Historical Sample from the Pens of Ethologists*, ed. by P. H. Klopfer and J. H. Hailman. New York: Addison-Wesley.

Lieblich, A. K., Symmes, D., Newman, J. D., and Shapiro, M. (1980) Development of the isolation peep in laboratory-bred squirrel monkeys. *Anim. Behav.* 28:1–9.

Marler, P. (1977) Development and learning of recognition systems. In *Recognition of Complex Acoustic Signals*, ed. by T. H. Bullock. Berlin: Dahlem Konferenzen.

Marler, P. (1987) Sensitive periods and the role of specific ands general sensory stimulation in birdsong learning. In *Imprinting and Cortical Plasticity*, ed. by J. P. Rauschecker and P. Marler. New York: John Wiley and Sons.

Marler, P. (1990) Innate learning preferences: Signals for communication. *Dev. Psychobiol.* 23:557–568.

Marler, P. (1991) The instinct for vocal learning: songbirds. In *Plasticity of Development*, ed. by H. S. Hall and R. J. Dooling. Cambridge, MA: MIT Press.

Marler, P. and Sherman, V. (1985) Innate differences in singing behavior of sparrows reared in isolation from adult conspecific song. *Anim. Behav.* 33:57–71.

Masataka, N. (1983a) Psycholinguistic analyses of alarm calls of Japanese monkeys (*Macaca fuscata*). *Am. J. Primatol.* 5:111–125.

Masataka, N. (1983b) Categorical responses to natural and synthesized alarm calls in Goeldi's monkeys (*Callimico goeldi*). *Primates* 24:40–51.

Masataka, N. (1985) Development of vocal recognition of mothers in infant Japanese monkeys. *Dev. Psychobiol.* 18:107–114.

Mitani, J. C. (1990) Experimental field studies of Asian ape social systems. *Int. J. Primatol.* 11:103–126.

Mitani, J. C. and Brandt, K. L. (1994) Social factors influence the acoustic variability in the long-distance calls of male chimpanzees. *Ethology* 96:233–252.

Nelson, K. (1973) Structure and strategy in learning to talk. *Monographs of the Society for Research in Child Development*, serial no. 149.

Newman, J. and Symmes, D. (1974) Vocal pathology in socially deprived monkeys. *Dev. Psychobiol.* 7:351–358.

Newman, J. and Symmes, D. (1982) Inheritance and experience in the acquisition of primate acoustic behavior. In *Primate Communication*, ed. by C. T. Snowdon, C. H. Brown, and M. H. Petersen. Cambridge: Cambridge University Press.

Nottebohm, F. (1991) Reassessing the mechanisms and origins of vocal learning in birds. *TINS* 14:206–211.

Oller, D. K. (1981) Infant vocalizations: Exploration and reflexivity. In *Language Behavior in Infancy and Early Childhood*, ed. by R. E. Stark. Amsterdam: Elsevier.

Owren, M. J. and Casale, T. M. (1994) Variation in fundamental frequency peak position in Japanese macaque (*Macaca fuscata*) coo calls. *J. Comp. Psych.* 108:291–297.

Owren, M. J. and Dieter, J. A. (1989) Infant cross-fostering between Japanese (*Macaca fuscata*) and rhesus macaques (*Macaca mulatta*). *Am. J. Primatol.* 18:245–250.

Owren, M. J., Dieter, J. A., Seyfarth, R. M., and Cheney, D. L. (1992) "Food" calls produced by adult female rhesus (*Macaca mulatta*) and Japanese (*M. fuscata*) macaques, their normally raised offspring, and offspring cross-fostered between species. *Behaviour* 120:218–231.

Owren, M. J., Dieter, J. A., Seyfarth, R. M., and Cheney, D. L. (1993) Vocalizations of rhesus (*Macaca mulatta*) and Japanese (*M. fuscata*) macaques cross-fostered between species show evidence of only limited modification. *Dev. Psychobiol.* 26:389–406.

Pinker, S. (1994) *The Language Instinct*. New York: W. W. Morrow.

Pusey, A. E. (1990) Behavioral changes at adolescence in chimpanzees. *Behaviour* 115:203–246.

Robinson, J. G. (1981) Vocal regulation of inter- and intragroup spacing during boundary encounters in the titi monkey, *Callicebus moloch*. *Primates* 22:161–172.

Roush, R. S. and Snowdon, C. T. (1994) Ontogeny of food associated calls in cotton-top tamarins. *Anim. Behav.* 47:263–273.

Seyfarth, R. M. (1987) Vocal communication and its relation to language. In *Primate Societies*, ed. by B. B. Smuts, D. L. Cheney, R. M. Seyfarth, R. W. Wrangham, and T. T. Struhsaker. Chicago: University of Chicago Press.

Seyfarth, R. M. and Cheney, D. L. (1980) The ontogeny of vervet monkey alarm calling behavior: A preliminary report. *Z. Tierpsychol.* 54:37–56.

Seyfarth, R. M. and Cheney, D. L. (1984a) Grooming, alliances, and reciprocal altruism in vervet monkeys. *Nature* 308:541–543.

Seyfarth, R. M. and Cheney, D. L. (1984b) The acoustic features of vervet monkey grunts. *J. Acoust. Soc. Am.* 75:1623–1628.

Seyfarth, R. M. and Cheney, D. L. (1986) Vocal development in vervet monkeys. *Anim. Behav.* 34:1640–1658.

Seyfarth, R. M. and Cheney, D. L. (1997) Some general features of vocal development in nonhuman primates. In *Social Influences on Vocal Development* (Ed. M. Husberger and C. T. Snowdon), pp. 249–273. Cambridge: Cambridge University Press.

Seyfarth, R. M. and Cheney, D. L. (1997) Behavioral mechanisms underlying vocal communication in nonhuman primates. *Anim. Learn. Behav.* 25, 249–267.

Seyfarth, R. M., Cheney, D. L., and Marler, P. (1980) Vervet monkey alarm calls: Semantic communication in a free-ranging primate. *Anim. Behav.* 28:1070–1094.

Smith, H. J., Newman, J. D. and Symmes, D. (1982) Vocal concomitants of affiliative behavior in squirrel monkeys. In *Primate Communication*, ed. by C. T. Snowdon, C. H. Brown, and M. H. Petersen. Cambridge: Cambridge University Press.

Snowdon, C. T. (1987) A comparative approach to vocal communication. *Neb. Symp. Motiv.* 35:145–200.

Snowdon, C. T. (1988) Communication as social interaction: Its importance in ontogeny and adult behavior. In *Primate Vocal Communication*, ed. by D. Todt, P. Goedeking, and D. Symmes. Berlin: Springer-Verlag.

Snowdon, C. T. (1990) Language capacities of nonhuman primates. *Yrbk. Phys. Anthrop.* 33:215–243.

Snowdon, C. T., Elowson, M., and Roush. R. S. (1997) Social influences on vocal development in New World monkeys. In *Social Influences on Vocal Development*, ed. by C. T. Snowdon and M. Hausberger. Cambridge: Cambridge University Press.

Snowdon, C. T., French, J. A., and Cleveland, J. (1985) Ontogeny of primate vocalizations: Models from bird song and human speech. In *Current Perspectives in Primate Social Dynamics*, ed. by D. Taub and F. King. New York: Van Nostrand Rheinhold.

Struhsaker, T. T. (1967) Auditory communication in vervet monkeys (*Cercopithecus aethiops*). In *Social Communication Among Primates*, ed. by S. A. Altmann. Chicago: University of Chicago Press.

Symmes, D., Newman, J. D., Talmadge-Riggs, G., and Lieblich, A. K. (1979) Individuality and stability of isolation peeps in squirrel monkeys. *Anim. Behav.* 27:1142–1152.

Takeda, R. (1965) Developmental of vocal communication in man-raised Japanese monkeys. I. From birth to 6 weeks. *Primates* 6:337–380.

Takeda, R. (1966) Development of vocal communication in man-raised Japanese monkeys. II. From seventh to thirteenth week. *Primates* 7:73–116.

Talmadge-Riggs, G., Winter, P., Ploog, D., and Mayer, W. (1972) Effects of deafening on the vocal behavior of the squirrel monkey (*Saimiri sciureus*). *Folia Primatol.* 17:404–420.

Tenaza, R. (1985) Songs of hybrid gibbons (*Hylobates lar* x *H. muelleri*). *Am. J. Primatol.* 8:249–253.

Winter, P., Handley, P., Ploog, D., and Schott, D. (1973) Ontogeny of squirrel monkey calls under normal conditions and under acoustic isolation. *Behaviour* 47:230–239.

15 Speech, Language, and the Brain: Innate Preparation for Learning

Patricia K. Kuhl

Thus, the question to be addressed is not "do innate mechanisms exist?" but rather, "what is the nature of the innate mechanisms for learning, by what mechanisms do they operate, and what provisions do they make for the interaction between organisms and their environments?" In other words, what are the ways in which innate mechanisms impinge on the pervasive plasticity that behavior displays in the course of its development?
—Peter Marler, Innate learning preferences

Nature, Nurture, and a Historical Debate

Forty years ago, there was a historic confrontation between a strong nativist and a strong learning theorist. Chomsky's (1957) reply to Skinner's (1957) *Verbal Behavior* had just been published, reigniting the debate on the nature of language. On Chomsky's (1965, 1981) nativist view, universal rules encompassing the grammars and phonologies of all languages were taken to be innately specified. Language input served to "trigger" the appropriate subset of rules, and developmental change in language ability was viewed as biological growth akin to other bodily organs, rather than learning. On the Skinnerian view, language was explicitly learned. Language was thought to be brought about in the child through a process of feedback and external reinforcement (Skinner 1957).

Both views made assumptions about three critical parameters: (i) the biological preparation that infants bring to the task of language learning, (ii) the nature of language input, and (iii) the nature of developmental change. Chomsky asserted, through the "poverty of the stimulus" argument, that language input to the child is greatly underspecified. Critical elements are missing; hence the necessity for innately specified information. Skinner viewed speech as simply another operant behavior, shaped through parental feedback and reinforcement like all other behaviors.

In the decades that have passed since these positions were developed, the debate has been played out for language at the syntactic, semantic, and phonological levels. It has also been played out for communication in animal models. Peter Marler's work on the acquisition of birdsong provides the quintessential example. Beginning with his theoretical writings in the 1970s, it was clear that Marler was a pioneer in promoting the epigenetic view that innate predispositions prepare organisms for learning (Marler 1970). Marler's (1991) view that an "instinct to learn" was key to both language and birdsong has been seminal to later discussions on the topic by many theorists.

In this chapter, I will concentrate primarily on language, using the elementary components of sounds—the consonants and vowels that make up words—to structure an argument about what is given by nature and gained by experience in the acquisition of language at the phonetic level. Studying the sound structure of language allows us to test the perception of language in infants just hours old and thereby to address the question of what language capacities are innate in infants. Then, by tracking the development of infants raised in various cultures listening to different languages, we can determine, again using tests of perception, when infants' use of language begins to diverge as a function of experience with a particular language. These methods provide a strong test of the historically opposing views, and the results of these tests deliver dramatic evidence of the interaction between biology and culture, leading to a new view. Parallels between speech and birdsong will be highlighted in describing this new approach (see also Doupe and Kuhl 1999).

Origins of Conceptual Distinctions and the Modern View

The discussion between linguists and psychologists regarding language is only one forum in which the nature-nurture issue has been debated. Begun by philosophers hundreds of years ago, the nativism-empiricism debate or the nativist-constructivist debate concerned the origins of knowledge and whether it stemmed from our native abilities or was empirically derived (Berkeley 1709; Locke 1690). The debate is of continuing interest across a wide variety of disciplines, fueled by arguments and data from ethology (Bateson 1991; Hauser 1996), neuroscience (Carew, Menzel, and Shatz 1998), language science (Kuhl 1994, 1998a; Pinker 1994), and developmental psychology (Bates and Elman 1996; Carey 1985; Gopnik and Meltzoff 1997; Karmiloff-Smith 1995).

These groups use different terms to distinguish complex behaviors that appear relatively immune from as opposed to wholly dependent on experience. The terminology reflects differences in emphasis between groups. In ethology, for example, the distinction has traditionally been drawn between *innate* or *instinctual* behaviors, considered to be genetically determined, and those *learned* as a function of exposure to the environment (Lorenz 1965; Thorpe 1959; Tinbergen 1951). The emphasis in early ethological writings was on explaining behaviors that existed at birth in the absence of experience (Lorenz's "innate release mechanisms").

In the early psychological literature on the mental development of the child (James 1890; Koffka 1924; Piaget 1954; Vygotsky 1962) and also in the neuroscience literature (Cajal 1906), the distinction has historically been drawn using the terms "development" and "learning." *Development* included changes in the organism over time that depend primarily on maturation or internal factors leading to the expression of

Conceptual relations between development and learning

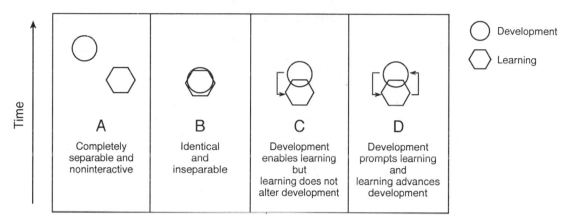

Figure 15.1
Conceptual relations between development and learning.

information specified in the genome. The term *development* and the term *innate* are
thus similar, but not identical. *Development* (as opposed to *innate*) emphasized complex behaviors, thought to be under genetic control, that unfolded well after birth
rather than those existing at birth (innate behavior). *Learning* encompassed processes
that depended on explicit experience producing long-lasting changes in the organism.

Modern writers in all the aforementioned fields agree that behavior unfolds under
the control of both a genetic blueprint and the environment, and that the debate now
centers on the precise nature of the interplay between the two. Using the develop-
ment-learning terminology, four alternatives can be conceptualized, as illustrated in
figure 15.1. The first two are not interactionist accounts, whereas the last two can be
described in this way.

Development and learning can be thought of as completely separable processes
(figure 15.1a). Development follows a maturational course guided by a genetic blueprint, and learning neither follows from nor leads to changes in the preestablished
course of development. Alternatively, they can be thought of as two processes so
inseparable that they cannot be pulled apart even conceptually (figure 15.1b).

More commonly, development and learning are thought of as separate and distin-
guishable processes that interact in one way or another (figure 15.1c–d). Developmental
psychologists, neuroscientists, and neurobiologists largely agree that the interactionist view is the correct one (Bonhoeffer and Shatz 1998; Carey 1985; Doupe 1998;

Doupe and Kuhl 1999; Fanselow and Rudy 1998; Gopnik and Meltzoff 1997; Karmiloff-Smith 1995; Kuhl 1994; Marler 1990, 1997). At issue, however, is exactly how the two systems interact, and particularly whether the interaction between development and learning is bidirectional.

Among the interactionist views, one model is that development enables learning, but that learning does not change the course of development, which unfolds more or less on its own timetable (figure 15.1c). Learning is seen as capitalizing on the achievements of development and as unable to occur unless a certain level of development has been achieved. The interaction is unidirectional, however. Development is not impacted by learning. In classical developmental psychology, this position is closest to the view of Piaget (1954). In modern neurobiology, the notion that there are "constraints" on learning, that development both prepares the organism and sets limits on learning, is consistent with this model (see Doupe 1998 and Marler 1974 for the case of birdsong). Greenough and Black's (1992) "experience-expectant" plasticity, wherein changes in neural development are thought to precede and prepare an organism to react to a reliably present environmental stimulus, provides a detailed example of this model. In each of these cases, development is conceived of as both enabling and limiting learning, but learning does not alter the course of development.

There is an alternative interactionist view. This model describes development and learning as mutually affecting one another (figure 15.1d). Development enables and even prompts learning, and learning in turn advances development. This view is closest to that developed by Vygotsky (1979). Vygotsky's theory, the "zone of proximal development" (ZPD), described development at two levels. One was the infant's actual developmental level, the level already achieved. The second was the level that was just within reach. The ZPD was the difference between the two. In Vygotsky's view, environmental stimulation slightly in advance of current development (in the ZPD) resulted in learning, and when this occurred, learning prompted development. Recent theories proposed by developmental psychologists to account for a wide variety of cognitive and linguistic tasks converge on the point that there is mutual interaction between development and learning (Carey 1985; Gopnik and Meltzoff 1997; Karmiloff-Smith 1991).

In linguistic theory, Chomsky's classic view, that the growth of language is largely determined by a maturational process, fits model C. Experience plays a role, but it is seen as triggering prespecified options, or as setting innately determined parameters (Chomsky 1981). The data reviewed here at the phonetic level of language come closer to the mutual interaction of model D. In the model of speech development I will describe, language input plays more than a triggering role in the process. Language input is mapped in a complex process that appears to code its subtle details.

Input thus goes beyond setting the parameters of prespecified options. Moreover, early mapping of the perceptual regularities of language input is argued to allow infants to recognize words and phrases, thus advancing development.

In summary, there is a great deal of support for interactionist views (models C and D) over noninteractionist views (models A and B). Although the relations between learning and development may differ across species and systems, there is an emerging consensus across diverse disciplines including neurobiology, psychology, linguistics, and neuroscience that development and learning are not independent entities. Both birdsong and speech fall clearly on the interactionist side. However, the form of the interaction remains a question, with a cutting-edge issue being whether (and how) learning can alter development. The model I will propose here on the basis of recent research on speech development goes some distance toward addressing this issue.

Explanations for Developmental Change in Speech

One of the puzzles in language development is to explain the orderly transitions that all infants go through. Infants the world over achieve certain milestones in linguistic development at roughly the same time, regardless of the language they are exposed to. Moreover, developmental change can also include cases in which infants' early skills exceed their later ones. Explaining these transitions is one of the major goals of developmental linguistic theory.

One of these transitions occurs in speech perception. At birth, infants discern differences between all the phonetic units used in the world's languages (Eimas, Miller, and Jusczyk 1987). All infants show these universal skills, regardless of the language environment in which they are being raised. Data on nonhuman animals' perception of speech suggest that the ability to partition the basic building blocks of speech is deeply rooted in our evolutionary history (Kuhl 1991a).

When do infants from different cultures begin to diverge in their perceptual abilities? Infants' initial language-universal perceptual abilities are highly constrained just one year later. By the end of the first year, infants fail to discriminate foreign-language contrasts they once discriminated (Werker and Tees 1984), resembling the adult pattern. Adults often find it difficult to perceive differences between sounds not used to distinguish words in their native language. Adult native speakers of Japanese, for example, have great difficulty discriminating American English /r/ and /l/ (Best 1993; Strange 1995), and American English listeners have great difficulty hearing the difference between Spanish /b/ and /p/ (Abramson and Lisker 1970).

Infants' abilities change over a 3-month period. A recent study we have just completed in Japan shows, for example, that at 7 months of age Japanese infants respond to the /r-l/ distinction and are as accurate in perceiving it as American 7-month-old infants. By 10 months, Japanese infants no longer demonstrate this ability, even though American infants at that same age have become even better at discriminating the two sounds (Kuhl, Kiritani, et al. 1997).

A similar transition occurs in speech production. Regardless of culture, all infants show a universal progression in the development of speech which encompasses five distinct phases: *cooing* (1–4 months), in which infants produce sounds that resemble vowels, *canonical babbling* (5–10 months), during which infants produce strings of consonant-vowel syllables, such as "babababa" or "mamamama," *first words* (10–15 months), wherein infants use a consistent phonetic form to refer to an object, *two-word utterances* (18–24 months), in which two words are combined in a meaningful way, and *meaningful speech* (15 months and beyond), in which infants produce both babbling and meaningful speech to produce long intonated utterances (Ferguson, Menn, and Stoel-Gammon 1992). Interestingly, deaf infants exposed to a natural sign language, such as American Sign Language (ASL), are purported to follow the same progression using a visual-manual mode of communication (Petitto and Marentette 1991).

Although infants across cultures begin life producing a universal set of utterances that cannot be distinguished, their utterances soon begin to diverge, reflecting the influence of the ambient language they are listening to. By the end of the first year of life, the utterances of infants reared in different countries begin to be separable; infants show distinct patterns of speech production, both in the prosodic (intonational patterns) and phonetic aspects of language, that are unique to the culture in which they are being raised (de Boysson-Bardies 1993). In adulthood, these distinctive speech motor patterns that we initially learned contribute to our "accents" when attempting to speak another language (Flege 1988).

The transitions in speech perception and production from a pattern that is initially universal across languages to one that is highly specific to one particular language present one of the most intriguing problems in language acquisition. What causes the transition? We know that it is not simply maturational change. In the absence of natural language input, as in the case of socially isolated children (Curtiss 1977) or deaf children not exposed to manual sign language and unable to hear oral language, full-blown linguistic skills do not develop. Linguistic input and interaction, provided early in life, appear to be necessary.

The thesis developed here at the phonetic level is that linguistic experience produces a special kind of developmental change. Language input alters the brain's processing of the signal, resulting in the creation of complex mental maps. The mapping "warps" underlying dimensions, altering perception in a way that highlights distinctive categories. This mapping is not like traditional psychological learning. In the psychological literature, learning involves explicit teaching. In the Skinnerian tradition (1957), for example, this kind of learning depended on the presence of external reinforcement (specific contingencies that rewarded certain responses), feedback about the correctness of the response, and step-by-step shaping of the response. The kind of learning reflected in language is just the opposite. Although it does depend on external information from the environment (language input), it does not require explicit teaching or reinforcement contingencies. Given exposure to language in a normal and socially interactive environment, language learning occurs, and the knowledge gained about a specific language is long-lasting and difficult to undo.

Language Experience Alters Perception

The thesis developed here for the phonetic level of language is that ambient language experience produces a "mapping" that alters perception. A research finding that helps explain how this occurs is called the "perceptual magnet effect." It is observed when tokens perceived as exceptionally good representatives of a phonetic category ("prototypes") are used in tests of speech perception (Kuhl 1991b). The notion that categories have "prototypes" stems from cognitive psychology. Findings in that field show that the members of common categories (like the category *bird* or *dog*) are not equal. An ostrich is not as representative of the category *bird* as is a robin; a Terrier is not as representative of the category *dog* as is a Collie. These "prototypes" or best instances of categories are easier to remember, result in shorter reaction times when identified, and are often preferred in tests that tap our favorite instances of categories (Rosch 1977). Because of this literature, we were motivated to test the concept that phonetic categories had "prototypes" or best instances, in the early 1980s.

Our results demonstrated that phonetic prototypes did exist (Grieser and Kuhl 1989; Kuhl 1991b), that they differed in speakers of different languages (Kuhl 1992; Näätänen et al. 1997; Willerman and Kuhl 1996), and that phonetic prototypes function like perceptual magnets for other sounds in the category (Kuhl 1991b). When listeners hear a phonetic prototype and attempt to discriminate it from sounds that surround it in acoustic space, the prototype displays an attractor effect on the surrounding sounds (figure 15.2). It perceptually pulls other members of the category toward it, making it difficult to hear differences between the prototype and surrounding stimuli. Poor instances from the category (nonprototypes) do not function in this way. A variety of experimental tasks produce this result with both consonants and vowels (Iverson and Kuhl 1995, 1996; Sussman and Lauckner-Morano 1995).

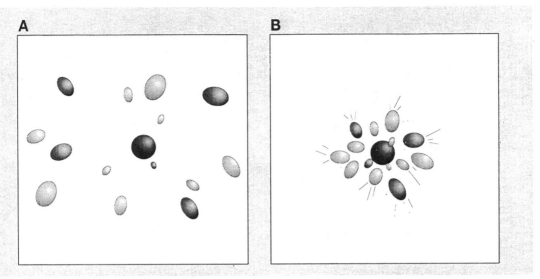

Figure 15.2
The perceptual magnet effect. When a variety of sounds in a category surround the category prototype (A), they are perceptually drawn toward the prototype (B). The prototype appears to function like a magnet for other stimuli in the category.

Other studies confirm listeners' skills in identifying phonetic prototypes and show that they are language-specific (Kuhl 1992; Miller 1994; Willerman and Kuhl 1996).

Developmental tests revealed that the perceptual magnet effect was exhibited by six-month-old infants for the sounds of their native language (Kuhl 1991b). In later studies, cross-language experiments demonstrated that the magnet effect is the product of linguistic experience (Kuhl et al. 1992). In the cross-language experiment, infants in the United States and Sweden were tested. The infants from both countries were tested with two vowel prototypes, an American English vowel prototype, /i/ (as in "peep"), and a Swedish vowel prototype, /y/ (as in "fye"). The results demonstrated that the perceptual magnet effect in six-month-old infants was influenced by exposure to a particular language. American infants demonstrated the magnet effect only for the American English /i/; they treated the Swedish /y/ like a nonprototype. Swedish infants showed the opposite pattern, demonstrating the magnet effect for the Swedish /y/ and treating the American English /i/ as a nonprototype. This is the youngest age at which language experience has been shown to affect phonetic perception.

The perceptual magnet effect thus occurs prior to word learning. What this means is that in the absence of formal language understanding or use—before infants utter

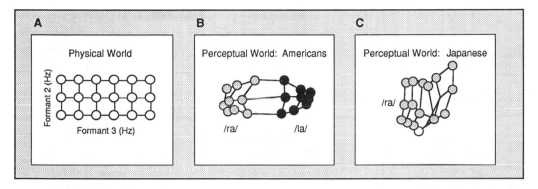

Figure 15.3
Physical (acoustic) versus perceptual distance. Consonant tokens of /r/ and /l/ were generated to be equally distant from one another in acoustic space (A). However, American listeners perceive perceptual space as "shrunk" near the best instances of /r/ (gray dots) and /l/ (black dots) and "stretched" at the boundary between the two (B). Japanese listeners' perceptual world differs dramatically; neither magnet effects nor a boundary between the two categories are seen (C).

or understand their first words—infants' perceptual systems strongly conform to the characteristics of the ambient language. We previously believed that word learning caused infants to recognize that phonetic changes that they could hear, such as the change that Japanese infants perceived between /r/ and /l/, did not change the meaning of a word in their language. This discovery was thought to cause the change in phonetic perception. We now know that just the opposite is true. Language input sculpts the brain to create a perceptual system that highlights the contrasts used in the language, while deemphasizing those that are not, and this happens prior to word learning. The change in phonetic perception thus assists word learning, rather than the reverse.

Further tests on adults suggested that the magnet effect distorted perception to highlight sound contrasts in the native language. Studies on the perception of the phonetic units /r/ and /l/ as in the words "rake" and "lake," illustrate this point. The /r-l/ distinction is one notoriously difficult for Japanese speakers and our studies sought to determine how adults from different cultures perceived these two sounds. To conduct the study, we used computer-synthesized syllables beginning with /r/ and /l/, spacing them at equal physical intervals in a two-dimensional acoustic grid (Iverson and Kuhl 1996) (figure 15.3a). American listeners identified each syllable as beginning with either /r/ or /l/, rated its category goodness, and estimated the perceived similarity for all possible pairs of stimuli using a scale from "1" (very dissimilar) to "7" (very similar). Similarity ratings were scaled using multidimensional scaling (MDS) techniques. The results revealed that perception distorts physical space. The physical (acoustic) differences between pairs of stimuli were equal; however, perceived distance was "warped" (figure 15.3b). The perceptual space around the best /r/ and the best /l/ was greatly reduced, as predicted by the perceptual magnet effect, while the space near the boundary between the two categories was expanded.

This experiment has now been done using Japanese monolingual listeners (Kuhl, Yamada, Tohkura, Iverson, and Stevens, submitted) and the results show a strong contrast in the way the /r-l/ stimuli are perceived by American and Japanese adults (figure 15.3c). Japanese adults hear almost all the sounds as /r/; there is no /l/ in Japanese. More striking is the complete absence of magnet and boundary effects in the Japanese MDS solution. The results suggest that linguistic experience induces the formation of perceptual maps specifying the perceived distances between stimuli. These maps increase internal category cohesion while maximizing the distinction between categories. The critical point for theory is that neither group perceives the physical reality, the actual physical differences between the sounds. For each language group, experience has altered perception to create a language-specific map of auditory similarities and differences, one that highlights the sound contrasts of the speaker's native language. These mental maps for speech are the front-end of the language mechanism. In this sense, they point infants in the direction needed to focus on the aspects of the acoustic signal that will separate categories in their own native language. They provide a kind of attentional network that may function as a highly tuned filter for language. Such a network would promote semantic and syntactic analysis.

The theoretical position developed here is that the mental maps for speech are developed early in infancy, prior to the development of word acquisition. The mapping of phonetic information is seen as enabling infants to recognize word candidates. For example, our work shows that Japanese infants fail to discriminate American English /r/ from /l/ at 10 months of age, though they did so perfectly well at 7 months of age (Kuhl et al. submitted). This is argued to assist Japanese infants in word recognition. The collapsing of /r/ and /l/ into a single category makes it possible for Japanese infants to perceive their parents' productions of /r/-like and /l/-like sounds as one entity at 10 months, when the process of word acquisition begins. If they did not do so, it would presumably make it more difficult to relate sound patterns to objects and events.

The view that phonetic mapping enhances the recognition of higher-order units is supported by data showing that slightly later in development infants use information about phonetic units to recognize wordlike forms. Work by Jusczyk and his colleagues shows that by 9 months of age, infants prefer word patterns that are typical of the native language, which requires recognition of native-language phonetic units (Jusczyk et al. 1993). Infants have also been shown to be capable of learning the statistical probabilities of sound combinations contained in artificial words (Saffran, Aslin, and Newport 1996). Infants' mapping at the phonetic level is thus seen as assisting infants in "chunking" the sound stream into higher-order units, suggesting that "learning" promotes "development." Infants' discovery of statistical regularities in language input suggests new ways of conceiving of learning. During the first year of life, infants come to recognize the recurring properties of their native language and mentally store those properties in some form. This occurs in the absence of any formal instruction or reinforcement of the infant's behavior. In this sense, the learning that transpires is outside the realm of the historic versions of learning described by psychologists.

A Theory of Speech Development

Given these findings, how do we reconceptualize infants' innate predispositions as preparing them for experience? One view can be summarized as a three-step model of speech development, called the *native language magnet* (NLM) model (Kuhl 1994). NLM describes infants' initial state as well as changes brought about by experience with language (figure 15.4). The model demonstrates how infants' developing native-language speech representations might alter both speech perception and production. The same principles apply to both vowel and consonant perception; the example developed here is for vowels.

Phase 1 describes infants' initial abilities. At birth, infants distinguish all the phonetic distinctions of all languages of the world. This is illustrated by a hypothetical F1/F2 coordinate vowel space partitioned into categories (figure 15.4a). These divisions separate perceptually the vowels of all languages. According to NLM, infants' abilities at this stage do not depend on specific language experience. The boundaries initially structure perception in a phonetically relevant way. However, they are not due to a "language module." This notion is buttressed by the fact that nonhuman animals also hear speech distinctions, displaying abilities that were once thought to be exclusively human (Kuhl 1991a; see also, e.g., Dooling, Best, and Brown 1995; Kluender, Diehl, and Killeen 1987 for demonstrations of speech perception abilities in nonhuman mammals).

Phase 2 describes the vowel space at six months of age for infants reared in three very different language environments, Swedish, English, and Japanese (figure 15.4b).

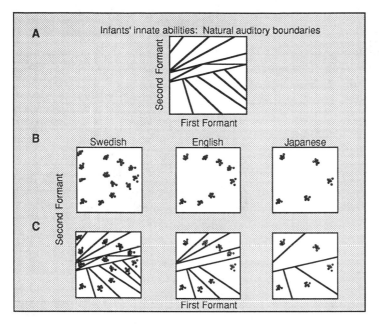

Figure 15.4
The native language magnet (NLM) model. (A) At birth, infants perceptually partition the acoustic space underlying phonetic distinctions in a language-universal way. They are capable of discriminating all phonetically relevant differences in the world's languages. (B) By 6 months of age, infants reared in different linguistic environments show an effect of language experience. Infants store incoming vowel information in memory in some form. The resulting representations (shown by the dots) are language-specific, and reflect the distributional properties of vowels in the three different languages. (C) After language-specific magnet effects appear, some of the natural boundaries that existed at birth "disappear." Infants now fail to discriminate foreign-language contrasts they once discriminated.

By six months of age, infants show more than the ability to perceptually separate all phonetic categories, as shown in phase 1. By six months, our informal calculations indicate that infants have heard many vowels. The distributional properties of vowels heard by infants being raised in Sweden, America, and Japan differ. According to NLM, infants mentally store this information in some way. As shown in figure 15.4b, infants' stored representations differ, reflecting the distributional differences between their languages. In each case, linguistic experience has produced stored representations that reflect the vowel system of the ambient language. Language-specific magnet effects, produced by the stored representations, are exhibited by infants at this stage.

An interesting question about phase 2 magnet effects is: How much language input does it take to develop these effects, and is all language heard by the child (including that from a radio or television) effective in producing this special kind of learning? This, in fact, was the question President Clinton asked me at the White House Conference on Early Learning and the Brain, in April of 1997. My answer was that at present we have little data suggesting how much language input it takes to show these effects, and we do not know whether language from a disembodied source (TV, radio) would be sufficient to produce it. By six months of age, the earliest age at which we have evidence of magnet effects, our estimates suggest that infants have heard thousands of instances of vowels in *en face* communication with their parents (Kuhl 1994), but we do not know what amount is necessary. These are exciting questions for future research, and we have studies underway at present that are providing some interesting information on these issues.

Phase 3 shows how magnet effects recursively alter the initial state of speech perception, and affect the processing of foreign-language stimuli. Magnet effects cause certain perceptual distinctions to be minimized (those near the magnet attractors) while others are maximized (those near the boundaries between two magnets). The consequence is that some of the boundaries that initially divided the space "disappear" as the perceptual space is reconfigured to incorporate a language's particular magnet placement (figure 15.4c). Magnet effects functionally erase certain boundaries—those relevant to foreign but not native languages.

In phase 3, a perceptual space once characterized by basic "auditory cuts"— boundaries that divide all speech categories and ones demonstrated in nonhuman animals—has been replaced by a dramatically warped space, dominated by magnet effects, that completely restructure the space. It is at this phase that infants fail to discriminate foreign-language contrasts that were once discriminable. The mapping of incoming speech has altered which stimulus differences infants respond to, producing a language-specific listener for the first time.

A natural question arising from these data is what happens to infants exposed to two different languages throughout phase 3. We are only beginning to study this issue, but the theory predicts that infants will develop magnet effects for the sound categories of both languages. Interestingly, preliminary data from studies underway suggest that development of two sets of magnet effects is particularly likely when the two languages are spoken by different speakers (mother speaks one language, father speaks another). Presumably having each language spoken by a different speaker allows infants to separate perceptually the maps for the two languages.

Infants at six months of age have no awareness of the fact that sound units are used contrastively in language to name things. Yet the infant's perceptual system organizes itself to reflect language-specific phonetic categories. At the next stage in linguistic development, when infants acquire word meanings by relating sounds to objects and events in the world, the language-specific mapping that has already occurred should greatly assist this process.

NLM theory offers an explanation for the developmental change observed in speech perception. A developing magnet pulls sounds that were once discriminable toward it, making them less discriminable. Magnet effects should therefore developmentally precede changes in infants' perception of foreign-language contrasts; preliminary data indicate that they do (Werker and Polka 1993). The magnet effect also helps account for the results of studies on the perception of sounds from a foreign language by adults (Best 1993; Flege 1993). For example, NLM theory may help explain Japanese listeners' difficulty with American /r/ and /l/. The magnet effect for the Japanese /r/ category prototype (which is neither American /r/ nor /l/) will attract both /r/ and /l/, making the two sounds difficult for native-speaking Japanese people to discriminate (Kuhl et al. submitted). NLM theory argues that early experience establishes a complex perceptual network through which language passes. On this view, one's primary language and the map that results from early experience will determine how other languages are perceived.

Reinterpreting "Critical Periods"

Evidence for the interaction between genetic programming and environmental stimulation is nowhere more predominant than in the literature on critical periods in learning (Marler 1970; Thorpe 1961). Critical periods are no longer viewed as strictly timed developmental processes with rigid cut-off periods that restrict learning to a specific time frame. Recent studies showing that learning can be stretched by a variety of factors has caused a shift in the terminology used to refer to this period. It is now understood that during "sensitive periods" exposure to specific kinds of information may be more effective than at other times, but that a variety of factors can alter the period of learning. Knudsen's work, for example, on the sound-localization system in the barn owl shows that the sensitive period for learning the auditory-visual map in the optic tectum can be altered by a variety of factors that either shorten or extend the learning period; the learning period closes much earlier, for instance, if experience occurs in a more natural environment (Knudsen and Brainerd 1995; Knudsen and Knudsen 1990).

The idea that sensitive periods define "windows of opportunity" for learning, during which environmental stimulation is highly effective in producing developmental change, remains well supported in both the human and the animal literature. Whether language or birdsong is the focus of inquiry, the ability to learn is not equivalent over time (Doupe and Kuhl 1999). The question is: What causes changes in the ability to learn throughout the individual's lifespan?

The sensitive period denotes a process of learning that is constrained primarily by time, or other factors (hormones, etc.)—factors outside the learning process itself (see Doupe and Kuhl 1999). There is an alternative possibility suggested by studies on speech. Later learning may be limited by the fact that learning itself alters the brain, and learning may produce a kind of "interference" effect that impacts later learning. To illustrate, if NLM's claim that learning involves the creation of mental maps for speech is true, this would mean that learning "commits" neural structure in some way. According to the model, ongoing processing of speech is affected by this neural structure, and future learning is affected as well. The mechanisms governing an organism's general ability to learn may not have changed. Rather, initial learning may result in a structure that reflects environmental input, and once committed, the learned structure may interfere with the processing of information that does not conform to the learned pattern. On this account, initial learning can alter future learning independent of a strictly timed period.

On this *interference* account, plasticity would be governed from a statistical standpoint. When additional input does not cause the overall statistical distribution to change substantially, the organism becomes less sensitive to input. Hypothetically, for instance, the infants' representation of the vowel /a/ might not change when the one millionth token of the vowel /a/ is heard. Plasticity might thus be independent of time, but be dependent on the amount and variability provided by experience. At some time in the lifetime of an organism, one could conceive of a point where new input no longer alters the underlying distribution, and this could, at least in principle, reduce the system's "plasticity."

The interference view may account for some aspects of second language learning. When acquiring a second language, certain phonetic distinctions are notoriously difficult to master both in speech perception and production. Take the case of the /r-l/ distinction for native speakers of Japanese. Hearing and producing the distinction is very difficult for native speakers of Japanese (Goto 1971; Miyawaki et al. 1975; Yamada and Tohkura 1992). According to NLM, this is because exposure to Japanese early in life altered the Japanese infant's perceptual system, resulting in magnet effects for the Japanese phoneme /r/, but not for American English /r/ or American English /l/. Once in place, the magnet effects appropriate for Japanese would not make it easy to process American English. Both American English /r/ and /l/ would be assimilated to Japanese /r/ (see also Best 1993). Teaching Japanese adults to distinguish /r/ and /l/ may require the use of stimuli that avoid the interference effect.

A second language learned later in life may require separation between the two systems to avoid interference. Data gathered using fMRI techniques indicate that adult bilinguals who learned both languages early in life activate overlapping regions of the brain when processing the two languages, whereas those who learned the second language later in life activate two distinct regions of the brain for the two languages (Kim, Relkin, Lee, and Hirsch 1997). This is consistent with the idea that the brain's processing of a primary language can interfere with the second language. This problem is avoided if both are learned early in development.

The general thesis is that acquiring new phonetic categories as adults is difficult because the brain's mental maps for speech, formed on the basis of the primary language, are incompatible with those required for the new language; hence interference results. Early in life, interference effects are minimal and new categories can be acquired because input continues to revise the statistical distribution. As mentioned earlier, limited evidence suggests that infants exposed to two languages do much better if each parent speaks one of the two languages, rather both parents speaking both languages. This may be the case because it is easier to map two different sets of phonetic categories (one for each of the two languages) if there is some way to keep them perceptually separate. Males and females produce speech in different frequency ranges, and this could make it easier to maintain separation.

These two factors—a maturationally defined temporal window and initial learning that makes later learning more difficult—could both be operating to produce constraints on learning a second language later in life. If a maturational process induces "readiness" at a particular time, input that misses this timing could reduce learning. At the same time, an "interference" factor might provide an independent mechanism that contributes to the difficulty in readily learning a second language in adulthood.

Vocal Learning

As Peter Marler has so clearly described, vocal learning—an organism's dependence on auditory input and feedback to acquire a vocal repertoire—is not common among mammals (see Snowdon and Hausberger 1997 for exceptions), but it is exhibited strikingly in songbirds. In certain songbirds, and in humans, young members of the species not only learn the perceptual properties of their conspecific communicative signals but become proficient producers of those signals. A great deal of research on birds (Marler 1990, 1997) and infants (Stoel-Gammon and Otomo 1986; Oller, Wieman, Doyle, and Ross 1976) has shown that input is essential to the development of vocalizations. Deaf infants, for example, do not babble normally (Oller and Mac-

Neilage 1983), nor do deafened birds (Konishi 1965; Nottebohm 1967). In the case of humans, the learned motor patterns that underlie speech become difficult to alter. Speakers who learn a second language later in life, for example, produce it with an "accent" typical of their primary language (Flege 1993). Most speakers of a second language would like to speak like a native speaker, without an accent, but this is difficult to do.

When do we adopt the indelible speech patterns that will mark us as native speakers of a particular language for our entire lives? Developmental studies suggest that by one year of age, language-specific patterns of speech production appear in infants' spontaneous utterances (de Boysson-Bardies 1993; Vihman and de Boysson-Bardies 1994). However, the fundamental capacity to reproduce the sound patterns one hears is in place much earlier. In a recent study, Kuhl and Meltzoff (1996) recorded infant utterances at 12, 16, and 20 weeks of age while the infants watched and listened to a video recording of a woman producing a vowel, either /a/, /i/, or /u/. Infants watched the video for five minutes on each of three consecutive days. Infants' utterances were analyzed both perceptually (phonetic transcription) and instrumentally (computerized spectrographic analysis).

The results showed that there was developmental change in infants' vowel productions between 12 and 20 weeks of age. The areas of vowel space occupied by infants' /a/, /i/, and /u/ vowels become progressively more tightly clustered at each age, and by 20 weeks, a "vowel triangle" typical of that produced in every language of the world had emerged in infants' own region of the vowel space (figure 15.5).

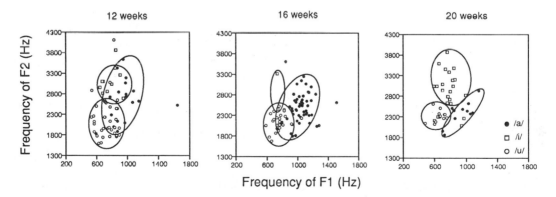

Figure 15.5
The location of /a/, /i/, and /u/ vowels produced by 12-, 16-, and 20-week-old infants. Infants' vowel productions show progressively tighter clustering in vowel space over the 8-week period and reflect differences between the three vowel categories seen in adults' productions.

This suggested the possibility that infants were listening to language and attempting to vocally imitate the sound patterns they heard (Kuhl and Meltzoff 1996).

Direct evidence that infants were vocally imitating was also obtained in the study. By 20 weeks, infants were shown to reproduce the vowels they heard. Infants exposed to /a/ were more likely to produce /a/ than when exposed to either /i/ or /u/; similarly, infants exposed to either /i/ or /u/ were more likely to produce the vowel in that condition than when listening to either of the two alternate vowels. The total amount of exposure to a specific vowel in the laboratory was only 15 minutes, yet this was sufficient to influence infants' productions. If 15 minutes of laboratory exposure to a vowel is sufficient to influence infants' vocalizations, then listening to ambient language for weeks would be expected to provide a powerful influence on infants' production of speech. These data suggest that infants' stored representations of speech not only alter infant perception but alter production as well, serving as auditory patterns that guide motor production. Stored representations are thus viewed as the common cause for both the tighter clustering observed in infant vowel production and the tighter clustering observed in infant vowel perception (figure 15.6).

This pattern of learning and self-organization, in which perceptual patterns stored in memory serve as guides for production, is strikingly similar for birdsong (Doupe 1998; Doupe and Kuhl 1999), in visual-motor learning in which nonspeech oral movements like tongue protrusion and mouth opening are imitated (Meltzoff and Moore 1977, 1994), and in language involving both sign (Petitto and Marentette 1991) and speech (Kuhl and Meltzoff 1996). In each of these cases, perceptual experience establishes a representation that guides sensory-motor learning. In the case of infants and speech, perception affects production in the earliest stages of language learning, which reinforces the idea that the speech motor patterns of a specific language are formed very early in life. Once learned, motor patterns may also further development by altering the probability that infants will acquire words that contain items they are capable of producing (see, e.g., Vihman 1993).

The Role of Vision in Speech Perception: Polymodal Speech Representation

The link between perception and production can be seen in another experimental situation in speech, and there is some suggestion that this is mirrored in birdsong learning. Speech perception in adults is strongly affected by the sight of a talker's mouth movements during speech, indicating that our representational codes for speech contain both auditory and visual information. One of the most compelling examples of the polymodal nature of speech representations is auditory-visual illu-

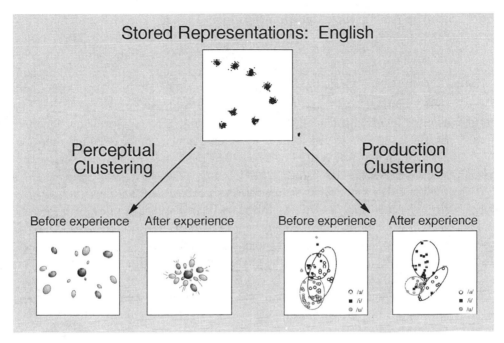

Figure 15.6
Stored representations of native-language speech affect both speech perception, producing the perceptual clustering evidenced by the magnet effect, as well as speech production, producing the increased clustering seen in infants' vocalizations over time.

sions that result when discrepant information is sent to two separate modalities. One such illusion occurs when auditory information for /b/ is combined with visual information for /g/ (McGurk and MacDonald 1976; Green, Kuhl, Meltzoff, and Stevens 1991; Kuhl, Tsuzaki, Tohkura, and Meltzoff 1994; Massaro 1987). Perceivers report the phenomenal impression of an intermediate articulation (/da/ or /tha/) despite the fact that this information was not delivered by or to either sense modality. This is a robust phenomenon and is readily obtained even when the information from the two modalities comes from different speakers, such as when a male voice is combined with a female face (Green et al. 1991). In this case, there is no doubt that the auditory and visual signals do not belong together. Yet the illusion is still unavoidable—our perceptual systems combine the multimodal information (auditory and visual) to give a unified percept.

Young infants are also affected by visual information. Infants just 18–20 weeks old recognize auditory-visual correspondences for speech, akin to what we as adults do when we lip-read; in these studies, infants looked longer at a face pronouncing a vowel that matched the vowel sound they heard, rather than at a mismatched face (Kuhl and Meltzoff 1982). Young infants demonstrate knowledge about both the auditory and visual information contained in speech, which supports the notion that infants' stored speech representations contain information of both kinds. Additional demonstrations of auditory-visual speech perception in infants suggest that there is a left-hemisphere involvement in the process (MacKain, Studdert-Kennedy, Spieker, and Stern 1983), and more recent data by Rosenblum, Schmuckler, and Johnson (1997) and Walton and Bower (1993) suggest that the ability to match auditory and visual speech is present in newborns.

Visual information thus plays a strong role in speech perception. Studies show that when listeners watch the face of the talker, perception of the message is greatly enhanced, in effect contributing the equivalent of a 20 dB boost (quite substantial) in the signal. This supports the view that speech in humans is polymodally represented. In birds, syllables from alien bird species' songs can be learned in the presence of the sight of a conspecific bird (Petrinovich and Baptista 1987). These visual effects suggest how strongly the visual-motor system is linked to perception in both birdsong and speech (see also Liberman 1993).

Nature of Language Input to the Child

Peter Marler's early studies (e.g., 1970) on birdsong learning highlighted the role of input by manipulating it. These studies showed the dramatic effects of input on song learning, as well as the birds' selectivity for certain kinds of signals. In the realm of language, attention is being increasingly devoted to understanding exactly how much and what kind of language input infants hear.

Estimates indicate that a typical listening day for a two year old includes 20,000–40,000 words (Chapman et al. 1992). Research has shown that the speech addressed to infants (often called "motherese" or "parentese") is unique: it has a characteristic prosodic structure that includes a higher pitch, a slower tempo, and exaggerated intonation contours, and it is syntactically and semantically simplified. Studies show that this speaking style is nearly universal in the speech of caretakers around the world, and that infants prefer it over other complex acoustic signals (Fernald 1985; Grieser and Kuhl 1989; Fernald and Kuhl 1987).

In recent studies, we have uncovered another modification made by parents when addressing infants that may be important to infant learning. We examined natural-language input at the phonetic level to infants in the United States, Russia, and

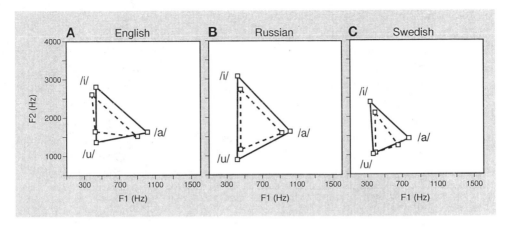

Figure 15.7
The vowel triangle of maternal speech directed toward infants (solid line) across three diverse languages shows a "stretching" relative to the adult-directed vowel triangle (dashed line), an effect that both makes vowels more discriminable and highlights the abstract features that infants must use to produce speech themselves.

Sweden (Kuhl, Andruski, et al. 1997). The study shows that across three very diverse languages, infant-directed speech exhibited a universal alteration of phonetic units when compared with adult-directed speech. Parents addressing their infants produced acoustically more extreme tokens of vowel sounds, resulting in a "stretching" of the acoustic space encompassing the vowel triangle (figure 15.7). A stretched vowel triangle not only makes speech more discriminable for infants, it also highlights critical spectral parameters that allow speech to be produced by the child. The results suggest that at the phonetic level of language, linguistic input to infants provides exceptionally well-specified information about the units that form the building blocks for words.

A stretched vowel space is not necessary from the standpoint of the infant's capacity to distinguish vowels. The formant frequency changes from adult-directed to infant-directed speech were substantial and would clearly be registered by the infant auditory system. Previous data on infants' capacities to discern subtle differences between vowels indicate that infants are capable of hearing differences a great deal smaller than those produced by mothers in the study (Kuhl 1991a).

If not required for infant discrimination, what function does a stretched vowel space serve? We hypothesized that stretching the vowel triangle could benefit infants in three ways. First, it increases the distance between vowels, making them more distinct from one another. In recent studies, language-delayed children showed substantial improvements in measures of speech and language after treatment in a program in which they listened to speech altered by computer to exaggerate phonetic differences (Merzenich et al. 1996; Tallal et al. 1996). Normally developing infants may benefit similarly from the enhanced acoustic differences provided in infant-directed speech.

Second, to achieve the stretching, mothers produce vowels that go beyond those produced in typical adult conversation. From both an acoustic and articulatory perspective, these vowels are "hyperarticulated" (Lindblom 1990). Hyperarticulated vowels are perceived by adults as "better instances" of vowel categories (Iverson and Kuhl 1995; Johnson, Flemming, and Wright 1993), and laboratory tests show that when listening to good instances of phonetic categories, infants show greater phonetic categorization ability. The present study shows that hyperarticulated vowels are a part of infants' linguistic experience and raises the possibility that they play an important role in the development of infants' vowel categories.

Third, expanding the vowel triangle allows mothers to produce a greater variety of instances representing each vowel category without creating acoustic overlap between vowel categories. Greater variety may cause infants to attend to non-frequency-specific spectral dimensions that characterize a vowel category, rather than to any one particular set of frequencies that the mother uses to produce a vowel, and this may assist learning (see Lively, Logan, and Pisoni 1993). Converting the formant values to spectral features shows that infant-directed speech maximizes the featural contrast between vowels (Kuhl, Andruski et al. 1997). This is especially critical for infants because they cannot duplicate the absolute frequencies of adult speech—their vocal tracts are too small (Kent and Murray 1982). To speak, infants must reproduce the appropriate spectral dimensions in their own frequency range (Kuhl and Meltzoff 1996). Our recent study indicates that maternal language input emphasizes these dimensions. It is unknown whether adult birds tutor their infants using a special kind of vocal signal, the equivalent of "songbird parentese."

Brain Correlates

Since the classic reports of Broca (1861) and Wernicke (1874) on patients with language deficits typical of aphasia, we have known that the two hemispheres are not equal in the extent to which they subserve language, and this had in the past been reported for birds as well (though see Doupe and Kuhl 1999 few recent data). In the 1960s, behavioral studies on language processing in normal adults contributed additional evidence of the left-hemisphere specialization for language (Kimura 1961). Using a method known as the "dichotic listening task," researchers sent two different speech signals simultaneously to the right and left ears and asked subjects to identify the stimuli they heard. The results demonstrated that people are significantly more accurate at identifying speech sent to the right ear than to the left ear, and that music showed a right-ear advantage; both were argued to be attributable to the increased strength of contralateral over ipsilateral fibers connecting the auditory input to the brain, and the fact that the left hemisphere (LH) of the brain was specialized for language, whereas the right hemisphere (RH) was specialized for music (Kimura 1961; Milner, Taylor, and Sperry 1968). The LH specialization was shown not only for spoken language but for individuals words, the consonants and vowel sounds contained in words, and even the phonetic features that formed the building blocks for phonemes (Studdert-Kennedy and Shankweiler 1970). These studies provided powerful evidence that the left hemisphere controlled language processing in adults, for units as small as the phonetic feature.

With the advent of modern neuroimaging techniques such as PET, positron emission tomography (Peterson, Fox, Snyder, and Raichle 1990; Posner, Peterson, Fox, and Raichle 1988), fMRI, functional magnetic resonance imaging, (Neville et al. 1998), ERP, event-related potentials (Neville, Mills, and Lawson 1992; Osterhout and Holcomb 1992), and MEG, magnetoencephalography (Näätänen et al. 1997), studies of the brain's organization of language have appeared in increasing numbers. It is early in this field, but there are some conclusions that take us beyond what early studies have shown regarding language and the brain. The new studies suggest, for example, that there is not one unified "language area" in the brain in which linguistic signals are processed. Different brain systems subserve different aspects of language processing, and the language-processing areas of the brain include many more regions than the classic Broca's and Wernicke's areas (see Binder 1994 for review).

The imaging studies support the dissociation for processing speech and nonspeech signals found in earlier behavioral studies. Zatorre, Evans, Meyer, and Gjedde (1992) used PET scans to examine phonetic as opposed to pitch processing. Subjects in the study had to judge the final consonant of the syllable in the phonetic task and the pitch of the syllable (high or low) in the pitch task. The results showed that phonetic processing engaged the LH whereas pitch processing engaged the RH. This dissociation between the phonetic and nonphonetic processing of auditory dimensions is mirrored in studies using vowels at different pitches and MEG, even though the lateralization of vowels was less strong than that shown for consonants, as might be expected from behavioral studies (Poeppel et al. 1997).

Studies of deaf individuals who communicate using sign language provide an interesting test for the hypothesis that the LH handles language processing. Because visual-spatial information is typically thought to involve right-hemisphere analysis, studies of sign-language processing by deaf speakers provided a method for examining whether language involves left-hemisphere analysis in speakers whose language is visual-spatial, a signal normally associated with right-hemisphere processing.

Studies of deaf individuals who have sustained cerebral damage and exhibit aphasia indicate that in such individuals the left hemisphere rather than right hemisphere is impaired (Bellugi, Poizner, and Klima 1989; Klima, Bellugi, and Poizner 1988). Studies using event-related potential methods show that in deaf individuals the left-hemisphere regions normally used for spoken language processing are active during processing of signed language signals (Neville, Mills, and Lawson 1992).

Given these results, an important question from the standpoint of development is when the left-hemisphere becomes dominant in the processing of linguistic information. Lenneberg (1967) hypothesized that the two hemispheres are equipotential for language until approximately two years of age, at which time left-hemisphere dominance begins to develop and continues until puberty. However, this theory was contradicted by data suggesting that children with LH versus RH damage at an early age displayed different deficits in language abilities; early LH damage affected language abilities more than early RH damage (Witelson 1987).

Behavioral studies established the right-ear advantage (REA) for speech for verbal stimuli and the left-ear advantage (LEA) for musical and environmental sounds using the dichotic listening task in children as young as 2.5 years of age (Bever 1971; Kimura 1963). But what of infants? Glanville, Best, and Levenson (1977) reported an REA for speech contrasts and a LEA for musical sounds using a cardiac orienting procedure in 3-month-olds. There have been only two studies providing data on infants' differential responses to speech and music at ages younger than two months. In one study, infants' discriminative capacities for speech and music were examined in 2-, 3-, and 4-month-old infants using a cardiac-orienting procedure. The results demonstrated a REA for speech discrimination in 3-month and 4-month-old infants, but not in 2-month-old infants. In addition, a LEA was shown for musical-note discrimination at all three ages. Finally, tests on 2-month-olds conducted by Vargha-Khadem and Corballis (1979) showed infants discriminated speech contrasts equally with both hemispheres. In other words, the results suggest that speech may not be lateralized in 2-month-old infants, but becomes so by 4 months of age.

This issue of the onset of laterality and the extent to which it depends on linguistic experience may be resolved with future research using techniques that can be used throughout the lifespan. One such technique is the mismatched negativity (MMN), a component of the auditorily evoked event-related potential (ERP). The MMN is automatically elicited by a discriminable change in a repetitive sound pattern and its generation appears to represent the detection of a change in the neural sensory-memory representation established by the repeated stimulus (see Näätänen 1990, 1992 for review). MMNs to a change in a speech stimulus have been well documented in adult listeners (see, e.g., Kraus et al. 1992). The MMN has been established in children (Kraus et al. 1993) and most recently in infants (Cheour-Luhtanen et al. 1995; Kuhl 1998b; Pang et al. 1998). In adult ERP studies, a left-hemisphere asymmetry is evident (Pang et al. 1998), but it has not been observed in newborns (Cheour-Luhtanen et al. 1995).

In summary, there is no strong evidence at present that the bias toward left-hemisphere processing for language is present at birth. The data suggest that it may take experience with linguistically patterned information to produce the left-hemisphere specialization. Thus there is support for a specialization for language in infancy, but one that develops, rather than one that exists at birth. Moreover, the input that is eventually lateralized to the left hemisphere can be either speech or sign, indicating that it is the linguistic or communicative significance of the signals, rather than their specific form, that accounts for the specialization.

Conclusions

As first suggested by Peter Marler (1970), birdsong and speech share a number of striking features: (i) evidence of innate perceptual predispositions that aid the acquisition of vocal communication; (ii) dramatic effects during sensitive periods to experience with conspecific communicative signals both in perception and production; (iii) vocal learning's dependence on auditory input; (iv) visual effects that enhance processing indicating perceptual-motor links and polymodal mapping of information; and (v) early brain correlates supporting the control of communication. Theories will be furthered by interactions between these two fields. In humans, theoretical progress is being made with detailed results of behavioral experiments on development. In birds, information regarding the neural substrates are providing detailed information, thus making the two fields highly complimentary.

To summarize these points: research has shown that in the first year of life infants learn a great deal about the perceptual characteristics of their native language, and this subsequently alters their perception and production of speech. According to the native language magnet model, perceptual learning early in life results in the formation of stored representations that capture native-language regularities. The theory emphasizes the role of linguistic input. Input does not act like a trigger for innately stored information. Rather, it is mapped in such a way as to "warp" the underlying acoustic space. Stored representations act like perceptual magnets for similar patterns of sound, resulting in maps that specify perceived distances between sounds and create categories. The map shrinks perceptual distances near a category's most typical instances and stretches perceptual distances between categories. Perceptual maps differ in adults who speak different languages and are polymodally mapped, containing auditory, visual, and motor information. The magnet effects and the mental maps they produce help explain how native-language speech develops, as well as our relative inability as adults to readily acquire a foreign language.

Acknowledgment

This essay was supported by grants to the author from the National Institutes of Health (DC00520, HD18286).

References

Abramson, A. S. and Lisker, L. (1970) Discriminability along the voicing continuum: Cross-language tests. In *Proceedings of the Sixth International Congress of Phonetic Sciences, Prague 1967*, pp. 569–573. Prague: Academia.

Bates, E. and Elman, J. (1996) Learning rediscovered. *Science* 274:1849–1850.

Bateson, P. (1991) Are there principles of behavioral development? In *The Development and Integration of Behaviour*, ed. by P. Bateson, pp. 19–39. Cambridge: Cambridge University Press.

Bellugi, U., Poizner, H., and Klima, E. S. (1989) Language, modality, and the brain. *Trends Neurosci.* 12:380–388.

Berkeley, G. (1709) *An Essay Toward a New Theory of Vision.* Dublin: Pepyat.

Best, C. T. (1993) Language-specific changes in non-native speech perception: A window on early phonological development. In *Developmental Neurocognition: Speech and Face Processing in the First Year of Life*, ed. by B. de Boysson-Bardies, S. de Schonen, P. Jusczyk, P. McNeilage, and J. Morton, pp. 289–304. Dordrecht, Netherlands: Kluwer Academic Publishers.

Bever, T. G. (1971) The nature of cerebral dominance in speech behavior of the child and adult. In *Language Acquisition: Models and Methods*, ed. by R. Huxley and E. Ingram. London: Academic Press.

Binder, J. R. and Rao, S. M. (1994) Human brain mapping with functional magnetic resonance imaging. In *Localization and Neuroimaging in Neuropsychology*, ed. by A. Kertesz, pp. 185–212. San Diego: Academic Press.

Bonhoeffer, T. and Shatz, C. J. (1998) Neurotrophins and visual system plasticity. In *Mechanistic Relationships between Development and Learning*, ed. by T. J. Carew, R. Menzel, and C. J. Shatz, pp. 93–112. New York: Wiley.

Broca, P. (1861) Nouvelle observation d'aphemie produite par une lesion de la motie posterieure des deuxieme et troiseme circonvolutions frontales. *Bulletin de la Societe d'Anatomique* 6:398–407.

Cajal, R. S. (1906 [1967]) The structure and connections of neurons. In *Nobel Lectures in Physiology or Medicine 1901–1921*, pp. 220–253. New York: Elsevier.

Carew, T. J., Menzel, R., and Shatz, C. J. (1998) *Mechanistic Relationships between Development and Learning.* New York: Wiley.

Carey, S. (1985) *Conceptual Change in Childhood.* Cambridge, MA: MIT Press.

Chapman, R. S., Streim, N. W., Crais, E. R., Salmon, D., Strand, E. A., and Negri, N. A. (1992) Child talk: Assumptions of a developmental process model for early language learning. In *Processes in Language Acquisition and Disorders,* ed. by R. S. Chapman, pp. 3–19. St. Louis, MO: Mosby Year Book.

Cheour-Luhtanen, M., Alho Kujala, K. T., Sainio Reinikainen, K. K., Renlund, M., Aaltonen, O., Eerola, O., and Näätänen, R. (1995) Mismatch negativity indicates vowel discrimination in newborns. *Hearing Research* 82:53–58.

Chomsky, N. (1957) A review of B. F. Skinner's *Verbal Behavior. Language* 35:26–58.

Chomsky, N. (1965) *Aspects of the Theory of Syntax.* Cambridge, MA: MIT Press.

Chomsky, N. (1981) *Rules and Representations.* New York: Columbia University Press.

Curtiss, S. (1977) *Genie: A Psycholinguistic Study of a Modern Day "Wild Child."* New York: Academic.

de Boysson-Bardies, B. (1993) Ontogeny of language-specific syllabic productions. In *Developmental Neurocognition: Speech and Face Processing in the First Year of Life,* ed. by B. de Boysson-Bardies, S. de Schonen, P. Jusczyk, P. McNeilage, and J. Morton, pp 353–363. Dordrecht, Netherlands: Kluwer Academic Publishers.

Dooling, R. J., Best, C. T., and Brown, S. D. (1995) Discrimination of synthetic full-formant and sine-wave /ra-la/ continua by budgerigars (*Melopsittacus undulatus*) and zebra finches (*Taeniopygia guttata*). *J. Acoust. Soc. Am.* 97:1839–1846.

Doupe, A. (1998) Development and learning in the birdsong system: Are there shared mechanisms? In *Mechanistic Relationships between Development and Learning,* ed. by T. J. Carew, R. Menzel, and C. J. Shatz, pp. 29–52. New York: Wiley.

Doupe, A. and Kuhl, P. K. (1999). Birdsong and speech: Common themes and mechanisms. *Annual Review of Neuroscience, 22,* 567–631.

Eimas, P. D., Miller, J. L., and Jusczyk, P. W. (1987) On infant speech perception and the acquisition of language. In *Categorical Perception: The Groundwork of Cognition,* ed. by S. Harnad, pp. 161–195. New York: Cambridge University Press.

Fanselow, M. S. and Rudy, J. W. (1998) Convergence of experimental and developmental approaches to animal learning and memory processes. In *Mechanistic Relationships between Development and Learning,* ed. by T. J. Carew, R. Menzel, and C. J. Shatz, pp. 15–28. New York: Wiley.

Ferguson, C. A., Menn, L., and Stoel-Gammon, C. (eds.) (1992) *Phonological Development: Models, Research, Implications.* Timonium, MD: York.

Fernald, A. (1985) Four-month-old infants prefer to listen to motherese. *Inf. Behav. Develop.* 8:181–195.

Fernald, A. and Kuhl, P. (1987) Acoustic determinants of infant preference for Motherese speech. *Infant Behavior and Development* 10:279–293.

Flege, J. E. (1988) Factors affecting degree of perceived foreign accent in English sentences. *J. Acoust. Soc. Am.* 84:70–79.

Flege, J. E. (1993) Production and perception of a novel, second-language phonetic contrast. *J. Acoust. Soc. Am.* 93:1589–1608.

Glanville, B. B., Best, C. T., and Levenson, R. (1977) A cardiac measure of cerebral asymmetries in infant auditory perception. *Develop. Psych.* 13:54–59.

Gopnik, A. and Meltzoff, A. N. (1997) *Words, Thoughts, and Theories.* Cambridge, MA: MIT Press.

Goto, H. (1971) Auditory perception by normal Japanese adults of the sounds "l" and "r." *Neuropsychologia* 9:317–323.

Green, K. P., Kuhl, P. K., Meltzoff, A. N., and Stevens, E. B. (1991) Integrating speech information across talkers, gender, and sensory modality: Female faces and male voices in the McGurk effect. *Perception & Psychophysics* 50:524–536.

Greenough, W. T. and Black, J. E. (1992) Induction of brain structure by experience: Substrates for cognitive development. In *The Minnesota Symposia on Child Psychology*, Vol. 24: *Developmental Behavioral Neuroscience*, ed. by M. Gunnar and C. Nelson, pp. 155–200. Hillsdale, NJ: Erlbaum.

Grieser, D. and Kuhl, P. K. (1989) Categorization of speech by infants: Support for speech-sound prototypes. *Develop. Psych.* 25:577–588.

Hauser, M. D. (1996) *The Evolution of Communication.* Cambridge, MA: MIT Press.

Iverson, P. and Kuhl, P. K. (1995) Mapping the perceptual magnet effect for speech using signal detection theory and multidimensional scaling. *J. of the Acoust. Soc. Am.* 97:553–562.

Iverson, P. and Kuhl, P. K. (1996) Influences of phonetic identification and category goodness on American listeners' perception of /r/ and /l/. *J. of the Acoust. Soc. of Am.* 99:1130–1140.

James, W. (1890 [1958]) *Principles of Psychology.* New York: Holt.

Johnson, K., Flemming, E., and Wright, R. (1993) The hyperspace effect: Phonetic targets are hyperarticulated. *Language* 69:505–528.

Jusczyk, P. W., Friederici, A. D., Wessels, J. M. I., Svenkerud, V. Y., and Jusczyk, A. M. (1993) Infants' sensitivity to the sound patterns of native language words. *J. of Mem. and Lang.* 32:402–420.

Karmiloff-Smith, A. (1991) Beyond modularity: Innate constraints and developmental change. In *The Epigenesis of Mind: Essays on Biology and Cognition*, ed. by S. Carey, and R. Gelman, pp. 171–197. Hillsdale, NJ: Erlbaum.

Karmiloff-Smith, A. (1995) Annotation: The extraordinary cognitive journey from foetus through infancy. *J. Child Psych. & Psychiat. & All. Disciplines* 36:1293–1313.

Kent, R. D. and Murray, A. D. (1982) Acoustic features of infant vocalic utterances at 3, 6, and 9 months. *J. of the Acoust. Soc. of Am.* 72:353–365.

Kim, K. H. S., Relkin, N. R., Lee, K. M., and Hirsch, J. (1997) Distinct cortical areas associated with native and second languages. *Nature* 388:172–174.

Kimura, D. (1961) Cerebral dominance and the perception of verbal stimuli. *Can J. Psych.* 15:166–171.

Kimura, D. (1963) Speech lateralization in young children as determined by an auditory test. *J. of Comp. and Physiol. Psych.* 56:899–901.

Klima, E. S., Bellugi, U., and Poizner, H. (1988) Grammar and space in sign aphasiology. *Aphasiol.* 2:319–327.

Kluender, K. R., Diehl, R. L., and Killeen, P. R. (1987) Japanese quail can learn phonetic categories. *Science* 237:1195–1197.

Knudsen, E. I. and Brainerd, M. S. (1995) Creating a unified representation of visual and auditory space in the brain. *Ann. Rev. Neurosci.* 18:19–43.

Knudsen, E. I. and Knudsen, P. F. (1990) Sensitive and critical periods for visual calibration of sound localization by barn owls. *J. Neurosci.* 10:222–232.

Koffka, K. (1924) *The Growth of the Mind.* New York: Harcourt Brace.

Konishi, M. (1965) Effects of deafening on song development in American robins and black-headed grosbeaks. *Z. Tierpsychol.* 22:584–599.

Kraus, N., McGee, T., Sharma, A., Carrell, T., and Nicol, T. (1992) Mismatch negativity event-related potential elicited by speech stimuli. *Ear and Hearing* 13:158–164.

Kraus, N., McGee, T., Micco, A., Sharma, A., Carrell, T., and Nicol, T. (1993) Mismatch negativity in school-age children to speech stimuli that are just perceptibly different. *Electroenceph. Clin. Neurophys.* 88:123–130.

Kuhl, P. K. (1991a) Perception, cognition, and the ontogenetic and phylogenetic emergence of human speech. In *Plasticity of Development*, ed. by S. E. Brauth, W. S. Hall, and R. J. Dooling, pp. 73–106. Cambridge, MA: MIT Press.

Kuhl, P. K. (1991b) Human adults and human infants show a "perceptual magnet effect" for the proto-types of speech categories, monkeys do not. *Perception & Psychophysics* 50:93–107.

Kuhl, P. K. (1992) Infants' perception and representation of speech: Development of a new theory. In *Proceedings of the International Conference on Spoken Language Processing*, ed. by J. J. Ohala, T. M. Nearey, B. L. Derwing, M. M. Hodge, and G. E. Wiebe, pp. 449–456. Edmonton, Alberta: University of Alberta.

Kuhl, P. K. (1994) Learning and representation in speech and language. *Current Opinion in Neurobiology* 4:812–822.

Kuhl, P. K. (1998a) The development of language. In C. von Euler, I. Lundberg, and R. Llinás (eds.), *Basic mechanisms in cognition and language*, pp. 175–195. New York: Elsevier.

Kuhl, P. K. (1998b) Effects of language experience on speech perception. Paper presented at the 135th meeting of the Acoustical Society of America, Seattle, WA.

Kuhl, P. K., Andruski, J. E., Chistovich, I. A., Chistovich, L. A., Kozhevnikova, E. V., Ryskina, V. L., Stolyarova, E. I., Sundberg, U., and Lacerda, F. (1997) Cross-language analysis of phonetic units in language addressed to infants. *Science* 277:684–686.

Kuhl, P. K., Kiritani, S., Deguchi, T., Hayashi, A., Stevens, E. B., Dugger, C. D., and Iverson, P. (1997) Effects of language experience on speech perception: American and Japanese infants' perception of /ra/ and /la/. *J. Acoust. Soc. Am.* 102:3135.

Kuhl, P. K. and Meltzoff, A. N. (1982) The bimodal perception of speech in infancy. *Science* 218:1138–1141.

Kuhl, P. K. and Meltzoff, A. N. (1996) Infant vocalizations in response to speech: Vocal imitation and developmental change. *J. Acoust. Soc. Am.* 100:2425–2438.

Kuhl, P. K., Tsuzaki, M., Tohkura, Y., and Meltzoff, A. N. (1994) Human processing of auditory-visual information in speech perception: Potential for multimodal human-machine interfaces. In *Proceedings of the International Conference on Spoken Language Processing*, pp. 539–542. Tokyo: Acoustical Society of Japan.

Kuhl, P. K., Williams, K. A., Lacerda, F., Stevens, K. N., and Lindblom, B. (1992) Linguistic experience alters phonetic perception in infants by 6 months of age. *Science* 255:606–608.

Lenneberg, E. H. (1967) *Biological Foundations of Language.* New York: Wiley.

Liberman, A. M. (1993) In the perception of speech, time is not what it seems. In *Temporal Information Processing in the Nervous System.* Annals of the New York Academy of Sciences, ed. by P. Tallal, A. M. Galaburda, R. R. Llinás, and C. von Euler, vol. 682, pp. 264–271. New York: The New York Academy of Sciences.

Lindblom, B. (1990) Explaining phonetic variation: A sketch of the H&H theory. In *Speech Production and Speech Modeling*, ed. by W. J. Hardcastle, and A. Marchal, pp. 403–439. Dordrecht, Netherlands: Kluwer Academic Publishers.

Lively, S. E., Logan, J. S., Pisoni, D. B. (1993) Training Japanese listeners to identify English /r/ and /l/. II. The role of phonetic environment and talker variability in learning new perceptual categories. *J. Acoust. Soc. Am.* 94:1242–1255.

Locke, J. (1690) *An Essay Concerning Human Understanding.* London: Bassett.

Lorenz, K. (1965) *Evolution and Modification of Behavior.* Chicago: Chicago University Press.

MacKain, K., Studdert-Kennedy, M., Spieker, S., and Stern, D. (1983) Infant intermodal speech percep-tion is a left-hemisphere function. *Science* 219:1347–1349.

Marler, P. (1970). A comparative approach to vocal learning: Song development in white-crowned spar-rows. *J. Comp. and Physiol. Psych.* 71:1–25.

Marler, P. (1974) Constraints on learning: Development of bird song. In *Ethology and Psychiatry*, ed. by W. F. Norman, pp. 69–83. Toronto: University of Toronto Press.

Marler, P. (1990) Innate learning preferences: Signals for communication. *Dev. Psychobiol.* 23:557–568.

Marler, P. (1991) The instinct to learn. In *The Epigenesis of Mind: Essays on Biology and Cognition*, ed. by S. Carey, and R. Gelman, pp. 37–66. Hillsdale, NJ: Erlbaum.

Marler, P. (1977) Three models of song learning: Evidence from behavior. *J. of Neurobiol.* 33:501–506.

Massaro, D. W. (1987) *Speech Perception by Ear and Eye: A Paradigm for Psychological Inquiry.* Hillsdale, NJ: Erlbaum.

McGurk, H. and MacDonald, J. (1976) Hearing lips and seeing voices. *Nature* 264:746–748.

Meltzoff, A. N. and Moore, M. K. (1977) Imitation of facial and manual gestures by human neonates. *Science* 198:75–78.

Meltzoff, A. N. and Moore, M. K. (1994) Imitation, memory, and the representation of persons. *Infant Behav. and Dev.* 17:83–99.

Merzenich, M. M., Jenkins, W. M., Johnston, P., Schreiner, C., Miller, S. L., and Tallal, P. (1996) Temporal processing deficits of language-learning impaired children ameliorated by training. *Science* 271:77–81.

Miller, J. L. (1994) On the internal structure of phonetic categories: A progress report. *Cognition* 50:271–285.

Milner, B., Taylor, L., and Sperry, R. W. (1968) Lateralized suppression of dichotically presented digits after commissural section in man. *Science* 161:184–186.

Miyawaki, K., Strange, W., Verbrugge, R., Liberman, A. M., Jenkins, J. J., and Fujimura, O. (1975) An effect of linguistic experience: The discrimination of [r] and [l] by native speakers of Japanese and English. *Percept. Psychophys.* 18:331–340.

Näätänen, R. (1990) The role of attention in auditory information processing as revealed by event-related potentials and other brain measures of cognitive function. *Behav. Brain Sci.* 13:201–288.

Näätänen, R. (1992) The mismatch negativity (MMN). In *Attention and Brain Function*, pp. 137–210. New Jersey: Erlbaum Assoc.

Näätänen, R., Lehtokoski, A., Lennes, M., Cheour, M., Huotilainen, M., Iivonen, M., Vainio, M., Alku, P., Ilmoniemi, RJ., Luuk, R., Allik, J., Sinkkonen, J., and Alho, K. (1997) Language-specific phoneme representations revealed by electric and magnetic brain responses. *Nature* 385:432–434.

Neville, H. J., Bavelier, D., Corina, D., Rauschecker, J., Karni, A., Lalwani, A., et al. (1998) Cerebral organization for language in deaf and hearing subjects: Biological constraints and effects of experience. *Proceedings of the Nat. Acad. Sci.* 95:922–929.

Neville, H. J., Mills, D. L., and Lawson, D. S. (1992) Fractionating language: Different neural subsystems with different sensitive periods. *Cerebral Cortex* 2:244–258.

Nottebohm, F. (1967) The role of sensory feedback in the development of avian vocalizations. *Proceedings of the 14th International Ornithological Congress*, pp. 265–280.

Oller, D. K. and MacNeilage, P. F. (1983) Development of speech production: Perspectives from natural and perturbed speech. In *The Production of Speech*, ed. by P. F. MacNeilage, pp. 91–108. New York: Springer-Verlag.

Oller, D. K., Wieman, L. A., Doyle, W. J., and Ross, C. (1976) Infant babbling and speech. *J. Child Lang.* 3:1–11.

Osterhout, L. and Holcomb, P. L. (1992) Event-related brain potentials elicited by syntactic anomaly. *J. Mem. Lang.* 31:785–806.

Pang, E. W., Edmonds, G. E., Desjardins, R., Khan, S. C., Trainor, L. J., and Taylor, M. J. (1998) Mismatch negativity to speech stimuli in 8-month-old infants and adults. *Int. J. Psychophysiol.* 29:227–236.

Petersen, S. E., Fox, P. T., Snyder, A. Z., and Raichle, M. E. (1990) Activation of extrastriate and frontal cortical areas by visual words and word-like stimuli. *Science* 249:1041–1044.

Petitto, L. A. and Marentette, P. F. (1991) Babbling in the manual mode: Evidence for the ontogeny of language. *Science* 251:1493–1496.

Petrinovich, L. and Baptista, L. F. (1987) Song development in the white-crowned sparrow: Modification of learned song. *Anim. Behav.* 35:961–974.

Piaget, J. (1954) *The Construction of Reality in the Child.* New York: Basic Books.

Pinker, S. (1994) *The Language Instinct.* New York: Morrow.

Poeppel, D., Phillips, C., Yellin, E., Rowley, H. A., Roberts, T. P., and Marantz, A. (1997) Processing of vowels in supratemporal auditory cortex. *Neurosci. Letters* 221:145–148.

Posner, M. I., Petersen, S. E., Fox, P. T., and Raichle, M. E. (1988) Localization of cognitive operations in the human brain. *Science* 240:1627–1631.

Rosch, E. H. (1977) Human categorization. In *Studies in Cross-cultural Psychology*, vol. 1, ed by N. Warren, pp. 1–49. San Francisco: Academic Press.

Rosenblum, L. D., Schmuckler, M. A., and Johnson, J. A. (1997) The McGurk effect in infants. *Percept. Psychophys.* 59:347–357.

Saffran, J. R., Aslin, R. N., and Newport, E. L. (1996) Statistical learning by 8–month-old infants. *Science* 274:1926–1928.

Skinner, B. F. (1957) *Verbal Behavior.* New York: Appleton-Century-Crofts.

Snowdon, C. T. and Hausberger, M. (eds.) (1997) *Social Influences on Vocal Development.* Cambridge: Cambridge University Press.

Stoel-Gammon, C. and Otomo, K. (1986) Babbling development of hearing-impaired and normally hearing subjects. *J. Speech and Hearing Disorders* 51:33–41.

Strange, W. (1995) *Speech Perception and Linguistic Experience: Issues in Cross-language Research.* Timonium, MD: York.

Studdert-Kennedy, M. and Shankweiler, D. (1970) Hemispheric specialization for speech perception. *J. Acoust. Soc. Am.* 48:579–594.

Sussman, J. E. and Lauckner-Morano, V. J. (1995) Further tests of the "perceptual magnet effect" in the perception of [i]: Identification and change/no-change discrimination. *J. Acoust. Soc. Am.* 97:539–552.

Tallal, P., Miller, S. L., Bedi, G., Byma, G., Wang, G., Nagarajan, S. S., Schreiner, C., Jenkins, W. M., and Merzenich, M. M. (1996) Language comprehension in language-learning impaired children improved with acoustically modified speech. *Science* 271:81–84.

Thorpe, W. H. (1959) Talking birds and the mode of action of the vocal apparatus of birds. *Proceedings Zoo. Soc. London* 132:441–455.

Thorpe, W. H. (1961) *Bird Song: The Biology of Vocal Communication and Expression in Birds.* New York: Cambridge University Press.

Tinbergen, N. (1951) *The Study of Instinct.* New York: Clarendon.

Vargha-Khadem, F. and Corballis, M. C. (1979) Cerebral asymmetry in infants. *Brain & Lang.* 8:1–9.

Vihman, M. M. (1993) Vocal motor schemes, variation and the production-perception link. *J. Phonetics* 21:163–169.

Vihman, M. M. and de Boysson-Bardies, B. (1994) The nature and origins of ambient language influence on infant vocal production and early words. *Phonetica* 51:159–169.

Vygotsky, L. S. (1962) *Thought and Language.* Cambridge, MA: MIT Press.

Vygotsky, L. S. (1979) Interaction between learning and development. In *Mind in Society: The Development of Higher Psychological Processes*, ed. by M. Cole, V. John-Steiner, S. Scribner, and E. Souberman, pp. 79–91. Cambridge, MA: Harvard University Press.

Walton, G. E. and Bower, T. G. R. (1993) Amodal representation of speech in infants. *Inf. Behav. Develop.* 16:233–243.

450 P. K. Kuhl

Werker, J. F. and Tees, R. C. (1984) Cross-language speech perception: Evidence for perceptual reorganization during the first year of life. *Inf. Behav. Develop.* 7:49–63.

Werker, J. F. and Polka, L. (1993) The ontogeny and developmental significance of language-specific phonetic perception. In *Developmental Neurocognition: Speech and Face Processing in the First Year of Life*, ed. by B. de Boysson-Bardies, S. de Schonen, P. Jusczyk, P. McNeilage, and J. Morton, pp. 275–288. Dordrecht, The Netherlands: Kluwer Academic Publishers.

Wernicke, C. (1874) *Der aphasische symptomenkomplex.* Breslau: Cohn and Weigert.

Willerman, R. and Kuhl, P. K. (1996) Cross-language speech perception: Swedish, English, and Spanish speakers' perception of front rounded vowels. *Proc. 1996 Int. Conf. Spoken Lang. Proc.* 1:442–445.

Witelson, S. F. (1987) Neurobiological aspects of language in children. *Child Develop.* 58:653–688.

Yamada, R. A. and Tohkura, Y. (1992) The effects of experimental variables on the perception of American English /r/ and /l/ by Japanese listeners. *Percept. Psychophys.* 52:376–392.

Zatorre, R. J., Evans, A. C., Meyer, E., and Gjedde, A. (1992) Lateralization of phonetic and pitch discrimination in speech processing. *Science* 256:846–849.

III EVOLUTION OF COMMUNICATION

Marc D. Hauser

Charles Darwin transformed our understanding of life's diversity by providing a powerful theory that is backed by an equally powerful method. He based the theory on the logic of natural selection, a blind pressure that requires for its operation heritable variation of replicating units. The logic of selection led him next to a focus on characters with adaptive design features, traits that promote fitness through survival and reproduction. To buttress his arguments, Darwin called on the power of the comparative method, one designed to illuminate the causes and consequences of interspecific similarities and differences. In his comparisons, Darwin covered a broad swath of taxonomic turf, looking at both closely and distantly related species. The importance of this approach was that it allowed for both a reconstruction of the evolutionary history of a character, as well as an explanation of why some species share certain traits even when they are distant relatives. In particular, to uncover nature's hierarchy, one must distinguish between shared characters that arise due to inheritance (homologies) and shared characters that arise from convergence (homoplasies). For the evolutionary biologist interested in the patterns that characterize the tree of life, homologies provide the requisite insights whereas homoplasies represent distractors. Cases of homology are of further interest because they highlight the conservative side of evolution, the fact that selection can maintain periods of stasis. An illustrative example comes from the recent work on hox genes, sequences of DNA that code for body segmentation and are carried by drosophila as well as by humans. Though homoplasies often derail systematists, they are of considerable interest to those concerned with the causes of adaptive phenotypes. Specifically, homoplasies show how and why adaptive design characteristics spring up in quite distantly related species, because for any given problem the solution set will be limited.

Darwin held a deep interest in the evolution of human and nonhuman animal communication. In his three major books on evolution (*Origins*, *Descent*, and *Expressions*), he discussed the design features of several communicative systems, showing how and why they differed or shared significant similarities. Thus he explored how changes in emotional state were related to changes in facial expression, how sexual selection favors exaggerated male displays designed to attract sexually receptive females, and how the human capacity for language—"an instinctive tendency to acquire an art"—was sculpted over time, "slowly and unconsciously developed by many steps." Since these writings, research on animal communication has played a central role in testing some of Darwin's intuitions. Such research has also led to several new theoretical insights, ones that build on Darwin's foundation and take advantage of modern techniques from neuroscience, molecular genetics, computer science, cognitive psychology, and animal behavior.

Perhaps the most important theoretical development since Darwin is the idea that selection favors gene replication. This insight, conceptualized in the late 1960s and early 1970s (Dawkins 1976; Hamilton 1964a,b; Maynard Smith 1964, 1965; 1974; Trivers 1971, 1972, 1974; Williams 1966) helped solve the problem of altruism, and as a result, it shed new light on the ultimate causes of communication. Thus, prior to the notion of selfish genes, it was commonly thought that communicative signals were designed to provide veridical information to other individuals. In the mid- to late-1970s, this view was challenged on two fronts. First, Dawkins and Krebs (1978; Krebs and Dawkins 1984) argued that the function of communication is to *manipulate* receivers for personal fitness gains; receivers, in turn, will be selected for their *mind-reading* capacities, perceptual skills that enable them to distinguish honest from dishonest signals. The logic underlying this radical position emerged from thinking about communication as a two-player game, and then imagining the conditions under which a particular strategy would remain stable over evolutionary time, immune to invasion from a mutant strategy. In general, if communication provides a veridical readout of what an individual will do next, then nothing will prevent an opponent from exaggerating—announcing, for example, that they will attack if threatened even though they lack the physical strength to carry out such a move. These ideas allow us to make sense of the extensive assessment periods preceding physical contact in a fight, the use of alarm calls in predator defense, and the production of food calls for recruiting conspecifics.

The second challenge, complementary to the first, was aimed at the problem of honesty, of working out the veridicality of the signal transmitted. What, specifically, would allow perceivers to mindread? The crucial insight into this problem was first articulated by Amotz Zahavi (1975, 1987), who argued that signals are honest if and only if they are costly to produce relative to current conditions and if the capacity to carry such costs is heritable. Although this claim—the *handicap principle*—was originally rejected because it couldn't be modeled using formal population genetics, it has recently been resuscitated on the basis of Grafen's (1990) game theory models, and a wealth of empirical work (reviewed in Hauser 1996; Bradbury and Vehrencamp 1997). Thus, for example, the handicap principle appears to explain the costliness of avian begging calls (an indicator of nutritional need), the antipredator stotting displays of ungulates (indicators of the ability to flee), and the lavish mating displays of males from a variety of species (indicators of genetic quality).

The theoretical insights that now guide research in animal communication are accompanied by a family of methodological tools. In particular, evolutionarily oriented biologists and psychologists are now using molecular phylogenies to address questions of origins and evolutionary change; neurobiological preparations to assess the constraints on signal production and perception; and experimental techniques from the cognitive sciences to understand the meaning (semantics and reference) of animal signals, as well as the mental states that accompany them. The chapters in this section represent state-of-the-art studies on the evolution of communication, studies that would certainly make Darwin smile.

In thinking about communication, we often consider modalities that humans are particularly good at processing, specifically, the visual and the auditory. This is, of course, a highly biased perspective, given that many species communicate in other modalities. Electric signaling is one such modality. In chapter 16, Carl Hopkins explores the production and perception ends of electric communication in fish, using an impressive combination of analytic techniques from neurobiology, functional morphology, behavioral ecology, systematics, molecular biology, and computer modeling. Focusing on one group in particular, the African Mormyridae, Hopkins shows that electric communication has evolved independently in several fish clades, but is restricted to those groups living in environments where the water provides a sufficient medium for passing electric currents. Some species come equipped with only receptive capacities for detecting electric signals, whereas others are equipped with both electric generating and receiving organs. This work highlights the importance of considering how environments function as selective forces on signal design, and how the coevolution of sender-receiver systems is constrained by neurophysiological mechanisms.

The integrative approach taken by Hopkins is continued by Andy Bass, Deana Bodnar, and Margaret Marchaterre in chapter 17. The theoretical core of this chapter is a slightly modified version of Tinbergen's (1952) methodological prescription for studying behavior. In particular, Bass and colleagues collapse Tinbergen's distinction between neurophysiological mechanisms and developmental processes into a single category (Mechanism), add on the dimension of life-history parameters, and then maintain the problems of adaptive function and phylogenetic history. Using this framework, they synthesize their research on an acoustically communicating teleost fish, the plainfin midshipman, focusing in particular on the patterns of mate choice as well as the causes and consequences of two phenotypic male morphs. As commonly revealed in life-history analyses, the two male morphs represent opposite endpoints of a continuum of energetic trade-offs, with one type investing in gonad mass whereas the other invests in body size and the early maturation of the vocal organ. Based on these analyses, Bass and colleagues go on to show that the vocal motor circuitry underlying midshipman vocalizations is a derived character, originating in an embryonic hindbrain segment that is responsible for generating a diversity of rhythmic behaviors. Here, then, is an elegant example of how phylogenetic reconstructions inform neurobiology, and conversely, of how the integration of work on behavior, ecology, and neurobiology informs phylogeny.

Some species occupy relatively narrow distributions, whereas others inhabit larger areas, often spanning several continents. Analyses of geographical variation in the expression of a character can provide important insights into the evolutionary process, allowing researchers to measure both random (e.g., drift) and nonrandom (e.g., selection) factors. In chapter 18, H. Carl Gerhardt uses his extensive knowledge of acoustical communication in frogs to explore the problem of reproductive character displacement, a process of species divergence that is caused by errors of signal recognition. In particular, he argues that divergence among species is often based on a combination of random processes that are intrinsic to the animal, as well as to environmental pressures that act upon signal design (e.g., habitat effects on signal transmission; predators that cue into acoustic signals; acoustic interference from other vocalizing species). Together, such factors provide the requisite genetic variation for sexual selection to act upon. Gerhardt supports his theoretical position with data from female mate choice experiments using both allopatric and sympatric species, and a variety of male characters. The resulting patterns deliver an important cautionary note for those focusing on univariate characters and single populations. Specifically, females often base their mating decisions on a suite of characters, and large differences in female selectivity are commonly found among allopatric populations, as well as between sympatric and allopatric populations.

A fundamental problem in sexual selection theory is to understand the reasons for female mate choice. When a female chooses a mate, is her decision based on direct fitness benefits (e.g., access to resources, help in parental care), or on indirect benefits that arise from picking a male with good genes? Given hundreds of mate-choice experiments involving manipulations of male-garnered resources, we now understand the sorts of direct benefits that females can accrue from being choosy. Less is known, however, about the causes and consequences of female mate choice when males have no direct real estate to offer. Mike Ryan and Stan Rand (chapter 19) provide one explanation for this puzzle by appealing to the theory of sensory exploitation, a theory that integrates neurobiological and phylogenetic analysis. Specifically, females are considered to have sensory biases that set up selective pressures on the design features of male signaling systems. Using mate-choice experiments with frogs from the genus *Physalaemus,* Ryan and Rand show that females may prefer calls that fall outside the range of species-typical variation if a particular characteristic of the call taps into an evolutionarily ancient sensory bias, a neural sweet spot so to speak. With this general result in place, they use the phylogeny of this group to recreate the ancestral call types, and then use these digitally synthesized calls in both a new round of mate-choice experiments as well as input to an artificial neural network model of female preference for male character coevolution. The mate-choice experiments consistently reveal evidence of female choice derived from the historical legacies of the past, preferences that ultimately may bias the pattern of male character evolution. The computational modeling approach reveals that when evolution was guided (constrained?) by preexisting sensory biases, recognition of call types was improved over an evolutionary process that was ahistorical, simply changing as a function of relatively random variations over time. As with the chapters by Hopkins and Bass et al., the work by Ryan and Rand emphasizes the power of an integrative biology of communication.

If a signal is communicative, then at some level it provides the perceiver with information, information that is presumed to reduce the uncertainty of the situation. Following signal detection, the animal must decide what to do with the information—fight or flee, mate or abstain, provide parental care or rest. When a signal is perceived, therefore, it is commonly placed into a category associated with a particular functional response. Some signals are packaged into discrete units, with each unit paired to a particular response type. The decision process under these conditions is relatively straightforward. Other signals, in contrast, are characterized by a physical continuum, thereby requiring perceivers to impose categorical boundaries for the purpose of choosing an appropriate response. Robert Wyttenbach and Ron Hoy (chapter 20) review the literature on categorical perception in humans and animals, using some of their own elegant work on crickets to illustrate both the difficulties associated with empirical work in this area, as well as the problems that face future inquiries into the nature of this perceptual process. Specifically, to distinguish categorical from continuous perception, studies must demonstrate that subjects not only *label* stimuli from different categories as different, but are able to *discriminate* between exemplars from different categories while failing to discriminate between exemplars from within the category. To date, few studies have documented both the labeling and discrimination components of this process, with work on humans and crickets providing important exceptions. Owing to the paucity of comparative work in this area, it is not yet possible to articulate the selective pressures that would have favored categorical over continuous perception, nor to recreate the phylogenetic history of this mechanism.

Like most other acoustic signaling systems, variation in oscine song exists at several levels, including within individuals, between individuals within populations, and between populations. What distinguishes the oscine song birds from such groups as the honey bees, electric fish, frogs, and microchiropteran bats is that much of the variation in song structure is due to their specialized capacity for vocal learning. In chapter 21, William Searcy and Stephen Nowicki explore the adaptive consequences of such variation using the song sparrow as a model system for field and laboratory research. Like other oscines, the song sparrow's song attracts females, stimulates their reproductive physiology, and repels potential male competitors. Some features of song sparrow song are species-typical, allowing for species recognition; manipulating these features beyond the normal range of variation causes female responsiveness to song to diminish. Selection therefore favors some level of signal stereotypy within an acoustic space, with perceptual mechanisms designed to reject signals that fall outside of this space. Paralleling the findings of Bass et al. on the midshipman and those of Gerhardt, Ryan, and Rand on frogs, a significant component of the variation in song structure plays a role in mate choice and intrasexual competition. Females generally prefer males with varied song repertoires, and males with different song types can more readily signal their level of arousal in addition to being able to match a neighbor's repertoire. These consequences are clearly functional, providing males with fitness advantages. In contrast, Searcy and Nowicki argue that geographic variation in song structure has no functional consequences. Although males may benefit from singing the local dialect, there is apparently no benefit associated with variation in dialects across the geographic range of the species. Their chapter, then, sends some of the same cautionary messages as Gerhardt's chapter on frogs, emphasizing the importance of broad sampling and subsequent testing of variability.

Brains are not general-purpose devices; rather they consist in specialized circuitry for solving tasks with adaptive consequences. The chapters in part 1 represent a testimony to this claim. In chapter 22, Marc Hauser explores the problem of specialization by looking at a peculiar feature of a number of vertebrate brains, specifically, asymmetries in hemispheric function. Although there is evidence of functional brain asymmetries in frogs, birds, bats, and rats, the bulk of this chapter focuses on primates, with an eye to reconstructing the evolution of hemispheric dominance in humans. Early work in this area led to the conclusion that although monkeys and apes show evidence of anatomical asymmetries, only humans show evidence of significant cognitive asymmetries. Studies of brain damaged patients, together with results from recent neuroimaging experiments, reveal that humans exhibit left-hemisphere dominance for language and expressions associated with positive emotion (e.g., smiling), and right-hemisphere dominance for expressions associated with negative emotion as well as the prosodic or melodic aspects of language. Hauser's research on rhesus monkey facial expressions, vocal articulations, and acoustic perception suggests significant parallels to the patterns emerging from humans. Thus when rhesus monkeys produce facial expressions associated with negative emotions, the left side of their face tends to start the expression earlier than the right and tends to be more expressive as well; this suggests that the right hemisphere plays a dominant role. In contrast, when facial expressions associated with positive emotion are produced, the right side of the face starts earlier and is more expressive, thereby implicating left hemisphere dominance. Furthermore, rhesus monkey adults, but not infants, tend to show a right-ear/left-hemisphere bias for listening to conspecific calls, but a left-ear/right-hemisphere bias (or no bias at all) for listening to sounds that fall outside the range of species-typical variation; the lack of hemispheric biases in infants may be the result of an immature brain, as well as a lack of sufficient experience with the range of acoustic variation in the system. At present, it is not possible to assess whether the similarities between monkeys and humans represent instances of homologies or homoplasies.

When animals vocalize, they typically convey some information about their affective state, whether they are aggressive, fearful, hungry, or friendly. Humans convey such information as well. But the kind of information conveyed by human language is not restricted to the affective states of the speaker. The power of human language comes from two sources, a system for generating an infinite variety of meaningful expressions that can refer to external objects and events, both imagined and real (i.e., the mental lexicon and universal grammar), together with a representational brain that operates on the basis of intentions, beliefs, and desires. In chapter 23, Dorothy Cheney and Robert Seyfarth explore the possibility that nonhuman primate vocalizations share some of these characteristics with human language. They begin with the problem of referential signaling and review both their classic studies with Peter Marler on the alarm calls of East African vervet monkeys, as well as more recent work on other monkey species. They conclude that for some nonhuman primates, and for some of their vocalizations, there is evidence of referentiality, that is, of calls designed to pick out such significant targets as predators, food, and social relationships. Although certainly falling short of the expressive power of most human words, these results provide some insights into the possible precursors of human language. In the second part of the chapter, Cheney and Seyfarth turn to the mental processes subserving vocal production and perception. Here, the similarities with human language break down. Though monkeys use their calls to manipulate social relationships, mediate spacing between individuals, and announce the discovery of food or predators, they fail to register the mental states of their potential audience when deciding whether or not to call and the kind of call to be used.

If we grant, for the moment, that human language represents a fundamentally unique form of communication, much like echolocation represents a unique form of communication for the microchiropteran bats and dolphins, then we are presented with a significant evolutionary challenge in uncovering its origins. Language doesn't fossilize, though there have been some attempts to make inferences about the presence of language in the fossil record based on changes in brain volume, the structure of the vocal tract, and the presence of fire, complex tools, and art. Leaving aside these attempts at reconstruction, one way to approach the problem is to assess whether animals have the conceptual apparatus needed to acquire language even if they can't acquire the formal structure of language, its semantics and syntax. In chapter 24, Tetsuro Matsuzawa uses laboratory and field studies to explore the cognitive abilities of our closest living relatives, the chimpanzees. In the first part of the chapter, he reviews work on "Ai," a female chimpanzee that was tutored and tested over the past 30 years on a variety of conceptual tasks. These studies, together with those conducted in other labs, reveal that under certain conditions, chimpanzees have the capacity to understand such language-relevant concepts as number (the count sequence from 0 to 10), same/different, and color terms. Moreover, chimpanzees exhibit some capacity for symbol comprehension and a much more limited ability for symbol production or generation. Importantly, however, there is currently no evidence that chimpanzees make use of such symbolic capacity within the constraints of their own communicative systems. In part two of the chapter, Matsuzawa turns to field observations and experiments on tool use, and in particular, the nut-cracking behavior of chimpanzees living in Bossou, New Guinea. This skill, which is acquired slowly over the course of the first 3–5 years of life, is complicated, involving first the search for a functional hammer and anvil, next the placement of a nut on the appropriate surface of the anvil, and then gripping the hammer at the appropriate end in order to maximize the surface area striking the nut; in a few rare cases where the anvil is unstable, a second stone is placed beneath it in order to stabilize the striking surface. Analyses of cultural variation in nut cracking, as well as other forms of tool use among chimpanzees, suggest strongly that social learning plays a significant role in both horizontal and vertical transmission among individuals.

References

Bradbury, J. W. and Vehrencamp, S. L. (1997). *Animal Communication.* Oxford: Blackwell.
Darwin, C. (1859) *On the Origin of Species.* London: John Murray.
Darwin, C. (1871) *The Descent of Man and Selection in Relation to Sex.* London: John Murray.
Darwin, C. (1872) *The Expression of the Emotions in Man and Animals.* London: John Murray.

Dawkins, R. (1976) *The Selfish Gene.* Oxford: Oxford University Press.

Dawkins, R. and Krebs, J. R. (1978) Animal signals: information or manipulation. In *Behavioural Ecology*, ed. by J. R. Krebs and N. B. Davies, pp. 282–309. Oxford. Blackwell Scientific Publications.

Grafen, A. (1990) Biological signals as handicaps. *J. Theor. Biol.* 144, 475–546.

Hamilton, W. D. (1964a) The evolution of altruistic behavior. *Am. Nat.* 97:354–356.

Hamilton, W. D. (1964b) The genetical evolution of social behavior. *J. Theor. Biol.* 7:1–52.

Hauser, M. D. (1996) *The Evolution of Communication.* Cambridge, MA: MIT Press.

Krebs, J. R. and Dawkins, R. (1984) Animal signals: mind-reading and manipulation. In *Behavioural Ecology*, ed. by J. R. Krebs and N. B. Davies, pp. 380–402. Sunderland, MA: Sinauer Associates Inc.

Maynard Smith, J. (1964) Group selection and kin selection. *Nature* 201:1145–1147.

Maynard Smith, J. (1965) The evolution of alarm calls. *Am. Nat.* 99:59–63.

Maynard Smith, J. (1974) The theory of games and the evolution of animal conflicts. *J. Theor. Biol.* 47:209–221.

Tinbergen, N. (1952) Derived activities: their causation, biological significance, origin, and emancipation during evolution. *Q. Rev. Biol.* 27:1–32.

Trivers, R. L. (1971) The evolution of reciprocal altruism. *Q. Rev. Biol.* 46:35–57.

Trivers, R. L. (1972) Parental investment and sexual selection. In *Sexual Selection and the Descent of Man*, ed. by B. Campbell, pp. 136–179 Chicago: Aldine Press.

Trivers, R. L. (1974) Parent-offspring conflict. *Am. Zool.* 14:249–264.

Williams, G. C. (1966) *Adaptation and Natural Selection.* Princeton: Princeton University Press.

Zahavi, A. (1975) Mate selection: A selection for a handicap. *J. Theor. Biol.* 53:205–214.

Zahavi, A. (1987) The theory of signal selection and some of its implications. In *International Symposium of Biological Evolution*, ed. by V. P. Delfino, pp. 305–327. Bari: Adriatica Editrice.

16 Signal Evolution in Electric Communication

Carl D. Hopkins

Peter Marler's observation of convergent similarity of alarm calls among several British birds (Marler 1955, 1957, 1967) has served as a model example for how selection, rather than arbitrary convention, can shape the form of vocal signals used for communication. The repetitive, broad-bandwidth ticking sounds, thought to be most easily locatable by conspecifics, are adaptive for use as mobbing calls; the high-frequency, narrow-bandwidth whistles, presumed difficult for predators to localize, are suited to aerial alarm. Marler developed an hypothesis to explain why these sounds differ in localizability based on human psychoacoustics. This hypothesis and his compelling observations stimulated efforts to understand other design features for sounds. His work also guided efforts to understand the mechanisms of sound localization. As ethologists have explored other systems of animal communication, many, including myself, have been guided by Marler's example.

The focus of my review is on the electrosensory modality and on electric signals used for communication among fish. I am interested in comparing adaptive features of communication signals in a sensory modality other than sound, and in examining the variety of selective influences that shape signal design. I shall first introduce important groups of organisms that use electric signals for communication, then discuss some of the selective influences that have shaped electric signal design, and finally review new evidence of the relation between signals and phylogeny in one group of electric fishes from Africa.

Background on the Evolution of Electric Communication in Fishes

By way of brief introduction to the literature on electric communication, I first examine the diversity of electric fishes before turning to design principles for signaling.

Electroreceptive and Electrogenic Fishes

Electric communication requires special electrosensory and electromotor capabilities which occur in only a few groups of freshwater and marine fishes. All of the electric species live in aquatic environments where the conductivity of the medium is sufficiently high to pass electric signals. The signals are transmitted from signaler to receiver as electrostatic fields that generate a three-dimensional pattern of current flow in the water. Signals are intercepted by electroreceptors embedded in the receiver's skin.

Electroreception Although electroreception is rare among aquatic organisms, it is pervasive and important among ancestral aquatic vertebrates including elasmobranchs, sarcopterygii, and chondrostei (Bullock and Heiligenberg 1986). The electric sense was apparently lost with the evolution of modern ray-finned fishes (*Teleostei*), only to reappear independently in two distantly related groups. These two are the *Otophysi* (Nelson 1976), which includes the electroreceptive gymnotiforms and catfish, and the *Osteoglossomorpha*, which includes the electroreceptive *Notopterids* (Braford 1982, 1986), *Gymnarchidae*, and the *Mormyridae* (Bell and Szabo 1986; Hopkins 1986).

Electrogenesis Electrogenesis among teleosts is more restricted than electroreception. It is confined to the mormyriforms (i.e., the *Mormyridae* and *Gymnarchidae*) from Africa, to the gymnotiforms with seven families from South America, and to a restricted number of catfishes belonging to different families including the electric catfishes, *Malapteruridae*, and several recently discovered weakly electric Mochokid and Clariid catfishes from Africa (Baron 1994; Baron et al. 1994; Hagedorn et al. 1990). The *Otophysi* and *Osteoglossomorpha* are phylogenetically distinct, and none of their common ancestors has either electroreceptive or electromotor capabilities, so it appears that these abilities evolved independently (Finger et al. 1986; Lissmann 1958; Lissmann and Machin 1958). The groups with the greatest diversity of electric communication signals are the gymnotiforms and the mormyriforms from the new- and old-world tropics. These two groups in particular provide fertile biological material in the search for adaptive principles of communication (Hopkins 1995), thus the focus in this paper.

Mormyriformes The African mormyriform fishes include about 200 species distributed among 18 genera in the family *Mormyridae*, and a single species of *Gymnarchus* belonging to the family *Gymnarchidae*. All mormyriforms have electric organs composed of numerous electrocytes that act in synchrony to produce the species-typical *electric organ discharge* (EOD) (Bass 1986c; Bennett 1971). All of the *Mormyridae* are pulse-generating species that fire brief electric discharges separated by comparatively long intervals. *Gymnarchus niloticus* is the only African species with a quasi-sinusoidal wavelike EOD.

    Mormyriforms have specialized cutaneous electroreceptors of three different morphological classes (Bullock and Heiligenberg 1986; Hopkins 1983a; Hopkins and Bass 1982; Szabo 1965; Zakon 1986), with strong evidence for functional specialization within the subclasses. Ampullary electroreceptors, which sense D.C. to 50Hz signals, are extremely sensitive and are used for passive electrolocation of prey or predators. Mormyromast electroreceptors, which are less sensitive and are tuned to higher frequencies, are used for active electrolocation of objects within close range. Knollenorgan receptors, which have low thresholds and are tuned to the energy spectrum of the EOD, appear to function in sensing the discharges of other fish in a communication role. The evidence for the functional segregation of the submodalities is presented elsewhere (Bell et al. 1983; Bell and Szabo 1986; Hopkins 1983b).

Gymnotiforms The gymnotiform fishes are restricted to neotropical freshwaters of South and Central America. The group comprises some 115 nominal species from 28 genera and 7 families (see recent reviews by Mago-Leccia 1994 and Alves-Gomes et al. 1995). The past decade has seen the discovery and description of many new gymnotiform species, some uncovered by recognizing the distinctive electric discharges of species that had been morphologically cryptic prior to the beginning of comparative studies of electric signals. Many come from previously unexplored habitats. One new genus, *Magosternarchus*, was discovered, for example, by making deepwater trawls in the central Amazon basin (Lundberg et al. 1996).

All gymnotiforms are electrogenic. The families *Eigenmanniadae*, *Sternopygidae*, and *Apteronotidae* are all wave-discharging species; the *Hypopomidae*, *Rhamphichthyidae*, *Electrophoridae*, and *Gymnotidae* are all pulse-discharging species like the mormyrids.

All gymnotiforms are electroreceptive and carry three subtypes of electroreceptors. Ampullary electroreceptors are extremely sensitive D.C. to 50Hz low-pass filters and appear to function again in prey and predator detection. P-type tuberous electroreceptor organs and T-type tuberous electroreceptors function both in active electrolocation and communication, and they appear to function together to detect the amplitude and temporal features of electric signals (Heiligenberg 1977, 1991). Ampullary receptors also detect certain types of electrical signals used in social communication (Metzner and Heiligenberg 1991).

Design Principles for Electric Signaling

Before discussing the specifics of electric signaling and its evolution, we should first review the selective forces that have shaped the design of electric signals used by electric fish. Are there advantages to certain types of electric signals compared to others in the context of social communication?

Signal Transmission Electric signals are fundamentally different from sounds in that they are transmitted from signaler to receiver not as propagated waves, but as a nonpropagating electrostatic field (Hopkins and Westby 1986). This difference is fundamental. It restricts the range of communication to a meter or less; it means that signals are not affected by reflection, refraction, and reverberation, as are acoustic signals (Michelsen and Larsen 1983; Wiley and Richards 1978, 1982); and it means that the temporal fine structure of electric signals is not altered in transmission, except by the addition of electrical noise. Because the temporal fine structure of electric signals is more predictable in transmission than that of sound, we might expect that cues encoded in the pulse waveform of electric discharges could have significance to receivers that might be lost if an equivalent acoustic signal were propagated through the air or water.

Distance   The signals of most electric fish can be approximated by an electrostatic dipole where the magnitude of the electric field decreases with the inverse cube of distance from the source (Heiligenberg 1975; Hopkins 1983b; Knudsen 1975). This severe rate of decrease brings high costs to long-distance communication. Each time the signaler attempts to double the communication distance, it has to multiply the amplitude at the source eightfold. This limit places premiums on both efficient signal production and optimal signal detection in the presence of noise. Ultimately, the distance of signaling is determined by the energy expenditure of signalers, sensitivity of receivers, and background noise in the environment. One rationale for documenting the diversity of electric signals used by electric fish is to characterize the biological background noise against which a given electric fish's signals must be detected in the natural environment.

Noise

There is considerable electrical noise in natural freshwater tropical environments. It is generated by distant lightning activity, which can produce continuous transient electrical clicks, whistles, pops, and tweeks within the detection range of electroreceptors. Lightning undoubtedly serves as the strongest source of continuous nonbiological background noise for communication (Hopkins 1973), although there may be other sources (Kalmijn 1974).

Signal Diversity in Natural Communities of Electric Fish

To illustrate the natural diversity of electric communication signals, we first turn to examples of communities of African electric fish for which there is now adequate information on signal diversity. Data of this type have been gathered for decades on communities of birds and primates (which communicate acoustically), but they are only now becoming available for electric fish.

EODs and SPIs   Mormyrids fire stereotyped electric organ discharges at about 2–10 impulses per second. The EOD waveform is the fixed part of the signal: it changes little over the course of days or weeks, often serving as a stereotyped, species-specific signature. The shape of the waveform is apparently controlled by the physiological and anatomical properties of the electric organ (Bass 1986a,c; Bennett 1970, 1971; Bennett and Grundfest 1961). The variable part of the signal is the sequence of pulse intervals (SPIs) produced by the pacemaker in the brain. Pulse intervals vary from second to second in patterns that serve as electrical displays, used for agonistic and reproductive behavior.

EOD Diversity for Mormyrids in Gabon   Figure 16.1 shows the diversity of EODs from the mormyrid fishes from the Ivindo River of Gabon in West Africa. For several species, males and females also differ, although sex differences are even more widespread than those illustrated in the figure.

There are three important dimensions to EOD diversity: wave shape, wave duration, and pulse polarity. For the majority of species, the wave shapes are biphasic, with an initial head-positive phase followed by a head-negative phase. Included in this category are *Boulengeromyrus knoepffleri*, *Pollimyrus marchei*, *Marcusenius moori*, *Ivindomyrus opdenboschi*, *Paramormyrops gabonensis*, the two *Petrocephalus* spp., *Brienomyrus kingsleyae*, *B. longicaudatus*, *B. curvifrons*, and *B. hopkinsi*. One species, *Brienomyrus* sp. 7 has a monophasic EOD in which most of the energy is contained in a single head-negative peak. Several species have triphasic EODs, including *Marcusenius conicephalus*, *Brienomyrus* sp. 1, *Brienomyrus* spp. 2, 3, and 6. In each of these, the first phase is head negative, although it may be so small that it can be seen on an oscilloscope trace only at high gain (Bass 1986c; Bennett 1971). One species, *Stomatorhinus walkeri*, has a 4 phase EOD. The differences in waveform are indicative of differing classes of cells within the electric organ itself, as has been partially explained for several of these species (Bass 1986a,c; Bennett 1971).

EOD waveforms vary widely in duration. The range illustrated for the Gabon mormyrids runs from about 100 microseconds for the two species of *Petrocephalus* to approximately 10 milliseconds for *Paramormyrops gabonensis*. The peak spectral energy varies correspondingly from 10,000Hz to 100Hz (Hopkins 1980). In several cases, males and females have distinctive EOD waveforms, but males always have the longer duration pulse. Sex differences are controlled by levels of circulating androgens, which act on the cells of the electric organ itself (Bass and Hopkins 1982, 1983, 1985) to prolong the action potentials that give rise to the EOD (Bass and Volman 1987).

EODs also vary in polarity, as two cases illustrate: *Mormyrops zanclirostris* and *Brienomyrus* sp. 8. For each, the largest peak-to-peak transition in the waveform is from head-negative to head-positive, although it goes from positive to negative in all others. In *M. zanclirostris*, the polarity inversion may be traced to the reversed anterior for posterior orientation of the electrocytes within the electric organ (Bass

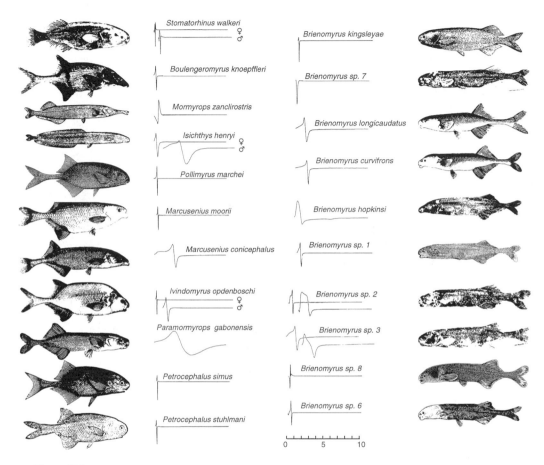

Figure 16.1
The mormyrid fish of northeastern Gabon and their electric organ discharges (EODs). The fish are arranged by genus and each species' EOD is plotted on the same time base with head-positivity upward. These EODs vary according to three different dimensions: overall waveform, polarity, and duration. Waveforms can be monophasic, biphasic, triphasic, or tetraphasic and can show a variety of inflection points and plateaus. Pulse polarity—defined by the largest peak to peak transition—usually goes from head positive to head negative, but is inverted in two species here. Duration varies over two orders of magnitude, from 100 microseconds to over 10 milliseconds and in many species is longer for males than for females. These fish generate these pulses many times per second for purposes of active electrolocation. As a consequence, the species-typical and sex-specific signal is broadcast nearly continuously. The diversity suggests that these fish exploit differences in waveforms, polarity and duration to identify the species and the sex of signalers and to attract mates. Modified from Hopkins 1986.

1986c). For *Brienomyrus* sp. 8, it is apparently due to the exaggeration of the first phase of a triphasic waveform and the diminution of the final phase.

The diversity of EODs within this community of mormyrids leads to the conclusion that the simple and short waveforms have communicative significance of their own, beyond that as a "carrier" of signals encoded by the rhythm of the discharge or sequence of pulse intervals. Indeed, differences in EODs have permitted discovery of new species previously overlooked by biologists who used morphological characters only (Crawford and Hopkins 1989; Hopkins 1986; Roberts 1989). This is especially well illustrated for species in the genus *Brienomyrus* from Gabon, where eleven new species have been uncovered by recording the distinctive electric organ discharges (Alves-Gomes and Hopkins 1997; Hopkins et al. in prep.-b; Teugels and Hopkins 1998; Teugels and Hopkins in prep.). Playback experiments using computer-synthesized EODs have confirmed the importance of EODs in reproductive isolation and in sex recognition (Hopkins and Bass 1981). There are now many examples of sex differences in EODs within populations of mormyrids (Hopkins 1980, 1981). There are even individual differences in EODs that are sufficient to permit the tracking of individuals and their movements in small streams monitored daily (Friedman and Hopkins 1996). The species-, sex-, and individual differences in EODs all rely upon subtle differences in the waveforms of the discharge.

A similar range of EOD diversity has been noted for other communities of electric fish from Africa. Although we still know very little about the signaling characteristics of fishes from the Congo River, a river basin of high diversity, recent studies by Lovell et al. (1997) indicate a surprising complexity of electric signals within one of its representative genera, *Campylomormyrus*, the elephant-snouted fish (see figure 16.2).

Systematists disagree on how many species there are in this genus (Poll et al. 1982; Roberts and Stewart 1976), but an analysis of the EODs of specimens imported through the aquarium trade suggests that the diversity may be greater than even the highest estimates given by systematists (Lovell et al. 1997). Figure 16.3 illustrates the EOD waveforms for some of these imported *Campylomormyrus*. The diversity of waveforms and durations match those for the *Brienomyrus* of Gabon. All of these fish have the same polarity to their discharges. This diversity has been noted for other river systems in Africa as well, including the Niger (Hopkins et al. in prep.-a).

Signal Diversity in South American Gymnotiforms   The gymnotiform fish exhibit a similarly impressive range of signal types comparable to that of mormyrids. Several field studies of communities of gymnotiform pulse fish confirm that EOD waveforms vary in duration, number of phases, and overall wave shape (Alves-Gomes et al.

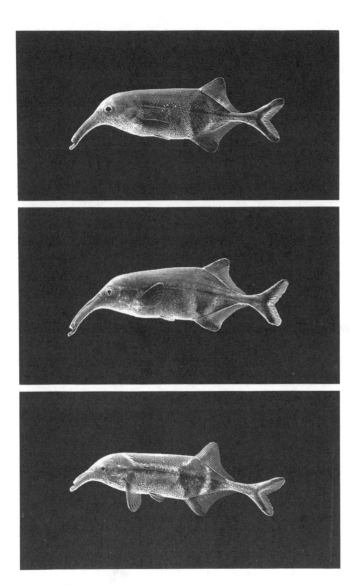

Figure 16.2
Three of the elephant-snouted mormyrids belonging to the genus *Campylomormyrus* which comes from the Congo River basin of Africa. From top to bottom, *Campylomormyrus* sp. B, *Campylomormyrus rhyncho-phorus*, and *Campylomormyrus tamandua*. Each of these individuals is approximately 150mm in length. (Photos by P. Lovell and C. D. Hopkins.)

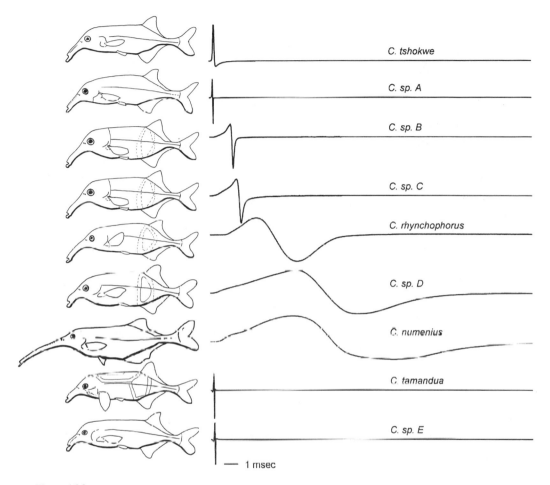

Figure 16.3
Systematists disagree on the number of species in the genus *Campylomormyrus*, but recent recordings of EOD waveforms suggest there may be even more species than the latest revision, which recognized 18 species (Poll et al. 1982). All EOD recordings were made with head-positivity upward from animals imported through commercial aquarium dealers. Only four of the nine species represented here can be unambiguously identified by reference to the type specimens, most of which are housed in the Musée Royal de l'Afrique Central in Tervuren, Belgium. The remainder represent forms whose identity is uncertain. Adapted from Lovell et al. 1997.

1995; Heiligenberg and Bastian 1980; Hopkins and Bass 1981; Hopkins and Westby 1986; Westby 1988). Signal diversity extends to sex differences, at least for several species within the family Hypopomidae (*Hypòpomus* and *Brachyhypopomus*). In all of these cases the waveforms of males are longer than those of females or juveniles (Hagedorn 1983, 1985; Hagedorn and Carr 1985; Hopkins et al. 1990; Shumway and Zelick 1988). The South American species appear to have developed a pattern of signal diversity that parallels that of the African fish.

For gymnotiforms, the generation of signal waveforms that are more complex than a simple biphasic EOD, which one expects from the sequential activation of caudal and rostral faces of a simple electrocyte, appears to be achieved by firing whole columns of electrocytes slightly out of phase with the rest of the electric organ (Bennett 1971; Caputi and Budelli 1993; Caputi et al. 1989b, 1993; Lorenzo et al. 1990, 1993a,b, 1988; Macadar 1993; Macadar et al. 1989). These columns of electrocytes are sometimes formed in a different part of the body as an accessory organ; otherwise they are integrated into the main organ. In the gymnotid fish, *Gymnotus carapo*, electrocytes within the main organ but near the head end of the fish have a specialized anterior innervation in addition to the more typical posterior innervation. This, plus the shorter pathway and conduction time from the pacemaker, ensures that the rostral faces of these electrocytes fire first, making the head go initially negative before the tail end. Electrocytes in the tail, innervated posteriorly, make the head go positive (Hopkins 1995). An elegant series of papers on *Gymnotus* has documented how the complexity of the electric organ results in the EOD waveform (Caputi and Budelli 1993; Caputi et al. 1989b, 1993; Lorenzo et al. 1990, 1993a,b, 1988; Macadar 1993; Macadar et al. 1989). Other gymnotiforms, such as *Steatogenys elegans*, *Hypopygus lepturus*, and *Rhamphichthys* species achieve multiphased EODs using electrocytes located in accessory electric organs on the head and trunk, in addition to the main electric organs in the tail.

Gymnotiforms produce a diversity of signals by varying the rhythm of their discharges. There is the distinction between wave and pulse discharges already mentioned, but there is also a wide range of modulations in the pulse rhythm generated by the pacemaker. For example, during courtship, male *Eigenmannia* generate interruptions or chirps. Males and females make infrequent chirps as threat signals (Hopkins 1974b; Kawasaki and Heiligenberg 1988a,b, 1990; Kawasaki et al. 1988). Subordinate *Eigenmannia* elevate their EOD frequency by a few Hz in "long rises" when attacked, and females "warble" their EOD frequency up and down when laying eggs (Hagedorn and Heiligenberg 1985). Similarly, pulse fish go silent, make long pauses, noisy silences (interruptions accompanied by hissing discharges), and a wide range of frequency modulations in social behavior (Hagedorn 1985; Hopkins 1974a; Kawasaki and Heiligenberg 1988a,b). Similar patterns have been reported for mormyrids (Kramer 1995; Moller 1995).

Sexual Selection and Signal Diversity Sexually dimorphic traits often result from female choice, with females choosing mates on the basis of signals that are costly to produce and are therefore honest indicators of male quality. This concept applies well to explain sex differences in EODs of the South American pulse fish, *Brachyhypopomus pinnicaudatus* (Hopkins et al. 1990). These males have EODs that are twice the duration of females. Since we expect that EODs of the same amplitude will have energetic costs in proportion to the integral of the squared voltage of the pulse over the duration of the EOD, male EODs should cost more to produce than female or juvenile EODs. However, male signals are measurably weaker than those of females when fish of the same body size are compared (Hopkins et al. 1990). Males compensate for the drop in amplitude of their discharge by growing their tails to be both thicker and longer so that they can generate greater current, at a higher source voltage for a given body size. These long tails are targets for predation, and males suffer greater tail damage than do females. Hopkins et al. (1990) concluded that female *Brachyhypopomus pinnicaudatus* select long-duration EODs over shorter ones because they know that these pulses are more costly to produce and put the male at greater risk to produce them. In essence, the female knows that males that produce long duration pulses must be of exceptional quality. This model is simply a restatement of the handicap principle of Zahavi (1977). This principle may apply equally well to African electric fish, which appear to have evolved similar sex differences in EODs, but this has yet to be tested quantitatively in this group of fish.

Avoidance of Electroreceptive Predators Since electric fish generate signals continuously, they advertise their location to any electroreceptive predators. Aside from predatory electric fish (Lundberg et al. 1996), the greatest danger may come from catfish, which have only ampullary electroreceptors. Most electric fish appear to avoid generating signals with a D.C. component, which would be detected by ampullary receptors, and instead generate signals where the positive and negative components of the discharge are balanced so there is no net D.C. For many of the pulse species in figure 16.1, the power spectrum of the EOD has very little energy at 0Hz and the numerical integration of the voltage waveform sums to zero. It was Bennett and Grundfest (1961) who first recognized the importance of the D.C. component of the discharges of pulse- and wave-discharging species. They demonstrated that both *Sternopygus* and *Eigenmannia*, which produce head-positive monophasic pulses, superimpose them on a head-negative baseline. The origin of the head-negative offset is unknown.

There are exceptions to the general rule that most fish appear to be attempting to minimize the D.C. component of their signal. Recently Metzner and Heiligenberg (1991) showed that *Eigenmannia*'s chirps and interruptions are cessations in the monophasic pulses only. The D.C. component continues, resulting in a sudden shift in the D.C. baseline whenever the fish turns its EOD off briefly, as it does during courtship displays. The resulting signal, a cessation in the EOD but a burst of D.C., creates a signal that may be conspicuous both to females but also to predatory catfish.

Interruptions in the wave discharge of virtually identical physical characteristics are produced by the African fish, *Gymnarchus*, in the context of threat behavior. Like those of *Eigenmannia*, these threat signals are composed of cessations of the main EOD. We expect these signals also to produce a large D.C. shift. We still do not understand the selection pressures that have led to the evolution of these signals, but the convergence on form as well as function again suggests that the signals are adaptive, not arbitrary.

Some electric fish may camouflage their signals by hiding behind the mask of electrical noise in the environment from lightning. Some fish appear to opt for signals that match the dominant frequencies of the ambient lightning discharges. Some fish with highly irregular discharges also appear to be camouflaging their SPIs against the irregular rhythms typical of lightning activity. When communicating with mates or intruders, pulse rhythms are "regularized" (Crawford 1992; Hopkins 1973; Moller 1995) and more conspicuous in a noisy background.

Selection for Electrolocation Performance   Some features of the EOD waveform may be uniquely important to active electrolocation and have no importance for communication. The capacitance of objects in the environment, for example, may influence the design of EOD waveforms. In environments where plants are common and where the capacitance of the environment is high, fish with longer duration signals may be better at discriminating differences in impedance based on capacitative properties. In environments where capacitative impedances are low, selection may favor shorter pulse durations, which emphasize higher spectral frequencies (Heiligenberg 1991; von der Emde and Bell 1994).

Animal density and spacing may have an effect on signal design. Fish in dense groups may favor short duration pulse discharges that are less likely to overlap and become jammed by neighbors. Solitary species may favor longer duration pulses that are distinctive (Hopkins 1980).

New Molecular Results Give Insights into the Evolution of Electric Signals

If we are to explain the evolution of signals, we must have a good understanding of the evolutionary relationships of the animals that produce them. Crucial to any comparative analysis of signals is a good understanding of the phylogenetic relationships between the organisms in question. With the advent of modern molecular biology and an explosive growth in methods of cladistics, there has been a transformation in our understanding of the phylogenetic relationships of species and genera that differ slightly in signal characteristics.

Gymnotiforms Among the gymnotiforms, Alves-Gomes et al. (1995) used mitochondrial DNA to construct a phylogeny for the gymnotiform fishes and to reexamine the relationships between the pulse-discharging genera. Albert (in press) used traditional morphological characters as well as brain morphology to construct a second recent phylogeny. Such evolutionary insights are of critical importance to issues such as the origin of pulse versus wave discharges, the origins of special features of electric organs, and the evolutionary history of muscle-versus neuronal-based electric organs.

For the pulse-discharging gymnotiforms belonging to the families *Gymnotidae*, *Electrophoridae*, *Hypopomidae*, and *Rhamphichthyidae*, there is a range of EOD diversity comparable with that seen for mormyrids. Unlike the mormyrids, however, the simple biphasic EODs are produced by the tail electric organs, while the more complex EOD waveforms are produced by distinct "accessory electric organs," which are usually in the head region and which are distinct from the electric organs in the tail. The function of these accessory electric organs is unknown, but an obvious hypothesis is that they serve to diversify the pulse waveform of the EODs at the species-specific level and thus play a role in identification. Alves-Gomes et al. (1995) recently reviewed the relationships between the pulse gymnotiforms and concluded that pulse discharges appear to have arisen independently in the families *Gymnotidae* and *Electrophoridae*, and then again in the *Hypopomidae* and *Rhamphichthyidae* clades. Especially interesting is the clade composed of the genera *Gymnorhamphich-thys*, *Rhamphichthys*, *Hypopygus*, and *Steatogenys*, all of which have accessory electric organs. All of these four genera produce complex EOD waveforms containing three or even four major peaks (figure 16.4). By contrast, fish in the genera *Hypo-pomus* and *Brachyhypopomus* (formerly *Hypopomus*) and *Microsternarchus* do not appear to have accessory electric organs, and their EODs are simple biphasic pulses. The revised phylogeny, based on molecular data, shows that these complex accessory electric organs may have had a single common evolutionary origin, rather than

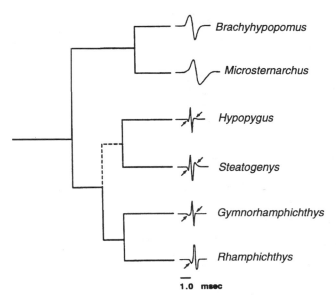

Figure 16.4
EOD waveforms of fishes belonging to the *Rhamphichthyoid* clade of gymnotiform fishes from South
America, organized according to a phylogeny derived from mitochondrial DNA sequences for 12s and 16s
rRNA. The EODs of *Hypopygus*, *Steatogenys*, *Gymnorhamphichthys*, and *Rhamphichthys* all have an early
head-negative phase preceding the main head-positive and head-negative phases. These early prepulses are
caused by accessory electric organs located on the underside of the head. A separate clade which includes
Brachyhypopomus and *Microsternarchus* lacks the prepulse and shows no indication of accessory electric
organs. Adapted from Alves-Gomes et al. 1995.

multiple origins as suggested by a traditional phylogeny. Even more recently, Sullivan has taken a closer look at the relationships between the *Rhamphichthyoids*,
probing even deeper the relationships between phylogeny and electric organ evolution (Sullivan 1997).

Mormyriforms Alves-Gomes and Hopkins (1997) provide a preliminary hypothesis
for the evolution of electric signals in the mormyriforms with a phylogeny based on
a survey of 12 species and 5 genera. Prior to this work, what was known about the
phylogeny of the group was derived from an osteological survey of mormyrids done
by Louis Taverne in the 1970s. Taverne (1969, 1971a,b, 1972) recognized 18 genera
of mormyrids, sorted through some 190 species, and developed a phylogeny that
recognized the families *Mormyridae* and *Gymnarchidae*. Within the *Mormyridae*,
Taverne recognized two subfamilies, the *Petrocephalinae*, which has a single genus
Petrocephalus, and the *Mormyrinae*, which has 17 genera and 165 species. However,

Taverne's work, and most of the subsequent systematic work on mormyrids, did not deal with relationships between the confusing genera. Since most of the prior work has been based on traditional methods that did not apply phylogenetic or cladistic reasoning, the Alves-Gomes and Hopkins (1997) study provides some of the first insights into evolutionary relationships in this group.

Electrocyte Structure Relates to Electric Organ Discharges among Mormyrids

Previous studies have reported on the anatomical characteristics of electric organs of mormyrids (Bass 1986a,b,c; Bennett 1970, 1971; Bennett and Grundfest 1961; Ogneff 1898), and there is generally a good understanding of the relationship between the cellular anatomy of electrocytes and physiological characteristics that lead to the EOD. However, attempts to understand the evolution of the electric organ have been confusing due to lack of information about evolutionary relationships and knowledge of functions of observed electrocyte design (Bass 1986a,b,c; Bennett 1971).

The cells or "electrocytes" that make up the electric organ are flattened multi-nucleated disks of several mm diameter but only 10–50 micrometers thickness. They lie in four parallel columns of about a hundred or more cells in the elongated and nearly cylindrical caudal peduncle of the fish. In sagittal sections, one sees that each electrocyte has a complex of stilt-root-like stalklets emerging from one flat face or the other (usually posterior face). These stalklets are smallest in diameter at the point where they fuse with the electrocyte face. They then repeatedly fuse with others, increasing the diameter of the stalklet until they form large stalk-like trunks, which receive synaptic input from the electromotor nerves in the caudal peduncle. This entire system of tubes has been called a "stalk" (Bennett and Grundfest 1961), or a "pédicule" (Szabo 1960, 1961).

In cross section (figure 16.5), it is clear how each electrocyte receives its innervation on the large-diameter portion of the stalk system. Innervation may be on either the anterior face or the posterior, depending on the species. In many cases, the stalks penetrate through the surface of the electrocyte to emerge on the opposite side; but in some there are double penetrations, so that the stalk first goes through from the innervated to the opposite side, then runs a short distance across the non-innervated side, and then turns and penetrates a second time to return to the innervated face where it divides profusely and spreads out to make contact with the surface of the cell on the same side as the innervation (figure 16.5e,f).

In *Gymnarchus*, innervation is on the posterior face of the electrocyte, which is lacking in a stalk system entirely.

Figure 16.5 summarizes with sagittal section diagrams six different types of electrocytes from mormyriforms, from the boxlike and stalkless cells of *Gymnarchus*

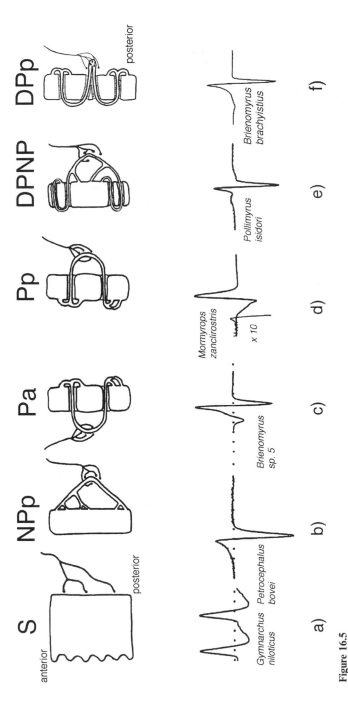

Figure 16.5

The electric organs of mormyriform fishes are composed of electrogenic cells called "electrocytes" of varying degrees of complexity illustrated in cross-section diagrams for six different morphological classes from different species. Each species has electrocytes of a single type, each of which is capable of generating the waveform of the whole-animal EOD.

(a) Stalkless electrocytes (S) are found in Gymnarchus niloticus and also in the larval electric organs of all mormyrids. The electrocytes are cylindrical in shape and are innervated only on their posterior surface. Only the posterior face fires a spike. The anterior face is deeply convoluted, is electrically inexcitable, but probably has high electrical capacitance. The resulting electric discharge is a head-positive monophasic pulse superimposed on a head-negative baseline. For Gymnarchus, the medullary pacemaker fires at a high repetition rate and the monophasic pulses merge to form a quasi-sinusoidal wave.

(b) Nonpenetrating stalk electrocytes with posterior innervation (NP$_p$) have a well-developed series of tiny tube-like stalklets emerging from the posterior face of the electrocyte. The stalklets repeatedly fuse with adjacent members to form stalks of greater and greater diameter. Innervation is on the largest stalk in the center of the cell. The entire stalk system lies on the posterior side of the electrocyte. After excitation by the nerve, an action potential in the stalk system propagates to excite the posterior face which is electrically active. The inward current on the posterior face generates a head-positive potential in the water. It also depolarizes the anterior face, which is also electrically excitable. After a delay, it generates an inward current which causes a head-negative phase to the ECD. All mormyrids with type NP_p electrocytes have biphasic EODs, although in some, like Brienomyrus batesii, the first phase may be small and visible only at high gain. Type NP_p electrocytes are found in all known species of Petrocephalus, Myomyrus, and Mormyrus, and in several members of other genera, including Brienomyrus, Marcusenius, and Campylomormyrus.

(c) Penetrating stalk electrocytes with anterior innervation (P_a). These cells have a well-developed system of stalklets that emerge from the posterior face of the electrocyte, fuse repeatedly to form stalks, but then penetrate through the cell to emerge on the opposite side. Innervation is on the largest stalks on the anterior face. The action potential is initiated in the stalk, but inward current has no effect until the action potential reaches the point of penetration. Then the inward current in the stalk is directed through the electrocyte, and posteriorly to create the first weak head-negative prepulse. When the spike reaches the posterior face which is electrically excitable, it spreads across the face, causing a head-positive peak in the EOD. This is followed by the anterior face firing, which generates the final head-negative phase. All species with P_a electrocytes have this initial head-negative prepulse, although it is small in some species.

(d) When the electrocyte is anatomically reversed, and the innervation is on the posterior side (P_p), the EOD is inverted in polarity compared to type P_a electrocytes. The light line shows a ×10 gain expansion for Mormyrops zanclirostris.

(e) Doubly penetrating and nonpenetrating stalked electrocytes (Type DPNP). In cells of this type, the stalk makes a double penetration through the face of the electrocyte. The stalk potential generates a complex prepulse, which may be head negative or head positive. The EOD in Pollimyrus isidori has an early head-positivity that precedes the main biphasic pulse. It is thought to arise from the anterior-directed current into the stalk on the posterior side of the electrocyte and the posterior directed flow on the anterior side. The main biphasic discharge that follows is probably produced by the posterior face and then anterior face of the electrocyte itself. From Hopkins 1995.

(f) Doubly penetrating stalked electrocytes with posterior innervation (type DP_p). In cells of this type, the stalk is innervated on the posterior side. It immediately penetrates through the cell to the anterior side, spreads out across the anterior surface, and then makes numerous penetrations through to the posterior side. This cell type is nearly identical to type P_a already mentioned, as is the EOD, which is triphasic.

niloticus (figure 16.5a) to the complex cell types with penetrating and nonpenetrating stalks for several of the mormyrid genera.

EODs of Mormyrids Used in Phylogenetic Analysis

Figure 16.6 shows electric organ discharges of 12 species of mormyriforms used in a phylogenetic analysis. Most of the specimens were taken from Gabon, but some are from the aquarium trade. Most mormyrids shown in this plot, except for *Petrocephalus*, have a sex difference in their EODs.

We extracted DNA and sequenced two mitochondrial gene fragments, the 12S and 16S mitochondrial rRNA, and from these we developed hypotheses for phylogenetic relationships using maximum parsimony, distance-based estimates based on neighbor joining, and maximum likelihood. All three analyses generated consistent hypotheses, which are illustrated in figure 16.7.

The Position of Gymnarchus

The molecular data places *Gymnarchus niloticus* at the base of the phylogenetic tree for mormyriforms, thereby confirming the osteological analysis of Taverne (1972). With its wavelike electric discharge (figure 16.6) and stalkless electrocytes (figures 16.5 and 16.7), this is reminiscent of the primitive position of the wave-discharging *Sternopygids* among the gymnotiform families (Alves-Gomes et al. 1995). It may well be the case that wave-discharging electric fish represent the ancestral condition for both groups, and the pulse-discharging condition the derived. The ancestral position of *Gymnarchus* also suggests that the relatively simple boxlike, stalkless electrocytes represent a primitive condition for the group. The posterior face of the electrocyte is the only innervated and electrically active face. The anterior face appears highly convoluted; it probably has great surface area which increases capacitance and decreases resistance, but the face appears inexcitable. Although this type of electric organ appears to be unique within the mormyriforms, as we shall see below, it arises also in the larval electric organs of the *Mormyridae*.

Petrocephalus   The sequence data places our representative of *Petrocephalus* at the base of the *Mormyridae*, thereby confirming Taverne's osteological results. Its electric organ is substantially different from *Gymnarchus* both in its position within the body and its electrocyte morphology. The electrocytes are stalked and innervated on the stalk itself on the posterior face of the cell. Action potentials arising in the stalk travel from the site of innervation to the posterior surface of the cell, which, when it fires, causes the first, head-positive phase of the EOD. The anterior face of the electrocyte, also electrically excitable, is activated by depolarizing current from the pos-

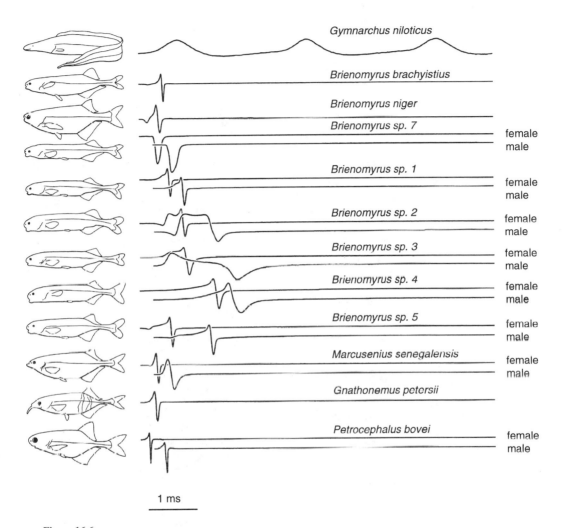

1 ms

Figure 16.6
These EODs are representative of the 12 species of mormyrids used for phylogenetic analysis with mitochondrial DNA. All EODs are plotted on the same time base with head-positivity upward. Representatives of each sex are illustrated only for those cases where the discharge has been recorded for males and females under field conditions. Sex differences do occur for *Gnathonemus petersii* and *Brienomyrus brachyistius* and *B. niger*, but these differences were compiled in laboratory studies involving animals treated with testosterone. From Alves-Gomes and Hopkins 1997.

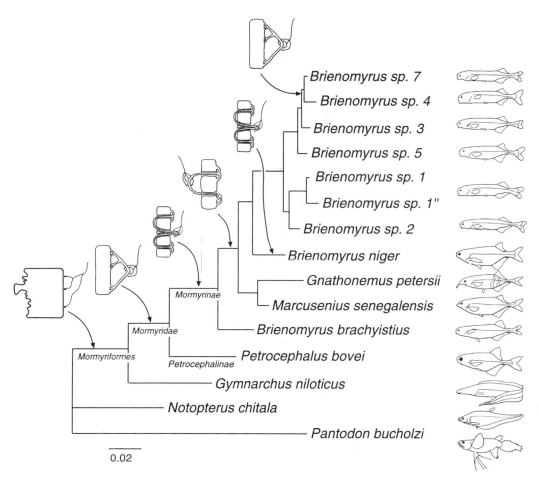

Figure 16.7
Phylogenetic hypothesis for the 12 mormyrids shown in figure 16.6 derived from mitochondrial sequence data from the 12S and 16S rRNA gene fragments. The topology shown here results from three independent approaches to phylogeny estimation: maximum likelihood, neighbor-joining, and maximum parsimony. Bars depict branch lengths for the maximum likelihood tree. Morphologies of the electrocytes for each lineage are depicted as insets. Adapted from Alves-Gomes and Hopkins 1997.

terior face, and when it fires, it generates the second head-negative phase. The electric organ discharge is biphasic. There are no known cases of sex difference in the EODs of this species, or in any other *Petrocephalus*.

Mormyrinae

The results of the DNA phylogeny depart from previous studies based on morphology when one considers the relationships within the subfamily *Mormyrinae*. Taverne had divided the subfamily into two major clades based on the presence of a single character: the lateral ethmoid bone (Taverne 1972). Under his hypothesis, *Gnathonemus* and *Brienomyrus* are placed in the same clade because they both lack the lateral ethmoid bone, and *Marcusenius* is placed into a different subgroup because it retains the bone. Contrary to Taverne's view, the DNA results suggest that *Marcusenius* and *Gnathonemus* are closely allied to each other, even more so than members of *Brienomyrus* are to each other. This implies that the lateral ethmoid may not be a reliable character to infer phylogenetic relationships between mormyrids.

The Genus Brienomyrus

The DNA results also contradict Taverne by suggesting that the genus *Brienomyrus* is not a monophyletic group. According to our findings, *Brienomyrus brachyistius*, which originates in West Africa, represents a different lineage from *Brienomyrus niger* and the *Brienomyrus* from Gabon. Although this result first seemed surprising, it has been supported now in several parallel studies, using other methods (S. Lavoué et al., personal communication). These results suggest that *Brienomyrus* from Gabon represents quite a separate lineage from *Brienomyrus* from West Africa, and that the morphological similarities must be due to either parallel or convergent evolution, probably due to retention of ancestral characters within the Gabon species complex.

Electrocyte Evolution   The phylogeny proposed in figure 16.7 is most interesting from the perspective of the electric organ morphology, which is illustrated as a series of insets on the cladogram. Nonpenetrating stalked electrocytes appear to be the primitive condition for the *Mormyridae*, best represented by the *Petrocephalus* in this cladogram, but also by members of the genus *Mormyrus* (not shown), which appears to be a monophyletic group, and all are characterized by nonpenetrating stalk electrocytes (see table 6 in Alves-Gomes and Hopkins 1997). Among the other genera presented here, however, including *Brienomyrus*, *Marcusenius*, and *Gnathonemus*, the majority of species have penetrating stalks on the electrocytes. Some, including two *Brienomyrus* (*brachyistius* and *niger*) have doubly penetrating stalks. Perhaps most interesting, two of the species of *Brienomyrus* that lie at the terminal branches of this tree carry nonpenetrating stalked electrocytes, as in the plesiomorphic condition.

The phylogeny derived from DNA analysis suggests an hypothesis for how the four types of electrocytes evolved (figure 16.7). First, type S electrocytes found in *Gymnarchus* appear to represent the primitive condition. One concludes this because *Gymnarchus* occupies a basal position on the phylogenetic tree in figure 16.7 and because the type S electrocytes bear some resemblance to the multinucleated muscle cells from which they are derived (Dahlgren 1914; Srivastava and Szabo 1972), and also because these stalkless cells are the simplest in design. Second, type NP_p electrocytes, as seen in all of the *Petrocephalinae* appear to be an early intermediate stage in evolution, but plesiomorphic for the *Mormyridae*. These electrocytes have a simple stalk system that is unadorned, lacking in penetrations, and lacking any evidence for sex differences. Third, the penetrating stalks seen in both type P_a and DP_p electrocytes seem to be a more derived condition within this group. Each has a complex system of penetrating stalks, well-developed sex differences, and highly complex waveforms differing widely in duration. It is unclear which of these two morphologies represents the more primitive condition, but figure 16.7 suggests that DP_p electrocytes are an intermediate stage for *B. brachyistius*, whereas DP_p electrocytes in *B. niger* represent a reversion. Finally, the occurrence of two closely related species of *Brienomyrus* with type NP_p electrocytes in this study (*Brienomyrus* sp. 4 and *B.* sp. 7) suggests that type NP_p electrocytes may also evolve as a reversion from P_a to an even simpler design.

Observations of the ontogeny of electrocytes suggest a mechanism for reversion to the ancestral condition, although the only data are studies done by Szabo (1960) on larval material collected in the field by J. Daget in the late 1950s. Studies by Denizot et al. (1978, 1982) were on laboratory-bred *Pollimyrus isidori*, a species with doubly penetrating and nonpenetrating stalks (type DPNP). Szabo (1960) examined larvae of *Mormyrops deliciosus* and *Hyperopisus occidentalis*, two species with penetrating stalks (both type P_a), and found that electrocytes in very young fish go through a three-stage development, starting with simple stalkless electrocytes, progressing to electrocytes with well-developed nonpenetrating stalks, and ending as an adult with electrocytes with penetrating, anterior innervated stalks. By contrast, *Mormyrus rume*, a species with type NP_p electrocytes, develops first stalkless and later nonpenetrating stalks, but never goes through a stage with penetrating stalks. Work in my laboratory has recently resulted in successful breeding of *Brienomyrus brachyistius* a fish with doubly penetrating stalks with posterior innervation (type DP_p). We have observed the development of their electrocytes from nonpenetrating electrocytes with posterior innervation to doubly penetrating electrocytes with posterior innervation.

Model for Electrocyte Development   Because we see nonpenetrating stalks as an earlier ontogenetic stage in several of the species with either singly penetrating or doubly penetrating stalks, we may speculate that the type NP_p electrocytes within the clade *Brienomyrus* must have evolved through paedomorphosis, the reversion to an earlier stage in development simply by arresting development at an earlier stage. The actual mechanism for development of penetrating stalks is unknown, although it has fascinated microscopists ever since Fritsch (1891). Alves-Gomes and Hopkins (1997) suggested two possible mechanisms to explain the ontogeny of penetrating stalks (figure 16.8). In the first, the developing stalk, already innervated on the posterior side, migrates medially to the edge of the electrocyte and then moves rostrally, to pull the smaller rootlets of the stalk through the edge of the cell. First the stalks pull through the edges, and later the membranes close back around the stalks. In the second model, the thickened middle part of the developing stalk pushes through the face in the electrocyte from the posterior side to create a doubly penetrating stalk system that is still innervated on the posterior side. Then the proximal end of the stalk migrates rostrally through the edge of the cell, pulling the innervated portion of the stalk entirely through to the anterior side.

According to the these models, arrested development may occur at two stages: failure to undergo any type of stalk migration at all causes a reversion to NP_p electrocytes, as seen in *Brienomyrus* sp. 7 and *Brienomyrus* sp. 4; failure to undergo a complete migration of the large proximal ends of the stalks results in DP_p morphology as seen in *B. niger*. In neither case does this imply a loss of other, more derived characteristics of the electric organ, such as the physiological response to sex-steroids, which appears to be retained within the *Brienomyrus* in our samples and also in several other *Brienomyrus* (see table 6 in Alves-Gomes and Hopkins 1997).

Larval Electric Organs in Mormyrids   Larval organs in mormyrids are probably homologous to adult electric organs in *Gymnarchus*. Mormyrids have a larval electric organ that is active well before the functioning of the main adult electric organ seen in the adult. Larval electric organs have been described for *Pollimyrus adspersus* (Westby and Kirschbaum 1977, 1978) and in several other species (see review in Kirschbaum 1995). In the case of mormyrids, the larval electric organ lies deep in the lateral body musculature in four longitudinal columns on each side of the body, but in a position far anterior to the caudal peduncle where the adult organ develops. Larval electrocytes bear close resemblance to the adult organ in *Gymnarchus*, both in

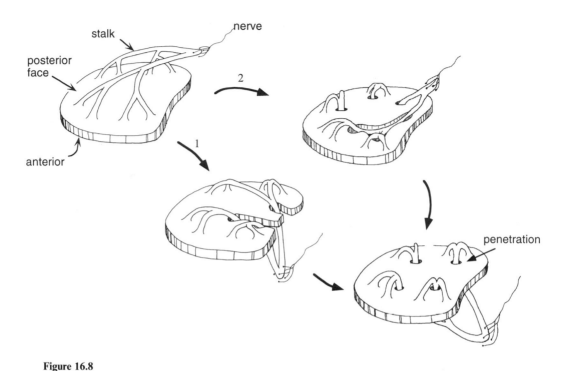

Figure 16.8
An hypothesis for the development of penetrating stalk electrocytes among mormyrids. The electrocyte
first develops a non-penetrating stalk system which is innervated on the posterior side (upper left).
According to the hypothesis, the stalk system migrates to the anterior side, pulling the stalks through the
edges of the electrocyte. The edges then reseal, leaving penetrations through the cell membrane. Two possible mechanisms are possible. In (1), the stalks pull through the edge of the electrocyte and the membrane
seals around the stalk as it migrates. In (2), the midregion of the stalk pushes through the membrane to
make a double penetration, but the thicker end of the stalk then pulls through the edges later to make a
penetration, shown in the lower right. Observations on larval electric organs in *Hyperopisus occidentalis*
and *Mormyrops deliciosus*, both of which have type P$_a$ electrocytes, have type NP$_p$ electrocytes in the
juvenile stages of development. From Alves-Gomes and Hopkins 1997.

the number of columns, the boxlike electrocyte morphology which is "stalkless," the
position within the body, and the physiology. Both larval electric organs and the
electric organs in *Gymnarchus* are electrically active only on the posterior (innervated) face. The noninnervated face is inexcitable. Kirschbaum (1995) has proposed
that the larval organ and the adult organ are homologous, with the larval electric
organ as plesiomorphic and the adult organ as apomorphic, whereas Fessard (1958)
thought that the electric organs in *Gymnarchus* and in adult mormyrids were distinct
and independently evolved. It is perhaps now more correct to state that the *Gymnarchus* electric organ is homologous to the larval electric organ in mormyrids, and

that the adult organ is an independently derived structure. In a similar fashion, the adult electric organ with nonpenetrating stalks is plesiomorphic, whereas the penetrating stalked electrocytes are apomorphic.

Future Directions

The revolution in modern biology brought about by improved methods for phylogenetic analysis has had its impact on many fields of biology, including the evolutionary analysis of animal communication signals. This is evident from recent studies on electric communication, and from studies of other communication systems in birds, frogs, primates, and insects. It is becoming increasingly valuable to study not only how signals are adaptive, but where they occur in the phylogeny of close relatives. The surveys of relationships between electric fish are just beginning, especially for the mormyrids, but these kinds of studies hold great promise for providing a framework for exploration of evolution of behavior. My lab and several others are actively working on a revision of the phylogenetic relationships for mormyrids, and there are several excellent phylogenetic studies of the gymnotiforms. It is evident that behavioral biologists will have to work closely with systematists in the future to chart a better understanding of the evolution of animal communication in the context of a modern evolutionary analysis.

This review has touched only briefly on some of the adaptive principles of signal design for the electrosensory modality of fish. Surprisingly, in spite of near 30 years of studies on electric fish and on electric communication, we still have very fragmentary knowledge of the diversity of signals and their natural context except for a few species. The difficulties of working with some of the more bizarre and difficult species, and the difficulty of maintaining them in captivity, has led to the fragmented nature of this knowledge. A truly comprehensive study of electric communication necessitates a broader comparative analysis of behavior and evidently will require more field work, especially long-term studies.

Electric fish have proven to be an excellent system on which to study the origin and adaptive significance of animal communication signals. The modality is relatively easy to study, and signals tend to be simple. Signals are easily recorded and reproduced, and the modality has evolved great diversity within several restricted groups of fishes. Although their mechanisms are unique and not well-represented among vertebrates, electric fish are rapidly becoming one of the better-studied systems, mechanistically, phylogenetically, and ethologically.

Dedication

This chapter is dedicated to Peter Marler, on the occasion of his retirement. Peter Marler has made an enormous contribution to the mechanistic study of animal communication, and his far-reaching influence extends from developmental psychology to neuroethology and animal behavior. As one of Peter's students at The Rockefeller University before the field station was built at Millbrook, I was fortunate to have my early career shaped by his broad perspective, his creative interdisciplinary thinking, and his enormous support and enthusiasm.

Acknowledgments

The research was supported in part by a grant from the National Institute of Mental Health (Grant MH37972). The paper was presented at a symposium held in Davis California on the occasion of Peter Marler's retirement. I thank Marc Hauser and Mark Konishi for their organization of a symposium and volume, Mr. Garry Harned for excellent technical help and for comments on the manuscript, and Ms. Lori Miller for help with the manuscript.

References

Albert, J. S. (in press) Phylogenetic systematics of the American knifefishes (*Teleostei: Gymnotiformes*). *Misc. Publ. Mus. Zool.*, Univ. Michigan.

Alves-Gomes, J. and Hopkins, C. D. (1997) Molecular insights into the phylogeny of mormyriform fishes and the evolution of their electric organs. *Brain, Behavior, and Evolution* 49:324–351.

Alves-Gomes, J. A., Orti, G., Haygood, M., Heiligenberg, W., and Meyer, A. (1995) Phylogenetic analysis of the South American electric fishes (Order *Gymnotiformes*) and the evolution of their electrogenic system: A synthesis based on morphology, electrophysiology, and mitochondrial sequence data. *Molecular Biology and Evolution* 12:298–318.

Baron, V. D. (1994) African *Clarias* catfish elicits long-lasting weak electric pulses *Experentia* 50:644–647.

Baron, V. D., Morshnev, K. S., Olshansky, V. M., and Orlov, A. A. (1994) Electric organ discharges of two species of African catfish (*Synodontis*) during social behaviour. *Animal Behaviour* 48:1472–1475.

Bass, A. H. (1986a) Electric organs revisited: evolution of a vertebrate communication and orientation organ. In *Electroreception*, ed. by T. H. Bullock and W. Heiligenberg, pp. 13–70. New York: Wiley.

Bass, A. H. (1986b) A hormone-sensitive communication system in an electric fish. *J. Neurobiol.* 17:131–156.

Bass, A. H. (1986c) Species differences in electric organs of mormyrids: Substrates for species-typical electric organ discharge waveforms. *Journal of Comparative Neurology* 244:313–330.

Bass, A. H. and Hopkins, C. D. (1982) Gonadal steroids modulate sex differences in an electric organ discharge waveform. *Society for Neuroscience Abstracts* 267:8.

Bass, A. H. and Hopkins, C. D. (1983) Hormonal control of sexual differentiation: Changes in electric organ discharge waveform. *Science* 220:971–974.

Bass, A. H. and Hopkins, C. D. (1985) Hormonal control of sex differences in the electric organ discharge (EOD) of mormyrid fishes. *Journal of Comparative Physiology* 156:587–605.

Bass, A. H. and Volman, S. F. (1987) From behavior to membranes: Testosterone-induced changes in action potential duration in electric organs. *Proceedings of the National Academy of Sciences* (USA) 84:9295–9298.

Bell, C. C., Libouban, S., and Szabo, T. (1983) Neural pathways related to the electric organ discharge command in mormyrid fish. *Journal of Comparative Neurology* 216:327–338.

Bell, C. C. and Szabo, T. (1986) Electroreception in mormyrid fish: central anatomy. In *Electroreception*, ed. by T. H. Bullock and W. Heiligenberg, pp. 375–421. New York: John Wiley & Sons.

Bennett, M. V. L. (1970) Comparative physiology: Electric organs. *Ann. Rev. Physiol.* 32:471–528.

Bennett, M. V. L. (1971) Electric organs In *Fish Physiology*, ed. by W. Hoar and D. J. Randall, pp. 347–491. New York: Academic Press.

Bennett, M. V. L. and Grundfest, H. (1961) Studies on the morphology and electrophysiology of electric organs III. Electrophysiology of electric organs in mormyrids. In *Bioelectrogenesis: A Comparative Survey of Its Mechanisms with Particular Emphasis on Electric Fishes*, ed. by C. Chagas and A. P. d. Carvalho, pp. 113–135. New York: Elsevier.

Braford, M. R. (1982) African, but not Asian notopterid fishes are electroreceptive: Evidence from brain characters. *Neuroscience Letters* 32:35–39.

Braford, M. R. (1986) In African knifefishes: the Xenomystines. *Electroreception*, ed. by T. H. Bullock and W. Heiligenberg, pp. 453–464. New York: John Wiley & Sons.

Bullock, T. H. and Heiligenberg, W. (1986) *Electroreception*. Wiley Series in Neurobiology. New York: John Wiley and Sons.

Caputi, A. and Budelli, R. (1993) A realistic model of the electric organ discharge (EOD) of *Gymnotus carapo*. *Journal of Comparative Physiology* A 173:751.

Caputi, A., Macadar, O., and Trujillo-Cenóz, O. (1989) Waveform generation of the electric organ discharge in *Gymnotus carapo*. III. Analysis of the fish body as an electric source. *J. Comp. Physiol.* A 165:361–370.

Caputi, A., Silva, A., and Macadar, O. (1993) Electric organ activation in *Gymnotus carapo*. Spinal origin and peripheral mechanisms. *J. Comp. Physiol.* A 173:227–232.

Crawford, J. D. (1992) Individual and sex specificity in the electric organ discharges of breeding mormyrid fish. *J. Exp. Biol.* 164:79–102.

Crawford, J. D. and Hopkins, C. D. (1989) Detection of a previously unrecognized mormyrid fish (*Mormyrus subundulatus*) by electric discharge characteristics. *Cybium* 13:319–326.

Dahlgren, U. (1914) Origin of the electric tissues of *Gymnarchus niloticus*. *Carnegie Inst. Wash. Publ.* 183:159–203.

Denizot, J. P., Kirschbaum, F., Westby, G. W. M., and Tsuji, S. (1978) The larval electric organ of the weakly electric fish *Pollimyrus (Marcusenius) isidori* (*Mormyridae, Teleostei*). *J. Neurocytol.* 7:165–181.

Denizot, J. P., Kirschbaum, F., Westby, G. W. M., and Tsuji, S. (1982) On the development of the adult electric organ in the mormyrid fish *Pollimyrus isidori* (with special focus on innervation). *J. Neurocytol.* 11:913–934.

Fessard, A. (1958) In Les organes électrique. *Traité de Zoologie*, ed. by P. P. Grassé, pp. 1143–1238. Paris: Masson.

Finger, T. E., Bell, C. C., and Carr, C. E. (1986) In Comparisons among electroreceptive teleosts: why are electrosensory systems so similar? *Electroreception*, ed. by T. H. Bullock and W. Heiligenberg. New York: John Wiley & Sons Inc.

Friedman, M. A. and Hopkins, C. D. (1996) Tracking individual mormyrid electric fish in the field using electric organ discharge waveforms. *Animal Behaviour* 51:391–407.

Fritsch, G. (1891) Zweiter Berich über neuere Untersuchungen an elektrischen Fischen. *Sitzber. k. Preuss. Akad. Wiss. Berlin, Phys. Math. Kl.* 1891:601–602.

Hagedorn, M. (1983) Social signals in electric fish. Ph.D thesis, San Diego: University of California, San Diego.

Hagedorn, M. (1985) Ecology and behaviour of a pulse-type electric fish, *Hypopomus occidentalis* (*Gymnotiformes, Hypopomidae*), in a fresh-water stream in Panama. *Copeia* 1985:324–335.

Hagedorn, M. and Carr, C. (1985) Single electrocytes produce a sexually dimorphic signal in South American electric fish, *Hypopomus occidentalis* (*Gymnotiformes, Hypopomidae*) *J. Comp. Physiol.* A. 156:511–523.

Hagedorn, M. and Heiligenberg, W. (1985) Court and spark: Electric signals in the courtship and mating of gymnotoid fish. *Anim. Behav.* 33:254–265.

Hagedorn, M., Womble, M., and Finger, T. (1990) Synodontid catfish: A new group of weakly electric fish. *Brain Behav. Evol.* 35:268–277.

Heiligenberg, W. (1975) Theoretical and experimental approaches to spatial aspects of electrolocation *J. Comp. Physiol.* 103:247–272.

Heiligenberg, W. (1977) In Principles of electrolocation and jamming avoidance in electric fish: a neuroethological approach. *Studies in Brain Function*, ed. by V. Braitenberg, pp. 1–85. New York: Springer-Verlag.

Heiligenberg, W. (1991) *Neural Nets in Electric Fish.* Cambridge, MA: MIT Press.

Heiligenberg, W. and Bastian, J. (1980) Species specificity of electric organ discharges in sympatric gymnotoid fish of the Rio Negro. *Acta. Biol. Venez.* 10:187–203.

Hopkins, C. D. (1973) Lightning as background noise for communication among electric fish. *Nature* 242:268–270.

Hopkins, C. D. (1974a) Electric communication in fish. *American Scientist* 62:426–437.

Hopkins, C. D. (1974b) Electric communication: Functions in the social behavior of *Eigenmannia virescens. Behaviour* 50:270–305.

Hopkins, C. D. (1980) Evolution of electric communication channels of mormyrids. *Behavioural Ecology and Sociobiology* 7:1–13.

Hopkins, C. D. (1981) On the diversity of electric signals in a community of mormyrid electric fish in West Africa. *American Zoologist* 21:211–222.

Hopkins, C. D. (1983) Neuroethology of species recognition in electroreception. In *Advances in Vertebrate Neuroethology*, vol. 56, pp. 871–881. New York: Plenum.

Hopkins, C. D. (1983a) In *Fish Neurobiology*, ed. by R. G. Northcutt and R. E. Davis, pp. 215–259. Ann Arbor, MI: University of Michigan Press.

Hopkins, C. D. (1983b) In *Animal Behaviour 2: Animal Communication*, ed. by T. R. Halliday and P. J. B. Slater, pp. 114–155. Oxford: Blackwell Scientific Publications.

Hopkins, C. D. (1986) In *Electroreception*, ed. by T. H. Bullock and W. Heiligenberg, pp. 527–576. New York: John Wiley & Sons.

Hopkins, C. D. (1995) Convergent designs for electrogenesis and electroreception. *Current Opinion in Neurobiology* 5:769–777.

Hopkins, C. D. and Bass, A. H. (1981) Temporal coding of species recognition signals in an electric fish. *Science* 212:85–87.

Hopkins, C. D. and Bass, A. H. (1982) Significance of electroreceptor tuning in the recognition of species specific signals in mormyrid electric fish. *Society for Neuroscience Abstracts* 167:2.

Hopkins, C. D., Comfort, N. C., Bastian, J., and Bass, A. H. (1990) A functional analysis of sexual dimorphism in an electric fish, *Hypopomus pinnicaudatus*, order Gymnotiformes. *Brain, Behavior and Evolution* 35:350–367.

Hopkins, C. D., Jacob, P., and Bénech, V. (in prep.-a) Reproductive ecology of mormyrid electric fishes in the Central Delta of the Niger River, lateral migration, electric discharges, and breeding ecology.

Hopkins, C. D., Teugels, G. G., and Rundell, R. (in prep.-b) A species flock of mormyrid electric fishes (*Osteoglossomorpha, Mormyridae*) from Central West Africa with descriptions of four new *Brienomyrus* in the "*sphecodes*" complex.

Hopkins, C. D. and Westby, G. W. M. (1986) Time domain processing of electric organ discharge waveforms by pulse-type electric fish. *Brain Behavior and Evolution* 29:77–104.

Kalmijn, A. J. (1974) On the detection of electric fields from inanimate and animate sources other than electric organs. *Handbook of Sensory Physiology III/3: Electroreceptors and Other Specialized Receptors in Lower Vertebrates*, ed. by A. Fessard, pp. 147–200. Berlin, Heidelberg, New York: Springer-Verlag.

Kawasaki, M. and Heiligenberg, W. (1988a) Distinct mechanisms of modulation in a neuronal oscillator generate different social signals in the electric fish *Hypopomus. Journal of Comparative Physiology* A 165:731–741.

Kawasaki, M. and Heiligenberg, W. (1988b) Individual prepacemaker neurons can modulate the pacemaker cycle of the gymnotiform electric fish, *Eigenmannia. Journal of Comparative Physiology* A 162:13–21.

Kawasaki, M. and Heiligenberg, W. (1990) Different classes of glutamate receptors and GABA mediate distinct modulations of a neuronal oscillator, the medullary pacemaker of a gymnotiform electric fish. *J. Neurosci.* 10:3896–3904.

Kawasaki, M., Maler, L., Rose, G. J., and Heiligenberg, W. (1988) Anatomical and functional organization of the prepacemaker nucleus in gymnotiform electric fish: The accommodation of two behaviors in one nucleus. *Journal of Comparative Neurology* 276:113–131.

Kirschbaum, F. (1995) In *Electric Fishes: History and Behavior*, ed. by P. Moller, pp. 267–301. London: Chapman & Hall.

Knudsen, E. I. (1975) Spatial aspects of electric fields generated by weakly electric fish. *J. Comp. Physiol.* 99:193–118.

Kramer, B. (1995) *Electroreception and Communication in Fishes.* Stuttgart: Georg Fischer Verlag.

Lissmann, H. W. (1958) On the function and evolution of electric organs in fish. *Journal of Experimental Biology* 35:156–191.

Lissmann, H. W. and Machin, K. E. (1958) The mechanisms of object location in *Gymnarchus niloticus* and similar fish. *Journal of Experimental Biology* 35:457–486.

Lorenzo, D., Sierra, F., Silva, A., and Macadar, O. (1990) Spinal mechanisms of electric organ discharge synchronization in *Gymnotus carapo. J. Comp. Physiol.* A 167:447–452.

Lorenzo, D., Sierra, F., Silva, A., and Macadar, O. (1993a) Spatial distribution of the medullary command signal within the electric organ of *Gymnotus carapo. J. Comp. Physiol.* A 173:221–226.

Lorenzo, D., Silva, A., Sierra, F., and Caputi, A. (1993b) Spatio-temporal analysis of electrogeneration in *Gymnotus carapo. J. Comp. Physiol.* A 173:750.

Lorenzo, D., Velluti, J. C., and Macadar, O. (1988) Electrophysiological properties of abdominal electrocytes in the weakly electric fish *Gymnotus carapo. J. Comp. Physiol.* A 162:141–144.

Lovell, P. V., Hopkins, C. D., and Harned, G. D. (1997) The diversity of electric organ discharges found in eight species of Campylomormyrus electric fish (Mormyridae) *27th Annual Meeting of the Society for Neuroscience, Part 1. Society for Neuroscience Abstracts* 23 (1–2): 249.

Lundberg, J. G., Fernandes, C. C., Albert, J. S., and Garcia, M. (1996) *Magosternarchus*, a new genus with 2 species of electric fishes (*Gymnotiformes, Apteronotidae*) from the Amazon river basin, South America. *Copeia* 1996:657–670.

Macadar, O. (1993) Motor control of waveform generation in *Gymnotus carapo. J. Comp. Physiol.* A 173:728–729.

Macadar, O., Lorenzo, D., and Velluti, J. C. (1989) Waveform generation of the electric organ discharge in *Gymnotus carapo. J. Comp. Physiol.* A 165:353–360.

Mago-Leccia, F. (1994) *Electric Fishes of the Continental Waters of America.* Caracas: Clemente.

Marler, P. (1955) The characteristics of certain animal calls. *Nature* 176:6–7.

Marler, P. (1957) Specific distinctiveness in the communication signals of birds. *Behaviour* 11:13–39.

Marler, P. (1967) Animal communication signals. *Science* 157:769–774.

Metzner, W. and Heiligenberg, W. (1991) The coding of signals in the electric communication of the gymnotiform fish *Eigenmannia*: From electroreceptors to neurons in the torus semicircularis of the midbrain. *J. Comp. Physiol.* 169:135–150.

Michelsen, A. and Larsen, O. N. (1983) In Strategies for acoustic communication in complex environments. *Neuroethology and behavioral physiology*, ed. by F. Huber and H. Markl, pp. 321–331. Berlin: Springer.

Moller, P. (1995) *Electric Fishes: History and Behavior.* London: Chapman & Hall.

Nelson, J. S. (1976) *Fishes of the World.* New York: John Wiley & Sons.

Ogneff, J. (1898) Einige Bermerkungen über den Bau des schwachen elektrischen Organs bei den Mormyriden. *Z. Wiss. Zool.* 64:565–595.

Poll, M., Gosse, J. P., and Orts, S. (1982) Le genre *Campylomormyrus* Bleeker 1874, étude systématique et description d'une espèce nouvelle (Pieces, Mormyridae). *Bull. Inst. r. Sci. nat. Belg.* 54:1–34.

Roberts, T. (1989) *Mormyrus subundulatus*, a new species of mormyrid fish with a tubular snout from West Africa. *Cybium* 13:51–54.

Roberts, T. and Stewart, D. J. (1976) An ecological and systematic survey of fishes in the rapids of the lower Zaire or Congo river. *Bull. Mus. Comp. Zool.* 147:239–317.

Shumway, C. A. and Zelick, R. D. (1988) Sex recognition and neuronal coding of electric organ discharge waveform in the pulse-type weakly electric fish, *Hypopomus occidentalis. J. Comp. Physiol.* A. 163:465–478.

Srivastava, C. B. L. and Szabo, T. (1972) Development of electric organs of *Gymnarchus niloticus* (Fam. Gymnarchidae). I. Origin and histogenesis of electroplates. *J. Morph.* 138:375–186.

Sullivan, J. P. (1997) A phylogenetic study of the neotropical hypopomid electric fishes (*Gymnotiformes, Rhamphichthyoidea*). *Department of Zoology*, pp. 1–335.

Szabo, T. (1960) Development of the electric organ of Mormyridae. *Nature* 188:760–762.

Szabo, T. (1961) In Les Organes Electriques des mormyrides. *Bioelectrogenesis*, ed. by C. Chagas and A. P. Carvalho, pp. 20–24. New York: Elsevier.

Szabo, T. (1965) Sense organs of the lateral line system in some electric fish of the *Gymnotidae, Gymnarchidae, and Mormyridae. J. Morph.* 117:229–250.

Taverne, L. (1969) Étude Ostéologique des genres Boulengeromyrus Taverne et Géry, Genyomyrus Boulenger, Petrocephalus Marcusen (Pisces Mormyriformes) *Musee Royal de l'Afrique Centrale Annales Series IN-8-Tervuren, Belg.* 174:1–85.

Taverne, L. (1971a) Note sur la systématique des poissons Mormyriformes. Le problème des genres *Gnathonemus* Gill, *Hippopotamyrus* Pappenheim, *Cyphomyrus* Myers et les nouveaux genres *Pollimyrus* et *Brienomyrus. Rev. Zool. Bot. Afr.* 84:99–110.

Taverne, L. (1971b) Ostéologie des genres *Marcusenius* Gill, *Hippopotamyrus* Pappenheim, *Cyphomyrus* Myers, *Pollimyrus* Taverne et *Brienomyrus* Taverne (Pisces, Mormyriformes). *Annals Mus. r. Afr. cent.* 188:1–144.

Taverne, L. (1972) Ostéologie des genres *Mormyrus* Linné, *Mormyrops* Müller, *Hyperopisus* Gill, *Isichthys* Gill, *Myomyrus* Boulenger, *Stomatorhinus* Boulenger et *Gymnarchus* Cuvier. Considérations générales sur la systématique des poissons d l'ordre des mormyriformes. *Musée Roy. de l'Afrique Centrale, Sciences Zoologique, Tervuren, Belgium* 200:1–194.

Teugels, G. and Hopkins, C. D. (1998) Morphological and osteological evidence for the generic position of *Mormyrus kingsleyae* in the Genus *Brienomyrus* (*Teleostei: Mormyridae*). *Copeia* 1998:199–204.

Teugels, G. G. and Hopkins, C. D. (in prep.) Morphometric and electric evidence for the description of a new species flock in the electric fish genus *Brienomyrus* (Osteoglossomorpha, Mormyridae) from West-Central Africa.

von der Emde, G. and Bell, C. C. (1994) Responses of cells in the mormyrid electrosensory lobe to EODs with distorted waveforms: Implications for capacitance detection. *J. Comp. Physiol.* A. 175:83–93.

Westby, G. W. M. (1988) The ecology, discharge diversity, and predatory behaviour of gymnotiform electric fish in the coastal streams of French Guiana. *Behavioural Ecology and Sociobiology* 22:341–354.

Westby, G. W. M. and Kirschbaum, F. (1977) Emergence and development of the electric organ discharge in the mormyrid fish, *Pollimyrus isidori*. I. The Larval Discharge. *J. Comp. Physiol.* A. 122:251–271.

Westby, G. W. M. and Kirschbaum, F. (1978) Emergence and development of the electric organ discharge in the mormyrid fish, *Pollimyrus isidori*. II. Replacement of the larval by the adult discharge. *J. Comp. Physiol.* A. 127:45–59.

Wiley, R. H. and Richards, D. G. (1978) Physical constraints on acoustic communication in the atmosphere: Implications for the evolution of animal vocalizations. *Behavioral Ecology and Sociobiology* 3:69–94.

Wiley, R. H. and Richards, D. G. (1982) In *Acoustic communication in Birds*, ed. by Donald Kroodsma, pp. 131–181. New York: Academic Press.

Zahavi, A. (1977) The cost of honesty (further remarks on the handicap principle). *J. Theoretical Biol.* 67:603–605.

Zakon, H. (1986) In The electroreceptive periphery. *Electroreception*, ed. by. T. H. Bullock and W. F. Heiligenberg, pp. 103–156. New York: John Wiley & Sons.

17 Complementary Explanations for Existing Phenotypes in an Acoustic Communication System

Andrew H. Bass, Deana Bodnar, and Margaret A. Marchaterre

A fundamental goal in biological research is to identify the causal factors that explain the existence of individual phenotypes. Recently, Sherman (1988) recast the various explanatory categories articulated by Tinbergen (1951, 1963) and Mayr (1961) into the "levels of analysis" (functional consequences, evolutionary origins, ontogenetic processes, mechanisms) and emphasized that complementary hypotheses can be proposed at different levels to explain an existing phenotype. As discussed in more detail below, Bass (1998) further modified this approach mainly by providing a more complete characterization of mechanisms (now inclusive of ontogenetic processes) and introducing life history as an explanatory level. The utility of this paradigm was demonstrated by proposing multiple explanations for the existence of behavioral and neurobiological phenotypes in a sound-producing teleost fish, the plainfin midshipman (*Porichthys notatus*).

Marler and Hamilton's textbook *Mechanisms of Animal Behavior* (1966) stands as a timely review of functional and evolutionary analyses in behavioral biology. This text essentially outlined many of the model systems that integrated the problem-solving approaches of field- and laboratory-oriented biologists. In particular, Marler's own work and that of his students and collaborators provided the groundwork for scientists from a diversity of disciplines who were interested in the how and why of acoustic communication. Here, we utilize the tools of bioacousticians, behavioral ecologists, and neurobiologists to identify the mechanisms underlying the expression of behavioral and neurobiological phenotypes in an acoustic communication system. Whereas a previous essay elaborated upon studies of the vocal motor system that establish the physical attributes of vocal behaviors in midshipman fish (Bass 1998), the current one focuses on acoustic mechanisms that may explain, in part, existing patterns of mate choice.

Complementary Explanations for Phenotypic Characters

Characters and Ecological Environments

Since a detailed description of the proposed theoretical framework for asking proximate and ultimate questions in behavioral and evolutionary neurobiology has been developed in an earlier essay (Bass 1998), it is reviewed only briefly here. An existing phenotype can be operationally defined by behavioral and structural characters that exist within an ecological environment. A character is "a feature of an organism's phenotype that may be described, figured, measured, weighed, counted, scored, or otherwise communicated by one biologist to other biologists" (Wiley 1981, p. 8). Behavioral characters are simply the "actions taken by organisms" (Wiley 1981, p. 319), the example mainly discussed here being animal vocalizations. Structural characters include a broad range of traits usually referred to as being either genetic, psychological, physiological, morphological, or biochemical; our discussion centers on structural characters of the nervous system, which may be further subdivided using the forementioned descriptors. "Ecological environment" is a phrase adopted from Williams (1966) that represents a vast range of abiotic and biotic factors external to an individual, which by example in the following discussion will mainly include nest sites and conspecifics in an aquatic environment.

Mechanisms and Complementary Explanations

Complementary explanations can best account for the existence of phenotypic characters. These explanations are specified as mechanisms, life history, fitness, and evolutionary history (Bass 1998). To illustrate the relationship between characters within this explanatory framework, Bass (1998) adopted a Venn-like diagram with three overlapping circles (figure 17.1). Each circle symbolizes the potential range of variation for either behavioral or structural characters, or the ecological environment. The existing organism or any one of its existing characters is represented by the center of the diagram, the single point of overlap for all three circles. The portions of the three circles outside of the center represent potential characters and environments.

Mechanisms either correlate or causally link characters with each other or with an ecological environment and are specified as structural-behavioral, behavioral-ecological, and ecological-structural (figure 17.1). Mechanisms, as used here, include Marler and Hamilton's (1966, p. vii) "processes that determine when behavior will occur and what form it will take." In this case, regions of overlap in the center of the Venn diagram now represent existing mechanisms, while their wings outside of the center represent potential mechanisms. Implicit to mechanistic explanations is that a character or an ecological environment may be represented either as a cause or as consequence by moving in either a clockwise or counterclockwise direction around the center of the diagram. The word orders for the mechanisms in figure 17.1, for example, "structural" followed by "behavioral," indicate the directions in which causal linkages are proposed here and in the previous essay (Bass 1998).

Behavioral-ecological mechanisms encompass the interactions of an individual's behavior with its surrounding environment, inclusive of conspecifics and heterospecifics. One relevant example is the exchange of reproductive-related acoustic signals (behavioral characters) mediating interactions between conspecifics (biotic

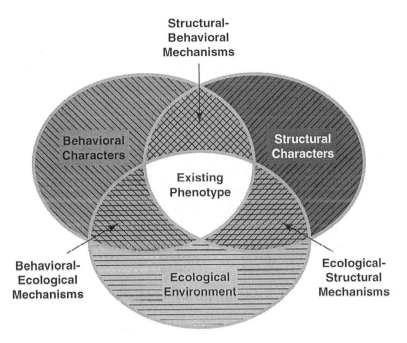

Figure 17.1
Three characters contribute to an individual's existing phenotype: behavioral, structural, and ecological. The relationships among characters are best described by a Venn diagram which has three overlapping circles; the potential range of variation for each character is represented by one of the circles. The center of the diagram, a point of overlap in all three circles, represents the existing phenotype. Mechanistic explanations are represented spatially by the overlap between two circles identified here as structural-behavioral, behavioral-ecological, and ecological-structural mechanisms.

ecological environment) during male-male competition and female choice behaviors (see Alcock 1998 for examples). Structural-behavioral mechanisms establish a causal relationship between structural characters and behavioral actions. A simple communication example is the demonstration that the geometry of electrocytes (structural characters), the spike-generating cells of the electric organ of weakly electric fish, can account for the number of phases and polarity in their electric organ discharge waveform (behavioral characters) (Bennett 1971; Bass 1986; Alves-Gomez and Hopkins 1997). Ecological-structural mechanisms include the influences of the abiotic environment on structural characters. An example important to acoustic signaling among ectotherms would be the influence of ambient water temperature (abiotic ecological environment) on the fundamental discharge frequency of the pacemaker-motoneuron circuit (structural characters) of sound-producing fish (Bass and Baker 1991).

Life History

A sequence of Venn diagrams moving along the temporal axis of age can represent an individual's entire life history (Bass 1998). The rotation of the circles of characters and the environment in the Venn diagram during an individual's lifetime can lead to new sets of characters and mechanisms that define a current phenotype such as those transformations that accompany the onset of sexual maturation. Ontogenetic "processes," such as neurogenesis or the onset of sex-specific behaviors at the time of reproductive maturation, would simply be included with respectively structural and behavioral characters.

Life-history explanations also introduce the concept of trade-offs. Stearns (1992) identified trade-offs as "constraining relationships" between "demographic traits"—birth, age, and size at maturity, number and size of offspring, growth and reproductive investment, length of life, and death. In a broader sense, trade-offs could also be considered to include developmental constraints, which may be further categorized as "disruptive developmental processes" or "lack of genetic variation" (see Reeve and Sherman 1993). Trade-offs in age and size at sexual maturity provide one explanation for the existence of divergent character sets, including alternative developmental trajectories, in two male reproductive morphs in midshipman fish (Bass 1996). One morph, the "type II" male, invests in gonad mass at an early age, while the alternative morph, the "type I" male, delays maturation and invests in body size and growth of the vocal motor system.

Fitness

The existence of characters and mechanisms can also be explained in terms of their relationship to reproductive success and survival, that is, to fitness (see Endler 1986). For example, the size of the song repertoire (behavioral characters) among male reed warblers has a consistent relationship with an individual's number of extrapair fertilizations and survival of their offspring (Hasselquist et al. 1996). By extension, the existing structural characters and structural-behavioral mechanisms that determine the physical appearance of a male's song repertoire could be explained in this same context.

Fitness explanations can also be applied to life-history patterns. Life-history theory traditionally explains the evolution of trade-offs in demographic characters in terms of fitness (see Stearns 1992), but this can be extended to cellular characters as well. For example, among midshipman fish, the adoption of a mate-calling, type I male phenotype involves trade-offs in both age and size at sexual maturity as well as growth of vocal neurons and muscles. The adoption of a type I male life-history strategy enables males to acoustically court gravid females, gain egg fertilizations, and guard nests against intruders (Bass 1996).

Evolutionary History

Explanations for existing phenotypes based on evolutionary history incorporate the temporal dimension of geologic time. Here, a sequence of Venn diagrams would represent past, present, and future interactions. Historical explanations often describe the origin and subsequent modification of a character based on a comparative analysis between extant species. For example, Bass and Baker (1997) recently proposed that the vocal motor circuitry across several vertebrate groups have common origins from embryonic hindbrain segments (rhombomeres) that form neurons establishing a diversity of rhythmic behaviors. Hence one explanation for the existence of shared vocal motor characters and mechanisms among vertebrates is that they reflect a phylogenetically conserved pattern of hindbrain characters and mechanisms.

This new framework differs from Sherman's (1988) "levels of analysis" in several ways:

1. A single new category of "structural characters" now encompasses "ontogenetic processes" and "mechanisms," which separately included cognitive, emotional and physiological processes.

2. Three categories of "mechanisms" (behavioral-ecological, structural-behavioral, ecological-structural) are now defined that can establish causal relationships between characters and an environment.

3. Diverse, but complementary explanations for an existing phenotype can now be formulated within a single "level," namely that of mechanisms.

4. "Life history" is now included as an explanatory level that introduces the concept of "trade-offs."

5. The term "fitness" replaces "functional consequences" and avoids the potential semantic problems with use of the term "consequences" (see Dewsbury 1992; Alcock and Sherman 1994).

6. There are now linkages between different explanatory levels (see earlier section on fitness). The interrelationships between explanations echo Marler and Hamilton's (1966, p. vii) comment: "Our aim is to elucidate the *interplay* [original emphasis] of such factors in the control and development of animal behavior."

Acoustic Communication Mechanisms in Midshipman Fish

Nonmammalian models of acoustic communication have provided unique and practical opportunities to identify the basic principles of operation for the auditory system of vertebrates. Our studies have focused on teleost fish, which is the largest group of extant vertebrates and includes both vocal and nonvocal species that have exploited a wide range of acoustic niches and have an auditory system resembling that of other vertebrates (Popper and Fay 1993). Sound-producing/vocalizing species generate a simple repertoire of species-specific signals that can be easily reproduced and manipulated using computer synthesis, and in some species, individuals produce stereotyped behavioral responses to acoustic playbacks of natural and computer-synthesized signals. A general review of vocal communication and hearing in teleost fish is beyond the goals of this essay; the reader is referred to recent and comprehensive surveys of the topic (Popper and Fay 1993; Ladich 1997). As mentioned at the beginning of this essay, the main goal here is to explain the existence of mate choice in midshipman fish in terms of acoustic sensory mechanisms.

Behavioral-vocal Characters and the Ecological Environment

A first step in identifying acoustic mechanisms that may explain patterns of mate choice is to define a relevant set of behavioral characters, in this case vocal signals. The vocal abilities of the plainfin midshipman fish, *Porichthys notatus*, have been reported since the early 1900s (review: Bass 1990). Large parental males, now known as type I males, excavate denlike nests under rocky shelters in the intertidal and subtidal zones along the western coast of the United States and Canada (all part of their abiotic ecological environment). We first distinguished two classes of males, type I and II, on the basis of structural characteristics—body size, gonad-to-body weight ratios, sonic motoneuron diameter, and sonic muscle mass and ultrastructure (Bass and Marchaterre 1989a,b). Later, observations of captive specimens showed that type I males and type II males also have distinct behavioral characteristics—spawning and vocalizations (Brantley and Bass 1994). Together, these and other studies established a suite of characteristics and ecological environments that distinguish each reproductive morph's sexuality (table 17.1; Bass 1992, 1996, 1998).

We have now studied plainfin midshipman vocalizations at two locales—Tomales Bay, California and Brinnon, Washington. There are at least three classes of acoustic signals generated by individuals. For all of the representative signals shown, the temperature was recorded inside the nest where a hydrophone was positioned (hydro-

Table 17.1
Sexually polymorphic traits.

	Type I Male	Type II Male	Female
Nest Building	yes	no	no
Egg-guarding	yes	no	no
Body size	Large	Small	Intermediate
Gonad size/Body size Ratio	Small	Large	Large (gravid); Small (spent)
Ventral Coloration	olive-gray	mottled yellow	bronze (gravid); mottled (spent)
Circulating steroids	testosterone; 11-ketotestosterone	testosterone	testosterone; estradiol
Vocal Behavior	Hums, Grunts	Isolated Grunts	Isolated Grunts
Vocal Muscle	Large	Small	Small
Vocal Neurons	Large	Small	Small
Vocal Discharge Frequency	High	Low	Low

phones from the Bioacoustics Program, Cornell Laboratory of Ornithology, Ithaca, NY; temperature loggers from DataLoggers, Onset Computer Corp., Pocasse, MA). Recording temperature is an important consideration since the fundamental frequency (F0) of midshipman signals varies with ambient temperature (Bass and Baker 1991; Brantley and Bass 1994). All recordings were done between dark and dawn, which is the time period for peak spawning and vocal activity (see Bass 1990; Brantley and Bass 1994). Recordings were digitized at 2KHz and 16-bit resolution; power spectra were calculated using a Fast Fourier transform size of 16K (0.11Hz frequency resolution) using Canary 1.1 (Program in Bioacoustics, Cornell University Laboratory of Ornithology). We first describe the physical attributes of midshipman vocalizations and then consider their functional significance in a social or ecological context.

(1) "Hums" are long-duration (minutes to over 1 hour), multiharmonic signals with a sinusoidal-like appearance and are produced by type I males (figure 17.2a). Hums were first reported by Ibara and colleagues (1983) and later by Brantley and Bass (1994). F0 is highly stable for individuals, as was first suggested by neurophysiolgical studies of the rhythmically active, vocal pacemaker circuit in midshipman (Bass and Baker 1990). The hum shown in figure 17.2a is a brief segment of one that lasted for 1 minute and 57 seconds. The F0 was measured for ten different segments and was consistently 102Hz (figure 17.2a). The hydrophone was placed immediately adjacent to a nest that contained only one type I male (21.5cm, standard

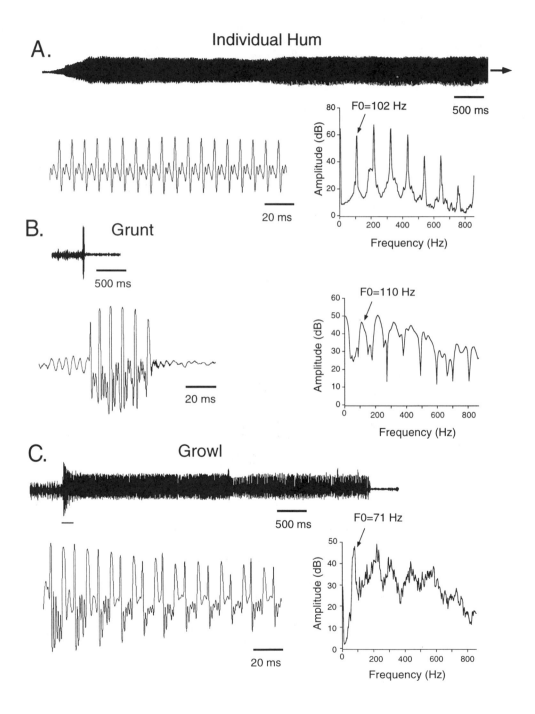

length) both the day before and the day after the recording was done; we assume his "ownership" of the signals.

(2) "Grunts" are brief duration signals that have a F0 similar to that of hums, but with wider bandwidths than hums (figure 17.2b). Grunts have been recorded from all adult reproductive morphs although they are of much lower amplitude in type II males and females (Brantley and Bass 1994). Grunts have often been reported when midshipman are picked up by hand (see Bass 1990); they were first described acoustically by Cohen and Winn (1967). For single grunts (n = 21) recorded from the individual's nest, shown in figure 17.2, the mean duration was 52msec (range 33.7 − 89; SE = 3.0) and the mean fundamental frequency (F0) was 107.6Hz (range = 99.6 − 110; standard error, SE = 0.7).

"Grunt trains" are only known to be generated by type I males and are defined as a rapid succession of single grunts at intervals of about 400msec (figure 17.3; records from a different male from that shown in figure 17.2; see also Brantley and Bass 1994).

(3) "Growls" are somewhat intermediate in their physical attributes between hums and grunts and are apparently produced only by type I males (figure 17.2c). We say "apparently" because these signals have not been recorded in captive populations where the individual source of the signal has been visually and acoustically confirmed, as it has been for hums and grunts (Brantley and Bass 1994). However, recordings of growls are restricted to nest sites where only midshipman fish are present, and they are of an amplitude comparable to that of type I male hums and grunts. These signals were first designated as growls by Lee and Bass (1994; see also Lee 1996), although they resemble the "buzzes" of Cohen and Winn (1967), who recorded sounds from the same locale in Washington state. Brantley and Bass (1994) also reported (but did not describe acoustically) buzzlike sounds evoked from hand-collected midshipman in California. Compared to a hum or a grunt, the F0 of a growl shows far greater variation (Lee and Bass 1994; Lee 1996). The growl in figure 17.4a was dissected into three segments (B–D; recorded from the same male represented in figure 17.2). F0 varies from 116Hz–70Hz–59Hz (figure 17.4b–d). The mean duration for growls (n = 10) recorded for the male shown in figures 17.2 and 17.4 was 3.5 sec (range = 0.542 − 8.0, SE = 0.7), and the mean F0 was 70.3Hz (range of 67.3 − 75.4; SE = 1.3).

Figure 17.2
Acoustic signals of plainfin midshipman fish. All signals were recorded from the same nest at 16.1 °C. The temporal waveform of each signal is shown on two different time scales along with its power spectrum (the fundamental frequency, F0, is indicated). Shown are representative examples of a hum (A), single grunt (B), and a growl (C).

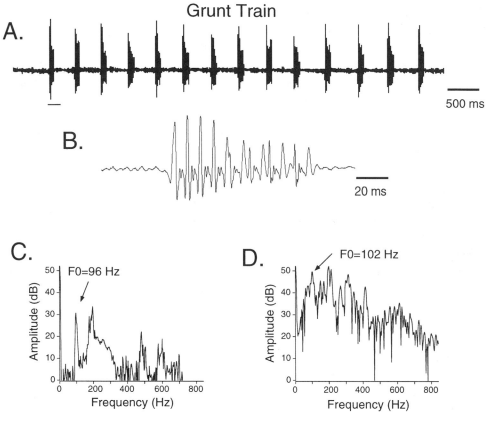

Figure 17.3
Type I males also produce trains of grunts when defending their nest against intruders. Shown here is an example of the temporal waveform of a segment of a grunt train that included 170 grunts over a period of 2.8sec (A), a single grunt from that train on an expanded scale (B), and the power spectrum of the entire train (C), and the single grunt (D). (Recorded from a different type I male than that shown in figure 17.2).

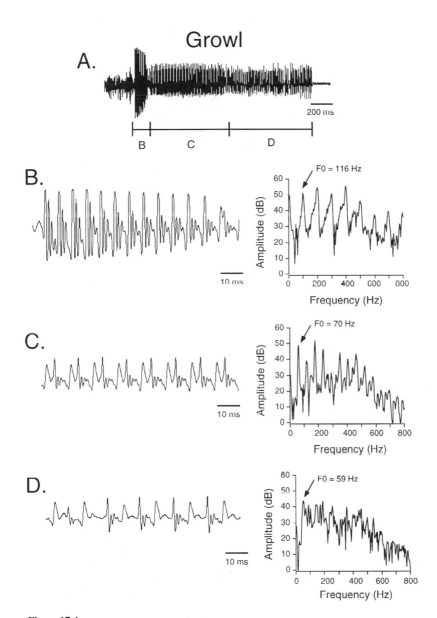

Figure 17.4
Dissection of a single growl (A) generated by the same male as shown in figure 17.2. The temporal waveform of each of three sections of the growl is shown on an expanded time scale along with its power spectrum (B–D). F0 varies from 116–59Hz for this growl.

Figure 17.5
Line drawings of a generalized spawning sequence of midshipman based on individuals that took up resi-
dence in artificial nests in aquaria (modified from Brantley and Bass 1994). Shown here, inside a nest, are a
type I male (left) and a gravid female (right) .with her ventrum up against the roof of the nest as she
deposits each individual egg onto the roof. Each egg has a cement disc which attaches it to the roof's surface. A type II male outside the nest (far right) "satellite-spawns" and fans sperm towards the inside of the
nest.

Behavioral-ecological Mechanisms

Behavioral-ecological explanations for midshipman acoustic communication signals
were first derived from studying the interactions of conspecifics in a reproductive
context (figure 17.5; Brantley and Bass 1994). To put it briefly, observations of captive specimens showed that type I males were the nest-building, egg-guarding males
identified in earlier studies (see Bass 1990) and that neither type II males nor females
build or guard nests. Instead, type II males lie perched along the outside wall of a
nest or sneak into a nest while a female is present, to compete with the type I male
for egg fertilizations. These studies also provided strong support for Ibara et al.'s
(1983) hypothesis that a type I male's humming behavior attracts females (part of
the biotic ecological environment) to a nest. Nesting males hum continuously until
just after a gravid female enters the nest. Once spawning is complete, a female leaves
the nest and the type I male hums the next evening to attract another female. These
same studies showed that grunt-trains function in an agonistic context, when a nesting, egg-guarding type I male is challenged by other males (Brantley and Bass 1994).
   A fourth class of vocalizations, identified as "acoustic beats," results from the
temporal overlap of the vocal behavior of two type I males. During the breeding
season, midshipman congregate in localized areas where two concurrent hums are
generated by neighboring type I males (M. Marchaterre and A. Bass, unpublished

data). Concurrent hums summate to produce acoustic beats at frequencies equivalent to the difference in fundamental frequencies (dF) between hums. For example, figure 17.6a,b shows the overlap of the hums from two type I males in nests separated by 16 feet, 8 inches (recording temperature at both nests was 16.1 °C). The F0s of the two males were 102Hz (same male as in figure 17.2a) and 100Hz; expansion of the power spectrum around the second harmonic facilitates recognition of the F0s (figure 17.6c,d). Difference frequencies for field-recorded specimens range from 2–10Hz (Figure 17.6e; Bodnar and Bass 1997). Midshipman acoustic beats are analagous in their physical attributes to the electric beats of gymnotid and gymnarchid fishes (see Heiligenberg 1991).

One- and two-choice playback experiments using underwater loudspeakers and computer-synthesized acoustic signals demonstrate conclusively the attraction function of hums (McKibben and Bass 1998). Gravid but not spent females show robust phonotaxis to playbacks of pure tones that have a fundamental frequency similar to that of natural hums. Only humlike signals, and not grunts or white noise, can attract females to a speaker. Females however, circle, swim back and forth in front of the speaker, or swim underneath touching the speaker, their movements resembling those of females in seminatural conditions (Brantley and Bass 1994). Some type I and type II males also demonstrate phonotaxis to a single hum, although their responsiveness does not compare to that of a female (McKibben and Bass, 1998).

Structural Characters

A complementary explanation for the existence of mate choice based on acoustic cues can be derived from hypotheses that establish a relationship between the structural characters of the "receiver's" auditory system and the attributes of a "sender's" vocalizations (structural-behavioral mechanisms). However, as with behavioral ecological mechanisms, we must first identify some of the relevant characters, which in this case are structural characters of the auditory system. As with most other teleost fish (Popper and Fay 1993), the principal organ of hearing in midshipman is the sacculus (Cohen and Winn 1967). The sacculus is a division of the inner ear that is characterized in midshipman by a relatively large otolith (SA, figures 17.7a,b). The sensory epithelium (macula) of the sacculus (m, figure 17.7b) is innervated by a branch of the eighth (octaval) cranial nerve (VIIIs, figure 17.7b). Neuroanatomical studies in midshipman fish have outlined the primary targets of eighth nerve/octaval afferents in the rostral medulla and have also shown linkages to the hindbrain vocal motor circuit (Bass et al. 1994). Both primary and secondary octaval nuclei of the medulla project to a midbrain auditory nucleus (nucleus centralis) positioned in the

Concurrent Hums

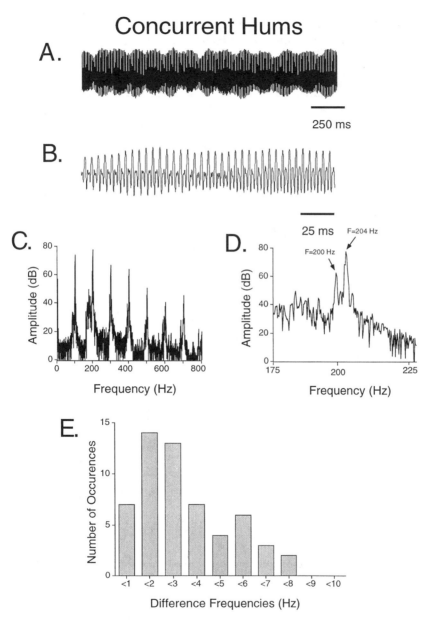

Figure 17.6
An example of the temporal waveform (A, B) and power spectrum of two, field recorded, concurrent hums. An expansion of the power spectrum (C) at the position of the second harmonic (D) permits an easier distinction of the two F0s of those signals which were 100Hz and 102Hz (the latter is from the same male as in figure 17.2). Both nests were at the same temperature (16.1 °C.). (E) The distribution of dFs for the fundamental frequencies (dF0s) of concurrent hums recorded in natural habitats (from Bodnar and Bass 1997). The recorded F0s ranged from 96–126Hz.

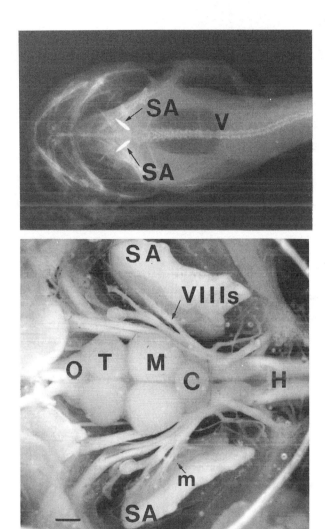

Figure 17.7
The sacculus is the division of the inner ear that is the main auditory organ in midshipman fish. It has the largest otolith within the inner ear. An X-ray image (A, ventrum on top) of a type I male shows the position of the otolith (SA). The otoliths appears to lie at a 90° angle relative to each other while both appear to lie perpendicular to the horizontal plane of the body. The vertebral column (V) is also indicated. Also shown (B) is a photograph of a dorsal view of the cranium of a type I male showing the position of both saccular otoliths. The sensory epithelium of the sacculus (macula, m) is innervated by a branch of the eighth (VIIIs) cranial nerve which emerges from the hindbrain (H). Abbreviations: C, cerebellum; M, midbrain; O, olfactory bulb; T, telencephalon. Bar scale represents 1mm.

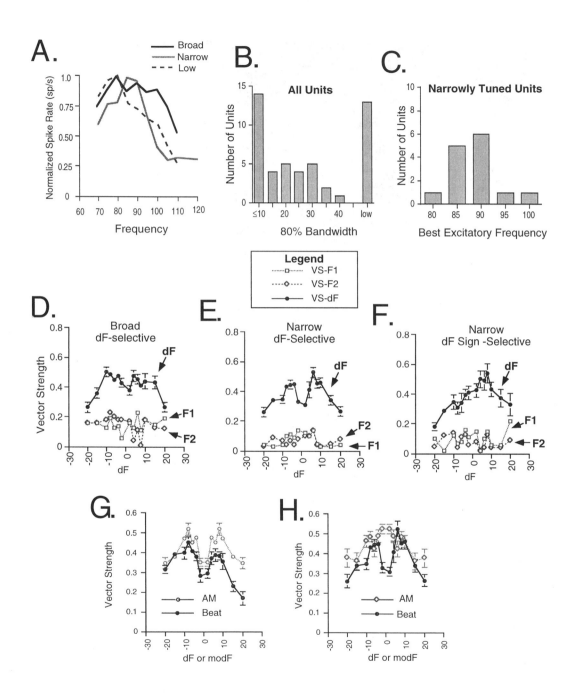

medial torus semicircularis, a homologue of the mammalian inferior colliculus (Bass et al. 1996). The physiological characters of the auditory system of teleosts have been mainly studied in nonvocalizing fish (see Popper and Fay 1993), although this area of study has recently been extended to sound-producing midshipman fish (see below) and weakly electric mormyrids (Crawford 1993, 1997).

Structural-behavioral Mechanisms

Studies of the auditory system of sonic vertebrates often define its physiological characters using stimuli whose design is guided by the temporal structure of a species' vocal signals, inclusive of their frequency, amplitude, and phase spectra. A main goal of auditory physiologists is therefore to understand how trains of action potentials generated by the peripheral and central nervous system code vocal behavior characters. Neurophysiologists use a number of tools to try to decipher this code including frequency tuning curves or isointensity profiles that characterize the frequency sensitivity of neurons. According to Fourier analysis, every periodic signal can be broken down into a constituent set of sinusoidal waveforms. In the case of a multiharmonic signal, the frequency composition is characterized by a fundamental frequency, F0, and a number of multiples of F0 (harmonics; see figures 17.2–17.4). Auditory neurons often exhibit correlations between their spike rates and/or synchronization characteristics and the spectral composition of a signal, and they are thus presumed to encode the F0 and harmonics of a vocal signal by a spike rate and/or temporal code (also see Simmons et al. 1993; Bodnar and Capranica 1994; Bodnar and Vrieslander 1997). As defined by spike rate, the majority of midbrain neurons in midshipmen have broad tuning properties. The 80% bandwidths, defined as the frequency at which the average spike rate fell below 80% of the maximum response, identified three categories of units: broad, narrow, and low (figure 17.8a,b). Among

Figure 17.8
(A)–(C) Frequency tuning of midshipman auditory midbrain units (modified from Bodnar and Bass 1997). (A) Representative isointensity curves of three units with broad, narrow, and low frequency tuning. (B) Distribution of the best excitatory frequencies of all units tested (n = 49) based on isointensity curves. (C) Distribution of the best excitatory frequency of narrowly tuned units. (D)–(F) Midshipman auditory midbrain responses to beat stimuli with low frequency dFs. Each beat stimulus is composed of F1, which in all cases is 90Hz, and F2 which is $90 \pm 2 - 20$Hz. Shown are plots of vector strength of synchronization for three units in which vector strength either does not significantly change (D) or does significantly change (E, F) with different dFs. Units exhibited low synchronization to the individual components (F1, F2) of a beat. (G), (H) Comparison of responses to beat stimuli with amplitude modulated (AM) signals. Plots show the vector strength of synchronization vs. dF for beats with F1 = 90Hz (filled circles) and vector strength vs. modF for AM signals with carrier frequency = 90Hz (open circles). AM modF values are plotted as both positive and negative to facilitate comparison with beat data. One example shows a unit with a significant effect of stimulus type on dF/modF synchronization, but no significant change in dF/modF selectivity for beats vs AM signals (G). A second example shows a unit with a significant change in dF/modF selectivity for beats vs AM signals (H).

the narrowly tuned units, best frequencies were centered near the F0s of vocal signals (figure 17.8c). Thus one structural-behavioral explanation of how an individual detects hums is that their auditory neurons are tuned to the F0s (structural characters) that characterize type I male hums (behavioral characters).

As mentioned earlier, midshipman fish regularly encounter acoustic beats in their natural environment. Phonotaxis experiments have shown that a gravid female will readily choose and directly approach the signal emitted from one speaker when two humlike tones with dFs comparable to natural beats are presented independently through two underwater speakers (McKibben and Bass, 1998). These results led us to investigate the hypothesis that midshipman fish must have a neural mechanism that permits them to segregate and discriminate between two signals on the basis of their fundamental frequencies. To date, our neurophysiological studies have focused on the separate and combined encoding of the F0s of the two pure tones that form simple beatlike signals. For these studies, the temporal coding characteristics of auditory neurons were quantified by their vector strength of synchronization (Goldberg and Brown 1969), which is a measure of the degree of phase locking for action potentials to a particular phase of an acoustic signal. Eighth-nerve auditory afferents exhibit a relatively high degree of synchronization to the individual tones of a beat and synchronize best to dFs $\geq$ 10Hz (McKibben and Bass 1996; McKibben 1998). In contrast, midbrain neurons display relatively low synchronization to the individual beat components and high synchronization to dFs of 2–10Hz (figure 17.8d–f; Bodnar and Bass 1997). Auditory midbrain vector strength compared with dF profiles shows two main response types for beat stimuli (spike rate profiles did not reflect dF tuning; Bodnar and Bass 1997). Single units exhibit either (1) moderate synchronization to all dFs between $\pm$ 10Hz ("broad dF-selective units," figure 17.8d) and no significant variations in their vector strength dF values or (2) distinct peaks at a particular dF ("narrow dF-selective" units, figure 17.8e,f). Among the narrow dF-selective units, a subset displays different responses to positive and negative dFs ("narrow dF sign-selective" units; figure 17.8f). Hence a stuctural-behavioral explanation of how individual midshipman fish choose one of two concurrent humlike signals that form an acoustic beat is that they have neurons with temporal-coding properties (structural characteristics) that permit the segregation and discrmination of each hum (behavioral characteristics).

One potentially confounding factor for the detection and segregation of concurrent hums is that the amplitude-modulations of acoustic beats are similar to those of amplitude-modulated (AM) signals such as grunt trains, which have a modulation frequency (modF) of about 2Hz (figure 17.3). For acoustic beats, AM periodicity is determined by the dF between the F0s of two hums. By contrast, the AM of grunt trains arises from modulation of a carrier frequency (Fc) by a modF that creates sidebands at Fc-modF and Fc+modF. The responses of single midbrain neurons to either beats or AM signals with the same dFs and modFs demonstrated that neurons are either (1) tuned to the same dFs and modFs (figure 17.8g) but differ significantly in their vector strength of synchronization (see Bodnar and Bass 1997), or (2) tuned to different dFs and modFs (figure 17.8h) with similar degrees of synchronization to dF and modF (see Bodnar and Bass 1997). Both of these spike train differences likely contribute to the behavioral discrimination of AM and beat signals. Thus, as with the discrimination of two concurrent hums, the available data suggest that the neurophysiological properties (structural characteristics) of midbrain neurons provide an explanation of how individuals discriminate beats from other acoustic signals (behavioral characteristics).

Ecological-structural Mechanisms

We have shown that an abiotic ecological factor, ambient temperature, directly influences a structural characteristic, the discharge frequency of the pacemaker-motoneuron circuit, which establishes the fundamental frequency of hums and grunts (Bass and Baker 1991; Brantley and Bass 1994). In the midshipman, the frequency preference of females also shifts with temperature, in accordance with changes in the F0 of hums (McKibben and Bass 1998). Hence females are attracted to playbacks through underwater speakers of computer-synthesized, humlike signals whose F0 more closely matches the F0 of natural hums at a particular ambient water temperature. Comparable behavioral effects have been shown in amphibians (Gerhardt and Doherty 1988) and crickets (Pires and Hoy 1992). Although temperature has been shown to affect the temporal selectivity of peripheral neurons in amphibians (Brenowitz et al. 1985), comparable data are unavailable for the midshipman; but such an ecological-structural explanation seems likely.

Concluding Comments

A fundamental behavioral phenotype common to all sexual species is that of mate preference. Figure 17.9 summarizes how our current data on midshipman acoustic signals, auditory neurons, and the ecological environment (e.g., water temperature and conspecifics) can be placed within an explanatory framework to consider the acoustic mechanisms underlying mate choice by the female midshipman. The final mate-preference of any single individual depends on all three mechanisms, and hence variation within the population can arise from variation in one or more characters or mechanisms.

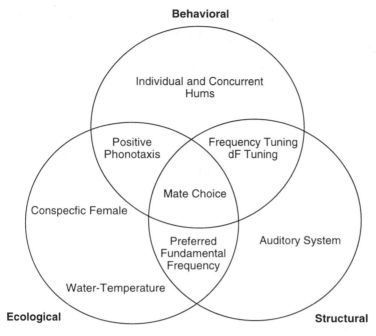

Figure 17.9
Summary of our current data on midshipman acoustic signals, auditory neurons and the ecological environment (e.g., water temperature and conspecifics) within the explanatory framework of figure 17.1 to consider acoustic mechanisms of mate preference.

Acknowledgments

Thanks to Mark Konishi and Marc Hauser for their invitation to be a participant in this symposium in honor of Peter Marler. Thanks also to M. C. Nelson and T. Natoli for help with the figures and manuscript. The original research reported here was supported by funds from NIH DC00092.

References

Alcock, J., ed. (1998) *Animal Behavior: An Evolutionary Approach*, sixth edition. Sunderland, MA: Sinauer Assoc.

Alcock, J. and Sherman, P. W. (1994) The utility of the proximate-ultimate dichotomy in ethology. *Ethology* 96:58–62.

Alves-Gomes, J. and Hopkins, C. D. (1997) Molecular insights into the phylogeny of mormyriform fishes and the evolution of their electric organs. *Brain. Behav. Evol.* 49:324–351.

Bass, A. H. (1986) Electric organs revisited: Evolution of a vertebrate communication and orientation organ. In *Electroreception,* ed. by T. H. Bullock and W. Heiligenberg, pp. 13–70. New York: John Wiley & Sons.

Bass, A. H. (1990) Sounds from the intertidal zone: Vocalizing fish. *Bioscience* 40:247–258.

Bass, A. H. (1992) Dimorphic male brains and alternative reproductive tactics in a vocalizing fish. *Trends Neurosci.* 15: 139–145.

Bass, A. H. (1996) Shaping brain sexuality. *Amer. Sci.* 84:352–363.

Bass, A. H. (1998) Behavioral and evolutionary neurobiology: A pluralistic approach. *Amer. Zool.* 38:97–107.

Bass, A. H. and Baker, R. (1990) Sexual dimorphisms in the vocal control system of a teleost fish: Morphology of physiologically identified neurons. *J. Neurobiol.* 21:1155–1168.

Bass, A. H. and Baker, R. (1991) Adaptive modification of homologous vocal control traits in teleost fishes. *Brain Behav. Evol.* 38:240–254.

Bass, A. H. and Baker, R. (1997) Phenotypic specification of hindbrain rhomberes and the origins of rhythmic circuits in vertebrates. *Brain Behav. Evol.* 50:3–16.

Bass, A. H., Bodnar, D. A., and Marchaterre, M. (1996) Auditory pathways in a vocal fish: Inputs to a midbrain nucleus encoding acoustic beats. *Soc. Neurosci. Abstr.* 22:447.

Bass, A. H. and Marchaterre, M. A. (1989a) Sound-generating (sonic) motor system in a teleost fish (*Porichthys notatus*): Sexual polymorphisms and general synaptology of a sonic motor nucleus. *J. Comp. Neurol.* 286:154–169.

Bass, A. H. and Marchaterre, M. A. (1989b) Sound generating (sonic) motor system in a teleost fish (*Porichthys notatus*): Sexual polymorphisms in the ultrastructure of myofibrils. *J. Comp. Neurol.* 286:141–153.

Bass, A. H., Marchaterre, M. A., and Baker, R. (1994): Vocal-acoustic pathways in a teleost fish. *J. Neurosci.* 14:4025–4039.

Bennett, M. V. L. (1971) Electric organs. In *Fish Physiology,* ed. by W. S. Hoar and D. J. Randall, pp. 347–484. New York: Academic Press.

Bodnar, D. A. and Bass, A. H. (1997) Temporal coding of concurrent acoustic signals in the auditory midbrain. *J. Neurosci.* 17:7553–7564.

Bodnar, D. A. and Capranica, R. R. (1994) Encoding of phase spectra by the peripheral auditory system of the bullfrog. *J. Comp. Physiol.* 174:157–171.

Bodnar, D. A. and Vrieslander, J. D. (1997) The contribution of changes in stimulus temporal features and peripheral nonlinearities to the phase sensitvity of auditory afferents in the bullfrog (*Rana catesbeiana*). *Audit. Neurosci.* 3:231–254.

Brantley, R. K. and Bass, A. H. (1994) Alternative male spawning tactics and acoustic signals in the plainfin midshipman fish, *Porichthys notatus* (*Teleostei, Batrachoididae*). *Ethology* 96:213–232.

Brenowitz, E., Rose, G., and Capranica, R. R. (1985) Neural correlates of temperature coupling in the vocal communication system of the gray treefrog (*Hyla versicolor*). *Brain Res.* 359:364–367.

Cohen, M. J. and Winn, E. W. (1967) Electrophysiological observations on hearing and sound production in the fish, *Porichthys notatus. J. Exper. Zool.* 165:355–370.

Crawford, J. D. (1993) Central auditory neurophysiology of a sound producing fish: The mesencephalon of *Pollimyrus isidori* (*Mormyridae*). *J. Comp. Physiol.* 172:139–152.

Crawford, J. D. (1997) Feature-detecting auditory neurons in the brain of a sound-producing fish. *J. Comp. Physiol.* 180:439–450.

Dewsbury, D. A. (1992) On the problems studied in ethology, comparative psychology, and animal behavior. *Ethology* 92:89–107.

Endler, J. A., ed. (1986) *Natural Selection in the Wild.* Princeton, NJ: Princeton University Press.

Gerhardt, H. C. and Doherty, J. A. (1988) Acoustic communication in the gray treefrog, *Hyla versicolor*: Evolutionary and neurobiological implications. *J. Comp. Physiol.* A 162:261–278.

Goldberg, J. M. and Brown, P. B. (1969) Response of binaural neurons of dog superior olive complex to dichotic tonal stimuli: Some physiological mechanisms of sound localization. *J. Neurophysiol.* 32:613–636.

Hasselquist, D., Bensch, S., and von Schantz, T. (1996) Correlation between male song repertoire, extra-pair paternity and offspring survival in the great reed warbler. *Nature* 381:229–232.

Heiligenberg, W., ed. (1991) *Neural Nets in Electric Fish.* Cambridge, MA: MIT Press.

Ibara, R. M., Penny, L. T., Ebeling, A. W., van Dykhuizen, G., and Cailliet, G. (1983) The mating call of the plainfin midshipman fish, *Porichthys notatus.* In *Predators and Prey in Fishes*, ed. by D. G. L. Noakes, D. G. Lindquist, G. S. Helfman, and J. A. Ward, pp. 205–212. The Hague: Dr. W. Junk Pubs.

Ladich, F. (1997) Agonistic behaviour and significance of sounds in vocalizing fish. *Mar. Fresh. Behav. Physiol.* 29:87–108.

Lee, A. (1996) Large mating advantage in the plainfin midshipman fish, *Porichthys notatus.* Masters Thesis, Cornell University.

Lee, A. O. and Bass, A. H. (1994) Acoustic behavior in the plainfin midshipman fish. Anim. Behav. Soc., 31st Ann. Mtg.

Marler, P. and Hamilton, W. J., III. (1966) *Mechanisms of Animal Communication.* New York: John Wiley and Sons.

Mayr, E. (1961) Cause and effect in biology. *Science* 134:1501–1506.

McKibben, J. (1998) A neuroethological analysis of acoustic communication in a vocalizing fish, the plainfin midshipman. Ph.D. Thesis, Cornell University.

McKibben, J. R. and Bass, A. H. (1996) Peripheral encoding of behaviorally relevant acoustic signals in a vocal fish. *Soc. Neurosci. Abstr.* 22:447.

McKibben, J. R. and Bass, A. H. (1998) Behavioral assessment of acoustic parameters relevant to signal recognition and preference in a vocal fish. *J. Acoust. Soc. Am.* 104:3520–3533.

McKibben, J. R., Bodnar, D., and Bass, A. H. (1995) Everybody's humming but is anybody listening: Acoustic communication in a marine teleost fish. *4th Int. Congr. Neuroethol.* 351.

Nelson, R., ed. (1995) *Behavioral Endocrinology.* Sunderland, MA: Sinauer Assoc.

Pires, A. and Hoy, R. (1992) Temperature coupling in cricket acoustic communication. I. Field and laboratory studies of temperature effects on calling song production and recognition in *Gryllus firmus. J. Comp. Physiol.* 171:69–78.

Popper, A. N. and Fay, R. R. (1993) Sound detection and processing by fish: Critical review and major research questions. *Brain Behav. Evol.* 41:14–38.

Reeve, H. K. and P. W. Sherman. (1993) Adaptation and the goals of evolutionary research. *Quart. Rev. Biol.* 68: 1–32.

Ryan, M. J. and Keddy-Hector, A. (1992) Directional patterns of female mate choice and the role of sensory biases. *Amer. Nat.* 139:S4–S35.

Sherman, P. (1988) The level of analysis. *Anim. Behav.* 36:616–619.

Simmons, A. M., Reese, G., and Ferragamo, M. G. (1993) Periodicity extraction in the anuran auditory nerve. II. Phase and temporal fine structure. *J. Acoust. Soc. Am.* 93:3374–3388.

Stearns, S. C., ed. (1992) *The Evolution of Life Histories.* Oxford: Oxford University Press.

Taborsky, M. (1994) Sneakers, satellites, and helpers: Parasitic and cooperative behavior in fish reproduction. In *Advances in the Study of Behaviour*, vol. 23, ed. by P. J. B. Slater, J. S. Rosenblatt, C. T. Snowdon, and M. Milinski, pp. 1–100. New York: Academic Press.

Tinbergen, N., ed. (1951) *The Study of Instinct.* New York: Oxford University Press.

Tinbergen, N. (1963) On aims and methods of ethology. *Z. f. Tierpsychol.* 20:400–440.

Wiley, E. O., ed (1981) *Phylogenetics: The Theory and Practice of Phylogenetic Systematics.* New York: John Wiley and Sons.

Williams, G. C., ed. (1966) *Adaptation and Natural Selection.* Princeton, NJ: Princeton University Press.

18 Reproductive Character Displacement and Other Sources of Selection on Acoustic Communication Systems

H. Carl Gerhardt

In my view, *Mechanisms of Animal Behavior* (Marler and Hamilton 1966) still stands as a model of how to approach the study of animal communication. Signals should be described objectively in terms of their physical properties, and their production and recognition examined in terms of the underlying mechanisms. Of equal importance, however, are questions about the biological function and evolution of communication.

In this paper, I discuss some environmental factors that account, at least in part, for evolutionary change in communication systems. I focus on geographical variation in acoustic communication and, in particular, on reproductive character displacement, wherein divergence in two species is driven by mistakes in signal identification. This topic was discussed in *Mechanisms of Animal Behavior* in a thorough and balanced way. Examples that did not support the hypothesis were discussed along with other results, including original work comparing the songs of island and mainland birds (Marler and Boatman 1951), which were consistent with the patterns expected from reproductive character displacement.

Mixed results are common in studies of evolution, which, by its very nature, is opportunistic. For any population, group of populations, or species, the forces of evolutionary change—mutation, selection, drift, and gene flow—vary in time and space. Thus, in principle, one cannot expect to find that some particular environmental variable always plays a major role in promoting or constraining evolutionary change in communication systems. For example, some mutations affecting signal structure, female preferences, or both are subject mainly to sexual selection, while the environment plays only an indirect role. In this sense, changes in communication systems caused by sexual selection can be thought of as intrinsic. One example of an indirect role for the environment in this context is the distribution of resources required for reproduction, which determines their defensibility and can therefore influence the dominant mode (intra- or intersexual) of sexual selection. By contrast, other environmental factors—both biotic and abiotic—can also serve as more direct sources of selection on communication systems by influencing signal transmission or the detectability of signals. These external factors interact with sexual selection: senders whose signals most effectively propagate in a given environment, for example, have an advantage over their sexual competitors.

Intrinsic Change in a Communication System

One example of intrinsic change involves the advertisement calls of four species of myobatrachid frogs found in southwestern Australia. As shown in figure 18.1,

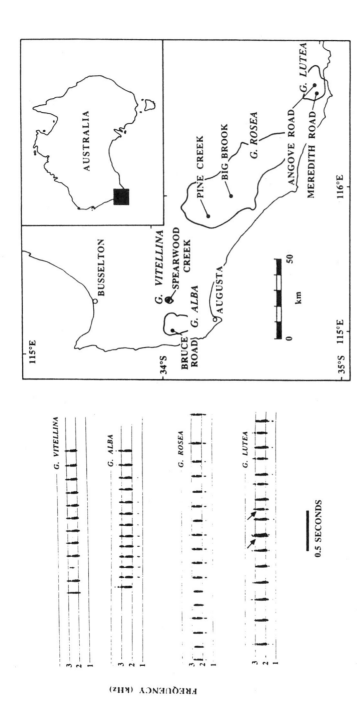

Figure 18.1

(A) Sonograms of the advertisement calls of four species of myobatrachid frogs of the genus *Geocrinia*. The arrows in the sonogram of *G. lutea* indicates the pulses produced by a second individual in the background. (B) Map showing the allopatric distributions of the four species in southwestern Australia. Notice that the species pairs with nearly contiguous distributions have the most similar calls. Modified from Roberts and Wardell-Johnson 1995.

Geocrinia alba and *G. vitellina* occur in the west and have shorter calls with slightly higher pulse rates than the calls of *Geocrinia rosea* and *G. lutea*, which occur in the east (Roberts and Wardell-Johnson 1995). Within each species, there is a high degree of genetic differentiation, maintained by extremely low rates of migration; substantial differences occur even between some populations that are separated by only a few kilometers (Driscoll et al. 1994). Driscoll et al. (1994) suggest that these differences and, by extension, speciation within this complex have resulted from range contraction and local extinctions, divergence in isolated populations, and subsequent range expansion. So far no significant ecological differences—in habitat, climate, or the acoustic community—have been documented that could reasonably be invoked to explain the call differences (Wardell-Johnson and Roberts 1993).

Thus, in my opinion, the most parsimonious view is that after establishment of the isolated populations that gave rise to the four recognized species, their calls diverged gradually by random mutation and drift. These changes would then be subject to sexual selection. The differences between the calls of the species with nearly contiguous ranges (*G. alba* and *G. vitellina* in the west and *G. rosea* and *G. lutea* in the east) are so trivial that they are unlikely to be discriminated by females; random mating would be expected if these geographically adjacent taxa became sympatric. The more substantial differences between the calls of the two eastern species vis-a-vis the calls of the two western species might reflect the initial fragmentation of an ancestral species. One scenario assumes that changes in calls arising by mutation are tested by females; very large changes might result in a call's not being perceived as a conspecific signal. Another scenario involves random changes in female preference that serve as preexisting biases for particular changes in calls that later arise by mutation (Ryan and Rand 1993). Changes in female preference should not, however, be so large that existing signals become ineffective in mate attraction.

Sources of Environmental Selection

In many systems, environmental factors must interact directly with intrinsic processes to bias evolutionary change in sexual signals and responses. Besides mistakes of signal identification that might lead to reproductive character displacement, which is discussed in detail below, there are two other sources of environmental selection.

First, local habitats can affect transmission so that signals with particular acoustic properties are distorted less or suffer less attenuation than signals with other properties. Individuals whose signals have such favorable properties should have increased success in attracting mates or repelling rivals. There are good examples of environmental effects on signal structure from comparisons of populations within wide-ranging species of anurans (Ryan and Wilczynski 1991) and songbirds (Nottebohm 1975; Handford 1981), although in both systems habitat acoustics do not explain all of the geographical variation. Moreover, we badly need studies of how such changes in signals affect the responses of receivers.

Second, acoustically orienting predators and parasites can also serve as sources of natural selection, favoring signal variants that are less likely to be detected or localized (Marler 1955; Klump and Shalter 1984). Recent comparative studies of the songs and singing patterns of different populations of the cricket *Teleogryllus oceanicus* are particularly informative. Males in populations where an acoustically orienting parasitoid occurs produce shorter, simpler songs than males in parasite-free populations (Zuk et al. 1993). Predators can also affect the evolution of hearing in their prey. For example, the ultrasonic sensitivity of many species of moths almost certainly evolved to detect the orientation signals of their bat predators (review by Fullard and Yack 1993).

Reproductive Character Displacement

Mistakes in the identification of conspecific signals because of confusion with those of other species have negative effects on the fitness of signalers, receivers, or both. Such mistakes are the driving force for reproductive character displacement. The processes that result in preferences for the signals of a particular conspecific mate or rival are, in principle, the same as those that result in preferences for the signals of conspecific individuals over those of heterospecific individuals. Except for certain hybrid zones, however, the consequences of mistakes involving heterospecific individuals are generally far more severe than mistakes involving choices between conspecific individuals. Responses to heterospecific signals result at least in increased assessment costs (e.g., loss of time and energy, risk of predation), and there might be a loss of gametes, which will almost always be a severe consequence for the female.

This form of selection should lead to patterns of geographical variation in which differences in the acoustic signaling system (including response selectivity) will be accentuated in areas of overlap between closely related species compared with differences in areas where only one of the two species occurs. In principle, interspecific masking, of which there are good examples from insects and anurans (see, e.g., Schwartz and Wells 1983; Römer et al. 1989), could have the same result by effectively decreasing the signal-to-noise ratio and hence increasing the chances of misidentification of signals (intra- and interspecific) used in mate choice. I am unaware, however, of any comparisons of the acoustic communication systems of different populations of a species based on whether or not masking species are present.

I apply the term *reproductive character displacement* to the pattern of enhanced divergence of signals, receiver selectivity, or both in sympatry and to the process (selection against mistakes in signal identification), but other definitions and terms (e.g., reinforcement) are also widely used (see, e.g., Butlin 1987; Howard 1993; Littlejohn 1997). Character release is another aspect of this phenomenon: in areas where other species with similar signals are absent, greater variance in signal structure or the dominance of some other form of environmental selection might be expected (Miller 1983).

Why Is Reproductive Character Displacement Rare?

There is a great deal of skepticism about the evolutionary significance of reproductive character displacement. One reason for this is that the conditions favoring the process and its documentation are restrictive. First, not only must there be areas of sympatry between the two taxa, but also areas of allopatry, which are required to calibrate the differences observed in sympatry (Grant 1972). Second, there must be some initial difference in signals, and yet some mistakes of identification, which are costly to the signaler, receiver, or both, must also occur, at least when sympatric contact is first established. Character displacement would not be expected if the communication systems of the interacting populations have diverged so much in disjunct allopatry that individuals hardly ever interact when sympatry is achieved. Indeed, one extreme view is that species can become sympatric only if they have diverged to such an extent (Paterson 1985). Character displacement based on acoustic signals alone might be expected to be rare in birds because many species rapidly learn to discriminate between appropriate and inappropriate signals on the basis of subtle acoustic differences; moreover, birds make extensive use of visual cues to identify prospective mates and rivals (Miller 1983; Lynch and Baker 1991). Third, character displacement is favored when genetic incompatibility of the interacting taxa reduces or eliminates gene exchange and hence recombination (Butlin 1987). Recombination can break down associations between the genes that promote assortative mating and those responsible for hybrid unfitness, thus requiring strong selection to cause divergence in the area of overlap (Barton and Hewitt 1981). Fourth, the conventional view is that restricted migration and hence limited gene flow from allopatry to sympatry will favor character displacement. That is, divergence caused by selection in sympatry could be diluted when individuals in lineages established within the zone of contact mate with naive individuals that move into he zone from outside. However, according to a recent model by Liou and Price (1994), gene flow may sometimes increase the likelihood of character displacement by rescuing from extinction the taxon with a lower population size or growth rate.

The second reason for skepticism about reproductive character displacement logically follows from the first: good examples are rare. Here there is a range of opinion about what are "good examples." On the one hand, Paterson (1985) would deny that there is any robust demonstration of reproductive character displacement, whereas Howard (1993) provides a long list of examples (see also Otte 1989). Miller (1983) offers a balanced and critical view that includes limited supporting evidence from some studies of birdsong, especially in the context of territorial defense. The following examples, which I consider the best available for acoustic signals, also serve to illustrate the difficulties of robustly demonstrating reproductive character displacement.

Two Examples of Sympatric Divergence in Acoustic Signals

Fouquette (1975) studied geographical variation in the pulse rate of advertisement calls, an acoustic property that reliably distinguishes two species of chorus frogs *Pseudacris nigrita* and *P. feriarum* found in the southeastern United States. In *P. feriarum*, there is an abrupt increase in pulse rate at the transition between allopatry and the overlap zone with *P. nigrita*. There is little evidence for such a shift within *P. nigrita*. This pattern, and the fact that *P. feriarum* may be expanding its range southward along the Appalachicola River system, supports the view of Littlejohn (1993, 1997) that changes in calls might be more likely in an invading species than in a species with an established range of distribution.

One strength of this study is that Fouquette (1975) extensively sampled areas of allopatry, thus providing baseline information about variation in pulse rate that might be expected in the noninteractive state. However, there are no estimates of the extent of mismating between the two species, nor are there experimental data concerning the minimum differences in pulse rate required for discrimination by females.

In another contact zone involving *P. nigrita* and *P. triseriata*, extensive interbreeding occurs in a narrow hybrid zone, and there is no evidence of reproductive character displacement (Gartside 1980). Gartside (1980) and Littlejohn (1997) suggest that the difference in the outcome of interactions in the two zones of contact might be caused by ecological factors. This counterexample underlines my caveat about the variability of evolutionary processes in time and space.

Littlejohn (1965) documented a striking divergence in sympatric areas between the pulse rates of the calls of *Litoria ewingii* and *L. verreauxii*, which are two treefrogs found in southeastern Australia. While the hypothesis of reproductive character displacement could be improved by additional sampling in areas of allopatry, additional studies provided critical information about the salience of the observed differences in calls to receivers. Littlejohn and Loftus-Hills (1968) showed that females of both species from the western part of the overlap zone discriminated between the calls of a conspecific male and a heterospecific male recorded in the same area; females did not, however, discriminate between local conspecific calls and heterospecific calls recorded in allopatry. Moreover, females of *L. verreauxii* from western sympatry preferred the call of a local conspecific male to that of a conspecific male from allopatry.

More recently, Littlejohn et al. (1993) provide evidence for character release (an increase in variance) in pulse rate in *L. ewingii* introduced from Tasmania to New Zealand. Additional details concerning these and other examples of reproductive character displacement of acoustic signals in anurans are provided by Littlejohn (1997).

Sympatric Divergence in Receiver Selectivity for Acoustic Signals without Divergence in Signals

Waage (1979) pointed out that reproductive character displacement might be more common than is generally accepted because most studies have focused only on signals and not on receiver selectivity. Enhanced divergence of signals is not always a necessary consequence of interspecific interactions in sympatry if, for example, the signals of two taxa were to become different enough to be discriminated during the noninteractive period of geographical separation. Selection on receivers should generally be strong because receivers usually have more to lose than signalers from a mating mistake in the case of females, or from unnecessary aggression in the case of territorial males. Data consistent with this view are available for several species of *Drosophila*, a katydid, and some songbirds (review in Gerhardt 1994). A particularly well-studied example is the subject of the rest of this chapter.

The Gray Treefrog Complex: A Model System

The gray treefrog, *Hyla chrysoscelis*, is a diploid species; there are two or more sibling species that are biparental tetraploids currently designated as *H. versicolor* (Ptacek et al. 1994). Mismatings result in sterile triploid offspring with reduced viability (Johnson 1963). Here I focus on geographical variation in the advertisement calls and female phonotactic selectivity of the diploid species.

Mate choice in these treefrogs is based solely on a single type of long-range acoustic signal, the advertisement call, which is produced only by males. Females

approach a speaker from which conspecific calls or appropriate synthetic calls are
played back, and there is no evidence of any kind of close-range assessment by either
sex prior to mating. There is only one mating by a female on any given night, and
usually only one mating per season (Ritke and Semlitsch 1991). Finally, males do
not displace other males from mating pairs, nor do males defend territories containing resources used by females. These are important attributes for testing for character
displacement. If other sensory cues were used, say, at close range, as they are in
many insects and birds (Miller 1983; Ewing 1989), then the selection for divergence
in acoustic signals would be weakened. Similarly, mating mistakes are potentially
more costly when there is only one chance for fertilization, as compared with insects,
for example, in which multiple matings might occur over short periods of time. If
males were to compete physically for females, or if females were to assess territorial
quality, then selection on signals and response selectivity would also be considerably
weakened.

As shown in figure 18.2, the calls of the two species have the same basic temporal
and spectral structure. They differ in two stereotyped properties: pulse rate (after
temperature correction), and the shape (= amplitude-time envelope) of the pulses.
On the one hand, females of both species discriminate between synthetic signals that
differ only in pulse rate by the average magnitude existing between the calls of the
two species in nature at the same temperature. On the other hand, females of both
species often show phonotactic approaches to a source of heterospecific advertisement calls when conspecific calls are unavailable (Gerhardt and Doherty 1988). That
is, females treat the calls of the other species as signals, and females sometimes make
mistakes in nature. The frequency of mismating at sympatric breeding sites in Missouri can be as high as 5% (Gerhardt et al. 1994), although some mistakes probably
do not involve misidentification of calls but rather a female's inadvertently moving
too close to a male of the wrong species. Again, some misidentification of signals
that reduces the fitness of signalers, receivers, or both favors reproductive character
displacement and is a requirement for its initial stages.

As shown in figure 18.3, there are widespread areas of stable sympatry with *H.
versicolor*; within these areas, the two species frequently breed synchronously at the
same breeding sites, although there may be some differentiation of calling sites within
such ponds (Ptacek 1992). As pointed out by Littlejohn (1993), the processes leading
to the establishment of sympatry are poorly understood, and the outcome of interactions between species (or groups of populations that are not formally recognized as
separate species) is often indeterminant, especially when there has been limited divergence of the ecology and communication systems during the period of disjunct allopatry. The widely separated areas of sympatry provide the opportunity to generalize

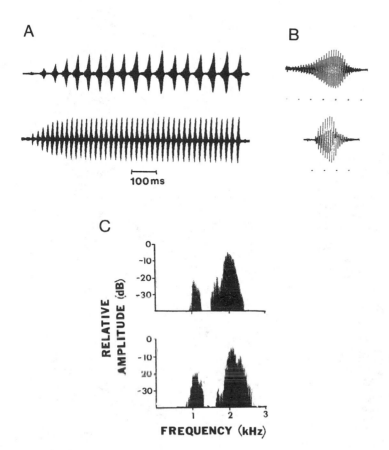

Figure 18.2
Oscillograms of (A) advertisement calls and (B) representative pulses from these calls of *Hyla versicolor* (top traces) and *II. chrysoscelis* (bottom traces). (C) power spectra of calls of *H. versicolor* (top) and *H. chrysoscelis* (bottom). The recordings were made at about 18°C at the same locality in Missouri. From Gerhardt 1982.

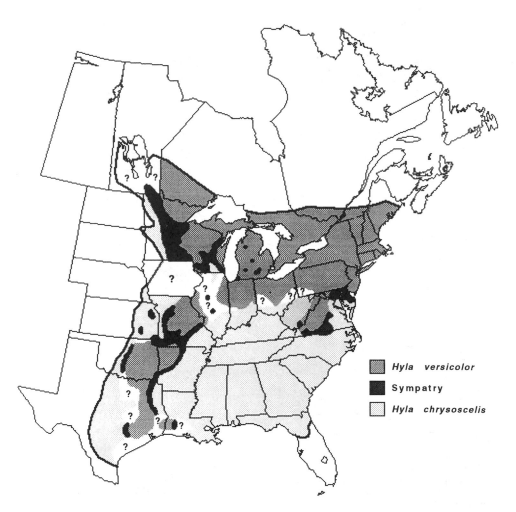

Figure 18.3
Map showing the geographical distribution of the diploid species of the gray treefrog (*Hyla chrysoscelis*) and its tetraploid sibling species (*H. versicolor*). There are likely to be areas of sympatry within some poorly sampled regions where the presence of only one species has been established.

about differences in the communication system of *H. chrysoscelis*, if any, that are associated with the presence of *H. versicolor*. The large areas of allopatry in the southeastern United States allow us to assess the degree of geographical variation in *H. chrysoscelis* that can occur in the absence of tetraploid species.

Finally, there are also data, based on chromosome polymorphisms (Wilcy et al. 1989), allozymes (Ralin and Selander 1979), and mtDNA sequences (Ptacek et al. 1994), that bear on genetic differentiation within both species. Thus strong tests of character displacement can be made by comparing sympatric and allopatric populations that show, by other criteria, minimal genetic divergence. Otherwise, differences between the communication systems of such populations could be interpreted as historical effects of past evolutionary divergence. For example, analyses of mtDNA sequences indicate that tetraploids have arisen independently multiple times from *H. chrysoscelis*, and the calls of all of the different lineages are very similar in pulse rate and shape (Ptacek et al. 1994). Moreover, females from the two lineages of *H. versicolor* that have been studied show preferences based on pulse shape; such preferences are absent in females of *H. chrysoscelis* (Gerhardt and Doherty 1988; Diekamp and Gerhardt 1995; Gerhardt, unpubl. data). These call differences, the new preference, or both could have arisen, in part, as a consequence of polyploidization. Bogart and Wasserman (1972) first proposed this hypothesis, and Ueda (1993) showed that artificially produced polyploids of the treefrog *Hyla japonica* produced calls with lower pulse rates than those of diploid controls. Preliminary results from similar experiments with *H. chrysoscelis* also show that autotriploid males produce calls with significantly lower pulse rates than diploid controls (Keller and Gerhardt, unpubl. data).

Geographical Variation in Pulse Rate

I focus on variation in pulse rate in *H. chrysoscelis* because females of this species show strong preferences based solely on differences in this acoustic property and because the extent of geographical variation in pulse rate is much greater than in *H. versicolor*. Advertisement calls were recorded along three major east-west transects, and mean pulse rates, corrected to a common temperature, are shown for many of these populations in figure 18.4. Mean pulse rates in sympatric populations are not consistently higher than those in populations in adjacent allopatry; indeed, greater differences in mean pulse rate are found among populations in remote allopatry along the southern transects (up to 12 pulses/s) (statistical analyses in Gerhardt et al., in preparation). These data indicate that, in terms of the current distributions of these frogs, geographical patterns of variation in mean pulse rate are inconsistent

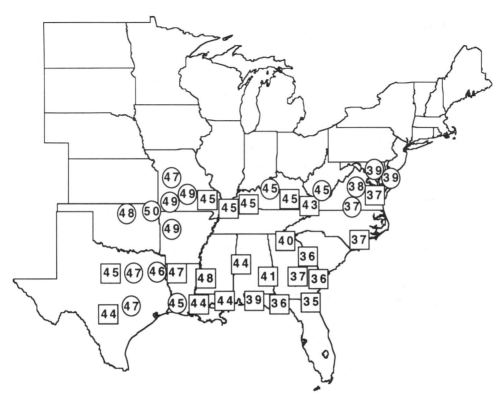

Figure 18.4
Map showing the geographical variation in pulse rate in the advertisement calls of males of *Hyla chrysoscelis*. Pulse rates are corrected to 20°C based on linear regressions for the population or a series of populations in the same region. There were only minor differences in the slopes of these regressions. Squares are localities where only *H. chrysoscelis* was found; circles are localities where *H. versicolor* was also calling. There were usually 10 or more frogs recorded per locality or area indicated by the symbols.

with the patterns expected from the operation of reproductive character displacement on the calls of *H. chrysoscelis*.

These data do not rule out the possibility that reproductive character displacement played a role in signal divergence in the past. Besides changes in the ranges of distribution that would obscure the expected pattern of geographical variation, interactions at the time that the tetraploids arose and became established could have caused major shifts in pulse rate in the diploid or the tetraploids. If call differences occurred as a consequence of polyploidization, for example, then strong selection against infertile hybrids could have rapidly enhanced the differences. In a theoretical analysis of reinforcement by Liou and Price (1994), for example, complete isolation could be achieved within 60 generations under some conditions, such as low recombination. An interesting feature of their model is the assumption that genetic correlations arise between signals and preferences, as in models of indirect sexual selection (Fisher 1930). Once started, further divergence could occur even in the absence of additional mating mistakes, being driven instead by Fisherian sexual selection.

Geographical Variation in Female Selectivity

If indirect sexual selection did play a role in the initial divergence of the communication systems of the diploid and tetraploid species, then present-day geographical variation in female preferences would be expected to parallel patterns of varation in male signals. Thus present-day sympatry with *H. versicolor* would not be expected to explain geographical differences in the pulse-rate selectivity of females of *H. chrysoscelis*, just as it explains little, if any, of the differences in pulse rate.

At one level of analysis, the expected correlation between variation in pulse rate and female preferences based on this property occurs in *H. chrysoscelis*. In figure 18.5, I summarize the results of experiments in which females were given choices between synthetic calls that differed only in pulse rate. Females from both sympatric and allopatric areas usually reject alternatives that have pulse rates that are about 50% higher or 20% lower than a *standard call*, defined as having a pulse rate equal to the mean value in the calls of males in the population from which the females were collected (Gerhardt 1994). Thus, all things being equal, even females from remote allopatric populations would be expected to discriminate against the calls of *H. versicolor*. Females should also discriminate against the calls of some males in their own population and against the calls of many males from some other populations (figure 18.4).

In nature, however, not all things are equal or average. First, many conspecific and heterospecific calls will differ by less than the average difference in some behaviorally relevant acoustic property (see also Littlejohn 1997, who derives a measure of differentiation between interacting taxa that considers the gap in the ranges of variation of call properties). Second, in the experiments just mentioned, not only were all other attributes of the synthetic calls held constant, but the pulse rate of the standard call corresponded to the mean value of a local male at 20°C, and females were tested at the same temperature. Temperature variation of the order of 5°C on the same night is common in breeding ponds (Gerhardt 1994). Thus, because pulse rate and female preferences for a particular pulse rate in both species are temperature-dependent (Gerhardt 1982; Gerhardt and Doherty 1988), females must often be confronted with choices of conspecific and heterospecific calls that are effectively

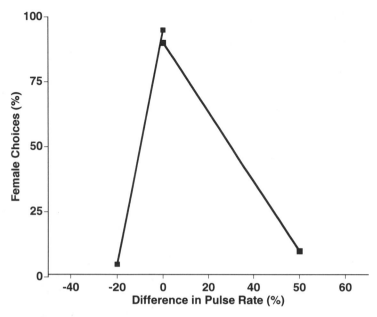

Figure 18.5
Current estimates of pulse-rate selectivity in females of *Hyla chrysoscelis* from throughout the range of geographic distribution. The points at the top of the figure show the average percentage of females that chose a standard synthetic call (0 = mean pulse rate of males from the same population at 20°C, which was also the test temperature); the points at the bottom of the figure show the average percentages of females that chose alternatives to the standard call that were either 20% lower or 50% higher in pulse rate. Females did not prefer the standard call over alternatives that were 10% lower or 25% higher. See Gerhardt (1994) for details concerning the playback experiments.

much less different in pulse rate than the average, temperature-corrected difference. Third, conspecific and heterospecific calls encountered in nature also vary in carrier frequency, duration, call rate, and sound pressure level (SPL), and variation in each of these properties also affects female preferences (Gerhardt 1975, 1994; Gerhardt et al. 1996). For example, the average call duration among males of both species varies by a factor of 300% or more in many populations (Gerhardt 1994), and females of both species prefer long calls to short calls, sometimes even when the source of short calls is closer and of greater amplitude (Gerhardt 1994; Gerhardt et al. 1996). Fourth, the relative amplitudes of the first conspecific and heterospecific signals that are detected by a female will obviously depend on where it enters a mixed-species chorus.

These considerations led me to design experiments that reflected the more difficult choices that some females would experience in nature. First, I reduced the difference in pulse rate between synthetic calls from the usual 40–60% to about 30%, a difference that has been documented in mixed-species choruses (Gerhardt 1994). Second, I either increased the duration of the alternative with the lower pulse rate (the "*H. versicolor*" stimulus) or lowered the SPL of the standard call. My strategy was, within the limits observed in nature, to favor the stimulus with the lower pulse rate to the extent that some females from sympatric populations chose the longer or louder calls. I could then compare the pulse-rate selectivity of females from these and other sympatric populations with the selectivity of females from allopatric populations in these more difficult and realistic choice-tests.

Earlier, I presented data showing that females from three sympatric areas were much more selective than females from two allopatric regions in experiments in which the standard call was shorter than the alternative stimulus of lower pulse rate (Gerhardt 1994). Since then, additional females from the same and different populations (one sympatric and two allopatric) have been tested, and the results for all sympatric and allopatric populations are summarized in figure 18.6a. The new data corroborate these earlier results. The highest proportion of females choosing these standard call from an allopatric population for which there were reasonable samples was about 65%, and the lowest proportion from a sympatric population was about 85%.

The proportions of allopatric and sympatric females that chose the standard call rather than the alternative with a higher SPL and lower pulse rate are also summarized in figure 18.6a. The results parallel those for the unequal-duration experiment, except that, as shown in figure 18.6b, about 75% of the females from allopatric areas in the southeastern part of the range chose the standard call. By contrast, only about 30% of the females from an allopatric population in Kentucky chose the standard call. This difference serves to reemphasize that multiple factors (including historical ones), and not just the presence or absence of another species, are likely to affect the evolution of communication systems.

These results have implications outside the context of character displacement. First, the data show differences in the potential for directional change in pulse rate. That is, the strength of stabilizing selection acting on pulse rate is weaker and more easily confounded by other acoustic variables in allopatric populations than in sympatric populations. Second, the existence of geographical variation in the strength of preferences and the relative importance of different acoustic properties means that neurobiologists interested in the underlying mechanisms must be concerned with the collecting sites of the animals they study. Findings from only one or two populations or from randomly sampled individuals from throughout an extensive geographical range are unlikely to be general for the whole species. For *H. chrysoscelis*,

A

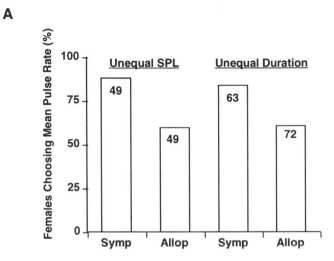

B

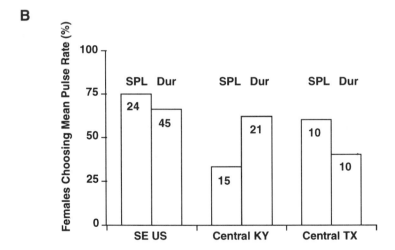

Figure 18.6
(A) Histograms summarizing the results of two-speaker playback experiments with females of *Hyla chrys-oscelis* from areas of sympatry and allopatry. The percentages of females choosing the standard synthetic call are shown. The alternative stimulus had a pulse rate that was approximately 30% lower, and either its sound pressure level (unequal SPL) was 12dB higher than that of the standard call (85dB versus 73dB) or its duration (Unequal Duration) was three times longer than that of the standard call (1.2 versus 0.4s). The numbers on the histograms indicate the numbers of frogs tested from either allopatric areas (Allop) or sympatric areas (Symp). These data include previously published results (Gerhardt 1994) for the Unequal Duration experiments, plus additional unpublished data for these experiments and the Unequal SPL experiments (Gerhardt, in preparation). (B) Histograms showing the data for three allopatric regions or

for example, we might expect to see geographical differences in the tuning properties ("best" pulse rate and cut-off values) of bandpass neurons in the midbrain (Rose et al. 1985).

This research is ongoing. Sample sizes need to be increased for some populations that have already been studied in order to improve our estimates of female selectivity, and, of course, additional populations must be studied. These additional populations should be chosen to increase the number of within-lineage comparisons, that is, pairs of sympatric and allopatric populations, which by other independent criteria show little genetic divergence. Moreover, because most comparisons of female selectivity have been between animals collected from sympatric areas and animals from remote allopatry, it will also be important to study females from populations that are intermediate in their geographical location in order to assess the possible effects on receiver selectivity of gene flow.

Summary

1. Intrinsic changes in communication systems may be subject mainly to sexual selection, with the environment (physical and biotic) playing only an indirect role of influencing the dominant mode of sexual selection.

2. Environmental sources of selection that can interact with intrinsic changes and sexual selection include: (a) habitat effects on signal structure and attenuation; (b) acoustically orienting predators and parasitoids; (c) reduced efficiency of communication caused by masking interference generated by the signals of other species; (d) negative consequences (loss of fitness) of misidentifying and responding to the signals of other species.

3. Good examples of reproductive character displacement are rare, reflecting the restrictive conditions favoring this process and the difficulty of documenting this phenomenon. In particular, additional divergence of signals in sympatry is unlikely to occur in taxa that use multiple cues (modalities) for mate identification or whose signals diverge sufficiently during allopatric disjunction to be readily discriminated.

Figure 18.6 (continued)
populations that were lumped in figure 18.6a. The data from the southeastern United States (SE US) included females collected at two localities in Florida, one in Georgia, two in South Carolina, and one in Alabama. The data from Central Kentucky (KY) were derived from females collected at a single locality, and the data from Central Texas (TX) were obtained from females collected at two localities (Gerhardt, in preparation).

4. One new perspective, exemplified by studies of the gray treefrog complex, emphasizes a multivariate approach to analyzing both the signals of the emitters and the mate-choice criteria used by receivers.

5. Gray treefrogs show patterns of geographical variation expected from reproductive character displacement in female preferences but not in male advertisement calls. However, the effects of sympatry on selectivity were detected only by offering females biologically realistic choices of acoustic stimuli.

6. There appear to be differences in selectivity between allopatric populations as well as between sympatric and allopatric ones, suggesting that generalizing from one or two populations is risky.

Acknowledgments

I am particularly grateful to M. J. Littlejohn for introducing me to this area of research in 1966, and for his extensive and helpful comments on two versions of this manuscript. M. Hauser, J. D. Roberts, W. J. Bailey, F. Breden, M. Keller, K. Shaw, and G. F. Watson also made helpful comments on the manuscript, and the NSF and NIMH provided generous support of my research. S. D. Tanner, M. L. Dyson, J. J. Schwartz, M. D. Keller, D. S. Forester, G. F. Watson, S. A. Perrill, B. Buchanan, S. Ronen, and M. B. Ptacek helped with the collection of or testing of female frogs, or both. I also thank M. Konishi and M. Hauser for inviting me to participate in the symposium honoring Peter Marler.

References

Barton, N. H. and Hewitt, G. M. (1981) Hybrid zones and speciation. In *Evolution and Speciation: Essays in Honor of M. J. D. White*, ed. by W. R. Atchley and D. S. Woodruff, pp. 109–145. Cambridge: Cambridge University Press.

Bogart, J. P. and Wasserman, A. O. (1972) Diploid-polyploid cryptic species pairs: A possible clue to evolution by polyploidization in anuran amphibians. *Cytogenetics* 11:7–24.

Butlin, R. K. (1987) Speciation by reinforcement. *Trends in Ecol. & Evolution* 2:8–13.

Diekamp, B. M. and Gerhardt, H. C. (1995) Selective phonotaxis to advertisement calls in the gray treefrog *Hyla versicolor*: Behavioral experiments and neurophysiological correlates. *J. Comp. Physiol.* A. 177:173–190.

Driscoll, D. A., Wardell-Johnson, G., and Roberts, J. D. (1994) Genetic structuring and distribution patterns in rare southwestern Australian frogs: Implications for translocation programmes. In *Reintroduction Biology of Australian and New Zealand Fauna*, ed. by M. Serena, pp. 85–90. Chipping Norton, NSW: Surrey, Beatty and Sons.

Ewing, A. W. (1989) *Arthropod Bioacoustics: Neurobiology and Behavior*. Ithaca, NY: Comstock Publishing Associates.

Fisher, R. A. (1930) *The Genetical Theory of Natural Selection*. Oxford: Oxford University Press.

Fouquette, M. J. (1975) Speciation in chorus frogs. I. Reproductive character displacement in the *Pseudacris nigrita* complex. *Syst. Zool.* 24:16–23.

Fullard, J. H. and Yack, J. E. (1993) The evolutionary biology of insect hearing. *TREE* 8:248–252.

Gartside, D. F. (1980) Analysis of a hybrid zone between chorus frogs of the *Pseudacris nigrita* complex in the southern United States. *Copeia* 1980:56–66.

Gerhardt, H. C. (1975) Sound pressure levels and radiation patterns of the vocalizations of some North American frogs and toads. *J. Comp. Physiol.* A 102:1–12.

Gerhardt, H. C. (1982) Sound pattern recognition in some North American treefrogs (*Anura: Hylidae*): Implications for mate choice. *Am. Zool.* 22:581–595.

Gerhardt, H. C. (1994) Reproductive character displacement of female mate choice in the gray treefrog *H. chrysoscelis*. *Anim. Behav.* 47:959–969.

Gerhardt, H. C. and Doherty, J. A. (1988) Acoustic communication in the gray treefrog, *Hyla versicolor*: Evolutionary and neurobiological implications. *J. Comp. Physiol.* A 162:261–278.

Gerhardt, H. C., Dyson, M. L., and Tanner, S. D. (1996) Dynamic acoustic properties of the advertisement calls of gray treefrogs: Patterns of variability and female choice. *Behavioral Ecology* 7:7–18.

Gerhardt, H. C., Ptacek, M. B., Barnett, L., and Torke, K. (1994) Hybridization in the diploid-tetraploid treefrogs *Hyla chrysoscelis* and *Hyla versicolor*. *Copeia* 1994:51–59.

Grant, P. R. (1972) Convergent and divergent character displacement. *Biol. J. Linn. Soc.* 4:39–68.

Handford, P. (1981) Vegetational correlates of variation in the song of *Zonotrichia capensis*. *Behav. Ecol. Sociobiol.* 8:203–206.

Howard, D. S. (1993) Reinforcement: Origin, dynamics and fate of an evolutionary hypothesis. In *Hybrid Zones and the Evolutionary Process*, ed. by R. G. Harrison, pp. 46–69. Oxford: Oxford University Press.

Johnson, C. F. (1963) Additional evidence of sterility between call-types in the *Hyla versicolor* complex. *Copeia* 1963:139–143.

Klump, G. M. and Shalter, M. D. (1984) Acoustic behaviour of birds and mammals in the predator context. *Z. Tierpsychol.* 66:189–226.

Liou, L. W. and Price, T. D. (1994) Speciation by reinforcement of premating isolation. *Evolution* 48:1451–1459.

Littlejohn, M. J. (1965) Premating isolation in the *Hyla ewingi* complex (*Anura: Hylidae*). *Evolution* 19:234–243.

Littlejohn, M. J. (1993) Homogamy and speciation: A reappraisal. In *Oxford Surveys of Evolutionary Biology*, ed. by D. Futuyma and J. Antonovics, pp. 135–164. Oxford: Oxford University Press.

Littlejohn, M. J. (1997) Variation in advertisement calls of anurans across zonal interactions: The evolution and breakdown of homogamy. In *Geographical Diversification of Behavior*, ed. by S. A. Foster and J. A. Endler, pp. 209–233. Oxford: Oxford University Press.

Littlejohn, M. J. and Loftus-Hills, J. J. (1968) An experimental evaluation of premating isolation in the *Hyla ewingi* complex (*Anura: Hylidae*). *Evolution* 22:659–663.

Littlejohn, M. J., Watson, G. F., and Wright, J. R. (1993) Structure of advertisement call of *Litoria ewingi* (*Anura: Hylidae*) introduced into New Zealand from Tasmania. *Copeia* 1993:60–67.

Lynch, A. and Baker, A. J. (1991) Increased vocal discrimination by learning in sympatry in two species of chaffinches. *Behaviour* 116:109–126.

Marler, P. (1955) Characteristics of some animal calls. *Nature* 176:6–8.

Marler, P. and Boatman, D. J. (1951) Observations on the birds of Pico, Azores. *Ibis* 93:90–99.

Marler, P. and Hamilton, W. J., III. (1966) *Mechanisms of Animal Behavior*. New York: John Wiley and Sons.

Miller, E. H. (1983) Character and variance shift in acoustic signals of birds. In *Acoustic Communication in Birds*, ed. by D. E. Kroodsma and E. H. Miller, pp. 253–295. New York: Academic Press.

Nottebohm, F. (1975) Continental patterns of song variation in *Zonotrichia capensis*: Some possible ecological correlates. *Am. Nat.* 109:605–624.

Otte, D. (1989) Speciation in Hawaiian crickets. In *Speciation and Its Consequences*, ed. by D. Otte and J. A. Endler, pp. 482–526. Sunderland, MA: Sinauer Associates.

Paterson, H. E. H. (1985) The recognition concept of species. In *Species and Speciation*, ed. by E. Vrba, pp. 21–29. Transvaal Museum Monograph no. 4, Pretoria.

Ptacek, M. B. (1992) Calling sites used by male gray treefrogs, *Hyla versicolor* and *H. chrysoscelis*, in sympatry and allopatry. *Herpetologica* 48:373–382.

Ptacek, M. B., Gerhardt, H. C., and Sage, R. D. (1994) Speciation by polyploidy in treefrogs: Multiple origins of the tetraploid, *Hyla versicolor*. *Evolution* 48:898–908.

Ralin, D. B. and Selander, R. K. (1979) Evolutionary genetics of diploid-tetraploid species of treefrogs of the genus *Hyla*. *Evolution* 33:595–608.

Ritke, M. E. and Semlitsch, R. D. (1991) Mating behavior and determinants of male mating success in the gray treefrog, *Hyla chrysoscelis*. *Can. J. Zool.* 69:246–250.

Roberts, J. D. and Wardell-Johnson, G. (1995) Call differences between peripheral isolates of the *Geocrinia rosea* complex (*Anura: Myobatrachidae*) in southwestern Australia. *Copeia* 1995:899–906.

Römer, H., Bailey, W. J., and Dadour, I. (1989) Insect hearing in the field. III. Masking by noise. *J. Comp. Physiol.* A 164:609–620.

Rose, G. J., Brenowitz, E. A., and Capranica, R. R. (1985) Species specificity and temperature dependency of temporal processing by the auditory midbrain of two species of treefrogs. *J. Comp. Physiol.* 157:763–769.

Ryan, M. J. and Rand, A. S. (1993) Sexual selection and signal evolution: The ghost of biases past. *Phil. Trans. R. Soc. Lond.* B. 340:187–195.

Ryan, M. J. and Wilczynski, W. (1991) Evolution of intraspecific variation in the advertisement call of a cricket frog (*Acris crepitans*, Hylidae). *Biol. J. Linnean Soc.* 44:249–271.

Schwartz, J. J. and Wells, K. D. (1983) An experimental study of acoustic interference between two species of neotropical treefrogs. *Anim. Behav.* 31:181–190.

Ueda, H. (1993) Mating calls of autotriploid and autotetraploid males in *Hyla japonica*. *Sci. Report Lab. Amphib. Biol. Hiroshima Univ.* 12:177–189.

Waage, J. K. (1979) Reproductive character displacement in *Calopteryx* (*Odonata: Calopterygidae*). *Evolution* 33:104–116.

Wardell-Johnson, G. and Roberts, J. D. (1993) Biogeographic barriers in a subdued landscape: The distribution of the *Geocrinia rosea* (*Anura: Myobatrachidae*) complex in south western Australia. *J. Biogeography* 20:95–108.

Wiley, J. E., Little, M. L., Romano, M. A., Blount, D. A., and Cline, G. R. (1989) Polymorphism in the location of the 18s and 28s rRNA genes on the chromosomes of the diploid-tetraploid treefrogs *Hyla chrysoscelis* and *H. versicolor*. *Chromosoma* 97:481–416.

Zuk, M., Simmons, L. W., Cupp, L. (1993) Calling characteristics of parasitized and unparasitized populations of the field cricket *Teleogryllus oceanicus*. *Behav. Ecol. Sociobiol.* 33:339–343.

19 Phylogenetic Inference and the Evolution of Communication in Túngara Frogs

Michael J. Ryan and A. Stanley Rand

Many biological phenomena engender issues that permeate various levels of analysis but which are often addressed in isolation. In contrast, Tinbergen's (1964) four questions describe a multidisciplinary approach to animal behavior in which issues of physiological mechanisms, ontogeny of behavioral acquisition, the adaptive significance of behavior, and its evolutionary history are addressed in an integrative manner. Studies of animal communication perhaps best exemplify how each of these questions impinge on the same general phenomenon.

Most studies of evolutionary history rely on interpreting the fossil record or deriving hypotheses about history from comparisons of extant taxa. The latter endeavor, which is the focus of phylogenetics, encompasses both studies of genealogical relationships and investigations of patterns by which characters have evolved. Ethological studies that have integrated phylogenetics and communication usually take one of two forms. One is the use of communication signals for taxonomic purposes. Animals themselves often rely on communication signals to identify conspecifics, and this is true for many taxonomists as well, especially when dealing with cryptic species. The other is the use of phylogenetics by ethologists to study the evolution of behavior, including how communication signals evolve. This approach is exemplified by Lorenz's (1941) studies of display evolution in ducks and Tinbergen's (1953) use of the comparative method to investigate the adaptive significance of social behavior.

The last decade has seen a resurgence in the use of explicit phylogenetic techniques to investigate behavioral evolution (see, e.g., Brooks and McLennan 1991; Harvey and Pagel 1991; Martins 1996). Many of these studies utilize hypotheses of phylogenetic relationships to derive the most parsimonious patterns by which behaviors have evolved (see, e.g., various chapters in Martins 1996), and to generate experimentally testable hypotheses about evolutionary processes (see examples discussed in Ryan 1996). The purpose of this chapter is to highlight some of these phylogenetic approaches to studying animal communication. To do so, we will introduce the acoustic communication system of the túngara frog, *Physalaemus pustulosus*. We will begin by reviewing studies that concentrate on the adaptive significance of this mate recognition system and the underlying mechanisms regulating it. The results of these studies suggest various hypotheses about the evolution of the communication system, which we then address using a variety of approaches combined with an underlying knowledge of the phylogenetic relationships of these frogs.

Natural Call Variation and Intraspecific Call Preference in Túngara Frogs

Studies with our colleagues of the mechanisms and evolution of acoustic mate recognition in the túngara frog and its close relatives have addressed animal behavior, neurobiology, molecular phylogenetics, physiological energetics, and functional morphology. These studies have provided information as to how females utilize acoustic cues to assess potential mates, the neural mechanisms that guide such mating preferences, how these preferences bias male mating success in nature, how these preferences cause the evolution of attractive male traits, how costs of such traits increase predation risk, elevate metabolism, and are correlated with hormonal changes, and how preferences and traits have evolved during the history of these frogs as estimated by molecular phylogenies. These studies have made the túngara frog system a valuable one for addressing various issues in sexual communication. Here we will concentrate on how we use various phylogenetic approaches to understand the evolution of this communication system.

The túngara frog is a small (ca. 30mm snout-vent length [SVL]), common species found throughout much of the lowland tropics from central Mexico, south through Middle America, across the Darien gap into northern Colombia, and east through the lowlands of Venezuela into Trinidad and western Guyana (Ryan 1985; Ryan et al. 1996). This frog is abundant in central Panama near the facilities of the Smithsonian Tropical Research Institute, where most of these studies have been conducted.

The call of this species is unusually variable for a frog. There are two components to the call: a whine and a chuck (figure 19.1). The whine initiates the call, is always present, and can be produced alone or may be followed by one or several chucks. Thus the call can vary in the number of components from a whine only to a call with multiple chucks; we classify these as simple and complex calls, respectively. A typical whine is a frequency-modulated component whose fundamental has an onset of 900Hz and sweeps to a final frequency of 430Hz in 300ms. The whine has several harmonics with detectable energy in the second to fourth harmonic, but most of the whine's energy is in the fundamental. The whine's dominant frequency, the frequency with the greatest concentration of energy, is about 600Hz (Rand and Ryan 1981; Ryan 1985).

The chuck has a much different acoustic structure. When chucks are added to the call they are appended near the end of the whine, although an ongoing study suggests that the chuck's position relative to the whine might not be critical to female preferences. Up to six chucks can be added to a call although one, two, or sometimes three chucks are the more common occurrence. The typical chuck is 35ms in duration, has a fundamental frequency of 250Hz, and is characterized by 14 harmonics,

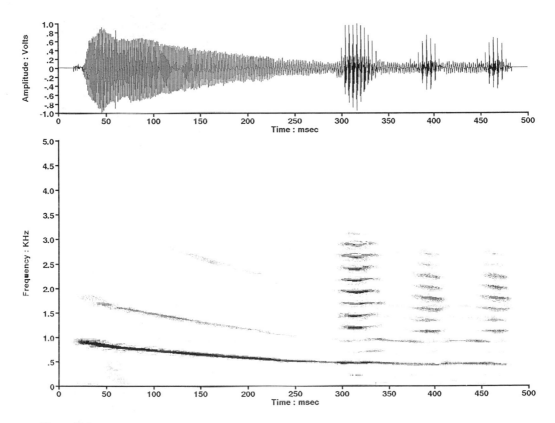

Figure 19.1
An advertisement call of the túngara frog, *Physalameus pustulosus*, consisting of a whine followed by three chucks.

thus having a frequency range from 250–3500Hz. More than 90% of the chuck's energy is within the higher half of the 14 harmonics, and the dominant frequency averages 2500Hz (Ryan 1985; Ryan et al. 1990).

Females are responsive to variation in call complexity. In nature, males call from stationary sites and females are free to move unimpeded throughout the chorus to choose a mate. As with most frogs, the call appears to be the primary cue used by females in mate location, assessment, and choice. Phonotaxis experiments in the laboratory offer a powerful tool to evaluate how the female's acoustic preferences might influence her choice of mates in nature. Phonotaxis experiments have shown that a whine is both necessary and sufficient to elicit female phonotaxis in controlled laboratory experiments. When females are given a choice between a whine only and a whine with chucks, they prefer the latter. The further addition of chucks can enhance call attraction, but the relationship is not linear (Rand and Ryan 1981; Rand et al. 1992; Wilczynski et al. 1995).

Although males produce calls to attract mates, they do not always produce the most attractive calls—that is, calls with chucks. When calling in areas isolated from others, a male will tend to produce simple calls. In choruses, however, most males produce complex calls. Males vary call complexity (the number of chucks added) in response to vocal stimulation from other males, and this effect can be elicited by broadcasting calls to evoke vocal responses in the wild or in the laboratory. A male producing a call without chucks will add chucks in response to the call of another male—simple or complex. Playbacks of more complex calls can cause further escalation in a male's call complexity. Thus call complexity can be varied by the male, and it appears that all males can produce calls with a full range of chucks (Rand and Ryan 1981; Ryan 1985).

There is also substantial variation in the advertisement call among populations. In a survey of 30 populations along a 5000km transect encompassing most of the species' range, we found that there were significant differences among populations in all 12 call parameters of the whine and chuck that we measured (Ryan et al. 1996). We are currently determining if females are attendant to this variation among populations.

It had been a paradox as to why males do not enhance call attractiveness by maximizing the number of chucks. This suggested there might be a cost to adding chucks that would balance the benefit of increased attractiveness. Although calling is energetically expensive, there is no detectable increase in oxygen consumption or lactate concentration that results from increasing call complexity (Bucher et al. 1982; Ryan et al. 1983). There does appear to be a predation cost, however. The bat, *Trachops cirrhosus*, is common in many areas in which túngara frogs breed. This bat feeds on frogs and locates them by homing in on the frogs' calls; it does not produce echolocation signals when approaching the frog, and it has a series of neuro-anatomical features that enhance its low-frequency sensitivity (Barclay et al. 1981; Bruns et al. 1989; Tuttle and Ryan 1981). The frog-eating bat responds to call variation in a manner similar to the female túngara frog. Bats approach a speaker broadcasting only the whine, but when given a choice the bat also prefers calls with chucks (Ryan et al. 1982). Males are safer from bat predation in larger choruses due to a selfish herd effect; since females are relatively more common in larger choruses, safety from predation is complimented by increased per capita mating success (Ryan et al. 1981). Thus the countervailing forces of sexual selection and bat predation appear to have been responsible for the evolution of the variably complex call of the túngara frog.

What is it about the chuck that makes the call more attractive? Females not only prefer calls with chucks but tend to prefer calls with lower-frequency chucks. In nature, larger males are more likely to be chosen by females, and there is a significant and negative correlation between the fundamental frequency of the chuck, which ranged from 200 270Hz, and male body size, which ranged from 26–33mm. In phonotaxis experiments, females preferred synthetic calls with lower fundamental frequencies (Ryan 1980, 1983, 1985). In these earlier experiments, the energy distribution across harmonics in the synthetic chucks were not controlled to reflect the natural variation among chuck harmonics. Later studies, in which the energy distribution among harmonics reflected this in a typical chuck, tended to be consistent with this lower-frequency preference although the preference was not as strong as previously suggested (P = 0.10 and P = 0.13 in two experiments; Wilczynski et al. 1995). In these studies the dominant frequency is in the upper harmonics, and the fundamental and dominant frequency were correlated (see below).

Behavioral preferences can result from an interaction of properties of the stimulus with sensory biases. We attempted to uncover some of these biases that might lead to low-frequency preference in túngara frogs. Frogs have two inner ear organs sensitive to airborne sound. In túngara frogs, as in most frogs, the amphibian papilla (AP) is maximally sensitive to frequencies below 1200Hz, and the basilar papilla (BP) is maximally sensitive to frequencies above 1200Hz (Ryan et al. 1990). The dominant frequency of the whine is close to the frequencies to which the AP are most sensitive, about 600Hz. Although the chuck encompasses a wide frequency range (250–3500Hz), more than 90% of its energy is concentrated in the higher frequencies (>1500Hz) to which the BP is more sensitive. This suggested that most of the processing of the chuck initially occurs through the BP—at least at amplitudes near threshold (Ryan et al. 1990). Phonotaxis experiments support this interpretation. Females were presented with a whine versus a whine with either the low half (<1500Hz) or the high half (>1500Hz) of the chuck's harmonics with the natural energy distribution; thus the whine/low-chuck had less energy than the whine/high-chuck. Females preferred a whine/high-chuck to a whine, but did not discriminate between a whine and a whine/low-chuck (Ryan and Rand 1990; Wilczynski et al. 1995). Thus the BP seems to be important in processing the chuck when the relative amplitudes of the chuck harmonics are greatly skewed to the higher harmonics, as they are in natural chucks. This is not to suggest that if more acoustic energy were invested in the low-chuck this would not enhance its attractiveness. That issue is addressed below.

Although the tuning of the AP and BP tends to match the dominant frequencies of the whine and chuck, respectively, the BP is tuned, on average, slightly below the dominant frequency of the average chuck in the population: 2100Hz for the BP versus 2500Hz for the chuck. This suggests that the female's behavioral preferences for chucks with a lower fundamental frequency, which also had a lower dominant frequency, might result from these calls effecting a better match to the BP's sensitivity. Computer models integrating an average tuning curve and digitized calls drawn at random from a population of túngara frogs support this contention. Chucks with lower dominant frequencies elicited greater excitation from the average tuning curve than did higher-frequency calls (Ryan et al. 1990). Phonotaxis experiments using single tones in place of the chuck, 2100Hz versus 3000Hz, offered qualified support for this hypothesis as well; more females preferred the lower-frequency tone, although the preference was not statistically significant ($P = 0.10$; Wilczynski et al. 1995). Similar results were also achieved with another species of frog, cricket frogs (*Acris crepitans*): female BP sensitivity is below the average call's dominant frequency, and females were preferentially attracted to lower-frequency calls (Ryan et al. 1992).

Acoustic Preferences and Sensory Exploitation

As discussed above, females prefer calls with chucks to calls without chucks, and there tends to be a weak preference for lower-frequency chucks over higher-frequency chucks. None of the other close relatives of the túngara frog, with the exception of a species in the jungles of Peru and Brazil that we tentatively identify as *P. freibergi*, adds a suffix to the call (Cannatella et al. 1998; Ryan and Rand 1993a,c, 1995; figure 19.2). Morphological studies have identified the exaggeration of a fibrous mass associated with the vocal cords as being partly responsible for the production of the chuck (Drewry et al. 1982), and a comparative analysis shows that the evolutionary elaboration of the fibrous mass is associated with the addition of a call suffix (Ryan and Drewes 1990). The addition of more taxa and more characters to the phylogenetic analysis continues to support this concordance (Cannatella et al. 1998).

So how did it come about that male túngara frogs produce calls with chucks and that the females prefer them? For a communication system to evolve there must not only be a change in signal structure, but the receiver must be able to interpret these new signals appropriately. Thus it is often assumed that signals and receivers coevolve. This is an assumption about past history. No degree of experimentation demonstrating the congruence of a signal and receiver within a species has any bearing on how this congruence came to be. Instead, one could utilize information on phylogenetic relationships to deduce past patterns of signal evolution. This infor-

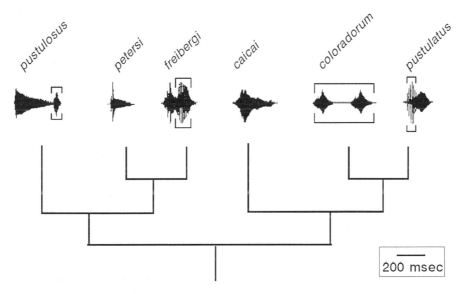

Figure 19.2
The phylogenetic relationships of taxa within the *Physalaemus pustulosus* species group. An oscillogram of the advertisement call of each species is shown. The brackets indicate derived call characters: *P. pustulosus*—chuck; *P. freibergi*—squawk; *P. colorodorum*—double calls; *P. pustulatus*—strongly amplitude-modulated prefix.

mation could then be used to design experiments that can test long-held assumptions about signal-receiver coevolution.

We utilized information on the phylogenetic relationships of these frogs to determine if, in fact, the female's preference for chucks evolved in concert with chucks (the coevolution hypothesis) or if females had a preexisting preference for chucks that was exploited by males (sensory exploitation hypothesis; Ryan 1990; Ryan et al. 1990; Ryan and Rand 1990; both hypotheses reviewed in Kirkpatrick and Ryan 1991; Andersson 1994; Ryan 1997). These hypotheses can be discriminated by reconstructing the phylogenetic history of the species group and inferring the historical sequence by which chucks and preferences for chucks evolved.

We utilized data on morphology, allozymes, and the sequences of the 12S ribosomal mitochondrial gene and the COI mitochondrial gene to estimate the phylogenetic relationships between the six species of the *Physalaemus pustulosus* group and three congeneric species that we used as outgroups (Cannatella et al. 1998; Ryan and Rand 1995; figures 19.2, 19.4). The six species in the species group comprise two smaller monophyletic groups. One group has a Middle American–Amazonian distribution and includes *P. pustulosus*, *P. petersi*, and *P. freibergi*. All of these species are north or east of the Andes. The other group has three species that are all west of the Andes, *P. coloradorum*, *P. pustulatus*, and *P. caicai*. The three outgroup species are *P. enesefae*, *P. ephippifer*, and an undescribed species that we refer to as *P.* "*roraima.*" Allozyme variation, differences in DNA sequence, and the geology of the Andes all suggest that these two groups within the *P. pustulosus* species group separated about 20 million years ago, coincident with the rise of the Andes (Cannatella et al. 1998).

As mentioned previously, a call suffix is present only in the Middle American–Amazonian group, in *P. pustulosus* (a chuck) and *P. freibergi* (a squawk). Call suffixes appear to be absent in the western Andes group and in the roughly 35 species in the genus that we have examined (figure 19.2). Thus the call suffix seems to have evolved after the Middle American–Amazonian group diverged from the western Andes group. We asked if female *P. coloradorum*, a member of the western Andes group, would prefer calls with chucks if they were to evolve. Several chucks from a túngara frog call were digitally appended to the whine-like species-specific call of *P. coloradorum*. When presented with such a choice in a phonotaxis experiment, females preferred calls with chucks to the normal species call, which lacks chucks (Ryan and Rand 1993b,c). The fact that *P. pustulosus* and *P. coloradorum* both prefer calls with chucks suggests that this preference is shared through a common ancestor, as opposed to the hypothesis that *P. coloradorum* females happened to evolve the same preference for traits not existing in their own males. The former hypothesis is more parsimonious because it requires fewer evolutionary changes: one instead of two, assuming that the lack of a chuck is ancestral. This possibility is now being investigated with studies of *P. enesefae* (Z. Tarano, personal communication). It must be cautioned that parsimony by itself does not prove that this preference did not evolve independently in *P. pustulosus* and *P. coloradorum* (Ryan 1996). But in the absence of other data allowing historical reconstruction, such as a fossil record, parsimony is an acceptable criterion to interpret data on evolutionary pattern.

If our interpretation of the shared ancestry of the preference for chucks in *P. coloradorum* and *P. pustulosus* is correct, we can ask when the preference for chucks arose relative to the chucks themselves. The molecular data suggest that the most recent common ancestor of these two taxa existed before the Middle American–Amazonian and the western Andes groups diverged (figure 19.2). If so, then this suggests that the preference for chucks existed prior to the evolution of the chucks. So it seems that males evolved chucks to exploit a preexisting preference for chucks. Analogous results in a variety of other taxa suggest that sensory exploitation is not merely restricted to this one group of frogs (e.g., crabs, Christy 1995; Christy and Salmon 1991; fish, Basolo 1990a,b, 1995a,b; Endler 1992; lizards, Fleishman 1992).

Although female túngara frogs prefer calls with chucks to those without chucks, they also have preferences for call components existing in other species but absent in their own. Call prefixes and multiple call groups exist in the western Andes species group (in *P. pustulatus* and *P. coloradorum*, respectively) but appear to be absent in the rest of the genus (figure 19.2). Túngara frog females prefer their own conspecific call to which a prefix from *P. pustulatus* has been added to the normal, whine only call. They also prefer calls in multiple groups, which their males do not produce but which are produced by male *P. coloradorum*, to single calls. Finally, female túngara frogs prefer the squawk of *P. freibergi* added to their own simple call to the same call without the squawk (Ryan and Rand 1993a,b,c); merely increasing the whine's duration does not duplicate this effect (unpublished data). Thus call components that evolved in other species enhance the attractiveness of the túngara frog's simple whine call.

Interestingly, these various call additions not only increase the attractiveness of the call analogous to adding a chuck but are as attractive to female túngara frogs as chucks (figure 19.3). Thus it appears that any of these three call additions that evolved first, a chuck, a prefix, or a squawk, might have been an evolutionarily stable strategy (ESS); that is, once fixed in the population none of these stimuli would have been invaded by one of the others, assuming other forces such as predation act on these components similarly. Furthermore, the chuck might be an ESS relative to other more complex stimuli since females did not exhibit a preference between a whine-chuck and a prefix-whine-chuck (figure 19.3).

Preexisting preferences are not restricted to stimuli that have evolved in closely related heterospecifics. Artificial stimuli added to the call also affect preferences. As mentioned above, in the natural call-energy distribution, a high-half chuck but not a low-half chuck increases call attractiveness, suggesting a role for the BP in the peripheral processing of the chuck. If the amplitude of the low-half chuck is increased to that of a full chuck, however, the low-half chuck increases call attractiveness; thus there is potentially plasticity in which of the two peripheral end organs could be implicated in chuck preferences (Ryan and Rand 1990). Furthermore, the precise acoustic structure of the chuck does not influence preferences in these phonotaxis experiments; white noise and single tones added to a simple whine with the amplitude of the full chuck also elicit enhanced call attractiveness from females (Ryan and Rand 1990; Wilczynski et al. 1995). It appears that female call preferences favored the evolution of the complex call in *P. pustulosus*, but that they might have been permissive relative to the types of sounds that increased call complexity. Aspects of the male's calling morphology, on the other hand, might have been more important in determining the precise sounds used to make the call more complex.

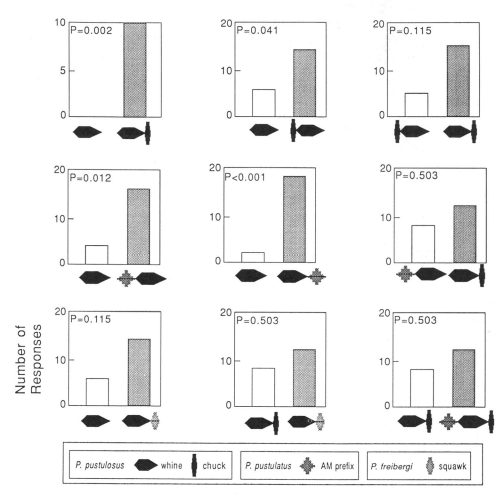

Figure 19.3
The results of phonotaxis experiments in which female túngara frogs were given a choice between pairs of stimuli that combined various call additions with the conspecific whine. In all experiments, except the whine versus whine-chuck with its sample size of 10, 20 females were tested. Exact binomial probabilities that test the null hypothesis of no preference are shown for each experiment.

It appears that there is a variety of stimuli that can enhance call attractiveness in túngara frogs, and that these stimuli are no less attractive than a natural chuck. Thus the female's acoustic preference space seems to be quite broad, encompassing a range of stimulus variation not exhibited by conspecific males, and even surpassing that exhibited by closely related heterospecifics. This observation has influenced how we now view the function and evolution of communication systems (see, e.g., Andersson 1994; Shaw 1995; Hauser 1996).

The concepts of sensory exploitation and preexisting biases are not nonadaptive (see, e.g., Dawkins and Guilford 1996; Ryan et al. 1998). If a preexisting bias had a direct, negative effect on female fitness, then selection should result in the evolution of the bias underlying the female preference (Kirkpatrick and Ryan 1991). Most hypotheses of adaptation, however, do not address the precise form of the phenotype that might result from selection. We suggest that knowledge of the evolutionary history of a lineage gives insights into those phenotypes that might plausibly evolve in response to selection. These studies provide an example.

Female túngara frogs gain some reproductive advantage by mating with larger males; more eggs are fertilized if the size difference between the typically larger female and the typically smaller male is minimized (Ryan 1985). To the extent that females are preferring lower-frequency chucks they are also preferring larger males (male size and chuck fundamental frequency are negatively correlated; Ryan 1980, 1985) and thus might be gaining a reproductive advantage derived from their call preference. If females had a different sensory bias and if males had a laryngeal morphology that biased them to other signal-phenotypes besides the chuck, then selection might still result in evolution and/or maintenance of female preference for sounds that signaled larger males. The resulting phenotype, however, could be quite different from the chuck; for example, males could add tones to the whine, or evolve visual displays that signaled body size. The inclusion of phylogenetic approaches that attempt to reconstruct evolutionary patterns of traits and preferences should be viewed as an addendum to and not an attack on hypotheses of adaptation.

Conspecific versus Heterospecific Preferences

By using phylogenetic information to design phonotaxis experiments, we have gained some insights into how sexual selection can influence the evolution of signal complexity. We have used this same approach to investigate the evolution of species-specific mate recognition in these frogs.

The túngara frog and all of the other species in the group produce whine-like frequency-modulated sweeps that appear to encode species-specificity and guide females toward conspecific males. Both *P. pustulosus* and *P. coloradorum* exhibit strong, near-unanimous preferences for the conspecific call over the calls of all the closely related species we tested. Females of both species, however, exhibit phono-taxis to some heterospecific calls when these calls are matched against white noise rather than the conspecific call (Ryan and Rand 1993b). These results suggest that like preferences for chucks, the female preferences for whines might be influenced by their historical legacy. Female call preferences are not deconstructed and recon-structed with every speciation event to result in a perfect match to the call of the newly evolved species. Instead, the precise forms that a newly evolved call and a call preference take are sensitive to their starting conditions or their ancestral states.

We utilized phylogenetic analyses to estimate the calls of ancestors of túngara frogs. We then asked if females discriminate between the calls of conspecifics and ancestors, and if calls of ancestors (when paired with white noise) are sufficient to elicit recognition from females (Ryan and Rand 1995). This analysis utilized differ-ences in DNA sequences as an estimate of phylogenetic relationships and rates of divergence, quantitative measures of salient call parameters of all the extant species, mathematical algorithms that estimate ancestral characters by minimizing the amount of evolutionary change over the phylogenetic tree, and digital synthesis of the ancestral calls using the estimates for each call parameter (figure 19.4). We asked to what degree overall call similarity and phylogenetic relatedness might influence female phonotaxis. Overall call similarity is a phenetic measure of the acoustic simi-larity of the target call to the túngara frog call based on a principal component analysis of call variables. Phylogenetic distance is the degree of relatedness, based on purported changes in the DNA sequence between the túngara frog and the species or purported ancestor of the call being examined. These two variables were not highly correlated (Ryan and Rand 1995).

The phonotaxis studies using ancestral calls highlight the role of historical effects on the female's preferences for the conspecific whine. Although female túngara frogs discriminated between the calls of conspecifics and those of most ancestors, as they did between conspecific and heterospecific calls, they did not discriminate between the conspecific call and the call of their most recent ancestor (node c, figure 19.4) even though these two calls differ statistically in all call parameters (i.e., each of the ancestral's call parameters are outside of the mean plus 95% confidence limits of the analogous parameter for the túngara frog calls). These results suggest that, as with chuck and chuck-preference evolution, the evolution of the whine and whine-preference are not tightly correlated with one another. Furthermore, a multiple re-

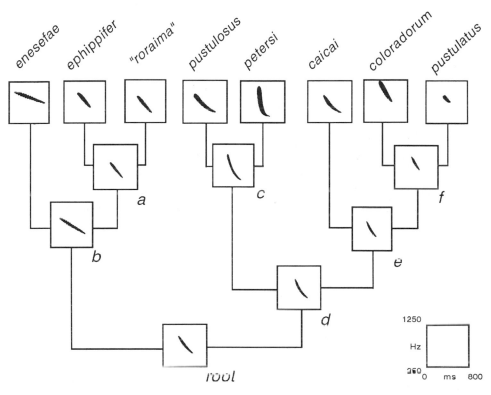

Figure 19.4
The tree illustrating the most parsimonious hypothesis for the relationships among members of the *Phys-alaemus pustulosus* species group and the three species we used as outgroups (note that *P. freibergi* was not used in this analysis, cf. figure 19.2). "roraima" is an undescribed species. Sonograms illustrate the synthetic advertisement calls for each taxon; the calls estimated for the ancestral nodes were derived from a local squared-change parsimony model assuming a gradual model of evolution (cf. FG, figure 19.5).

gression analysis of phylogenetic distance and overall call similarity regressed on phonotaxis preference showed that phylogenetic distance was a more important predictor of female preference than overall call similarity.

We also asked to what degree females would recognize a heterospecific call by presenting it in a phonotaxis experiment paired with white noise. A number of calls elicited statistically significant female phonotaxis. In contrast with the findings of the discrimination experiments, the overall call similarity between the conspecific call and the heterospecific call rather than phylogenetic distance better predicted female responses in the recognition experiments.

How Robust Is the Phylogenetic Approach?

Behavioral interpretations based on phylogenetic hypotheses are only as strong as the phylogenetic foundation upon which they are based. One approach to estimating the robustness of such behavioral interpretations is to vary the assumptions underlying the phylogenetic hypothesis and ask to what extent changing such assumptions alters the behavioral interpretations.

In the previous study of female preferences for ancestral mating calls, we used one model of evolution to estimate calls at ancestral nodes. This model was based on the following characteristics: the most parsimonious tree topology (a bifurcating tree [two monophyletic groups] within the species group), the local squared-change parsimony algorithm, an assumption of gradual evolution, and inclusion of all three of the outgroups. We repeated the above procedure to determine how sensitive the results and conclusions of the previous study were to the particular model used to estimate the ancestral call characters (Ryan and Rand 1999). We asked: (1) if different models gave different call estimates for the same nodes; (2) if different call estimates at the same node were meaningful to females; and (3) if differences in female responses influenced conclusions from the previous study. We used seven different models that varied in at least one of the following parameters: tree topology (bifurcating versus pectinate tree), algorithms (local squared-change versus squared-change parsimony), tempo (gradual or punctuated evolution), and outgroups (two or three outgroup taxa used). In summary, we found that: (1) 51% of the 48 calls estimated at the various ancestral nodes differed by at least 10% in at least one of the eight call characters estimated at the same node; (2) 28% of the separate sets of female choice experiments revealed that different call estimates for the same node were perceived as meaningfully different by the females; and (3) these meaningful differences to females did not influence any of the major conclusions from the previous study (figure 19.5).

One conclusion of our previous study, for example, was based upon the female response to the ancestral call at a single node: the immediate ancestor of *P. pustulosus* and *P. petersi*, node c. In the previous study, females did not show a strong preference for the conspecific call versus the call estimated for the immediate ancestor (13 to conspecific versus 7 to ancestral call; two-tailed exact binomial probability $P = 0.263$). In the other 13 tests in this study, there was always a significant preference for the conspecific call; in one case $P = 0.045$ and in 12 cases $P < 0.001$ ($N = 20$ for all tests). The seven different models of evolution gave two different call estimates for node c. The pectinate tree gave one estimate, and the six models that varied in some assumptions but always used the most parsimonious tree topology

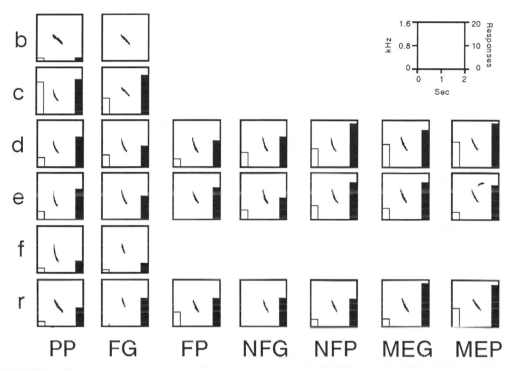

Figure 19.5
Call estimates derived from different models of evolution (columns) for advertisement calls at the same ancestral node (rows). Only calls at the same node that vary by more than 10% in any single call character are shown (e.g., call estimates at node a were essentially the same). The critical attributes of the different models of evolution used were: PP—pectinate tree, local squared-change parsimony, gradual; FG—squared-change parsimony, gradual; FP—squared-change parsimony, punctuated; NFG—tree without *P. enesefae*, squared-change parsimony, gradual; NFP, tree without *P. enesefae*, squared-change parsimony, punctuated; MEG—local squared-change parsimony (squared-change parsimony), gradual; MEP—local squared-change parsimony, punctuated. FG is the model used to estimate the calls shown in figure 19.4. In each box the open bars show the number of females that responded to the heterospecific call when it was paired with the conspecific call, and the closed bars the number of females that responded to the heterospecific call when it was paired with a white noise stimulus. In all experiments the sample size was 20.

gave another estimate. The results of the G test, when not adjusted for experiment-wide error, suggest that the females responded to these two estimates differently in the discrimination tests. Using the call estimated from the pectinate tree, fewer females were attracted to the conspecific call. Only 6 females were attracted to the conspecific call, while 14 were attracted to the ancestral call ($P = 0.115$), versus 13 to 7 in the previous experiment. Although the strength of female response differs between the two experiments, both fail to reject the hypothesis of statistically significant preference for the conspecific call. Although we would not argue strongly for a true lack of discrimination when $P = 0.115$, we point out that the trend in preference is actually in the opposite direction than would be predicted—more females were attracted to the call estimate for the immediate ancestor than to the conspecific call! This result offers an especially compelling argument for how the evolution of signals and receivers can proceed at different rates.

How General Are Sensory Biases? A Neural Network Study

In the studies described above, the receiver (i.e., the female túngara frog) was an experimental constant and we measured its response to calls that varied over evolutionary time. We reached the conclusion that the receiver had biases toward other stimuli that might result from the historical legacy of this species. We took this approach one step further to explicitly address both how responses to heterospecific calls might be incidental consequences of conspecific recognition, and the degree to which historical effects influence these receiver biases. We did this by utilizing a technique from computational neurobiology: artificial neural networks.

Previously, Enquist and Arak (1993) showed that when a network was trained to a simple visual stimulus, such as a cross, there were a variety of hidden preferences for novel stimuli, including supernormal preferences. In another series of studies, Enquist and Arak (1994) and Johnstone (1994) showed that preference for signal symmetry can also emerge despite no specific selection on networks to recognize symmetric signals. The authors suggested that these results might be analogous to selection to recognize species-specific traits, and that they were in accord with studies of animal communication that showed hidden or preexisting preferences. There have been some criticisms of these studies, mostly based on the artificiality of the systems (Dawkins and Guilford 1995).

Phelps and Ryan (1998, in review) recently used neural networks to ask two questions: Would such artificial and relatively simple models predict the biases of female túngara frogs? And, would evolutionary history affect the models similarly to how it affects female túngara frogs? We used a simple neural network that consisted of an input layer, a hidden layer, a recurrent layer, and an output (figure 19.6). As with other neural network models, the response of the network varied with the strength of the weights of the connections; these weightings were subject to selection, recombination, and mutation. We used synthetic calls that included all the heterospecific and ancestral calls used in Ryan and Rand (1995) as well as other stimuli with which females were tested. The other stimuli were from an ongoing study in which we tested female preferences to stimuli that were intermediate between the conspecific call and various heterospecific calls. These calls were digitized and presented to the networks in small time increments. The networks' performance was measured by comparing the strengths of response to the call and to noise; the greater the difference (favoring the call), the higher the value of call recognition.

Twenty populations of 100 networks per population were trained to recognize the túngara frog call. Most recognized the call at our arbitrary criterion after a thousand or so generations. The network that best recognized the call in each of the 20 populations was then tested with other stimuli (heterospecific, ancestral calls) with which female túngara frogs had already been tested. The results show that the response of the neural networks to these calls, with which they had no experience, predicts a significant and substantial amount of the variation in the biases of real túngara frogs ($r^2 = 0.65$; Phelps and Ryan 1998).

These studies show that for a simple neural architecture, the task of learning a túngara frog call generates a variety of responses, some weak and some strong, for stimuli with which the network has had no previous experience. The emergence of hidden biases, as mentioned above, was also found in more artificial studies of neural network recognition of visual stimuli. The notable result from this study, however, is that these emergent biases of the artificial network explain a substantial proportion of the response biases of real females. The fact that these neural networks are far simpler systems than the frog's auditory system makes this result more rather than less interesting. In theoretical modeling in general, the simplicity of the model is a strength, increasing its generality and applicability. Although the frog's peripheral end organs and various auditory nuclei in the brain allow the latitude for various complex combinatorial analyses of signal structure, the neural net models suggest that these processes need not be overly complex. These models of course do not prove this assertion.

One limitation of the neural net model in the above simulations is that, unlike a real animal receiver, nets have no history of its ancestors having had to recognize different acoustic stimuli; that is, they are ahistorical. Our studies of preferences of real female túngara frogs for ancestral calls were designed to address the concern

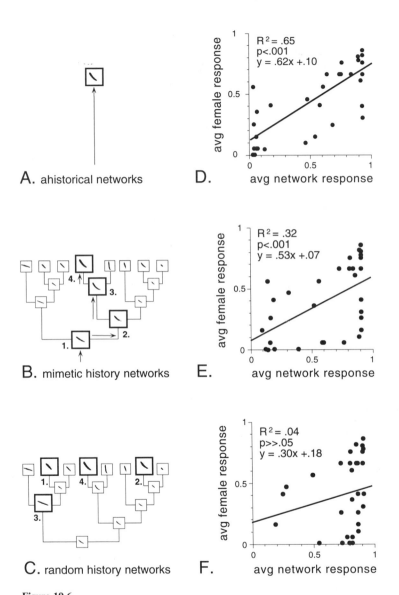

Figure 19.6
The relationships between the responses of female túngara frogs and the responses of neural networks to a variety of heterospecific and synthetic stimuli. Networks were trained either only to the túngara frog call (A, D), to a series of calls along the evolutionary pathway from the most ancestral call to the túngara frog (B, E), or to a series of random histories that always ended with the túngara frog call (one example of which is shown in C, the responses of these networks compared to responses of females are in F).

that the history of the signal-receiver system could introduce hidden biases and pre-existing preferences into the receivers of extant species. We used the neural network studies to explore further the influence of history on female biases. We trained the neural networks to a series of calls representing our best estimate of the actual evolutionary history of the túngara frog call (the "mimetic" history) and compared how well these networks predicted female biases relative to a series of networks that were tested with random evolutionary histories.

In the mimetic-history simulations, networks were selected to respond to the root call (figure 19.6). When populations reached the response criterion, they were then trained on the call that was immediately descendent on the evolutionary pathway to the túngara frog—this is the node at the divergence of the two clades within the *Physalaemus pustulosus* species group. When those networks reached response criterion, they were trained to the call that was the immediate ancestor to *P. pustulosus* and *P. petersi*. Finally, these networks were trained to the túngara frog call. We also trained networks to random evolutionary histories (figure 19.6). As with the mimetic history, the networks were trained to a series of four calls, the last always being the túngara frog call. The previous three calls, however, were randomly chosen from the 15 heterospecific and ancestral calls in the call phylogeny. After the evolutionary simulations were completed, that is, were selected to respond to the túngara frog call, we measured their responses to the same set of heterospecific and ancestral stimuli that were used in the initial tests of the neural networks. We found that the networks with the mimetic evolutionary history better predicted the responses of female túngara frogs ($r^2 = 0.45$ vs. $r^2 = 0.11$; figure 19.6).

The neural networks that were trained only to the túngara frog call (ahistorical) and those that were trained to other calls prior to being trained to the túngara frog call (historical) were all eventually able to recognize the túngara frog call. The response biases in these networks, that is, how they responded to other calls, differed, however. A similar phenomenon might be expected in the evolution of receiver systems of real animals. For example, although most species show a preference for conspecific courtship signals over heterospecific ones, species might differ in the manner in which they respond to signals outside of the species' range, and these response biases might be influenced by the receiver's evolutionary history, that is, by the types of signals that the receivers of ancestors had evolved to decode. We make this interpretation because, as we discussed earlier, female call preferences are not deconstructed and reconstructed with every speciation event to result in a perfect match to the call of the newly evolved species. Instead, the precise forms that a newly evolved call and a call preference take are sensitive to their starting conditions or their ancestral states. This interpretation is supported by the results of the neural network models that show that those neural networks with the history more closely resembling that of the túngara frog better predicts the responses biases of túngara frog females than those networks having the random history. We note that the neural network with the mimetic evolutionary history, however, did not predict female biases as well as did the ahistorical network in the initial study.

These studies show that neural network modeling can be used effectively to predict unintended response biases that occur in real animal communication systems. Furthermore, these models can be subject to evolution and the specific effects of history on these response biases can be quantified. With some obvious exceptions, such as information theory and game theory, animal communication has not benefited greatly from theoretical modeling. Artificial neural networks seem to offer the dual advantage of achieving generality by applying simple and artificial constructs to "hard" problems, as well as providing the advantage of hypothesis testing and assessing biological reality that comes from applying these models to specific communication signals and evolutionary histories.

Summary

Our earlier studies of túngara frogs concentrated on the adaptive significance of the acoustic mate recognition system and the mechanisms that underlie receiver responses and signal generation. These studies provided substantial detail about the functions and mechanisms of communication in this system, but could not address questions about its evolutionary history. By deriving hypotheses of the phylogenetic relationships of the túngara frog and its close relatives, however, we were able to design experiments that explicitly tested hypotheses about evolutionary history. The phylogenetically based phonotaxis and neural network studies reveal that the evolutionary history of the communication system generates response biases to stimuli that are not part of the conspecific repertoire. In some cases, these response biases might be the starting point of sexual selection for new signals. We emphasize that these studies do not challenge the notion that female preferences and male signals are adaptive, but instead give insights into the phenotypes that are likely to evolve in response to selection. These insights could not have been gained without addressing the evolution of the communication system in an explicitly phylogenetic context. Since all communication systems have an evolutionary history, we believe a full understanding of any system can only be achieved when phylogenetic approaches are invoked.

Phylogenetic approaches by themselves, however, will offer little insight into the evolution of communication. Instead, we urge the development of more in-depth model systems for a better understanding of animal communication. We feel that the success of the phylogenetic approach in our studies of túngara frogs depends, in part, upon our detailed understanding of the adaptive significance and sensory and morphological mechanisms underlying this communication system. Studies utilizing newly developed phylogenetic analyses in animal behavior will be lacking without otherwise detailed information about the behaviors in question. We will better understand the phenomenon of animal communication when we understand more systems that integrate Tinbergen's four questions of ontogeny, mechanisms, adaptive significance, and evolutionary history. Then we will have what we should be striving for—a general biology of animal communication (see also Hauser 1996).

Acknowledgments

We appreciate logistical support from the Smithsonian Tropical Research Institute, financial support from the Smithsonian Institution's Scholarly Studies Program, the National Science Foundation (IBN 93-16185), and the University of Texas. We especially thank F. Bolonos, M. Briadorolli, M. Dantzker, L. Dries, J. Ellingson, M. Gridi Papp, A. S. Kapfer, N. Kime, D. Lombicdo, K. Mills, M. Monsivais, G. More, G. Rosenthal, S. Rodriguez, M. Sasa, Z. Tarana, and S. Yoon for assistance with the female choice tests.

References

Andersson, M. (1994) *Sexual Selection*. Princeton, NJ: Princeton University Press.

Barclay, R. M. R., Fenton, B., Tuttle, M. D., and Ryan, M. J. (1981) Echolocation calls produced by *Trachops cirrhosus* (*Chiroptera: Phyllostomatidae*) while hunting for frogs. *Canadian J. Zool.* 59:150–153.

Basolo, A. L. (1990a) Female preference for male sword length in the green swordtail, *Xiphophorus helleri* (*Pisces: Poeciliidae*). *Anim. Behav.* 40:332–338.

Basolo, A. L. (1990b) Female preference predates the evolution of the sword in swordtail fish. *Science* 250:808–810.

Basolo, A. L. (1995a) A further examination of a pre-existing bias favouring a sword in the genus *Xiphophorus*. *Anim. Behav.* 50:365–375.

Basolo, A. L. (1995b) Phylogenetic evidence for the role of a pre-existing bias in sexual selection. *Proc. Royal Soc.* B 259:307–311.

Brooks, D. R. and McLennan, D. A. (1991) *Phylogeny, Ecology, and Behavior*. Chicago: University of Chicago Press.

Bruns, V., Burda, H., and Ryan, M. J. (1989) Ear morphology of the frog-eating bat (*Trachops cirrhosus*, Family *Phylostomidae*): Apparent specializations for low-frequency hearing. *J. Morphol.* 199:103–118.

Bucher, T. L., Ryan, M. J., and Bartholomew, G. W. (1982) Oxygen consumption during resting, calling, and nest building in the frog *Physalaemus pustulosus*. *Phys. Zool.* 55:10–22.

Cannatella, D. C., Hillis, D. M., Chippindale, P., Weigt, L., Rand, A. S., and Ryan, M. J. (1998) Phylogeny of frogs of the *Physalaemus pustulosus* species group, with an examination of data incongruence. *Syst. Biol.* 47:311–335.

Christy, J. H. (1995) Mimicry, mate choice, and the sensory trap hypothesis. *Am. Nat.* 146:171–181.

Christy, J. H. and Salmon, M. (1991) Comparative studies of reproductive behavior in mantis shrimp and fiddler crabs. *Amer. Zool.* 31:329–337.

Dawkins, M. S. and Guilford, T. (1995) An exaggerated preference for simple neural network models of signal evolution? *Proc. Royal Soc. London* B 261:184–200.

Dawkins, M. S. and Guilford, T. (1996) Sensory bias and the adaptiveness of female choice. *Am. Nat.* 14:937–942.

Drewry, G. E., Heyer, W. R., and Rand, A. S. (1982) A functional analysis of the complex call of the frog *Physalaemus pustulosus. Copeia* 1982:636–645.

Endler, J. A. (1992) Signals, signal conditions, and the direction of evolution. *Am. Nat.* 131:S125–S153.

Enquist, M. and Arak, A. (1993) Selection of exaggerated male traits by female aesthetic senses. *Nature* 361:446–448.

Enquist, M. and Arak, A. (1994) Symmetry, beauty, and evolution. *Nature* 372:169–170.

Fleischman, L. J. (1992) The influence of the sensory system and the environment on motion patterns in the visual displays of anoline lizards and other vertebrates. *Am. Nat.* 139:S36–S61.

Harvey, P. and Pagel, M. D. (1991) *The Comparative Method in Evolutionary Biology*. Oxford: Oxford University Press.

Hauser, M. (1996) *The Evolution of Communication*. Cambridge, MA: MIT Press.

Johnstone, R. A. (1994) Female preference for symmetrical males as a by-product of selection for mate recognition. *Nature* 372:172–175.

Kirkpatrick, M. and Ryan, M. J. (1991) The paradox of the lek and the evolution of mating preferences. Nature 350:33–38.

Lorenz, K. (1941) Vergleichende Bewegungstudien an Anatien. *J. Ornithol.* 89:194–294.

Martins, E. (1996) *Phylogenies and the Comparative Method in Animal Behavior*. Oxford: Oxford University Press.

Phelps, S. M. and Ryan, M. J. (1998) Neural networks predict response biases in female túngara frogs. Proc. Roy. Soc. B 265:279–285.

Phelps, S. M. and Ryan, M. J. (in review) History influences signal recognition: Neural network models of túngara frogs.

Rand, A. S. and Ryan, M. J. (1981) The adaptive significance of a complex vocal repertoire in a Neotropical frog. *Z. Tierpsychol.* 57:209–214.

Rand, A. S., Ryan, M. J., and Wilczynski, W. (1992) Signal redundancy and receiver permissiveness in acoustic mate recognition by the túngara frog, *Physalaemus pustulosus. Amer. Zool.* 32:81–90.

Ryan, M. J. (1980) Female mate choice in a Neotropical frog. *Science* 209:523–525.

Ryan, M. J. (1983) Sexual selection and communication in a Neotropical frog, *Physalaemus pustulosus. Evolution* 39:261–272.

Ryan, M. J. (1985) *The Túngara Frog: A Study in Sexual Selection and Communication*. Chicago: University of Chicago Press.

Ryan, M. J. (1990) Sensory systems, sexual selection, and sensory exploitation. *Oxford Surv. Evol. Biol.* 7:157–195.

Ryan, M. J. (1996) Phylogenetics and behavior: Some cautions and expectations In *Phylogenies and the Comparative Method in Animal Behavior*, ed. by E. Martins, pp. 1–21. Oxford: Oxford University Press.

Ryan, M. J. (1997) Sexual selection and mate choice. In *Behavioural Ecology: An Evolutionary Approach*, ed. by J. R. Krebs, and N. B. Davies, pp. 179–202. Oxford: Blackwell Science.

Ryan, M. J., Autumn, K., and Wake, D. B. (1998) Integrative biology and sexual selection. *Integrative Biology* 1:68–72.

Ryan, M. J., Bartholomew, G. W., and Rand, A. S. (1983) Reproductive energetics of a Neotropical frog, *Physalaemus pustulosus. Ecology* 64:1456–1462.

Ryan, M. J. and Drewes, R. C. (1990) Vocal morphology of the *Physalaemus pustulosus* species group (Family Leptodactylidae): Morphological response to sexual selection for complex calls. *Biol. J. Linn. Soc.* 40:37–52.

Ryan, M. J., Fox, J. H., Wilczynski, W., and Rand, A. S. (1990) Sexual selection for sensory exploitation in the frog *Physalaemus pustulosus. Nature* 343:66–67.

Ryan, M. J., Perrill, S. A., and Wilczynski, W. (1992) Auditory tuning and call frequency predict population-based mating preferences in the cricket frog, *Acris crepitans. Am. Nat.* 139:1370–1383.

Ryan, M. J. and Rand, A. S. (1990) The sensory basis of sexual selection for complex calls in the túngara frog, *Physalaemus pustulosus* (sexual selection for sensory exploitation). *Evolution* 44:305–314.

Ryan, M. J. and Rand, A. S. (1993a) Phylogenetic patterns of behavioral mate recognition systems in the *Physalaemus pustulosus* species group (*Anura: Leptodactylidae*): The role of ancestral and derived characters and sensory exploitation. In *Evolutionary Patterns and Processes*, ed. by D. R. Lees and D. Edwards, pp. 251–267. Linnean Society Symposium Series, no. 14. London: Academic Press.

Ryan, M. J. and Rand, A. S. (1993b) Species recognition and sexual selection as a unitary problem in animal communication. *Evolution* 47:647–657.

Ryan, M. J. and Rand, A. S. (1993c) Sexual selection and signal evolution. The ghost of biases past. *Phil. Trans. Roy. Soc.* B 340:187–195.

Ryan, M. J. and Rand, A. S. (1995) Female responses to ancestral advertisement calls in the túngara frog. *Science* 269:390–392.

Ryan, M. J. and Rand, A. S. (1999) Phylogenetic influences on mating call preferences in female túngara frogs (*Physalaemus pustulosus*). *Anim. Behav.* 57:915–956.

Ryan, M. J., Rand, A. S., and Weigt, L. A. (1996) Allozyme and advertisement call variation in the túngara frog, *Physalaemus pustulosus. Evolution* 50:2435–2453.

Ryan, M. J., Tuttle, M. D., and Taft, L. K. (1981) The costs and benefits of frog chorusing behavior. *Behav. Ecol. Sociobiol.* 8:273–278.

Ryan, M. J., Tuttle, M. D., and Rand, A. S. (1982) Sexual advertisement and bat predation in a Neotropical frog. *Am. Nat.* 119:136–139.

Shaw, K. (1995) Phylogenetic tests of the sensory exploitation model of sexual selection. *Trends Ecol. Evol.* 10:117–120.

Tinbergen, N. (1953) *The Social Behaviour of Animals*. London: Butler and Tanner.

Tinbergen, N. (1964) On aims and methods in ethology. *Z. Tierpsychol.* 20:410–433.

Tuttle, M. D. and Ryan, M. J. (1981) Bat predation and the evolution of frog vocalizations in the Neotropics. *Science* 214:677–678.

Wilczynski, W., Rand, A. S., and Ryan, M. J. (1995) The processing of spectral cues by the call analysis system of the túngara frog, *Physalaemus pustulosus. Anim. Behav.* 49:911–929.

20 Categorical Perception of Behaviorally Relevant Stimuli by Crickets

Robert A. Wyttenbach and Ronald R. Hoy

In an animal's sensory world, stimuli must be parsed into behaviorally salient categories. This is a trivial task for stimuli that activate different sensory modalities, but for stimuli within the same modality, assessing the behavioral equivalence or difference of a pair of stimuli may demand a high degree of sensitivity. Moreover, the neural basis of this assessment may lie as much in the brain as in the sensory organ itself. Nonetheless, many animals have been shown to possess the ability to differentiate between physically very similar stimuli and to place them in different response categories. There are two ways in which this may be done. An animal may perceive minute differences between many stimuli and then group them into a small number of categories for response. Alternatively, the perceptual system may lump groups of stimuli together into categories before they are perceived, in which case the animal will be able to perceive differences between stimuli only when they fall into different categories. This second mode of perception, categorical perception, is the one that will concern us here. To distinguish categorical perception from continuous perception, it is essential to determine not only how an animal *labels* stimuli (its behavioral response), but also how it *discriminates* between stimuli. One can state that categorical perception occurs only if the animal fails to discriminate between stimuli drawn from the same category. The experimenter's ability to study this discrimination is greatly facilitated when the subject can simply tell the experimenter how it perceives experimental stimuli, and so most of the work on categorical perception is done on humans, particularly within the domain of human speech, in which it was first discovered. There is a voluminous literature on categorical perception in humans (reviewed by Harnad 1987), but the number of documented cases of categorical perception in other animals is rather small (reviewed by Hauser 1996).

Some interesting examples of categorical perception in nonhuman vertebrates come from the work of Kuhl and Miller on chinchillas (1975, 1978), Kuhl and Padden on macaques (1982, 1983), and by Dooling et al. on birds (Dooling and Brown 1990; Dooling 1992; Dooling et al. 1995). In these studies, the investigators showed that these animals were able to differentiate between some sounds of human speech in a way that suggests that the same phonetic cues are used by humans, macaques, chinchillas, and birds. This raises the possibility that the basis of categorical perception lies in features common to vertebrate auditory systems in general. To the neuroethologist, however, a crucial question is whether animals also perform categorical perception on sounds with clear adaptive value, such as conspecific communication signals or the sounds of predators. Peter Marler and his students have made great contributions in the area of how animals classify natural signals. There is, for example, the large body of work by Dorothy Cheney and Robert Seyfarth (1990) on classification of primate vocalizations, following work done with Marler (Seyfarth et al. 1980a,b). Marler himself, with his student Douglas Nelson, demonstrated categorical perception of conspecific songs in the swamp sparrow, using note duration as a cue (Nelson and Marler 1989). They used a habituation paradigm in their experiments, a paradigm that has also been used to investigate discrimination in human infants. As will be seen, the demonstration of categorical perception in animals other than talking humans can be tricky, because it is easy to misinterpret a measure of preference (labeling) as a measure of discrimination. We might call this the "labeling fallacy."

There is little doubt that vertebrate animals other than humans perform categorical perception of salient, adaptive stimuli. But what about the invertebrates, which compose most of the species and biomass of the animal kingdom? Do animals possessing brains with vastly fewer neurons perform such a seemingly demanding task as categorical perception? We suggest that the problem may not be one of the capability of the animal, but of the ability of the experimenter to demonstrate the phenomenon. We have found categorical perception in an insect, a field cricket (Wyttenbach et al. 1996). As we describe below, the trick is to find a repeatable robust behavioral act with which to work, so that the same kinds of psychophysical tests of categorical perception can be applied to an insect as are applied to vertebrates.

Like humans, Polynesian field crickets (*Teleogryllus oceanicus*) face the problem of responding differently to parts of a continuous spectrum. In their case, this is the frequency of sound: conspecific crickets call at 4–5kHz, while predatory bats produce ultrasound (typically 25–80kHz) to echolocate their prey. A flying cricket must make the critical choice between flying toward another cricket's call and escaping from a bat. Although the temporal pattern of sound pulses provides a cue for calling song, this choice can be made based on frequency alone, since a temporal pattern that attracts at 4–5kHz repels at ultrasonic frequencies (Moiseff et al. 1978; Nolen and Hoy 1986). Although attraction (positive phonotaxis) requires a train of pulses in an appropriate temporal pattern, escape (negative phonotaxis) can be elicited by a single pulse of ultrasound. A single pulse at the frequency of calling song does not elicit any behavioral response. Because there is a transition from positive to negative phonotaxis between 10–20kHz (Moiseff et al. 1978), there is a possibility that phonotactic responses result from categorical perception of frequency.

In 1970, Studdert-Kennedy et al. proposed four operational criteria for absolute categorical perception of human speech: (a) distinct labeling categories with sharp boundaries; (b) no discrimination between stimuli from the same category; (c) a peak

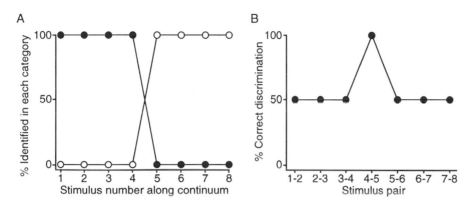

Figure 20.1
Idealized labeling and discrimination functions for categorical perception (after Studdert-Kennedy et al. 1970). (A) Labeling of stimuli distributed along a continuum. (B) Discrimination between equally spaced pairs of stimuli along the continuum.

in discrimination at category boundaries; and (d) close agreement between actual discrimination performance and that predicted from the labeling results assuming absolute categorization. To test these criteria, one must determine both how a subject labels stimuli varying along a continuum and how well that subject discriminates between pairs of stimuli along that continuum. If these criteria are met, the results of labeling and discrimination tests should be as shown in figure 20.1.

Labeling Tests

We tested the crickets' category labeling by presenting synthesized calling-song-like patterns of sound pulses in which only the carrier frequency varied. At the normal carrier frequency, this pattern has been shown to be equally as attractive as the natural song (Pollack and Hoy 1981). If a cricket labels a stimulus as attractive (in the "song" category), it should turn toward the speaker; if it labels a stimulus as repulsive (in the "bat" category), it should turn away from the speaker. There is also the possibility that the cricket does not respond at all.

Methods

This experiment used female *Teleogryllus oceanicus* reared in the laboratory. Crickets were tethered to a thin wire and flown upright in wind stream of 0–3m/s (the normal flight speed). All crickets were pretested for negative phonotaxis to 20kHz and positive phonotaxis to 2.5kHz pulse trains.

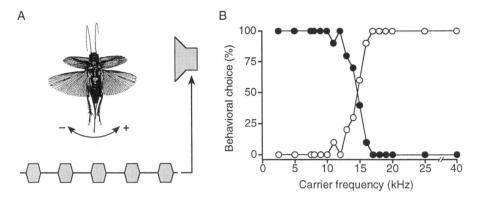

Figure 20.2
Labeling tests. (A) A calling-song-like pattern of pulses is presented and a cricket turns towards or away form the speaker. The carrier frequency of the pulses varies between 2.5–40kHz. (B) When presented with the stimuli in (A), crickets turned toward (filled circles) or away from (open circles) the speaker. There is an abrupt shift from attraction to escape between 13–16kHz, indicating a categorical boundary (N = 10).

The calling song of this species consists of a series of chirps and trills of 4.7kHz, but these crickets respond equally well to a "continuous chirp" song (Pollack and Hoy 1981). The artificial continuous chirp song we used consisted of a 5s train of 30ms pulses with 5ms rise and fall times at a rate of 15 pulses per second (figure 20.2a). All stimuli were presented at 80dB SPL. Carrier frequencies from 2.5–40kHz were presented from the right or left in a randomized order.

During prolonged steering, either toward an attractive stimulus or away from a repulsive one, the forewings bank into the turn and the abdomen swings, rudderlike, toward the turn. Since these tests used trains of stimuli, forewing tilt was used as a measure of steering. Because this is a continuous response, tilt could be monitored visually (on video tapes) and was scored as a turn to the right or to the left, without regard to the magnitude of the turn. All crickets responded with a clear turn toward or away from the speaker at each frequency tested.

Results

If a cricket labeled a stimulus as attractive, it turned toward the speaker; if it labeled a stimulus as repulsive, it turned away from the speaker. The third possibility, that intermediate frequencies would evoke no response, did not occur. The labeling function for 10 crickets (figure 20.2b) shows a sharp transition from attraction to escape between 13–16kHz. Thus the first criterion for categorical perception, distinct labeling categories, is met.

Discrimination Tests

As shown above, testing an animal's labeling along a continuous spectrum merely requires presenting a set of stimuli varying along that spectrum and recording how the response of the subject changes as the stimuli vary. This is relatively simple in animals and has been done several times (reviewed by Ehret 1987). However, determining the sensory discrimination ability of an animal is more problematic. With adult humans, discrimination tests involve some variation of asking whether pairs of stimuli are the same or different and relying on a verbal response. Obviously, this cannot be done directly with nonverbal animals. Conditioning paradigms such as that used by Kuhl and Miller (1978) for chinchillas come closest to this, with the subject motivated to make the best discrimination possible. With animals that cannot be trained, or when unconditional responses to natural stimuli are of interest, this becomes more difficult. Although some studies have attempted to infer discrimination from an animal's choice between two stimuli, such an inference is invalid. The inference that two stimuli are discriminated if one is preferred to another may be correct, but the inference that no preference means no discrimination is not.

In research on human infants, habituation-dishabituation paradigms have been established to circumvent this problem (Miller and Morse 1976); these have also been used to investigate discrimination in monkeys (Morse and Snowdon 1975) and birds (Nelson and Marler 1989). As a stimulus is presented repeatedly, the response of the subject declines. That is, the subject becomes *habituated* to that stimulus. If a second stimulus is then presented, followed by one more repetition of the first stimulus, the response to the last repetition of the first stimulus may show recovery from habituation. That is, the subject is *dishabituated*. Dishabituation occurs only if the second stimulus is perceived by the subject as a novel stimulus. Thus dishabituation can be used as a measure of sensory discrimination, since dishabituation can occur only if the two stimuli are discriminated. In the literature on human infants, this is often referred to as a variety of "same-different" test.

The ultrasound-induced escape response of crickets decrements with repetition in a way consistent with standard criteria for habituation (Thompson and Spencer 1966). It declines nearly exponentially, recovers spontaneously, declines more rapidly with higher repetition or lower amplitude, and recovers following the presentation of a novel stimulus (May and Hoy 1991). Thus dishabituation of the escape response can be used as a "same-different" test for crickets just as it has been used with human infants and other animals. A frequency that is discriminated from the habituating ultrasound will cause dishabituation, while a stimulus that is not discriminated from that frequency of ultrasound will not. This allows us to test frequency discrimination within the ultrasound category and between the ultrasound and song categories.

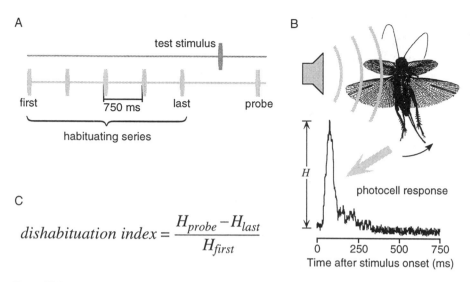

Figure 20.3
Dishabituation tests. (A) Five pulses of ultrasound were presented to habituate the cricket, followed by a test pulse, followed by a final ("probe") pulse of ultrasound. All pulses are 750ms apart. (B) The photocell trace of a hind leg swing resulting from a single pulse of ultrasound. (C) Calculation of the amount of dishabituation based on the responses to pulses shown in (A).

Methods

Subjects were chosen and tethered as before, except that males were used and pre-testing was done only with ultrasound. Stimuli consisted of single 10ms pulses with 1ms rise and fall times. The threshold intensity required to evoke an escape response was determined for each cricket before experiments. A single pulse of 20kHz was repeated 5 times with a 750ms interval to let the escape response habituate. After another 750ms, a single 10ms pulse of the test frequency was presented, followed after another 750ms by a final pulse of 20kHz (figure 20.3a). Pulses of 20kHz were 10dB above the previously determined behavioral threshold; the test pulse was another 10dB greater than this amplitude. The side of the habituating pulses (left or right) varied from trial to trial. Test pulses could come either from the same side as the habituating series or from the opposite side. All crickets were tested for habituation to 20kHz and for dishabituation with 20kHz from the side opposite the habituating pulse. For each test frequency used, at least 5 crickets were tested with at least 2 trials per cricket with the test pulse coming from either the same side as the habituating pulses or from the opposite side. Each cricket was not tested at each frequency. Instead, trials continued as long as a cricket continued to fly and to have a stable threshold for ultrasound response.

Habituation-dishabituation tests used single pulses of sound, so only the fast swing of the metathoracic leg could be used as an indicator of steering. Furthermore, measuring habituation and dishabituation requires that all responses be quantitatively recorded. For this, we used a photoresistor that produced a signal proportional to the amount of leg swing. After each habituation trial, all responses (figure 20.3b) were normalized to the first response and a dishabituation index was calculated (figure 20.3c). This amounts to the difference between the probe pulse and the last habituating pulse after both have been normalized to the first of the habituating pulses.

Results

The degree of habituation occurring after 5 pulses of 20kHz varied from trial to trial and between individuals, but the response to the fifth habituating pulse was reduced to 10–50% of the initial response. There may or may not have been any response to the test pulse, and the extent to which the response to the final pulse of 20kHz dishabituated depended on the frequency of the test pulse (figure 20.4). If the test pulse was replaced with silence, the probe pulse recovered by .01 ± .02 units (mean ± SEM), showing that the absence of ultrasound in that position was not sufficient to cause dishabituation or significant recovery from habituation. Furthermore, a 10dB increase in amplitude of the test pulse did not itself cause dishabituation, as is shown by the 20kHz response in figure 20.5a.

When presented from the side opposite the 5 habituating pulses, a test pulse of any frequency caused dishabituation (figure 20.5b). This test was required to show that all frequencies tested were perceived and capable of producing dishabituation. Of the frequencies tested, only those below 16kHz caused significant dishabituation when presented from the same speaker as the habituating train (figure 20.5a). Thus there is sharp between-category discrimination but no discrimination within the ultrasound category, satisfying the remaining criteria for categorical perception. Dishabituation could not be used to test discrimination within the calling-song category, however, because attraction to calling song builds up slowly and habituates irregularly if at all (Moiseff et al. 1978).

Discussion

Categorical Perception in Crickets

Labeling results show an abrupt transition from positive to negative phonotaxis, meeting the criterion of distinct labeling categories with a sharp boundary. The dishabituation results meet the criteria of no discrimination within the ultrasound

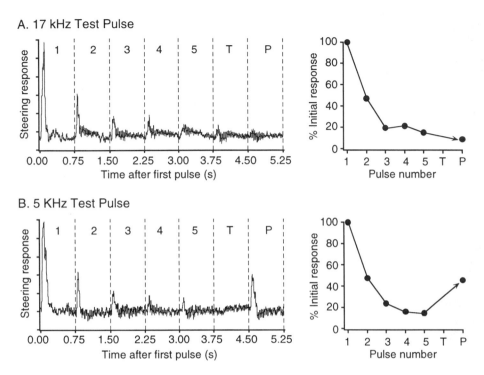

A. 17 kHz Test Pulse

B. 5 KHz Test Pulse

Figure 20.4
Habituation and dishabituation. Left panels show photocell traces during a single trial of one cricket; right panels show the measured and normalized responses. The habituating and probe pulses are all 20kHz. (A) The test pulse is 17kHz, which results in no dishabituation (index $= -0.08$). (B) A test pulse of 5kHz evokes significant dishabituation (index $= +0.31$).

category and sharp discrimination between categories. Both tests of categorical perception show a categorical boundary between 13–16kHz. This is an interesting and perhaps surprising result, given that this range has no known behavioral significance to this species (Libersat et al. 1994). Communication calls of *Teleogryllus* spp. are 4–5kHz with relatively little energy at higher harmonics; echolocation cries of bats are between 25–80kHz. There is a large gap between these two ranges, and one might expect either that the frequencies between them would elicit no behavioral response or that attraction and avoidance would grade into each other over this range, given that there is no clear selective pressure to avoid 16–25kHz or to be attracted to 7–13kHz. It has been suggested that categorical perception in general functions to allow fast and accurate perceptual decisions (Rosch 1978); this is plausible in the case of the cricket, in which a rapid choice between attraction and escape is crucial to survival.

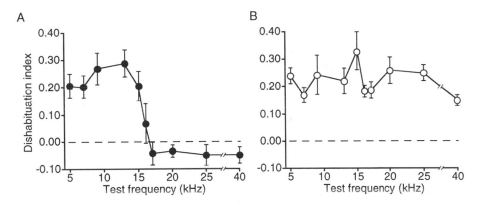

Figure 20.5
Frequency discrimination. (A) When habituating and test pulses were presented from the same speaker, only frequencies below 16kHz evoke dishabituation. Thus only these frequencies were discriminated from 20kHz. (B) When the habituating and test pulses were presented from opposite speakers, any frequency evokes dishabituation. Thus the crickets did perceive all frequencies and could discriminate them on the basis of location. (Mean ± SEM; 5–8 crickets per point).

There is a slight mismatch between the boundaries found by the labeling and dishabituation tests. The labeling tests show 15kHz to be an ambiguous stimulus (60% negative phonotaxis) and 16kHz to be a clearly negative stimulus (90% negative). The dishabituation tests, on the other hand, show that 15kHz is clearly discriminated from ultrasound and 16kHz is an ambiguous stimulus. Such a mismatch is not uncommon in categorical perception (Pastore 1987). In this case, there may be a simple explanation based on the temporal characteristics of the stimuli used. Labeling stimuli were presented in an attractive temporal pattern mimicking that of calling song, while discrimination stimuli were presented as single pulses, which are never attractive. If 15 and 16kHz are in fact both ambiguous stimuli, it is likely that the attractive pattern would bias both of them toward positive phonotaxis in the labeling tests, while the single-pulse pattern would bias both toward negative phonotaxis in the discrimination tests.

The Dishabituation Test

The dishabituation paradigm was originally developed for studies of perception in human infants because they could not give verbal answers of "same" or "different" when presented with pairs of stimuli. Our experiments illustrate that this technique is also useful with crickets. There are several advantages of this method. First, only the stimulus used in the habituating series must elicit a measurable behavior. The test stimulus need not elicit a behavior itself, because its effects are seen instead in the response to the final probe pulse. Second, it is possible to show that two stimuli are discriminated even though both may give rise to the same magnitude and orientation of behavior. In this case, if crickets had been able to discriminate between 20–25kHz, both would give rise to a turn away from the speaker but there would still have been dishabituation of the final response. This point became more important later when we applied the habituation-dishabituation test to sound localization (Wyttenbach and Hoy 1997).

A limitation of this approach, which is evident in these experiments, is that it is possible to test discrimination only in cases in which one of the stimuli to be tested can elicit behavior with a single presentation and in which that behavior habituates. This meant that we were restricted to testing discrimination between ultrasound frequencies and between ultrasound and low frequency. We could not test discrimination between 5–10kHz, for example, because neither of those frequencies elicits a behavior with a single pulse. Thus our experiments leave open the possibility that crickets can distinguish frequencies within the low frequency calling-song category.

Although widely used, dishabituation is not well understood, and its use as a discrimination test involves several assumptions. The main difficulty lies in the interpretation of no dishabituation. It is assumed that dishabituation occurs when stimuli are discriminated and that lack of dishabituation indicates lack of discrimination. The best verification of these assumptions is to show that the results of dishabituation tests conform with results of other discrimination tests. In the absence of that, we have at least shown (1) that dishabituation does not require that the test stimulus evoke a behavior different from the habituating stimuli or even that it evoke any behavior at all (single pulses of 5kHz dishabituate but evoke no behavior); and (2) that lack of dishabituation is not due to test stimuli not being perceived at all (ultrasound test pulses that do not dishabituate still evoke negative phonotaxis), being of too low an intensity (ultrasound test pulses were 10dB over habituating pulses), or being incapable of causing dishabituation under any circumstances (all frequencies cause dishabituation when presented contralaterally to the habituating stimuli).

Other "Dishabituation" Tests

Most of the discrimination tests described in the literature as dishabituation tests are in fact tests of the generalization of habituation and do not involve dishabituation at all. Dishabituation refers to recovery of the response to the *original habituating stimulus* after presentation of a novel stimulus. Generalization refers to attenuation of the response to a *novel stimulus* presented after habituation (Thompson and Spencer 1966).

In a true test of dishabituation, a series of stimuli is presented to habituate the subject, followed by a test stimulus, followed by another presentation of the original habituating stimulus, as in figure 20.6a. If the test stimulus is sufficiently novel relative to the habituating stimulus, then the response to the final presentation of the habituating stimulus increases beyond that expected if habituation had continued. That is, the response was dishabituated. The inference, again, is that dishabituation occurs when the test and habituating stimuli are discriminated but not when they are not discriminated.

In a test of generalization of habituation, a series of stimuli is presented to habituate the subject, followed by a test stimulus, as in figure 20.6b. If the response to the test stimulus is attenuated, then habituation was generalized between the two stimuli, and the inference may be that they were not discriminated. If the response to the test stimulus is normal, then habituation was not generalized, and the inference may be that the two stimuli were discriminated. This failure of generalization is often, but incorrectly, referred to as dishabituation.

Does it matter whether a discrimination test stops after the test stimulus and measures generalization or returns to the original habituating stimulus and measures dishabituation? There is at least one case in the cricket in which the two tests give different results: habituation generalizes between two stimuli but dishabituation still occurs. We have used dishabituation to test the spatial acuity of cricket hearing (Wyttenbach and Hoy 1997). This involved habituating the cricket with ultrasound from a speaker at one location and presenting a test pulse from a speaker at another location. An unhabituated cricket makes left turns of equal magnitude away from ultrasound presented from either 67° or 112° to the right of the midline. If a cricket is habituated to ultrasound from 67° and then tested with ultrasound from 112°, the response to the test stimulus is attenuated, and so habituation is generalized between the two stimuli. However, the response to a subsequent stimulus from 67° shows recovery from habituation, and so a stimulus from 112° does dishabituate the response to a stimulus from 67° (figure 20.6c). Thus, in this case, generalization seems to occur between stimuli that give rise to the same behavioral decision (right turn or left turn), while dishabituation indicates that those stimuli are discriminated.

This suggests is that as a discrimination test, dishabituation is much more sensitive than generalization of habituation. It should not be surprising that generalization is not very sensitive as a discrimination test, given the results of several primate studies using natural calls. Cheney and Seyfarth (1988), for example, showed that vervet monkeys generalize habituation between calls that are acoustically quite distinct, as long as the caller and meaning of call were the same. Similarly, Hauser (1998) shows that rhesus monkeys generalize habituation between acoustically distinct calls

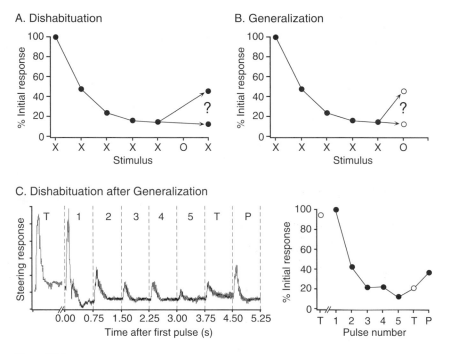

Figure 20.6
Habituation tests. (A) In a true dishabituation test, the subject is first habituated with one stimulus (X), presented with a test stimulus (O), and then with another of the original habituating stimulus (X). If the final response increases significantly above the habituated level, then dishabituation occurred. (B) In a test of generalization of habituation, the subject is first habituated with one stimulus (X) and then presented with a test stimulus (O). If the response to the test stimulus is attenuated, then habituation was generalized between the two stimuli. (C) When habituation is generalized between two stimuli, dishabituation can still occur. In this case, the habituating stimulus is ultrasound from 67° to the right of the cricket and the test stimulus is ultrasound from 112° to the right. The first trace in the left panel and the first open circle in the right panel show the response to 112° without any prior stimuli. The next five responses (1–5, filled circles) show habituation of the response to 67°. The next response (T, open circle) is to 112°, showing that this habituation was generalized. The final response (P, filled circle) is to 67° again, and shows dishabituation due to the 112° test pulse.

that have the same referent. In neither of these studies is it argued that the subjects cannot discriminate between the acoustically distinct but referentially similar calls. Rather, it is argued that generalization of habituation is based on classification instead of discrimination. It would be interesting to know what would have happened in these experiments if a full dishabituation trial had been presented. If primates are anything like crickets in this regard, acoustically dissimilar calls should cause dishabituation whether or not habituation had generalized between them.

This is not to suggest that there is anything wrong with the generalization test as such, or with the many studies that have used it, as long as it is understood that this is not a very sensitive test of discrimination, and as long as the proper term is used to describe it. Indeed, we think much could be learned by comparing dishabituation with generalization, and would urge that those who use generalization tests go ahead and repeat the habituating stimulus after the test stimulus to see whether true dishabituation occurs.

The "Labeling Fallacy"

Most cases of categorical labeling are probably not due to categorical perception. In such cases, an animal is able to discriminate between stimuli that evoke the same behavioral response. To demonstrate categorical perception, one must show not only that a broad range of stimuli evokes one response while an adjacent range evokes a different response, but also that stimuli that evoke the same response do so because they are not discriminated. In practice, it is impossible to prove beyond doubt that an animal cannot discriminate between two stimuli. The best that one can do is apply the most sensitive discrimination test available for the animal in question. In the case of the cricket, we were fortunate that the startle response showed dishabituation after a novel stimulus. However, it is generally difficult to design a true discrimination test for an animal that cannot be conditioned, and it is easy to be led astray by experiments that look like discrimination tests but that are in fact merely preference tests. This can be illustrated by two examples.

The first example comes from our own examination of categorical perception in crickets. After performing the labeling experiments (figure 20.2b) and getting results similar to those theoretically required for categorical perception (figure 20.1a), we attempted to replicate, as closely as possible, the human discrimination experiments that give rise to the sort of result shown in figure 20.1b. In these experiments, a subject is presented with pairs of equally spaced stimuli and asked whether they are the same or different. If discrimination is categorical, the results are as in figure 20.1b, with a peak in discriminability at the category boundary; if discrimination is continuous, discriminability is relatively flat across the stimulus continuum. We presented

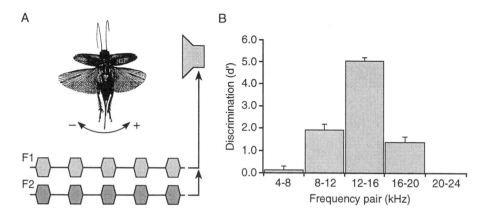

Figure 20.7
A misleading discrimination function. (A) Each cricket was tested with a pair of frequencies. Responses were scored as explained in the text. (B) "Discrimination" within each frequency pair is shown as d', a calculated measure in which a higher d' means better discrimination (e.g., the highest d' shown here, 5, corresponded to a 95% correct "discrimination"). (Mean ± SEM; 6 crickets; 6 trials per cricket per test pair.)

pairs of frequencies in a two-interval-same-different paradigm (Macmillan et al. 1977). In this paradigm, for each pair of stimuli A and B, the cricket was tested with pairs A + A, A + B, B + A, and B + B. If the cricket responded the same to A + A or B + B, this was scored as a "hit," while if it responded the same to A + B or B + A, it was scored as a "false alarm." From the proportion of hits and false alarms, we calculated d' (a measure of discrimination) from the tables of Kaplan et al. (1978). This gave the discrimination function of figure 20.7, which corresponded nicely to the labeling results of figure 20.2b, and which seemed to complete the demonstration of categorical perception. However, on closer examination, it became clear that we had not actually performed a discrimination test, but only a succession of preference tests. A cricket merely chose independently for each stimulus of the pair whether to fly toward or away from it, without making any judgment of "same" or "different" between the two stimuli. Just because a cricket made the same choice for both stimuli of a pair did not mean that it could not discriminate between them, but only that it labeled them in the same way.

A similar situation occurs in work said to demonstrate categorical perception of mouse pup distress calls by lactating female mice (Ehret 1992; Ehret and Haack 1981). The mouse pup distress call consists of band-limited ultrasound noise bursts. In Ehret's experiments, a lactating female mouse was allowed to run toward one of two speakers broadcasting natural or simulated calls. First, a simple (pure 20kHz) artificial call was tested against a natural call, and there was a clear preference for the natural call. Next, a series of artificial calls varying in bandwidth was tested against the simple call from the first experiment. This showed that artificial calls with narrow bandwidths were preferred over the simple call, while artificial calls with wider bandwidths were not, and that there was a sharp boundary between the two categories. Thus there are two categories of artificial calls, attractive and unattractive, with a sharp boundary between them, which is suggestive of categorical perception. As a discrimination test, pairs of stimuli were presented in which both calls had previously been judged attractive or unattractive or in which one of the pair had been judged attractive and the other unattractive. In these tests, the female mice showed a clear preference for the attractive call when the other call had previously been judged unattractive; when both calls of the pair were attractive or both were unattractive, there was no preference. This was interpreted as showing that within-category pairs were not discriminated and that between-category pairs were discriminated (Ehret and Haack 1981). However, like our d' test, this was merely another preference, or labeling, test, not a discrimination test. All it proves is that the attractive calls were equally attractive, the unattractive calls equally unattractive, and the attractive calls more attractive than the unattractive calls. There is as yet no evidence for lack of discrimination between equally attractive or equally unattractive calls and thus no demonstration of categorical perception. Of course, it remains an open question whether the female mice do perceive distress calls categorically. Because mice should be amenable to conditioning paradigms using these stimuli, it should still be possible to answer this question with a more sensitive discrimination test.

Why Categorical Perception?

We started by noting that there are two ways in which an animal could produce categorical responses to continuous stimuli: it could perceive minute differences along the stimulus continuum and then make categorical decisions, or it could do the categorization early in sensory processing, before perceiving the differences. Although categorical perception has been found in a diverse set of animals since its initial discovery in humans, it does not appear to be ubiquitous. More accurately, we should state that it is not yet clear whether categorical perception is ubiquitous, for it has been subjected to rigorous testing in only a very small number of animals. Clearly not all cases of categorical *responses* are due to categorical *perception*, so what is special in those cases that are? Attempting to understand categorical perception in an evolutionary context raises two questions. First, what in general is the adaptive benefit of categorical perception; what is it good for? Second, why is categorical perception found in some cases of categorical response but not in others; what is the trade-off of costs and benefits of categorical perception that produced this pattern?

The major benefit of categorical perception is generally assumed to be speed of decision making. By categorizing stimuli directly, before bothering to perceive minute differences between them, an animal is able to respond much more quickly. This is a reasonable, though probably untestable, assumption that we will accept for now.

What accounts for the presence of categorical perception in some cases and its absence in others? An ethological approach suggests that we should look for categorical perception in situations in which there is selective pressure for categorical distinctions and, perhaps more importantly, in which there is no significant pressure against nondiscrimination of same-category stimuli. Because of the long association of categorical perception with perception of speech and other complex signals, a cricket might be the last animal in which one would expect to find categorical perception. However, the cricket may also be the nonhuman animal in which it is easiest to explain the adaptive value of the phenomenon. To a cricket, the frequency of sound within a category carries no information that is crucial to survival: ultrasound means a bat, and it doesn't matter what kind of bat, while the species-specificity of cricket calling songs is determined by the temporal pattern rather than the frequency of the song. Thus the cricket meets our two conditions: adaptive necessity of rapid categorization and low cost of nondiscrimination within each category.

In the case of human perception of human speech sounds, categorical perception can be understood as a means of making distinctions between the many complex sounds that make up speech. The benefit of categorical perception is speed and accuracy in making these discriminations. There is also, presumably, a cost to categorical perception, in that it should cause failure to discriminate certain nonspeech sounds. This has apparently not been tested, but the cost does not appear to be great. The same argument can be made for animals in which categorical perception of communication signals has been found, although the sets of stimuli involved are considerably smaller.

When we ask this question about other animals in which categorical perception has been found, the situation is much less clear. Why should chinchillas or birds perceive the sounds of human speech categorically? These are not, after all, sounds with known behavioral relevance to the animals in question. One suggestion is that these animals simply share with humans certain common features of a vertebrate auditory system, and that this includes categorical perception of some of the same stimuli. As neuroethologists, we find this explanation unsatisfying. Clearly vertebrate auditory systems are structurally similar, but why should this result in categorical perception of the same stimulus features by humans, in which those stimuli form part of the set of communication signals, and by chinchillas and birds, for which these stimuli have no obvious innate behavioral relevance? The answer may lie in the nature of the stimulus features themselves. The task is to pare speech stimuli down to their essentials to determine just which features cause them to be perceived categorically by these animals. For example, many of the speech sounds that have been tested on animals vary primarily in temporal structure. Categorical perception of these sounds by animals may be due to temporal auditory processing normally done in other circumstances. If so, categorical perception of these strictly temporal features should also occur with nonspeech stimuli that may be more behaviorally relevant to the animal.

We conclude by reiterating the desire, earlier stated by Ehret (1987), that categorical perception be put in an evolutionary framework in all of the animals in which it has been found, from crickets through birds, chinchillas, and monkeys, to humans. Only when we understand the function and origins of this important form of perception can we make informed hypotheses about the evolution of speech itself.

References

Cheney, D. L. and Seyfarth, R. M. (1988) Assessment of meaning and the detection of unreliable signals by vervet monkeys. *Anim. Behav.* 36:477–486.

Cheney, D. L. and Seyfarth, R. M. (1990) *How Monkeys See the World: Inside the Mind of Another Species.* Chicago. Chicago University Press.

Dooling, R. J. (1992) Perception of speech sounds by birds. *Adv. Biosci.* 83:407–413.

Dooling, R. J. and Brown, S. D. (1990) Speech perception by budgerigars *Melopsittacus undulatus*: Spoken vowels. *Percept. Psychophys.* 47:568–574.

Dooling, R. J., Best, C. T., and Brown, S. D. (1995). Discrimination of synthetic full-formant and sine-wave /ra-la/ continua by budgerigars (*Melopsittacus undulatus*) and zebra finches (*Taeniopygia guttata*). *J. Acoust. Soc. Am.* 97:1839–1846.

Ehret, G. (1987) Categorical perception of sound signals: Facts and hypotheses from animal studies. In *Categorical Perception: The Groundwork of Cognition*, ed. by S. Harnad, pp. 301–331. New York: Cambridge University Press.

Ehret, G. (1992) Categorical perception of mouse-pup ultrasounds in the temporal domain. *Anim. Behav.* 43:409–416.

Ehret, G. and Haack, B. (1981) Categorical perception of mouse pup ultrasound by lactating females. *Naturwissenschaften* 68:208–209.

Harnad, S., ed. (1987) *Categorical Perception: The Groundwork of Cognition.* New York: Cambridge University Press.

Hauser, M. D. (1996) *The Evolution of Communication.* Cambridge, MA: The MIT Press.

Hauser, M. D. (1998) Functional referents and acoustic similarity: Field playback experiments with rhesus monkeys. *Anim. Behav.* 55:1647–1658.

Kaplan, H. L., MacMillan, N. A., and Creelman, C. D. (1978) Methods and designs: Tables of d' for variable-standard discrimination paradigms. *Behav. Res. Meth. Inst.* 10:796–813.

Kuhl, P. K. and Miller, J. D. (1975) Speech perception by the chinchilla: Voiced-voiceless distinction in alveolar plosive consonants. *Science* 190:69–72.

Kuhl, P. K. and Miller, J. D. (1978) Speech perception by the chinchilla: Identification functions for synthetic VOT stimuli. *J. Acoust. Soc. Am.* 63:905–917.

Kuhl, P. K. and Padden, D. M. (1982) Enhanced discriminability at the phonetic boundaries for the voicing feature in macaques. *Percept. Psychophys.* 32:542–550.

Kuhl, P. K. and Padden, D. M. (1983) Enhanced discriminability at the phonetic boundaries for the placd feature in macaques. *J. Acoust. Soc. Am.* 73:1003–1010.

Libersat, F., Murray, J. A., and Hoy, R. R. (1994) Frequency as a releaser in the courtship song of two crickets, *Gryllus bimaculatus* (de Geer) and *Teleogryllus oceanicus*: A neuroethological analysis. *J. Comp. Physiol.* 174:485–494.

Macmillan, N. A., Kaplan, H. L., and Creelman, C. D. (1977) The psychophysics of categorical perception. *Psych. Rev.* 84:452–471.

May, M. L. and Hoy, R. R. (1991) Habituation of the ultrasound-induced acoustic startle response in flying crickets. *J. Exp. Biol.* 159:489–499.

Miller, C. L. and Morse, P. A. (1976) The "heart" of categorical speech discrimination in young infants. *J. Speech Hearing Res.* 19:578–589.

Moiseff, A., Pollack, G. S., and Hoy, R. R. (1978) Steering responses of flying crickets to sound and ultrasound: Mate attraction and predator avoidance. *Proc. Natl. Acad. Sci.* (USA) 75:4052–4056.

Morse, P. A. and Snowdon, C. T. (1975) An investigation of categorical speech discrimination by rhesus monkeys. *Percept. Psychophys.* 17:9–16.

Nelson, D. A. and Marler, P. (1989) Categorical perception of a natural stimulus continuum: Birdsong. *Science* 244:976–978.

Nolen, T. G. and Hoy, R. R. (1986) Phonotaxis in flying crickets. I. Attraction to the calling song and avoidance of bat-like ultrasound are discrete behaviors. *J. Comp. Physiol.* 159:423–439.

Pastore, R. E. (1987) Categorical perception: Some psychophysical models. In *Categorical Perception: The Groundwork of Cognition*, ed. by S. Harnad, pp. 301–331. New York: Cambridge University Press.

Pollack, G. S. and Hoy, R. R. (1981) Phonotaxis to individual rhythmic components of a complex cricket calling song. *J. Comp. Physiol.* 144:367–373.

Rosch, E. (1978) Principles of categorization. In *Cognition and Categorization*, ed. by E. Rosch, and B. B. Lloyd, pp. 27–48. Hillsdale, NJ: Erlbaum.

Seyfarth, R. M., Cheney, D. L., and Marler, P. (1980a) Monkey responses to three different alarm calls: Evidence of predator classification and semantic communication. *Science* 210:801–803.

Seyfarth, R. M., Cheney, D. L., and Marler, P. (1980b) Vervet monkey alarm calls: Semantic communication in a free-ranging primate. *Anim. Behav.* 28:1070–1094.

Studdert-Kennedy, M., Liberman, A., Harris, K. S., and Cooper, F. S. (1970) Motor theory of speech perception. *Psych. Rev.* 77:234–249.

Thompson, R. F. and Spencer, W. A. (1966) Habituation: A model phenomenon for the study of neuronal substrates of behavior. *Psych. Rev.* 173:16–43.

Wyttenbach, R. A. and Hoy, R. R. (1997) Spatial acuity of ultrasound hearing in flying crickets. *J. Exp. Biol.* 200:1999–2006.

Wyttenbach, R. A., May, M. L., and Hoy, R. R. (1996) Categorical perception of sound frequency by crickets. *Science* 273:1542–1544.

21 Functions of Song Variation in Song Sparrows

William A. Searcy and Stephen Nowicki

Almost any animal signal varies from performance to performance, both within and between individuals. Human speech offers one set of examples, and birdsong another, with some interesting parallels between the two. The same words produced by people in separate geographic areas often show systematic "dialect" differences; just so, birdsong typically varies geographically within a species. People within a geographic neighborhood also differ in speech, such that individuals can be recognized by their speech patterns; in the same way, individual birds can be recognized by their songs. Finally, one person often varies the production of a single word or phrase between performances. At this level, the parallel between birdsong and speech becomes hazier, because strict analogues to human words or phrases do not exist in birdsong, but clearly song production also may vary considerably within individual birds.

In this chapter, we address the functional importance of variation in birdsong at each of the above levels: within individuals, between individuals within populations, and between populations. We use as our model organism the song sparrow (*Melospiza melodia*), a species in which song variation is particularly marked. In our analysis of function, we keep two assumptions in mind. First, to be relevant to the evolution of signal characteristics, a selective advantage for signal variation must benefit the signaler, rather than the receiver or population (Dawkins and Krebs 1978); this assumption simply extends the primacy of individual selection to signal variation. Second, song variation at some levels may not be functional at all. Mechanisms of genetic and cultural transmission of song across generations, as well as production error, serve to introduce variation; therefore song may vary because selection in favor of stereotypy is not strong enough to eliminate these sources of variation, rather than because variation is beneficial.

Song-sparrow song appears to fulfill the typical functions of song in passerine birds, of attracting and stimulating females (Nice 1943; Searcy and Marler 1981) and repelling other males from the singer's territory (Nowicki et al. 1998a). To fulfill these functions, song-sparrow song presumably must be recognized by other song sparrows as a conspecific signal. Song sparrows of both sexes respond preferentially to song-sparrow song relative to songs of other species, and gross alteration of either the pattern of phrases or the syllable makeup of the song causes response to diminish (Peters et al. 1980; Searcy et al. 1981). Research on other species has shown that particular acoustic features of song must remain within certain limits for the song to be recognized by conspecifics. In the field sparrow (*Spizella pusilla*), for example, male response to modified songs falls off when features such as note duration and frequency are altered by two to three standard deviations relative to the mean of natural songs (Nelson 1988). Thus, to fulfill its functions in territory defense and mate attraction, song-sparrow song must retain certain features that label it as the song of a song sparrow. These features define a volume in a "signal space" (Nelson and Marler 1990), and selection for stereotypy occurs because songs that vary outside that volume will not be recognized and therefore will not be fully functional. The features that define this signal volume are subject to evolutionary change, but we assume that at any given time (such as the present), they are almost certainly held in stasis by stabilizing selection.

Within-male Variation

Saunders (1924) made systematic records of song-sparrow song, using handwritten notations, and concluded that "each individual has a number of totally distinct songs, and often minor variations of the same song." Later workers used sonagraphic analysis to confirm these observations (Mulligan 1963, 1966; Borror 1965). We use the term "song types" for the totally distinct songs, and "variants" for the minor variations. Male song sparrows typically have repertoires of 5–14 song types (Borror 1965; Searcy 1984). Figure 21.1 shows the song types in one male's repertoire together with examples of variants.

Some authors have emphasized the magnitude of within-song-type variation in song sparrows (Wheeler and Nichols 1924; Stoddard et al. 1988), with the effect of casting doubt on the validity of song types as categories. Song type classifications are vulnerable to criticism because they typically have been formed by the subjective sorting of songs into categories by human observers. Three recent lines of evidence, however, combine to support the validity of such classifications. First, Podos et al. (1992) developed an objective method for classifying songs to song types. Songs are broken into "minimal units of production" or "MUPs," representing the smallest invariant elements in a male's repertoire. The proportion of MUPs shared between two songs is used to measure the similarity of those songs. Cluster analysis is performed on the set of songs recorded from a given male, and songs are assigned to song types at the level of clustering at which groups are maximally isolated. Podos et al. (1992) classified the songs of 12 males using both MUP analysis and the traditional subjective sorting method and found the two analyses on average agreed on the classification of 96.5% of recorded songs.

Second, Stoddard et al. (1992a) trained two male song sparrows to peck a key (GO) in response to playback of one set of 32 song types and to refrain from pecking

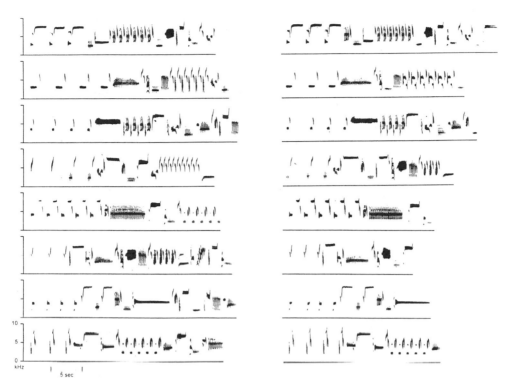

Figure 21.1
The repertoire of one male song sparrow, illustrating his eight song types in the left hand column, with a second variant of each type in the right hand column. Note the typical form of song sparrow song, in which strings of repeated syllables ("trills") alternate with groups of unrepeated notes ("note complexes").

(NOGO) for a second set of 32 song types. Once this discrimination was learned, the birds were presented with new variants of a subset of the GO and NOGO song types. The subjects generalized their training to the new variants with little drop in performance, showing that song sparrows tend to classify variants of the same song type together.

Third, Searcy et al. (1995) exposed individual males to hour-long playbacks of a single variant of one song type followed by six minutes of either a second variant of the same song type or six minutes of a new song type. Mean distance of subjects to the speaker decreased over the first two three-minute playback periods and then slowly increased over the next 18 periods as the subjects habituated to playback (figure 21.2). Recovery was seen as a renewed approach to the speaker after the switch

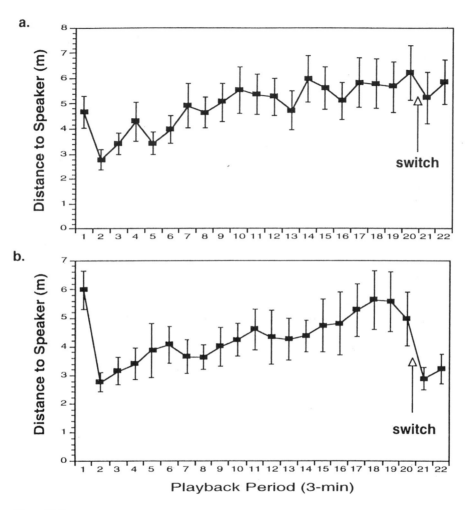

Figure 21.2
Response of male song sparrows to a switch to either (a) a new variant or (b) a new song type. A base song was played to a male on his territory for 60 minutes; playback then switched to a second variant of the same song type or to a new song type from the same male. Response was measured as the subject's distance to the speaker. Recovery was significantly greater for switches between song types than for switches between variants. Data from Searcy et al. 1995.

in playback songs. Significant recovery occurred for both between-type and between-variant switches, but it was significantly greater for the former. These results indicate that song sparrows regard song types as being more distinctive than variants.

Function of Song Type Repertoires

One approach to studying the function of a trait is to examine patterns of use, under the assumption that the context in which the trait is used can reveal its functions. Using this approach, Kramer and Lemon (1983) showed that as the context of singing becomes more aggressive, male song sparrows switch between song types with increasing frequency. Switching frequencies increase steadily between solo singing, countersinging, and pre- and postfight singing. Kramer et al. (1985) manipulated context experimentally and confirmed that switching rates are higher in more aggressive contexts. These patterns suggest that male song sparrows use switching between song types to signal level of aggressive motivation.

Song sparrows also use their repertoires in matched countersinging. Song type matching, in which a male responds to another singer by singing the same song type, is thought to be a method of directing a signal at a particular rival (Bremond 1968). In a Washington population, Stoddard et al. (1992b) found that males matched playback of stranger and their own song significantly more often than expected by chance, but matched neighbor song at only chance levels. Close resemblance between song types is found mainly among neighbors in this population (Beecher et al. 1994a, 1996), yet males rarely match neighbor song, which suggests that song type matching is unimportant. Beecher et al. (1996) proposed instead that song sparrows reply to a neighbor not with the song type the neighbor has just sung, but with any shared song type, a behavior they term "repertoire matching." In playback experiments, Washington males replied to neighbor song with repertoire matches during 87.5% of trials, significantly more often than expected from the 42% sharing of song between neighbors.

If repertoire matching is advantageous in allowing stronger signals of aggression to neighbors, then singing multiple song types would be advantageous in allowing matching with more than one neighbor. Therefore "it may be sharing of song types with several neighbors, rather than the number of song types *per se*, that is the target of selection" in the evolution of repertoires (Beecher et al. 1994a). One problem with this hypothesis is that song type sharing between neighbors is rare in some song sparrow populations, which nonetheless have song repertoires. In our Pennsylvania study population, the mean percentage of the repertoire shared between pairs of neighbors is only 3% (Hughes et al. 1998), compared with 42% in Washington (Beecher et al. 1996). In Pennsylvania, fewer than 20% of neighbor pairs share any song types, compared with approximately 100% in Washington. The Pennsylvania pattern of low song sharing seems to hold for most of the populations for which there are data, that is, in Maine (Borror 1965), northern California (Mulligan 1966; Baker 1983), and Quebec (Harris and Lemon 1972). Levels of sharing appear intermediate in southern California (Eberhardt and Baptista 1977). In areas where most pairs of neighbors do not share song types, repertoire matching cannot be a common strategy. Because male song sparrows have repertoires whether or not sharing is frequent enough to allow repertoire matching, it seems unlikely that matching has been central to the evolution of repertoires.

A second method for studying function is to manipulate a signal experimentally and measure short-term effects on the signal's efficacy. We used this approach to study the function of song repertoires in signaling to females. Searcy and Marler (1981) showed that female song sparrows primed with estradiol perform more copulation solicitation display in response to playback of 32 songs of 4 song types than to 32 songs of a single song type (figure 21.3). Further experiments showed that females respond more to playback of 8 song types than to 4, and more to 16 song types than to 8 (figure 21.3) (Searcy 1984). Potency of songs in eliciting courtship from females is known to correlate with male success in copulation in brown-headed cowbirds (*Molothrus ater*) (West et al. 1981), and song repertoire size is known to correlate

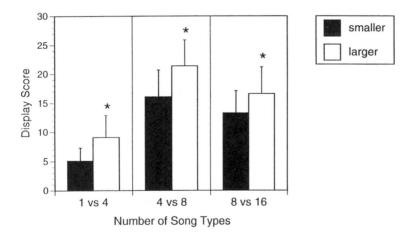

Figure 21.3
Response of female song sparrows to playback of larger or smaller repertoires of song types. Display score combines the number and intensity of copulation solicitation displays performed by captive females in response to playback. Means $\pm$ s.e. are shown. An asterisk indicates a significant difference at $P < 0.05$. Data from Searcy and Marler 1981 and Searcy 1984.

with success in extrapair fertilization in great reed warblers (*Acrocephalus arundinaceus*) (Hasselquist et al. 1996). Neither of these relationships has yet been demonstrated in song sparrows, but it is a reasonable inference from the laboratory results that song repertoires function in increasing male copulatory success in this species.

Hiebert et al. (1989) applied a third approach to studying the function of song sparrow repertoires, in which natural variation in the trait is related to fitness. In a sample of 16 males from an island population in British Columbia, repertoire size showed an astonishingly high correlation with lifetime reproductive success (LRS), with variation in repertoire size accounting for 50% of the variation in LRS. Although the relationship between fitness and repertoire size was clear, the cause of the relationship was not. A strong correlation existed between repertoire size and years of territory tenure, but repertoire size still showed a strong relationship with LRS when territory tenure was controlled ($r^2 = .38$). Repertoire size also was strongly correlated with annual reproductive success. Hiebert et al. (1988) concluded they could not determine "whether the relationship between repertoire size and reproductive success is due (1) to direct effects of repertoire size on the abilities of males to acquire and hold territories and/or attract and stimulate females, or (2) to a correlation between repertoire size and male traits that in turn produce these benefits" (p. 271).

We believe that the strong link between LRS and song repertoire size may be explained by an effect of early nutrition on song learning. Nowicki et al. (1998b) propose that nutrition during the period of dependence on parental care affects the development of the brain centers responsible for song learning and production. Learned features of song, including repertoire size, should therefore reflect nutrition during this crucial period. Nutrition also affects development of the phenotype in general. According to this hypothesis, the correlation between repertoire size and LRS should be largely indirect: good early nutrition causes males to have high phenotypic quality and therefore have high LRS, and it also causes them to develop large song repertoires. A direct causal component may enter the correlation as well, because repertoire size should serve as an indicator of male quality and might therefore affect female choice. The same hypothesis can be applied to the great tit (*Parus major*), in which repertoire size has also been shown to correlate strongly with fitness (McGregor et al. 1981; Lambrechts and Dhondt 1986), and to the many species in which song repertoire size affects female choice (Searcy and Yasukawa 1996).

Function of Within-song Type Variation

Relatively little attention has been paid to possible functions of within-song type variation, in song sparrows or any other species. We know that song sparrows perceive within-type variation, at least in certain circumstances. Stoddard et al. (1988)

presented to territorial males playbacks consisting of either 18 repetitions of a single song, 6 repetitions of each of 3 song types, or 3 repetitions of each of 6 variants of one type. Aggressive response during playback was similar for all three treatments, but after playback it fell off more quickly for the single song than for either the multiple types or multiple variants. Our habituation/recovery experiments with male song sparrows constitute a second test for perception of variants (Searcy et al. 1995). Subjects in these experiments showed significant recovery in approach following switches to new variants, though the magnitude of the recovery was considerably less than for switches to new song types (figure 21.2). Neither of these experiments, however, provides evidence that within-type variation is functional, because of the nature of the territorial playback design used in these studies. Song functions in communication between males as a signal from a territory owner to other males, repelling them from the territory. Territorial playback, however, measures the reaction of the territory owner rather than of intruders, and songs score well if they elicit approach and aggression rather than avoidance.

Laboratory playback studies with females provide a better method of assessing function, as it is undoubtedly advantageous to males to induce females to court and copulate. We have tested estradiol-treated, captive females for response to playback of multiple variants and single variants. Females responded no more strongly to multiple variants than to single variants (Searcy and Nowicki unpublished data). In a second set of playbacks, female courtship habituated to repetition of one song, but did not show any recovery when playback switched to a new variant (Searcy and Nowicki unpublished data). We thus are unable to find any evidence of a female preference for within-song type variation.

Moreover, within-type variation has two characteristics that we might expect to find in production error. First, the number of variants in a male's repertoire appears to be open-ended, in the sense that the number of variants identified increases with the number of songs analyzed with no asymptote (Podos et al. 1992). Second, transitions between variants tend to occur between the most similar ones (Nowicki et al. 1994), a pattern we might expect if changes between variants are accidental.

Although we have advanced some evidence that within-type variation is functionless, we can suggest some reasons for not abandoning functional hypotheses altogether. First, as noted above, male song sparrows do attend to within-type variation in territorial playbacks. This type of response is not direct evidence of a function, but it does suggest that an intrasexual function is possible. Second, we also have evidence that within-type variation influences song learning. Nowicki et al. (unpublished data) tape-tutored young male song sparrows with both variable and invariant song types and found that the subjects learned the variable types preferentially. We do not suggest that it is advantageous for a male to have others learn his songs, but these results show that another class of listeners attends to within-type variation, which opens the possibility that within-type variation produces some response in these listeners that is beneficial to the singer. Finally, we have evidence that the extent of within-type variation varies geographically in song sparrows. We have measured within-type variation in four song sparrow populations, in Maine, Pennsylvania, North Carolina, and Washington. The average similarity of variants of the same song type differs significantly across the four populations, with higher similarity (and thus lower variability) in Maine and Pennsylvania than in North Carolina and Washington. Geographic variation in a trait is often associated with geographically varying selection pressures, though other explanations are possible.

In conclusion, within-type variation leaves us with a puzzle. On the one hand, we have negative results from a standard paradigm for assessing function, the solicitation display assay, as well as our observation that patterns of within-type variation approximate what we might expect from production error. On the other hand, we have some interesting hints of functionality from territorial playbacks, learning experiments, and patterns of geographical variation. Moreover, it is our impression that other species with comparable song repertoires do not vary their song types to the same extent as do song sparrows, and it is difficult to see why song sparrows would be more prone to error than other species. More work needs to be done; comparative research on song variation in other species might be especially profitable.

Between-individual Variation

Between-individual variation can best be introduced by discussing its antithesis: song sharing. Song sharing occurs when two males in a population sing a highly similar song type. If the frequency of song sharing approaches 100%, and the degree of similarity in song types approaches identity, then between-individual variation disappears. In song sparrows, the highest known level of sharing occurs in the Washington population studied by Beecher et al. (1994a, 1996), where neighbors share on average 40% of their repertoires. Thus even in Washington sharing is far below the 100% level that would negate individual variation. In other song sparrow populations, with lower sharing, between-individual differences are more extreme.

Direct evidence for individuality in song comes from studies demonstrating individual recognition via song. Stoddard et al. (1991) tested the response of male song sparrows to the song of a specific neighbor broadcast either from the boundary with that neighbor or from the opposite boundary. Playback songs were chosen randomly, so they might or might not have been shared with other neighbors. Aggressive response

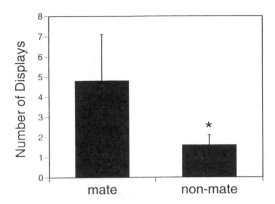

Figure 21.4
Response of female song sparrows to playback of mate song vs. song of another male from the same population. Response is measured as the number of solicitation displays performed. Means $\pm$ s.e. are shown. An asterisk indicates a significant difference at the 0.05 level by a one-tailed test.

was weaker to the neighbor song broadcast from the correct boundary than to the same song broadcast at the opposite boundary, or to the song of a stranger broadcast from either boundary. These results indicate male song sparrows can discriminate one neighbor from all other males by song alone, even if song sharing is high in the population.

Female song sparrows also can recognize individuals by song alone. We tested estradiol-treated female song sparrows on two days each for response to 16 repetitions of one of their mate's songs and to 16 repetitions of a song of another male from the same population, using 10 females captured in New York. Females gave approximately three times as many displays for their mate's song as for the other male's song (figure 21.4). The difference in response was significant (Wilcoxon $T = 6$, $N = 8$ untied observations, $P < 0.05$ one-tailed). O'Loghlen and Beecher (1997) obtained similar results using females captured in Washington. Females thus recognize the song of their own mate and prefer it over other songs.

Function of Between-individual Variation

Various advantages have been proposed for the ability to recognize other individuals by song. For example, the ability to recognize neighbors by song may be advantageous to a territory owner, allowing him to save time and energy by ignoring his neighbors when they sing from their own territories. Any benefit to recognizing others is irrelevant, however, to the question of why males sing individually specific songs, because such a benefit is accrued by listeners rather than by singers. In considering whether and how individual variation is advantageous, we need to concentrate on why it might be advantageous to the singer to be recognized as an individual, rather than on why it is advantageous for others to recognize him.

The female preference for own-mate songs does not necessarily indicate any advantage to males of being recognizable. Imagine a population of males all singing identical songs, in which one male with a distinctive, recognizable songs appears. The distinctive male will reap an advantage, in that his mate will be better able to confine her mating to him alone, but he will also bear a disadvantage, in that all females mated to other males will be better able to discriminate against him in mating. By this reasoning, on average the cost and benefit of individuality cancel, but being recognizable might still be advantageous to especially attractive males. Furthermore, males might benefit from being recognized by females in contexts other than courtship and copulation. For example, it may be easier to coordinate activities during parental care if the female can recognize the male's song and use it to keep track of his location.

In addition, neighbor recognition among territorial males may be advantageous to singers as well as to receivers, in which case the phenomenon would be relevant to the evolution of individuality. Fisher (1954) suggested that territorial birds "are bound firmly ... to their next door neighbours by what in human terms would be described as a dear enemy or rival friend situation...." What Fisher had in mind was an advantage to proximity with neighbors because of mutual stimulation, an advantage that now seems doubtful. Others, however, have since pointed to benefits of dear enemy relationships in competition for territory. Getty (1987) proposed that because peaceful relations with a neighbor can only be established after a period of costly negotiation over boundaries, it may benefit a resident to have familiar, established neighbors. The relationship between a territory owner and a neighbor would be negative, but less negative than between the owner and intruders from outside the neighborhood. The owner might therefore have an interest in maintaining the familiar neighbor in place, leading to mutual defense of the neighborhood, with neighboring males acting either alone or jointly to expel intruders (Getty 1987). The mutually beneficial relationship between the neighbors can only be maintained if each of the neighbors is recognizable to the other, so they can avoid attacking their "dear enemy" while continuing to attack outsiders. This scenario thus provides to the singer a benefit from possessing distinctive and recognizable songs in territory defense.

Although we can posit advantages to being recognizable, it may be that such hypotheses are unnecessary. Instead, individual distinctiveness may be inevitable, if each male has distinctive "voice" characteristics that make him recognizable even when singing exactly the same song as another male. Individual voice characteristics could be produced, for example, by individual differences in the size or shape of vocal tract structures known to affect the acoustic properties of song (Nowicki and Marler 1988). However, a direct experimental test for recognition by voice characteristics in song sparrows gave negative evidence of this (Beecher et al. 1994b). Five song sparrows were trained to respond to one set of songs and not to respond to another set. The subjects were then tested for response to unrewarded test probes of two types: voice probes, which were new song types from the same males as produced the training songs, and match probes, which were new song types that resembled one of the training songs but from a different singer. Subjects responded appropriately to match probes significantly more often than chance, but showed only chance responses to voice probes. The experimental evidence on voice recognition in song sparrows, then, is so far negative.

Geographic Variation

Song-sparrow songs from separate locales often sound different to human observers, but specifying the nature of the underlying acoustic differences is difficult. In some classic cases of geographic variation, as in the white-crowned sparrow (*Zonotrichia leucophrys*) (Marler and Tamura 1962), songs from particular locales are marked by obviously distinctive features such as particular syllables or phrases. Mulligan (1963, 1966) studied geographic differences in song sparrow populations in the San Francisco Bay area and concluded that geographic variation in this sense did not exist. Instead, the great variability of songs within populations tended to obscure differences between populations (Mulligan 1963). In white-crowned sparrows, transitions from one form of song to another tend to occur abruptly, at discrete boundaries (Marler and Tamura 1962; Baptista 1975). Song-sparrow songs, by contrast, seem to change gradually over space, without abrupt boundaries.

Despite the difficulty of defining the nature of geographic variation in song-sparrow song, the existence of such variation can be easily shown by playback experiments. Harris and Lemon (1974) tested male song sparrows in Quebec for discrimination between songs recorded at sites separated by as little as 37km. In all cases, males responded more strongly to local songs than to foreign ones. We have shown that female song sparrows also respond more strongly to local than to foreign songs (Searcy et al. 1997). We tested females captured at a Pennsylvania site with local songs and songs recorded at a New York site approximately 500km distant. In each of two experiments, females gave almost five times as many courtship displays for local songs as for foreign songs. Males from this population also discriminated between local and foreign songs.

Studies with several other species of song birds have shown that female birds court more in response to local than to foreign songs, both in species with discrete dialects (e.g., white-crowned sparrows, Baker et al. 1982, 1987) and in species, like the song sparrow, with more gradual patterns of geographic variation (e.g., red-winged blackbirds [*Agelaius phoeniceus*], Searcy 1990). Male birds also commonly discriminate between local and foreign songs (see, e.g., McGregor 1983; Brenowitz 1983; Balaban 1988).

Function of Geographic Variation Catchpole and Slater (1995) divide hypotheses on the function of geographic variation in song into three categories: social adaptation, habitat matching, and genetic adaptation. Social adaptation suggests that convergence on local songs enables males to interact more effectively with their neighbors. Young males, for example, might mimic the songs of a particular older male so that others might mistake them for that male; the mimic might thereby gain an advantage in territory defense or mate attraction. Payne (1981) proposed this hypothesis for indigo buntings (*Passerina cyanea*), a species in which males sing a single song type that usually resembles closely the song of some neighboring male. Young male indigo buntings have greater mating and reproductive success if they share the song of an older neighbor than if they do not (Payne 1982; Payne et al. 1988), but the processes bringing about this correlation are not clear (Payne 1983). Social mimicry seems unlikely to apply to song sparrows, given the low degree of sharing between males in most populations.

Habitat matching proposes that geographical variants of song are matched to the sound transmission properties of the local habitat. Habitats differ in transmission properties, such that particular frequencies and temporal patterns transmit better in some habitats than in others (Wiley 1991). Some songbird species have been found to possess geographic variation in song properties that parallels variation in habitat, notably the rufous-collared sparrow (*Zonotrichia capensis*). In this species, the rate of syllable repetition in the terminal trill appears adapted to the local habitat, being slower in forests than in grasslands, and intermediate in woodland (Nottebohm 1975; Handford 1988). Male rufous-collared sparrows sing only a single song type each, and their songs vary relatively little within local populations. A system of adaptation to local sound transmission conditions seems less workable in a species like the song sparrow, with a much higher degree of song variation within populations. Moreover, song sparrows occupy similar habitats throughout much of their range. The habitats occupied by song sparrows in our Pennsylvania study sites are closely similar in terms of vegetation structure to those they occupy at our New York sites, but songs nevertheless differ between the two areas. Some adaptation of song to habitat characteristics is possible in song sparrows, but this hypothesis seems unlikely to explain the bulk of geographic variation in song-sparrow song.

Genetic adaptation hypotheses suggest that populations of songbirds are genetically adapted to local conditions, and that geographic variation in song serves to facilitate mating within the population, thus preserving local adaptation (Nottebohm 1969, 1972). Females are predicted to prefer mating with males singing local songs, and males are predicted to be repelled from areas where foreign songs are sung. Genetic adaptation thus receives some support in song sparrows from the results on female preference for local songs. Whether the male results accord with genetic adaptation is less certain. Male song sparrows also respond more strongly to local songs than to foreign ones, but their response is measured as the aggressive reaction of territorial males, and it is not obvious that a strong aggressive response by territory owners to a particular song implies that the song will weakly repel local males seeking territories.

Although the pattern of response by female song sparrows is as predicted by the genetic adaptation hypothesis, this result alone does not confirm the hypothesis. We do not know the extent to which song sparrow populations are locally adapted, and thus we do not know whether female song sparrows benefit by mating within the local population. Moreover, the question of whether females benefit by preferring males singing local songs is irrelevant to the question of whether geographic variation in song is adaptive, because (again) females do not produce the song variation.

A functional explanation for geographic variation in song has to suggest an advantage to males, since they are the ones producing the behavior. Such a hypothesis must explain both why it is advantageous to a male to sing songs resembling those of other local males, and why it is advantageous to a male to sing songs different from those of foreign males, as both phenomena are necessary to produce geographic variation. The evidence that local females prefer local songs supports the first requirement, but to satisfy the second requirement we would have to show that it is advantageous to a male to be rejected by foreign females. The advantage to a male in being rejected by a foreign female would lie in the opportunity to produce superior offspring by mating instead with a local female; this hypothetical advantage has to be weighed against the possibility of not mating at all if a male is rejected by a foreign female and then fails to attract another female of any origin. In any event, encounters with foreign females must be rare in song sparrows, because of philopatry. Genetic data yield estimates of dispersal distance in song sparrows on the order of 3–6km (Zink and Dittman 1993), considerably less than the distances over which song variation has been shown. Encounters with foreign females, in the sense of females familiar with different song traditions, may be relatively more common in species with sharp dialect boundaries, such as the white-crowned sparrow.

Geographic variation in song thus seems unlikely to benefit male song sparrows in their relations with females. Geographic variation could be advantageous to males in their relations with other males only if males benefit from doing a better job in repelling foreign males than in repelling local males (or vice versa); again, any such benefit seems unlikely.

If we reject adaptive hypotheses for song variation, we are left with the hypothesis that geographic variation is the product of chance historical factors (Catchpole and Slater 1995). In song sparrows, as in other oscines, the details of song are transmitted from generation to generation by learning (Marler and Peters 1977). Change can occur between generations owing to either mistakes in copying or improvisation, and both these processes ought to occur independently in different locales. Accumulation of change due to mistakes and improvisation would account for geographic variation. Individuals from areas 40km apart (or even less) must seldom encounter one another, and so selection for increased stereotypy over such distances must be weak.

Conclusions

When we ask whether song variation is functional, we are really asking whether it is advantageous to the singer to produce a different song, different from what he himself has produced previously, or different from what other males produce. Within-individual variation at the level of song types is clearly functional in this sense. By singing different song types, a male is able to signal his level of arousal or aggressiveness to other males, and to direct attention to particular males by repertoire matching. The ability to sing multiple song types also increases a male's ability to stimulate females to copulate with him. Repertoires seem to have not one but several functions in song sparrows.

At the opposite extreme, geographic variation in song seems unlikely to be functional. Males benefit by singing local songs, but they do not seem to benefit from singing songs that differ from foreign songs; that is, they would be just as well off if their local song was sung throughout the species' range. Geographic variation in the song of song sparrows may simply be the product of the accumulation of chance changes that occur during song learning combined with insufficient selection for stereotypy among populations of individuals that rarely come into contact. A function for geographic variation is perhaps more likely in species with abrupt dialect boundaries, but conclusive evidence of such a function is not available for any species (Catchpole and Slater 1995).

A better case can be made for a function of variation between individuals within populations. Here there seems to be an advantage to singing songs that differ from those of other individuals, in that differences make the singer recognizable to his partners in cooperative relationships. Cooperative relationships may extend to neighboring territory owners as well as to the mated female. At this level, a male would not be as well off if all individuals in the local population sang the same songs as he does, because then cooperating individuals could not recognize and aid him in preference to others. Evidence for individual recognition of song is available for other species besides the song sparrow, but in all cases the evidence for advantages of individuality is indirect.

Within-song-type variation is the most enigmatic level in terms of function in the song sparrow, and it has been little studied in other species. Song sparrows perceive variation at this level, and there seems to be no logical reason that this kind of variation cannot have the same types of function as between-song-type variation. Our evidence thus far indicates that within-song-type variation does not function to stimulate females in courtship, but we cannot definitively disprove this or other functions.

Acknowledgments

We would first like to thank Peter Marler, who got us both started working on song in song sparrows. We also thank all the others who have collaborated with us in this work, including especially Susan Peters, and also Melissa Hughes, Jeff Podos, Cindy Hogan, Mike Beecher, Preston Few, Matt Lovern, and Alicia Maynard. Financial support was provided by the National Science Foundation through grants IBN-9523635 to WAS and IBN-9408360 to SN.

References

Baker, M. C. (1983) Sharing of vocal signals among song sparrows. *Condor* 85:482–490.

Baker, M. C., Bjerke, T. K., Lampe, H. U., and Espmark, Y. O. (1987) Sexual response of female yellowhammers to differences in regional song dialects and repertoire sizes. *Anim. Behav.* 35:395–401.

Baker, M. C., Spitler-Nabors, K. J., and Bradley, D. C. (1982) The response of female mountain white-crowned sparrows to songs from their natal dialect and an alien dialect. *Behav. Ecol. Sociobiol.* 10:175–179.

Balaban, E. (1988) Cultural and genetic variation in swamp sparrows (*Melospiza georgiana*). II. Behavioral salience of geographic song variants. *Behaviour* 105:292–321.

Baptista, L. F. (1975) Song dialects and demes in sedentary population of the white-crowned sparrow (*Zonotrichia leucophrys nuttalli*). *Univ. Calif. Publ. Zool.* 105:1–52.

Beecher, M. D., Campbell, S. E., and Stoddard, P. K. (1994a) Correlation of song learning and territory establishment strategies in the song sparrow. *Proc. Nat. Acad. Sci.* (USA) 91:1450–1454.

Beecher, M. D., Campbell, S. E., and Burt, J. M. (1994b) Song perception in the song sparrow: Birds classify by song type but not by singer. *Anim. Behav.* 47:1343–1351.

Beecher, M. D., Stoddard, P. K., Campbell, S. E., and Horning, C. L. (1996) Repertoire matching between neighbouring song sparrows. *Anim. Behav.* 51:917–923.

Borror, D. J. (1965) Song variation in Maine song sparrows. *Wilson Bull.* 77:5–37.

Bremond, J. C. (1968) Recherches sur la sémantique et les éléments vecteurs d'information dans les signaux acoustiques du rouge-gorge (*Erithacus rubecula* L.). *Terre Vie* 2:109–220.

Brenowitz, E. A. (1983) The contribution of temporal song cues to species recognition in the red-winged blackbird. *Anim. Behav.* 31:1116–1127.

Catchpole, C. K. and Slater, P. J. B. (1995) *Bird Song: Biological Themes and Variations.* Cambridge: Cambridge University Press.

Dawkins, R. and Krebs, J. R. (1978) Animal signals: Information or manipulation? In *Behavioural Ecology*, ed. by J. R. Krebs and N. B. Davies, pp. 282–309. Sunderland, MA: Sinauer.

Eberhardt, C. and Baptista L. F. (1977) Intraspecific and interspecific song mimesis in California song sparrows. *Bird-Banding* 48:193–205.

Fisher, J. (1954) Evolution and bird sociality. In *Evolution as a Process*, ed. by J. Huxley, A. C. Hardy, and E. B. Ford, pp. 71–83. London: Allen and Unwin.

Getty, T. (1987) Dear enemies and the prisoner's dilemma: Why should territorial neighbors form defensive coalitions? *Amer. Zool.* 27:327–336.

Handford, P. (1988) Trill rate dialects in the rufous-collared sparrow, *Zonotrichia capensis*, in northwestern Argentina. *Can. J. Zool.* 66:2658–2670.

Harris, M. A. and Lemon, R. E. (1972) Songs of song sparrows (*Melospiza melodia*): Individual variation and dialects. *Can. J. Zool.* 50:301–309.

Harris, M. A. and Lemon, R. E. (1974) Songs of song sparrows: Reactions of males to songs of different localities. *Condor* 76:33–44.

Hasselquist, D., Bensch, S., and von Schantz, T. (1996) Correlation between male song repertoire, extra-pair paternity, and offspring survival in the great reed warbler. *Nature* 381:229–232.

Hiebert, S. M., Stoddard, P. K., and Arcese, P. (1989) Repertoire size, territory acquisition, and reproductive success in the song sparrow. *Anim. Behav.* 37:266–273.

Hughes, M., Nowicki, S., Searcy, W. A., and Peters, S. (1998) Song-type sharing in song sparrows: Implications for repertoire function and song learning. *Behav. Ecol. Sociobiol.* 42:437–466.

Kramer, H. G. and Lemon, R. E. (1983) Dynamics of territorial singing between neighboring song sparrows (*Melospiza melodia*). *Behaviour* 85:198–223.

Kramer, H. G., Lemon, R. E., and Morris, M. J. (1985) Song switching and agonistic stimulation in the song sparrow (*Melospiza Melodia*): Five tests. *Anim. Behav.* 33:135–149.

Lambrechts, M. and Dhondt, A. A. (1986) Male quality, reproduction, and survival in the great tit (*Parus major*). *Behav. Ecol. Sociobiol.* 19:57–63.

Marler, P. and Peters, S. (1977) Selective vocal learning in a sparrow. *Science* 198:519–521.

Marler, P. and Tamura, M. (1962) Song "dialects" in three populations of white-crowned sparrows. *Condor* 64:368–377.

McGregor, P. K. (1983) The response of Corn Buntings to playback of dialects. *Z. Tierpsychol.* 62:256–260.

McGregor, P. K., Krebs, J. R., and Perrins, C. M. (1981) Song repertoires and lifetime reproductive success in the great tit (*Parus major*). *Am. Nat* 118:149–159.

Mulligan, J. A. (1963) A description of song sparrow song based on instrumental analysis. *Proc. XIII Int. Ornith. Congr.* 272–284.

Mulligan, J. A. (1966) Singing behavior and its development in the song sparrow *Melospiza melodia. Univ. Calif. Publ. Zool.* 81:1–76.

Nelson, D. A. (1988). Feature weighting in species song recognition by field sparrows (*Spizella pusilla*). *Behaviour* 106:158–182.

Nelson, D. A. and Marler, P. (1990) The perception of bird song and an ecological concept of signal space. In *Comparative Perception*, ed. by W. C. Stebbins and M. A. Berkely, vol. 2, pp. 443–478. New York: Wiley.

Nice, M. M. (1943) Studies in the life history of the song sparrow, part 2. *Trans. Linn. Soc. N.Y.*, no. 6.

Nottebohm, F. (1969) The song of the chingolo, *Zonotrichia capensis*, in Argentina: Description and evaluation of a system of dialects. *Condor* 71:299–315.

Nottebohm, F. (1972) The origins of vocal learning. *Am. Nat.* 106:116–140.

Nottebohm, F. (1975) Continental patterns of song variability in *Zonotrichia capensis*: Some possible ecological correlates. *Am. Nat.* 109:605–624.

Nowicki, S. and Marler, P. (1988) How do birds sing? *Music Perception* 5:391–426.

Nowicki, S., Podos, J., and Valdes, F. (1994) Temporal patterning of within-song type and between-song type variation in song repertoires. *Behav. Ecol. Sociobiol.* 34:329–335.

Nowicki, S., Searcy, W. A., and Hughes, M. (1998a) The territory defense function of song in song sparrows: A test with the speaker occupation design. *Behaviour* 135:615–628.

Nowicki, S., Peters, S., and Podos, J. (1998b) Song learning, early nutrition, and sexual selection in songbirds. *Am. Zool.* 38: 179–190.

O'Loghlen, A. L. and Beecher, M. D. (1997) Sexual preferences for mate song types in female song sparrows. *Anim. Behav.* 53:835–841.

Payne, R. B. (1981) Population structure and social behavior: Models for testing the ecological significance of song dialects in birds. In *Natural Selection and Social Behavior*, ed. by R. D. Alexander and D. W. Tinkle, pp. 108–120. New York: Chiron Press.

Payne, R. B. (1982) Ecological consequences of song matching: Breeding success and intraspecific song mimicry in indigo buntings. *Ecology* 63:401–411.

Payne, R. B. (1983) The social context of song mimicry: Song matching dialects in indigo buntings (*Passerina cyanea*). *Anim. Behav.* 31:788–805.

Payne, R. B., Payne, L. L., and Doehlert, S. M. (1988) Biological and cultural success of song memes in indigo buntings. *Ecology* 69:104–117.

Peters, S. S., Searcy, W. A., and Marler, P. (1980) Species song discrimination in choice experiments with territorial male swamp and song sparrows. *Anim. Behav.* 28:393–404.

Podos, J., Peters, S., Rudnicky, T., Marler, P., and Nowicki, S. (1992) The organization of song repertoires in song sparrows: Themes and variations. *Ethology* 90:89–106.

Saunders, A. A. (1924) Recognizing individual birds by song. *Auk* 41:242–259.

Searcy, W. A. (1984) Song repertoire size and female preferences in song sparrows. *Behav. Ecol. Sociobiol.* 14:281–286.

Searcy, W. A. (1990) Species recognition of song by female red-winged blackbirds. *Anim. Behav.* 40:1119–1127.

Searcy, W. A. and Marler, P. (1981) A test for responsiveness to song structure and programing in female sparrows. *Science* 213:926–928.

Searcy, W. A., Marler, P., and Peters, S. S. (1981) Species song discrimination in adult female song and swamp sparrows. *Anim. Behav.* 29:997–1003.

Searcy, W. A., Nowicki, S., and Hughes, M. (1997) The response of male and female song sparrows to geographic variation in song. *Condor* 99:651–657.

Searcy, W. A., Podos, J., Peters, S., and Nowicki, S. (1995) Discrimination of song types and variants in song sparrows. *Anim. Behav.* 49:1219–1226.

Searcy, W. A. and Yasukawa, K. (1996) Song and female choice. In *Ecology and Evolution of Acoustic Communication in Birds*, ed. by D. E. Kroodsma and E. H. Miller, pp. 454–473. Ithaca, NY: Cornell University Press.

Stoddard, P. K., Beecher, M. D., and Willis, M. S. (1988) Response of territorial male song sparrows to song types and variations. *Behav. Ecol. Sociobiol.* 22:125–130.

Stoddard, P. K., Beecher, M. D., Loesche, P., and Campbell, S. E. (1992a) Memory does not constrain individual recognition in a bird with song repertoires. *Behaviour* 122:274–287.

Stoddard, P. K., Beecher, M. D., Campbell, S. E,. and Horning, C. L. (1992b) Song-type matching in the song sparrow. *Can. J. Zool.* 70:1440–1444.

Stoddard, P. K., Beecher, M. D., Horning, C. L., and Campbell, S. E. (1991) Recognition of individual neighbors by song in the song sparrow, a species with song repertoires. *Behav. Ecol. Sociobiol.* 29:211–215.

West, M. J., King, A. P., and Eastzer, D. H. (1981) Validating the female bioassay of cowbird song: Relating differences in song potency to mating success. *Anim. Behav.* 29:490–501.

Wheeler, W. C. and Nichols, J. T. (1924) The song of the song sparrow (a systematic study of its construction). *Auk* 41:444–451.

Wiley, R. H. (1991) Associations of song properties with habitats for territorial oscine birds of eastern North America. *Am. Nat.* 138:973–993.

Zink, R. M. and Dittman, D. L. (1993) Gene flow, refugia, and evolution of geographic variation in the song sparrow (*Melospiza melodia*). *Evolution* 47:717–729

22 The Evolution of a Lopsided Brain: Asymmetries Underlying Facial and Vocal Expressions in Primates

Marc D. Hauser

Structural and functional brain asymmetries exist in nonhuman vertebrates. It is no longer tenable to view brain lateralization as an exclusively, or even primarily, human attribute. Yet the animal data fail to suggest a general principle relating brain lateralization to behavior.
—M. Hiscock and M. Kinsbourne, Phylogeny and Ontogeny of cerebral lateralization

General Overview

The evolution of the primate brain is most aptly characterized by a suite of neural refinements, rather than by changes in gross neuroanatomy such as the addition of completely new structures (reviews in Jerison and Jerison 1988; Deacon 1991; Changeux and Chavaillion 1995). However, over the course of this evolutionary process, the human brain underwent two important changes. First, a highly modular brain emerged, with different components associated with domain-specific cognitive tasks (Cosmides and Tooby 1994; Hirschfeld and Gelman 1994). And second, particular cognitive functions became asymmetrically distributed in the brain, such that the right and left hemispheres took on different computational operations (Davidson and Hugdahl 1995). To understand the origins of and selection pressures on human brain evolution, it is necessary to adopt the comparative method and examine the cognitive functions of our closest living relatives, the nonhuman primates. In this chapter, the comparative method is used to assess whether rhesus monkeys (*Macaca mulatta*) show hemispheric asymmetries for two species-typical traits—facial expressions and vocalizations. In a wide variety of taxa, such communicative signals play a critical role in the maintenance of species integrity and often in the initiation of the speciation process (Otte and Endler 1989; Ryan and Rand 1993). Thus one would expect selection to have favored neural specializations designed to meet the demands of this evolutionarily significant process.

Humans typically show left-hemisphere specialization for language production and perception and right-hemisphere specialization for face processing (reviewed in Hellige 1993; Kimura 1993). Studies of nonhuman animals, including anurans, songbirds rats, mice, macaques, and chimpanzees show asymmetries for the perception and production of species-typical vocalizations (Goller and Suthers 1995; reviewed in Corballis 1991; Bradshaw and Rogers 1993; Hellige 1993; Hiscock and Kinsbourne 1995; see chapter by R. Suthers, this volume), with less information on nonvocal expressions (Hauser 1993a). From a phylogenetic perspective, aimed at revealing the evolutionary precursors to human hemispheric function, data on nonhuman primates are most critical. Unfortunately, and in contrast to studies of other taxonomic groups, the comparative data on nonhuman primate asymmetries for processing facial expressions and vocalizations are rather limited (Hamilton and Vermeire 1991; Hauser 1993a; Hauser and Andersson 1994; Heffner and Heffner 1984; Hopkins et al. 1991; Perrett et al. 1988; Petersen et al. 1978). This stands in striking contrast to the wealth of data on nonhuman primate handedness (Mac-Neilage et al. 1987; MacNeilage 1991; Ward and Hopkins 1993).

Specific Background on Lateralization

Several neuroscientists (Corballis 1991; Hellige 1993; Hiscock and Kinsbourne 1995) have argued that although nonhuman animals show evidence of neuroanatomical asymmetries and even some evidence of behavioral asymmetries, only humans exhibit extensive differentiation of cognitive function between the hemispheres, with evidence of asymmetry at the population level. Specifically, most humans exhibit left-hemisphere dominance for language processing and right-hemisphere dominance for spatial reasoning, emotional perception and expression (see reviews in Bradshaw and Rogers 1993; Davidson and Hugdahl 1995; Hellige 1993). As research in this area has developed over the past ten years, however, it is clear that the original claims regarding hemispheric dominance were far too general—that the dichotomies for right- and left-hemisphere dominance covered up important overlap in function (Efron 1990; see the chapters in Davidson and Hugdahl 1995). For example, although the left hemisphere is dominant with regard to the semantics and formal combinatorial properties of language (e.g., grammar), the right hemisphere appears dominant for processing the paralinguistic features of language such as melody and changes in pitch (see, e.g., Ross et al. 1988; but see also Peretz and Babai 1992). Thus the right hemisphere is certainly not *silent* during language processing, and in some cases of damage to the left hemisphere, there is evidence that the right hemisphere can take on a number of significant linguistic functions.

Recent EEG data suggest that the right hemisphere may play a dominant role in negative/withdrawal emotion whereas the left hemisphere appears dominant for positive/approach emotion (see, e.g., Davidson 1992, 1995; but see also Lee et al. 1990 for the reverse pattern of emotional valence and hemisphere bias using epileptic patients receiving intracarotid administration of sodium amobarbital). Thus, for example, when people are given explicit instructions to move their face into a Duchenne smile—what Ekman and colleagues (1988, 1990) consider to be the only true or honest smile—they exhibit far greater left hemisphere activation than right (Ekman et al. 1990a,b). Moreover, Gazzaniga and Smiley (1991) provide important information on split-brain patients, showing that there are much greater asymmetries in smiling on the left side of the face than on the right.

As a result of an exponentially increasing quantity of empirical data on human laterality (most recently reviewed in Davidson and Hugdahl 1995), an emerging theme is that *both* hemispheres are typically involved (i.e., activated) in cognitive function, although the particular computational operations of each hemisphere may be different, and one hemisphere may be more *naturally* dominant. This perspective has led some researchers to propose a new and slightly more flexible approach, which looks at hemispheric asymmetries in terms of global versus local features of the incoming signal, independently of sensory modality (reviewed in Hellige 1993; Brown and Kosslyn 1995). Thus, for example, results from PET scans and visual-half-field studies of adults and infants (Levine 1989; Sergent et al. 1992; de Schonen et al. 1993) indicate that the right hemisphere may be specialized for extracting the configural (global) properties of the face (e.g., eyes located above the nose) whereas the left hemisphere appears specialized for processing the distinctive (local) and presumably familiar features of the face (e.g., shape of the eyes, nose, mouth).

The pattern of hemispheric asymmetry demonstrated for human adults is, in some domains, different from that demonstrated for human children. For example, Carey and colleagues (Carey and Diamond 1977; Leehey et al. 1979) have shown that children under the age of ten years represent faces in terms of piecemeal features, not global configural features. In addition, in young infants, the right side of the face is more expressive than the left (Best and Queen 1989). This pattern is the reverse of what has been demonstrated for normal human adults, where a left side of the face bias is typically observed (Levy et al. 1983; Sackheim et al. 1978). Regarding language, both infants and adults show a left-hemisphere advantage for processing consonants. In contrast, whereas adults show no hemispheric specialization for processing vowels, infants show a right-hemisphere bias (reviewed in Best 1988).

If we are to understand how and why hemispheric specialization evolved, it is important to look more closely at the neural specializations of our closest living relatives, the monkeys and apes. This movement has already begun, thanks in part to MacNeilage, Studdert-Kennedy, and Lindblom (1987), who critically examined the evidence for hand preferences in nonhuman primates. This work (see review by MacNeilage 1991) demonstrated that in several nonhuman primate species, individuals use one hand more than the other in both unimanual and bimanual tasks (Ward and Hopkins 1993); in general, most primates are left-handed. Data on handedness, coupled with work on asymmetries in nonhuman primate neuroanatomy (e.g., Cheverud et al. 1991; Falk 1987; Falk et al. 1990; Heilbroner and Holloway 1988; Perrett et al. 1988) and cognitive function (e.g., Hamilton and Vermeire 1991; Hopkins et al. 1990, 1991; Vauclair et al. 1993) are important in that they provide some insights into the phylogenetic precursors of human hemispheric specialization (for recent synthetic discussions of this point, see Bradshaw and Rogers, 1993; Hauser 1996).

To date, significantly less research has focused on the possibility of nonhuman primate hemispheric specialization for cognitive function, especially asymmetries in processing species-typical visual and auditory signals. And yet, some of the most fascinating findings on human hemispheric asymmetries come from studies that have examined the neural specializations underlying language and facial expression—our own species-typical signals.

A word of caution. The discussion of hemispheric specialization has focused on nonhuman primates. This is intentional. There is strong evidence of lateralization in rats and birds, in terms of both motor output (e.g., song production in Passerine birds: Nottebohm 1972, 1977; Nowicki and Capranica 1986; Hartley and Suthers 1990, Suthers 1994; Goller and Suthers 1995; this volume; spatial ability in rats: Sherman et al. 1980; LaMendola and Bever 1997) and the perception of biologically meaningful stimuli (song perception in Passerine birds: Nottebohm et al. 1990; perception of ultrasonic pup calls: Ehret 1987). And as Marler (1970) pointed almost 30 years ago, some of these finding provide striking parallels (homoplasies) to human speech processing. In this proposal, however, the evolution of hemispheric specialization is explored from a phylogenetic perspective aimed at revealing possible homologous processes. Consequently, comparisons between closely related ancestral species are likely to lead to the greatest insights (Hodos and Campbell 1990). The following discussion, therefore, concentrates on empirical findings emerging from studies of nonhuman primates, a group of organisms that show clear genetic affiliation with our own species, *Homo sapiens sapiens*.

Face Recognition

Faces are interesting visual stimuli because they represent a composite of highly invariant features such as the relative spatial location of the eyes, nose, and mouth, together with a suite of highly variant features such as the color of the eyes, the shape of the mouth and nose, and so forth. Studies of humans indicate that faces presented to the right hemisphere (i.e., left visual field) tend to be processed more rapidly than faces presented to the left hemisphere (Hilliard 1973). In contrast, in some experiments, nonface stimuli are processed more rapidly by the left hemisphere, whereas in other experiments, focusing especially on spatial tasks, a right-hemisphere bias is observed (see review by Hillger and Koenig 1991; Ungerleider 1995). Further evidence for a face-specific asymmetry in processing comes from studies using rotated (e.g., inverted) or scrambled faces, where significant distortion is imposed upon the most salient facial features (Carey and Diamond 1977; Leehey et al. 1979). Specifically, the right-hemisphere bias for face recognition disappears when faces are rotated, or when features such as the eyes and nose are rearranged so that they appear in spatially inappropriate locations (see, e.g., Yin 1969). Studies of prosopagnosics (individuals who have typically experienced injury to the occipito-temporal region of the brain, and who show significant deficits in recognition of familiar faces; see chapters by R. Adolphs and by D. Perrett, this volume) provide further evidence of right-hemisphere specialization for face processing, but they also illustrate the importance of bilateral involvement, with suggestive evidence of a right-hemisphere bias for global features and a left-hemisphere bias for local features (see, e.g., Damasio and Damasio 1986).

Research on nonhuman primates has revealed that the superior temporal sulcus consists of cells that are highly responsive to faces (Gross and Sergent 1992; reviewed by Perrett, this volume), but not comparably complex nonface visual stimuli, with some cells responding to such subtle facial features as the direction of eye gaze and the vertical orientation of the head (see, e.g., Desimone 1991, Harries and Perrett 1991). Most observations of hemispheric asymmetries in processing visual stimuli, including faces and nonfaces, come from rhesus macaques (reviews in Perrett et al. 1988; Perrett, this volume; Hamilton and Vermeire 1991), with more limited research on chimpanzees (Hopkins et al. 1990) and baboons (Vauclair et al. 1993). Some studies report a lack of hemispheric specialization for face recognition (see, e.g., Hamilton et al. 1974; Overman and Doty 1982) and the failure to detect an inversion effect (i.e., familiar faces presented upside down are either not recognized as familiar faces or are processed more slowly; Bruce 1982). More recent research on rhesus macaques, however, suggests that nonface visual forms are processed more rapidly by the left hemisphere (Hopkins et al. 1990), faces are processed more rapidly by the right hemisphere (Hamilton and Vermeire 1991), and processing (i.e., reaction) time increases when faces are distorted, either through scrambling or through rotation (Perrett et al. 1988). Face rotation tends to eliminate hemispheric biases in processing time. In summary, therefore, data on visual processing of faces in macaques provides evidence of hemispheric asymmetry, but the degree and direction of asymmetry may differ from the pattern documented in humans.

Facial Expression

In contrast with work on face recognition in nonhuman primates, relatively little is known about hemispheric biases in the *production* of facial expressions. Ifune and colleagues (1984) presented split-brain rhesus monkeys with videotaped sequences of human and nonhuman primates, in addition to sequences of other animals and scenes. Significantly more facial expressions, both submissive and aggressive, were elicited during right-hemisphere activation than during left-hemisphere stimulation.

To fill in this empirical gap, recordings of facial expressions were obtained from free-ranging adult rhesus macaques living on the island of Cayo Santiago, Puerto Rico; table 22.1 describes a sample of the most common rhesus monkey facial expressions, including the corresponding articulation and measures of expressiveness. The first set of analyses (Hauser 1993a) focused on four different facial expressions produced by adults. Three expressions were associated with negative/withdrawal emotion (i.e., "fear grimace," "open mouth threat," and "ear flap threat") and one, the "copulation grimace" given by adult males, was ambiguous with regard to its

Table 22.1
Rhesus monkey facial expression, articulations, and measures of expressiveness.

Facial Expression	Kinematic Description	Expressiveness Measures
Fear grimace	Lips are retracted, teeth either clenched or separated.	1. Relative height of lip retraction 2. Number of skin folds btw. lower portion of eye and cheek bone
Copulation grimace	Lips are retracted, teeth are typically clenched.	1. Relative height of lip retraction 2. Number of skin folds btw. lower portion of eye and cheek bone
Ear Flap Threat	Ears are moved back and flattened against the side of the head	1. The extent to which the ear makes contact with the back of the head
Eyebrow flash	The area above the eye is raised, thereby causing the eyes to open wider and for the area above the eye, which is lighter in pigmentation, to be revealed.	1. Relative height of the raised brow
Open mouth threat	Lips are protruded and placed into an O-shaped position.	1. Relative bias in the extent of mouth opening on each side.
Muzzle up	Lips protruded as the male dips his head down and then up in a semicircle.	1. Relative side biases in the extent of the lip protrusion
Lip smacks	Lips are smacked together repeatedly, often accompanied by a smacking noise.	1. Relative side bias in the side of lip contact during smacking.
Play face	Mouth opened wide into an O-shaped configuration, with less lip protrusion than in the open mouth threat.	1. Relative bias in the extent of mouth opening on each side.

emotional substrate; although copulation involves approach, and may be considered a positive emotional context, mating is commonly associated with aggression, and in particular, aggression targeted at the copulating male (Hauser 1993b).

Video records were obtained from individuals engaged in natural social interactions associated with facial expressions. To determine facial asymmetries from the video record, it is necessary to obtain footage of individuals who are facing the camera. Asymmetries in expression were only scored from video records where the subject faced the camera straight on, and thus both sides of the face could be clearly seen.

For each expression, measures of asymmetry in timing (i.e., whether one side of the face initiated the gesture before the other) and expressiveness were obtained. Timing asymmetry is limited to the resolution of our video equipment, a minimum difference of one frame or 33msec. A preliminary analysis of some of the footage revealed that this level of resolution would be sufficient to detect some asymmetries in facial expression; it is, of course, possible that this measurement underestimates the degree of asymmetry present in some expressions, where one side starts less than a frame earlier than the other. Expressiveness is measured in a number of ways and depends on the particular kinematics of the expression.

For timing (Hauser 1993a), all expressions except the copulation grimace showed a highly significant left side of the face bias; the copulation grimace was relatively symmetrical with respect to timing. For the fear and copulation grimaces, two measures of expressiveness (number of skin folds and height of the lip retraction) revealed a significant left side of the face bias. These results suggest that the right hemisphere may play a dominant role in the production of facial expressions, at least those expressions with an underlying negative/withdrawal emotion.

To build on our analyses and add an ontogenetic component, we have recently looked at a facial expression associated with positive/approach emotion: the "play face." This expression, given during play or play initiation, is most commonly given by infants and juveniles, but is occasionally given by adults as well. To contrast with the play face, we also analyzed a new sample of fear grimaces for adults, juveniles, and infants; for purposes of analysis, and owing to the relatively small sample of expressions per individual and age group, we have pooled the data for adults and juveniles and contrasted this sample with those for infants. Recall that in human infants under the age of one year, there is a right side of the face bias for facial expressions, both positive (smiling) and negative (crying).

Though our current sample size is small, some intriguing trends have emerged from the analyses. Figure 22.1 shows the results for adults, juveniles, and infants. For the adult/juvenile class, a significant proportion of individuals reveals a left side of the face timing bias for fear grimaces (sign test: $p < 0.01$), but a right side of the

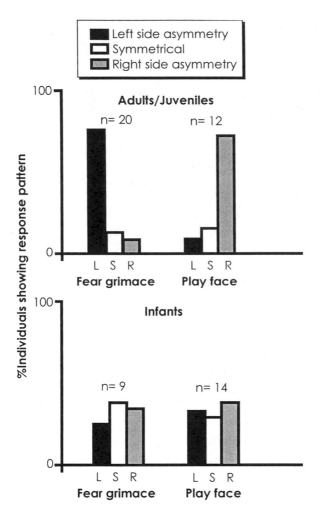

Figure 22.1
Asymmetries in facial expression for the adult/juvenile class (top pane) and the infant class (bottom panel). The proportion of individuals showing a particular pattern of expression (symmetrical or asymmetrical on the right/left) is plotted on the y-axis, with the type of expression plotted on the x-axis.

face bias for the play face (sign test: $p < 0.01$). The fear grimace data provide a replication of the earlier results (Hauser 1993a). The play face data reveal that for a positive/approach emotion, the bias in timing flips to the opposite side from the fear grimace, a negative/withdrawal expression of emotion. In contrast with adults and juveniles, infants show no significant response bias for either the fear grimace or the play face (sign test: $p > 0.05$). Thus infants do not appear to exhibit significant hemispheric dominance for facial expression. These data suggest that up until the age of one year, neither hemisphere is dominant with regard to facial expression. This pattern must be treated cautiously, however, owing to the small sample of individuals and types of facial expressions.

Perception of Vocalizations

Human language consists of both highly variant and invariant features. Neuroimaging studies of normal human subjects, in addition to observations of brain damaged patients, have shown that in right-handers, the left hemisphere plays a dominant role in language processing (Kolb and Whishaw 1985; reviewed in Kimura 1993). Although the aphasia literature, combined with more recent imaging results, indicates high levels of variation across subjects in the neural circuitry subserving language, the pathway that leads from Broca's to Wernicke's area via the arcuate fasciculus is clearly important. The observed left-hemisphere specialization is primarily restricted to the more formal properties of language such as phonetics, phonology, semantics, and syntax. The right hemisphere, in contrast, may play a more dominant role in processing the paralinguistic features of language such as prosody and affective expression

At the perceptual level, early neurobiological investigations of squirrel monkeys and macaques (reviewed in Pandya, Seltzer, and Barbas 1988) failed to find areas that were selectively responsive to specific acoustic features of a signal. Most of this work, however, was carried out with pure tones or broad band noise as stimuli, though a few experiments used species-typical vocalizations (Newman and Wollberg 1973a,b). A recently published experiment using single-unit recording techniques has, however, revealed that at a perceptual level, cells within the superior temporal gyrus of rhesus monkeys are selectively responsive to species typical vocalizations as opposed to spectrally matched pure tones or broad band noise (Rauschecker, Tian and Hauser 1995). This area appears to be homologous to Brodmann Areas 42 and 22 in humans, cortical areas that are critically involved in speech processing.

The first attempt to assess hemispheric biases in acoustic perception in primates took advantage of a detailed field study and psychophysical techniques. The empirical foundation for this research was Green's (1975) in-depth analyses of wild Japanese macaque vocalizations, and in particular, their "coo" vocalizations. This call type is acoustically variable, with much of the variation resulting from modulations in the fundamental frequency contour. For example, coos with one frequency contour pattern were given during group progressions, whereas coos with a different contour were given by estrous females. Experiments by Petersen et al. (1978) showed that Japanese macaques, but not closely related species (an exception was one vervet monkey), responded faster in a discrimination task when the call was played into the right ear (left hemisphere) than when it was played into the left ear (right hemisphere). Follow-up studies by Heffner and Heffner (1984, 1990) indicated that lesioning the left temporal lobe, but not the right, caused subjects to lose the ability to discriminate coos on the basis of their characteristic frequency contours; although this deficit was observed early on, subjects with left hemisphere lesions recovered quite rapidly. In general, these results have been taken as support for the view that in addition to humans, monkeys also show a left hemisphere bias for processing species-typical vocal signals.

There are two potential problems with the interpretation offered for the Japanese macaque data. First, only one call type was used, and thus we do not yet understand whether the perceptual bias extends to other calls within the repertoire. Second, the claim that Japanese macaques show a pattern of hemispheric bias that is comparable to that shown for humans processing language hinges on the assumption that coos are language-like—that they convey, at some level, semantic information. And yet, studies of this call type in both Japanese macaques (Owren et al. 1992, 1993) and the closely related rhesus macaque (Hauser 1991) suggest that the information conveyed is likely to be entirely emotive (i.e., there is currently no evidence that the call conveys even functionally referential information, *sensu* Marler et al. 1992).

To address some of the concerns raised above, a field study of rhesus macaques was conducted (Hauser and Andersson 1994). Playback experiments were carried out with a large number of adults and infants (< 12 mos), using most of the call types from the repertoire. The experiment involved placing a speaker 180 degrees behind an individual, and then playing back a single exemplar of a call type. The logic underlying the experimental design was that if subjects preferentially turned their right ear toward the speaker, they would preferentially bias the intensity of the input to the left hemisphere. In contrast, if subjects turned the left ear, they would preferentially bias the input to the right hemisphere. Note that in this procedure, both ears receive acoustic input, but there will be an interaural time and intensity difference due to the orienting bias. Results showed that for all conspecific calls played, adults consistently showed a right-ear bias; and this orienting bias was observed despite an overall left-hand motor preference for reaching and manipulating objects in this population (Hauser et al. 1991), and no correlation between handedness and orienting bias in a subset of the subjects tested. In contrast, no ear bias was observed in infants for any of the call types played back. Moreover, when the alarm call of a local bird (ruddy turnstone) was played, adults preferentially turned the left ear, whereas infants failed to show a bias; the turnstone's call is familiar to rhesus macaques, but represents a signal that is clearly not from a conspecific. Together, these results provide additional support for the idea that in macaques, there is a right-ear bias for the perception of conspecific signals, suggesting that the left hemisphere plays a dominant role in processing conspecific calls.

To determine which acoustic features of a signal influence the preferential head-turning response, and thus the suggested hemispheric bias underlying perception in rhesus macaques (Hauser and Andersson 1994), two sets of playback experiments have recently been conducted. In the first experiment, digital signal editing tools (Beeman 1996) were used to modify the structure of naturally produced calls. The idea, in a nutshell, is this. Call types within the repertoire are characterized by a suite of parametric features, including both temporal and spectral features. We hypothesized that when particular features of a signal are manipulated beyond the range of natural variation, such signals will no longer be perceived as conspecific calls; call types within the repertoire will differ in terms of their characteristic defining features, and consequently, no single manipulation is likely to be meaningful across all call types, except at extremes. Given the observation that rhesus macaques respond to playbacks of one avian species' alarm call by preferentially turning their left ear to listen (Hauser and Andersson 1994), we predicted that playbacks of rhesus calls that have been acoustically shifted *outside* of the species-typical range will also elicit a left-ear bias; such manipulations may also result in no response bias if the acoustic signal causes significant activation in both hemispheres, but for different causal factors. Calls that have been manipulated, but remain *inside* the species-typical range, will continue to elicit a right-ear bias—that is, will continue to be classified as a conspecific call.

The first experiment (Hauser, Agnetta, and Perez 1990) focused on the importance of *temporal parameters* in call classification, and the design is sketched in figure 22.2. All three call types used (see below) are characterized by pulses of energy separated by silence. For each call type, we start with a naturally recorded call consisting of three pulses, together with pulse and interpulse intervals that fall close to the population mean. We then shrink as well as stretch interpulse intervals to create four additional stimuli. Calls with reduced interpulse intervals have been reduced to the minimum observed in the population or have been completely eliminated. Calls with

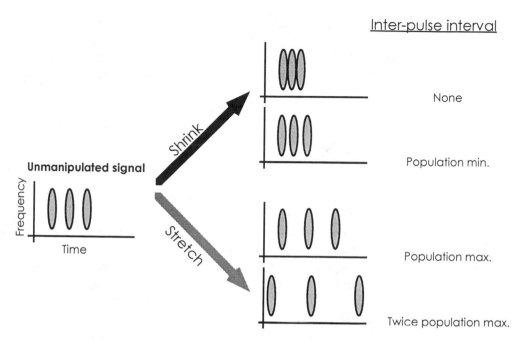

Figure 22.2
Experimental design for playback experiments on asymmetries in the orienting response. For each call type, an unmanipulated signal was modified in four ways: shrink inter-pulse to (1) the population minimun or (2) zero; stretch interpulse interval to (3) the population maximum or (4) twice the population maximum.

stretched interpulse intervals have been increased to the maximum in the population or twice the maximum.

For each call type, five naturally recorded exemplars were obtained and manipulated as per the design in figure 22.2. Thus the total stimulus set for this experiment is 3 call types and 25 exemplars per call type, for a total of 75 playback stimuli. Multiple exemplars of each call type are necessary so that we can more confidently interpret our results at the level of functionally distinctive call types.

Figure 22.3 provides representative spectrograms of the three call types used in this experiment: grunt, shrill bark, and copulation scream (Hauser 1993b; Hauser and Marler 1993a; Bercovitch et al. 1995). Three factors guided our decision to use these particular call types. First, each call type is produced in a context that can be clearly identified. Thus grunts are produced during affiliative interactions involving food or a conspecific (Hauser and Marler 1993a). Shrill barks are given exclusively in the context of alarm, and for rhesus monkeys on Cayo Santiago, represent their

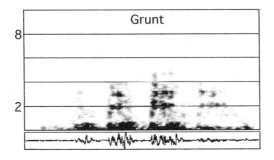

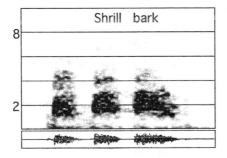

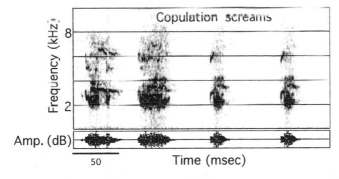

Figure 22.3
Sound spectrograms (top) and time-amplitude wavefoms (bottom) of the three call types used in the laterality experiments. The y-axis is frequency in kilohertz for the spectrograms and amplitude in decibels for the time-amplitude waveform; the x-axis is time in milliseconds.

only alarm vocalization (Hauser and Marler 1993a; Bercovitch et al. 1995). Copulation screams are only given by adult males during copulation, and in no other context (Hauser 1993b). Second, quantitative acoustic analyses were already available, both from published results (Hauser 1993b; Hauser and Marler 1993a) and from unpublished data. Thus we have a good understanding of the range of acoustic variation both at the population level and in terms of specific features of the call. Third, in manipulating the structure of a call away from its species-typical morphology, we need to ensure that we are not changing its structure into that of a different call from within the repertoire. Thus, for example, if we took a rhesus coo and gradually increased the frequency modulation of the terminal portion of the call, we would move outside of the coo's normal range of variation, but move into the range of variation typical of the "harmonic arch," a call given during food discovery (Hauser and Marler 1993a). For grunts, shrill barks, and copulation screams, manipulating interpulse interval does not result in the generation of different call types from within the repertoire.

Having manipulated one parameter of the call, we then conducted playback experiments using the design of our previous experiments (Hauser and Andersson 1994). In brief, we conceal a speaker in dense foliage, approximately 180 degrees and 10–12m behind one side of a chow dispenser; there are three dispensers on the island. We then wait for an individual to sit and feed at the appropriate dispenser location, or to sit near the dispenser. When the individual's back completely faces the speaker and the camera is lined up with the speaker and subject, the playback is initiated and the subject's head orienting response recorded on video. Recording the response on video enables us to assess unambiguously which direction the subject turns to listen. Three responses are possible: turn right, turn left, or no detectable response.

Figure 22.4 presents the results from playbacks of each call type. For all three call types, playbacks of unmanipulated exemplars, and exemplars with interpulse interval reduced to the population minimum subjects showed a highly significant right-ear bias ($p < 0.05$ to 0.001), thereby replicating our earlier results. For grunts and shrill barks, eliminating interpulse interval eliminated the orienting bias, with some individuals turning to the right, some to the left, and some not responding at all; for copulation screams, however, the right-ear bias was preserved. When interpulse interval was stretched to the maximum in the population, there was a tendency for subjects to orient with the left ear leading for both grunts and shrill barks, but this pattern was not statistically significant; for copulation calls, the right-ear bias was preserved. Last, when interpulse interval was stretched to two times the maximum,

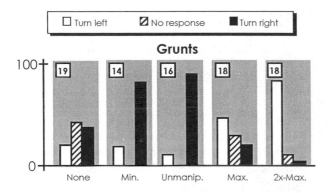

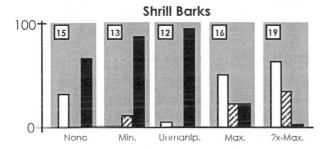

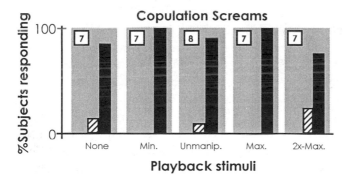

Figure 22.4
Results from laterality playbacks of unmanipulated and manipulated calls. For each call type, the proportion of subjects responding by turning with the right ear leading (black), left ear leading (white) or not responding at all (striped) is shown. The type of call played is indicated on the x-axis. The numbers in the upper left hand corner of each histogram panel indicate the number of individuals tested in each condition.

subjects showed a statistically significant left-ear bias for the grunt and shrill bark, but a right-ear bias was preserved for the copulation scream.

These results indicate that for grunts and shrill barks, manipulating interpulse interval beyond the species-typical range of variation (at least for this population) causes a shift from a right-ear bias to either no bias (eliminating interpulse interval) or to a significant left-ear bias (two times the maximum interpulse interval). This pattern of change was not, however, observed in playbacks of copulation screams. Why did manipulations of the interpulse interval have a detectable effect on responses to grunts and shrill barks, but no effect on responses to copulation screams? A closer inspection of the natural variation in acoustic morphology provides a clue. Whereas grunts and shrill barks are produced with no *less* than two pulses, copulation screams are produced with one or more pulses. Thus, although the number of pulses and interpulse interval in a copulation scream may be relevant to male quality (see, e.g., Hauser 1993b), such temporal features do not appear to be important in terms of classifying the call as a rhesus copulation scream. In summary, then, we appear to have identified at least one feature that defines a rhesus monkey call, and to have demonstrated that altering this feature causes a shift in the direction of orientation.

As a first step in addressing the role of spectral features in perceptual orientation, we synthesized (Beeman 1996) two rhesus vocalizations—a tonal scream given by subordinates (Gouzoules et al. 1984) and a harmonic arch given by individuals finding rare, high-quality food. The sounds were synthesized using a procedure developed by Evan Balaban that extracts the fundamental frequency contour and the amplitude envelopes of each harmonic. The signal can then be manipulated by changing the parameters of either the fundamental or the amplitude envelope. Figure 22.5 shows two natural exemplars and one synthetic for each of the call types.

To determine whether rhesus monkeys perceive a difference in the natural and synthetic exemplars, we (Hauser and Fitch in prep.) needed to run a habituation-discrimination procedure. The design of our experiment, schematically illustrated in figure 22.6, followed previous tests with rhesus monkeys (Hauser 1996, 1998). Specifically, multiple exemplars of, for example, a tonal scream were played back to a target subject until they failed to respond on two consecutive trials and responded to at least the first two playback trials. Having failed to respond to the presentation of natural exemplars, we played back a single exemplar of a synthetic tonal scream and recorded the response. If subjects failed to respond to the synthetic, we ran a post-test trial using a different call type: a copulation scream. The motivation for the post-test trial was to insure that failure to respond to the test stimulus was not due to habituation to the test area. It is conceivable, of course, that having heard a series of calls from one area, the target subject will habituate to the general activity in that area. If this were to occur, then we would expect subjects to transfer habituation (i.e., fail to respond) to all calls played back from this area. In contrast, if subjects were to respond to the post-test stimulus, then we would have greater confidence in our interpretation that transfer of habituation was due to perceptual clustering of calls in the habituation and test trials.

We tested a total of 18 animals using the habituation-discrimination procedure, half receiving tonal screams and the other half receiving harmonic arches. Only one subject responded in the test trial. All others transferred habituation, even though they all responded to the post-test stimulus. This provides evidence that synthetic exemplars are perceived as valid rhesus vocalizations. Thus we are now in the position to manipulate spectral parameters and explore how such changes influence the pattern of orienting bias.

Production of Vocalizations

Neurophysiological studies of squirrel monkeys and several macaque species have revealed homologues to Broca's and Wernicke's areas (reviewed in Jürgens 1990; Deacon 1991). When the homologue to Broca's area is lesioned in these species, however, no detectable differences in the acoustic morphology of the vocal repertoire are observed (reviewed in Sutton and Jürgens 1988; reviewed in Hauser 1996). These results have led to the conclusion that in nonhuman primates, the locus of control for the production of species-typical vocalizations is the limbic system. A problem with this interpretation is that in both studies, relatively crude measurements of pre- and postoperative effects on call structure were obtained (Kirzinger and Jürgens 1982). Specifically, spectrographic differences in call structure were assessed qualitatively, rather than quantitatively using detailed acoustic analyses. Given that damage to Broca's and Wernicke's areas can lead to quite subtle linguistic effects in humans, it is possible that comparably subtle effects would emerge among nonhuman primates as well. Moreover, the potential effects of these experimental lesions were only measured over a short period of time; production and perception deficits may not reveal themselves immediately following injury. In sum, the importance of higher cortical structures in nonhuman primate vocal production remains ambiguous.

Studies of cortical physiology aside, there has been considerable interest in the possibility that the fundamental units of human language (e.g., phonemes, words) have evolved from a nonhuman primate ancestor. For example, MacNeilage (1994)

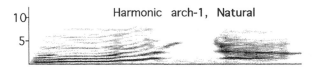

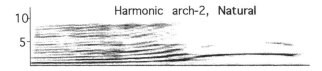

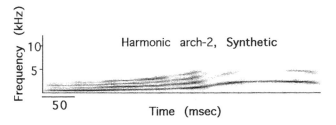

Figure 22.5
Representative exemplars of natural and synthesized rhesus monkeys calls—a tonal scream given by subordinates and a harmonic arch given by an individual who has found high quality/rare food. Frequency is indicated on the y-axis in kilohertz, time on the x-axis in milliseconds.

has suggested that syllables evolved from primate lipsmacks and other communicative mandibular cyclicities. Thus far, however, no study has explored whether non-human primates exhibit asymmetries during vocal articulation. In humans, Graves and his colleagues (1982, 1985, 1988, 1990) have demonstrated that during speech production, the right side of the mouth opens wider than the left. Moreover, in aphasics with damage to the left hemisphere, a right side of the mouth bias is observed for spontaneous speech, repetition, and word list generation, whereas a left side of the mouth bias is observed for serial speech (counting to ten) and singing (familiar rhymes). This difference suggests that when an automatic motor sequence is enlisted for vocal production, the right hemisphere is dominant. In contrast, even aphasics show left-hemisphere dominance for nonautomatic vocal articulations, spe-

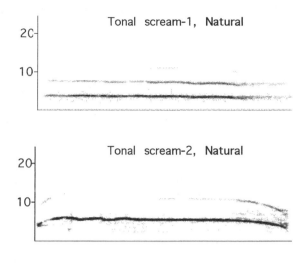

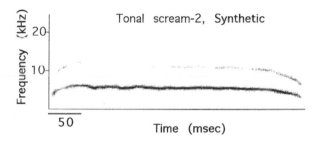

Figure 22.5 (continued)

cifically those involving speech articulation. Studies such as those conducted by Graves and colleagues on humans are now critically needed for nonhuman primates. Given our increasing knowledge of primate vocal communication, including its function, acoustic architecture, and the mechanisms underlying its production (Jürgens 1990; Cheney and Seyfarth 1990; Snowdon 1990; Hauser et al. 1993; Hauser 1993b, Hauser and Schön Ybarra 1994), we are in an excellent position to examine hemispheric biases underlying the production of species-typical vocalizations.

Parallel to our analyses of facial expressions, assessment of articulatory gestures is also derived from two measures. First, for each vocalization (the acoustics and visual articulation captured on video), we score whether or not one side of the mouth opens up or shuts down before the other—a timing measure. An articulation is scored as

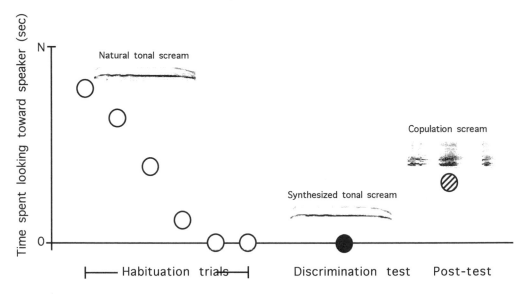

Figure 22.6
Experimental design for habituation-discrimination test for assessing potential differences in perception of natural as opposed to synthetic calls. Here, an example of a seession with tonal screams is provided; in the post-test trial the subject receives a single copulation scream.

asymmetric if one side of the mouth starts or ends the articulation at least one frame earlier than the other side. Second, we score, frame-by-frame, which side of the mouth is open wider at the start of articulation as well as the midpoint of the call. Specifically, a frame is digitized with the Adobe Premier (v 4.0) software and the frame imported into Image (v 1.50). Within the Image environment, the mouth is divided down the middle, and the number of pixels on the right and left side derived. For both the timing clips and the digitized frames, half of the exemplars are flipped in the horizontal plane so that observers are blind with regard to the original orientation of the subject. The end product of this analysis is an overall assessment of articulatory asymmetry and its production time course. Below, I focus on the results of the timing measure.

The first set of analyses focused on three call types: coos, screams, and grunts. Coos and grunts are produced by lip protrusion and an open mouth, whereas screams are produced by lip retraction. Results (figure 22.7) from 3 adult males and 2 adult females (5 to 9 call exemplars per individual) indicate that for coos, the articulation appears highly symmetrical, with only a small proportion of exemplars showing a left- or right-side bias. In contrast, for both screams and grunts, there is a

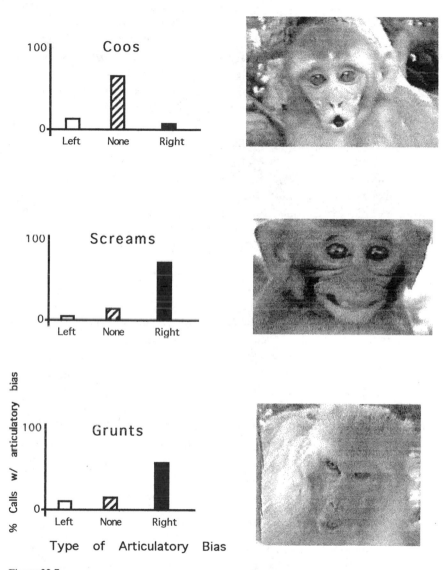

Figure 22.7
Differences in articulatory timing bias for three call types, the coo, scream and grunt. The y-axis plots the proportion of individuals with a particular articulatory bias and the x-axis shows the type of articulatory bias (white = left; striped = none; black = right).

significant right side of the face bias ($p < 0.05$ to 0.01). These results are promising, not only because they reveal directional biases for some calls and not others, but because the measurement technique works well. Moreover, the results on screams are particularly interesting when compared with the asymmetry data for fear grimaces (Hauser 1993a). Specifically, fear grimaces and screams are both produced by retracting the lips. When fear grimaces are produced, there is a left side of the face bias, whereas a right side of the face bias is observed for screams. If screams were merely expressions of affective state (e.g., fear), then we would expect a left side of the face bias (right hemisphere), as shown for fear grimaces. Given that screams are produced with a right-side bias, we suggest that this provides further support for the idea that they convey referential information. Specifically, observations and experiments by Gouzoules, Gouzoules, and Marler (1984) indicate that the rhesus monkey's scream system consists of functionally referential signals that map onto variation in the details of the social interaction (e.g., aggressive interactions with kin or non-kin).

General Discussion and Future Directions

In this chapter, I have reviewed current evidence for hemispheric biases in the production and perception of primate facial and vocal expressions. In contrast with earlier views, it appears that at least some nonhuman primates evidence cerebral asymmetries during communication, either sending a signal or perceiving one. Although preliminary, some of the data from rhesus macaques suggest that early in development, infants show little evidence of hemispheric biases; recall that infants under the age of one year showed no asymmetries during either the production of facial expressions or the perception of vocalizations. In this concluding section, I would like to point to some potentially fruitful avenues for future research. My comments are based on the general patterns presented in the previous sections and summarized in table 22.2.

Communicating with the Face

Results from our analyses of adult rhesus monkeys indicate that individuals evidence a left side of the face bias during the production of facial expressions associated with negative/withdrawal emotions. In contrast, when adults produce expressions associated with positive/approach emotions, they evidence a right side of the face bias. It was argued that such observable patterns provide insights into the underlying mechanisms of neural control, and in particular, the direction of hemisphere bias. There are several problems with this argument that I would like to flesh out here.

Table 22.2
Summary of asymmetries underlying rhesus communication.

Species-specific Communication	Age	Direction of hemispheric dominance		
		Left	Right	None
Face recognition	Adults		X	
	Infants	—	—	—
Facial expression	Adults	$X_{p/a}$	$X_{n/w}$	
	Infants			X
Vocal recognition	Adults	X		
	Infants			X
Vocal expression	Adults	X_{fr}		X_a
	Infants	—	—	—

—: No data
p/a: positive/approach emotion
n/w: negative/withdrawal emotion
fr: signals that appear functionally referential
a: signals of affective state

The first two problems can be remedied quite easily. Currently, our sample size for adults is relatively small, both in terms of the number of individuals recorded and the number of exemplars per individual per expression. Until we increase our samples, we can only provide tentative conclusions with respect to the probability of population-wide asymmetries in facial expression. Second, to understand the pattern of development, we need to increase the number and types of expressions for infants, as well as for juveniles. Current analyses suggest that infants under the age of one year lack consistent directional biases in facial expression. To determine the onset of asymmetries in facial expression, we will require a finer titration along the developmental continuum from infancy to adulthood. It will also be important to pay attention to the possibility of sex differences, since in the Cayo population, females reach reproductive maturity at around three years whereas males reach reproductive maturity at around four years. The third problem is more difficult. A fundamental assumption underlying our analyses of facial expression is that attributions of positive/negative or approach/withdrawal are accurate. At present, however, we have no independent measure for extracting the correct emotional substrate. Two solutions are possible. Under field conditions, we can extract more detailed information on the socioecological factors preceding and following each interaction involving a facial expression. Additionally, we can score other actions associated with the facial expression, such as body posture (e.g., hair bristling, tail position) and the presence or absence of urination and defecation; these responses will fine-tune our assessment of emotional state. In the laboratory, it might be possible to generate situations that would elicit facial expressions, and if so, we could conceivably use autonomic measures (heart rate, galvanic skin response) to quantify the underlying emotional substrate.

Communicating with the Voice

Our playback experiments were designed to assess whether rhesus monkeys show an ear bias in orienting toward acoustic signals, and if so, whether the directional bias is affected by the type of signal and the age of the perceiver. Results showed that for adults, a large and significant proportion of subjects turned with the right ear leading in response to calls falling within the natural range of acoustic variation for this rhesus population. In contrast, adults turned with the left ear leading (or showed no asymmetry) in response to the ruddy turnstone's alarm call (heterospecific), as well as to grunts and shrill barks with interpulse intervals exceeding the range of natural variation. These results suggest that for adult rhesus monkeys, the left hemisphere is dominant for processing conspecific calls. Although both ears receive auditory input when a sound is played from a position 180 degrees behind the subject, by turning one ear toward the sound source, subjects bias the intensity of the input to that ear, thereby creating an interaural time and intensity difference.

To increase our understanding of lateral biases in perception, there are several directions for future research, including additional field studies combined with laboratory experiments. In the field, our success with synthetic vocalizations places us in an ideal position to alter the spectral structure of conspecific vocalizations and thereby determine which features are associated with a right-as opposed to a left-ear bias. In the temporal domain, we plan to return to the structure of pulses and manipulate the number of pulses beyond the population maximum for each call type, using two different interpulse intervals. Specifically, for each call type (i.e., grunts and shrill barks) we will add one, two, or three additional pulses to the maximum for this population. For one set of these stimuli, we will maintain interpulse intervals at the population mean. The result of this manipulation is that for grunts and shrill barks with more than six pulses, call duration exceeds the population maximum. Thus this particular manipulation confounds pulse number with overall call duration. To examine this problem, we create a second set where interpulse intervals are restricted to the population minimum. Here, changes in pulse number result in exemplars that fall within the population range for call duration.

A second set of playback experiments, currently underway, uses the same procedures as outlined above, but instead of manipulating the acoustic structure of rhesus calls, we play back other heterospecific vocalizations as well as nonbiological but familiar sounds. In our previous experiments (Hauser and Andersson 1994), we used the alarm call of the ruddy turnstone because we anticipated that this call would elicit an orienting response from the rhesus. Our expectation was based on the fact that the turnstone's call is both familiar and potentially meaningful, since it is commonly given in situations that are relevant to rhesus (e.g., alarm calls to personnel working on the island). Although the turnstone's alarm call is structurally different from all rhesus calls, its spectral and temporal properties fall well within the range of the rhesus repertoire. In the proposed experiments, we will play back pieces of human speech. Human speech is acoustically familiar (i.e., rhesus hear humans speaking all the time), but from a distantly related heterospecific. The second category, familiar nonbiological signals, is used to explore the possibility that the right-ear bias has more to do with familiarity than species-specificity. Although the left-ear bias observed to the turnstone's call rules this out to some extent, playing back familiar nonbiological sounds (e.g., the sounds of the motorboat approaching the dock, or the truck that runs on the island) will provide a stronger test of this hypothesis. As in our experiments with edited rhesus calls, playbacks of heterospecific calls and familiar nonbiological sounds will also be used to assess biases in the head orienting response. We predict that if the left hemisphere bias for conspecific calls is robust, then the rhesus will exhibit a significant right-hemisphere bias (orienting to the left) for heterospecific calls and familiar nonbiological sounds, or no bias at all.

Recent experiments on rhesus monkeys using single-unit recording techniques suggest that there are cells in the lateral belt areas of the primary auditory cortex that are selectively responsive to rhesus monkey vocalizations, but not spectrally matched artificial signals (Rauschecker et al. 1995). To determine whether there are hemispheric biases, two sets of experiments must be run. First, single- and multiunit recordings must be carried out in the right and left hemispheres, matched for brain areas. Second, perceptual discrimination experiments should be run using either a lesion technique such as the one implemented by Heffner and Heffner (1984) or, slightly less invasive, the infusion of muscimol to temporarily "silence" a particular area of the brain; the infusion of muscimol provides a temporary but reversible lesion, thereby enabling the subject to run multiple discrimination trials, altering one side first and then the other. Although these experiments will help illuminate the extent to which lateral biases in perception can be detected at the neuron level, the patterns observed need not match the patterns observed under field conditions. Specifically, the field studies have been designed to assess biases in sound localization, whereas the laboratory work assesses asymmetries in response specificity and discrimination.

Our studies of articulation are truly in their infancy. Before a clear picture can be presented, we need to collect far more data, both to assess inter- and intraindividual variation, as well intercall type variation. For some call types, such as screams, coos, copulation screams, and barks, we are confident that a sufficient sample size can be readily obtained, owing in part to the high rates at which such calls are produced. These calls are also some of the more telling representatives of the repertoire, given the hypotheses being considered. There are two reasons for this claim. First, for vocalizations such as screams and barks, the kinematics of the articulation appear to be fundamentally similar to those used during contextually matched facial expressions. Thus, for example, screams and fear grimaces are both produced by individuals being attacked and for both the call and facial expression, the motor gesture observed is extensive lip retraction. Second, studies by Gouzoules, Gouzoules, and Marler (1984) have already hinted at the possibility that like human words, screams are functionally referential in that they appear to designate external events—in the case of screams, the event is a particular type of social relationship (e.g., physical aggression from a higher ranking individual). Given this suggestion, we would expect such calls to be preferentially processed by the left hemisphere, whereas more emotionally grounded calls such as coos would be preferentially processed by the right hemisphere or show no bias at all. From an articulatory perspective, our expectations about hemispheric control or dominance lead to the following predictions: (a) calls that are primarily emotive, in that they convey information about the signaler's affective state, should exhibit a left side of the face bias during articulation; (b) calls that are primarily language-like, in that they convey meaningful information about external objects and events, should exhibit a right side of the face bias during articulation; (c) symmetry during articulation may result from the lack of hemispheric dominance or from bilateral involvement that relates to the potentially varied sources of information in the signal (e.g., both affective and referential).

A second direction for future research on vocal articulation is to perturb the system. Earlier work on vocal production suggested that rhesus monkeys engage the supralaryngeal vocal tract to modify formant structures (Hauser et al. 1993; Hauser and Schön Ybarra 1994; Fitch 1997). In one study (Hauser and Schön Ybarra 1994), xylocaine (a form of novocaine) was injected into the upper and lower lips to block lip protrusion. This manipulation had a significant impact on formant structure, but not on fundamental frequency. Given the success of this procedure, it is possible to repeat the injections, but administer them only to one side of the mouth at a time. The prediction, following Graves and colleagues, is that injections to the right side of the mouth will have a more deleterious effect on the precision of articulation than injections on the left side of the mouth. Such expected effects can be measured both by analyzing the kinematics of the gesture and especially by comparing the acoustic morphology of signals produced while one side of the mouth is anesthetized.

In conclusion, studies of lateral biases in nonhuman primate communication are still in their infancy, especially when compared with studies of humans and songbirds. However, the patterns emerging are intriguing and suggest interesting parallels to those that have been suggested for human facial expressions and vocalizations. By increasing our understanding of nonhuman primates, both those that are closely related to humans and those that are more distantly related, we will be in a better position to understand how hemispheric biases for communication evolved over time.

Acknowledgments

When I was in high school I read Peter Marler's 1970 paper in *Scientific American*. In that paper, he provided a foundation for comparing animal communication with human speech. I told my teacher at the time that I wanted to do research on this kind of problem and, in particular, wanted to study with Marler. Sometimes dreams come true. I feel extremely fortunate to have been able to work with Peter. I have never encountered a person with Peter's insight, and passion for knowing. It is contagious. I thank him for sharing such talents, and for making my own science that much better. I also thank Peter and Judith for being such good friends during my travels to and from Davis.

References

Andrew, R. J. (1962) The origin and evolution of the calls and facial expressions of the primates. *Behaviour* 20:1–109.

Beeman, K. (1992) *SIGNAL User's Guide*, Belmont, MA: Engineering Design.

Bercovitch, F., Hauser, M. D., and Jones, J. (1995) The endocrine stress response and alarm vocalizations in rhesus macaques. *Anim. Behav.* 49:1703–1706.

Best, C. T. (1988) The emergence of cerebral asymmetries in early human development: A literature review and a neuroembryological model. In *Brain Lateralization in Children*, ed. by D. L. Molfese and S. J. Segalowitz, pp. 5–34. New York: The Guilford Press.

Best, C. T. and Queen, H. F. (1989) Baby, it's in your smile: Right hemiface bias in infant emotional expressions. *Dev. Psychol.* 25:264–276.

Bradshaw, J. L. (1989) *Hemispheric Specialization and Psychological Function*. New York: John Wiley and Sons.

Bradshaw, J. L. and Rogers, L. (1993) *The Evolution of Lateral Asymmetries, Language, Tool Use, and Intellect*. San Diego, CA: Academic Press.

Brown, H. D. and Kosslyn, S. K. (1995) Hemispheric differences in visual object processing: Structural versus allocation theories. In *Brain Asymmetry*, ed. by R. Davidson and K. Hugdahl, pp. 77–97. Cambridge, MA: MIT Press.

Bruce, C. (1982) Face recognition by monkeys: Absence of an inversion effect. *Neuropsychologia* 20:515–521.

Carey, S. and Diamond, R. (1977) From piecemeal to configurational representation of faces. *Science* 195:312–314.

Changeux, J.-P. and Chavaillion, J. (1995) *Origins of the Human Brain*. Oxford: Oxford University Press.

Cheney, D. L. and Seyfarth, R. M. (1990) *How Monkeys See the World: Inside the Mind of Another Species*. Chicago: University of Chicago Press.

Cheverud, J., Falk, D., Hildebolt, C., Moore, A. J., Helmkamp, R. C., and Vannier, M. (1991) Heritability and association of cortical petalias in rhesus macaques (*Macaca mulatta*). *Brain Behav. Evol.* 35:368–372.

Corballis, M. (1991) *The Lopsided Ape*. Oxford: Oxford University Press.

Cosmides, L. and Tooby, J. (1994) Origins of domain specificity: The evolution of functional organization. In *Mapping the Mind: Domain Specificity in Cognition and Culture*, ed. by L. A. Hirschfield and S. A. Gelman, pp. 85–116. Cambridge: Cambridge University Press.

Damasio, A. and Damasio, H. (1986). *Lesion Analysis in Neuropsychology*. New York: Oxford University Press.

Davidson, R. J. (1992) Emotion and affective style: Hemispheric substrates. *Psychological Science* 3(1):39–43.

Davidson, R. J. (1995) Cerebral asymmetry, emotion, and affective style. In *Brain Asymmetry*, ed. by R. J. Davidson and K. Hugdahl, pp. 361–389. Cambridge, MA: MIT Press.

Davidson, R. J. and Hugdahl, K., eds.(1995) *Brain Asymmetry*. Cambridge, MA: MIT Press.

Deacon, T. W. (1991) The neural circuitry underlying primate calls and human language. In *Language Origin: A Multidisciplinary Approach*, ed. by J. Wind, pp. 131–172. Dordrecht, the Netherlands: Kluwer Academic Publishers.

Delis, D. C., Robertson, L. C., and Efron, R. (1986) Hemispheric specialization of memory for visual hierarchical stimuli. *Neuropsychologia* 24:205–214.

de Schonen, S., Deruelle, C., Mancini, J., and Pascalis, O. (1993) Hemispheric differences in face processing and brain maturation. In *Developmental Neurocognition: Speech and Face Processing in the First Year*, ed. by B. De Boysson-Bardies, S. de Schonen, P. Jusczyk, P. MacNeilage, and J. Morton, pp.149–163. Dordrecht, The Netherlands: Kluwer Academic Publishers.

Desimone, R. (1991) Face-selective cells in the temporal cortex of monkeys. *J. Cog. Neurosci.* 3:1–8.

Efron, R. (1990) *The Decline and Fall of Hemispheric Specialization*. Hillsdale, NJ: Lawrence Erlbaum Associates.

Ehret, G. (1987) Left hemisphere advantage in the mouse brain for recognizing ultrasonic communication calls. *Nature* 325:249–251.

Ekman, P., Davidson, R. J., and Friesen, W. V. (1990a) The Duchenne smile: Emotional expression and brain physiology *J. Pers. Soc. Psychol.* 58:342–353.

Ekman, P., Davidson, R. J., and Friesen, W. V. (1990b) Emotional expression and brain physiology. II. The Duchenne smile. *J. Pers. Soc. Psychol.* 58:112–133.

Ekman, P., Friesen, W. V., and O'Sullivan, M. (1988) Smiles while lying. *J. Pers. Soc. Psychol.* 54:414–420.

Falk, D. (1987) Brain lateralization in primates and its evolution in hominids. *Yearbook of Physical Anthropology*. 30:107–125.

Falk, D., Hildebolt, Cheverud, J., Vannier, M., Helmkamp, R. C., and Konigsberg, L. (1990) Cortical asymmetries in frontal lobes of rhesus monkeys (*Macaca mulatta*). *Brain Res.* 512:40–45.

Fitch, W. T. (1997) Vocal tract length and formant frequency dispersion correlate with body size in rhesus macaques. *J. Acous. Soc. Am.* 102:1213–1222.

Gautier-Hion, A., Bourliere, F., Gautier, J.-P., and Kingdon, J. (1988) *A Primate Radiation: Evolutionary Biology of the African Guenons*. Cambridge: Cambridge University Press.

Gazzaniga, M., and Smiley, C. S. (1991) Hemispheric mechanisms controlling voluntary and spontaneous facial expressions. *Journal of Cognitive Neuroscience* 2, 239–245.

Goller, F. and Suthers, R.A. (1995) Implications for lateralization of bird song from unilateral gating of bilateral motor patterns. *Nature* 373:63–66.

Gouzoules, S., Gouzoules, H., and Marler, P. (1984) Rhesus monkey (*Macaca mulatta*) screams: Representational signalling in the recruitment of agonistic aid. *Anim. Behav.* 32:182–193.

Graves, R., Goodglass, H., and Landis, T. (1982) Mouth asymmetry during spontaneous speech. *Neuropsychologia* 20:371–381.

Graves, R. and Landis, T. (1985) Hemispheric control of speech expression in aphasia: A mouth asymmetry study. *Archives of Neurology* 42:249–251.

Graves, R. and Landis, T. (1990) Asymmetry in mouth opening during different speech tasks. *Internat. J. Psych.* 25:179–189.

Graves, R., Strauss, E. H., and Wada, J. (1990) Mouth asymmetry during speech of epileptic patients who have undergone corotid amytal testing. *Neuropsychologia* 28:1117–1121.

Graves, R. E. and Potter, S. M. (1988) Speaking from two sides of the mouth. *Visible Language* 22:129–137.

Green, S. (1975) Variation of vocal pattern with social situation in the Japanese monkey (*Macaca fuscata*): A field study. In *Primate Behavior*, vol. 4, ed. by L. A. Rosenblum, pp. 1–102. New York: Academic Press.

Gross, C. G. and Sergent, J. (1992) Face recognition. *Curr. Opin. Neurobiol.* 2:156–161.

Hamilton, C. R., Tieman, S. B., and Farrell, W. S., Jr. (1974) Cerebral dominance in monkeys? *Neuropsychologia* 12: 193–198.

Hamilton, C. R., and Vermeire, B. A. (1991) Functional lateralization in monkeys. In *Cerebral Laterality*, ed. by F. L. Kitterle, pp. 19–34. Cambridge: Cambridge University Press.

Harries, M. H. and Perrett, D. I. (1991) Visual processing of faces in temporal cortex: Physiological evidence for a modular organization and possible anatomical correlates. *J. Cog. Neurosci.* 3:9–24.

Hartley, R. J. and Suthers, R. A. (1990) Lateralization of syringeal function during song production in the canary. *J. Neurobiol.* 21:1236–1248.

Hauser, M. D. (1991) Sources of acoustic variation in rhesus macaque vocalizations. *Ethology* 89:29–46.

Hauser, M. D. (1992) Articulatory and social factors influence the acoustic structure of rhesus monkey vocalizations: A learned mode of production? *J. Acoust. Soc. Am.* 91:2175–2179.

Hauser, M. D. (1993a) Right hemisphere dominance for production of facial expression in a monkey. *Science* 261:475–477.

Hauser, M. D. (1993b) Rhesus monkey (*Macaca mulatta*) copulation calls: Honest signals for female choice? *Proc. Roy. Soc. Lond.* 254:93–96.

Hauser, M. D. (1996) *The Evolution of Communication*. Cambridge, MA: MIT Press.

Hauser, M. D. (1998) Functional referents and acoustic similarity: Field playback experiments with rhesus monkeys. *Anim. Behav.* 55:1647–1658.

Hauser, M. D., Agnetta, B., and Perez, C. (1998) Orienting asymmetries in rhesus monkeys: The effect of time-domain changes on acoustic perception. *Anim. Behav.* 56:41–47

Hauser, M. D. and Andersson, K. (1994) Left hemisphere dominance for processing vocalizations in adult, but not infant rhesus monkeys: Field experiments. *Proc. Natl. Acad. Sci.* 91:3946–3948.

Hauser, M. D., Evans, C. S., and Marler, P. (1993) The role of articulation in the production of rhesus monkey (*Macaca mulatta*) vocalizations. *Anim. Behav.* 45:423–433.

Hauser, M. D. and Marler, P. (1993a) Food-associated calls in rhesus macaques (*Macaca mulatta*). I. Socioecological factors influencing call production. *Behav. Ecol.* 4:194–205.

Hauser, M. D. and Marler, P. (1993b) Food-associated calls in rhesus macaques (*Macaca mulatta*). II. Costs and benefits of call production and suppression. *Behav. Ecol.* 4:206–212.

Hauser, M. D., Perry, S., Manson, J., Ball, H., Williams, M., Pearson, E., and Berard, J. (1991) It's all in the hands of the beholder: New data on handedness in a free-ranging population of rhesus macaques. *Behav. Brain Sci.* 14:342–344.

Hauser, M. D. and Schön Ybarra, M. (1994) The role of lip configuration in monkey vocalizations: Experiments using xylocaine as a nerve block. *Brain and Language* 46:232–244.

Heffner, H. E. and Heffner, R. S. (1984) Temporal lobe lesions and perception of species-specific vocalizations by macaques. *Science* 226:75–76.

Heffner, H. E. and Heffner, R. S. (1990) Role of primate auditory cortex in hearing. In *Comparative Perception*, vol. 2: *Complex Signals*, ed. by M. A. Berkley, and W. C. Stebbins, pp. 136–159. New York: J. Wiley and Sons.

Heilbroner, P. L. and Holloway, R. L. (1988) Anatomical brain asymmetries in New World and Old World Monkeys: Stages of temporal lobe development in primate evolution. *Am. J. Phys. Anthro.* 76:39–48.

Hellige, J. B. (1993) *Hemispheric Asymmetry: What's Right and What's Left.* Cambridge, MA: Harvard University Press.

Hershkovitz, P. (1977) *Living New World Monkeys (Platyrrhini).* Chicago: University of Chicago Press.

Hillger, L. A. and Koenig, O. (1991) Separable mechanisms in face processing: Evidence from hemispheric specialization. *J. Cog. Neurosci.* 3:42–58.

Hilliard, R. D. (1973) Hemispheric laterality affects on a facial recognition task in normal subjects. *Cortex* 9:246–258.

Hirschfeld, L. A. and Gelman, S. A. (1994) *Mapping the Mind: Domain Specificity in Cognition and Culture.* Cambridge: Cambridge University Press.

Hiscock, M. (1988) Behavioral asymmetries in normal children. In *Behavioral Asymmetries in Normal Children*, ed. by D. L. Molfese and S. J. Segalowitz, pp. 134–182. New York: The Guilford Press.

Hiscock, M. and Kinsbourne, M. (1995) Phylogeny and ontogeny of cerebral lateralization. In *Brain Asymmetry*, ed. by R. J. Davidson and K. Hugdahl, pp. 535–578. Cambridge, MA: MIT Press.

Hodos, W. and Campbell, C. B. G. (1990) Evolutionary scales and comparative studies of animal cognition. In *Neurobiology of Comparative Cognition*, ed. by R. P. Kesner and D. S. Olton, pp. 1–20. Hillsdale, NJ: Lawrence Erlbaum.

Hopkins, W. D., Washburn, D. A., and Rumbaugh, D. (1990) Processing of form stimuli presented unilaterally in humans, chimpanzees (*Pan troglodytes*) and monkeys (*Macaca mulatta*). *Behav. Neurosci.* 104:577–582.

Hopkins, W. D., Morris, R. D., and Savage-Rumbaugh, E. S. (1991) Evidence for asymmetrical hemispheric priming using known and unknown warning stimuli in two language-trained chimpanzees (*Pan troglodytes*). *J. Exp. Psychol.* 120:46–56.

Ifune, C. K., Vermeire, B. A., and Hamilton, C. R. (1984) Hemispheric differences in split-brain monkeys viewing and responding to videotape recordings. *Behav. Neur. Biol.* 41:231–235.

Ivry, R. B. and Lebby, P. C. (1993) Hemispheric differences in auditory perception are similar to those found in visual perception. *Psychol. Sci.* 4(1):41–45.

Jerison, H. and Jerison, I. (1988) *The Evolutionary Biology of Intelligence.* New York: Academic Press.

Jürgens, U. (1990) Vocal communication in primates. In *Neurobiology of Comparative Cognition*, ed. by R. P. Kesner and D. S. Olton, pp. 51–76. Hillsdale, NJ: Lawrence Erlbaum.

Kimura, D. (1993) *Neuromotor Mechanisms in Human Communication.* Oxford: Oxford University Press.

Kirzinger, A. and Jürgens, U. (1982) Cortical lesion effects and vocalization in the squirrel monkey. *Brain Res.* 358:150–162.

Kolb, B. and Whishaw, I. Q. (1985) *Fundamentals of Human Neuropsychology*, 2nd edition. San Francisco: Freeman.

Kosslyn, S. M., Koenig, O., Barrett, A., and Cave, C. B. (1989) Evidence for two types of spatial representations: Hemispheric specialization for categorical and coordinate relations. *J. Exp. Psychol.* 15:723–735.

Kuhl, P. K. (1992) Infants' perception and representation of speech: Development of a new theory. In *Proceedings of the International Conference on Spoken Language Processing*, ed. by J. Ohala, T. Neary, B. Derwing, M. Hodge, and G. Wiebe, pp. 449–456. Edmonton: University of Alberta Press.

LaMendola, N. P. and Bever, T. G. (1997) Peripheral and cerebral asymmetries in the rat. *Science* 278:483–486.

Lee, G. P., Loring, D. W., Meader, K. J., and Brooks, B. B. (1990) Hemispheric specialization for emotional expression: A reexamination of results from intracarotid administration of sodium amobarbital. *Brain Cog.* 12:267–280.

Leehey, S. C., Carey, S., Diamond, R., and Cohn, A. (1979) Upright and inverted faces: The right hemisphere knows the difference. *Cortex* 14:411–419.

Levine, S. C. (1989) The question of faces: Special in the brain of the beholder. In *Handbook of Research in Face Processing*, ed. by A. W. Young and H. D. Ellis, pp. 37–40. Hillsdale, NJ: Lawrence Erlbaum.

Levy, J., Heller, W., Banich, M. T., and Burton, L. A. (1983) Asymmetry of perception in free viewing of chimeric faces. *Brain Cog.* 2:404–419.

MacNeilage, P. F. (1991) The "postural origins" theory of primate neurobiological asymmetries. In *Biological Foundations of Language Development*, ed. by N. Krasnegor, D. Rumbaugh, M. Studdert-Kennedy, and R. Schiefelbusch, pp. 165–188. Hillsdale, NJ: Lawrence Erlbaum

MacNeilage, P. F. (1994) Proegomena to a theory of the sound patterns of the first language. *Phonetica* 51:184–194.

MacNeilage, P. F., Studdert-Kennedy, M. G., and Lindblom, B. (1987) Primate handedness reconsidered. *Behav. Brain Sci.* 10:247–303.

Marler, P. (1970) Birdsong and speech development: could there be parallels? *Am. Sci.* 58.669–673.

Marler, P., Evans, C. S., and Hauser, M. D. (1992) Animal signals? Reference, motivation, or both? In *Nonverbal Vocal Communication: Comparative and Developmental Approaches*, ed. by H. Papoucek, U. Jürgens, and M. Papoucek, pp. 66–86. Cambridge: Cambridge University Press.

Masataka, N. and Fujita, K. (1989) Vocal learning of Japanese and rhesus monkeys. *Behaviour* 109:191–199.

Newman, J. D. and Wollberg, Z. (1973a) Multiple coding of species-specific vocalizations in the auditory cortex of squirrel monkeys. *Brain Res.* 54:287–304.

Newman, J. D. and Wollberg, Z. (1973b) Responses of single neurons in the auditory cortex of squirrel monkeys to variants of a single call type. *Exp. Neurol.* 40:821–824.

Nottebohm, F. (1972) Neural lateralization of vocal control in a Passerine bird. II. Subsong, calls, and a theory of vocal learning. *J. Exp. Zool.* 179:35–50.

Nottebohm, F. (1977) Asymmetries in neural control of vocalization in the canary. In *Lateralization in the Nervous System*, ed. by S. Harnad, R. W. Doty, L. Goldstein, J. Jaynes, and G. Krauthamer, pp. 23–44. New York: Academic Press.

Nottebohm, F., Alvarez-Buylla, A., Cynx, J., Kirn, J., Ling, C. Y., and Nottebohm, M. (1990) Song learning in birds: The relation between perception and production. *Phil. Trans. Royal Soc.* (London) B 292:205–211.

Nowicki, S. and Capranica, R. R. (1986) Bilateral syringeal interaction in vocal production of an oscine bird sound. *Science* 231:1297–1299.

Otte, D. and Endler, J. A. (1989) *Speciation and Its Consequences*. Sunderland, MA: Sinauer Press.

Overman, W. H. and Doty, R. W. (1982) Hemispheric specialization displayed by man but not macaques for analysis of faces. *Neuropsychologia* 20:113–128.

Owren, M. J., Dieter, J. A., Seyfarth, R. M., and Cheney, D. L. (1992) "Food" calls produced by adult female rhesus (*Macaca mulatta*) and Japanese (*M. fuscata*) macaques, their normally raised offspring, and offspring cross-fostered between species. *Behaviour* 120:218–231.

Owren, M. J., Dieter, J. A., Seyfarth, R. M., and Cheney, D. L. (1993) Vocalizations of rhesus (*Macaca mulatta*) and Japanese (*M. fuscata*) macaques cross-fostered between species show evidence of only limited modification. *Dev. Psychobiol.* 26:389–406.

Pandya, D. P., Seltzer, B., and Barbas, H. (1998) Input-output organization of the primate cerebral cortex. In *Comparative Primate Biology: Neurosciences*, ed. by H. D. Steklis and J. Erwin. New York: Liss. Yin, R. U. Looking at upside down faces. *Jorunal of Experimental Psychology* 81, 141–148.

Peretz, I. and Babai, M. (1992) The role of contour and intervals in the recognition of melody parts: Evidence from cerebral asymmetries in musicians. *Neuropsychologia* 30:277–292.

Perrett, D. I., Mistlin, A. J., Chitty, A. J., Smith, P. A. J., Potter, D. D., Broennimann, R., and Harries, M. (1988) Specialized face processing and hemispheric asymmetry in man and monkey: Evidence from single unit and reaction time studies. *Behav. Brain Res.* 29:245–258.

Petersen, M. R., Beecher, M. D., Zoloth, S. R., Moody, D. B., and Stebbins, W. C. (1978) Neural lateralization of species-specific vocalizations by Japanese macaques. *Science* 202:324–326.

Rauschecker, J. P., Tian, B., and Hauser, M. (1995) Processing of complex sounds in the macaque non-primary auditory cortex. *Science* 268:111–114.

Rosch, E. (1975) Cognitive reference points. *Cog. Psychol.* 7:532–547.

Ross, E. D., Edmondson, J. A., Seibert, G. B., and Homan, R. W. (1988) Acoustic analysis of affective prosody during right-sided wada test: A within-subjects verification of the right hemisphere's role in language. *Brain and Language* 33:128–145.

Ryan, M. J. and Rand, A. S. (1993) Phylogenetic patterns of behavioral mate recognition systems in the *Physalaemus pustulosus* species group (*Anura: Leptodactylidae*): The role of ancestral and derived characters and sensory exploitation. In *Evolutionary Patterns and Processes*, ed. by D. Lees and D. Edwards, pp. 251–267. London: Academic Press.

Sackheim, H. A., Gur, R. C., Saucy, M. C. (1978) Emotions are expressed more intensely on the left side of the face. *Science* 202:434–436.

Sergent, J. S., Ohta, S., and MacDonald, B. (1992) Functional neuroanatomy of face and object processing: A positron emission tomography study. *Brain* 115:15–36.

Sherman, G. F., Garbanati, J. A., Rosen, G. D., Yutzey, D. A., and Dennenberg, V. H. (1980) Brain and behavioral asymmetries for spatial preferences in rats. *Brain Res.* 192:61–67.

Snowdon, C. T. (1990) Language capacities of nonhuman animals. *Yearbook of Physical Anthropology* 33:215–243.

Sutton, D. and Jürgens, U. (1988) Neural control of vocalization. In *Comparative Primate Biology*, vol. 4: *Neuroscience*, ed. by J. Erwin, pp. 625–647. New York, NY: Alan Liss.

Suthers, R. A. (1994) Variable asymmetry and resonance in the avian vocal tract: Astructural basis for individually distinct vocalizations. *J. Comp. Physiol.* A 175:457–466.

Ungerleider, L. G. (1995) Functional brain imaging studies of cortical mechanisms for memory. *Science* 270:769–775.

Vauclair, J., Fagot, J., and Hopkins, W. D. (1993) Rotation of mental images in baboons when the visual input is directed to the left cerbral hemisphere. *Psychol. Sci.* 4(2):99–103.

Ward, J. P. and Hopkins, W. D. (1993) *Primate Laterality: Current Behavioral Evidence of Primate Asymmetries.* New York: Springer-Verlag.

23 Mechanisms Underlying the Vocalizations of Nonhuman Primates

Dorothy L. Cheney and Robert M. Seyfarth

During the 1960s and 1970s it was generally assumed that the vocalizations of non-human primates conveyed information primarily about the signaler's affective state (see examples provided by Marler 1975, 1992; see also Hockett 1960, Snowdon et al. 1982). Only animals that had been explicitly tutored by humans were thought to be capable of symbolic communication (Premack 1975). In 1967, however, Struhsaker described a possible exception to prevailing dogma. East African vervet monkeys (*Cercopithecus aethiops*), he reported, gave a variety of acoustically distinct alarm calls in response to different classes of predators, suggesting that at least some animal signals might function to signal information about specific features of the environment. It became apparent that the dichotomy between animal signals and human language might not be as clear-cut as had been assumed (Marler 1967).

In the 30 years since Struhsaker's initial report, a number of studies have shown that at least some nonhuman primate vocalizations function to designate objects or events in the external world (see review by Hauser 1996). In the case of vervet monkeys, for example, playback experiments have revealed that the animals' acoustically different alarm calls evoke qualitatively different responses from nearby listeners. For instance, alarm calls given to leopards (*Panthera pardus*) cause vervets to run into trees, while alarm calls given to martial and crowned eagles (*Polemaetus bellicosus* and *Stephanoaetus coronatus*) cause vervets to look up or run into bushes. Moreover, tape recordings of the alarm calls alone elicit the same responses as do the predators themselves, even when an actual predator is absent (Seyfarth et al. 1980a,b).

The Classification of Calls by Monkeys

Vocalizations like vervet monkey alarm calls may function as referential signals, but how similar are they to human words? For many years, it was assumed that animals respond to vocal signals simply on the basis of the calls' physical features, or acoustic properties (see, e.g., Morton 1977). Humans, by contrast, make judgments about the similarity or difference between words on the basis of an abstraction, their meaning. For example, when asked to compare the words "treachery" and "deceit," we typically ignore the fact that the two words have different acoustic properties and describe them as similar because they have similar meanings. "Treachery" and "lechery," on the other hand, are judged as different because, despite their acoustic similarity, they mean different things. In making these judgments, we implicitly recognize the referential relation between words and the things for which they stand.

The "ape language" projects provide a number of elegant cases in which chimpanzees (*Pan troglodytes*) and bonobos (*Pan paniscus*) have learned to assess and compare signs according to their meaning (see, e.g., Premack 1976; Savage-Rumbaugh 1986; Boysen 1996). This ability, however, may not be not restricted to captive apes that have been trained in the use of artificial signs. Vervet monkeys also appear to have some mental representation of what their vocalizations stand for: when responding to calls, they seem to compare and assess them according to their meanings, and not just their acoustic properties.

When a vervet subject is repeatedly played a tape-recording of another individual's leopard alarm call when there is no leopard in the vicinity, she soon habituates to the call and ceases responding to it. If, however, the subject is then played the same individual's eagle alarm call, she responds strongly to it, in the same way that she would if an eagle had been sighted. Apparently, because the two calls have different referents, the subject does not transfer habituation across call types (Cheney and Seyfarth 1988).

Vervets do transfer habituation, however, between call types that appear to have similar referents. Vervet monkeys are hostile toward the members of neighboring groups (Struhsaker 1967b; Cheney 1981). When females encounter another group encroaching on their range, they often utter a loud, long, trilling call (termed a "wrr"), which seems to function to alert other individuals of the encroachment. Roughly 45% of all intergroup encounters involve only the exchange of wrrs; others, however, escalate into aggressive chases and fights. When groups come together under these more aggressive conditions, females often give an acoustically different "chutter." The two calls, wrrs and chutters, therefore, are acoustically different but seem to share a similar referent: another group. Moreover, vervets seem to treat the two calls as being, roughly speaking, synonymous. If a subject has habituated to repeated playback of another individual's intergroup wrr, she shows a similarly low level of response when played that individual's intergroup chutter. Apparently, she transfers habituation from one call type to another because, despite their different acoustic properties, the two calls have the same general meaning (Cheney and Seyfarth 1988).

Another example of the ways in which monkeys seem to classify calls according to their meaning comes from studies of the predator alarm calls of diana monkeys (*Cercopithecus diana*). Like vervets, male and female diana monkeys give acoustically different, sex-specific alarm calls in response to leopards. If the monkeys are played tape-recordings of a leopard's growl, males and females respond by giving alarm calls. Similarly, when played a male diana monkey's leopard alarm call, females respond with their own, acoustically different, leopard alarm call (Zuberbuhler et al. 1997). If, however, females are played a male diana monkey's leopard alarm call shortly after hearing a leopard's growl, the call no longer evokes a vocal response, apparently because the alarm call is redundant (Zuberbuhler et al. 1999). Diana monkeys, therefore, appear to judge a leopard's growl, a male diana monkey's leopard alarm call, and a female diana monkey's leopard alarm call as designating the same class of danger, even though the three calls are acoustically distinct.

What are the mental mechanisms that underlie the classification and comparison of calls by monkeys? On the one hand, monkeys might classify acoustically different calls as synonymous because the calls evoke the same mental concept (e.g., an intruding group or a leopard), in much the same way that humans judge different-sounding words because they carry the same meaning. On the other hand, two calls could be judged as equivalent simply because they are associated with the same stimulus and/or response (Thompson 1995).

This explanatory impasse can be partially resolved by considering other, complementary sorts of evidence. For example, in captivity monkeys readily learn to classify objects according to sameness or oddity (see, e.g., Davis et al. 1967; Burdyn and Thomas 1984), suggesting, at the very least, that free-ranging monkeys are capable of forming relative class concepts and comparing calls according to their meanings. Equally important, under natural conditions vocal signals like vervets' intergroup calls do not consistently elicit the same responses, nor are they always elicited by the same stimuli. Depending on the context in which they occur, the same call can evoke a number of different responses, ranging from apparent indifference to hostile chases and fights. Similarly, the call can be given to single individuals or entire groups. Intergroup calls may also function to tag the status of immigrant males. Female vervets often give calls normally associated with intergroup encounters to males when they first enter a group, but they gradually shift to other call types as they become more integrated into the social structure (Cheney and Seyfarth 1990b).

Observations such as these suggest that vervets' intergroup calls designate a type of event rather than a specific behavioral response or stimulus. When one vervet hears another calling, she appears to form some sort of mental representation of what the call means. And if, shortly thereafter, she hears a second call, the two calls are compared on the basis of their meaning, and not just their acoustic properties.

Intentional Communication

The comprehension of words by humans involves more than just a recognition of the referential relation between sounds and the objects or events they denote. As listeners, we interpret words not just as signs for things but also as representations of the speaker's knowledge. We attribute mental states like knowledge or ignorance to others, and we recognize the causal relation between mental states and behavior. We are, as a result, acutely sensitive to the relation between words and the mental states that underlie them. If, for example, we detect a mismatch between what another person says and what he thinks, we immediately consider the possibility that he is trying to deceive us.

H. P. Grice (1957) is one of many philosophers who have tried to clarify the distinction between human speech and simpler signaling systems that can nevertheless convey sophisticated, complex information. Grice distinguished the "nonnatural" meaning of linguistic phenomena, in which the speaker intends to modify both the behavior and beliefs of his audience, from the "natural" meaning of many other types of signs, in which, for example, thunder and lightning mean that it will soon rain (see also Bennett 1976; Tiles 1987). According to Grice's definition, truly linguistic communication does not occur unless both signaler and recipient take into account each other's states of mind—unless, in other words, both signaler and recipient take what the philosopher Dennett (1987) has called the "intentional stance."

All observations and experiments conducted to date suggest that monkeys do not attribute knowledge and beliefs different from their own to other individuals, though the evidence from chimpanzees is more equivocal (reviewed by Cheney and Seyfarth 1990b; Povinelli 1993; van Hooff 1994; Byrne 1995; Tomasello and Call 1997). Grice's definition of communication, therefore, may be irrelevant when applied to most cases of animal communication. Nevertheless, his definition is useful and provocative because it reminds us that there can be communication systems that are complex and even semantic but that may not qualify as language because they fail to meet the criteria of language on intentional grounds.

The Social Function of Primate Vocalizations

Only a small proportion of the vocalizations given by monkeys and apes occur in the form of alarm or intergroup calls. Instead, the most common calls given by non-human primates are low amplitude grunts, coos, or trills that are given at close range and occur in the context of social interactions or group movement. Many of these calls appear to function to initiate and facilitate social interactions. For example, female baboons (*Papio cynocephalus ursinus*) utter low amplitude tonal grunts during many of their social interactions. The majority of grunts occur in the context of handling other females' infants, but females may also grunt as they approach one another, as they feed near or groom one another, or as they move into new areas of their range. As is true also of many other nonhuman primates' calls (e.g., cotton-top tamarins, *Saguinus oedipus*: Cleveland and Snowdon 1982; squirrel monkeys, *Saimiri sciureus*: Boinski 1992; Japanese macaques, *Macaca fuscata*: Blount 1985, Masataka 1989, Sakuro 1989; stump-tailed macaques, *M. arctoides*: Bauers 1993; vervet monkeys: Cheney and Seyfarth 1982; mountain gorillas, *Gorilla gorilla*: Harcourt et al. 1993; Seyfarth et al. 1994; reviewed by Hauser 1996), baboons' grunts appear to function at least in part to facilitate social interactions. Dominant females that grunt as they approach more subordinate individuals are less likely to supplant these individuals, and are more likely to handle their infants, than females that remain silent (see also Cheney et al. 1995).

From a functional perspective, baboon grunts are interesting because they are in many ways analogous to human speech. Typically, there is no obvious behavioral response to the calls from nearby listeners, and it certainly seems as if these vocalizations, like many human conversations, function simply to mediate social interactions and grease the social wheels. Note, however, that it is difficult to describe the function of these calls without adopting an intentional vocabulary on behalf of the signaler. If a call serves to mollify a subordinate mother, it seems almost essential that the signaler be able to recognize her partner's anxiety and to signal her own benign intent.

Dominant female baboons also grunt to their former victims after about 13% of aggressive interactions. Although these calls seem to serve a reconciliatory function, this is difficult to determine from observations alone because grunts often occur in conjunction with other friendly behavior like grooming or infant handling. To test the hypothesis that vocalizations lead to reconciliation even in the absence of any other friendly interactions, we designed a playback experiment in which we attempted to mimic vocal reconciliation by playing the grunt of a former opponent to a victim in the minutes immediately following a fight (for details, see Cheney and Seyfarth 1997). The experiment's aim was to determine whether an apparently reconciliatory call has any influence on victims' subsequent behavior toward their former opponents.

Victims were played their opponents' grunts in the minutes immediately following a fight and then observed for half an hour. After hearing these "reconciliatory" grunts, victims approached their former opponents and also tolerated their opponents' approaches at significantly higher rates than they did under baseline conditions (figure 23.1; two-tailed Wilcoxon matched-pairs signed ranks sign, $P < 0.005$). They were also supplanted by their opponents at significantly lower rates ($P < 0.001$). By contrast, playbacks of reconciliatory grunts had no effect on opponents' tendencies to approach their victims or to initiate friendly interactions with them (Cheney and Seyfarth 1997). This was no doubt due to the fact that "reconciliatory"

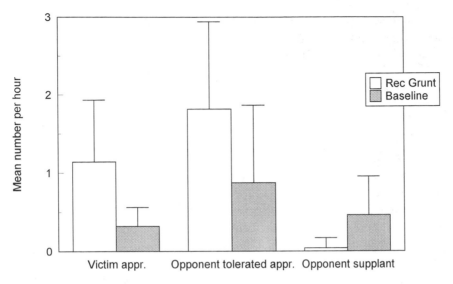

Figure 23.1
The mean hourly rate that victims approached their opponent, tolerated their opponent's approach, or were supplanted by their opponent after hearing a playback of their opponent's "reconciliatory" grunt, compared with baseline conditions. Baseline rates were obtained from focal animal samples conducted in the absence of a recent fight between a victim and a given opponent. Histograms show means and standard deviations for 20 victims (90 dyads) (see Cheney and Seyfarth 1997 for additional data).

grunts were not actually produced by the opponents themselves, but were instead mimicked through artificial playbacks. From the perspective of the victim, reconciliation had apparently occurred, while from the perspective of her opponent it had not. As a result, although dominant females tolerated their former victims' more frequent approaches, they were not necessarily inclined either to initiate a friendly interaction or to signal in some way their willingness to accept such an interaction.

The Cognitive Mechanisms Underlying Monkeys' Calls

These experiments suggest that vocalizations have a strong causal influence on victims' behavior and constitute a major component of reconciliatory behavior in female baboons. What, however, are the mechanisms underlying apparently reconciliatory grunts? Do dominant females give grunts with the intent of appeasing their former victims? One explanation for the prevalence of vocalizations following conflicts is that dominant females grunt in order to alleviate their opponent's anxiety and to reassure them that they are no longer angry. An equally plausible explanation, however, is that dominant females simply grunt to their victims because they now wish to interact with their opponents or their infants.

Although these two explanations are functionally equivalent, they are based on quite different underlying cognitive mechanisms. The first focuses on the signaler and assumes that calling individuals recognize that their audience may have different mental states (e.g., anxiety) than their own. The second explanation focuses on the audience and assumes that listeners respond to calls on the basis of behavioral contingencies. This latter explanation requires that subordinate females learn, through experience, that grunts signal a low probability of attack; as a result, their anxiety is diminished when a dominant female grunts to them.

Despite their functional equivalence, the distinction between these two explanations is crucially important to any discussion concerned with the evolution of language. If, as Grice and others have argued, true linguistic communication cannot occur unless both speaker and listener take into account each other's states of mind, then monkeys cannot be said to communicate unless they use calls like reconciliatory grunts with the intent of influencing each other's beliefs and emotions. By contrast, if monkeys are incapable of recognizing the causal relationship between behavior and beliefs, a call that functions to reconcile an opponent will be based on fundamentally different underlying mental mechanisms than reconciliation in the human sense of the term, in which individuals deliberately act to appease or overcome the distrust or animosity of another. In fact, there is very little evidence that monkeys or other animals ever take into account their audience's knowledge when calling to one another.

Consider alarm calls, for example. The alarm calls of many birds and mammals are not obligatory, but depend on social context. Individuals often fail to give alarm calls when there is no functional advantage to be gained by alerting others; for instance, when they are alone or in the presence of unrelated individuals (e.g., ground squirrels, *Spermophilus beldingi*: Sherman 1977; downy woodpeckers, *Picoides pubescens*: Sullivan 1985; vervet monkeys, Cheney and Seyfarth 1985; roosters, *Gallus gallus*: Gyger et al. 1986). However, although this "audience effect" clearly requires that a signaler monitor the presence and behavior of group companions, it does not demand that he also distinguish between ignorance and knowledge on the part of his audience (Marler et al. 1988). Indeed, in all species studied thus far, signalers call regardless of whether their audience is already aware of danger. Vervet monkeys, for example, will continue to give alarm calls long after everyone in their group has seen the predator and retreated to safety.

Experiments with captive rhesus (*Macaca mulatta*) and Japanese macaques have demonstrated that mothers do not alter their alarm-calling behavior depending upon the knowledge or ignorance of their offspring. When given the opportunity to alert ignorant offspring of potential danger, they do not change their alarm-calling behavior (Cheney and Seyfarth 1990a). Similarly, vervet monkeys do not instruct their offspring in the appropriate use of alarm calls. Infant vervets give eagle alarm calls to many bird species, like pigeons, that pose no danger to them. Adults, however, never correct their offspring when they make inappropriate alarm calls, nor do they selectively reinforce them when they give alarm calls to real predators, like martial eagles. Instead, infant vervets seem to learn appropriate usage simply by observing adults (Seyfarth and Cheney 1986, this volume). Finally, adult vervets are more likely to give alarm calls at predators like leopards, to which they themselves are vulnerable, than to predators like baboons, to which their offspring—but not adults—are vulnerable (Cheney and Seyfarth 1981).

In summary, there is no doubt that the alarm calls given by monkeys function to inform nearby listeners of quite specific sorts of danger. They seem, however, simply to mirror the intent and state of the signaler, and they fail to take into account their audience's knowledge or ignorance.

A similar disregard for one's audience's knowledge and beliefs seems to characterize the contact and food-associated calls given by many species of animals. Despite numerous attempts to test the hypothesis that foraging animals share information about the location of food or each other's relative positions in the group progression, no study has yet been able to demonstrate that individuals deliberately inform one another. For example, although carrion birds and bats that feed on widely dispersed food sources could potentially share information at common roosting sites, individuals appear to locate food either by following others or by simply finding it themselves (e.g., crows, *Corrus corone*: Richner and Marclay 1991; turkey vultures, *Cathartes aura*: Prior and Weatherhead 1991; bats, *Nycticeius humeralis*: Wilkinson 1992; red kites, *Milvus milvus*: Hiraldo et al. 1993).

Even in the case of nonhuman primates, evidence for intentional information sharing is lacking. There is no indication that signalers selectively answer the calls of separated individuals, or that they call more upon discovering a new food source than upon returning to a tree that was recently visited by many group members. For example, capuchins (*Cebus capucinus*) and squirrel monkeys (*Saimiri sciureus*) give progression calls primarily when they themselves are moving or about to move (Boinski 1991, 1993). Spider monkeys (*Ateles geoffroyi*) call when they arrive at a fruiting tree, but the calls function to recruit other subgroups only a small proportion of the time (Chapman and Levebre 1990). Similarly, although chimpanzees often give pant hoots upon arrival at large unoccupied fruiting trees, parties that call are not joined more than parties that remain silent (Clark and Wrangham 1994), nor are individuals that remain silent punished for failing to alert others. These observations have forced some revision of the hypothesis that calls such as chimpanzees' pant hoots function to alert others to food (Wrangham 1977). Indeed, current evidence suggests that the calls may instead function to signal the caller's status (Mitani and Nishida 1993; Clark and Wrangham 1994). Although listeners may use calls to maintain contact with signalers or to locate food resources, therefore, the proximate cause of the calls appears to be the current state or status of the signaler.

Baboon Contact Barks

When moving through wooded areas, female and juvenile baboons often give loud barks that can be heard up to 500 meters away (Cheney et al. 1996; see also Byrne 1981). These "contact barks" can function to maintain group cohesion because, upon hearing one or more barks, an individual that has lost contact with others knows immediately where at least some group members are.

Because contact barks are typically temporally clumped, with many individuals giving calls at roughly the same time, baboons often appear to be answering one another. What is not clear, however, is whether baboons give such calls with the intent of maintaining contact with each other, or whether the calls simply reflect the signaler's own circumstances (e.g., separated from the group). Hypotheses based on mental-state attribution predict that individuals will answer the contact barks of others even when they themselves are in the center of the group progression and at no risk of becoming separated from others. If, however, baboons are incapable of understanding that other individuals' mental states can be different from their own, they should be unable to recognize when another individual has become separated from the group unless they themselves are also peripheral and at risk of becoming separated. Under these circumstances, contact barks will simply reflect the state and location of the signaler.

In fact, closer inspection of the contact barks given by female baboons indicates that the calls are clumped in time not because females are answering one another but because females typically give calls in bouts. Playback experiments further suggest that females "answer" the contact barks of their close relatives primarily when they themselves are peripheral and at risk of becoming separated from the group (for details, see Cheney et al. 1996). Subjects are significantly more likely to "answer" their relatives' contact barks when they are in the last third of the group progression than when they are at the front or middle. They are also more likely to give answering barks when there are no other females within 25 meters than if there is at least one other female nearby (figure 23.2).

Both observations and experiments suggest, therefore, that baboons do not give contact barks with the intent of sharing information, even though the calls may ultimately function to allow widely separated individuals to maintain contact with one

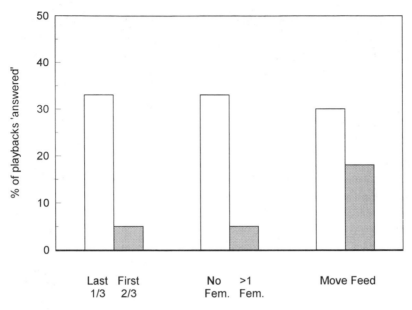

Figure 23.2
The proportion of playback experiments that elicited "answering" barks from subjects in different contexts. Histograms compare subjects in the last third versus the first two thirds of the group progression, in the vicinity of no other versus at least one other female, and moving as opposed to feeding. Data are based on 36 trials involving 18 subjects (see Cheney et al. 1996 for additional data).

another. Like the progression, contact, and food calls given by other species of primates, baboon contact barks appear to reflect the signaler's own state and position rather than the state and position of others.

Discussion

The vocalizations of nonhuman primates share a number of similarities with human speech. Many of the calls given by vervet monkeys, for example, are functionally semantic and serve to denote objects or events in the external world. Vervets seem to compare and classify calls according to their meaning, and not just their acoustic properties. They judge some acoustically different calls to be the same when the calls refer to similar events. The monkeys behave, in other words, as if they recognize the referential relation between calls and the things for which they stand.

The calls given by monkeys during social interactions also appear to serve many of the same purposes as human speech, in the sense that they act to mediate social interactions, to appease, and to reconcile. Other calls function to inform individuals about the caller's location and to maintain group contact and cohesion.

Despite these functional similarities, however, the mental mechanisms underlying nonhuman primate vocalizations appear to be fundamentally different from the mechanisms underlying adult human speech. When calling to one another, monkeys seem to lack one of the essential requirements of human language: the ability to take into account their audience's mental states.

Explanations based on mental-state attribution make quite specific predictions about the pattern and context of calls. A vervet or macaque that attributes to others beliefs different from her own should adjust her alarm or intergroup calls according to her audience's knowledge, and she should selectively inform ignorant individuals more than knowledgeable ones. She should also correct her offspring when it gives alarm calls to inappropriate species. A dominant female baboon that attributes emotions to others should grunt to a subordinate victim in order to alleviate her victim's anxiety even though, being dominant, she feels no anxiety herself. Similarly, a baboon capable of attributing confusion or anxiety to others should answer other individuals' contact barks regardless of her own position in the group progression.

Despite a variety of tests, however, there is no evidence that monkeys attribute mental states like knowledge or ignorance to one another. Monkeys appear not to call with the intent of providing information or influencing listeners' beliefs. Instead, listeners appear to respond to calls based on learned behavioral contingencies.

Although vervet monkeys, like many other species of birds and mammals, may vary their rates of alarm calling depending upon the composition of their audience, they do not act deliberately to inform ignorant individuals more than knowledgeable ones (Cheney and Seyfarth 1990a,b). A vervet's alarm call alerts other animals regardless of whether or not they are already aware of the danger. In a like manner, infant vervets are not explicitly instructed to respond to some prey species rather than others. Instead, they learn to recognize their predators by observing the behavior of adults (Seyfarth and Cheney 1986).

In the case of baboons' reconciliatory grunts, it seems likely that dominant females grunt to their former victims because they wish to interact in a friendly way with them, usually because these individuals have young infants (Cheney et al. 1995; Silk et al. 1996). Through past experience, and perhaps also by observing the interactions of others, the victims learn that grunts honestly signal a low probability of aggression. They therefore alter their behavior toward their opponents after hearing their "reconciliatory" grunts.

Similarly, baboons give contact barks when they are at the group's periphery and at risk of becoming separated from others. Through experience, listeners learn that they can maintain contact with at least a subset of the group simply by listening to other individuals' calls.

In all cases, listeners are able to extract relevant information about a call's function based on their own experiences. Their responses need not take into account the signaler's knowledge and beliefs at all. Indeed, in each case, the meaning and function of the calls are to a large part determined by the listener rather than the signaler (Marler 1961; Smith 1977). Upon hearing a vervet's intergroup call, the listener deduces that another group is nearby, and this representation allows her to ignore any subsequent intergroup vocalizations, even those with different acoustic properties. Upon hearing a dominant baboon's grunt, the subordinate listener deduces that she will not be attacked. Upon hearing another baboon's contact bark, the listener deduces the group's location and direction of travel. In each case, the listener extracts rich, semantic information from a signaler who may not, in the human sense, have intended to provide it.

Even in the case of apes, evidence for the intentional sharing of information is lacking. Although apes can be more easily trained than monkeys to attend to information-sharing gestures like pointing, there is little indication that they distinguish between knowledgeable and ignorant informants (Povinelli et al. 1990, 1992a,b). Similarly, although apes seem better than monkeys at recognizing the causal relation between tools and their function (Boesch 1991; Limongelli et al. 1995), they do not go out of their way to teach tool-using skills to ignorant individuals, or to inform others about their use (Boesch 1991; Tomasello 1996; Tomasello and Call 1997).

From the listener's perspective, then, nonhuman primate vocalizations share many similarities with human semantic signals. Not only do calls function to inform others of specific features of the environment and the signaler's emotions and intentions, but they also appear to be judged and classified according to the representations that they instantiate in the listener's mind.

From the signaler's perspective, however, there are striking discontinuities between nonhuman primate vocalizations and human language. These discontinuities are based not so much on the formal properties of the calls themselves than on the mental mechanisms underlying call production. In marked contrast to adult human language, the calls of monkeys do not seem to take into account listeners' mental states. As a result, monkeys cannot communicate with the intent of appeasing those who are anxious or informing those who are ignorant.

There is no doubt that the vocal communication of nonhuman primates mediates complex social relationships and results in the transfer of quite specific sorts to information. Equally clearly, nonhuman primate vocalizations affect listeners' mental states, in the sense that they change what other individuals know about the world and affect what they are likely to do. Compared with human language, however, the vocalizations of monkeys achieve this end almost by accident, without individuals' being aware of the features of the system in which they are participating. Monkeys, and perhaps also apes, are skilled at monitoring each other's behavior. There is little evidence, however, that they are equally adept at monitoring each other's states of mind. A challenge for the future will be to identify the selective factors that might have favored the evolution of mental-state attribution in the language and behavior of our early ancestors.

Acknowledgments

We are grateful to the Republics of Botswana and Kenya for permission to conduct research. Research was supported by the National Geographic Society, NSF, NIH, and the University of Pennsylvania.

References

Bauers, K. A. (1993) A functional analysis of staccato grunt vocalizations in the stumptailed macaque (*Macaca arctoides*). *Ethology* 94:147–161.

Bennett, J. (1976) *Linguistic Behaviour*. Cambridge: Cambridge University Press.

Blount, B. (1985) "Girney" vocalizations among Japanese macaque females: Context and function. *Primates* 26:424–435.

Boesch, C. (1991) Teaching in wild chimpanzees. *Anim. Behav.* 41:530–532.

Boinski, S. (1991) The coordination of spatial position: A field study of the vocal behaviour of adult female squirrel monkeys. *Anim. Behav.* 41:89–102.

Boinski, S. (1992) Ecological and social factors affecting the vocal behavior of adult female squirrel monkeys. *Ethology* 92:316–330.

Boinski, S. (1993) Vocal coordination of troop movement among white-faced capuchin monkeys, *Cebus capucinus. Am J. Primatol.* 30:85–100.

Boysen, S. T. (1996) Representation of quantities by apes. In *Advances in the Study of Behavior*, vol. 26, ed. by P. J. B. Slater, J. S. Rosenblatt, C. T. Snowdon, and M. Milinski, pp. 326–349. San Diego, CA: Academic Press.

Burdyn, L. E. and Thomas, R. K. (1984) Conditional discrimination with conceptual simultaneous and successive cues in the squirrel monkey (*Saimiri sciureus*). *J. Comp. Psych.* 98:405–413.

Byrne, R. W. (1981) Distance vocalizations of Guinea baboons (*Papio papio*) in Senegal: An analysis of function. *Behaviour* 78:283–313.

Byrne, R. W. (1995) *The Thinking Ape: Evolutionary Origins of Intelligence*. New York: Oxford University Press.

Chapman, C. A. and Levebre, L. (1990) Manipulating foraging group size: Spider monkey food calls at fruiting trees. *Anim. Behav.* 39:891–896.

Cheney, D. L. (1981) Inter-group encounters among free-ranging vervet monkeys. *Folia Primatol.* 35:124–146.

Cheney, D. L. and Seyfarth, R. M. (1981) Selective forces affecting the predator alarm calls of vervet monkeys. *Behaviour* 76:25–61.

Cheney, D. L. and Seyfarth, R. M. (1982) How vervet monkeys perceive their grunts: Field playback experiments. *Anim. Behav.* 30:739–751.

Cheney, D. L. and Seyfarth, R. M. (1985) Vervet monkey alarm calls: Manipulation through shared information? *Behaviour* 93:150–166.

Cheney, D. L. and Seyfarth, R. M. (1988) Assessment of meaning and the detection of unreliable signals in vervet monkeys. *Anim. Behav.* 36:477–486.

Cheney, D. L. and Seyfarth, R. M. (1990a) Attending to behaviour versus attending to knowledge: Examining monkeys' attribution of mental states. *Anim. Behav.* 40:742–753.

Cheney, D. L. and Seyfarth, R. M. (1990b) *How Monkeys See the World: Inside the Mind of Another Species.* Chicago: University of Chicago Press.

Cheney, D. L. and Seyfarth, R. M. (1997) Reconciliatory grunts by dominant female baboons influence victims' behavior. *Anim. Behav.* 54:409–481.

Cheney, D. L., Seyfarth, R. M., and Palombit, R. A. (1996) The function and mechanisms underlying baboon contact barks. *Anim. Behav.* 52:507–518.

Cheney, D. L., Seyfarth, R. M., and Silk, J. B. (1995) The role of grunts in reconciling opponents and facilitating interactions among adult female baboons. *Anim. Behav.* 50:249–257.

Clark, A. P. and Wrangham, R. W. (1994) Chimpanzee arrival pant-hoots: Do they signify food or status? *Int. J. Primatol.* 15:185–205.

Cleveland, J. and Snowdon, C. T. (1982) The complex vocal repertoire of the adult cotton-top tamarin (*Saguinus oedipus oedipus*). *Z. Tierpsychol.* 58:231–270.

Davis, R. T., Leary, R. W., Stevens, D. A., and Thompson, R. F. (1967) Learning and perception of oddity problems by lemurs and seven species of monkey. *Primates* 8:311–322.

Dennett, D. C. (1987) *The Intentional Stance.* Cambridge, MA: MIT Press/Bradford Books.

Grice, H. P. (1957) Meaning. *Phil. Rev.* 66:377–388.

Gyger, M., Karakashian, S. J., and Marler, P. (1986) Avian alarm-calling: Is there an audience effect? *Anim. Behav.* 34:1570–1572.

Harcourt, A. H., Stewart, K. J., and Hauser, M. D. (1993) Functions of wild gorilla 'close' calls: I. Repertoires, context, and interspecific comparison. *Behaviour* 124:89–122.

Hauser, M. D. (1996) *The Evolution of Communication.* Cambridge, MA: MIT Press/Bradford Books.

Hauser, M. D. and Marler, P. (1993) Food-associated calls in rhesus macaques (*Macaca mulatta*). II. Costs and benefits of call production and suppression. *Behav. Ecol.* 4:206–212.

Hiraldo, F., Heredia, B., and Alonso, J. C. (1993) Communal roosting of wintering red kites, *Milvus milvus*: Social feeding strategies for the exploitation of food resources. *Ethology* 93:117–124.

Hockett, C. F. (1960) Logical considerations in the study of animal communication. In *Animal Sounds and Communication*, ed. by W. E. Lanyon and W. N. Tavolga, pp. 292–340. Washington, DC: American Institute of Biological Sciences.

Limongelli, L., Boysen, S. T., and Visalberghi, E. (1995) Comprehension of cause-effect relations in a tool-using task by chimpanzees (*Pan troglodytes*). *J. Comp. Psych.* 109:18–26.

Marler, P. (1961) The logical analysis of communication. *J. Theor. Biol.* 1:295–317.

Marler, P. (1967) Animal communication signals. *Science* 157:769–774.

Marler, P. (1975) On the origin of speech from animal sounds. In *The Role of Speech in Language*, ed. by J. F. Kavanaugh and J. E. Cutting, pp. 114–131. Cambridge, MA: MIT Press.

Marler, P. (1992) Functions of arousal and emotion in primate communication: A semiotic approach. In *Topics in Primatology*, vol. 1: *Human Origins*, ed. by T. Nishida, W. C. McGrew, P. Marler, M. Pickford, and F. B. M. de Waal, pp. 225–232. Tokyo: Tokyo University Press.

Marler, P., Karakashian, S., and Gyger, M. (1988) Do animals have the option of withholding signals when communication is inappropriate? The audience effect. In *Cognitive Ethology: The Minds of Other Animals*, ed. by C. Ristau and P. Marler, pp. 187–208. Hillsdale, NJ: Lawrence Erlbaum.

Masataka, N. (1989) Motivational referents of contact calls in Japanese macaques. *Ethology* 80:265–273.

Mitani, J. and Nishida, T. (1993) Contexts and social correlates of long-distance calling by male chimpanzees. *Anim. Behav.* 45:735–746.

Morton, E. S. (1977) On the occurrence and significance of motivation-structural rules in some bird and animal sounds. *Am. Nat.* 111:855–869.

Povinelli, D. J. (1993) Reconstructing the evolution of mind. *Am. Psychol.* 48:493–509.

Povinelli, D. J., Nelson, K. E., and Boysen, S. T. (1990) Inferences about guessing and knowing by chimpanzees (*Pan troglodytes*). *J. Comp. Psych.* 104:203–210.

Povinelli, D. J., Nelson, K. E., and Boysen, S. T. (1992a) Comprehension of role reversal in chimpanzees: Evidence of empathy? *Anim. Behav.* 43:633–640.

Povinelli, D. J., Parks, K. A., and Novak, M. A. (1992b) Role reversal by rhesus monkeys, but no evidence of empathy. *Anim. Behav.* 44:269–281.

Premack, D. (1975) On the origins of language. In *Handbook of Psychobiology*, ed. by M. S. Gazzaniga and C. B. Blakemore, pp. 219–237. New York: Academic Press.

Premack, D. (1976) *Intelligence in Ape and Man.* Hillsdale, NJ: Lawrence Erlbaum.

Prior, K. A. and Weatherhead, P. J. (1991) Turkey vultures foraging at experimental food patches: A test of information transfer at communal roosts. *Behav. Ecol. Sociobiol.* 28:385–390.

Richner, H. and Marclay, C. (1991) Evolution of avian roosting behaviour: A test of the information centre hypothesis and of a critical assumption. *Anim. Behav.* 41:433–438.

Sakuro, O. (1989) Variability in contact calls between troops of Japanese macaques: A possible case of neutral evolution of animal culture. *Anim. Behav.* 38:900–902.

Savage-Rumbaugh, E. S. (1986) *Ape Language: From Conditioned Response to Symbol.* New York: Columbia University Press.

Seyfarth, R. M. and Cheney, D. L. (1986) Vocal development in vervet monkeys. *Anim. Behav.* 34:1640–1658.

Seyfarth, R. M., Cheney, D. L., Harcourt, A. H., and Stewart, K. J. (1994) The acoustic features of gorilla double grunts and their relation to behavior. *Am. J. Primatol.* 33:31–50.

Seyfarth, R. M., Cheney, D. L., and Marler, P. (1980a) Monkey responses to three different alarm calls: Evidence for predator classification and semantic communication. *Science* 210:801–803.

Seyfarth, R. M., Cheney, D. L., and Marler, P. (1980b) Vervet monkey alarm calls: Semantic communication in a free-ranging primate. *Anim. Behav.* 28:1070–1094.

Sherman, P. W. (1977) Nepotism and the evolution of alarm calls. *Science* 197:1246–1253.

Silk, J. B., Cheney, D. L., and Seyfarth, R. M. (1996) The form and function of reconciliation among baboons, *Papio cynocephalus ursinus. Anim. Behav.* 52:259–268.

Smith, W. J. (1977) *The Behavior of Communicating: An Ethological Approach.* Cambridge, MA: Harvard University Press.

Snowdon, C. T., Brown, C. H., and Peterson, M. R., eds. (1982) *Primate Communication.* Cambridge: Cambridge University Press.

Struhsaker, T. T. (1967a) Auditory communication among vervet monkeys (*Cercopithecus aethiops*). In *Social Communication among Primates*, ed. by S. A. Altmann, pp. 281–324. Chicago: University of Chicago Press.

Struhsaker, T. T. (1967b) Social structure among vervet monkeys. *Behaviour* 29:83–121.

Sullivan, K. (1985) Selective alarm-calling by downy woodpeckers in mixed-species flocks. *Auk* 102:184–187.

Thompson, R. (1995) Natural and relational concepts in animals. In *Comparative Approaches to Cognitive Science*, ed. by H. Roitblat and J. A. Meyer, pp. 278–294. Cambridge, MA: MIT Press.

Tomasello, M. (1996) Do apes ape? In *Social Learning in Animals: The Roots of Culture*, ed. by C. M. Heyes and B. G. Galef, pp. 256–269. New York: Academic Press.

Tiles, J. E. (1987) Meaning. In *The Oxford Companion to the Mind*, ed. by R. L. Gregory, pp. 450–454. Oxford: Oxford University Press.

Tomasello, M. and Call, J. (1997) *Primate Cognition*. Oxford: Oxford University Press.

van Hooff, J. A. R. A. M. (1994) Understanding chimpanzee understanding. In *Chimpanzee Cultures,* ed. by R. W. Wrangham, W. C. McGrew, F. B. M. de Waal, and P. G. Heltne, pp. 267–284. Cambridge, MA: Harvard University Press.

Wilkinson, G. S. (1992) Information transfer at evening bat colonies. *Anim. Behav.* 44:501–518.

Wrangham, R. W. (1977) Feeding behaviour of chimpanzees in Gombe National Park, Tanzania. In *Primate Ecology*, ed. by T. H. Clutton-Brock, pp. 178–212. New York: Academic Press.

Zuberbuhler, K., Noe, R., and Seyfarth, R. M. (1997) Diana monkey long-distance calls: Messages for conspecifics and predators. *Anim. Behav.* 53:589–604.

Zuberbuhler, K., Cheney, D. L., and Seyfarth, R. M. (1999) Conceptual Semantics in a non-human primate. *J. Comp. Psychol.* 113:33–42.

24 Communication and Tool Use in Chimpanzees: Cultural and Social Contexts

Tetsuro Matsuzawa

Humans seem to have special characteristics: language, advanced technology, culture, and so forth. The word "language" has connotations of being something more than the vocal communication we observe in nonhuman primates. Similarly, "advanced technology" is at a glance in quite a different league from wild chimpanzees' termite fishing using a twig. However, the cognitive functions of humans should be considered in the light of an evolutionary background, and thus as sharing some aspects with living nonhuman primates (Hauser 1996; Tomasello and Call 1997). To examine the unique features of *Homo sapiens*, one of about 170 living species of primates, we need to have such an evolutionary perspective: we must look not only at humans but also at their immediate relatives, the nonhuman primates.

I have been studying chimpanzees, the closest relatives of humans within the order of primates, both in captivity and in the wild. The first part of this chapter will deal with two main questions: one, what are the similarities and differences in the perceptual/cognitive capabilities of humans and chimpanzees? and two, what are the similarities and differences between symbol use by captive chimpanzees and human language? For the remaining part of the chapter, I would like to focus on cultural and social influences on material intelligence. I believe that a view incorporating a cultural and social perspective will provide valuable inspiration for theories on the evolution of the unique system of communication in humans.

First, I would like to briefly outline a framework for discussing various intellectual behaviors, including human language and technology. From a behavioral and biological viewpoint, "intelligence" can be defined as a way of modulating behavior to adapt to an ever-changing ecological environment. "Culture" may be defined as a set of behaviors that are shared by members of a community and are transmitted from one generation to the next through nongenetic channels. In a naive categorization of the world from an egocentric perspective, the perceptual world may be divided into three parts: self, conspecifics (other individuals of the same species), and others (either animate or inanimate). Following this scheme (Matsuzawa 1996, 1998), intelligence possessed by "self" can be broken down into three constituent aspects: social intelligence, material intelligence, and intelligence about the intelligence of other individuals.

Social intelligence is the intelligence underlying the modulation of social relationships with other members of a group. In many primate societies, the repertoire of behaviors in such social contexts includes communication, alliance formation, reassurance to others (de Waal 1989), and so forth. Field studies have shown that nonhuman primates are able to recognize the relationships between the self and other individuals, as well as those betwen others (Cheney and Seyfarth 1990; Ogawa 1995a,b). The second aspect of intelligence, material intelligence (equivalent to technological intelligence; Byrne and Whiten 1988), is the intelligence implicated in utilizing objects in the environment, such as in tool manufacture and tool use. The third is the intelligence to perceive and understand other individuals' social and material intelligence. This type of intelligence was first formulated by David Premack and his colleagues (Premack and Woodruff 1978), who named it a "theory of mind." Such intelligence of intelligence is, in other words, a knowledge of another's knowledge.

Human language and advanced technology is shaped in each culture through education or the social transmission of information from one individual to the next. This means that the unique intelligence of humans, in its social as well as technological aspects, is shaped in cultural and social contexts. This chapter focuses mainly on tool use rather than symbol use or communication in chimpanzees. The reasons are as follows. First, although there exists a large number of studies on chimpanzee social intelligence, chimpanzee communication—especially symbolic communication—is still open to question and needs more research in the future. Second, the extensive amount of data on chimpanzees' material intelligence (such as tool use), provides a case in point for demonstrating the importance of social contexts and cultural influences. These points taken together suggest that cultural and social contexts, interacting with both social intelligence and material intelligence, may have played a key role in the emergence of intelligence of conspecifics' intelligence.

Cognitive Abilities and Symbol Use in Chimpanzees

This section summarizes the cognitive capabilities of chimpanzees, as revealed by a long-term laboratory study that I and my colleagues have been conducting (Matsuzawa 1985a,b, 1996). The study was launched in 1978, and it has been dubbed the "Ai-project" after its principal subject, a female chimpanzee named Ai who is now 22 years old. Eleven chimpanzees including Ai live as a group in a seminatural outdoor compound at the Primate Research Institute of Kyoto University. The main aim of the project has been to compare directly the perceptual/cognitive performance of chimpanzees with that of humans under identical test conditions, following strictly objective methods. The general procedure requires subjects to face a computer system that tries and evaluates their performance in a variety of cognitive tasks.

For a rough outline of chimpanzee perception/cognition, consider the following findings. Chimpanzees are trichromatic, and through learning to use specially constructed visual symbols, they can express how they perceive various colors (Matsu-zawa 1985b). The categories of color classification have been found to be similar to and as stable as those of humans. Form perception and visual acuity are also comparable to those of humans (Matsuzawa 1990; Tomonaga and Matsuzawa 1992). We have found no significant differences between the species in the fundamental perception of such things as color and form. The "constructive matching-to-sample" procedure (which involves making a copy of a sample pattern by assembling it from scratch from its constituent elements) has made it possible to analyze the detailed processes of pattern perception (Fujita and Matsuzawa 1990; Matsuzawa 1989). When a complex geometric pattern is presented as a sample, humans as well as chimpanzees prefer to produce a copy of this sample pattern beginning with the outer contour first, even when the order of reproduction is the subject's own choice. This has been taken to suggest that both humans and chimpanzees perceive patterns starting with the outer contour.

Comparisons of higher cognitive functions have revealed some interesting differences between the two species. The chimpanzee can easily recognize chimpanzee faces, but has somewhat more difficulty identifying human faces (Matsuzawa 1990). Furthermore, upside-down pictures and forms are recognized faster by the chimpanzee than by human subjects (Tomonaga et al. 1993). This may reflect the chimpanzees' adaptation to their ecological environment.

Fundamental perceptual abilities are similar between humans and chimpanzees not only in visual but also in auditory aspects (Kojima 1990). The auditory range has been found to be almost identical in the two species, although chimpanzees appear to be slightly insensitive at around the 2–4kHz band. This gives a W-shaped wave-length discrimination curve of chimpanzee auditory perception, which contrasts with the U-shaped curve of humans, most sensitive in the 2–4kHz zone. Thus chimpanzees lack the fine perception of human voices that frequently use the 2–4kHz range, in addition to the absence of a vocal tract needed to produce the various sounds contained in human speech. Together, these observations may serve to explain why several attempts at training two-way vocal communication in chimpanzees have met with so little success.

Symbol use is thought to be a feature uniquely associated with human cognitive processes. Human language has a highly developed hierarchical structure of generating and perceiving complex signs and signals, whether it is based on a manual-visual or vocal-auditory mode. However, previous studies on so-called ape-language have revealed that the Great Apes have the ability to master a language-like skill. The cases of Washoe, Sarah, Lana, Nim, as well as ongoing research with Ai (Matsuzawa 1985a; 1996), Kanzi (Savage-Rumbaugh and Lewin 1994), and other chimpanzees (Boysen and Berntson 1989), continue to confirm that the chimpanzee (genus *Pan*) is capable of processing "symbols" to some extent. If, however, one closely examines the details, language-like skills acquired by chimpanzees and other great apes differ from human language on at least three counts.

First, there is a contrast in the ease with which apes and humans handle two distinct skills—productive use and receptive comprehension of "symbols." These two aspects of symbol use are equivalent and symmetrical in human language, but not fully so in chimpanzees (Kojima 1984) or in retarded human children. Second, all previous "ape language" studies show that subjects' vocabulary of "symbols" may reach several hundred, but never exceed one thousand: a level below that of a three-year-old human infant. Mean utterance length (MUL), or the average number of "symbols" used consecutively in a communicative context, is less than two (Patterson 1978). In other words, apes tend to use one "symbol" only in most cases, and they seldom use them in a combination. Third, there is no clear evidence demonstrating the existence of grammatical rules. Whether chimpanzees can combine "symbols" following grammatical rules to create "sentences" (Greenfield and Savage-Rumbaugh 1993; Matsuzawa 1985a; Terrace et al. 1979) remains controversial.

Overall, therefore, based on perceptual/cognitive capabilities similar to those of humans, it may be concluded that chimpanzees can acquire rudimentary forms of language-like skills provided that they have been reared in a human cultural environment. In interaction with humans, they may learn to use visual signs or vocal sounds for communication. In turn, such abilities shed light not only on the potential scope of chimpanzee cognition, but also on the importance of the cultural environment in general. In a sense, in the present context we may infer that the cultural environment is instrumental in shaping the language-like skill that represents an adaptive behavior for captive chimpanzees.

Cognitive Behavior in Wild Chimpanzees

The necessity for language in cultural constructions and the transmission of information has been argued for extensively in the past. Following Peter Marler's classic study analyzing the vocal behavior of wild chimpanzees (Marler 1969; Marler and Hobbett 1975), there have been a number of surveys of chimpanzee communication in their natural habitat. To my knowledge, however, there is no corresponding language-like skill found in the vocal/gestural repertoire of communication in the wild, with a few exceptions (Boesch 1991c). For now, I believe that we are still very much in need of more evidence if we are to demonstrate and accept the possibility of symbolic communication between wild chimpanzees.

Laboratory studies have given us much insight into various aspects of perceptual and cognitive abilities in chimpanzees. The question that now arises is as follows: How is the same intelligence utilized in the chimpanzees' own cultural environment and natural habitat? The most important issue in investigating the ontogenetic development of chimpanzee intelligence is the role of culture, or cultural environment. Field studies that have recently attracted special attention focus on the existence and nature of cultural differences between communities of wild chimpanzees. Such communities may differ from each other in a variety of ways, including communication (Mitani et al. 1992), tool use, feeding habits, and so on. Researchers who have compared findings from two or more chimpanzee communities have found many behavioral differences that appear to be culturally based (McGrew 1992): Chimpanzees must individually learn the unique cultural traditions of their community, thereby maintaining the continuity as well as the distinctiveness of the latter.

There are five research sites across Africa at which long-term studies on chimpanzee behavior have been carried out: two Tanzanian communities in East Africa, Gombe (Goodall 1986) and Mahale (Nishida 1990), about 150km apart, Kibale Forest in Uganda (Chapman and Wrangham 1993), and two communities in West Africa, Bossou (Sugiyama and Koman 1979) and Tai Forest, about 200km apart. A large number of differences between the communities have been found and confirmed on the basis of long-term studies, including food repertoires, responses to water, grooming postures, and so forth. In addition, close attention to detail has also revealed some very fine distinctions, such as the differences in behavioral topography or preferred characteristics of tools employed in seemingly analogous tasks at distinct sites.

The diversity shown in the manufacture and use of tools has been analyzed in an attempt to gain an understanding of the cultural influence on cognitive abilities of chimpanzees in the wild, and it is illustrated in part in the following section. The present chapter illustrates an attempt to synthesize studies of tool use from (1) field observation in the natural habitat, (2) field experiments in an outdoor laboratory, and (3) simulation experiments in a seminatural laboratory setting.

Unique Tool Use at Bossou, West Africa

This section provides a description of the unique cultural attributes of a single community of chimpanzees. A small group of chimpanzees living at Bossou, Republic of Guinea, West Africa, has been studied by Sugiyama and his colleagues since 1976. Bossou is located at $7° 39'$ north latitude and $8° 30'$ west longitude, at an altitude of 550–700m. The forest area at Bossou is isolated from the nearby large forest of the Nimba Mountains by an approximately 4km stretch of savanna vegetation. The group's home range covers a mosaic of primary, secondary, riverine, and scrub forest, as well as areas of farmland. The following descriptions of tool-using behavior are based on my own field observations since 1986, collected during visits of one to three months' duration to Bossou each year.

A tool can be defined as a detached object that is used in some way to arrive at an apparent goal. For the purposes of this chapter, I would like to divide object manipulation into two categories: one, manipulation of an object toward another object (e.g., in termite fishing, a twig serves a tool that is related to the termite to be fished), and two, the manipulation of an object toward another individual. In other words, in the latter case the object is used in the context of a social interaction. For example, in aimed throwing, a branch is thrown toward another individual in an attempt to frighten or intimidate.

Some of the unique tools of the Bossou community are described below, focusing first on examples of object-to-object manipulation. Bear in mind that the nature of these kinds of tool entails relating one thing to another.

Nut-cracking with Stones   Chimpanzees at Bossou are known to use a pair of stones as a hammer and anvil to crack open oil-palm nuts, *Elaeis guineensis* (Sugiyama and Koman 1979). Such stone tools are used exclusively by chimpanzees in West Africa. Oil-palm nuts and stones are also available in East Africa, but chimpanzees in that region have never been observed to utilize stones as tools. Interestingly, Gombe chimpanzees eat the fresh, red, soft outer tissue of oil-palm nuts, but never crack them open to obtain the kernel inside. Mahale chimpanzees never eat any part of the nuts. The details of stone tool use are illustrated in figure 24.1.

Ant-dipping   Bossou chimpanzees use a variety of tools in addition to stones. For example, the use of "wands" (prepared by breaking off a twig or a grass stem, breaking it further in half, and then removing its leaves by biting or by hand) aids in obtaining Safari ants (*Dorylus* sp.). Ant-catching wands at Bossou measure 46.7cm on the average ($N = 60$) in length, with the mean diameter being 6.8mm at the top (Sugiyama et al. 1988; Sugiyama 1995a). In their typical fashion of manipulating these slim objects, Bossou chimpanzees keep the wand between their index and middle fingers, and catch the insects by slowly moving the wand back and forth. This technique is quite different from that associated with "ant-dipping" in Gombe chimpanzees (Goodall 1986).

Termite-fishing   In the first reported case of chimpanzee tool use, Goodall (1964) observed that Gombe chimpanzees fish for *Macrotermes* termites with twigs. We

Figure 24.1
A chimpanzee at Bossou cracks open a nut of the oil palm with a pair of stones used as a hammer and anvil.

have so far believed that Bossou chimpanzees do not obtain *Macrotermes* termites in this manner; instead of luring them from their nests, the insects are caught directly by hand. However, a recent observation (T. Humle, 1999) confirmed that termite fishing is not absent at Bossou. Two chimpanzees, a mother and her 6-year-old son, were observed using a short flexible stalk of a terrestrial herbaceous plant (genus *Megaphrynium*). The individuals were seen biting off the distal end of the stalk, thus discarding the single leaf possessed by this plant, and using the remainder as a probing tool. As at Gombe, termites inside the mound attacked the intruding object, so that upon withdrawing the tool the chimpanzees could use their lips to nibble at the seized nest-defenders. This constitutes the first record of termite-fishing for ground-dwelling termites with tools by Bossou chimpanzees. How this new tool emerged is still unclear.

Use of Leaves for Drinking Water   Bossou chimpanzees use leaves for drinking water accumulated in tree-holes (Sugiyama 1995b). A technique referred to as "leaf folding" (Tonooka et al. 1995) represents the first step: a leaf is broken off (or leaves in some cases), put in the mouth with one hand, folded inside the mouth, taken out, and inserted into a hole in a tree. Once soaked with water, the folded leaf is then returned to the mouth. This technique is different from that of leaf sponging (Goodall 1986), used by the Gombe community for drinking water. Chimpanzees show a marked preference for selecting the leaves of *Hybophrynium braunianum* as tools for drinking water, and it is interesting to note that this leaf is also utilized by the local people of the region when drinking from small streams; they make a cup out of the leaf, however, instead of folding it. On one occasion, a 4-year-old female was observed performing combined sequential use of two tools to drink water. She was drinking water from a tree hollow with a narrow opening. As the water level became low after repeated drinking and the leaf could no longer reach the moisture, she climbed up the tree to break off a small branch, then inserted it through the opening to push the leaf further down the hole. She then retrieved the leaf soaked in water with the stick, drank the water, and proceeded to repeat the procedure.

Pestle-pounding Bossou chimpanzees have recently been observed to first pound and then excavate the centers of oil-palm crowns with "pestles." They make a hole through which they obtain the soft and juicy pulp from inside; as a pestle, they use a petiole of the oil palm (Sugiyama 1994; Yamakoshi and Sugiyama 1995). The part of the plant ingested is the apical meristem at the base of the young shoots. This type of tool use, "pestle-pounding," has never been reported from any other study site.

Algae-scooping In the summer of 1995, the chimpanzees at Bossou were first observed using a twig or a grass stem to scoop algae (*Spirogyra* sp.) floating on a pond surface (Matsuzawa et al. 1996, figure 24.2). Although the manufacturing process of the tool itself is similar to that involved in preparations for ant-dipping, the variety of materials used in the two activities do not overlap. Furthermore, the manipulating techniques applied to the processed tools are also different: chimpanzees hold the stick in one hand to scoop, as opposed to gripping it between fingers as in the case of ant-dipping. Two kinds of sticks are used. One is a thick and relatively long stick made from plants such as *Costus diestelli* and *Alcornia cordiforia* that is used to gather large amounts of algae at one time. The second is a thin and shorter stick with hooks formed by the removal of side leaves from a Polypodiaceae plant (*Cyclosurus afer*), used for retrieving spots of floating algae. The discovery of algae-scooping contributes a completely new item to the existing list of tools, as well as a new addition to the chimpanzees' food repertoire—neither has ever been found at other research sites.

Leaf cushion Bossou chimpanzees arrange large leaves on wet ground as cushions to sit on in order to avoid contact with the moist surface (Hirata et al. 1998). The

Figure 24.2
A chimpanzee at Bossou uses a stick to scoop algae floating on a pond.

leaves of the parasol tree (*Musanga cecropioides*) or the leaves of carapa trees (*Carapa procera*) are used as material. This example adds to the few instances of nonsubsistence, elementary technology shown by wild chimpanzees.

Exploratory Probing Chimpanzees at Bossou have been observed to pick up a stick, hold it in one hand, and push it into a tree-hole. After retrieving the stick, they normally sniff the tip and then probe it through the hole again to repeat the process. This behavior possibly has the function of exploring inaccessible hidden crooks and crevices.

We now turn to the second category of tools introduced above: the "social tools" of the Bossou community. The following three instances of habitual social tool use might aid to clarify what is meant by this term.

Leaf Clipping Similarly to those at Mahale, male chimpanzees at Bossou hold a leaf in one hand which they clip with their lips as part of a very distinctive courtship display. Facing a female in estrus, leaf-clipping males normally sit on a branch showing their erect penis, while rhythmically stamping one heel against the tree and occasionally shaking branches with the hand.

Aimed Throwing   Chimpanzees at Bossou as well as other sites often throw a branch toward another individual as part of a display or in the context of fighting. In some cases targets have included the human observers themselves. At the nut-cracking site, a hammer stone held by a chimpanzee may also be used as a missile.

Charging Display   Again, similarly to those other sites, chimpanzees at Bossou use branches and rocks in their charging displays. Dragging pieces of wood or rolling large stones or rocks is the typical routine. In one case at Bossou, the alpha male of the troop used the mummified carcass of a dead infant chimpanzee as a tool in the context of a charging display (Matsuzawa 1997).

Each community of chimpanzees has its own unique tools. Rain hats and branch dragging in Wamba bonobos in Zaire (Ingmanson 1996), sandals in chimps in Sierra Leone, symbolic use of leaves at Kibale in Uganda, brush-stick for digging and catching termites in Cameroon chimpanzees—all these reports make up an extensive catalogue of wild chimpanzees' tool manufacture and use. The transmission of these behaviors from one generation to the next is believed to be culturally based.

Field Experiments on Tool Use at an Outdoor Laboratory

The previous section has provided an outline of tool use by chimpanzees, focusing on a single community. It should be noted that there are very few instances of symbolic use of tools in the wild, with the overwhelming majority of tools being employed in subsistence ecology.

Field observation of tool use behavior has brought us a long way to understanding how material intelligence is utilized by wild chimpanzees in their natural habitat. The accumulation of reported episodes in the field is important and useful for understanding patterns of behavior. However, a considerable drawback of such accounts of tool manufacture and tool use is that they lack the control traditionally associated with experimental approaches. This section will illustrate our attempts to conduct a "field experiment" in an outdoor laboratory in the wild.

Almost all of the various kinds of tool use that chimpanzees at Bossou demonstrate are unique to the community if one carefully examines (1) the tool material, (2) the manufacturing process, (3) the manipulating skill, and (4) the target object. However, most of these behavioral patterns are examples of subsistence tool use for obtaining food, and they follow the rule of "a tool related to a target item." The rare exception is nut cracking: instead of a single tool being related to the target, a *set* of tools—hammer and anvil stones—is necessary. Nut cracking thus involves multiple objects that combine to serve as a single tool and is a good example of complex tool use exhibited by wild chimpanzees.

When attempting, however, to study nut-cracking behavior in the natural habitat at Bossou, one encounters considerable difficulties. The reasons are twofold. First, the bush beneath the palm trees is so dense that the behavior is not clearly visible to the observer. Second, the chimpanzees are extremely shy of humans in locations where oil-palm nuts are naturally available, since the palms which supply the nuts grow in secondary and scrub forests close to a village.

To investigate detailed aspects of the nut-cracking behavior, we created an outdoor laboratory for field experiments (Matsuzawa 1994, 1996; Inoue-Nakamura and Matsuzawa 1997). The laboratory was set at the top of a small hill in the chimpanzees' home range, and we regularly transported stones and oil-palm nuts to the site. Oil-palm nuts are oblong and round, similar in shape to rugby balls. They weigh 7.2g on average, and inside the hard shell is an edible kernel that weighs approximately 2.0g. The nutritional energy of each kernel is 663kcal per 100g, close to that of walnuts, and is rich in fat. A chimpanzee cracks open a nut to obtain its kernel by placing the nut on an anvil stone with one hand, then cracking it with a hammer stone held in the other.

In general, about 50 stones and approximately 2–5kg of oil-palm nuts were provided at the outdoor laboratory. The observer hid behind a screen made of grass about 20m from the experimental cracking site and remained in position continuously from 7 A.M. until 6 P.M., monitoring activity at the cracking site for the duration of the entire day. All episodes of nut-cracking behavior at this outdoor laboratory were thus observed directly, as well as being video-recorded as they occurred.

The advantages of such a field experiment over field observation are threefold. First, it provides not just one-off anecdotal cases witnessed by an observer only, but objective data, as all observations are fully recorded on videotape and can be analyzed repeatedly. Second, the experimenter can control variables, such as the availability of stones and nuts in this case. Third, one can greatly increase the opportunity for and duration of observations (several hundred times in the case of nut cracking), as well as maintain the same location for observations at all times. These features make an outdoor laboratory highly suitable for collecting objective data on cognitive behavior in the wild.

We began the preliminary field experiment at several sites in the group's ranging area in 1988 (Sakura and Matsuzawa 1991), then settled at one particular location in 1990. Since that time, we have continued the study of nut cracking at this site, making observations each year. Table 24.1 provides a summary of data from 10

Table 24.1

Summary of stone-tool use by chimpanzees in the wild at Bossou, Guinea. The hand used for the hammer stone in the nut-cracking behavior has been recorded since the project began in 1988. In general, the data were collected from January to March in the dry season of each year.

Name	Sex	Age in 1997	Mother	Year observed								
				1988	1990	1991	1992	1993	1994	1995	1996	1997
Tua	m	adult	unknown	?	L	L	L	L	L	L	L	L
Kai	f	adult	unknown	?	R	R	R	R	R	R	R	R
Nina	f	adult	unknown	?	X	X	X	X	X	X	X	X
Fana	f	adult	unknown	?	L	L	L	L	L	L	R	R
Jire	f	adult	unknown	?	L	L	L	L	L	L	L	L
Velu	f	adult	unknown	?	R	R	R	R	R	R	R	R
Yo	f	adult	unknown	?	L	L	L	L	L	L	L	L
Pama	f	adult	unknown	?	X	X	X	X	X	X	X	X
Kie*	f	21	Kai	?	R	R	—	—	—	—	—	—
Foaf	m	16.5	Fana	?	R	R	R	R	R	R	R	R
Puru*	m	16.5	Pama	R	R	R	—	—	—	—	—	—
Vube*	f	15	Velu	?	L	—	—	—	—	—	—	—
Ja	f	14	Jire	?	R	R	R	R	—	—	—	—
Yunro	f	13	Yo	?	X	X	X	X	—	—	—	—
Na	m	12.5	Nina	?	R	R	R	R	R	R	—	—
Kakuru*	f	11.5	Kie	?	A	R	—	—	—	—	—	—
Vui	m	11.5	Velu	?	X	X	L	L	L	L	L	L
Pili	f	11	Pama	—	X	R	R	R	R	R	R	R
Jokro	f	9	Jire	—	X	X	X	—	—	—	—	—
Yela*	f	8.5	Yo	—	X	—	—	—	—	—	—	—
Fotayu	f	6.5	Fana	—	—	—	X	X	X	AR	R	R
Vuavua	f	6.5	Velu	—	—	—	X	X	X	AL	L	L
Yoro	m	6	Yo	—	—	—	X	X	X	X	L	L
Poni	f	5	Pama	—	—	—	—	X	X	X	R	R
Nto	m	4.5	Nina	—	—	—	—	—	X	X	X	R
Julu	f	4	Jire	—	—	—	—	—	X	X	X	X
Pokru	m	1.5	Pili	—	—	—	—	—	—	—	—	X
Fanle	f	0	Fana	—	—	—	—	—	—	—	—	—

Notes: * = The individual had disappeared or died by February 1997. L = always used left hand for hammer. R = always used right hand for hammer. A = ambidextrous use of hammer. X = no successful hammer use but eating nuts cracked by others. ? = data unavailable because no observation at the cracking site. — = data unavailable because the subject was not yet born, disappeared, or died in the research period. Age represents the estimate as of February 1997. Fana injured her left arm in 1995. Yunro used left hand to hit a nut without holding a hammer stone.

Source: Matsuzawa 1998, 1991, 1992, 1993, 1994, 1995, 1996, and 1997; Fushimi et al. 1990 data.

years of research at Bossou, focusing on the acquisition of the nut-cracking skill and hand preference. Our field experiments have revealed many interesting characteristics of Bossou chimpanzees' nut-cracking behavior (Matsuzawa 1994), some of which are outlined below.

Flexibility of Nut-cracking Behavior   Chimpanzees appear to understand the relationship between tools and their functions. Stones were used flexibly, serving as hammers and/or anvils according to their shape, size, or some other characteristic. Chimpanzees selected nuts that were neither too old nor too fresh. They were able to use not only stones but also tree trunks as anvils, and wooden clubs as hammers, when the availability of stones was limited by the experimenter.

Hand Preference   Laterality of manual skills is an important issue in considering the origins of the left-hemisphere specialization of human language (see chapter by M. Hauser in this volume). Each individual chimpanzee always used the same hand, either right or left, as the hammer-holding hand. Adult chimpanzees' hand preference was complete in the case of hammering at Bossou (Sugiyama et al. 1993; Matsuzawa 1994): each individual used only one hand for hammering at any time. This contrasts with nut cracking using clubs and stones by Tai chimpanzees in Cote d'Ivoire, who sometimes use two hands for hammering. We found no significant left or right bias at the community level (12 right-handers vs. 9 left-handers). These findings are generally consistent with those reported from laboratory studies on chimpanzees' hand preference in reaching and various other tasks (Bard et al. 1990; Finch 1941; Tonooka and Matsuzawa 1995) and in tool use in the wild (Boesch 1991a; McGrew 1992). Lateral preference in chimpanzees is one of the most important research topics under consideration in the endeavor to reveal the origins of human hemispheric lateralization (Hopkins and Morris 1993; MacNeilage et al. 1987; Ward and Hopkins 1993; McGrew and Marchant 1997). The long-term study of hand preference further revealed the following interesting finding. As figure 24.3 shows, hand preference was not always congruent between mothers and their offspring; however, among siblings it was consistent without exception (9 out of 9 pairs). A plausible explanation for this new finding shall not be considered here.

Metatool Use   The most complex form of chimpanzee tool use in the wild was first observed at our outdoor laboratory, as performed by three chimpanzees (an adult female, a 6.5-year-old male, and a 10.5-year-old male). A stone, weighing 4.1kg and with a slanted upper surface, was available at the laboratory site. Although many chimpanzees had attempted to use the stone as an anvil, they remained unsuccessful because nuts could not be balanced on top long enough for the hammer stone to

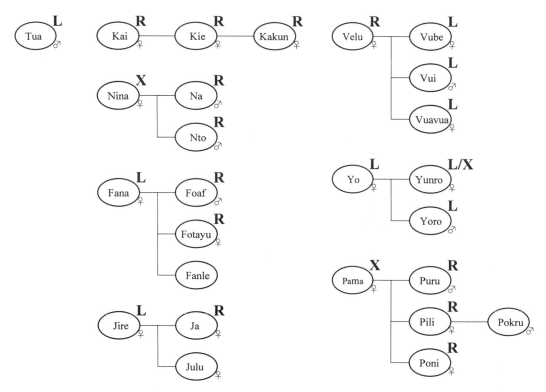

Figure 24.3
Laterality of hammering hand following family lines. Only maternal kinship was known. There was no concordance in hand laterality between mother and offspring; all possible left-right combinations appeared. There was, however, perfect concordance in hand laterality among siblings.

strike. The three chimpanzees solved this problem by using a third stone as a wedge to level and stabilize the upper surface of the anvil stone. To describe a tool with such a role, a new term was coined: "metatool" refers to a tool that itself serves as a tool for yet another tool (Matsuzawa 1991, 1994).

Developmental Change and Critical Period   Young chimpanzees at Bossou first succeeded in using stone tools between the ages of 3.5 and 5 years (table 24.1). On the basis of these data, we consider this age range to represent the critical period for acquiring the skill. Cognitive development was reflected in a change in the ways individuals manipulated stones and/or nuts. A pattern of behavior typical of the first step was one-object manipulation. A stone or a nut was manipulated by the hands, the feet, or the mouth: a single action toward a single object. In the second step, multiple actions on multiple objects appeared, with all possible combinations of two of the three required objects (the nut and the two stones) being represented. A stone was hit by a nut; a nut on the ground was hit by a stone; a stone was hit by another stone in the absence of a nut. Finally, in the ultimate step, a nut placed on a stone was hit by another stone. Just prior to this stage, infants usually began to pound a nut resting on the stone with an empty hand, without actually holding a hammer stone. The developmental change in nut/stone manipulation is thus a step-by-step process, which is never reversed.

Observational Learning and Imitation   Active teaching is a much-discussed topic associated with the acquisition of nut-cracking behavior by wild chimpanzees, following reports by Boesch (1991b). However, such instances of "teaching" are very rare in Boesch's observation (only two cases), and there is scope for alternative interpretations of the teaching-like behavior. Field experiments at Bossou clearly show that through direct experience as well as observational learning from community members, chimpanzees can acquire the skills of using stone tools. During our period of twelve years' long-term observation, we never encountered a case of active teaching. A mother was never seen to give a stone or a nut to her infant, nor did she mold the hands of her offspring to encourage the appropriate hitting action. However, mothers appeared very tolerant towards their infants when the latter stole kernels from nuts that had just been opened up by their mothers. Infants sometimes stole the nut-to-be-cracked that the mother had placed on the anvil stone and proceeded to crack it by themselves. Infants would also pick up a nut and place it directly on the mother's anvil stone; she would then crack it open, subsequently allowing her infant to take the kernel. All these episodes illustrate altruistic aspects—rather than "teaching"—from the mothers' side in the close interaction of mother and infant during the acquisition of the nut-cracking skill. Not only mothers but also other members of the community, especially elder brothers or sisters, may often play this same role for the infant.

Discrepancy between Mother and Offspring   We encountered three individuals who did not know how to use stone tools: two adult females (Pama and Nina) and one 7-year-old juvenile female (Yunro). They merely picked up broken kernels produced by other community members and ate them. As mentioned earlier, mothers are usually tolerant toward offspring less than 4 years old, but we have also witnessed some cases (figure 24.4) where a mother (Nina) took a kernel from the anvil of her 4-year-old daughter (Nto). Although the two adults, Pama and Nina, had never used stone tools, each of their four offspring (Puru, Pili, Na, and Nto) succeeded to acquire the

Figure 24.4
An adult chimpanzee, Nina, takes a kernel from the anvil of her 4-year-old daughter, Nto, as Nto looks on.

skill. In contrast, an offspring (Yunro) failed to learn the technique from his nut-cracking mother (Yo). These facts clearly show that transmission is not exclusively from mother to offspring, and that the skill may also be acquired from other members of the community.

Possession We found that each chimpanzee had his or her own favorite stone tools, which tended to be used at their favorite spot of the site—in some cases, chimpanzees even transported the stones to these favored locations. In addition, chimpanzees have on occasion been observed to chase away subordinate individuals and take over their hammer and anvil. For example, the eldest female, Kai, had her own set of favorite stones and was seen retrieving them from her 5-year-old grand-daughter who happened to have been using them. These observations may indicate a rudimentary form of possession.

Deception A mother chimpanzee, Fana, demonstrated deceptive behavior in taking over the tool used by her son (figure 24.5). Fana came to the outdoor laboratory, where her adolescent son, 9-year-old Foaf, had already started cracking nuts with a pair of stones. She approached Foaf and stopped nearby, with the side of her body

Figure 24.5
In a possible example of deceptive behavior, a mother, Fana, arrives at the nut-cracking site and appears to request being groomed by her son, Foaf (*top*). Foaf complies (*middle*), but five seconds later Fana suddenly snatches his stones (*bottom*) and sets off to crack nuts by herself.

toward him: a behavior that often indicates a request for grooming. Compliant, Foaf put his nut cracking on hold and began grooming his mother. Fana continued to stand on four legs instead of settling down as we had expected, then five seconds later she suddenly snatched the stones from in front of her son, her lips retracted and teeth showing in the process. This remarkable episode might constitute a good example of tactical deception in the wild. It also demonstrates the advantage of field experiments that enable the video-recording of such rare occurrences.

Manufacturing Tools   Chimpanzees manufacture tools when using leaves for drinking water and wands for catching ants. Tool use in chimpanzees implies some form of tool manufacture in most cases. In the case of nut cracking, the active production of stone tools, however, is more difficult to imagine. Nevertheless, we observed several episodes in which a hammer or an anvil stone was broken into pieces by hard hitting. On four occasions, the broken pieces were then put to use as reliable hammers. Without referring to "intention" or implying any goals, we may consider such transformation from anvil to hammer an example of manufacturing in the realm of stone tool use.

Direct Comparison with Human Children   To compare chimpanzee and human performance, 28 human children (1–13 years old) served as subjects. Nuts and stones were provided following the procedure used for the chimpanzees' test condition. We found that children less than 3 years old did not succeed in using stones as tools; much the same age limit as we had seen in chimpanzees. A 6-year-old boy showed the metatool technique of using a third stone as a wedge to keep the anvil stone flat and stable. Although the absolute age in chimpanzees cannot be compared directly to that in humans (but corresponds to roughly 1.5 times the latter), we surmised that the developmental course of nut/stone manipulation and stone tool use was fundamentally similar in the two species.

Cultural Transmission   To explore the important issue of cultural differences between communities, we also carried out a field survey of the chimpanzees of Mount Nimba, Cote d'Ivoire. The distance between the two communities at Bossou and Nimba is approximately 10km. We found a number of behavioral differences between the neighboring groups (Matsuzawa and Yamakoshi 1996), and we devised a field experiment on cultural transmission to analyze these differences (Matsuzawa 1994; Matsuzawa and Yamakoshi 1996). We provided a group of Bossou chimpanzees with unfamiliar *Coula* nuts which, unlike oil-palm nuts, are encased within a thick fruit. Most of the chimpanzees examined the fruits and tried to bite them, but they did not attempt to crack them, despite being skilled oil-palm nut crackers. One adult female named Yo, however, immediately placed the *Coula* nut on her stone anvil, cracked it, and ate it. A group of juveniles gathered around and peered at what she was doing. None tried to take the *Coula* nuts. The next day a 6-year-old male named Vui, unrelated to Yo, successfully cracked open a nut without any prior practice. Four days later, a 5-year-old female named Pili followed suit. Both of these juveniles cracked a nut open, sniffed its kernel, chewed it, then spat it out. Although we provided *Coula* nuts continuously for another two weeks, Vui and Pili were the only group members who learned to crack them. In general, adult chimpanzees had a tendency simply to neglect the new nuts, whereas youngsters observed Yo's novel behavior and proceeded to try their hands at opening the unfamiliar fruit. Our interpretation of the above results is as follows: the *Coula*-cracking female, Yo, was born in another community, such as Mount Nimba, 10km away from Bossou, where a tradition of cracking *Coula* nuts had already existed. She grew up and learned to crack *Coula* nuts there, before migrating to Bossou (adolescent female chimpanzees emigrate from their natal groups). Once at Bossou she would have no further opportunity to crack the same nuts because no *Coula* trees grew in the vicinity. Our experimental manipulation reintroduced her to *Coula* nuts; as a result, she functioned as an innovator by introducing a new kind of nut cracking to the Bossou community. A previously unseen behavior was thus transmitted from an immigrant female to other members of her receiving community, demonstrating moreover the flow of knowledge from one generation to the next. Although all the Bossou chimpanzees had access to *Coula* nuts, only younger chimpanzees learned to crack them in the initial stage, and they did so only after observing the informant, an adult female.

Other Examples of Tool Use in the Outdoor Laboratory   The outdoor laboratory provided an opportunity to closely examine nut-cracking behavior that used a set of stones. We applied the same idea to other tools, including ant dipping and the use of leaves for drinking water. For the latter purpose, a hole was artificially drilled in a large tree trunk, (damage to the tree was minimal). Water was subsequently supplied by the experimenter. Chimpanzees who came to the outdoor laboratory found that the artificial tree-hole contained water, and began to drink with the aid of leaves (figure 24.6). Such an experimental approach dramatically increased observation opportunity, not only in terms of duration, but also the chance to videotape and carefully analyze individual episodes. The detailed technique involved in leaf folding was thus uncovered and the selective preference for leaves of *Hybophrinuim braunianum* confirmed. In the case of ant dipping, a variety of efforts were necessary before

Figure 24.6
Nut cracking and the use of leaves for drinking water in an outdoor laboratory set in the natural habitat.
Two kinds of tool use are seen here performed at the same time and same place in the course of a field
experiment. The mother and her daughter in front are cracking open oil-palm nuts with stones. The large
tree in the background has a tree hollow filled with water. An adult male uses his left hand to obtain the
water by leaf folding. A young male is observing the behavior.

we recognized that fresh oil-palm nuts laid out on the ground of the laboratory made
excellent bait for safari ants. The ants attracted by the fresh nuts were discovered by
the chimpanzees, who were yet again encouraged to use tools under close observation in our outdoor laboratory.

Acquisition Age Depending on the Types of Tools   Through the comparison of various types of tool use in the outdoor laboratory, it has become clear that the minimum age of acquisition depends on the tool. Level 1 tools (relating one object to
another), according to the present author's definition (Matsuzawa 1996), such as ant
dipping or the use of leaves for drinking water, are acquired by the age of two. For
level 2 tools (relating one object to another, and then relating this set to a third
object) such as nut cracking, the minimum age of acquisition is between 3.5–5 years.
In the case of level 3 tools (relating one object to another, relating this set to a third,
then further to a fourth object) such as the use of metatools in nut cracking, the
minimum age appears to be 6.5 years.

Laboratory Simulation in Captive Chimpanzees

Field observation has taught us a great deal about cultural differences in the ways tools are traditionally used in each chimpanzee community. Field experiments have revealed the developmental process and other details associated with tool use and tool-making behavior. However, we have very little information regarding the origin of these behaviors and the mechanism of propagation in the social context. How did a particular type of tool use emerge? What kind of learning process is involved in the acquisition of the skills? How can the skills be transmitted from one individual to another in a social context, or from one generation to the next in a cultural context? To answer questions along these lines, we have begun a new series of experiments on tool use in captive chimpanzees.

A "dome," or outdoor experimental booth, was built in the compound that is home to a community of eleven chimpanzees in Inuyama, Japan. The traditional set-up has thus been reversed: the experimenter and the apparatus are now kept inside an experimental chamber and the chimpanzees are free to engage in any activity in a daily life situation (figure 24.7). We examined the use of leaves for drinking in this captive setting by supplying chimpanzees with orange juice filled into acrylic cylinders (Tonooka et al. 1997). This simulation allowed us to observe closely the behavior of each individual chimpanzee from the first day that the cylinders were introduced into their environment, and to track the changes that occurred in their tool-making and using skills (figure 24.8). The study provided clear evidence for the processes involved in the emergence of a new drinking tool and its propagation. Two chimpanzees of the Inuyama community initiated the manufacture and use of a new drinking tool, a twig of *Thuja occidentalis*. Other chimpanzees then shifted to use the same plant as the favored drinking tool, even though 28 different species of tree and several kinds of grass were available in the compound. This juice-drinking behavior simulates the high degree of selectivity for *Hybophrynium* leaves as water-drinking tools of Bossou chimpanzees. The social interactions leading to a convergence in the preferred tool has been analyzed in detail (Tonooka et al. 1997).

We also performed simulation experiments to investigate nut cracking with stones. We used macadamia nuts as the target food instead of oil-palm nuts, while the stones that were to serve as tools were brought from Bossou, West Africa. Of the three captive chimpanzees whom we have tested, one immediately copied the nut-cracking behavior demonstrated by a human model on only one occasion. For the other two, imitating human actions proved difficult, and it took them a long time to develop the skill.

Figure 24.7
Outdoor compound for chimpanzees at the Primate Research Institute, Kyoto University. A group of 11 chimpanzees lives in a semi-natural environment in which they have free access to planted trees, grass, a stream of water, and so forth. There is an outdoor booth for experiments which is connected by an underground tunnel to the adjacent building.

In addition, the ant-catching skill of Mahale chimpanzees (catching ants inside tree trunks by a short, thin probing stick; Nishida 1990) was also studied in a laboratory simulation: short, thin probing objects needed to be inserted into a small hole of 5mm diameter drilled into the center of an acrylic panel. Through the hole, chimpanzees could gain access to honey (rather than ants) in a small container attached behind the panel. Although no particulars are given here, simulation experiments of this sort will provide us with valuable information on the emergence and propagation of tool use by chimpanzees.

Importance of Cultural and Social Contexts

All living primates, including prosimians, are highly social animals. They possess social intelligence as shown in their ability to manipulate other individuals. However, most of the living nonhuman primates lack the material and technological intelligence to manipulate detached objects: they seldom use tools. The only excep-

Figure 24.8
Outdoor booth experiment on tool use for drinking juice contained in a cylinder. The cylinder has a hole for access to the juice, and is connected by a tube to a bottle manipulated by the experimenter inside the booth. *Top*: The chimpanzee on the left tries to use her right hand to obtain juice. *Bottom*: A chimpanzee uses a *Thuja* twig to gain access to the juice.

tion are hominoids (humans and the great apes), and therefore it may be a valid assumption that it was the common ancestor of hominoids who began to develop material intelligence, based on its already existing social intelligence.

Examples of chimpanzee tool use are many. However, recent findings from different research sites in Africa tell us that each community of chimpanzees has its own unique cultural tradition of tool use as well as food repertoire. Consider an analogy in humans: the Japanese use chopsticks to eat sashimi, but not all nations eat raw fish with a pair of sticks. When we talk about tool use, we must acknowledge that every chimpanzee community will use certain tools that are in some way unique to the community. One cannot refer to behaviors in different communities collectively as "termite fishing," "ant catching," "nut cracking." Such labels simply tell us that there are common features in terms of the target food, yet the most important point to remember is that tool materials, tool manufacure, and tool-using technique may differ greatly between communities. Simply, then, they must be regarded as different tools. The marked difference between communities, along with very little within-group variance in tool materials, manufacture, and technique means that social and cultural contexts play a role of extreme importance in the convergence of tool-use and tool-making behavior of chimpanzees in the same community.

This chapter has contributed a cultural context to tool manufacture and use by wild chimpanzees. It has also illustrated ways of analyzing details of cognitive behavior by experimental manipulation. I believe it has become clear that the study of chimpanzee tool use should no longer be limited to considerations of material intelligence, but should be reviewed in the light of social intelligence in social and cultural contexts. Further research will focus on the emergence and social transmission of such cognitive behaviors. Studies of tool use shed light on social and material aspects of intelligence in chimpanzees, as well as the extent to which knowledge from one individual can be translated to another—topics of interest that share characteristics with issues in communication, symbol use, and human language.

Acknowledgments

This study was financed by grants from the Ministry of Education, Science, and Culture, Japan (#07102010 to Matsuzawa, and #01041058 to Sugiyama for field research). I would like to thank Dr. Yukimaru Sugiyama. I also thank my colleagues for their assistance in my field work: Osamu Sakura, Rikako Tonooka, Noriko Inoue-Nakamura, Gen Yamakoshi, Masako Myowa, and Satoshi Hirata. Thanks are also due to the government of Guinea (DNRST) and the people at Bossou: Jeremie Koman, Guanou Goumy, Tino Camara, Paquile Cherif, and Glabota

Goumy, and to the government of Côte d'Ivoire and the people at Yealé for their assistance in the field work. I wish to thank Dora Biro for her helpful comments and the revision of the English, and Marc Hauser and Mark Konishi for their encouragement and patience.

References

Bard, K., Hopkins, W., and Fort, C. (1990) Lateral bias in infant chimpanzees (*Pan troglodytes*). *J. Comp. Psych.* 104:309–321.

Boesch, C. (1991a) Handedness in wild chimpanzees. *Int. J. Primatol.* 12:541–558.

Boesch, C. (1991b) Teaching among wild chimpanzees. *Anim. Behav.* 41:530–532.

Boesch, C. (1991c) Symbolic communication in wild chimpanzees? *Hum. Evol.* 6:81–90.

Boesch, C. and Boesch, H. (1989) Hunting behavior of wild chimpanzees in the Tai National Park. *Am. J. Phys. Anthropol.* 78:547–573.

Boesch, C., Marchesi, P., Marchesi, N., Fruth, B., and Joulian, F. (1994) Is nut cracking in wild chimpanzees a cultural behaviour? *J. Hum. Evol.* 26:325–338.

Boysen, S. and Berntson, G. (1989) Numerical competence in a chimpanzee (*Pan troglodytes*). *J. Comp. Psych.* 103:23–31.

Byrne, R. and Whiten, A. (1988) *Machiavellian Intelligence: Social Expertise and the Evolution of Intellect in Monkeys, Apes, and Humans.* Oxford: Oxford University Press.

Chapman, C. and Wrangham, R. (1993) Range use of the forest chimpanzees of Kibale: Implications for the understanding of chimpanzee social organization. *Am. J. Primatol.* 31:263–273.

Cheney, D. L. and Seyfarth, R. M. (1990) *How Monkeys See the World.* Chicago: University of Chicago Press.

de Waal, F. (1989) *Peacemaking among primates.* Cambridge: Harvard University Press.

Finch, G. (1941) Chimpanzee handedness. *Science* 94:117–118.

Fujita, K. and Matsuzawa, T. (1990) Delayed figure reconstruction by a chimpanzee and humans. *J. Comp. Psych.* 104:345–351.

Goodall, J. (1964) Tool-using and aimed throwing in a community of free-living chimpanzees. *Nature* 201:1264–1266.

Goodall, J. (1986) *The Chimpanzees of Gombe: Patterns of Behavior.* Cambridge: Harvard University Press.

Greenfield, P. M. and Savage-Rumbaugh, E. S. (1993) Comparing communicative competence in child and chimp: The pragmatics of repetition. *J. Child Lang.* 20(1):1–26.

Hauser, M. (1996) *The Evolution of Communication.* Cambridge, MA: MIT Press.

Hirata, S., Myowa, M., and Matsuzawa, T. (1998) Use of leaves as cushions to sit on wet ground by wild chimpanzees. *Am. J. Primatol.* 44:215–220.

Hopkins, W. and Morris, R. (1993) Handedness in Great apes: A review of findings. *Int. J. Primatol.* 14:1–26.

Ingmanson, E. (1996) Tool-using behavior in wild *Pan paniscus*: Social and ecological considerations. In *Reaching into Thought*, ed. by A. Russon, K. Bard, and S. Parker, pp. 190–210. Cambridge: Cambridge University Press.

Inoue-Nakamura, N. and Matsuzawa, T. (1997). Development of stone tool use by wild chimpanzees (*Pan troglodytes*). *J. Comp. Psych.* 111:159–173.

Kojima, S. (1990) Comparison of auditory functions in the chimpanzee and human. *Folia primatol.* 55:62–72.

Kojima, T. (1984) Generalization between productive use and receptive discrimination of names in an artificial visual language by a chimpanzee. *Int. J. Primatol.* 5:161–182.

MacNeilage. P., Studdert-Kennedy, M., and Lindblom, B. (1987) Primate handedness reconsidered. *Behav. Brain Sci.* 10:247–303.

Marler, P. (1969) Vocalizations of wild chimpanzees, an introduction. In *Proceedings of the 2nd International Congress of Primatology* (Atlanta 1968), 1:94–100.

Marler, P. and Hobbett, L. (1975) Individuality in a long-range vocalization of wild chimpanzees. *Z. Tierpsychol.* 38:97–109.

Matsuzawa, T. (1985a) Use of numbers by a chimpanzee. *Nature* 315:57–59.

Matsuzawa, T. (1985b) Color naming and classification in a chimpanzee (*Pan troglodytes*). *J. Hum. Evol.* 14:283–291.

Matsuzawa, T. (1989) Spontaneous pattern construction in a chimpanzee. In *Understanding Chimpanzees*, ed. by P. Heltne and L. Marquardt, pp. 252–265. Cambridge: Harvard University Press.

Matsuzawa, T. (1990) Form perception and visual acuity in a chimpanzee. *Folia Primatol.* 55:24–32.

Matsuzawa, T. (1991) Nesting cups and metatools in chimpanzees. *Behav. Brain Sci.* 14:570–571.

Matsuzawa, T. (1994) Field experiments on use of stone tools by chimpanzees in the wild. In *Chimpanzee Cultures*, ed. by R. Wrangham, W. McGrew, F. B. M. de Waal, and P. Heltne, pp. 351–370. Cambridge: Harvard University Press.

Matsuzawa, T. (1996) Chimpanzee intelligence in nature and in captivity: Isomorphism of symbol use and tool use. In *Great Ape Societies*, ed. by W. H. McGrew, T. Nishida, and L. Marchant, pp. 196–209. Cambridge: Cambridge University Press.

Matsuzawa, T. (1997) The death of an infant chimpanzee at Bossou, Guinea. *Pan African News* 4:4–6.

Matsuzawa, T. (1998) Chimpanzee behavior: A comparative cognitive perspective. In *Comparative Psychology*, ed. by G. Geenberg and M. H. Haraway, pp. 360–375. New York: Garland.

Matsuzawa, T. and Yamakoshi, G. (1996) Comparison of chimpanzee material culture between Bossou and Nimba, West Africa. In *Reaching into Thought*, ed. by A. Russon, K. Bard, and S. Parker, pp. 211–232. Cambridge: Cambridge University Press.

Matsuzawa, T., Yamakoshi, G., and Humle, T. (1996) A newly found tool-use by wild chimpanzees: Algae scooping. [In Japanese] *Prim. Res.* 12:283.

McGrew, W. (1992) *Chimpanzee Material Culture*. Cambridge: Cambridge University Press.

McGrew, W. and Marchant, L. (1997) On the other hand: Current issues in and meta-analysis of the behavioral laterality of hand function in nonhuman primates. *Yrbk. Phys. Anthropol.* 40:201–232.

Mitani, J., Hasegawa, T., Gros-Louis, J., Marler, P., and Byrne, R. (1992) Dialects in wild chimpanzees? *Am. J. Primatol.* 27:233–243.

Nishida, T. (1990) *The Chimpanzees of the Mahale Mountains*. Tokyo: University of Tokyo Press.

Ogawa, H. (1995a) Bridging behavior and other affiliative interactions among male Tibetan macaques (*Macaca thibetana*). *Int. J. Primatol.* 16:707–729.

Ogawa, H. (1995b) Triadic male-female-infant relationships and bridging behavior among Tibetan macaques (*Macaca thibetana*). *Folia Primatol.* 64:153–157.

Patterson, F. (1978) The gestures of a gorilla: Language acquisition in another pongid. *Brain Lang.* 5:72–97.

Premack, D. and Woodruff, G. (1978) Does the chimpanzee have a theory of mind? *Behav. Brain Sci.* 1:515–526.

Sakura, O. and Matsuzawa, T. (1991) Flexibility of wild chimpanzee nut-cracking behavior using stone hammers and anvils: An experimental analysis. *Ethology* 87:237–248.

Savage-Rumbaugh, S. and Lewin, R. (1994) *Kanzi: The Ape at the Brink of the Human Mind*. New York: John Wiley and Sons.

Sugiyama, Y. (1994) Tool use by wild chimpanzees. *Nature* 367:327.

Sugiyama, Y. (1995a) Tool-use for catching ants by chimpanzees at Bossou and Mount Nimba, West Africa. *Primates* 36:193–205.

Sugiyama, Y. (1995b) Drinking tools of wild chimpanzees at Bossou. *Am. J. Primatol.* 37:263–269.

Sugiyama, Y., Fushimi, T., Sakura, O., and Matsuzawa, T. (1993) Hand preference and tool use in wild chimpanzees. *Primates* 34:151–159.

Sugiyama, Y. and Koman, J. (1979) Tool-using and making behavior in wild chimpanzees at Bossou, Guinea. *Primates* 20:513–524.

Sugiyama, Y., Koman, J., and Sow, M. B. (1988) Ant-catching wands of wild chimpanzees at Bossou, Guinea. *Folia Primatol.* 51:56–60.

Terrace, H. S., Petitto, L. A., Sanders, F. J., and Bever, T. G. (1979). Can an ape create a sentence? *Science* 206:891–900.

Tomasello, M. and Call, J. (1997) *Primate Cognition*. Oxford: Oxford University Press.

Tomonaga, M., Itakura, S., and Matsuzawa, T. (1993) Superiority of conspecific faces and reduced inversion effect in face perception by a chimpanzee. *Folia Primatol.* 61:110–114.

Tomonaga, M. and Matsuzawa, T. (1992) Perception of complex geometric figures in chimpanzees and humans: Analyses of visual similarity on the basis of choice reaction time. *J. Comp. Psych.* 106:43–52.

Tonooka, R., Inoue, N., and Matsuzawa, T. (1995) Leaf-folding behavior for drinking water by wild chimpanzees at Bossou, Guinea: A field experiment and leaf selectivity. [In Japanese with English summary] *Prim. Res.* 10:307–313.

Tonooka, R. and Matsuzawa, T. (1995) Hand preferences of captive chimpanzees in simple reaching for food. *Int. J. Primatol.* 16:17–35.

Tonooka, R., Tomonaga, M., and Matsuzawa, T. (1997) Acquisition and transmission of tool making and use for drinking juice in a group of captive chimpanzees (*Pan troglodytes*). *Jap. Psychol. Res.* 39:253–265.

Ward, J. and Hopkins, W. (1993) *Primate Laterality: Current Behavioral Evidence of Primate Asymmetries*. New York: Springer-Verlag.

Yamakoshi, G. and Sugiyama, Y. (1995) Pestle-pounding behavior of wild chimpanzees at Bossou, Guinea: A newly observed tool-using behavior. *Primates* 36:489–500.

Contributors

Ralph Adolphs
The University of Iowa
Division of Cognitive Science
Department of Neurology
Iowa City, IA

Gregory F. Ball
Johns Hopkins University
Department of Psychology
Behavioral Neuroendocrinology Group
Baltimore, MD

Andrew H. Bass
Cornell University
Section of Neurobiology and Behavior
Ithaca, NY

Deana Bodnar
Cornell University
Section of Neurobiology and Behavior
Ithaca, NY

Dorothy L. Cheney
University of Pennsylvania
Departments of Psychology and Biology
Philadelphia, PA

Allison J. Doupe
University of San Francisco
Keck Center for Integrated Neuroscience and
Departments of Psychiatry and Physiology
San Francisco, CA

Carl H. Gerhardt
University of Missouri
Division of Biological Sciences
Columbia, MO

Marc D. Hauser
Harvard University
Department of Anthropology and
Psychology
Program in Neuroscience
Cambridge, MA

Carl D. Hopkins
Cornell University
Section of Neurobiology and Behavior
Ithaca, NY

Ronald R. Hoy
Cornell University
Neurobiology and Behavior
Ithaca, NY

Kathleen Hunt
University of Washington
Department of Zoology
Seattle, WA

Jerry D. Jacobs
University of Washington
Department of Zoology
Seattle, WA

Jagmeet S. Kanwal
Georgetown University Medical Center
GICCS, Research Building
Washington, DC

Darcy B. Kelley
Columbia University
Department of Biological Sciences
New York, NY

Mark Konishi
California Institute of Technology
Division of Biology
Pasadena, CA

Donald E. Kroodsma
University of Massachusetts
Department of Biology
Amherst, MA

Patricia K. Kuhl
University of Washington, Seattle
Department of Speech and Hearing
Sciences
Seattle, WA

Donna L. Maney
University of Washington
Department of Zoology
Seattle, WA

Margaret A. Marchaterre
Cornell University
Section of Neurobiology and Behavior
Ithaca, NY

Peter Marler
University of California, Davis
Department of Neurobiology
Physiology and Behavior
Davis, CA

Tetsuro Matsuzawa
Kyoto University
Primate Research Institute
Inuyama, Aichi, Japan

Simone Meddle
University of Washington
Department of Zoology
Seattle, WA

Axel Michelsen
Odense University
Centre for Sound Communication
Institute of Biology
Odense, Denmark

Paul C. Mundinger
Queens College
Department of Biology
Flushing, NY

Fernando Nottebohm
The Rockefeller University
Field Research Center
New York, NY

Stephen Nowicki
Duke University
Department of Zoology
Durham, NC

David I. Perrett
The University of St. Andrews
School of Psychology
Fife, Scotland

Marilyn Ramenofsky
University of Washington
Department of Zoology
Seattle, WA

Stanley A. Rand
Smithsonian Tropical Research Institute
Washington, DC

Michael J. Ryan
University of Texas-Austin
Department of Zoology
Austin, TX

William A. Searcy
University of Miami
Department of Biology
Coral Gables, FL

Robert M. Seyfarth
University of Pennsylvania
Departments of Psychology and Biology
Philadelphia, PA

Michele M. Solis
University of San Francisco
Keck Center for Integrated Neuroscience
and Departments of Psychiatry and
Physiology
San Francisco, CA

Kiran Soma
University of Washington
Department of Zoology
Seattle, WA

Kimberly Sullivan
Utah State University
Department of Biology
Logan, Utah

Roderick A. Suthers
Physiology Section
Medical Sciences
Indiana University
Bloomington, IN

Martha L. Tobias
Columbia University
Department of Biological Sciences
New York, NY

John C. Wingfield
University of Washington
Department of Zoology
Seattle, WA

Deborah Wisti-Peterson
University of Washington
Department of Zoology
Seattle, WA

Robert A. Wyttenbach
Cornell University
Neurobiology and Behavior
Ithaca, NY

Name Index

Subject Index